D1107302
W
E
S

A BOOK
ABOUT THE BIBLE

✠

A BOOK ABOUT THE BIBLE

BY

GEORGE STIMPSON

HARPER & BROTHERS PUBLISHERS

New York and London

A BOOK ABOUT THE BIBLE

FIFTH EDITION

K-U

To

W. M. Kiplinger

FOREWORD

✠

More copies of the Bible are distributed on the average every year, and fewer destroyed, than of any other book. It is estimated that more than a billion Bibles have been printed. Bibles are preserved, not only because they are regarded as sacred books, but also because they are widely used for family records of births, baptisms, marriages and deaths. Consequently, there are more copies of the Bible in existence than of any other book.

Christianity, Judaism and Islam all derive directly or indirectly from the Bible or parts of it. Many people look upon the Bible merely as a source of spiritual inspiration and religious doctrine. It is much more than that. The Bible is also the source of many secular beliefs, customs, moral precepts, stories, illustrations, figures of speech and phrases. It contains a treasury of literature, history, biography, poetry, drama, orations, epigrams, proverbs, psalms, anecdotes, elegies, letters, common sayings, maxims and general wisdom.

The Bible contains a larger collection of apt and striking comments on the behavior of human beings than any other book, and accordingly it is the most widely quoted of all books. Our daily speech is rich in references and allusions to the Bible. It has had, and still has, a profound influence on our speech, customs, and daily conduct. Our laws, government, art, literature and folklore all have been greatly influenced by the Bible. Such has been its influence on our culture that it might be said that no person not familiar with it can regard himself as really educated.

The purpose of the author in writing this book is to supply reliable and adequate answers to a great number of popular questions asked about the Bible. Hundreds of questions are answered specifically and thousands of others incidentally.

Perhaps the basic characteristic of this book is the fact that the questions are such as continually occur to all sorts and conditions of people. Nonetheless the author has tried to impart to it another characteristic in the reliability of the answers.

Two essential processes entered into the writing of this book. First, questions with a wide range of interest were chosen; and, second, the answers to these questions were based on the most reliable information available. Thus the author has sought to give the book a distinctive character both in the wide appeal of its questions and in the authenticity of its answers.

Of course, no one could answer all the questions about the Bible to the entire satisfaction of everybody. The author has selected for discussion questions that are most frequently asked at the present time and particularly those that have been asked persistently through the years. He has included "out of his treasure things new and old." These are such questions as are asked by the great mass of Bible readers as well as by those with a slighter knowledge and lesser interest. Since the questions have a general rather than merely a special and passing interest, this book, it is believed, will supply the answers to the majority of all questions most commonly asked about the Bible.

A Book About the Bible is much more than simply a question-and-answer book. The questions themselves are the substance rather than the exact words of the questions as they are generally asked. In fact they are in the nature of headings. Questions are used to challenge the reader's attention and to present information in the most effective manner. Often several related and equally important subjects are grouped together and discussed under one leading question. The book is, in fact, a series of short essays on many Biblical matters, ranging in length from a sentence or two to several pages. It is not a commentary, concordance, dictionary, encyclopedia or a new interpretation of the Bible, but it embraces some of the characteristics of all of them. The author has tried to observe the rule, set forth in a foreword to the original King James Version, not to "weary the unlearned, who need not know so much" nor to "trouble the learned, who know it already."

Many questions are included not because they are essentially Biblical but because the subjects are alluded to in the Bible. It is surprising how many things are popularly attributed to the Bible that are not in it. Folklore about the Bible and homespun Scripture result from the popular practice of making the Bible say things it does not say and distorting things that it does say.

Some of the problems dealt with are controversial and hardly susceptible of definite answers. In many cases, however, it seems to be worth while to give the authentic information available on the subject. The fact that the authorities have not found an adequate and satisfactory answer to a question is in itself often valuable to the general reader. The author has tried to be objective, impartial, clear and as brief as is consistent with the nature of the questions dealt with. He has left purely theological questions to the theologians.

This book has been considerably expanded because the author has quoted freely from the Bible to give the reader the actual text under consideration and some of the flavor of the style. He has obeyed the injunction of Jesus to "Search the scriptures" and wherever possible has let the Bible speak for itself. A certain amount of duplication of fact and quotation has been necessary to avoid distracting cross references. Some of the material has been previously published in books, magazines and newspapers, during the last twenty-five years, but all such parts have been carefully revised or completely rewritten for the present purpose.

This book is the result of much reading and research. Half a library has been turned over in writing it. Sometimes a hundred or more sources have been consulted to answer a single question. It contains the essence of the researches and thought of thousands of Bible students and secular scholars. The author has made use of what appear to be the correct conclusions and most plausible findings of those who have spent much time and talent on the subject. In each case he has tried to give the most authentic information afforded by scholarship and sound research.

The author does not profess to have read all the books and articles written about the Bible, not even all the important ones. It would be physically impossible for any one person to do that. For instance, although virtually all the original information available about Jesus is in the Bible, more than two thousand "biographies" of him have been published.

The author would like to give the source and authority for every statement made in this book. He would also like to acknowledge individually the services of the many persons who have helped him. But so many sources and authorities have been consulted, and so many persons have helped, that it is impracticable even to try to list them.

To simplify the plan of the book, all quotations are from, and all citations are to, the King James Version of the Bible as currently printed, unless otherwise indicated. This appeared to be a practical way to proceed. Although many distinctive versions of the Bible in

English are available, the King James Version, with those on which it was based and those based on it, has a wider circulation than any other English version. Most reference systems are based on it. There is not so much difference between the various English versions as may be commonly supposed, particularly for the purposes of such a book as this.

The King James Version has been described as "a miracle in prose" and as "the great English classic." Its unsurpassed beauty and simplicity of style are generally conceded. This version was made at a time when the English language was young, flexible in grammar, vivid in vocabulary and fresh and original in expression. Although there are many archaic words in the King James Version, it contains comparatively few obsolete words. There are two reasons for this. The revisers and translators of the version of 1611 were careful in choosing words already firmly fixed in the language and the popularity of the work had a tendency to keep alive all words in it.

In fact the language of the King James Version has become so much a part of our language and thought that many people have difficulty in realizing that it was not originally composed in English. The old humorous saying, "The English language was good enough for St. Paul and it is good enough for me," summarizes this close link between the language and the thought of the Bible in the minds of many English-speaking people.

Because most of the questions in this book defy classification, there is no general scheme of arrangement, unless a deliberate disarrangement may be regarded as such. Each question is answered as if it were the only one under consideration at the moment. It is believed that the random order, the sudden change from topic to topic, presents the information in the most direct and interesting manner. No index is ever entirely satisfactory, but the author trusts the one at the back of this book will satisfy all reference needs.

George Stimpson

March 7, 1945
Washington, D. C.

A BOOK
ABOUT THE BIBLE

✠

A BOOK ABOUT THE BIBLE

*

When was Jesus born?

The exact date of the birth of Jesus has never been determined for certain and probably never can be. There is not a single contemporaneous reference to Jesus in existence, either in or out of the Bible, and all specific and definite conclusions on the subject of the date of his birth rest upon a pyramid of presumptions. The Gospels, probably written between fifty and one hundred years after the birth of Jesus, are vague and general in their references to historical persons, events and facts. Attempts to determine the date of Jesus' birth from historical, archaeological and astronomical data have resulted in doubtful success. The Jews and Romans had different methods of reckoning time and dating historical events. In all the Bible there is not one single date in the modern sense of the word. The solution of the problem of the birth date of Jesus hinges on a very few events in the Gospels that can be determined with a fair measure of certainty. From *Matthew 2:1* we learn that "Jesus was born in Bethlehem of Judaea in the days of Herod the king." History tells us that this Herod, surnamed the Great, died sometime in 4 B.C., according to our present calendar. Therefore Jesus must have been born in or before that year. The year of his birth has been placed by different authorities all the way from 4 B.C. to 20 B.C. Many suppose that Jesus was born at least two years before Herod's death. This is based on *Matthew 2:16*, which says that Herod, in his attempt to destroy Jesus, slew all the children "from two years old and under," indicating that the king thought that Jesus might be as much as two years of age at that time. We have no way of knowing, however, that this incident occurred during the last year of Herod's life. In *Luke 2:1-2* we are told that in the days when Jesus was born "there went out a decree from Caesar Augustus, that all the world should be taxed" and that "this taxing was first made when Cyrenius was governor of Syria." This Cyrenius is generally believed to have been

Publius Sulpicius Quirinius, who, we learn from Roman history, occupied important positions in Syria, which included Judaea, three different times—6-4 B.C., 3-2 B.C. and 6-9 A.D. It is known that Augustus Caesar in 23 B.C. started the practice of making an enrollment of the taxpayers every fourteen years. Accordingly such an enrollment would have been due in Syria in 9 B.C. Such enrollments, however, probably required more than one year, and in some cases they may have been postponed a year or two for various reasons. Probably an enrollment took place sometime between 9 B.C. and 6 B.C., possibly the first year that Quirinius was proconsul of "Asia," which suggests 6 B.C. as the year of the birth of Jesus. There is not enough evidence to justify a definite conclusion. The best that can be said is that Jesus was probably born before 4 B.C., and very likely several years earlier. There is no evidence whatever to indicate what time of the year, month or day he was born.

What two chapters of the Bible are alike?

No two chapters of the Bible are exactly alike, as often supposed. There is very little difference, however, between *Isaiah 37* and *II Kings 19*. These are the two chapters that are frequently spoken of as being alike. But *Isaiah 37* contains 38 verses, while *II Kings 19* contains only 37, and there are other minor variations. Large portions of *Ezra 2* and *Nehemiah 7* are also identical. *Psalm 14* and *Psalm 53* are substantially alike in matter, though not in form. Some of these duplications of parts of the Bible may have been owing to mistakes made by the early copyists of the manuscripts or to quotations that were not clearly indicated. Similarities in *Matthew, Mark* and *Luke* are explained in a different manner. The authors of these "synoptical" gospels were telling essentially the same story and used many of the same sources. Matthew apparently borrowed from Mark, and Luke no doubt borrowed from both Mark and Matthew. There are also many repetitions in *Psalms*. For instance, in *Psalms 107* Verses 8, 15, 21 and 31 are identical.

How do the Protestant and Catholic Bibles differ?

The Protestant and the Catholic Bibles differ considerably in the contents of the Old Testament. At the Council of Trent (1546-1563) the Roman Catholic church enumerated the books that should be regarded as "sacred and canonical" and consequently as parts of the Bible. This list comprises the present Catholic Bible and includes all but three—*Esdras I*, and *Esdras II* and the *Prayer of Manasses*—of the books and portions of books which are not found in the Jewish traditions of the Old Testament and which Protestants generally denominate the Apocrypha. Accordingly the Catholic Bible comprises all of the Old Testament books accepted as canonical by Protestants, and in addition *Tobias, Judith, Wisdom of Solomon, Ecclesiasticus, Baruch, Maccabees I, Maccabees II,* and certain fragments of *Esther* and *Daniel.* Strictly speaking, the Apocryphal books are not essential parts of the Protestant Bible, although they were formerly printed between the Testaments in nearly all Protestant editions, and the Bibles on the lecterns of the Anglican church and the Protestant Episcopal church of the United States contain these books, and lessons are taken from them on certain days of the Church Year. Thus, it will be seen that the chief difference between the Protestant and the Catholic Bibles is that the Catholics regard all but three of the so-called Apocryphal books and parts of books as canonical and essential parts of the Scriptures, while the Protestants read them merely for inspiration and edification and do not use them to establish points of doctrine.

Who divided the Bible into chapters and verses?

Early editions of the Bible were not divided into chapters and the smaller sections now known as verses. They did not contain even perceptible spaces between words. The division into chapters and verses was a gradual process that started during the Middle Ages. Tertullian, who died before 240 A.D., referred to some sort of sections in the New Testament. Later the Gospels were divided into what were known as the Ammonian-Eusebian sections, which were smaller divisions than our present chapters. Euthalius, a deacon and bishop who lived about the middle of the fifth century, divided parts of the New Testament into minute portions similar to the present verses. About 1226 Cardinal Hugo de Sancto-Caro of France divided the entire Latin Vulgate into chapters and verses somewhat similar to those of today. But even the early printed Bibles, such as the Gutenberg Bible, were not divided into chapters and verses. The first printed New Testament with such divisions was issued in 1527 at Lyons by Sanctus Pagninus. Robert Stephens followed a similar arrangement in his edition of the New Testament printed at Geneva in 1551. This was a two-volume work with the Greek text in the center of the page and with the Latin of Erasmus on one side and the Latin Vulgate on the other. Stephens, whose French name was Robert Estienne, was a member of a famous family of scholars and printers in France. In the preface to his concordance, the son of Robert Stephens says his father worked out the system of chapters and verses for his edition of the New Testament while he was journeying on horseback from Paris to London. His system of dividing the Bible into chapters and verses was adopted by William Whittingham and his associates in the Geneva or Breeches Bible, the New Testament of which was first printed in 1557 and the Old Testament in 1560. An introductory note to the reader of that Bible says: "The argumentes bothe for the booke and for the chapters with the nombre of the verse are added." The Geneva Bible is the first English version with the chapter and verse enumeration as we now know them. It should be borne in mind that the Greek classics and other ancient books were likewise arbitrarily divided into sections for convenience and reference. The general plan appears to have been to include each separate sentence or its equivalent in a verse, but this plan was not always followed. Both chapters and verses often disregard natural divisions of thought and are misleading. For instance, the first three verses of *Genesis 2* are clearly the conclusion of the narrative in *Genesis 1*. But the chapters and verses are now definitely fixed and are regarded as virtually parts of the Bible. Although the arrangement sometimes obscures the sense and interrupts the flow of the narrative, it is so convenient for reference and citation that its elimination would destroy the usefulness of thousands of concordances and other reference books and make millions of citations meaningless. The Revisers of 1885 tried to solve this problem by printing the chapter and verse numbers in the margin.

How did *poor as Job's turkey* originate?

Poor as Job's turkey was apparently suggested by the older phrase *patient as Job*. In *James 5:11* it is said that "Ye have heard of the patience of Job." This, of course, refers to the patriarch whose history is related in the *Book of Job* and whose patience is proverbial. Some writers suppose that *poor as Job's turkey* was originated by Thomas Chandler Haliburton in *The Clockmaker: or the Sayings and Doings of Samuel Slick of Slickville*. Haliburton, a native of Nova Scotia and a noted Canadian humorist and historian, described a turkey gobbler that was so poor that he had only one feather in his tail and so weak that he had to lean against a fence to gobble. This condition was attributed to the gobbler's persistent efforts to hatch chicks from eggs that didn't have chicks in them. *Turkey*, however, was popularly associated with Job in phrases before the Sam Slick stories appeared in 1837. In 1824 the *Sentinel* of Troy, New York, quoted the following extract from a paper called the *Microscope*: "We have seen fit to say the *patience of Job's turkey,* instead of the common phrase, *as patient as Job.* And so it must go for this time at any rate. 'Twould worry out the patience of Job's turkey to be picked and pillaged from in this way." Although *turkey* is of Old World origin, Job could not have had a bird of the species we call turkey, because this branch of the pheasant family was native to America. In the New Testament Job is mentioned by name only in *James 5:11,* quoted above, but *The Book of Job* is quoted in *I Corinthians 3:19,* which says in part, "For it is written, He taketh the wise in their own craftiness," which is from *Job 5:13.*

What did Balaam's ass say?

In *Genesis 3* the serpent speaks. In *Numbers 22* we are told of Balaam's speaking ass. These instances are unique in the Bible so far as dumb creatures are given the power of human speech. When the Israelites, after wandering forty years in the wilderness, appeared on the borders of Moab, King Balak of the Moabites sent messengers to Balaam at Pethor near the Euphrates to ask him to come and curse the invaders. At first Balaam refused, because God told him the Israelites were a blessed people. But Balak sent more honorable messengers to Balaam and repeated the request with offers of larger rewards. This time God told Balaam to go but to do only what he was instructed to do. The incident of the speaking ass followed. *Numbers 22:21-33* says: "And Balaam rose up in the morning, and saddled his ass, and went with the princes of Moab. And God's anger was kindled because he went: and the angel of the Lord stood in the way for an adversary against him. Now he was riding upon his ass, and his two servants were with him. And the ass saw the angel of the Lord standing in the way, and his sword drawn in his hand: and the ass turned aside out of the way, and went into the field: and Balaam smote the ass, to turn her into the way. But the angel of the Lord stood in a path of the vineyards, a wall being on this side, and a wall on that side. And when the ass saw the angel of the Lord, she thrust herself unto the wall, and crushed Balaam's foot against the wall: and he smote her again. And the angel of the Lord went further, and stood in a narrow place, where was no way to turn either to the right hand or to the left. And when the ass saw the angel of the Lord, she fell down under Balaam: and Balaam's anger was kindled, and he smote the ass with a staff. And the Lord opened the mouth of the ass, and she said unto Balaam, What have I done unto thee, that thou hast smitten me these three times? And Balaam said unto the ass, Because thou hast mocked me: I would there were a sword in mine hand, for now would I kill thee. And the ass said unto Balaam, Am not I thine ass, upon which thou has ridden ever since I was thine unto this day? was I ever wont to do so unto thee? And he said, Nay. Then the Lord opened the eyes of Balaam, and he saw the angel standing in the way, and his sword drawn in his hand: and he bowed down his head, and fell flat on his face. And the angel of the Lord said unto him, Wherefore hast thou smitten thine ass these three times? behold, I went out to withstand thee, because thy way is perverse before me: and the ass saw me, and turned from me these three times: unless she had turned from me, surely now also I had slain thee, and saved her alive." An interesting feature about this narrative is the fact that Balaam did not show the least surprise that his faithful female ass should suddenly start speaking. Another interesting feature is that the ass could see the angel with sword in hand while Balaam could not.

What was Sir Walter Scott's tribute to the Bible?

Sir Walter Scott died September 21, 1834, at Abbotsford on the Tweed. For some months his health had been declining, but several weeks before his death he appeared to be recovering. "One morning," wrote John Gibson Lockhart, the novelist's son-in-law and biographer, "after again enjoying the Bath chair for perhaps a couple of hours out of doors, he desired to be drawn into the library, and placed by the central window, that he might look down upon the Tweed. Here he expressed a wish that I should read to him, and when I asked from what book, he said—'Need you ask? There is but one.' I chose the 14th chapter of St. John's Gospel; he listened with mild devotion, and said when I had done—'Well, this is a great comfort. I have followed you distinctly, and feel as if I were yet to be myself again.' " The chapter read to Sir Walter by his son-in-law on that occasion opens as follows: "Let not your heart be troubled: ye believe in God, believe also in me. In my Father's house are many mansions: if it were not so, I would have told you. I go to prepare a place for you. And if I go and prepare a place for you, I will come again, and receive you unto myself; that where I am, there ye may be also. And whither I go ye know, and the way ye know." Some authorities say this passage is the most popular and widely read in the New Testament. Incidentally, more copies of *John* and *Psalms* have been circulated than any other books in the Bible. There are so many beautiful passages in the Bible that it would be difficult to say which one is the most beautiful, but, speaking from the purely literary point of view, many critics assign that honor to *Isaiah 40,* which opens with the words: "Comfort ye, comfort ye my people, saith your God."

How did "he who runs may read" originate?

The common expression, "he who runs may read," is a misquotation or altered form of a passage in the Old Testament. According to the King James Version, *Habakkuk 2:2* says: "And the Lord answered me, and said, Write the vision, and make it plain upon tables, *that he may run that readeth it.*" This is an approximate literal translation of the Hebrew version, which is supposed to date back in its original form to about 590 B.C. The last part of the verse, "that he may run that readeth it," is almost always quoted, "that he who runs may read." In sense the Biblical quotation and the popular misquotation are essentially the same. The popular version of the expression is not of recent origin. In his *Tirocinium,* published in 1784, William Cowper wrote:

> Shine by the side of ev'ry path we tread
> With such a lustre, he that runs may read.

And Alfred Lord Tennyson wrote in *The Flower*:

> Read my little fable;
> He that runs may read.

It is possible that the expression, "he that runs may read," was current in English before the publication of the King James Version in 1611. In 1604 Joshua Sylvester published a translation of *The Divine Weeks of the World's Birth,* by Guillaume de Salluste du Bartas, French Huguenot poet, soldier and diplomat. One line of the English poet's translation is:

> And reads, though running, all these needful motions.

Is *In God We Trust* in the Bible?

In God We Trust, the motto on all United States coins, is not in the Bible, but it may have been suggested indirectly by various Biblical phrases. According to *Psalms 56:11,* David sang: "In God have I put my trust: I will not be afraid what man can do unto me." In *Job 13:15* the patriarch says of the Almighty: "Though he slay me, yet will I trust him." And according to *Matthew 27:43* the chief priests, scribes and elders, mocking Jesus on the cross, said: "He trusted in God; let him deliver him now, if he will have him: for he said, I am the Son of God." The underlying thought of *In God We Trust,* though not expressed in these exact words, was current long before the motto was first placed on United States coins. Francis Scott Key's *The Star-Spangled Banner*, first printed in *The Baltimore Patriot* September 20, 1814, under the title *Defense of Fort McHenry*, contains the couplet:

> Then conquer we must, for our cause it is just,
> And this be our motto: "In God is our trust."

In a letter dated April 25, 1861, and addressed to Cassius Lee, Robert E. Lee acknowledged that mediation between the Northern and Southern States was impossible and declared that "In God must be our trust." It was during that same year that the Reverend W. R. Watkinson, a minister at Ridleyville, Pennsylvania, wrote to Secretary of the Treasury Salmon P. Chase suggesting that the Deity be recognized in some form on American coins. Acting upon this suggestion, Secretary Chase instructed James Pollock, director of the United States Mint at Philadelphia, to have prepared without delay a device with a motto expressing such national recognition of the Deity. Secretary Chase wrote that "no nation can be strong except in the strength of God or safe except in His defense. The trust of our people in God should be declared on our national coins." Owing to legal difficulties Pollock did not submit his designs until 1863. One of the mottoes suggested was *God Our Trust*. Chase approved the designs, but suggested the motto be changed to *In God We Trust*. At a cabinet meeting during that same year it was proposed to place *In God We Trust* on paper money as well as on coins. President Lincoln, however, observed dryly that if a legend was to be engraved on the greenbacks he would suggest that of Peter in *Acts 3:6*: "Silver and gold have I none; but such as I have give I thee." In 1864 Congress passed an act authorizing the coinage of the two-cent piece, and it was upon these bronze two-cent pieces that the motto *In God We Trust* first appeared. It will thus be seen that Chase was responsible for the exact wording of the motto. No doubt Pollock and Chase were both influenced by the motto in *The Star-Spangled Banner*. Later Congress passed an act giving the proper officials authority to place the motto on all coins that would admit of the inscription. During the second administration of Theodore Roosevelt, Augustus St. Gaudens, the sculptor, prepared some designs for new coins with a view to improving the coinage from an artistic standpoint. When the double eagle and eagle of the new designs appeared in 1907, the motto *In God We Trust* was omitted. President Roosevelt objected to the motto on the coins on the ground that such use of the beautiful sentiment tended to cheapen it. A storm of criticism all over the country was the result. Once a design for a coin is approved and accepted, it cannot be changed under the law within twenty-five years without an act of Congress. Therefore an act of Congress was necessary to restore *In God We Trust* on the eagle and the double eagle. This was done by a bill that passed Congress in 1908, providing that "the motto *In God We Trust* heretofore inscribed on certain denominations of the gold and silver coins of the United States of America, shall hereafter be inscribed upon all such gold and silver coins of said denominations as heretofore." *In God We Trust* is the State motto of Florida.

Who was the first convert to Christianity in Europe?

So far as the Bible informs us, a woman named Lydia at Philippi in Macedonia was the first convert made to Christianity in Europe. *Acts 16:14-15* says: "And a certain woman named Lydia, a seller of purple, of the city of Thyatira, which worshipped God, heard us: whose heart the Lord opened, that she attended unto the things which were spoken of Paul. And when she was baptized, and her household, she besought us, saying, If ye have judged me to be faithful to the Lord, come into my house, and abide there. And she constrained us." After Paul and Silas were scourged, imprisoned and set free by divine power, they "entered into the house of Lydia." Paul does not once refer to Lydia by name in all his epistles, a fact that suggests it may not have been her personal name, but the designation of her native country, since she came from Thyatira in *Lydia* in Asia Minor. It is generally assumed, however, that there were many Christian converts among the Jews in Rome and perhaps elsewhere in Europe before Paul visited that continent.

What caused the walls of Jericho to fall?

The taking of the fortified city of Jericho by the Israelites under Joshua is related in *Joshua 6*. There we are told: "And Joshua rose early in the morning, and the priests took up the ark of the Lord. And seven priests bearing seven trumpets of rams' horns before the ark of the Lord went on continually, and blew with the trumpets: and the armed men went before them; but the rereward came after the ark of the Lord, the priests going on, and blowing with the trumpets. And the second day they compassed the city once, and returned into the camp: so they did six days. And it came to pass on the seventh day, that they rose early about the dawning of the day, and compassed the city after the same manner . . . only on that day they compassed the city seven times. And it came to pass at the seventh time, when the priests blew with the trumpets, Joshua said unto the people, Shout; for the Lord hath given you the city. . . . So the people shouted when the priests blew with the trumpets: and it came to pass, when the people heard the sound of the trumpet, and the people shouted with a great shout, that the wall fell down flat, so that the people went up into the city, every man straight before him, and they took the city." This is one of the Bible miracles that many attempt to explain as a natural phenomenon. Jericho lies in a region subject to numerous earth tremors and a favorite theory is that the walls of the heathen city were shaken down by an earthquake. Another theory, more ingenious, explains the phenomenon by what is known as synchronism. The notion is that the trumpet blasts and the shouts of the multitude, if in the proper rate of vibration, could have set up sufficient oscillation in the poorly constructed walls of Jericho and caused them to shake until they collapsed. This theory is akin to the notion that dogs and cats endanger suspension bridges. According to that belief, the even tread of a small animal walking over a large suspension bridge will sometimes cause sufficient vibration to endanger the structure. Many people believe that cats and dogs are not permitted to cross long bridges of this type. It is a fact that a comparatively small force, applied at regular intervals under favorable circumstances, will occasionally set up considerable oscillation in such a structure, but it is improbable that a modern suspension bridge would be affected to a dangerous extent by a cat or dog, although the vibration produced might be appreciable. Experts testify that a few soldiers marching over a long bridge in regular step might produce more vibration than a whole regiment out of step. That is why troops are generally ordered to *route step* before starting over a bridge. Two hundred and twenty-six men lost their lives in 1850 when a suspension bridge over the Marne at Angers, France, broke down under 487 marching soldiers. The crash was caused by the vibration of the men in step, combined with their great weight. But the theory that the walls of Jericho were shaken down by vibration caused by the trumpets and shouting is merely an interesting speculation. We know nothing about the construction of the walls of Jericho. It is supposed that Jericho fell to the Israelites about 1407 B.C., but a study of pottery, archaeology, astronomy and history have shed little light on the Bible story. The authors of the Old Testament obviously believed in miracles, they were not concerned with the scientific aspects of such probiems, and they took it for granted that the collapse of the walls when the trumpets sounded and the people shouted was a miraculous intervention by Jehovah in behalf of the children of Israel. Only Eriha, a village of some three hundred huts and hovels, now stands on the site of ancient Jericho.

Why is mint sauce eaten with lamb?

The custom of eating mint sauce with lamb, which is virtually unknown on the European continent and which Americans borrowed from the English, is possibly a relic of the Jewish practice of eating bitter herbs with the lamb slain and eaten at the Passover. Referring to the paschal lamb, *Exodus 12:8* says: "And they shall eat the flesh in that night, roast with fire, and unleavened bread; and with bitter herbs they shall eat it." The bitter herbs originally may have been an allusion to the bitter bondage endured by the Israelites in Egypt.

Does the Bible mention cats?

The cat is nowhere mentioned in the King James Version of the Bible. It is mentioned once (Chapter 4, Verse 21) in *Baruch,* which is accepted by the Roman Catholics but rejected by the Protestants. The original Hebrew text of that book has been lost and there is no indication what the Hebrew word translated *cat* was. Many commentators believe that the Hebrews had no such word in the time when the Old Testament was composed, and that the word so translated in *Baruch* referred to another animal. The cat apparently played no part in the lives of the Israelites. Although the domestic cat was familiar to the Egyptians from the dawn of history, it seems to have been unknown to the Assyrians and the Babylonians, and even to the Greeks and Romans, until after the conquest of Egypt. The common domesticated cat is believed to have sprung from the long-tailed wild cat of North Africa and to have been first tamed and domesticated by the Egyptians thousands of years before Christ. Perhaps several wild breeds were interbred with the original domesticated variety. At any rate, the cat has been domesticated for so many centuries that its wild progenitor can not be identified for certain. Among the ancient Egyptians the cat was a peculiarly sacred animal, and to kill one was a crime punishable by death. The historian Diodorus tells of a Roman ambassador who was put to death in Egypt for killing a cat. When a sacred cat died it was embalmed, placed in a case neatly carved and often inlaid with precious metals, and interred with elaborate funeral services. Hundreds of thousands of these cat mummies were discovered in a cat cemetery in the Beni Hassan grottoes in Egypt in 1890. They had laid there since the days of the Pharaohs, thousands of rows of them on shelves, each one in a neatly carved mummy case. Some of these cat corpses were carried away by neighboring villagers and some were sold to tourists as souvenirs after being stripped of their gold and jeweled ornaments. An interprising merchant of Alexandria shipped about 280,000 of them to England and they were sold at auction in Liverpool at about fifteen dollars a ton to be used as fertilizer. The species venerated by the ancient Egyptians is known as the Caffer cat (*Felis chaus*). One authority suggests that the Egyptians may have introduced the cat into their country from Nubia to the south and that the cat religion resulted from the services of this animal in controlling the hordes of field mice that otherwise would have destroyed all the grain in the delta of the Nile. But Herodotus tells us that virtually all animals were sacred to the Egyptians. The Hebrews must have come in contact with the cat during their long sojourn in Egypt. Since the cat was peculiarly sacred to the Egyptians, it is possible that the Israelites associated the animal with pagan idolatry and image worship and therefore looked upon it with disfavor. There is some evidence that the Greeks and Romans at first regarded the cat with disgust for similar reasons.

What language did Jesus speak?

It is generally supposed that the Galilean dialect of the Aramaic or Syriac language was the native tongue of Jesus, as well as of the twelve apostles, with the possible exception of Judas, who may have been a Judaean. Four principal languages were in use in Palestine in the time of Jesus—Hebrew, Aramaic, Greek and Latin. Hebrew, the original language of the ancient Israelites in which most of the Old Testament books were composed, began to pass out of use as the vernacular of the Jews after their dispersion by the Babylonians. *Aramaic* is derived from *Aram,* an old Semitic geographical term that was applied to Syria, Mesopotamia and adjacent regions, although it did not originally include Palestine. Aramaic was spoken by the northern Semitic groups and was closely related to Hebrew and Chaldean. It was probably introduced into Palestine in several ways. To some extent Aramaic was acquired by the Jews during their captivity in the East; it was the native tongue of the colonists whom the Babylonians settled in Samaria after the removal of the Israelites, and it was the prevailing language of most of the peoples with whom the early Israelites came into contact. It may have been the native tongue of

Abraham himself. For various reasons the march of Aramaic was from the East toward the West. Some time between the sixth and third centuries B.C. it gradually began to supplant Hebrew as the spoken language of the Jews. By the time of Augustus Caesar, Aramaic in one form or other had spread over all Palestine and was the everyday language of the Jews from Babylon to the River of Egypt. Naturally Aramaic in Palestine absorbed many Hebrew words and expressions, and by the time of Jesus the vernacular spoken by the Jews bore a relation to Hebrew somewhat similar to the relation that modern Yiddish bears to medieval German. Most Jews could no longer speak the language of the Old Testament, although Hebrew remained the literary, sacred and ritual language of the Jews. Even the sacred books themselves had been translated or paraphrased in the vulgar tongue. Aramaic continued to be the vernacular of Palestine and Syria until about the thirteenth century A.D., when it was almost completely displaced by Arabic, which is closely related to both Hebrew and Aramaic. The Galileans probably spoke Aramaic with a peculiar accent that distinguished them from the people in other parts of Palestine. In *Matthew 26:73* we read: "And after a while came unto him they that stood by, and said to Peter, Surely thou also art one of them; for thy speech betrayeth thee." There is no reason to suppose that Jesus spoke Latin, a language confined chiefly to the Romans. It is likely that he used the vernacular of the district and his mother tongue in speaking to his disciples and countrymen. In fact he would be obliged to do so in order to be understood. Some authorities suggest that Jesus may have also spoken Greek, which was then the "international" language of commerce and literature in the Roman Empire, of which Palestine was a part. Alexander the Great and his Macedonians had conquered Palestine in the fourth century B.C., and the Greeks had continued in authority there after a fashion until they were succeeded by the Romans under Pompey in 63 B.C. Greek was in everyday use in the eastern part of the Roman Empire during the first century A.D. and it was the common means of communication among different classes and nationalities. Presumably most of the upper-class Jews spoke Greek in addition to Hebrew and Aramaic. Since it is probable that Pilate spoke and understood only Latin and Greek, and since the Gospels mention no interpreter, some authorities infer that Greek was the language used at the trial of Jesus before the Roman procurator. There is nothing improbable in the supposition that Jesus had become acquainted with Greek in Galilee and that he may have replied to Pilate in that language. According to *Luke 23:38*, the inscription on the cross was in Greek, Latin and Hebrew so that all could read. Whether *Hebrew* there refers to Hebrew proper or to Aramaic is not clear, because the latter was generally referred to as Hebrew or the Hebrew vernacular, and consequently writers often confused the two languages. It should be borne in mind that Aramaic was written with Hebrew characters and in writing looked more like Hebrew than it actually was. Most of the allusions to Hebrew in the New Testament are really to Aramaic. Since Hebrew was not a spoken language at that time, there is every reason to believe that the *Hebrew* inscribed on the cross was Aramaic and not classical Hebrew. Although Greek was at that time spoken and read in Palestine and was understood by most persons of even an ordinary degree of intelligence in Jerusalem and the other larger cities, it does not seem probable that the simple fishermen and village folk of Galilee were familiar with Greek or any language other than Aramaic. Even if Jesus himself understood Greek it is not probable that his disciples and other listeners did. In *Luke 4:16-17* we are told that Jesus went into the synagogue at Nazareth and "stood up for to read." He then proceeded to read from the prophet Isaiah. Whether this particular synagogue copy of the Scriptures was written in Hebrew, Aramaic or Greek we have no means of knowing. Jesus may have read in any one of these languages, for the sacred writings were available at that time in all three of them. There is no direct evidence that Jesus ever wrote a line himself. The only reference to his writing is in *John 8* in connection with the incident of the woman taken in adultery. In *John 8:6* we are told: "But Jesus stooped down, and with his finger wrote on the ground, as though he heard them not." And *John 8:8*: "And again he stooped down, and wrote on the ground." This, however, suggests that Jesus may have merely made marks on the ground with his finger, a common practice in the Near East. The Gospels indicate that Jesus was reputed to be a man without formal schooling or education. *John 7:15* says: "And the Jews marvelled, saying, How knoweth this man letters, having never learned?" And yet, according to *Matthew 7:29*, "he taught them as one having authority, and not as the scribes."

Why does the Bible use *throughly* for *thoroughly*?

When the King James Version of the Bible was made *throughly* was the usual spelling of the word that we now spell *thoroughly*. For instance, in *Matthew 3:12*, John the Baptist is quoted as saying: "Whose fan is in his hand, and he will *throughly* purge his floor, and gather his wheat into the garner." In *II Corinthians 11:6* St. Paul says, "though I be rude in speech, yet not in knowledge; but we have been *throughly* made manifest among you in all things." Again in *II Timothy 3:17*: "That the man of God may be perfect, throughly furnished unto all good works." Originally *thorough* and *through* were merely variant spellings of the same word, but they have become completely differentiated in modern usage. Now *throughly* is regarded as archaic and in many modern printings of the Bible *thoroughly* is substituted for it. *Thoroughfare,* which literally means "through way," was formerly spelled *throughfare.*

How were Jesus and John the Baptist related?

In *Luke 1:36* the angel Gabriel, in speaking to Mary, is quoted as referring to Elizabeth as "thy cousin." If Elizabeth and Mary were first cousins, then their sons, John and Jesus, were second cousins. But the Greek word rendered *cousin* here probably means merely *kinswoman* or *relative* and it is rendered *kinswoman* in the Revised Version. Consequently the degree of relationship between Jesus and John the Baptist cannot be determined for certain. The account in *Luke 1* suggests that John the Baptist was six months older than Jesus. There is nothing in the Bible to indicate that Jesus and John were personally acquainted before Jesus went "from Galilee to Jordan unto John, to be baptized of him.'

Why was John the Baptist taken for Elijah?

The belief that the prophet Elijah would return to earth as the herald of the Messiah was based largely on *Malachi 4:5-6,* the last two verses in the Old Testament, which reads: "Behold, I will send you Elijah the prophet before the coming of the great and dreadful day of the Lord: and he shall turn the heart of the fathers to the children, and the heart of the children to their fathers, lest I come and smite the earth with a curse." The author of *Malachi* is believed to have lived during the Persian period about 450 B.C. Long before the birth of Jesus the belief that Elijah would return as the forerunner of the ideal king had become an integral part of the Messianic hope among the Jews. Elijah, one of the outstanding figures in the Old Testament, lived in the ninth century B.C. and was the prophet of zeal and fire and the worker of miracles. In the New Testament *Elijah* occurs as *Elias*. According to *Luke 1:17,* the angel Gabriel told Zacharias that his unborn son John should go before the Lord "in the spirit and power of Elias, to turn the hearts of the fathers to the children, and the disobedient to the wisdom of the just; to make ready a people prepared for the Lord." References to John's raiment of camel's hair, the leathern girdle about his loins, and his meat of locusts and wild honey, are an obvious attempt to portray the Baptist as a "second Elijah." When the Jews sent priests and Levites from Jerusalem to ask John whether he was Elias, according to *John 1:21*, he answered, "I am not" and "No." But *Matthew 11:14* quotes Jesus as saying, after he had referred to John as the messenger of whom the prophets had spoken: "And if ye will receive it, this is Elias, which was for to come." *Luke 9:7-9* tells us that Herod the tetrarch, after he had beheaded John the Baptist, was perplexed "because that it was said of some, that John was risen from the dead; and of some, that Elias had appeared." Jesus himself seems to have been mistaken by some to be Elias. When Jesus asked his disciples, "Whom say the people that I am?", they answered: "John the Baptist; but some say, Elias; and others say, that one of the old prophets is risen again." *Matthew 17:1-3* says: "And after six days Jesus taketh Peter, James, and John his brother, and bringeth them up into an high mountain apart, and was transfigured before them: and his face did shine as the sun, and his raiment was white as the light. And, behold, there appeared unto them Moses and Elias talking with him." Later in the same chapter the disciples asked Jesus: "Why then say the scribes that Elias must first come?" Jesus replied: "Elias truly shall first come, and restore all things. But I say unto you, that Elias is come already, and they knew him not, but have done unto him whatsoever they listed." The author of the gospel adds: "Then the disciples understood that he spake unto them of John the Baptist." This suggests that Jesus looked upon John as the reincarnation of Elijah. Even at the crucifixion Elijah was in the minds of many present. *Matthew 27:46-49* says: "And about the ninth hour Jesus cried with a loud voice, saying Eli, Eli, lama sabachthani? that is to say, My God, my God, why hast thou forsaken me? Some of them that stood there, when they heard that, said, This man calleth for Elias. And straightway one of them ran, and took a spunge, and filled it with vinegar, and put it on a reed, and gave him to drink. The rest said, Let be, let us see whether Elias will come to save him."

Does the Bible say Herodias' daughter was named Salome?

Nowhere in the Bible is it said that *Salome* was the name of the daughter of Herodias who, instructed by her mother, requested of Herod and received the head of John the Baptist in a charger as the reward for her dancing. The Scriptural accounts do not give the name of Herodias' daughter, referring to her simply as "the damsel."

Matthew 14:3-11 says: "For Herod had laid hold on John, and bound him, and put him in prison for Herodias' sake, his brother Philip's wife. For John said unto him, It is not lawful for thee to have her. And when he would have put him to death, he feared the multitude, because they counted him as a prophet. But when Herod's birthday was kept, the daughter of Herodias danced before them, and pleased Herod. Whereupon he promised with an oath to give her whatsoever she would ask. And she, being before instructed of her mother, said, Give me here John Baptist's head in a charger. And the king was sorry: nevertheless for the oath's sake, and them which sat with him at meat, he commanded it to be given her. And he sent, and beheaded John in the prison. And his head was brought in a charger, and given to the damsel: and she brought it to her mother." Of this same event *Mark 6:17-28* says: "For Herod himself had sent forth and laid hold upon John, and bound him in prison for Herodias' sake, his brother Philip's wife: for he had married her. For John had said unto Herod, It is not lawful for thee to have thy brother's wife. Therefore Herodias had a quarrel against him, and would have killed him; but she could not: for Herod feared John, knowing that he was a just man and an holy, and observed him; and when he heard him, he did many things, and heard him gladly. And when a convenient day was come, that Herod on his birthday made a supper to his lords, high captains, and chief estates of Galilee; and when the daughter of the said Herodias came in, and danced, and pleased Herod, and them that sat with him, the king said unto the damsel, Ask me whatsoever thou wilt, and I will give it thee. And he sware unto her, Whatsoever thou shalt ask of me, I will give it thee, unto the half of my kingdom. And she went forth, and said unto her mother, What shall I ask? And she said, The head of John the Baptist. And she came in straightway with haste unto the king, and asked, saying, I will that thou give me by and by in a charger the head of John the Baptist. And the king was exceeding sorry; yet for his oath's sake, and for their sakes which sat with him, he would not reject her. And immediately the king sent an executioner, and commanded his head to be brought: and he went and beheaded him in the prison, and brought his head in a charger, and gave it to the damsel: and the damsel gave it to her mother." Luke and John do not mention the incident. It is not from the Bible, but from the Jewish historian Josephus that we learn Herodias had a daughter named Salome by her first husband, who was Herod's brother Philip. This Salome first married her first cousin and step-brother, Herod Philip, tetrarch of Ituraea, and afterwards became the wife of

Aristobulus, king of Chalcis. It is merely a conjecture that she was the damsel who asked for the head of John the Baptist. Some authorities, however, suppose that damsel to have been Herod Antipas's own daughter and that she bore the same name as her mother, Herodias. There was a woman named Salome mentioned in *Mark 15:40* and *16:1* as being present at the crucifixion and visiting the sepulchre on the morning of the resurrection. A comparison of the parallel passage of *Matthew 27:56* indicates that this Salome was the wife of Zebedee and the mother of the apostles James and John.

Who said soldiers should be content with their wages?

Although the quotation is often attributed to Jesus, it was John the Baptist who told the soldiers to be content with their wages. According to *Luke 3:14*, when the soldiers asked what they should do, John said to them: "Do violence to no man, neither accuse any falsely; and be content with your wages."

Did John the Baptist found a religious sect?

There is reason for supposing that John the Baptist made a greater impression on his contemporaries than even Jesus did. He remained a power in Judaea after his death and many of his followers continued to baptize in his name. Some of John's disciples joined Jesus, but others appear to have perpetuated the teachings of John independently of the followers of Jesus. According to *John 1*, when John baptized Jesus and proclaimed him the Messiah two of his disciples followed Jesus. One of these was Andrew, Simon Peter's brother, and the other is believed to have been John, the disciple whom Jesus loved. Later, however, *John 4:1* tells us: "Jesus made and baptized more disciples than John." Some authorities think that a sect composed of the followers of John the Baptist continued to exist along the Jordan for generations after their leader's death. They were known as *Sabians*, a word of Aramaic origin meaning "to immerse" or "to baptize." That the influence of John the Baptist did not die with him is indicated by *Acts 18:24-25*, where we learn that an Alexandrian Jew named Apollos, "an eloquent man, and mighty in the scriptures," knew "only the baptism of John." At Ephesus, according to *Acts 19:2-3*, some twelve disciples told Paul that they had not "so much as heard whether there be any Holy Ghost" and said they had been baptized "unto John's baptism." The earliest reference to John the Baptist in any writing outside the Bible is in Josephus's *Antiquities of the Jews*, written about 95 A.D. The historian of the Jews said: "Now some of the Jews thought that the destruction of Herod's army came from God, and that very justly, as a punishment of what he did against John, that was called the Baptist; for Herod slew him, who was a good man, and commanded the Jews to exercise virtue, both as to righteousness toward one another, and piety toward God, and so to come to baptism; for that the washing would be acceptable to him, if they made use of it, not in order to the putting away of some sins, but for the purification of the body, supposing still that the soul was thoroughly purified beforehand by righteousness. Now when others came in crowds about him, for they were very greatly moved by hearing his words, Herod, who feared lest the great influence John had over the people might put it into his power and inclination to raise a rebellion, for they seemed ready to do any thing he should advise, thought it best, by putting him to death, to prevent any mischief he might cause, and not bring himself into difficulties, by sparing a man who might make him repent of it when it should be too late. Accordingly he was sent a prisoner, out of Herod's suspicious temper, to Macherus, the castle I before mentioned, and was there put to death. Now the Jews had an opinion that the destruction of the army was sent as a punishment upon Herod, and a mark of God's displeasure to him."

Did John the Baptist eat insects?

"And the same John," says *Matthew 3:4*, "had his raiment of camel's hair, and a leathern girdle about his loins; and his meat was locusts and wild honey." This is clearly a reference to *I Kings 1:8*, where Elijah the Tishbite is described as "an hairy man, and girt with a girdle of leather about his loins." The author of *Matthew* merely emphasized the fact that John the Baptist dressed simply, ate humble fare and lived close to nature like the prophets of old. His raiment of camel's hair may have been either a robe of camel's skin or cloth woven from camel's hair, which would be a humble habit compared with the luxurious robes of soft wool worn by the fashionable and great of the time. The wild honey that he ate may have been either true honey made by wild bees in the crevices of the rocks and in hollow trees, or the sticky, sugary liquid popularly known as tree-manna or honeydew, which is excreted by aphids or plant lice and deposited on certain plants, or which is exuded by the leaves themselves. Enough has been written to make a sizable volume on the question whether the locusts eaten by John the Baptist were insects or vegetable matter of some kind. Some Bible commentators suppose the locusts referred to in *Matthew 3:4* were the pods of the carob or locust tree which contain a sweetish pulp and are used as food for stock and are sometimes eaten by man. Hence these pods are popularly called St. John's bread. The evidence, however, tends to support the belief that the locusts eaten by John the Baptist were insects resembling grasshoppers. It seems improbable that honey would be eaten with the locust bean, which is itself very sweet. There are many species of migratory locusts or grasshoppers in Palestine and adjacent regions. In that part of the world locusts migrate in myriads and eat up every green thing in their path. Their ravages in southwestern Asia and northeastern Africa are so notable that the insects have become the symbol of famine, plague and destruction. Covering the land with locusts was one of the ten plagues of Egypt in the time of Moses. The Greek word translated *locust* in the New Testament is *akris,* the plural of which is *akrides,* and does not mean the fruit of a tree but a species of insect. Locusts and grasshoppers were classed in the law of Moses among the flying creeping things that might be eaten by the Israelites. *Leviticus 11:22* says: "Even these of them ye may eat; the locust after his kind, and the bald locust after his kind, and the beetle after his kind, and the grasshopper after his kind." Oddly enough, however, there is no reference in the Old Testament to the actual eating of locusts or grasshoppers. Several different Hebrew words there are rendered *locust* in English translations. There is nothing startling in the statement that the locusts eaten by John the Baptist were insects. Locusts are widely eaten today in many parts of the world and even considered a delicacy in some places. They daily appear in the markets of Arabia, Syria, Egypt, Madagascar, China, India, Iraq and Iran. In the Near East they are particularly eaten by the poor in time of famine or food shortage. There the locusts are preserved in brine or dried in the sun and exported as an article of commerce. The insects are usually caught in the early morning when the dew is heavy and the air chilly. Under such conditions the insects can be literally shoveled into baskets. After the wings and the long hopping legs are removed the locusts are dipped in salt. They are then roasted, fried, stewed, mixed with flour and pounded fine, or boiled in water. It is said that the Bedouins string locusts together and eat them with unleavened cake and butter or oil while on their journeys over the desert. Travelers report that in Arabia where locusts form an important part of the diet the dish is quite palatable. David Livingstone, who ate locusts with the natives of Africa, pronounced them superior to shrimp. Although the Jews and Christians in Palestine do not now eat locusts, as the Bedouins do in time of food scarcity, they may have done so in ancient times. John the Baptist, who was an ascetic, probably ate locusts in imitation of the Arabs on the skirt of the desert "beyond Jordan." Honey is still often eaten with locusts, as it was in the day of John the Baptist. The ancient Greeks called some of the Ethiopian tribes *Acridophagi,* because they ate locusts. Herodotus, referring to the Masamonians, "a numerous people" in western North Africa, wrote: "They also chase the locusts, and, when caught, dry them in the sun, after which they grind them to powder, and, sprinkling this upon their milk, so drink it." In China locusts are candied. It is not necessary to search in foreign lands for people who eat locusts. Grasshoppers played an important part in the diet of many American Indian tribes, especially on the Pacific Coast and in the arid regions of the West. Even the Pawnees, during the grasshopper season, would dig a hole on the prairie and then start a fire around it at a distance of several hundred yards. Grasshoppers could be scooped from the hole by the bushel. As a rule the Indians dried the insects, pounded them into meal and mixed them with vegetable products to make a sort of cake or bread. As a matter of fact, not only locusts but hundreds of different species of insects have been, and still are, eaten by different peoples in different parts of the world.

Was Jesus descended from David?

The New Testament clearly represents Jesus as a descendant of David. Prophecy foretold that the Messiah would be a descendant of David and "the Son of David" had been the accepted title of the Messiah among the Jews for generations. In the Gospels Jesus is frequently referred to as the Son of David. *Matthew 1:18* says: "Now the birth of Jesus Christ was on this wise: When as his mother Mary was espoused to Joseph, before they came together, she was found with child of the Holy Ghost." *Luke 3:23* refers to Jesus as "being (as was supposed) the son of Joseph." Since Joseph was not the blood father of Jesus, the inference is that Mary as well as Joseph "was of the house and lineage of David," although the New Testament nowhere says so specifically. *Luke 1:27* says the angel Gabriel was sent "to a virgin espoused to a man whose name was Joseph, of the house of David; and the virgin's name was Mary." This, however, may refer to the genealogy of Joseph rather than of Mary. But in *Romans 1:3* Paul says Jesus "was made of the seed of David according to the flesh." According to *Luke 1:32,* Gabriel told Mary that the Lord would give unto her son "the throne of his father David," and *Revelation 22:16* refers to Jesus as "the root and the offspring of David." The Davidic descent of Mary has been assumed since Apostolic times and the passages quoted indicate that Jesus was descended from David through his mother. Among the Israelites it was customary to trace descent only through the male line, and the supposition that Jesus was born of a virgin presented difficulties to the authors of the Gospels when they came to give his genealogy. The genealogies in both *Matthew 1* and *Luke 3* trace the descent of Joseph from David, but neither includes the genealogy of Mary. That in *Matthew* closes with: "And Jacob begat Joseph the husband of Mary, of whom was born Jesus, who is called Christ."

Why doesn't the Christian Era begin on Christmas?

The Christian Era theoretically begins with the birth of Jesus, but the calendar year begins January 1 instead of December 25, the traditional birthday of Jesus. This anomalous situation is due to the fact that the Christian Era was not calculated until the sixth century and was not generally accepted in Christendom until about the year 1000. Consequently the beginning of the Era was projected into the past. The Romans reckoned time from the legendary date of the founding of Rome. The starting point in Roman chronology was *Anno Urbis Conditae* (A.U.C.), which literally means "in the year of the founded city." About 532 A.D., after Christianity had become dominant in the old Roman Empire, a learned monk of Rome named Dionysius Exiguus worked out a Christian system of chronology to take the place of the then prevalent pagan system. He concluded that Jesus was born December 25, 753 A.U.C. During the first centuries of Christianity there was little uniformity in the date observed as the nativity. Christmas (*Christ-mass*) was first celebrated on December 25 in Rome about 350 A.D. But this was regarded as a legendary rather than an exact date and Christmas was observed on different days in different parts of Christendom. Logically Dionysius should have begun the new Era with December 25, but he decided to begin it with January 1 because he wanted to leave the Roman year and months intact and did not want to upset and confuse the established and accepted chronology. Accordingly he began the Christian Era with the first day in 754 A.U.C. His system was adopted gradually and did not completely supplant the old system in the Western World until about 1000 A.D. Emperor Charles III of Germany was the first sovereign to adopt the new system of chronology. In 879 A.D. he adopted *Anno Domini*, "in the year of the Lord," and that in the course of centuries became the accepted mode of designating the year in all Christian countries. Modern scholars believe Dionysius was off several years in fixing the date of the birth of Jesus and consequently we have the anomalous situation of Christ's having been born at least four or five years before the date beginning the Era that bears his name. After the Christian calendar and the Christian Era had become firmly established, with December 25 as Christmas, it was found impractical to change it and to upset the entire system of historical chronology. As a matter of fact, the Christian world is not yet in agreement even on the traditional date of the birth of Jesus. While Roman Catholics and Protestants generally observe Christmas on December 25, Orthodox Greek Catholics observe it on January 6 and the Armenian church on January 19. The epoch beginning with the birth of Jesus is often called the Common Era, particularly by orthodox Jews, who are compelled to recognize it for practical purposes but who object to referring to it as the Christian Era on the ground that such notice might be interpreted as a recognition of its founder. Strict Jews who use the Christian date seldom add the letters A.D. At least that was formerly true. The Jewish calendar reckons time from the year 3761 B.C., the traditional date of creation. This calendar, which assumed its present form in the fourth century A.D. in the time of Hillel II, is based on the motions of both the sun and the moon and in consequence the Jewish New Year and other holidays, festivals and fasts do not fall on the same date each year according to the Gregorian calendar. Although Christmas is a fixed date in the Christian calendar, Easter and certain other church days are variable dates and are determined somewhat after the manner of the Jewish calendar.

How much older than Mary was Joseph?

The age of neither Mary nor Joseph is given in the Bible. The common belief that Joseph was considerably older than Mary is only a general inference from the Gospel narratives and is not based upon any particular passage. That Mary was quite young when she was espoused to Joseph was undoubtedly suggested by an association of two facts: in Palestine girls matured rather young and were generally married in their middle teens, and *virgin* is used in the English Bible to render Hebrew and Greek words meaning a young unmarried woman. The authors of the Gospels related *Isaiah 7:14* to Jesus as the Messiah foretold in the Old Testament. That verse reads: "Therefore the Lord himself shall give you a sign; Behold, a virgin shall conceive, and bear a son, and shall call his name Immanuel." The Hebrew word translated *virgin* in this passage is *almah,* the root of which signifies "mature." It was applied by Hebrew writers simply to a young woman of marriageable age without any reference to her being married or not. If the author of *Isaiah 7:14* had wished to convey the idea that Immanuel was to be born of a virgin in our sense of the term he could have employed *bethulah,* the root of which signifies "separated" and which imparts definitely the idea of virginity. Although Mary is mentioned as being still alive at the time of the crucifixion, Joseph is not again mentioned after the time that Jesus at the age of twelve was lost from his parents among the crowds in the temple at Jerusalem. It is presumed that Joseph was already dead when Jesus began his public ministry.

Was Jesus born in a manger?

There is nothing in the Bible to justify the popular belief that Jesus was actually born in a manger. Allusions to the place of the nativity of Jesus are few and obscure in the Scriptures. *Matthew 2:11* says that when the wise men "were come into the *house,* they saw the young child with Mary his mother, and fell down, and worshipped him." *Manger* is used three times in *Luke.* In Chapter 2, Verse 7, we read: "And she brought forth her first-born son, and wrapped him in swaddling clothes, and laid him in a manger; because there was no room for them in the inn." According to *Luke 2:12* the angel said to the shepherds: "Ye shall find the babe wrapped in swaddling clothes, lying in a manger." *Luke 2:16* says: "And they came with haste, and found Mary, and Joseph, and the babe lying in a manger." A manger, properly speaking, is a trough or box from which domestic animals eat. The Greek word rendered *manger* in the passages quoted above is derived from a verb meaning "to eat" and literally means "feeding-place." Some authorities suppose that the manger in which Mary laid her child was in the court of an inn or caravansary. The typical Near Eastern inn of that day consisted of a rude, unfurnished shelter surrounding a court in which the camels, horses and other beasts of burden were picketed. It should be noted that the Bible nowhere mentions a stable in this connection. Pictures representing the wise men worshiping Jesus in a stable surrounded by cattle and horses are not based on Scripture. A local tradition dating back at least to the second century places the manger and nativity in a grotto or cave near Bethlehem. In 165 A.D. St. Justin wrote: "Having failed to find any lodging in the town, Joseph sought shelter in a neighboring cavern of Bethlehem." About half a century later the celebrated ecclesiastical writer Origen declared that "at Bethlehem is shown the grotto where he first saw the light." This grotto, it is supposed, was used as a shelter by the shepherds and their flocks. St. Helena, mother of Constantine the Great, identified a grotto near Bethlehem as the birthplace of Jesus and had it converted into a chapel. Later a basilica was erected over the grotto.

What is the doctrine of Immaculate Conception?

Many people confuse the doctrine of Immaculate Conception with that of the Virgin Birth. These two doctrines are entirely different. Although *Virgin Birth* does not occur in the Bible, the doctrine described by the phrase is founded on Biblical passages and refers to the fact that Jesus was miraculously begotten of God and born of a virgin mother. In *Matthew I* we read: "Now the birth of Jesus Christ was on this wise: When as his mother Mary was espoused to Joseph, before they came together, she was found with child of the Holy Ghost." In the same chapter it is related that the angel of the Lord appeared to Joseph in a dream, saying: "Joseph, thou son of David, fear not to take unto thee Mary thy wife: for that which is conceived in her is of the Holy Ghost." *Luke 1:34-35* says: "Then said Mary unto the angel, How shall this be, seeing I know not a man? And the angel answered and said unto her, The Holy Ghost shall come upon thee, and the power of the Highest shall overshadow thee: therefore also that holy thing which shall be born of thee shall be called the Son of God." "Then," according to *Matthew 1:24-25*, "Joseph being raised from sleep did as the angel of the Lord had bidden him, and took unto him his wife: and knew her not till she had brought forth her firstborn son: and he called his name Jesus." "Now all this was done," says *Matthew 1:22-23*, "that it might be fulfilled which was spoken of the Lord by the prophet, saying, Behold, a virgin shall be with child, and shall bring forth a son, and they shall call his name Emmanuel, which being interpreted is, God with us." The quotation is from *Isaiah 7:14*, which reads, "Therefore the Lord himself shall give you a sign; Behold, a virgin shall conceive, and bear a son, and shall call his name Emmanuel," and which the Jews probably did not regard as Messianic but which the author of *Matthew* took to be applicable to the Messiah. The Immaculate Conception, on the other hand, in no way concerns the birth of Jesus, but the conception of the Virgin Mary by her mother, whose name is not given in the Bible but which traditionally was Anna. The doctrine of the Immaculate Conception holds that the Virgin Mary, by a singular privilege and grace granted by God, was preserved exempt and immaculate from all stain of original sin. All other descendants of Adam, save only Jesus, have been born with original sin on their souls. Mary, according to this doctrine, was immune from original sin at the moment her soul was created and infused into her body. The doctrine does not refer to Mary's physical conception by her parents, who had the usual part in the formation of her body. The Immaculate Conception of the Virgin Mary was a subject of controversy for about six hundred years. Finally, in 1854, it was proclaimed a Catholic article of faith by Pope Pius IX.

Is Nazareth mentioned in the Old Testament?

The Old Testament does not mention Nazareth, where Jesus spent most of his childhood, all of his youth and most of his manhood. It is believed that in the time of Jesus the village of Nazareth was inhabited chiefly by Samaritans. Both Joseph and Mary lived there before their espousal. *Luke 1:26-27* says: "And in the sixth month the angel Gabriel was sent from God unto a city of Galilee, named Nazareth, to a virgin espoused to a man whose name was Joseph, of the house of David; and the virgin's name was Mary." *Luke 2:3-5* says: "And all went to be taxed, every one into his own city. And Joseph also went up from Galilee, out of the city of Nazareth, into Judaea, unto the city of David, which is called Bethlehem; (because he was of the house and lineage of David:) to be taxed with Mary his espoused wife, being great with child." In *Matthew 2:22-23* we are told that after Joseph returned from Egypt to the land of Israel with the young child and his mother and heard "that Archelaus did reign in Judaea in the room of his father Herod, he was afraid to go thither: notwithstanding, being warned of God in a dream, he turned aside into the parts of Galilee: and he came and dwelt in a city called Nazareth: that it might be fulfilled which was spoken by the prophets, He shall be called a Nazarene." This passage indicates that Joseph and Mary had originally intended to settle at Bethlehem or elsewhere in Judaea. No prophecy saying that the Messiah should be called a Nazarene is found in the Old Testament. Some Jewish authorities suppose *Nazarene* here to be merely a play upon one of two Hebrew words translated *Branch,* a term applied by the old prophets to the Messiah. *Jeremiah 23:5* says: "Behold, the days come, saith the Lord, that I will raise unto David a righteous Branch, and a King shall reign and prosper, and shall execute judgment and justice in the earth." And in

Isaiah 11:1 we read: "And there shall come forth a rod out of the stem of Jesse, and a Branch shall grow out of his roots." At any rate, in consequence of the decision made by Joseph and Mary, their first-born child came to be known as "Jesus of Nazareth." *Nazarene* occurs nowhere again in the King James Version of the New Testament except in *Acts 24:5*, where a certain orator named Tertullus, in his accusation against Paul before Felix at Jerusalem, is quoted as saying: "For we have found this man a pestilent fellow, and a mover of sedition among all the Jews throughout the world, and a ring-leader of the sect of the Nazarenes." It is merely the common rendering of the Greek word translated elsewhere as "of Nazareth." For some unknown reason Nazareth appears to have been held in contempt in the time of Jesus, for *John 1:46* says: "And Nathanael said unto him, Can there any good thing come out of Nazareth? Philip saith unto him, Come and see." *Nazarene* and *Nazarite* are often confused. Nazarite occurs frequently in the Old Testament. It is from a Hebrew word meaning "to dedicate" or "consecrate." Among the Israelites a Nazarite was a devotee or consecrated person, man or woman, who was prohibited from drinking wine, cutting the hair or touching a corpse. The conditions of being a Nazarite were subject to minute regulations. Although the term itself does not occur in the New Testament, it is supposed that both John the Baptist and St. Paul took the vows of a Nazarite. It is barely possible that the reference to Jesus in *Matthew 2:23*, "He shall be called a Nazarene," is a mistake for, "He shall be called a Nazarite."

Were the shepherds and wise men the same persons?

Some authorities incline toward the opinion that the shepherds who visited the new-born Jesus were the same persons as the wise men who came from the East. Only *Matthew* records the story of the wise men, and only *Luke* records the story of the shepherds. *Mark* and *John* refer to neither the shepherds nor the wise men. *Luke 2:8-20* says: "And there were in the same country shepherds abiding in the field, keeping watch over their flock by night. And, lo, the angel of the Lord came upon them, and the glory of the Lord shone round about them: and they were sore afraid. And the angel said unto them, Fear not: for, behold, I bring you good tidings of great joy, which shall be to all people. For unto you is born this day in the city of David a Saviour, which is Christ the Lord. And this shall be a sign unto you; ye shall find the babe wrapped in swaddling clothes, lying in a manger. And suddenly there was with the angel a multitude of the heavenly host praising God, and saying, Glory to God in the highest, and on earth peace, good will toward men. And it came to pass, as the angels were gone away from them into heaven, the shepherds said one to another, Let us now go even unto Bethlehem, and see this thing which is come to pass, which the Lord hath made known unto us. And they came with haste, and found Mary, and Joseph, and the babe lying in a manger. And when they had seen it, they made known abroad the saying which was told them concerning this child. And all they that heard it wondered at those things which were told them by the shepherds. But Mary kept all these things, and pondered them in her heart. And the shepherds returned, glorifying and praising God for all the things that they had heard and seen, as it was told unto them." This passage, the only information we have about the shepherds who visited the new-born Jesus, has many points in common with the story of the wise men related in *Matthew 2:1-12*. Although some authorities regard the two as merely different versions of the same event, there is not sufficient evidence to establish the conclusion that these shepherds and the wise men were the same persons. The conventional opinion is that they were not the same.

What was the slaughter of the innocents?

The slaughter (or *massacre*) *of the innocents* is the popular name given to the destruction of the infants by order of Herod the king in his attempt to destroy the young child Jesus, who was saved by being taken secretly into Egypt by Joseph and Mary. The phrase itself occurs nowhere in the Bible, and the incident is related only in *Matthew 2:16-18,* which reads: "Then Herod, when he saw that he was mocked of the wise men, was exceeding wroth, and sent forth, and slew all the children that were in Bethlehem, and in all the coasts thereof, from two years old and under, according to the time which he had diligently inquired of the wise men. Then was fulfilled that which was spoken by Jeremy the prophet, saying, in Rama was there a voice heard, lamentation, and weeping for her children, and would not be comforted, because they are not." That is the only information we have on the subject. There is no reference whatever to this act of Herod in the history and records of the time. Even Josephus, in his long, rather detailed and unfavorable accounts of the life of Herod the Great, does not mention it. It is particularly strange that Josephus would omit all reference to this cruel and brutal act when he takes such great pains to record so many barbarous enormities committed by Herod. Although it is remarkable that the Roman authorities would have permitted the puppet king of Judaea to commit such a wholesale slaughter of children, it is not doubted that Herod was capable of such cruelty and brutality. At the time he had, with the permission of Rome, put three of his own sons to death, was virtually insane, and was extremely suspicious of any person who might be mentioned as a possible successor to him as King of the Jews. Contrary to a popular notion, the Biblical account does not say that the destruction was limited to male children. It merely says "all the children that were in Bethlehem, and in all the coasts thereof, from two years old and under." "In Bethlehem, and in all the coasts thereof" probably means that Herod's order applied only to a district around Bethlehem rather than all Judaea. Throughout the centuries various commentators have "estimated" the number of children destroyed by Herod all the way from 144,000 to only a dozen or fifteen. Of course, there is no information whatever on which to base such figures and they are meaningless guesses. Since all the children "from two years old and under" were destroyed, some authorities suppose this act of barbarity was committed about two years after the birth of Jesus. At an early date the Christian church recognized these innocent children slain by order of Herod as the first Christian martyrs, and Holy Innocents' Day, or Childermas as it is called in England, is observed as a festival in the Roman Catholic church on December 28 and in the Greek Orthodox church on December 29 (O.S.) in commemoration of the massacre of the Holy Innocents. Childermas, according to an old superstition, is the unluckiest day in the entire year. Centuries ago the superstitious never married on Childermas-day. The coronation of Edward IV in 1461 was postponed a day to avoid having it fall upon this day of ill omen. Children were whipped in bed by their parents early on the morning of Holy Innocents' Day to impress upon them with actual pain the horror of Herod's massacre of the infants. Processions of children marched through the streets and recited verses commemorating the event. In Great Britain *slaughter of the innocents* is applied facetiously in Parliamentary circles to the bills left over at the end of a session for want of time to take them up.

Who were the Three Wise Men from the East?

The names, number and nationality of the wise men from the East who followed the star of the new-born Jesus to Jerusalem and Bethlehem are not given in the Bible. This beautiful story is told in *Matthew 2:1-12*: "Now when Jesus was born in Bethlehem of Judaea in the days of Herod the king, behold, there came wise men from the east to

Jerusalem, saying, Where is he that is born King of the Jews? for we have seen his star in the east, and are come to worship him. When Herod the king had heard these things, he was troubled, and all Jerusalem with him. And when he had gathered all the chief priests and scribes of the people together, he demanded of them where Christ should be born. And they said unto him, In Bethlehem of Judaea: for thus it is written by the prophet, and thou Bethlehem, in the land of Juda, art not the least among the princes of Juda: for out of thee shall come a Governor, that shall rule my people Israel. Then Herod, when he had privily called the wise men, inquired of them diligently what time the star appeared. And he sent them to Bethlehem, and said, Go and search diligently for the young child; and when ye have found him, bring me word again, that I may come and worship him also. When they had heard the king, they departed; and, lo, the star, which they saw in the east, went before them, till it came and stood over where the young child was. When they saw the star, they rejoiced with exceeding great joy. And when they were come into the house, they saw the young child with Mary his mother, and fell down, and worshipped him: and when they had opened their treasures, they presented unto him gifts; gold, frankincense, and myrrh. And being warned of God in a dream that they should not return to Herod, they departed into their own country another way." That is all the information there is in the Bible about the wise men. Early writers fixed their number at three, probably because three gifts are mentioned. A legend, apparently dating from the second or third century, refers to them as kings. Later legends give them names—Gasper (white), Melchior (light) and Balthasar (lord of the treasury house). Many Bible scholars suppose the three wise men to have been Magi, members of a priestly caste in Persia. This opinion is supported by two circumstances: in Palestine *the east* generally referred to Persia; and the religion of the Magi, which was similar to that of Zoroaster, included belief in the advent of a messiah. The book of travels dictated by Marco Polo about 1299 A.D. contains the following interesting reference to this subject: "In Persia there is a city that is called Saba, whence were the three Magi who came to adore Christ in Bethlehem; and the three are buried in that city in a fair sepulchre, and they all three are entire with their beards and hair. One was called Balthasar, the second Gasper, and the third Melchior. Marco inquired often in that city concerning the three Magi, and nobody could tell him anything about them, except that the three Magi were buried there in ancient times." A medieval legend speaks of them as "the three kings of Cologne." According to this legend, Helena, the mother of Constantine the Great, discovered the bones of the Magi in Persia and took them to Constantinople. In 1162 the Emperor Frederick Barbarossa took them from Milan to the Cologne cathedral where the skulls have been exhibited for many centuries. The names of the three kings were widely used as a charm, and it was believed that those who touched the bones would be healed of all diseases.

Does the Bible say Jesus was a carpenter?

The popular impression is that Jesus was a carpenter by trade and that he spent his youth and early manhood working in his father's carpenter shop. There is only one reference in the Bible indicating that Jesus, like Joseph, was himself a carpenter, and that reference may be owing to a mistake in the text. In connection with a visit made by Jesus to Nazareth, *Mark 6:2-3* says: "And when the sabbath day was come, he began to teach in the synagogue: and many hearing him were astonished, saying, From whence hath this man these things? and what wisdom is this which is given unto him, that even such mighty works are wrought by his hands? Is not this the carpenter, the son of Mary, the brother of James, and Joses, and of Juda, and Simon? and are not his sisters here with us? And they were offended at him." But in *Matthew 13:55-56,* where the same incident is apparently referred to, the old neighbors of Jesus ask: "Is not this the carpenter's son? is not his mother called Mary? and his brethren, James, and Joses, and Simon, and Judas? And his sisters, are they not all with us?" These are the only references in the entire Bible about Jesus and Joseph being carpenters. The natural inference is that Joseph ran a carpenter shop and that Jesus worked with him. All indications are that Joseph died long before Jesus started out on his public ministry. Perhaps Jesus and his young brothers continued to work in the shop after the father's death. Apparently Jesus was still making his home at Nazareth when he went down to the Jordan to be baptized by John, for *Matthew 4:12-13* says: "Now when Jesus had heard that John was cast into prison, he departed into Galilee; and leaving Nazareth, he came and dwelt in Capernaum." This is further confirmed by the fact that his mother and brethren went with him when he removed from Nazareth to Capernaum. *John 2:12* says: "After this he went down to Capernaum, he, and his mother, and his brethren, and his disciples: and they continued there not many days." This seems to answer the oft-asked question as to what Jesus did between the time he was twelve until he began to be about thirty years old. That Jesus was reared in the home of his parents is indicated by *Luke 2*, which, after relating the incident of the twelve-year-old boy being left behind in the temple, tells us that Jesus went down with his parents to Nazareth, "and was subject to them." It is probable that at that time there was very little building in a village like Nazareth and that most of the work of a carpenter consisted in repairing houses and in making household and farm implements such as tables, benches, cabinets, wooden plows and yokes. The parable of the men who built houses on a rock and on the sand may have been suggested by the experience of Jesus as a carpenter.

How long did Jesus live in Egypt?

Nothing whatever is positively known about the sojourn of Jesus in Egypt except what is related in *Matthew*. It is not referred to in the other three Gospels or elsewhere in the New Testament. *Matthew 2:13-15* says: "And when they [the wise men] were departed, behold, the angel of the Lord appeareth to Joseph in a dream, saying, Arise, and take the young child and his mother, and flee into Egypt, and be thou there until I bring thee word: for Herod will seek the young child to destroy him. When he arose, he took the young child and his mother by night, and departed into Egypt: and was there until the death of Herod: that it might be fulfilled which was spoken of the Lord by the prophet, saying, Out of Egypt have I called my son." Again in *Matthew 2:19-22* we are told: "But when Herod was dead, behold, an angel of the Lord appeareth in a dream to Joseph in Egypt, saying, Arise, and take the young child and his mother, and go into the land of Israel: for they are dead which sought the young child's life. And he arose, and took the young child and his mother, and came into the land of Israel. But when he heard that Archelaus did reign in Judaea in the room of his father Herod, he was afraid to go thither: notwithstanding, being warned of God in a dream, he turned aside into the parts of Galilee." The prophecy referred to in *Matthew* is generally supposed to be from *Hosea 11:1*, which reads: "When Israel was a child, then I loved him, and called my son out of Egypt." If this is correct, it could be no more than a figurative or symbolical application, because Hosea obviously was making a simple historical allusion to the deliverance of the Israelites from Egypt. But the author of *Matthew* seems to be motivated by the conception of Jesus as "the second Moses" or "a prophet like unto Moses" and in his narrative there are several parallels between the life of Jesus and the Moses epic. Some authorities reject the story of the journey of Jesus into

Egypt as factual history and regard it merely as an attempt by the author of *Matthew* to fit his narrative to supposed Old Testament predictions. Bible scholars who accept the story as factual history have estimated the length of the sojourn of Jesus in Egypt from a few months to several years. The Bible does not answer this question and there are no other sources on the subject. Many authorities have questioned the authenticity of the account in *Matthew* on the ground that it is improbable. But there is nothing improbable in the story itself. Previously Palestine had been subject to the Greek Ptolemies of Egypt, and at that very time both Palestine and Egypt were parts of the Roman Empire. There were hundreds of thousands of Jews in Egypt, who had their own governor and who governed their community by laws recognized by the Roman senate and Emperor. The caravan route between Judaea and Egypt was well known to the Jews and many of them had traveled it. Joseph and his family may very well have stayed with relatives or friends in Egypt during the virtual reign of terror that occurred in Palestine immediately before and after the death of Herod the Great. The theory that Jesus was a year or two old when his parents fled with him to Egypt is suggested by the fact that Herod's order for the massacre of infants included all children two years old and under. The theory that he remained in Egypt for a considerable time is based on the historical fact that the Roman authorities did not permit Archelaus to succeed immediately to the kingship over Judaea after the death of his father, 4 B.C. Under Herod's will the territory over which he had ruled as vassal king was to be distributed among several of his sons. Augustus Caesar ratified this will reluctantly and with reservations. It was a period of civil war, tumults, rioting and commotion in Palestine. There were several contenders for the throne. The Roman garrison was besieged in the citadel in Jerusalem by mobs. Roving bands of patriots shouted for a return to the ancient liberties and independence of the Jews. Some favored and some opposed Archelaus. Rome finally permitted Archelaus to become ethnarch of Judaea, Idumaea and Samaria with the promise that he might become king in room of his father if he made good in his government. Herod Antipas, another son of Herod the Great, became tetrarch of Galilee and Paraea and occupied that position throughout the rest of the life of Jesus. By going to Nazareth in Galilee instead of to Judaea, Joseph and his family became subjects of Herod Antipas rather than of Archelaus, who turned out to be an unsatisfactory ethnarch and after eight or ten years was exiled by Caesar. In view of these conditions, what would have been more natural than for Joseph and his wife to take their first-born down to Egypt and seek safety there among friends or relatives in the large Jewish colony, and then to return to settle in the quieter and more secure domain of Herod Antipas in Galilee?

Did Jesus have brothers and sisters?

Whether Jesus had blood brothers and sisters is a disputed question upon which even the early church fathers differed. Several passages in the New Testament refer to the *brother of the Lord* and the *brethren of the Lord*. For instance, *Matthew 13:55-56* says in part: "Is not this the carpenter's son? is not his mother called Mary? and his brethren, James, and Joses, and Simon, and Judas? And his sisters, are they not with us?" Again in *Mark 3:31-32*: "There came then his brethren and his mother, and, standing without, sent unto him, calling him, and the multitude sat about him, and they said unto him, Behold, thy mother and thy brethren without seek thee." Thus it will be seen that the Bible mentions by name four *brethren of the Lord*, while it merely refers to his sisters, without giving their names or number. Apparently, according to oriental custom, the names of the sisters were not considered worthy of mention. The exact relationship intended in these passages, as well as in others, is not clear, owing chiefly to the fact that *brother* and *brethren* were employed in the Scriptures to indicate various degrees of relationship, such as that between blood brothers and sisters, brothers-in-law and sisters-in-law, cousins, and even more distant relatives. The Catholic church, which believes in the perpetual virginity of Mary, the mother of Jesus, holds that the sisters and brethren of the Lord were his cousins. Many ingenious theological arguments have been advanced in support of this position. They are, however, largely determined by an accepted and established doctrine. The Eastern church regards the brethren of the Lord as the children of Joseph by a former marriage, which would make them step-brothers of Jesus and his seniors. Protestants, however, as well as most independent scholars, generally believe that James, Joses, Simon, and Judas, and *his sisters* mentioned in *Matthew 13*, were blood brothers and sisters who were born to Mary and Joseph after the birth of Jesus. Several references in the Epistles of Paul and in *Acts* are the basis of the accepted belief that after the crucifixion of Jesus his brother James succeeded to the leadership of the Christian community in Jerusalem. The idea of family succession was so firmly established that it is likely that the followers of Jesus assumed that his next oldest brother alone would be worthy to succeed him as the head of the new Jewish sect. In *Galatians 1:19* Paul the Apostle says: "But other of the apostles saw I none, save James the Lord's brother." This apparently was the same person mentioned by Paul in *I Corinthians 15:7,* which says: "After that, he was seen of James; then of all the apostles," where the context indicates that this James was not one of the twelve. *John 7:7* says: "For neither did his brethren believe in him." This leads to the supposition that the James mentioned by Paul was a brother of Jesus, but did not believe in his brother's teachings until after the resurrection. In *Acts 1* James "and Judas the brother of James" are listed among those who returned to Jerusalem after the resurrection and in an upper room "continued with one accord in prayer and supplication, with the women, and Mary the mother of Jesus, and with his brethren." In the list of the brothers of Jesus in *Mark 6:3* the name of one of them is spelled *Juda* (or *Judah*) instead of *Judas.* The James mentioned by Peter in *Acts 12:17* in connection with the story of his imprisonment is supposed to be the brother of Jesus, for the context indicates that James the brother of John, had already been killed by Herod the king. In *Corinthians 9:5* Paul, maintaining his right to be considered an apostle because he had seen Jesus in a vision, says: "Have we not power to lead about a sister, a wife, as well as other apostles, and as the brethren of the Lord, and Cephas?" This suggests that at least two of the brothers of Jesus reached manhood, married and had children. In *Acts 15* James is clearly represented as one of the leaders of the Christian community in Jerusalem, and in *Galatians 2:9* Paul says: "And when James, Cephas, and John, who seemed to be pillars, perceived the grace that was given unto me, they gave to me and Barnabas the right hands of fellowship; that we should go unto the heathen, and they unto the circumcision." Verse 12 of the same chapter shows clearly that James was looked upon as the leader of the Jewish Christians. Most authorities identify this James as the brother of Jesus who Josephus says was summoned before the Sanhedrin about the year 62 A.D., tried on charges of breaking the sacred laws, found guilty and stoned to death. The instigator of this action was Ananus, a Sadducee high priest, who was the son of the Annas who held that office when Jesus was crucified. James was called "the Just," a title applied earlier to Jesus himself. Who succeeded James, the brother of Jesus, as head of the Jewish Christians in Jerusalem is not known. It may have been one of the other three brothers of Jesus. Whether the author of *The General Epistle of Jude,* who refers to himself modestly as "Jude, the servant of Jesus Christ, and brother of James," was the same as the Judas and

Judah mentioned in the Gospels as one of the Lord's brethren is a disputed question. Eusebius, the church historian, records a tradition that two grandsons of Jude, the brother of Jesus, were living toward the end of the first century. Emperor Domitian (81-96 A.D.) had them arrested because they were suspected of being pretenders to the throne of David, but they were released when it was discovered they were merely simple peasants in Palestine. Virtually nothing is known of Simon and Joses, the other two referred to as brethren of the Lord. *Matthew 27:56* says: "Among which was Mary Magdalene, and Mary the mother of James and Joses." *Mark 15:40* also includes among the women who watched the crucifixion "Mary the mother of James the less and Joses." Some writers make a point of the fact that in *Matthew 1:25* Jesus is called "the firstborn son" of Mary, but this in itself does not prove that she had other children. Likewise, *only begotten son* was sometimes used in the sense of *best beloved son.*

Does the Bible call Jesus "The Prince of Peace"?

The phrase, "The Prince of Peace," occurs nowhere in the New and only once in the Old Testament. *Isaiah 9:6* says: "For unto us a child is born, unto us a son is given: and the government shall be upon his shoulder: and his name shall be called Wonderful, Counseller, The mighty God, The everlasting Father, The Prince of Peace." Christians regard this passage in *Isaiah* as a reference to the Messiah and therefore refer to Jesus as The Prince of Peace. In the New Testament Jesus is several times referred to as a prince; as, "the Prince of life" (*Acts 3:15*), "a Prince and a Saviour" (*Acts 5:31*), and "the prince of the kings of the earth" (*Revelation 1:5*). Over a period of twenty years beginning in 1904, William Jennings Bryan hundreds of times delivered his famous lecture entitled "The Prince of Peace," which did much to popularize the phrase in America.

Was Jesus a Roman citizen?

So far as known Jesus was not a Roman citizen, as the term is generally used, although he was a Roman national or subject. Citizenship then, as now, carried with it certain rights and privileges as well as duties. Palestine in the time of Jesus had the status of a conquered province, which was divided into several principalities with varying degrees of autonomy. At that time comparatively few of the inhabitants, whether Gentiles or Jews, had acquired Roman citizenship. Galilee, where Jesus lived, was part of a tetrarchy, which also included Peraea, and Herod Antipas was the tetrarch throughout the life of

Jesus. This tetrarchy was in the nature of a vassal state and the tetrarch was a puppet king with very restricted local powers. Judaea and Samaria during most of the lifetime of Jesus constituted a Roman province attached directly to the Empire and was governed by a series of procurators or governors, of whom Pontius Pilate was the sixth. Very few Jews at that time were Roman citizens. Most of them probably would not have accepted Roman citizenship if it had been offered to them. Both the Roman Republic and the Roman Empire developed from the old city-state of Rome. The only full-fledged Roman citizens were the privileged classes in the city of Rome. All members of the Roman senate had to be residents of the city, and a Roman citizen could exercise his franchise only within the limits of the capital. In the time of Jesus the number of Roman citizens in the Empire was only a few million in a total population of about 120,000,000. Roman citizens outside the city of Rome enjoyed certain privileges and civil rights not enjoyed by mere nationals. They had the right to appeal to Caesar from decisions of the local authorities, and if condemned to death they could not be executed by crucifixion. During the reign of Claudius (41-54 A.D.), who became emperor about twelve years after the crucifixion of Jesus, the rights of Roman citizens living outside Rome and Italy were increased and such citizens were permitted to sit as members of the Roman senate. Sometimes, as a mark of special consideration, civil rights were conferred upon entire cities and communities outside Italy. Pompey granted the protection of Roman citizenship to Tarshish and this was confirmed by Julius Caesar. Thus Paul, as well as his father before him, was a Roman citizen. In connection with the arrest of Paul and Silas at Philippi, "the chief city of that part of Macedonia, and a colony," *Acts 16:35-38* says: "And when it was day, the magistrates sent the serjeants, saying, Let those men go. And the keeper of the prison told this saying to Paul, The magistrates have sent to let you go: now therefore depart, and go in peace. But Paul said unto them, They have beaten us openly uncondemned, being Romans, and have cast us into prison; and now do they thrust us out privily? nay verily; but let them come themselves and fetch us out. And the serjeants told these words unto the magistrates: and they feared, when they heard that they were Romans." From *Acts 22* we learn that Paul was free born in Tarsus (Tarshish), a city of Cilicia, and that his parents were Jews. The chief captain who ordered Paul bound and scourged at Jerusalem admitted that he himself had paid a great sum for citizenship. Historians inform us that the sale of civil rights to foreigners and nationals was at that time the source of considerable revenue to the Roman government. In *Philippians 3:5* the Apostle to the Gentiles says he was of "the stock of Israel, of the tribe of Benjamin, a Hebrew of the Hebrews." Thus it is clear that Jews living in the Roman provinces were permitted to enjoy the status of Roman citizens and what was known as "the freedom of the city." Paul finally appealed directly to Caesar in Rome, which was one of the prerogatives of Roman citizenship in certain cases. According to tradition, when Paul was later condemned to death in Rome, he could not be scourged and crucified because he was a Roman citizen; but Peter, who was not a Roman citizen, suffered both of these humiliations and tortures. Jesus was not a Roman citizen, but lived and died a Roman national. Not being a Roman citizen, he could not appeal from Pilate's decision, and he was scourged and crucified as a Roman subject without civil rights.

Is *Abraham's bosom* in the Old Testament?

Neither this phrase nor the thought expressed by it occurs in the Old Testament, which has nothing to say about Heaven or Hell and contains only vague hints relating to life after death. In the Old Testament the customary phrases for recording deaths were simply "he died" or "he was gathered to his fathers." *Genesis 25:8* gives us a typical Old Testament death notice: "Then Abraham gave up the ghost, and died in a good old age, an old man, full of years; and was gathered to his people." According to *Genesis 15:15*, the Lord had said to Abraham in a vision: "And thou shalt go to thy fathers in peace; thou shalt be buried in a good old age." In Old Testament times the hope of a life after death was linked solely with the resurrection that would occur with the coming of the Messiah. But by the time of Jesus the idea of Heaven, Hell and Abraham's bosom were already common among members of certain sects of Jews. According to *Luke 16:22-23*, in the parable of the rich man and Lazarus, Jesus said: "And it came to pass, that the beggar died, and was carried by the angels into Abraham's bosom: the rich man also died, and was buried; and in hell he lift up his eyes, being in torments, and seeth Abraham afar off, and Lazarus in his bosom." From this passage *Abraham's bosom* has become synonymous with Heaven.

What manner of man was Jesus physically?

The Bible gives no description of the physique of Jesus and there is no known contemporaneous description of him in existence. Accordingly we have no means of knowing his height, weight, complexion, the color of his eyes, whether he wore a beard or was clean-shaven, how he dressed, or anything else about his physical appearance. The inference is that he was an average man in size and strength. Speaking of his childhood, *Luke 2:52* says Jesus "increased in wisdom and stature." In his youth he worked as a carpenter and his public ministry was spent largely in the open air. He fasted forty days in the wilderness, taught multitudes in the mountains and in the valleys, sailed on the fishing craft of his followers, and made many long journeys on foot. Every action of his recorded by the Gospels indicates that he was a man of strong physique, physical courage and outdoor activity. The Synoptic Gospels tell us that Simon of Cyrene was compelled to bear the cross of Jesus, but this is not conclusive evidence that Jesus was unable to carry the cross, for *John 19:17* says he "bore his cross," which probably means that he bore it part way to Calvary. According to tradition, members of the house of David were light-complexioned. Since Jesus was a descendant of that family and lineage, artists have generally portrayed Jesus as a blond. But even the earliest extant pictures of Jesus appear to be conventional representations rather than realistic likenesses. A picture of him in the Roman catacombs, said to date from the second century, represents him with long, curled hair, short, neatly-trimmed beard and mustache, and shaven lips. In his "Last Judgment" Michelangelo represented Jesus as beardless. From time to time reports have been published of the finding of a new description or portrait of Jesus made by a contemporary writer or artist, "who probably was an eye-witness to the crucifixion," but none of these have proved genuine. One of the most interesting of these is the Lentulus letter. This curious document purports to be a description of Jesus written in the form of a letter to the Roman senate by Publius Lentulus, "governor of Judaea in the reign of Tiberius Caesar." It has been quoted as genuine so often that it is worth reproducing here. It reads: "There hath appeared in these our days, a man of great virtue, named Jesus Christ, who is yet living among us, and of the Gentiles is accepted as a Prophet, but his disciples call him the Son of God. He raiseth the dead, and cures all manner of diseases; a man of stature somewhat tall and comely, with very reverent countenance, such as the beholders both love and fear; his hair the color of chestnut, full ripe, plain to his shoulders. In the midst of his head is a seam or a partition of his hair after the manner of the Nazarites; his forehead plain and very delicate; his face without a spot or wrinkle, beautiful with a most lovely red; his nose and mouth so formed that nothing can be reprehended; his beard thickish, in color like his hair, not very long but forked; his look, innocent and mature; his eyes, gray, clear and quick. In reproving he is terrible; in admonishing, courteous, and fair spoken; pleasant in conversation, mixed with gravity. It cannot be remarked that any one saw him laugh, but many have seen him weep. In proportion of body, most excellent; his hands and arms most delicate to behold. In speaking, very temperate, modest, and wise. A man, for his singular beauty, surpassing the children of men." This so-called "letter" has been traced back to the eleventh century, a copy having been found in the manuscript writings of St. Anselm, archbishop of Canterbury from 1093 to 1109. The description of Jesus in this document bears a striking resemblance to one in the writings of Nicephorus, who lived early in the fourteenth century and who was the last of the Greek ecclesiastical historians. It is now generally agreed that the Lentulus letter was written during the Middle Ages either as a deliberate forgery or as fiction. There is no probability whatever that it is genuine. No such person as Publius Lentulus was governor or procurator of Judaea, and the style, spirit and other internal evidence all stamp it as apocryphal. It is interesting only because it is the most ancient of the many purported descriptions of the personal appearance of Jesus.

Which is correct, *Saviour* or *Savior*?

This word is derived through Old French from Latin *salvator,* meaning one who saves, preserves, rescues or delivers from destruction, danger or peril. When used as a title of God, and especially of Jesus as the Redeemer of mankind, it is always capitalized and spelled *Saviour,* with the *u.* In American usage, when used in the ordinary sense of one who saves it is not capitalized and is spelled without the *u—savior.* In British usage, however, the word is always spelled *Saviour,* whether applied to the Deity or used in the ordinary sense. "Of agent nouns," says H. W. Fowler in *Modern English Usage,* "*saviour* (with its echo *paviour*) is perhaps the only one that now retains—*our, governor* being the latest to shed its—*u*—." Noah Webster, whose *American Dictionary of the English Language* was first published in 1828, was largely responsible for the American practice of omitting the *u* in many words such as *saviour, governour, labour, honour, favour, ardour, succour, armour,* etc. At the time the King James Version was made, *Saviour* was the only recognized spelling of this term regardless of sense or application. In the Old Testament *saviour* is generally applied only to the Deity, but occasionally it is used in the ordinary sense of deliverer from worldly trouble. In

Nehemiah 9:27 the Levites, standing on the stairs before the whole congregation, are reported as saying: "Therefore thou deliveredst them into the hand of their enemies, who vexed them: and in the time of their trouble, thou heardest them from heaven; and according to thy manifold mercies thou gavest them *saviours,* who saved them out of the hand of their enemies." In the New Testament the term invariably refers to God or to Jesus.

Did Jesus have the power of making himself invisible?

Passing unseen through the multitude who sought to kill him is often listed among the miracles performed by Jesus. For instance, the *Oxford Cylopedic Concordance* includes "When Christ passed unseen through the multitude" under "Miracles of our Lord" and cites *Luke 4:30* as the reference. That Jesus possessed and exercised the power of making himself invisible to others is only faintly suggested by several passages in the New Testament. We are told in *Luke 4* that all those in the synagogue at Nazareth, after they had heard Jesus compare his mission with those of Elijah and Elisha, were filled with wrath, and rose up, and thrust him out of the city, and led him to the brow of the hill whereon their city was built, that they might cast him down headlong. Verse 30 of that chapter then adds: "but he passing through the midst of them went his way." *John 8:59* says: "Then took they up stones to cast at him: but Jesus hid himself, and went out of the temple, going through the midst of them, and so passed by." Perhaps these passages denote nothing more than that Jesus withdrew from the scene quietly and inobtrusively. Speaking of a time immediately after the Resurrection, *Luke 24:31* says: "he vanished out of their sight." It is often stated that both Elijah and Elisha had the power of making themselves invisible or partially so, but this is not borne out by any passage in the Bible.

How does *Messiah* differ from *Christ*?

Messiah is from a Hebrew word meaning "anointed." At first it was used simply as a title in the sense of the Anointed One. *I Samuel 24:5-6* says: "And it came to pass afterward, that David's heart smote him, because he had cut off Saul's skirt. And he said unto his men, The Lord forbid that I should do this thing unto my master, the Lord's anointed, to stretch forth mine hand against him, seeing he is the anointed of the Lord." Priests and prophets, as well as kings, were anointed in Israel as a sign of their elevation to high functions. In *Psalms 105:15* the term is applied to the patriarchs as the chosen people. The Lord suffered no man to do them wrong, even reproved kings for their sakes, and said: "Touch not mine anointed, and do my prophets no harm." Later the prophets applied the term *Messiah* or the Anointed One to an ideal king, a descendant of David, who was vaguely referred to as the Deliverer, the Prince of Peace, the Son of God, a Branch from the stem of David, the Elect of the Lord, the Servant of Jehovah, the Saviour, the Everlasting King, and the spiritual and perhaps temporal ruler and leader who would at some undetermined time deliver the broken and scattered tribes of Israel. The conviction that such a Messiah would come was firmly fixed and widespread among the Jews by the time of Jesus' birth. In the King James Version of the Old Testament, *Messiah* is used only in *Daniel 9:25-26*, which reads: "Know therefore and understand, that from the going forth of the commandment to restore and to build Jerusalem unto the Messiah the Prince shall be seven weeks, and threescore and two weeks: the street shall be built again, and the wall, even in troublous times. And after threescore and two weeks shall Messiah be cut off, but not for himself: and the people of the prince that shall come shall destroy the city and the sanctuary: and the end thereof shall be with a flood, and unto the end of the war desolations are determined." Except in two instances, in the New Testament the word for Messiah is rendered by *Christos*, the Greek equivalent, from which came Latin *Christus* and English *Christ*. *John 1:41* says: "He first findeth his own brother Simon, and saith unto him, We have found the Messias, which is, being interpreted, the Christ." According to *John 4:25*, the woman of Samaria at Jacob's well said to Jesus: "I know that Messias cometh, which is called Christ: when he is come, he will tell us all things." John Wycliffe and later translators, following the Latin Vulgate, used the form *Messias* in these two passages. The form *Messiah* was invented by the translators of the Geneva Bible of 1560, perhaps because they thought it looked more Hebraic, and eventually it became the prevalent form of the word in English. *Messianic* (generally pronounced *mess-i-ANN-ick*) is an adjective which means pertaining to the Messiah and was formed from the older form *Messias*.

Why did Jesus call himself the Son of Man?

In the Gospels Jesus refers to himself more than eighty times as the Son of Man. Authorities differ widely as to why he chose that title. Jesus often permitted himself to be called the Son of God by others, but he applied that title to himself only by implication. He seems to have used *Son of Man* very much as he used *I* or as he might have used his own name in the third person. A Hebrew term rendered *son of man* occurs in singular and plural in *Psalms, Ecclesiastes, Proverbs, Isaiah, Jeremiah, Ezekiel, Job, Daniel* and other parts of the Old Testament. There, except in *Daniel,* it generally means a human being, a mortal, mere man, or frail humanity. Ezekiel, conscious of his own mortality and frailty, applies *son of man* to himself about ninety times. Some authorities suppose that Jesus, out of modesty and humiliation, referred to himself as the son of man merely in the general sense of that term as used in the Old Testament. But the Greek term rendered *son of man* in the New Testament has no clear and obvious counterpart in Aramaic, the language that Jesus is supposed to have spoken. Aramaic *bar enash* signifies "son of man" only in the literal sense. For that reason even the authenticity of the phrase in the Gospels has been questioned. Other authorities suppose this title had some special Messianic significance, although there is no positive evidence that it was so understood by the Jews in the time of Jesus. But Jesus undoubtedly borrowed it from Old Testament usage. *Psalms 8:4* says: "What is man, that thou art mindful of him? and the son of man, that thou visitest him?" In *Daniel 7:13-14* the prophet "saw in the night visions, and, behold, one like the Son of man came with the clouds of heaven, and came to the Ancient of days, . . . and there was given him dominion, and glory, and a kingdom, that all people, nations, and languages, should serve him." These passages were sometimes interpreted as alluding to the Messiah and may have been the source of the title as used by Jesus. When Jesus says in *Matthew 16:28,* "Verily I say unto you, There be some standing here, which shall not taste of death, till they see the Son of man coming in his kingdom," he is undoubtedly alluding to the passage in *Daniel* just cited. Also in *Mark 14:62,* in answer to the high priest's question whether he was the Christ, Jesus said: "I am: and ye shall see the Son of man sitting on the right hand of power, and coming in the clouds of heaven." In *Daniel* "one like the Son of man" is indefinite and appears to denote that this vision was in human form as contrasted with the brute forms in the preceding visions. But in the Gospels, where *the son of man* is used continually and only by Jesus, the title is individualized and definitely identified with Jesus himself. Jesus may have adopted this particular phrase to hide his identity with the Messiah from some and to reveal it to others. *Son of man* is specifically identified with the Messiah in the Apocryphal *Book of Enoch,* but it is not certain that those writings antedate Jesus. If *Enoch* was in circulation at that time, Jesus may have obtained the title from that book, which is quoted in *The General Epistle of Jude,* generally ascribed to his brother of that name.

What does *corban* mean?

According to *Mark 7:9-12,* Jesus said to the Pharisees and scribes: "Full well ye reject the commandment of God, that ye may keep your own tradition. For Moses said, Honour thy father and thy mother; and, Whoso curseth father or mother, let him die the death: but ye say, If a man shall say to his father or mother, It is Corban, that is to say, a gift, by whatsoever thou mightest be profited by me; he shall be free. And ye suffer him no more to do ought for his father or his mother." *Corban* is an Anglicized form of Hebrew *qorban,* literally meaning "that which is brought near." In the Hebrew Bible the term signifies "a sacrificial offering," "gift" or "oblation" and is so translated in the English Bible except in the passage just quoted. Later *corban* was applied to any gift set apart for God, especially in performance of a vow, and therefore not to be appropriated to any other use. In New Testament times *corban* was little more than a formula for making a vow. For instance, when a devout Jew said, "Corban to me is wine for a year," he meant that he vowed to abstain from wine for that period. Likewise, a son might say to his parents, "Corban is whatever you might have profited by me," signifying that he vowed not to help them no matter what their need. Technically, whatever the son might have given the parents in the way of support was dedicated as a gift to God. By this legal fiction the son could avoid his filial responsibilities while doing a formal religious act. The scribes held that such a vow excused the son from giving to his parents what he had dedicated to God. Jesus clearly implies that some who had no intention of delivering the corban to God adopted this device merely to avoid complying with the commandment and shirking their parental responsibilities.

Why is Jesus called the Good Shepherd?

The Good Shepherd as a title of Jesus is from *John 10:11* and 14, which reads: "I am the good shepherd: the good shepherd giveth his life for the sheep," and, "I am the good shepherd, and know my sheep, and am known of mine." Jesus is also popularly called *The Good Physician* in allusion to *Mark 2:17,* which says: "When Jesus heard it, he saith unto them, They that are whole have no need of the physician, but they that are sick: I came not to call the righteous, but sinners to repentance." In the New Testament more than thirty different names, titles and descriptive phrases are applied to Jesus. The most common are as follows: Emmanuel; Jesus of Nazareth; the Nazarene; Messiah (Messias); Son of David; Son of God; Son of Man; Christ; Jesus Christ; Christ Jesus; Lord; Master; Christ the Lord; Lord's Christ; Lord Jesus Christ; Lord Jesus; King of the Jews; Lamb of God; Son of the Highest; Saviour; Redeemer; Light of the World; Holy One of God; Just One; the Comforter; Holy One; and Rock.

What is meant by new wine in old bottles?

According to *Luke 5:37-38,* Jesus said: "And no man putteth new wine into old bottles; else the new wine will burst the bottles, and be spilled, and the bottles shall perish. But new wine must be put into new bottles; and both are preserved." This passage occurs in substantially the same form in *Matthew 9:17* and *Mark 2:22.* In everyday speech "putting new wine in old bottles" signifies typical incongruity or incompatibility. English *bottle* is really the diminutive of *butt,* a wine cask or skin, and literally means "little butt." Glass bottles are not mentioned in the Bible. In those days bottles and "butts" for wine were made of animal skins. The usual wine bottle consisted of the complete skin of a goat or kid with the neck of the animal forming the bottleneck. This skin was tanned with oak bark and seasoned with smoke to give the wine a special flavor. "I am become like a bottle in the smoke," says *Psalms 119:83.* The point of the passage quoted is that the after-fermentation of new wine would break the unelastic leather of old bottles. Jesus probably meant that the new spiritual doctrine he taught could not be made to fit into the rigid forms and rituals of the old religion.

What does "Let the dead bury their dead" mean?

In popular parlance, "Let the dead bury their dead" means let bygones be bygones, forget the past, or don't rake up old grievances. *Matthew 8:21-22,* says: "And another of his disciples said unto him, Lord, suffer me first to go and bury my father. But Jesus said unto him, Follow me; and let the dead bury their dead." This puzzling passage, peculiar to *Matthew,* is hard to explain. It may mean just what it appears to mean; namely, Jesus regarded his work as so important and urgent that it could not wait and he desired the disciple to leave every worldly thing and follow him. Jewish funerals and mourning periods lasted several weeks and some authorities suppose the passage to mean that it would be better for the father to remain unburied than for the disciple to delay the work of the Lord by attending the funeral. Others see in the passage a purely spiritual meaning and interpret it as signifying that the disciple should attend to the Lord's work and let unbelieving relations bury the father. Still others suggest that possibly the father was not yet dead and that the disciple asked to remain with him during his latter years, thus postponing indefinitely the spiritual mission.

What is meant by a *red and lowering sky*?

In *Matthew 16:1-3* it is said of Jesus: "The Pharisees also with the Sadducees came, and tempting desired him that he would shew them a sign from heaven. He answered and said unto them, When it is evening, ye say, It will be fair weather: for the sky is red. And in the morning, It will be foul weather to day: for the sky is red and lowring. O ye hypocrites, ye can discern the face of the sky; but can ye not discern the signs of the times?" This passage indicates the antiquity of the popular belief that a red sky in the morning is a sign of foul weather and a red sky in the evening is a sign of fair weather. An old rhyme says:

Evening red and morning gray
Will set the traveler on his way;
But evening gray and morning red
Will bring down rain upon his head.

Such weather signs are far from infallible. Nevertheless, meteorologists tell us, they have a slight scientific basis and rightly interpreted may serve as fairly good weather indicators. It is hard to make a scientific distinction between a sky that is red and one that is "red and lowring." The English translators of the Bible in the passage quoted above used *lowring* when *louring* or *lowering* would be used in present-day English. *Lowring* and *lowering* are merely variants of *louring*. *Lour* is an old English verb meaning "to frown," "scowl" or "look angry or sullen." Whether spelled *lour, lowr* or *lower,* it is pronounced to rhyme with *hour, dower* and *sour*. In origin and meaning it has no connection with *lower* as the comparative of *low*. A louring or lowering sky is one that looks dark, gloomy, threatening. Meteorologists recognize two kinds of red skies—a pale or pinkish red, common in the evening; and a much darker red often associated with broken clouds. The former is said to be common during fair weather; the second shortly before a rain. A pale or pinkish-red sky in the evening usually means that the atmosphere contains very little moisture and that rain is improbable within the next twenty-four hours. When the evening sky is overcast with uniform gray the dust particles in the air have become loaded with moisture, giving rise to the proverb, "If the sunset is gray, the next will be a rainy day." On the other hand, a gray morning sky generally justifies the expectation of a fair day. In the morning, however, it is a red sun, rather than a red sky, which is the sign of rain. Any modified appearance of the sun is most conspicuous when it is near the horizon, because the solar orb is then seen through a greater distance of atmosphere. The rays at the red end of the spectrum are refracted to the eye by increased moisture in the atmosphere, and accordingly when the air is heavily charged with dust particles laden with moisture the sun often appears as a fiery red ball, whether it is morning or evening.

Who gave the Golden Rule its name?

Matthew 7:12 quotes Jesus as saying: "Therefore all things whatsoever ye would that men should do to you, do ye even so to them: for this is the law and the prophets." *Luke 6:31* gives a slightly different version: "And as ye would that men should do to you, do ye also to them likewise." "Do as you would be done by," is a homelier but more popular way of expressing the same thought, which is generally known as the Golden Rule of Life. Who first called this precept the Golden Rule is not known for certain. The *London Encyclopedia*, published in 1845, attributed it to Isaac Watts (1674-1748), the British theologian and hymn writer. Watts frequently employed the word *golden* when he desired to express quality of great value. In *Logick, or the Right Use of Reason in the Enquiry after Truth*, published in 1725, he wrote: "In matters of equity between man and man, our Saviour has taught us an effectual means of guarding against this prejudice, and that is;—to put my neighbor in the place of myself, and myself in the place of my neighbor, rather than be bribed by the corrupt principle of self-love to do injury to my neighbors. Thence arises that *Golden Rule* of dealing with others as we would have others deal with us." This is the earliest known application of *Golden Rule* to the famous precept of Jesus. But Clement Ellis, an English churchman, indirectly applied *golden* to the rule fourteen years before Watts was born. In an address delivered in 1660 he said: "The Gentleman is too much a man to be without all passion, but he is not so much a beast as to be governed by it. In this moderation and empire over himself . . . the just rule he goes by, is not opinion, but knowledge; not that *leaden* one, which is so easily bent and made crooked, or melted and dissolved by the heat of passion . . . but that other *golden* one, which lies so close and firm, as it is made straight and even." In 1674 Robert Godfrey, in his *Physics,* wrote: "whilst forgetting that *Golden Law,* 'do as you would be done by,' they make self the center of their actions." But the earliest known use of *Golden Rule* referred to a proposition in mathematics, not to the famous precept of Jesus. In *The Grounde of Arts,* published in 1540, Robert Recorde wrote: "The rule of proportion which, for excellency, is called the *Golden Rule.*" Gabriel Harvey, in his Pierce's *Supererogation,* published in 1593, said: "The finest methodists, according to Aristotle's *golden rule* of artificial bounds, condemn geometrical precepts in arithmetic, or arithmetical precepts in geometry, as irregular and abusive." In 1635 Daniel Featley in his *Clavis Mystica* wrote: "The rule of three, or *golden rule,* as it is called in sacred algebray." Jesus did not originate the thought embodied in the Golden Rule. The Golden Rule had been previously taught, almost in the same words, by many great teachers in different parts of the world. Five centuries before the time of Jesus the great Chinese philosopher laid down a similar precept. In the twenty-third chapter of the *Analects of Confucius* appears this passage: "Tszeking asked, saying, Is there one word which may serve as a rule of practice for all one's life? The master said, Is not *reciprocity* such a word? What you do not want done to yourself, do not do to others." Although this saying of Confucius is stated negatively, in it is easily recognizable the essence of the precept that Jesus regarded as the law and the prophets. Isocrates, Aristotle, Epictetus and other ancient Greeks had expressed the same thought. Writing about 150 years B.C., Diogenes Laertius said: "The question was once put to Aristotle how we ought to behave to our friends; and his answer was, 'As we should wish them to behave to us.'" The *Mahabharata,* one of the great epics of the Hindus dating from about 150 B.C., contains this passage: "This is the sum of all true righteousness: deal with others as thou wouldst thyself be dealt by. Do nothing to thy neighbor which thou wouldst not have him do to thee hereafter." The Talmudic form of the Golden Rule, like that of Confucius, is stated negatively. In the maxims of Hillel, a Jewish rabbi of Babylonian origin who taught in Jerusalem about 30 B.C., we find the following: "What is unpleasant to thyself that do not to thy neighbor; this is the whole law, all else is but exposition." In the Apocryphal *Book of Tobit,* Tobit admonishes his son: "What is displeasing to thyself, that do not unto any other." The difference between the Golden Rule when stated negatively and when stated positively is more apparent than real. In the final analysis, the essence of the Golden Rule is found in *Leviticus 19:18*, which reads: "Thou shalt not avenge, nor bear any grudge against the children of thy people, but thou shalt love thy neighbour as thyself: I am the Lord." The ancient Israelites probably restricted *neighbour* here to other Israelites. In the parable of the Good Samaritan Jesus extended the term to outcaste Jews, if not to all people. Jesus also went far beyond the Golden Rule of the ancients in his teachings. In *Matthew 5:43-44* Jesus is quoted as saying: "Ye have heard that it hath been said, Thou shalt love thy neighbour, and hate thine enemy. But I say unto you, *Love your enemies*, bless them that curse you, do good to them that hate you, and pray for them which despitefully use you, and persecute you."

Did Jesus baptize?

Whether Jesus himself personally baptized with water is not made entirely clear in the New Testament. *John 3:22* says: "After these things came Jesus and his disciples into the land of Judaea; and there he tarried with them, and baptized." Again it is related in *John 3:25-26*: "Then there arose a question between some of John's disciples and the Jews about purifying. And they came unto John, and said unto him, Rabbi, he that was with thee beyond Jordan, to whom thou barest witness, behold, the same baptizeth, and all men come to him." But *John 4:1-3* says: "When therefore the Lord knew how the Pharisees had heard that Jesus made and baptized more disciples than John, (Though Jesus himself baptized not, but his disciples,) he left Judaea, and departed again into Galilee." Some authorities take these passages to mean that Jesus personally administered the rite of baptism during the early days of his ministry. The Synoptics—*Matthew*, *Mark* and *Luke*—are silent on the subject. *Matthew 3:13-17* tells us: "Then cometh Jesus from Galilee to Jordan unto John, to be baptized of him. But John forbad him, saying, I have need to be baptized of thee, and comest thou to me? And Jesus answering said unto him, Suffer it to be so now: for thus it becometh us to fulfill all righteousness. Then he suffered him. And Jesus, when he was baptized, went up straightway out of the water: and lo, the heavens were opened unto him, and he saw the Spirit of God descending like a dove, and lighting upon him: and lo a voice from heaven, saying, This is my beloved Son, in whom I am well pleased." Apparently the Pharisees expected the Messiah to baptize, perhaps from certain hints in the prophets, for *John 1:25* says: "And they asked him, and said unto him, Why baptizest thou then, if thou be not that Christ, nor Elias, neither that prophet?" John answered that he baptized with water, but that there stood among them one who "baptizeth with the Holy Ghost." *Matthew 3:11* quotes John as saying: "I indeed baptize you with water unto repentance: but he that cometh after me is mightier than I, whose shoes I am not worthy to bear: he shall baptize you with the Holy Ghost, and with fire." *Luke 12:49-50* quotes Jesus: "I am come to send fire on the earth; and what will I, if it be already kindled? But I have a baptism to be baptized with; and how am I straitened till it be accomplished!" According to *Mark 10:38-39*: "But Jesus said unto them, Ye know not what ye ask: can ye drink of the cup that I drink of? and be baptized with the baptism that I am baptized with? And they said unto him, We can. And Jesus said unto them, Ye shall indeed drink of the cup that I drink of; and with the baptism that I am baptized withal shall ye be baptized." It appears from these passages that, while Jesus administered the rite of baptism with water in the early days of his ministry, it was merely a temporary practice and not a vital part of his mission.

What does *beatitude* mean?

Beatitude is not in the English Bible. It is an Anglicized form of Latin *beatitudo,* meaning "happiness" or "blessedness." The Latin adjective is *beatus,* "happy" or "blessed." Since the sixteenth century at least the plural form *Beatitudes* has been applied to *Matthew 5:3-11,* which are the nine verses in the Sermon on the Mount that begin with the words "Blessed are." A similar introductory formula is found in *Psalms 1:1, Psalms 41:1* and *Psalms 65:4,* which begin, "Blessed is the man that," "Blessed is he that" and "Blessed is the man whom."

Does *sermon on the mount* occur in the Bible?

Sermon, a word of Latin origin and signifying "talk" or "discourse," is found nowhere in the Bible. The name *Sermon on the Mount* was given to the fifth, sixth and seventh chapters of *Matthew* as early as the fourth century, when St. Augustine wrote his commentary on the subject. These chapters open with, "And seeing the multitudes, he went up into a mountain: and when he was set, his disciples came unto him: and he opened his mouth, and taught them, saying," and are followed with, "When he was come down from the mountain, great multitudes followed him." Many authorities suppose that the Sermon on the Mount is largely a compilation of the sayings of Jesus that were uttered at different times in different places and that were later collected and arranged as if they composed one discourse. This is based upon parallel sayings in other connections in the Gospels and certain internal evidence that they are not preserved in their original connection. A somewhat similar arrangement of the sayings of Jesus is recorded in *Luke 6:20-49*. This is sometimes called the *Sermon on the Plain*, because in *Luke 6:17* Jesus is represented as standing "in the plain" when he spoke.

What was the value of the widow's mite?

Strictly speaking, we should refer to the widow's *mites*, instead of *mite*, because according to the Bible story she cast two mites into the treasury. *Luke 21:1-4* says: "And he looked up, and saw the rich men casting their gifts into the treasury. And he saw also a certain poor widow casting in thither two mites. And he said, Of a truth I say unto you, that this poor widow hath cast in more than they all: for all these have of their abundance cast in unto the offerings of God: but she of her penury hath cast in all the living that she had." *Mark 12:41-44* relates the same incident as follows: "And Jesus sat over against the treasury, and beheld how the people cast money into the treasury: and many that were rich cast in much. And there came a certain poor widow, and she threw in two mites, which make a farthing. And he called unto him his disciples, and saith unto them, Verily I say unto you, That this poor widow hath cast more in, than all they which have cast into the treasury: for all they did cast in of their abundance; but she of her want did cast in all that she had, even all her living." The value of ancient coins cannot be given exactly in terms of modern money. It is supposed that the Greek *lepton*, which is rendered *mite* in English translations of the New Testament, was worth about one-sixth of a United States one-cent piece and one-thirteenth of an English penny. If this is correct, the widow's two mites would be roughly worth a little more than one-third of a cent in American money and one-sixth of a penny in English money. Since foreign coins were forbidden as Temple offerings, it is assumed that the money dropped into the box by the widow consisted of the smallest Maccabean coins, which bore Hebrew symbols and inscriptions. *Mite*, it seems, was never the name of a specific coin in England. The original mite (Dutch *mitj*) was a Flemish copper coin of very small value, being worth, according to some early Flemish writers. only one-third of a penning. It is improbable, says the Oxford Dictionary, that *mite* was ever in English mercantile use, although in books of commercial arithmetic during the sixteenth and seventeenth centuries it appears as the lowest denomination of English money of account, generally one twenty-fourth of a penny. *Mite* was used rather as a general name for the smallest current unit of money, in the same manner that the French use *sou* and Americans use *mill.* The popular belief that a mite is half a farthing is based entirely on the use of these words in translations of *Mark 12:42,* quoted above. In this particular instance *farthing* is used to translate the Greek *kodrantes,* which was a Roman coin believed to be worth about three-tenths of a cent and three-twentieths of a penny.

How many hairs does the average head contain?

This oft-asked question is no doubt prompted by the statement of Jesus, quoted in both *Luke 12:7* and *Matthew 10:30,* that even "the very hairs of your head are all numbered." Oddly enough, numerous attempts have been made to estimate the average number of hairs on the human head. Taking several of these counts as a basis for the calculation, it is estimated that the number of hairs on the average human head is about 110,000, or about 1,000 to the square inch of the scalp. The actual number varies considerably with age, sex and the color of the hair. Women have a greater number of hairs on their heads than men, and the heads of blonds contain a greater number of hairs because blond hair is generally of finer texture. Some blond heads contain as many as 150,000 hairs. Brunets generally contain several thousand fewer than blonds, the average for them being fewer than 100,000. Red hair is a form of blondness, but as a rule red-haired heads have fewer hairs than other blonds, the average for them being fewer than 75,000.

Did Jesus ever offer sacrifices?

There is nothing in the Bible to indicate that Jesus himself ever offered sacrifices according to the law of Moses. But the silence of the New Testament on this subject is not particularly significant, because it was possible for an individual Israelite to observe the Mosaic law and still go through life without ever being obliged to offer sacrifices for himself. The New Testament, however, makes it clear that Joseph and Mary offered a sacrifice for Jesus when he was a child. *Luke 2:21-24* says: "And when eight days were accomplished for the circumcision of the child, his name was called JESUS, which was so named of the angel before he was conceived in the womb. And when the days of her purification according to the law of Moses were accomplished, they brought him to Jerusalem, to present him to the

Lord; (As it is written in the law of the Lord, Every male that openeth the womb shall be called the holy of the Lord;) And to offer a sacrifice according to that which is said in the law of the Lord, a pair of turtledoves, or two young pigeons."

What does *straining at a gnat* mean?

Matthew 23:24, according to the King James Version, quotes Jesus as saying to the scribes and Pharisees: "Ye blind guides, which strain at a gnat, and swallow a camel." This appears to have been a misprint in the edition of 1611 that has been permitted to remain to the present time. The original Greek clearly means "strain *out* a gnat." That is the way it is rendered in the Geneva, Coverdale's and Tyndale's Bibles, all of which formed the basis for the King James Version, and that is also the way it is rendered in the Revised Version. "Strain *at* a gnat, and swallow a camel" conveys the idea of a person swallowing a minute particle like a gnat with great difficulty while readily gulping down a large object like a camel. This obviously is not the meaning intended. Jesus was addressing this to the scribes and Pharisees and he undoubtedly alluded to the practice among strict Jews of straining their wine through linen or gauze to prevent swallowing unawares some unclean insect forbidden by the Mosaic or the Oral Law. In the preceding verse Jesus had accused the scribes and Pharisees of emphasizing observance of the minor matters of the law at the expense of the weightier matters of the law. The idea clearly seems to be that the scribes and Pharisees very properly observed the letter of the law to the minutest details but in doing so neglected the spirit of the law—judgment, mercy and faith. *Gnat* occurs nowhere else in the English Bible. Both gnats and mosquitoes are common pests in Palestine and the Greek word rendered *gnat* may refer to either of these insects.

What does *legion* in the Bible mean?

The expression, "their name is legion," meaning "they are innumerable," is of Biblical origin. According to *Mark 5:9*, when Jesus asked a man possessed with the devil what his name was, he replied: "My name is Legion: for we are many." In common speech this proverbial saying has been twisted inaccurately into "their name is legion." In the time of Jesus the legion was a Roman military unit consisting of from five thousand to six thousand soldiers, all Roman citizens, divided into ten cohorts of six centuries each. *Legion* came to be used in Greek, Hebrew and Aramaic in the sense of many, a multitude, a great number or a vast host. This figurative significance of the term is better illustrated by Luke's version of the passage quoted from Mark. *Luke 8:30* says: "And Jesus asked him, saying, What is thy name? And he said, Legion; because many devils were entered into him." *Legion* has a similar sense in *Matthew 26:53,* which reads: "Thinkest thou that I cannot now pray to my Father, and he shall presently give me more than twelve legions of angels?"

Is the mustard seed the least of all seeds?

In *Matthew 13:31-32* Jesus is quoted as saying: "The kingdom of heaven is like to a grain of mustard seed, which a man took, and sowed in his field: which indeed is the least of all seeds: but when it is grown, it is the greatest among herbs, and becometh a tree, so that the birds of the air come and lodge in the branches thereof." And in *Matthew 17:20* Jesus says: "If ye have faith as a grain of mustard seed, ye shall say unto this mountain, Remove hence to yonder place; and it shall remove; and nothing shall be impossible to you." *Mustard* and *mustard seed* occur nowhere in the Bible except in these passages and the corresponding passages in *Mark* and *Luke.* Although the mustard plant is compared to a tree, it is believed that herb, not the so-called mustard tree, is referred to. In Palestine this annual herb, a common source of spice, often attains a height of ten or twelve feet and certain birds do actually nest in its branches. The mustard seed is not literally the smallest of all seeds, but it was so regarded in popular parlance. Among the rabbis "the quantity of a mustard seed" was the proverbial way of expressing the smallest possible quantity, and in the *Koran* Mohammed employed the same figure of speech.

What were the husks in the prodigal son parable?

It is presumed that the husks referred to in the Biblical passage popularly known as the parable of the prodigal son were the sweetish pods of the carob or locust tree. The pods, known also as locust beans and St. John's bread, are called husks because they contain the carob or locust seeds. Analysis shows that the seeds themselves have practically no food value. The husks, however, contain some starch and sugar and in the Near East they are fed to stock and are sometimes eaten by the poor. Unripe carob husks are also used to give water a pleasant taste. It should be noted that the Bible does not say that the prodigal son actually ate husks. In *Luke 15,* the only place in the Bible where this story is told, we read that the wanton "would fain have filled his belly with the husks that the swine did eat." From this we need not necessarily infer that he was starving to death. It appears to mean merely that the prodigal had been so far reduced in poverty that he began to think seriously of eating locust pods, which he was feeding the hogs and which the poor in that region ate when they could get nothing else. Popularly, however, it is generally presumed that the prodigal actually ate husks. In Shakespeare's *I Henry IV* Sir John Falstaff, describing his company of recruits to Bardolph, says that "you would think that I had a hundred and fifty tattered prodigals lately come from swine-keeping, from eating draff and husks"; and in *As You Like It* Orlando asks his brother bitterly, "Shall I keep your hogs, and eat husks with them?"

Does salt lose its flavor?

This question is often raised because the subject is referred to several times in the New Testament. For instance, *Matthew 5:13* quotes Jesus as saying: "Ye are the salt of the earth; but if the salt have lost his savour, wherewith shall it be salted? It is thenceforth good for nothing, but to be cast out, and to be trodden under foot of men." And *Luke 14:34-35*: "Salt is good: but if the salt have lost his savour, wherewith shall it be seasoned? It is neither fit for the land, nor yet for the dunghill; but men cast it out." *Savor* (still *savour* in British usage) is derived indirectly from a Latin root meaning "to taste." The King James translators of the New Testament employed the term in the sense of essential virtue or property rather than taste or flavor. Common salt is a definite chemical combination of two elements, sodium and chlorine, and it cannot lose any of its properties, not even its flavor or savor. However, it can be rendered useless by mixing with foreign matter, and undoubtedly that is the meaning of the loss of savor in the beautiful figure ascribed to Jesus. The salt used in Palestine in the time of Jesus was obtained from the Dead Sea by means of a crude process, and often it was poorly cleaned and seriously adulterated with other substances. In those days salt was about the only condiment available to the common people with which to season their humble food. There was a heavy tax on salt in the Roman Empire and the product was relatively quite expensive. Consequently salt was regarded as precious among the people to whom Jesus spoke. The metaphor used by Jesus is more striking when we recall that salt was widely used in connection with Hebrew sacrifices and was the symbol of purity and permanence, because it preserves food from putrefaction. "For every one shall be salted with fire, and every sacrifice shall be salted with salt," said Jesus, according to *Mark 9:49-50*. "Salt is good: but if the salt have lost his saltness, wherewith will ye season it? Have salt in yourselves, and have peace one with another." There are at least a score of different interpretations of this passage. *Leviticus 2:13* says: "And every oblation of thy meat offering shalt thou season with salt; neither shalt thou suffer the salt of the covenant of thy God to be lacking from thy meat offerings; with all thine offerings thou shalt offer salt." In *Numbers 18:19* we read: "All the heave offerings of the holy things, which the children of Israel offer unto the Lord, have I given thee, and thy sons and thy daughters with thee, by a statute for ever: it is a covenant of salt for ever." Here salt as a preservative clearly typifies that which is lasting and abiding. "To eat salt together" was a sign of friendship among the Hebrews as well as many other ancient peoples. "Have salt in yourselves, and have peace one with another," alludes to the use of salt in sacrifices and eating salt together as a symbol of friendship, harmony, goodwill and peace. On the theory that a man's table has the sacredness of the altar, the Jews adopted the custom of dipping bread in salt for the grace before meals. In *Colossians 4:6* Paul says: "Let your speech be always with grace, seasoned with salt, that ye may know how ye ought to answer every man." The probable general meaning of, "For every one shall be salted with fire, and every sacrifice shall be salted with salt," is that every believer shall be purified and prepared for the future by trials and afflictions.

Did Jesus say, "The spirit is willing, but the flesh is weak"?

This is a popular version of a saying of Jesus in *Matthew 26:41*. The exact words of the verse are: "Watch and pray, that ye enter not into temptation: the spirit indeed is willing, but the flesh is weak." These words were uttered by Jesus on the night of the arrest in the place called Gethsemane on the Mount of Olives after he had asked the three disciples with him to tarry and watch while he went "a stone's cast" aside to pray, but returned an hour later to find them asleep. This particular saying was addressed to Peter. *Mark 14:38* renders it: "The spirit truly is ready, but the flesh is weak."

When is the eleventh hour?

The eleventh hour or *at the eleventh hour* means the latest possible time or just in time. This usage was suggested by the parable told by Jesus about the householder who hired laborers to work in his vineyard. In *Matthew 20:1-16* Jesus is quoted as saying: "For the kingdom of heaven is like unto a man that is an householder, which went out early in the morning to hire labourers into his vineyard. And when he had agreed with the labourers for a penny a day, he sent them into his vineyard. And he went out about the third hour, and saw others standing idle in the market-place, and said unto them; go ye also into the vineyard, and whatsoever is right I will give you. And they went their way. Again he went out about the sixth and ninth hour, and did likewise. And *about the eleventh hour* he went out, and found others standing idle, and saith unto them, Why stand ye here all the day idle? They say unto him, Because no man hath hired us. He saith unto them, Go ye also into the vineyard; and whatsoever is right, that shall ye receive. So when even was come, the lord of the vineyard saith unto his steward, Call the labourers, and give them their hire, beginning from the last unto the first. And when they came that were hired *about the eleventh hour,* they received every man a penny. But when the first came, they supposed that they should have received more; and they likewise received every man a penny. And when they had received it, they murmured against the goodman of the house, saying, These last have wrought but one hour, and thou hast made them equal unto us, which have borne the burden and heat of the day. But he answered one of them, and said, Friend, I do thee no wrong: didst not thou agree with me for a penny? Take that thine is, and go thy way: I will give unto this last, even as unto thee. Is it not lawful for me to do what I will with mine own? Is thine eye evil because I am good? So the last shall be first, and the first last: for many be called, but few chosen." Among the Jews in the time of Jesus the day was twenty-four hours long, but it was not divided into twenty-four parts or hours of sixty minutes. The day proper was an integral part of time and was reckoned from sunrise to sunset, which was divided into twelve varying periods called hours. That the day was regarded only as the period of daylight is shown in *John 11:9,* where Jesus, when his disciples warned him against returning to Judaea, replied: "Are there not twelve hours in the day? If any man walk in the day, he stumbleth not, because he seeth the light of this world." Likewise the night proper was a distinct division of time and was measured from sunset to sunrise, which was divided into four watches of three varying hours each. Our modern hour is a fixed period of time of sixty minutes, but the Jewish hour was not a fixed period of time. It varied in length as successive days and nights varied in length at different seasons of the year. Accordingly, under the Jewish system the first hour of the day was the first twelfth of daylight after sunrise, while the eleventh hour was the last twelfth of daylight just before sunset. Presumably the laborers who came into the vineyard at the eleventh hour worked only one hour. It is possible, however, that in Jesus' parable *eleventh hour* meant the next to the last hour of daylight and that the laborers who came in at the eleventh hour worked two hours. No mention of hours is made in the Old Testament except in the portions of *Daniel* that are in Aramaic in the original.

What did Jesus mean by the *eye of a needle*?

Many Bible students have attempted to prove that when Jesus said, "It is easier for a camel to go through the *eye of a needle,* than for a rich man to enter the kingdom of heaven," the phrase *eye of a needle* referred to the small gate that was opened in the great gate of an Oriental city when the latter was closed for the night. They say it is difficult, but possible, for a camel to pass through such a gate. There is no positive evidence to support this theory and it is apparently without foundation, although many students of the Scriptures accept it. The author has been unable to find a particle of evidence that such a gate was called *the eye of a needle* or *the needle's eye* in the time of Jesus. This figurative use of *the eye of a needle* occurs in all three of the Synoptics—*Matthew 19:24, Mark 10:25,* and *Luke 18:25.* Some writers believe that Jesus wished merely to point out the difference between what is possible with men and what is possible with God. It is recorded that the disciples were astonished out of measure by the statement of Jesus. They asked: "Who then can be saved?" Jesus replied: "With men it is impossible, but not with God: for with God all things are possible." It is more probable, however, that Jesus was illustrating something actually impossible, *rich man* meaning a person selfishly bound up in his riches. That such was the meaning of Jesus is becoming more and more the accepted theory among Bible scholars. In *Mark 10:24* it is recorded that Jesus said: "How hard is it for them that trust in riches to enter into the kingdom of God." After relating the parable of the sower, Jesus, according to *Mark 9:14,* said: "And the cares of this world, and the deceitfulness of riches, and the lusts of other things entering in, choke the word, and it becometh unfruitful." *Luke 18:22* tells us that Jesus told the ruler who was rich but who had kept the commandments: "Yet lackest thou one thing; sell all that thou hast, and distribute unto the poor, and thou shalt have treasure in heaven." There are other passages in the Gospels illustrating the same attitude toward worldly riches. It is probable that the saying about the camel and the needle's eye was proverbial already in the time of Jesus. Mohammed used it six centuries later. The *Koran* says: "The impious shall find the gates of heaven shut, nor shall he enter till a camel pass through the eye of a needle." Which is another way of saying that the impious shall not enter at all. Some suppose the Greek words for *camel* and *rope* were confused, and *cable* for *camel* occurs in a few versions, but early texts do not support the theory, which is generally rejected. *Needle* occurs nowhere else in the Bible, although *needlework* does.

Why was the woman taken in adultery brought to Jesus?

The story of the woman taken in adultery and brought before Jesus is one of the most widely cited passages in the entire Bible. In many respects it is one of the most beautiful and remarkable stories in the New Testament. It is found only in the Gospel according to St. John and is not so much as alluded to in the three Synoptic Gospels. The incident occurred while Jesus sat in the temple and taught the people early in the morning. *John 8:3-11* says: "And the scribes and Pharisees brought unto him a woman taken in adultery; and when they had set her in the midst, they say unto him, Master, this woman was taken in adultery, in the very act. Now Moses in the law commanded us, that such should be stoned: but what sayest thou? This they said, tempting him, that they might have to accuse him. But Jesus stooped down, and with his finger wrote on the ground, as though he heard them not. So when they continued asking him, he lifted up himself, and said unto them, He that is without sin among you, let him first cast a stone at her. And again he stooped down, and wrote on the ground. And they which heard it, being convicted by their own conscience, went out one by one, beginning at the eldest, even unto the last: and Jesus was left alone, and the woman standing in the midst. When Jesus had lifted up himself, and saw none but the woman, he said unto her, Woman, where are those thine accusers? hath no man condemned thee? She said, No man, Lord. And Jesus said unto her, Neither do I condemn thee: go, and sin no more." The authenticity of this incident has been attacked with more vigor than almost any other part of the Bible. Higher critics are almost unanimous in saying that this passage was not a part of the original Fourth Gospel, that it is not in the style of the author of the rest of *John*, that it breaks the normal sequence of the discourse of Jesus at that point, and that it contains several discrepancies and improbabilities. For these reasons the passage was printed within brackets in the Revised Version of the New Testament. They insist that strangulation, not stoning, was the historic Hebrew method of executing adulterers; that the death penalty for adultery was obsolete in the time of Jesus; that it was not the legal function of the scribes and Pharisees to accuse and bring to judgment a woman guilty of adultery, but that of the husband and the proper judges; that such a case would not be brought before Jesus for a decision, and that it is inconsistent with the rest of the Gospels for Jesus to have undertaken to judge a civil case of this kind. Those who insist upon the authenticity of the passage say that it dates back to Apostolic times, even if it was not a part of some early copies of *John*; that the woman taken in adultery may have been only betrothed, not actually married; that the sin of a betrothed woman was equivalent to a species of adultery according to rabbinic interpretation; that the enemies of Jesus wished to make him unpopular with the people by inducing him to revive an obsolete law; that they sought to embroil him with the Romans who would not permit death penalties without their approval, and that they expected only an opinion and not a legal decision. Whatever the truth, the story of the woman taken in adultery has been a part of the Bible for a long time and it is one of the most familiar and popular passages in the Scriptures. Some scholars believe that it was originally a part of *Luke* rather than *John*.

What is meant by a beam in the eye?

In *Matthew 7:3-5* Jesus says: "And why beholdest thou the mote that is in thy brother's eye, but considerest not the beam that is in thine own eye? Or how wilt thou say to thy brother, Let me pull out the mote out of thine eye; and, behold, a beam is in thine own eye? Thou hypocrite, first cast out the beam out of thine own eye; and then shalt thou see clearly to cast out the mote out of thy brother's eye." With slight variations the same observation occurs in *Luke 6:41-42*: "And why beholdest thou the mote that is in thy brother's eye, but perceivest not the beam that is in thine own eye? Either how canst thou say to thy brother, Brother, let me pull out the mote that is in thine eye, when thou thyself beholdest not the beam that is in thine own eye? Thou hypocrite, cast out first the beam out of thine own eye, and then shalt thou see clearly to pull out the mote that is in thy brother's eye." It is believed that this comparison of a *mote* and *beam* in the eye is an allusion to a Jewish proverbial saying that was familiar to the people to whom Jesus was speaking. The Greek word translated *mote* signifies "dried twig" or "splinter." English *mote* is similar in origin and meaning and is probably related to Dutch *mot* and Low German *mut,* "dust" or "grit." A mote is a small dry twig or stalk, an atom, a trifle, a minute dust particle, a speck seen floating in a sunbeam, especially an irritating particle in the eye or throat. Literally *beam* means one of the main timbers of a building or other wooden structure. In the Icelandic Bible of 1540 the *beam* in *Matthew 7:3-5* and *Luke 6:41-42* is translated *vagle,* which is an old Scandinavian word meaning "beam" and which is supposed to be the source of *wall* in *wall-eyed.* Jesus merely employed *mote* and *beam* figuratively to contrast a small fault and a great fault.

Who were the Twelve Apostles?

It is surprising how few persons, even when they are generally familiar with the Bible, are able to name the Twelve Apostles or disciples of Jesus. Many, when asked to name the Twelve Apostles, will start by naming Matthew, Mark, Luke and John. But Mark and Luke were not among the original Twelve Apostles and it is not known that either one of them ever knew Jesus personally. The New Testament itself is vague as to the identity of several of the Twelve Apostles and virtually nothing definite is known about them. *Apostle* is not restricted to the original twelve disciples of Jesus. Paul, for instance, was not one of the twelve disciples, but he continually calls himself an apostle and is generally known as the Apostle to the Gentiles. The term is derived from Greek *apo,* "off" and *stello,* "send," and signifies "envoy," "messenger" or "missionary." *Disciple* is from Latin *discipulus,* meaning "student" or "pupil." The original Twelve Apostles, that is, the original twelve disciples of Jesus, were: Simon (also called Peter), Andrew (Simon's brother), James (called James the greater or the elder), John (brother of James the elder), Philip, Bartholomew (also called Nathanael), James (also called James the less or the younger), Jude (the same as Thaddaeus and Labbeus), Thomas, Matthew (Levi), Simon (known as Simon the Canaanite or Zelotes), and Judas Iscariot. There were really thirteen original Apostles, because, after Judas Iscariot betrayed his Master and committed suicide, the other eleven cast lots to determine who should fill the vacancy and the lot fell upon Matthias. Of the original Twelve, the deaths of only Judas Iscariot and James the Greater are recorded in the Bible. In *Acts 12* it is related that Herod the king stretched forth his hand to vex certain of the church and killed James, the brother of John, with the sword. John, although one of the original Twelve, is known as St. John the Divine. Tradition says he died peacefully at a great age and was the only one of the original Twelve who did not meet a violent death. He is also almost unique among the Apostles and great saints in never having been important as a patron saint. Certain Christian writers who lived in the time of the Apostles are known as "the Apostolic Fathers." Matthew, Mark, Luke and John, the reputed authors of the Four Gospels, are called Evangelists, although the term does not occur in that sense in the New Testament. *Evangelist,* derived from Greek *eu,* "well," and *angelistes,* "messenger," signifies "a bearer of the *gospel,*" which itself is from Anglo-Saxon *god-spell,* literally meaning "good news" or "glad tidings." *Disciple* is applied in the New Testament to others as well as the Twelve. *Mark 3:14* says Jesus "ordained twelve, that they should be with him, and that he might send them forth to preach." These Twelve Apostles were chosen from a larger number of disciples. *Luke 10:1* tells us that "after these things the Lord appointed other seventy also, and sent them two and two before his face into every city and place, whither he himself would come." Apparently the number twelve was chosen in reference to the twelve tribes of Israel, for Jesus promised them, according to *Luke 22:30,* that they would "sit on thrones judging the twelve tribes of Israel." The number seventy for the larger group was probably chosen in reference to the seventy elders appointed by Moses in the wilderness. Some of the disciples of Jesus deserted him, for *John 6:66* says: "From that time many of his disciples went back, and walked no more with him."

Who was doubting Thomas?

Doubting Thomas, meaning one who will not believe until he sees, an incredulous person or a habitual doubter, is not in the Bible, but the phrase was suggested by the fact that the Apostle Thomas refused to believe in the resurrection of Jesus until he had seen him with his own eyes. This incident is related only in *John 20:24-29,* which reads: "But Thomas, one of the twelve, called Didymus, was not with them when Jesus came. The other disciples therefore said unto him, We have seen the Lord. But he said unto them, Except I shall see in his hands the print of the nails, and put my finger into the print of the nails, and thrust my hand into his side, I will not believe. And after eight days again his disciples were within, and Thomas with them: then came Jesus, the doors being shut, and stood in the midst, and said, Peace be unto you. Then saith he to Thomas, Reach hither thy finger, and behold my hands; and reach hither thy hand, and thrust it into my side: and be not faithless, but believing. And Thomas answered and said unto him, My Lord and my God. Jesus saith unto him, Thomas, because thou hast seen me, thou hast believed: blessed are they that have not seen, and yet have believed." Because of this passage this Apostle has come down through the centuries as Doubting Thomas, the typical pessimist and skeptic. On at least one other occasion Thomas is a doubter. According to *John 14:4-5*, after Jesus had said, "Whither I go ye know, and the way ye know," Thomas said to him, "Lord, we know not whither thou goest; and how can we know the way?" In *Matthew, Mark* and *Luke* he is called simply Thomas, but in *John* he is referred to as "Thomas, called Didymus." *Didymus* is merely a literal Greek translation of the Aramaic form of *Thomas* and signifies "twin." Some authorities suppose that Didymus alluded to his doubting propensities and in some versions it is rendered "double-minded." Others, however, suppose that *Didymus* was originally an editor's note to explain the meaning of the name. Since the names of Thomas and Matthew are linked together in the lists of the Twelve Apostles in *Matthew, Mark* and *Luke,* one theory is that they may have been twin brothers, but in *Acts 1:13* Thomas's name is separated from that of Matthew by Bartholomew.

What was the value of the betrayal money?

It is impossible to determine in terms of modern money the value of the "thirty pieces of silver" that Judas received from the chief priests for betraying Jesus. The Hebrew equivalent of *piece of silver* appears to have been applied at various times to different coins and weights of monetary metal. In the time of Jesus it probably was merely a popular name for the most common silver coin in circulation. *Exodus 21:32* says: "If the ox shall push a manservant or maidservant; he shall give unto their master thirty shekels of silver, and the ox shall be stoned." One authority states that the value of a piece of silver was one sum in the Pentateuch, another in the prophets, and still another in the other Old Testament writings. *Matthew,* the only one of the Gospels to refer to the price of betrayal as "thirty pieces of silver," relates the actual amount to a prophecy of Jeremiah. Apparently this was an error for *Zechariah 11:12-13*, which reads: "And I said unto them, If ye think good, give me my price; and if not, forbear. So they weighed for my price thirty pieces of silver. And the Lord said unto me, Cast it unto the potter: a goodly price that I was prised at of them. And I took the thirty pieces to the potter in the house of the Lord." If a piece of silver was the prevalent silver coin of the time, the money received by Judas was probably thirty Tyrian shekels, which were the customary temple offerings and which were worth about fifty cents apiece in American money. If this is true, Judas betrayed his Master for only about fifteen dollars. Some have supposed that it must have been a larger sum, because after Judas returned the money it was used by the priests to buy the potter's field. This, however, is not conclusive, because we have no means of knowing what the potter's field was or what it was worth. It may have been a comparatively worthless piece of property. There simply is not sufficient information on the subject to form a conclusion. *Thirty pieces of silver* has become the proverbial name for a bribe or for "blood money."

Was Judas treasurer of Jesus and his disciples?

The popular notion that Judas Iscariot acted as treasurer or steward for Jesus and his disciples rests on two passages in the New Testament. *John 12:4-6,* in connection with Mary's anointing the feet of Jesus with a pound of costly ointment of spikenard, says: "Then saith one of his disciples, Judas Iscariot, Simon's son, which should betray him, Why was not this ointment sold for three hundred pence, and given to the poor? This he said, not that he cared for the poor; but because he was a thief, and had the bag, and bare what was put therein." At the Last Supper Jesus gave Judas a sop and said to him, "That thou doest, do quickly." *John 13:28-29* says: "Now no man at the table knew for what intent he spake this unto him. For some of them thought, because Judas had the bag, that Jesus had said unto him, Buy those things that we have need of against the feast; or, that he should give something to the poor." The Greek word translated *bag* in these two passages really means "box" rather than "bag." *Matthew, Mark* and *Luke* make no allusion to the fact that Judas acted as treasurer and steward for Jesus and his disciples.

What is the origin of *potter's field*?

Potter's field, signifying "a burial ground for the poor and for strangers," was suggested by the following passage in *Matthew 27*: "Then Judas, which had betrayed him, when he saw that he was condemned, repented himself, and brought again the thirty pieces of silver to the chief priests and elders, saying, I have sinned in that I have betrayed the innocent blood. And they said, What is that to us? see thou to that. And he cast down the pieces of silver in the temple, and departed, and went and hanged himself. And the chief priests took the silver pieces, and said, It is not lawful for to put them into the treasury, because it is the price of blood. And they took counsel, and bought with them the *potter's field,* to bury strangers in. Wherefore that field was called, The field of blood, unto this day. Then was fulfilled that which was spoken by Jeremy the prophet, saying, And they took the thirty pieces of silver, the price of him that was valued, whom they of the children of Israel did value; And gave them for the *potter's field,* as the Lord appointed me." The saying ascribed to Jeremiah in *Matthew 27:9-10* is not in the *Book of Jeremiah* in its present form. This quotation appears rather to be a paraphrase of *Zechariah 11:12-13,* which reads: "And I said unto them, If ye think good, give me my price; and if not, forbear. So they weighed my price thirty pieces of silver. And the Lord said unto me, Cast it unto the potter: a goodly price that I was prised at of them. And I took the thirty pieces of silver, and cast them to the potter in the house of the Lord." Bible scholars have offered several explanations to account for this discrepancy. It may have been due to a lapse of the original writer, the first transcriber, or a later copyist. The quotation may be from a lost part of *Jeremiah* or from a complete lost book of that prophet. Perhaps an early copyist merely confused the passage in *Zechariah* with *Jeremiah 18:1-4,* which reads: "The word which came to Jeremiah from the Lord, saying, Arise, and go down to the *potter's house* and there I will cause thee to hear my words. Then I went down to the *potter's house,* and, behold, he wrought a work on the wheels. And the vessel that he made of clay was marred in the hand of the potter: so he made it again another vessel, as seemed good to the potter to make it." Another explanation is that the quotation in *Matthew 27:9-10* was ascribed to Jeremiah because the prophecies of that prophet stood first in the particular book of the prophets from which it was taken. Some commentators suggest that the place near Jerusalem referred to as the *potter's field* in *Matthew* may have been the very *potter's house* mentioned by Jeremiah. Just what this original potter's field was before it was converted into a cemetery for strangers will probably never be known. Evidently the field purchased by the chief priests with the thirty pieces of silver for which Judas Iscariot betrayed Jesus and then cast down in the temple was either the site of a potter's workshop or the place where the potter obtained his clay. *Acts 1:18-19* indicates this place was called "the field of blood" because Judas committed suicide there rather than because it was bought with the betrayal money. That passage reads: "Now this man purchased a field with the reward of iniquity; and falling headlong, he burst asunder in the midst, and all his bowels gushed out. And it was known unto all the dwellers at Jerusalem; insomuch as that field is called in their proper tongue, Aceldama, that is to say, The field of blood." In Jerusalem, south of the valley of Hinnom and opposite Mount Zion, there is an eminence known at the present time as the Hill of Evil Counsel. According to legend this is where Judas bargained for the betrayal of Jesus and on the slope of the hill is the traditional Aceldama or "field of blood."

What was the name of Pilate's wife?

There is only one direct reference to the wife of Pontius Pilate in the New Testament and that does not give her name. In connection with the trial of Jesus before the Roman procurator, *Matthew 27:19* says: "When he was set down on the judgment seat, his wife sent unto him, saying, Have thou nothing to do with that just man: for I have suffered many things this day in a dream because of him." History is equally silent on the name of Pilate's wife. Later Christian tradition gives her the name Claudia Procula or Procla and says that she was inclined toward Judaism, if not actually a Jewish proselyte of the gate and was a secret follower of Jesus. Some authorities, with little justification, have identified Pilate's wife with the Claudia mentioned by Paul in *II Timothy 4:21,* which reads: "Do thy diligence to come before winter. Eubulus greeteth thee, and Pudens, and Linus, and Claudia, and all the brethren." This Claudia was probably a Roman Christian and a freedwoman of the Claudian clan. In Christian tradition she is regarded as a relative of either Pudens or of Linus, who became Bishop of Rome and is listed second, next to Peter, among the Popes. On the strength of the tradition that Pilate's wife was a secret follower of Jesus and that her name was Claudia she was canonized as a saint by the Greek Orthodox church and her feast day is October 27.

How did Judas die?

There are two accounts of the death of Judas in the Bible. *Matthew 27:3-10* says: "Then Judas, which had betrayed him, when he saw that he was condemned, repented himself, and brought again the thirty pieces of silver to the chief priests and elders, saying, I have sinned in that I have betrayed the innocent blood. And they said, What is that to us? see thou to that. And he cast down the pieces of silver in the temple, and departed, and went and hanged himself." *Acts 1:18*, however, says of Judas: "Now this man purchased a field with the reward of iniquity; and falling headlong, he burst asunder in the midst, and all his bowels gushed out." These two passages seem to present a serious discrepancy which Bible scholars have attempted to reconcile with more ingenuity than success. According to *Matthew*, Judas hanged himself, but according to *Acts* he was killed by a fall. Probably the discrepancy is best explained by the supposition that the author of *Acts* spoke only figuratively of Judas's end and did not intend to specify the actual manner of his death. There is a further discrepancy in the two accounts. *Matthew* says that with the thirty pieces of silver the priests bought a field in which to bury strangers, while *Acts* says Judas himself purchased a field with the reward of iniquity. Notwithstanding the obscure passage in *Acts*, it has always been popularly assumed that Judas hanged himself. *Judas tree* is applied to the species of tree on which Judas, according to legend, committed suicide by hanging himself. In legend the tree is variously identified as the fig tree, the elder, a leguminous tree of southern Europe that flowers before the leaves appear, and the red bud. One story has it that the small tree known as the rosebud originally had white flowers, but after Judas hanged himself upon it they turned to bright purple red. Only one other Biblical character committed suicide by hanging himself. *II Samuel 17:23* says: "And when Ahithophel saw that his counsel was not followed, he saddled his ass, and arose, and gat him home to his house, to his city, and put his household in order, and hanged himself, and died, and was buried in the sepulchre of his father."

Who first referred to Pilate as "jesting Pilate"?

Pontius Pilate, the Roman procurator of Judaea at the time Jesus was crucified, was first called "jesting Pilate" by Francis Bacon. In his essay entitled *Of Truth* Lord Bacon wrote: "What is truth? said jesting Pilate; and would not stay for an answer." The Biblical passage to which this alludes is found only in *John 18:37-38*, which reads: "Pilate therefore said unto him, Art thou a king then? Jesus answered, Thou sayest that I am a king. To this end was I born, and for this cause came I into the world, that I should bear witness unto the truth. Every one that is of the truth heareth my voice. Pilate saith unto him, What is truth? And when he had said this, he went out again unto the Jews, and saith unto them, I find in him no fault at all." This passage is generally explained on the theory that Pilate, like many other Romans of his day, had come to scoff at all mention of the search for truth because the Empire was infested with all sorts of Greek sophists and Oriental theosophists who claimed to have a monopoly on the truth. Pilate's question was probably rhetorical and no answer was expected. Whether the Roman procurator was asking the question flippantly or seriously is not clear. The New Testament does not represent Pilate as a scoffer or jester. He was in a difficult position and may have spoken superficially, but there is nothing in the Bible to indicate that he was jesting. The Gospels are remarkably lenient in their portrayal of the character and acts of Pilate. Philo, Josephus and other ancient historians of the same period portray the Roman procurator as stubborn, cruel, vindictive and tyrannical, while the authors of the Gospels treat him with dignity, forbearance and without the slightest trace of ill feeling. What happened to Pilate is the subject of several legends. He became procurator of Judaea about 26 A.D. and continued in the office until about 36 A.D., six years after the crucifixion of Jesus. In the latter year he was summoned to Rome to answer official charges, but the Emperor Tiberius Caesar died before he reached the Roman capital. That is the last authentic information we have about Pilate. On the basis of later legends that he became a Christian, he was canonized as a saint by the Abyssinian church and is numbered among the martyrs by the Coptic church.

What does *washing one's hands of* allude to?

Washing the hands of, meaning "to disown responsibility for, to disclaim interest in or to renounce further connection with an act," was originally an allusion to Pilate's washing his hands before the multitude who accused Jesus. Like many other popular phrases of Biblical origin, the exact words do not occur in the Scriptures. *Matthew 27:24-25* says: "When Pilate saw that he could prevail nothing, but that rather a tumult was made, he took water, and washed his hands before the multitude, saying, I am innocent of the blood of this just person: see ye to it. Then answered all the people, and said, His blood be on us, and on our children." The incident of Pilate's washing his hands is not related in the other Gospels. Pilate probably could not speak the language of the majority of the people present and therefore adopted a piece of ancient Jewish symbolism to make himself intelligible to the crowd. This washing of hands to symbolize innocence of bloodshed is an obvious allusion to the ancient Hebrew rite of sacrificing a heifer in expiation of an untraced murder. *Deuteronomy 21:1-9* says: "If one be found slain in the land which the Lord thy God giveth thee to possess it, lying in the field, and it be not known who hath slain him: then thy elders and thy judges shall come forth, and they shall measure unto the cities which are round about him that is slain: and it shall be, that the city which is next unto the slain man, even the elders of that city shall take an heifer, which hath not been wrought with, and which hath not drawn in the yoke; and the elders of that city shall bring down the heifer unto a rough valley, which is neither eared nor sown, and shall strike off the heifer's neck there in the valley: and the priests the sons of Levi shall come near; for them the Lord thy God hath chosen to minister unto him, and to bless in the name of the Lord; and by their word shall every controversy and every stroke be tried; and all the elders of that city, that are next unto the slain man, shall wash their hands over the heifer that is beheaded in the valley: and they shall answer and say, Our hands have not shed this blood, neither have our eyes seen it. Be merciful, O Lord, unto thy people Israel, whom thou hast redeemed, and lay not innocent blood unto thy people of Israel's charge. And the blood shall be forgiven them. So shalt thou put away the guilt of innocent blood from among you, when thou shalt do that which is right in the sight of the Lord." In *Psalms 26:6* David, adopting the same symbolism, sings: "I will wash mine hands in innocency: so will I compass thine altar, O Lord." The priests always washed their hands before approaching the altar in the temple, and washing the hands has since ancient times been a common ritual and symbol of innocence among the Jews.

When did Jesus ask his disciples to arm themselves?

According to *Luke 22:36*, Jesus at the last supper said to the Twelve Apostles: "He that hath no sword, let him sell his garment, and buy one." Previously Jesus had spoken of the sword in the symbolical sense. For instance, in *Matthew 10:34* he is quoted as saying: "Think not that I am come to send peace on earth: I came not to send peace, but a sword." But in *Luke 22* he appears to have spoken literally, for Verse 38 adds: "And they said, Lord, behold, here are two swords. And he said unto them, It is enough." Presumably it was with one of these swords that Peter cut off the right ear of the servant of the high priest in the garden of Gethsemane on the night that Jesus was arrested. There are four different versions of the sword incident in the Gospels. *Mark 14:46-47* says simply: "And they laid their hands on him, and took him. And one of them that stood by drew a sword, and smote a servant of the high priest, and cut off his ear." *Matthew 26:51-54* says: "And, behold, one of them which were with Jesus stretched out his hand, and drew his sword, and struck a servant of the high priest's, and smote off his ear. Then said Jesus unto him, Put up again thy sword into his place: for all they that take the sword shall perish with the sword. Thinkest thou that I cannot now pray to my Father, and he shall presently give me more than twelve legions of angels?" *Luke 22:49-51* says: "When they which were about him saw what would follow, they said unto him, Lord, shall we smite with the sword? And one of them smote the servant of the high priest, and cut off his ear. And Jesus answered and said, Suffer ye thus far. And he touched his ear, and healed him." John supplies the name of the person who cut off the servant's ear as well as that of the servant. *John 18:10-11* says: "Then Simon Peter having a sword drew it, and smote the high priest's servant, and cut off his right ear. The servant's name was Malchus. Then said Jesus unto Peter, Put up thy sword into the sheath: the cup which my Father hath given me, shall I not drink it?" It has been suggested that Matthew, Mark and Luke suppressed the name of the person who cut off the ear of the high priest's servant in order to protect Peter, who may have still been living when they wrote, while John, writing after the death of "the first disciple," felt free to be more specific. Only Luke mentions that Jesus healed the servant's ear. This sword incident is one of the most difficult in the New Testament to explain. It is hard to believe that *Luke 22:38* means literally that Jesus asked his little band to arm themselves with a view to resisting the authorities. Such a conclusion seems to be inconsistent with the words and spirit of the rest of the Gospels. Yet the text indicates clearly that Jesus was talking about real swords and that the disciples produced two, one of which was used by Peter in a defensive act. In *Revelation 13:10* we are told "he that killeth with the sword must be killed with the sword."

Who was Barabbas?

Barabbas was a prisoner whom Pilate pardoned because the mob preferred his release to that of Jesus. *Bar,* equivalent to Aramaic *ben,* was a Chaldean loan-word meaning "son." *Barabbas* literally means "son of the father or master." In some manuscript copies and ancient versions of *Matthew* Barabbas's first name is given as Jesus. The Gospels say it was customary for the Roman governor to release at the Passover any one prisoner whom the people desired. There is no other authority for this custom, which appears to have been comparable to birthday pardons granted by monarchs. Such an act of clemency would be appropriate to the Passover, a commemoration of the deliverance from bondage. Barabbas was "a notable prisoner" who "lay bound with them that had made insurrection with him, who had committed murder in the insurrection." He had been cast into prison "for a certain sedition made in the city" and was "a robber" as well as a murderer. Pilate was willing to release Jesus of Nazareth, but "the chief priests and elders persuaded the multitude that they should ask Barabbas, and destroy Jesus." Barabbas had led a rebellion against Rome and was probably popular with the zealots. So Pilate, "willing to content the people, released Barabbas unto them," and "delivered Jesus unto their will." Very likely the two malefactors crucified with Jesus belonged to the rebels under Barabbas. The Gospels are silent on what became of Jesus Barabbas whose life was spared at the expense of Jesus of Nazareth.

Who was the young man who fled naked?

Mark 14:50-52, in connection with the arrest of Jesus, says: "And they forsook him, and fled. And there followed him a certain young man, having a linen cloth cast about his naked body; and the young men laid hold on him: and he left the linen cloth, and fled from them naked." This interesting but unimportant detail is mentioned only by Mark. There is no way of ever knowing who this "young man" was, but there is good reason for supposing that he was no other than Mark himself. In *Acts 12:12* we are told that after Peter had been miraculously delivered from Herod's prison in Jerusalem, "he came to the house of Mary the mother of John, whose surname was Mark; where many were gathered together praying." From *Colossians 4:10* we learn that Mark was closely related to Barnabas. There is nothing very improbable about the supposition that as a youth he may have been with Jesus on the night of the arrest. Other conjectures are that the young man who fled from them naked was John, the disciple whom Jesus loved; James, the brother of Jesus; a youth who lived at the house where the Last Supper was eaten, and an unknown youth of no importance but whose unhappy experience was long remembered because of its unusual aspect.

Who was Simon of Cyrene?

Other than what is in the Bible, we know nothing about Simon of Cyrene, whom the Roman soldiers compelled to carry the cross on which Jesus was crucified. *Matthew 27:32* says: "And as they came out, they found a man of Cyrene, Simon by name: him they compelled to bear his cross." And *Mark 15:21*: "And they compel one Simon a Cyrenian, who passed by, coming out of the country, the father of Alexander and Rufus, to bear his cross." Simon of Cyrene is often popularly supposed to have been a Negro, probably because he was a native of Africa and was made to bear the burden of another. There is, however, no valid reason for believing that he was a member of the colored race. In all probability he was a Hellenistic Jew who resided at Cyrene in Libya and who happened to be in Palestine for one reason or another at the time of the crucifixion of Jesus. Cyrene, his home city in northern Africa, was the metropolis and capital of ancient Cyrenaica, a province that had been governed successively by Egyptians, Greeks and Romans for six centuries preceding the Christian Era. The Cyrenians were chiefly of Greek stock and were noted for their intellectual activity and business ability. Cyrene was founded about 700 B.C. by Greek refugees from the islands of the Aegean Sea, and at one time it had a population of at least 100,000, when it was known as "The Athens of Libya," because of its happy combination of merchants and men of culture. Its buildings were noted for their architectural beauty; its medical school was one of the most famous in ancient times; and from its inhabitants sprang artists, poets and philosophers, who attracted the attention of the entire civilized world. At the time of the crucifixion of Jesus there was a considerable colony of Jews living in Cyrene. Jerusalem was then the religious, cultural and social capital of the Jews who lived throughout the entire Roman Empire, not only of those who lived in Palestine. In those days Jews from all over the Empire made frequent pilgrimages to Jerusalem, if they could afford it, to worship in the temple, offer sacrifices, to visit with their friends and relatives, and to transact business. Simon of Cyrene was probably a Jew who happened to be in or around Jerusalem for such a purpose. From the Gospels we learn simply that Simon was a Cyrenian, that he was the father of Rufus and Alexander, that the mob met him coming in from the country soon after they left Pilate's judgment hall with Jesus on their way to the place of execution, and that they stopped the passerby and compelled him to carry the cross the remainder of the way. There is nothing in the Bible that tells us this Simon was a Jew or that he had any particular interest in Jesus. In *Romans 16:13* St. Paul salutes "Rufus chosen in the Lord, and his mother" and it may be that this Rufus and his mother were the son and wife of Simon of Cyrene. Some of the Gnostics of the early part of the Christian era taught the curious belief that Simon was mistakenly crucified in place of Jesus. Upon their arrival at Golgotha, declared the Gnostics, Simon assumed the outward form of Jesus and Jesus that of Simon, and during the crucifixion Jesus mingled with the crowd and laughed at them. With more justice, some apocryphal writers related that it was Judas, not Simon the Cyrenian, who was thus substituted. Cyrene, after the Roman occupation in 96 B.C., gradually declined, and in the fourth or fifth century A.D. it was abandoned to the elements. In modern times the site of ancient Cyrene has provided one of the favorite workshops of archaeologists from many countries.

Does the Bible mention Mt. Calvary?

The popular notion is that Jesus was crucified on a hill or elevated place at Jerusalem. References to this belief are common in hymns, sermons and other religious literature. The place of the crucifixion has been referred to as the hill of calvary or "Mt. Calvary" since the fifth century. But the Bible does not contain a single reference or allusion to the place of crucifixion as a hill, mount or elevated place. It certainly was not a mountain. The references to the place of crucifixion in the Gospels are as follows: "And when they were come unto a place called Golgotha, that is to say, a place of a skull."—*Matthew 27:33*. "And they bring him unto the place Golgotha, which is, being interpreted, The place of a skull"—*Mark 15:22*. "And when they were come to the place, which is called Calvary, there they crucified him."—*Luke 23:33*. "And he bearing his cross went forth into a place called the place of a skull, which is called in the Hebrew Golgotha; where they crucified him."—*John 19:17-18*. In *John 19:20* we are told that "the place where Jesus was crucified was nigh to the city." *Hebrews 13:12* says: "Wherefore Jesus also, that he might sanctify the people with his own blood, suffered without the gate." *Golgotha* and *Calvary* are merely Anglicized forms of the Hebrew and Latin words meaning "a skull." Some authorities suppose the place was so called because it was the regular place for public executions; others, because of a tradition connecting it with the skull of Adam, and still others, because its contour suggested a skull. The exact site of the place of crucifixion has never been identified beyond question. We have no means of determining the correctness of the conventional and popular notion that it was on a hill or elevated spot. The Biblical accounts give us the impression that the place where Jesus was crucified and the tomb in the garden where he was buried were close together. One tradition places the original Golgotha on a skull-shaped hillock above Jeremiah's grotto just outside the Damascus gate of Jerusalem. Another tradition places it on the elevated site of the Church of the Holy Sepulchre within the walls of the modern city. All we know for certain is that it was a place near Jerusalem outside the gate. It was probably near a road. Whether or not the original Golgotha may have been the site of the Church of the Holy Sepulchre depends upon the location of the city wall at that time. Some authorities say that archaeological and other evidence discovered in recent times indicates that this site in the time of Jesus lay beyond the second wall, which was the outer wall at the date of the crucifixion. They also say that theory is further corroborated by the discovery of several rock tombs in the vicinity. Some authorities reject both the traditional sites referred to and say that the crucifixion took place in a valley near Jerusalem. But the popular notion that Jesus was crucified on the summit of a hill has become so fixed in legend, literature and art that it is not likely to be shaken by anything short of conclusive evidence to the contrary.

Did Jesus know he would be crucified?

According to the Gospels, Jesus knew he would suffer martyrdom by crucifixion. *Matthew 26:2* quotes Jesus as saying to his disciples: "Ye know that after two days is the feast of the passover, and the Son of man is betrayed to be crucified." In *John 12:32* he says: "And I, if I be lifted up from the earth, will draw all men unto me." The next verse explains: "This he said, signifying what death he should die." Even without assuming that Jesus had a divine foreknowledge of the future, there is nothing improbable in the statement that he had a premonition not only that he would be put to death but also that the method would be crucifixion. Under the Romans that was the common mode of execution of persons condemned to death who were not Roman citizens. As Jesus traveled through Judaea, Samaria and Galilee he must have often seen the bodies of the condemned hanging on crosses along the roads and outside the gates of the towns and cities. He would naturally realize that if the authorities in Jerusalem condemned him to death the mode of execution would be crucifixion. The Romans required the condemned to carry his own cross to the place of execution. *Cross* in the sense of *burden* occurs in the Gospels several times previous to the crucifixion of Jesus. *Matthew 10:38* quotes Jesus as saying: "And he that taketh not his cross, and followeth after me, is not worthy of me." According to *Luke 9:23*, he said: "If any man will come after me, let him deny himself, and take up his daily cross and follow me." Some writers, assuming that *cross* did not acquire the meaning of *burden* until after the crucifixion of Jesus, suppose these references to be anachronisms; that is, the authors of the Gospels ascribed to Jesus a figure of speech that would have been meaningless at the time he used it. That may be true, but it is not certain.

How old was Jesus when he was crucified?

The date of the crucifixion of Jesus is not known definitely, and since the date of his birth is uncertain, it is doubly difficult to determine his age at the time he was crucified. Nobody has yet been able to make a calendar of the life of Jesus that is generally acceptable to Biblical scholars themselves. *Luke 3:23* says that "Jesus himself began to be about thirty years of age." This was at the outset of his public ministry and shortly after he had been baptized by John the Baptist. John was six months older than Jesus, and, according to *Luke 3:1-2*, began to preach in the wilderness of Judaea "in the fifteenth year of the reign of Tiberius Caesar." We are also told in that same passage that Pontius Pilate was governor of Judaea; Herod (Antipas), tetrarch of Galilee; his brother Philip (Herod), tetrarch of Ituraea and Trachonitis; Lysanias, tetrarch of Abilene, and Annas and Caiaphas, the high priests. Tiberius succeeded Augustus during the year 14 A.D., and the fifteenth year of his reign would have been in 29 A.D. This suggests that Jesus was about thirty years old in 29 A.D., which would place his birth in 1 B.C., or three years after the death of Herod the Great. It is generally agreed that Luke is substantially correct in his other historical facts. Herod Antipas, Philip, Lysanias II, and Annas and Caiaphas all held the positions indicated in the fifteenth year of the reign of Tiberius, although it appears that Caiaphas was actually the high priest then; but Annas, his father-in-law, still retained much influence in the Jewish hierarchy as a former high priest. Some authorities point out that Luke, being a Greek, would not necessarily be aware of the fact that a Jew in those days would have to be a man of at least forty or fifty before he would be accepted as a prophet and teacher by his people. Accordingly they suppose that Luke merely conjectured that Jesus was about thirty at the time he began his public ministry. *John 8:57* says: "Then said the Jews unto him, Thou art not yet fifty years old, and hast thou seen Abraham?" Some authorities put considerable stock in this as indicating that Jesus was much older than he is generally supposed to have been. They argue that John, who was born and reared a Jew, would be more likely to be correct about his age than would Luke, who was not familiar with Jewish thought and customs. But the mocking question of his enemies proves little, except possibly that Jesus appeared to them as an older man than one in his early thirties, or that he was rather young to be taken seriously as a prophet. If Jesus was nearly fifty at that time he must have been born nearly 20 B.C. According to *John 2:20,* referring to a period early in the ministry of Jesus, the Jews said: "Forty and six years was this temple building." There is some historical evidence that Herod the Great began to rebuild the temple about 20 B.C. Forty-six years later would be 26 A.D. Assuming that Luke was correct, this would mean that Jesus was about thirty in that year, which agrees with the supposition he was born about 4 B.C. The duration of the ministry of Jesus is equally uncertain. Estimates range all the way from one to fifteen years. Three is generally accepted, chiefly because three Passovers seem to be mentioned during that period. It was long supposed that the three Passovers in the ministry of Jesus were those of the years 27, 28 and 29 A.D., which implies that Jesus was crucified in the spring of 29 A.D. The Gospel sources seem to agree that the crucifixion took place on Friday and that this Friday fell either on the day immediately preceding or the day immediately following the Passover. Recent investigators maintain that a scientific comparison of the Jewish calendar, inscriptions on Babylonian tablets, Biblical and historical references and other available data show that there was only one year during Pilate's regime in Judaea when the Passover could have met these conditions, and that this was the year 30 A.D. Accordingly they fix the exact date of the crucifixion on April 7, 30 A.D. But in the New Testament *Passover* is used in a sense so vague that we cannot be entirely certain that the Passover and the Sabbath fell on the same day in the year Jesus was crucified, although there is good reason for supposing that it did. The Synoptics and *John* appear not to be in complete agreement on this point. The best information points to the conclusion that the public ministry of Jesus lasted between one and three years and that he was probably thirty-four years old and possibly several years older when he was crucified.

Who were the two thieves crucified with Jesus?

The names of the two thieves crucified with Jesus are not given in the Biblical accounts. Nothing whatever is known about these two malefactors except what is related in the Four Gospels. *Matthew 27:38* says: "Then were there two thieves crucified with him, one on the right hand, and another on the left." *Luke 23* tells us that "there were also two other malefactors, led with him to be put to death," which emphasizes the fact that the Roman and Jewish authorities regarded Jesus as a common malefactor. "And when they were come to the place, which is called Calvary," says Luke, "there they crucified him, and the malefactors, one on the right hand, and the other on the left." *John 19:17* says: "And he bearing his cross went forth into a place called the place of a skull, which is called in the Hebrew Golgotha: where they crucified him, and two other with him, on either side one, and Jesus in the midst." Matthew and Mark imply that both of the thieves were impenitent at first. *Matthew 27:44* says that "the thieves also, which were crucified with him, cast the same in his teeth," while *Mark 15:32* says that "they that were crucified with him reviled him." Only Luke tells about the penitent thief. *Luke 23:39-43* says: "And one of the malefactors which were hanged railed on him, saying, If thou be Christ, save thyself and us. But the other answering rebuked him, saying, Dost not thou fear God, seeing thou art in the same condemnation? And we indeed justly; for we receive the due reward of our deeds: but this man hath done nothing amiss. And he said unto Jesus, Lord, remember me when thou comest into thy kingdom. And Jesus said unto him, Verily I say unto thee, Today shalt thou be with me in paradise." John adds one more detail about the two thieves. *John 19:32* says: "Then came the soldiers, and brake the legs of the first, and of the other which was crucified with him." According to early Christian tradition, the name of the penitent thief was Dysmas. He is regarded as a saint and his relics are claimed for Bologna in Italy. In some church calendars his feast day is commemorated March 25. The "good thief" is represented in art with a cross beside him. At the outskirts of the Judaean hills in Palestine is a village now called Latrun. Originally the name was Natrun, but during the Middle Ages it was confused with Latin *latro*, "robber," and from this circumstance there grew up a legend that Latrun was the birthplace of the penitent thief. According to the apocryphal Gospel of Nicodemus, the impenitent thief crucified with Jesus was named Gestas.

Why was Jesus offered vinegar at the crucifixion?

The purpose of the drink offered Jesus on the cross is not made clear by the Bible narratives. According to the Gospels, Jesus was offered drink twice. One of these offers of drink may have been made by the Jews and the other by the Romans. *Mark 15:23* says that when they brought Jesus to Golgotha "they gave him to drink wine mingled with myrrh: but he received it not." *Mark 15:34-36* says: "And at the ninth hour Jesus cried with a loud voice, saying, Eloi, Eloi, lama sabachthani? which is, being interpreted, My God, my God, why hast thou forsaken me? And some of them that stood by, when they heard it, said, Behold, he calleth Elias. And one ran and filled a spunge full of vinegar, and put it on a reed and gave him to drink, saying, Let alone; let us see whether Elias will come to take him down." *Matthew* confirms the double offer of a drink, once before Jesus was placed on the cross and once after, but says that he tasted the drink the first time. *Matthew 27:33-34* says: "And when they were come into a place called Golgotha, that is to say, a place of a skull, they gave him vinegar to drink mingled with gall: and when he had tasted thereof, he would not drink." Referring to a later time *Matthew 27:47-49* says: "Some of them that stood there, when they heard that, said, This man calleth for Elias. And straightway one of them ran, and took a spunge, and filled it with vinegar, and put it on a reed, and gave him to drink. The rest said, Let be, let us see whether Elias will come to save him." The other two Gospels say nothing about the first offer of a drink. In *Luke 23:36-37* we are told simply: "And the soldiers also mocked him, coming to him, and offering him vinegar, and saying, If thou be the king of the Jews, save thyself." *John,* however, indicates that Jesus after being put on the cross asked for drink. *John 19:28-30* says: "After this, Jesus knowing that all things were now accomplished, that the scripture might be fulfilled, saith, I thirst. Now there was set a vessel full of vinegar: and they filled a spunge with vinegar, and put it upon hyssop, and put it to his mouth. When Jesus therefore had received the vinegar, he said, It is finished: and he bowed his head, and gave up the ghost." The scriptural prophecy alluded to by John is apparently *Psalms 69:21,* which reads: "They gave me also gall for my meat; and in my thirst they gave me vinegar to drink." The *hyssop* in *John* appears to correspond with the *reed* in *Matthew* and *Mark*. This implies that it was necessary to put the spunge on a stick to reach the mouth of Jesus on the cross. There seems to be no merit to the suggestion that the hyssop was a spice added to the vinegar to make it quench thirst better. Just what the *vinegar* was and for what purpose it was offered to Jesus are not entirely clear. The Hebrew word rendered *vinegar* in the Old Testament appears to refer to what we now know as vinegar; that is, wine in which the alcohol has changed to acetic acid. In fact, *vinegar* is derived from Old French *vin,* "wine," and *aigre,* "sour." In *Numbers 6:3* the Nazarite was required to "separate himself from wine and strong drink" and was forbidden to drink "vinegar or wine, or vinegar of strong drink." Solomon, in *Proverbs 10:26,* said: "As vinegar to the teeth, and as smoke to the eyes, so is the sluggard to them that send him." But Boaz, according to *Ruth 2:14*, said to Ruth: "At mealtime come thou hither, and eat of the bread, and dip thy morsel in the vinegar." Obviously undiluted vinegar was too strong to drink straight. Even if we assume that the vinegar of the Old Testament was vinegar in the modern sense, it is not certain that *vinegar* means the same thing in the New Testament, where the term occurs only in connection with the crucifixion. There are three theories as to what the vinegar offered to Jesus was and as to why it was offered. One is that it was real vinegar and was offered to him to mock him and further afflict him. Another is that the drink consisted of a mixture of wine and myrrh such as kind and pious people were accustomed to offer a condemned person just before his execution to stupefy him and to prevent unnecessary suffering. Still another is that those charged with his crucifixion merely wished to offer him a drink out of kindness and sympathy. From sources outside the Bible we learn that it was a custom among the Jews of that day to give a stupefying mixture of light wine and frankincense and myrrh to a person about to be executed in order to prevent all unnecessary pain. We are told that this benumbing and stupefying draught was regularly supplied at Jerusalem by a charitable organization of Jewish women. This was undoubtedly the kind of drink offered to Jesus just before he was placed on the cross. It was an act of mercy on the part of the Jews. Jesus may have merely tasted it, or refused to drink it, because he desired to remain conscious to the end and to demonstrate to his followers that he could suffer the supreme penalty without flinching. The second drink offered to Jesus, just before his death on the cross, was probably the *posca* or sour wine ordinarily drunk by Roman soldiers. It is said that a drink of this sour wine was the privilege of any person who was crucified. The Roman soldiers naturally would have with them "a vessel of vinegar" (sour wine) as part of their regular rations. This theory seems to be borne out by the meaning of the Greek word translated *vinegar* in the New Testament. Therefore it seems reasonable to suppose that the first drink was offered by the Jews and the second by the Romans, and that both were customary acts of mercy on such occasions.

Were the feet of Jesus nailed to the cross?

That the feet as well as the hands of Jesus were nailed to the cross is a popular presumption that is not supported by any passage in the New Testament. In art and literature Jesus is almost always represented as having been fastened to the cross by nails driven through both hands and feet. Shakespeare, in *I King Henry IV*, has the English monarch yearning to visit "those holy fields, over whose acres walk'd those blessed feet, which fourteen hundred years ago were nail'd for our advantage on the bitter cross." In the fourteenth century tales attributed to Sir John Mandeville we read: "He had two in his hondes, and two in his feet; and of one of these the emperour Constantynoble made a brydille to his hors, to bere him in bataylle; and throughe vertue thereof he overcam his enemyes." The Four Gospels have little to say on this subject. Matthew and Mark mention neither hands nor feet in connection with the crucifixion. St. John tells us that one of the soldiers pierced the side of the body of the Saviour with a spear after it was taken down. When Jesus appeared to some of his disciples, who had assembled in secret for fear of the Jews, according to *John 20:20*, he "shewed unto them his hands and his side." Later, we are told in *John 20:25*, Thomas, who was not present at the first meeting, said: "Except I shall see in his hands the print of the nails, and put my finger into the print of the nails, and thrust my hand into his side, I will not believe." Eight days later, according to *John 20:27*, Jesus said to Thomas: "Reach hither thy finger, and behold my hands: and reach hither thy hand, and thrust it into my side." St. Luke does mention the feet of Jesus, but he says nothing to indicate that they were wounded. In *Luke 24:39* Jesus is represented as saying: "Behold my hands and my feet, that it is myself: handle me, and see; for a spirit hath not flesh and bones, as ye see me have." Clearly here Jesus was not calling attention to his wounds, but merely identifying himself and trying to satisfy his disciples that it was he in body and not in spirit. Under the customary Roman method of crucifixion at that time the body of the victim was fastened to the cross by nails driven into the hands. Sometimes the feet were also nailed to the cross, but the more general practice was merely to bind them with cords. The idea that the feet of Jesus were nailed to the cross was probably suggested by an Old Testament passage. In *Psalms 22:16* we are told that "they pierced my hands and my feet." It is clear that the compilers of the Gospels supposed this chapter to allude to the Messiah and consequently they connected it with Jesus as the Christ. More than a dozen nails alleged to have been used in the crucifixion of Jesus are preserved as relics in different parts of the world. According to legend, Empress Helena, the mother of Constantine, found the nails used at the crucifixion at the same time and at the same place at Calvary where was discovered the true cross. Another legend has it that the Empress once calmed the Adriatic during a terrific storm by throwing one of these nails into the sea. The finch known as a crossbill has sharply curved mandibles that cross each other, and a medieval story says these characteristics were bestowed upon the bird by Jesus because it attempted to release him from the cross by trying to pull out the nails with its beak.

When was the cross first used as a religious emblem?

The cross is among the oldest of all sacred symbols and there is evidence that it was used in various forms as a religious emblem by widely separated peoples long before the beginning of the Christian Era. Many centuries before the time of Jesus the ancient Egyptians venerated the cross and carved it on monuments and mummy cases and put it on sacred cakes eaten as part of a religious ritual. In Egypt the cross may have acquired its sacred character because a cross-like device was used to measure the depth of the waters of the Nile. The cross was a religious emblem among the ancient Scandinavians, Druids, Etruscans, Sabines, Phrygians, Greeks, Romans and Hindus. The swastika, used as a mystic symbol among the ancient Aryans, is a modified cross. When Europeans first came to the New World they found the cross an object of veneration among the Aztecs of Mexico, the Incas of Peru and other native American peoples. It is believed, however, that the cross as the Christian emblem originated with the crucifixion of Jesus and had no direct connection with its earlier use as a mystic and sacred symbol.

What kind of wood was the cross made of?

There is no authentic information as to the composition of the cross on which Jesus was crucified. Most of the alleged fragments of the cross preserved as sacred relics are composed of pine. Legends on the subject are legion. According to one, the original Christian cross was made of four kinds of wood—palm, cedar, olive and cypress—representing the four quarters of the earth. A poetic legend has it that the true cross was made of aspen, which accounts for the almost constant quivering of the leaves of that species of tree. Helena, mother of Constantine the Great, first Christian emperor of the Roman Empire, spent a great deal of time and money in the fourth century in efforts to find the true cross. In 326 A.D. the news was dispatched from Jerusalem by fast couriers that the original cross had been found. The story is that Helena was guided to Golgotha by an aged Jew. An excavation was made and at a considerable depth three crosses were discovered lying side by side. Near by was also found the inscription in Hebrew, Latin and Greek that had been placed above the head of Jesus when he was crucified. According to the legend, the identity of the true cross was determined, upon the suggestion of Bishop Macarius of Jerusalem, by having sick persons touch the three crosses. One of the crosses imparted miraculous cures to those who touched it. The Church of the Holy Sepulchre was built over the excavation and in it was deposited the greater part of the true cross. The remainder of this cross was sent to Byzantium, capital of the Eastern Empire. Later this sacred relic was taken to Rome and placed in the Church of Santa Croce in Gerusalemme, which was built especially to receive it. In the twelfth century the authenticity of this relic was attested in a bull issued by Pope Alexander III. The Invention of the Cross, or the Feast of the Finding of the Holy Cross, is still celebrated on May 3 by the Roman Catholic church in commemoration of the finding of the true cross by Helena.

How many crucifixions are mentioned in the Bible?

Although crucifixion had been a common mode of execution in Palestine for centuries when the last books of the Bible were composed, it is an interesting fact that it contains no mention of any crucifixions except those of Jesus and the two malefactors crucified with him. Crucifixion as a form of capital punishment was unknown to ancient Hebrew law. A form of impaling after execution by stoning is referred to in *Deuteronomy 21:22-23*, which reads in part: "If a man have committed a sin worthy of death, and he be to be put to death, and thou hang him on a tree: his body shall not remain all night upon the tree, but thou shalt in any wise bury him that day." *Joshua 10:26-27* tells us that Joshua, after capturing the five kings in a cave, "smote them, and slew them, and hanged them on five trees: and they were hanging upon the trees until evening." According to *Numbers 25:4*, the Lord commanded Moses to take the heads of certain rebellious leaders "and hang them up before the Lord against the sun." This obviously refers to the provision in the law that the body of any person so hanged was to be taken down and buried before sundown. Josephus confirms certain New Testament passages relating to the crucifixion of Jesus when he says the Jews were so careful about burying the dead "that they took down those that were condemned and crucified, and buried them before the going down of the sun." These Old Testament references are not to crucifixion in the sense of nailing the condemned alive to a cross and leaving him there until he died, but rather to a primitive form of posthumous indignity. But crucifixion was introduced into Palestine by the Gentiles at an early date. Josephus says Cyrus of Persia commanded that all persons who refused to help the Jews rebuild the temple at Jerusalem should be "caught and hung upon a cross." King Demetrius of Syria, after capturing Jerusalem, crucified eight hundred Jews. Apparently some of the Maccabean Jewish kings imitated their Greek rivals in this respect, for Josephus tells us that Alexander Jannaeus, king of Judaea about 100 B.C., had eight hundred of his subjects crucified in Jerusalem.

Who crucified Jesus?

The Gospels clearly show that Jesus was crucified by the Romans on charges preferred and pressed by the Jewish authorities in Jerusalem. In Palestine crucifixion was a Roman, not a Jewish, penalty. There is no contemporaneous evidence on the arrest, trial, conviction and execution of Jesus. Our only information on the subject is in the New Testament, composed long after the events. Even the year when Jesus was crucified is merely conjectural. Judaea had been subject to Rome nearly a century and at that time was a Roman province. The ruling class in Jerusalem had become more or less Romanized. It was a period of political unrest in Judaea and the actual political and legal status of the Jews at that time was changing. Herod the Great, "the half-Jewish" king, had put to death many members of the Great Sanhedrin and restricted Jewish independence. Later Roman procurators had virtually destroyed the Jewish independence established under the Maccabees. The so-called Jewish council and the high priest were probably mere tools of Pilate and Rome. *John 18:31* says: "Then said Pilate unto them, Take ye him, and judge him according to your law. The Jews therefore said unto him. It is not lawful for us to put any man to death." According to *John 19:10,* Pilate said to Jesus: "Knowest thou not that I have power to crucify thee and have power to release thee?" It is undoubtedly true that the Jewish authorities had been shorn of their political and legal powers and had only a shadowy jurisdiction over purely local and religious affairs. The power of life and death had been taken from them and vested solely in the Roman procurator, who had the authority to intervene in and to review all capital cases. It is clear in the Gospels that Jews initiated the action against Jesus, arrested him, tried him in the first instance and recommended the death penalty. Jesus was a Jew in nationality, race and religion and was so regarded by both the Roman and Jewish authorities. *Mark 10:33* quotes Jesus as saying "the Son of man shall be delivered unto the chief priests, and unto the scribes; and they shall condemn him to death, and shall deliver him to the Gentiles." *John 18:35* says: "Pilate answered, Am I a Jew? Thine own nation and the chief priests have delivered thee unto me." Apparently the Jewish authorities were interested chiefly in the charge that Jesus, in claiming to be the Messiah, had committed blasphemy, a purely religious offense. On the other hand, the Roman authorities were probably interested chiefly in the charge that Jesus, in claiming to be a king in the line of David, had committed treason, a purely political offense. But the dual system of government caused the two charges to be confused. The Jewish authorities wanted to maintain their religious system and the Romans wanted to maintain law and order and Roman supremacy. We are told in the Gospels that Judas "went unto the chief priests" and that Jesus was arrested by "a great multitude" from "the chief priests and elders of the people." According to *Luke 22:52*, this group included "the chief priests, and captains of the temple, and the elders." *John 18:3* tells us that Judas had "received a band of men and officers from the chief priests and Pharisees." "Then," says *John 18:12*, "the band and the captain and officers of the Jews took Jesus, and bound him." These passages indicate that the arrest of Jesus was purely a Jewish action. After preliminary hearings before Jewish officials, a Jewish council tried Jesus and found him guilty of blasphemy. It appears that the confession of Jesus that he was the Messiah and the Son of God was regarded by the Jewish authorities as sufficient evidence to convict him on the charge of blasphemy. But Judaea was a Roman province and the Jewish authorities could not carry out their sentence. *Luke 23:2* gives us the gist of the charges preferred by the Jewish authorities against Jesus before Pilate: "And they began to accuse him, saying, We found this fellow perverting the nation, and forbidding to give tribute to Caesar, saying that he himself is Christ a King." When Pilate found no fault in the accused, "they were the more fierce, saying, He stirreth up the people, teaching throughout all Jewry, beginning from Galilee to this place." Upon this hint, Pilate, wishing to extricate himself from a difficult situation, sent Jesus to Herod Antipas, whose tetrarchy included Galilee and who happened to be in Jerusalem. This scheme did not work and Herod sent the prisoner back to Pilate. According to the Gospels, Pilate was willing to let Jesus off with a scourging, but the accusers demanded his crucifixion. When Pilate persisted the accusers cried out, "Thou art not Caesar's friend." This was too much for the vacillating Roman procurator, who apparently did not have the political courage to decide against the local authorities. Therefore, after washing his hands of the whole case, he said: "Take ye him, and crucify him, for I find no fault in him." This can hardly mean that Pilate expected the Jewish authorities themselves to crucify Jesus. Under the local Jewish law the witnesses in capital cases were also the legal executioners, and one might suppose that the order was directed to the Jewish rulers, but stoning, not crucifixion, was the Jewish method of execution, and the context makes it clear that Jesus was crucified by a detail of Roman soldiers commanded by a centurion. Who these soldiers were, we have no means of knowing. Josephus says the Roman garrison in Judaea at the time of the death of Herod the Great was composed of Romans, Thracians, Germans, Gauls and Galatians. It was probably such a mixed company that crucified Jesus in the Roman fashion. There may have been some Romanized Jews among the soldiers, but that is improbable. The title on the cross—"JESUS KING OF THE JEWS"—indicates that the Romans crucified Jesus on a charge of treason. One gets the impression from the Gospels that the arrest, trial, conviction and execution of Jesus was more a mob than a legal action. It seems to have been a hasty affair, which took place at night and in the early part of the day and which involved trumped-up charges, false witnesses, political trickery and a confusion of Jewish and Roman legal procedure. It should be borne in mind that uprisings in Judaea and Galilee were frequent in those days and the Roman and Jewish authorities, which were really both part of the same government, feared the commotion about Jesus would start another rebellion among the zealots. In later times it became customary among Christians to say that "the Jews" crucified Jesus. Much of the confusion and bitterness on this question arose from the fact that the New Testament uses *Jew* in several different senses. Since Jesus and most of his early followers, as well as the authors of the New Testament, were Jews, obviously *Jew* in this connection refers to the Jewish authorities in Jerusalem and not the Jewish people. This distinction is generally made clear in the New Testament. Naturally the Jewish people as a whole were not responsible even indirectly for the crucifixion of Jesus. It is not probable that most of the three or four million Jews in the Roman Empire at the time even heard of the event until long afterwards. There is not a single reference to the subject in any Jewish or Roman contemporary writing. As a matter of fact, the Gospels themselves indicate that some members of the Jewish council in Jerusalem were friendly to Jesus. Both Nicodemus, who came to Jesus by night, and Joseph of Arimathaea, who buried Jesus, were members of the Jewish council. When the early Jewish Christians accused "the Jews" of being responsible for the crucifixion of Jesus they meant the Jewish-Roman authorities in Jerusalem. This is shown by the fact that in *I Thessalonians 2:14-15* Paul, who elsewhere calls himself "an Hebrew of the Hebrews," accuses Jews of having killed Jesus; but in *Acts 13:27-28* the Apostle to the Gentiles, speaking in the Jewish synagogue at Antioch, said: "For they that dwell at Jerusalem, and their rulers, because they knew him not, nor yet the voices of the prophets which are read every sabbath day, they have fulfilled them in condemning him. And though they found no cause of death in him, yet desired they Pilate that he should be slain." Paul himself, before his conversion, stood by and held the garments of those who stoned Stephen to death. For fifteen hundred years Christians have been repeating, in the Apostles' Creed, that Jesus "suffered under Pontius Pilate."

Who invented crucifixion?

The Romans did not invent crucifixion as a form of execution, as often stated. *Crucify* is derived from Latin *crux*, "cross," and "figere," "to fix," and literally means "to fix on a cross." Crucifixion was probably of Oriental origin and was practiced by the ancient Assyrians, Persians, Egyptians, Phoenicians, Carthaginians and Greeks before it was by the Romans. Legend attributes the invention of crucifixion to Queen Semiramis of Assyria, who is reputed to have reigned at Babylon about 900 B.C. The earliest and simplest form of crucifixion probably consisted of impaling a condemned person to a standing tree and was merely one form of hanging. Herodotus cites numerous cases of crucifixion among the Persians and Greeks. He says that after Cyrus of Persia captured Babylon about 538 B.C. he crucified three thousand of the leading citizens as an example to the rest of the inhabitants. The Romans appear to have borrowed this form of capital punishment from the Greeks, who in turn had borrowed it from the Persians. According to the Twelve Tables, a code of Roman laws framed in the fifth century B.C., traitors were crucified in the Forum by being nailed to trees. After the suppression of the slave uprising led by Spartacus, the Thracian gladiator, six thousand of his followers were crucified in 71 B.C. on the high road between Capua and Rome. The Jews were the victims of mass crucifixions after each one of several uprisings in Judaea and Galilee from the time of Herod the Great until the last Jewish rebellion led by Bar Cochba in 132-135 A.D.

Varus, governor of Syria when Jesus was a boy of ten or twelve, crucified two thousand Jews in Jerusalem after the suppression of a revolt. Josephus says that during the Jewish rebellion of 66-70 A.D., the Romans under Titus crucified so many Jews outside the walls of Jerusalem that "room was wanting for crosses, and crosses were wanting for bodies."

When did the Romans discontinue crucifixions?

Crucifixion continued to be the usual mode of executing slaves and malefactors in the Roman Empire until the fourth century A.D. Constantine the Great, emperor from 307-337 A.D., issued an edict abolishing crucifixion as a method of capital punishment. After that there were comparatively few executions by this method in Christendom. Although the cross had been previously used as an emblem by the Christians themselves, it was not until about this same time that it began to be used publicly as the generally acknowledged symbol of the Christian religion. Constantine, the first Christian emperor of Rome, attached great importance to the cross. Legend says that he himself was converted to Christianity by a vision of a cross in the sky. His mother, Helena, claimed to have found in Jerusalem the original cross on which Jesus was crucified. By Constantine's time the Christians were rapidly becoming the dominant religious group in the Empire and Rome had become cross conscious.

Why are criminals executed on Friday?

The custom of executing criminals on Friday, which in Europe dates back at least to the Middle Ages, is supposed by some authorities to have arisen from the fact that Jesus was executed by crucifixion on Friday, the sixth day of the week according to the old Jewish calendar. Although the practice is not so prevalent as formerly, an examination of current newspaper files indicates that Friday is still the favorite day in the United States for the execution of persons condemned to capital punishment. No adequate explanation has ever been offered as to why the sixth day of the week should be preferred as the day for executions. It is generally assumed, with some reason, that the ill luck associated with Friday by superstitious people arose from the connection of that day with the crucifixion of Jesus; but the assertion that the old practice of setting that day for executions resulted from this belief is mere speculation. Friday is popularly known as hangman's day. Whether the superstition associated with Friday was suggested by the fact that it was hangman's day, or whether condemned criminals were put to death on that day because of the ill luck already associated with it, we have no present means of determining. Curiously enough, the ancient Scandinavians, as well as the Hindus, regarded Friday as the luckiest day of the week.

What is the origin of *criss-cross*?

Criss-cross is merely a modified form of *Christ's cross,* the customary name of the Christian cross several hundred years ago. Formerly the alphabet was known as *Christ-cross row* from the figure of a Maltese-like figure of a cross at the beginning and the end of the alphabet in the old English horn-books. This name was first corrupted into *Chriss-cross* and finally into *Criss-cross.* In the course of time the origin and meaning of the term was lost sight of and it was treated as a reduplication of *cross* and taken to signify *cross-cross.* Now *criss-cross* means a transverse crossing, intersections, or marked or covered with crossed lines. Fox and geese, a children's game played on a slate, is called *criss-cross.*

What became of the robe worn by Jesus?

The dress worn by Jesus is frequently mentioned in the Gospels but never specifically described. It may be assumed that Jesus wore the customary Jewish dress of the time. This probably consisted of a kerchief to cover the head, coarse linen undergarments, a long loose outer garment variously called a coat, cloak, mantle or robe, a leathern girdle and sandals. On special ceremonial or dress occasions Jewish men wore a loose robe with short sleeves in place of the usual girdled robe. It was probably such a robe that Jesus laid aside when he washed the feet of the disciples after the Last Supper. *John 13:4* says: "He riseth from supper, and laid aside his garments; and took a towel, and girded himself." That Jesus wore the regulation Jewish costume is indicated by references to the hem of his garment. *Matthew 9:20-22* says: "And, behold, a woman, which was diseased with an issue of blood twelve years, came behind him, and touched the hem of his garment. For she said within herself, If I may but touch his garment, I shall be whole. But Jesus turned him about, and when he saw her, he said, Daughter, be of good comfort; thy faith hath made thee whole. And the woman was made whole from that hour." And *Matthew 14:34-36*: "And when they were gone over, they came into the land of Gennesaret. And when the men of that place had knowledge of him, they sent out into all that country round about, and brought unto him all that were diseased; and besought him that they might only touch the hem of his garment: and as many as touched were made perfectly whole." *Hem* in these passages should really be rendered *borders* or *tassels.* In *Numbers 15:39* the Israelites were bidden to "make them fringes in the borders of their garments throughout their generations, and that they put upon the fringe of the borders a ribband of blue: and it shall be unto you for a fringe, that ye may look upon it, and remember all the commandments of the Lord, and do them." Nothing was more natural for Jews who believed in the miraculous powers of Jesus to seek to touch that part of his garment that they regarded as the most holy. *Matthew 17:2* tells us that when Jesus was transfigured before Peter, James and John on a high mountain apart "his face did shine as the sun, and his raiment was white as the light." Referring to the same occasion, *Luke 9:29* says that "as he prayed, the fashion of his countenance was altered, and his raiment was white and glistering." *Mark 9:3* says "his raiment became shining, exceeding white as snow: so as no fuller on earth can white them." In *Matthew 27:28* we are told that the soldiers, after Pilate had delivered Jesus to them to be crucified, "stripped him, and put on him a scarlet robe." But after they had mocked him and ill treated him as a pretender to the throne of Israel, "they took the robe off from him, and put his own raiment on him." *Mark* says they "clothed him with purple" and afterwards "took off the purple from him, and put his own clothes on him." But *Luke 23:11* says it was Herod and his men of war who "arrayed him in a gorgeous robe, and sent him again to Pilate." *John* suggests that it was the Roman soldiers of Pilate who "put on him a purple robe." A scarlet or purple robe was the emblem of royalty and therefore appropriate for their mockery of one whom they charged had pretended to be King of the Jews. These passages indicate clearly that Jesus was wearing his usual clothes when he was crucified. *Matthew 27:35* says: "And they crucified him, and parted his garments, casting lots: that it might be fulfilled which was spoken by the prophet, They parted my garments among them, and upon my vesture did they cast lots." The words ascribed to "the prophet" are a paraphrase of *Psalms 22:18,* a song of David interpreted as referring to the Messiah, which reads: "They part my garments among them, and cast lots upon my vesture." *Luke 23:34* says simply "they parted his raiment, and cast lots," but by the position of the passage indicates that the soldiers cast lots for the raiment of Jesus before he died. John gives the most detailed account of the incident. *John 19:23-24* says: "Then the soldiers, when they had crucified Jesus, took his garments, and made four parts, to every soldier a part; and also his coat: now the coat was without seam, woven from the top throughout. They said therefore among themselves, Let us not rend it, but cast lots for it, whose it shall be: that the scripture might be fulfilled, which saith, They parted my raiment among them, and for my vesture they did cast lots. These things therefore the soldiers did." This refers to the fact that in those days the garments of a condemned person were the perquisites of the executioners. The passage indicates that there were four soldiers in immediate charge of the crucifixion of Jesus. Nothing whatever is known of the fate of these garments. What became of the seamless coat of Jesus for which the soldiers cast lots is the theme of *The Robe*, a novel by Lloyd Douglas, published in 1942.

Why were the followers of Jesus called Christians?

Acts 11:25-26 says: "Then departed Barnabas to Tarsus, for to seek Saul. And when he had found him, he brought him unto Antioch. And it came to pass, that a whole year they assembled themselves with the church, and taught much people. And the disciples were called Christians first in Antioch." *Christian* is the English form of a Latinized adjective based on Greek *Christos*, "Christ." It seems very unlikely that the earliest adherents of the new faith would call themselves Christians. It seems more likely that the term was at first applied to them by the heathen at Antioch in mild contempt. Antioch, the third city of the Roman Empire, like Alexandria, the second city, was famous for nicknames. At first the followers of Jesus were regarded merely as a Jewish sect. Like other Jews, they continued to meet in the regular synagogues, worshipped in the Temple when in Jerusalem, and generally observed all the rites and laws of the Jewish faith. The sole difference between the followers of Jesus and other Jews at first was that the former believed the Christ or Messiah had come in the person of Jesus while the other Jews said he was yet to come. Even as late as the persecutions under Nero the Christians were probably regarded by the Romans merely as particularly objectionable Jews who made converts among the Gentiles. But this one point of difference between the adherents of Jesus and the other Jews was a tremendous one and it led to a rapid separation of the two groups. Although there was a large Jewish colony in Antioch, it was predominantly a Greek city and by far the largest number of converts to the new faith there came from the Gentiles rather than from the adherents of Judaism. This was natural, because many Greeks had already joined the Jews in their worship and were regular attendants at the synagogues where Paul and Barnabas first preached the Gospel. Accordingly it is not surprising that the rapidly growing Jewish sect should have first attracted general notice and have been differentiated as a new faith in Antioch. Probably called Christians at first in derision, the adherents of Jesus gradually adopted the name and regarded it as a compliment rather than one of contempt or reproach. There are parallels to this in Quaker, Methodist and the names of several other religious denominations. But on the other hand, even to this day the Moslems resent being called Mohammedans. In addition to *Acts 11:26*, *Christian* occurs only twice in the New Testament: once in Agrippa's famous saying, "Almost thou persuadest me to be a Christian," in *Acts 26:28*, and once in *I Peter 4:16*, which reads: "Yet if any man suffer as a Christian, let him not be ashamed; but let him glorify God on this behalf." It is generally assumed that the first Christian church or organized community was founded in Jerusalem and the second at Antioch.

Does the Bible mention the Assumption of Mary?

No reference to the death of the mother of Jesus is found in the Bible. Both the Catholic church and the Eastern Orthodox church teach that the Virgin Mary was received directly into heaven. "The Assumption of the Blessed Virgin Mary" is commemorated by a special feast August 15. *Assumption* is derived from Latin *ad*, "to," and *sumere*, "to take," and the Assumption of the Virgin Mary refers to the assumption of her body into heaven upon her death. Titian's "Assumption of the Virgin" is regarded as one of the finest oil paintings in the world. When Napoleon was looting the art treasures of Italy to enrich his galleries in Paris, this priceless canvas in the Church of the Frari at Venice was so blackened by candle smoke that the French art commissioners decided that it was not worth taking away.

Does the Bible say Luke was a physician?

Our information that Luke, reputed author of one of the Gospels and of *Acts*, was a doctor by profession rests solely upon a single phrase used by Paul. In *Colossians 4:14* the Apostle to the Gentiles says: "Luke, the beloved physician, and Demas, greet you." It is supposed that Luke was a native of Antioch and was a Gentile Christian of Greek culture. There is nothing improbable in the statement that he was a physician. Some authorities think this is borne out by internal evidence in the writings ascribed to him, such as his use of "medical terms" and his emphasis upon mercy and the healing art. Others, however, say that Luke's references to these matters are no more than could be expected of any person of Greek culture who was possessed of the general scientific, philosophical, theological and artistic knowledge of the time. Paul is believed to have suffered throughout life from some physical affliction. If that is true, what would be more natural than for him to take as the companion on his missionary journeys a Greek doctor who had early become an adherent of the new faith? Nor is there anything improbable in the church legend that Luke was also a painter and sculptor. A picture of the Virgin found in Jerusalem and now in Rome is traditionally attributed to him. There is no evidence that Luke ever knew Jesus personally.

Who composed the Apostles' Creed?

The religious formula known as the Apostles' Creed is one of the most ancient and widely accepted rules of Christian faith and was so called either because its composition was traditionally ascribed to the Twelve Apostles themselves or because it was regarded as an epitome of their teachings. In 108 simple words it contains all the essential elements of the Christian religion in twelve statements or articles. When, where, why, by whom and in what language it was originally composed are matters merely for speculation rather than positive proof. According to a legend that seems to date back only to the Middle Ages the creed was written on the day of Pentecost and each Apostle contributed one article. This, of course, was after Matthias had been chosen to fill the vacancy among the Twelve caused by the desertion and suicide of Judas. Whether or not the Apostles authorized the creed, its substance was derived from the Gospels and the other Apostolic writings. It may have been suggested by Peter's confession in *Matthew 16:16*, which reads: "And Simon Peter answered and said, Thou art the Christ, the Son of the living God." A somewhat similar formula existed in Greek in the second century. It is mentioned by St. Irenaeus, who died in 202 A.D. The Apostles' Creed had assumed substantially its present form in Latin about 400 or 500 A.D. Perhaps originally it was a profession of faith that candidates for baptism were required to learn, recite and subscribe to. The English translation now employed by the Roman Catholic church and, with minor changes, by most Protestant churches is as follows: "I believe in God, the Father Almighty, Creator of Heaven and earth; and in Jesus Christ, His only Son, our Lord; who was conceived by the Holy Ghost, born of the Virgin Mary, suffered under Pontius Pilate, was crucified, dead, and buried; He descended into Hell; the third day he rose again from the dead; He ascended unto Heaven, sitteth at the right hand of God the Father Almighty; from thence He shall come to judge the living and the dead. I believe in the Holy Ghost, the Holy Catholic Church, the communion of saints, the forgiveness of sins, the resurrection of the body, and life everlasting. Amen."

How did *church* originate?

English *church* is derived from Anglo-Saxon *cirice.* The successive stages in the development of the word were *circe, circ, chirche, churche, church.* The Scotch *kirk* is from the same source. *Church,* singular and plural, occurs many times in the New Testament. The earliest use of the term is in *Matthew 16:18,* where Jesus is quoted as saying: "And I say also unto thee, That thou art Peter, and upon this rock I will build my church; and the gates of hell shall not prevail against it." The only other occurrence of the term in the Gospels is in *Matthew 18:17,* where Jesus, speaking of a trespassing brother, says: "And if he shall neglect to hear them, tell it unto the church: but if he neglect to hear the church, let him be unto thee as an heathen man and a publican." The translators of the Greek Septuagint sometimes employed *ecclesia,* which in ancient Greece meant an assembly of citizens called together by the public crier, to render the Hebrew term signifying "congregation" or "assembly." About the fourth or fifth century Western Christianity adopted the Greek *kyriakon* in place of *ecclesia,* the original Greek and Latin name for church. *Kyriakon* is the neuter form of the adjective *kyriakos,* meaning "of or belonging to the Lord." Thus *kyriakon* came to mean "house of the Lord," as well as the whole body of Christians. In the English Bible it was rendered church. But the King James translators retained *congregation* in the Old Testament to denote the assembly of God's people.

What bird is named after one of the Twelve Apostles?

Petrel, the name of several species of small sea-birds, is the diminutive of *Peter,* "little Peter." This name was suggested by the Apostle Peter's walking upon the Sea of Galilee and alludes to the peculiar manner these birds have of paddling along the surface of the waves. The story of Peter walking on the water is related in *Matthew 14:22-32,* which reads: "And straightway Jesus constrained his disciples to get into a ship, and to go before him unto the other side, while he sent the multitudes away. And when he had sent the multitudes away, he went up into a mountain apart to pray; and when the evening was come, he was there alone. But the ship was now in the midst of the sea, tossed with waves: for the wind was contrary. And in the fourth watch of the night Jesus went unto them, walking on the sea. And when the disciples saw him walking on the sea, they were troubled, saying, It is a spirit; and they cried out for fear. But straightway Jesus spake unto them, saying, Be of good cheer; it is I; be not afraid. And Peter answered him and said, Lord, if it be thou, bid me come unto thee on the water. And he said, Come. And when Peter was come down out of the ship, he walked on the water, to go to Jesus. But when he saw the wind boisterous, he was afraid; and beginning to sink, he cried, saying, Lord, save me. And immediately Jesus stretched forth his hand, and caught him, and said unto him, O thou of little faith, wherefore didst thou doubt? And when they were come into the ship, the wind ceased." *Mother Carey's chickens* is the popular name given to the "stormy petrels," which are often seen around ships in rough weather and are looked upon by many sailors as a sign of a storm. It is supposed that *Mother Carey* is a queer Anglicization of Latin *Mater Cara,* meaning "Dear Mother," a term often applied to the Virgin Mary.

Is "Love thy neighbour" in the Decalogue?

Matthew 22:34-40 says: "But when the Pharisees had heard that he had put the Sadducees to silence, they were gathered together. Then one of them, which was a lawyer, asked him a question, tempting him, and saying, Master, which is the great commandment in the law? Jesus said unto him, Thou shalt love the Lord thy God with all thy heart, and with all thy soul, and with all thy mind. This is the first and great commandment. And the second is like unto it, Thou shalt love thy neighbour as thyself. On these two commandments hang all the law and the prophets." In *Luke 10:27* the reference to this commandment is made by "a certain lawyer," who prompted the parable of the Good Samaritan by asking Jesus, "And who is my neighbour?" On several other occasions Jesus referred to "Thou shalt love thy neighbour as thyself" as one of the great commandments. Curiously enough, because of the emphasis given to it by Jesus, many people are surprised to learn that it is of Old rather than New Testament origin, while others are equally surprised to learn that it is not one of the Ten Commandments. "Thou shalt love thy neighbour as thyself" is one of the greatest provisions found in the law of Moses and it is in a sense the progenitor of the Golden Rule. The Ten Commandments—known as the Decalogue—are given in the first part of *Exodus 20* and repeated in *Deuteronomy 5,* while the Golden Rule of Judaism, which Jesus referred to as the second great commandment, does not occur until *Leviticus 19:18,* where it is found among various miscellaneous commands. That verse reads: "Thou shalt not avenge, nor bear any grudge against the children of thy people, but thou shalt love thy neighbour as thyself: I am the Lord." What is even more interesting is the fact that what Jesus regarded as the first and great commandment is also not found in the Ten Commandments. It is found, however, several times in *Deuteronomy,* which has been aptly described as "the book with a heart." *Deuteronomy 6:5* says: "And thou shalt love the Lord thy God with all thine heart, and with all thy soul, and with all thy might." In *Deuteronomy 10:12* we read: "And now, Israel, what doth the Lord thy God require of thee, but to fear the Lord thy God, to walk in all his ways, and to love him, and to serve the Lord thy God with all thy heart and with all thy soul."

Does the Bible say all people are of one blood?

In *Acts 17:26* Paul, speaking to the men of Athens on Mars' Hill, says that God "hath made of one blood all nations of men for to dwell on all the face of the earth, and hath determined the times before appointed, and the bounds of their habitation." The Apostle to the Gentiles apparently was rebuking the arrogance of the Greeks, who generally divided all mankind into only two groups—Greeks and barbarians. Among the Greeks at that time only the Stoics believed in the spiritual equality of all mankind.

Does *Holy Ghost* occur in the Old Testament?

In the King James Version of the Bible *Holy Ghost* occurs more than eighty times in the New Testament, but not once in the Old Testament. *Holy Spirit* is used several times in the Old Testament for certain phases of the action of God upon nature and man. "Cast me not away from thy presence; and take not thy holy spirit from me," says *Psalms 51:11. Isaiah 63:10-11* says: "But they rebelled, and vexed his holy Spirit: therefore he was turned to be their enemy, and he fought against them. Then he remembered the days of old, Moses, and his people, saying, Where is he that brought them up out of the sea with the shepherd of his flock? where is he that put his holy Spirit within him?" *Spirit* originally meant "breath." *Holy Spirit,* as well as *Holy Ghost,* occurs in the New Testament. For instance, in *Luke 11:13* Jesus is quoted as saying: "If ye then, being evil, know how to give good gifts unto your children: how much more shall your heavenly Father give the Holy Spirit to them that ask him?"

How did Sunday become the Christian Sabbath?

Adoption of Sunday as the Christian Sabbath was gradual. *Sunday,* which occurs nowhere in the Bible, is derived from Anglo-Saxon *Sunnandaeg,* "day of the sun," the first day of the week having been dedicated to the sun by the pagans. The commandment, "Remember the Sabbath day, to keep it holy," referred to the ancient Jewish Sabbath, which was the seventh day of the week according to the Hebrew calendar. That the New Testament writers clearly distinguished between the Sabbath and the first day of the week is shown by several passages in which the first day is mentioned as following the Sabbath. Although Jesus himself observed the Sabbath, St. Paul seems to have placed observance of this day among the customs not obligatory on Christians. "Let no man therefore," he says in *Colossians 2:16,* "judge you in meat, or in drink or in respect of an holy day, or of the new moon, or of the Sabbath days." This passage indicates that the question of the Christian's relation to the Jewish Sabbath was raised at an early date, although it is not certain that the passage refers to the weekly Sabbath. In *Romans 14:5-6* Paul says: "One man esteemeth one day above another: another esteemeth every day alike. Let every man be fully persuaded in his own mind. He that regardeth the day, regardeth it unto the Lord; and he that regardeth not the day, to the Lord he doth not regard it." Whatever the true meaning of these passages, from the beginning many of the Christians commemorated the first day of the week as Resurrection day, the day on which Jesus rose from the dead. Aside from the Sabbath, the days of the week did not bear special names in Palestine in the time of Jesus. They were generally referred to simply as the first day, the second day, the third day, etc. In the Gospels the sixth day, that is, the day preceding the seventh or the Sabbath, is called "the preparation." Originally Sunday as a holy day had no connection with the Sabbath. *Lord's day* first occurs in *Revelation 1:10*: "I was in the Spirit on the Lord's day." *I Corinthians 16:2* says: "Upon the first day of the week let every one of you lay by him in store, as God hath prospered him, that there be no gatherings when I come." This seems to imply some sort of observance of the first day of the week among the Christians in the time of Paul. There is, however, no evidence in the New Testament itself that the first day was originally intended as a substitute for the Jewish Sabbath. In fact it appears that most of the early Christians observed both the Sabbath and the Lord's day, and this was the tendency as long as the Christian community was composed chiefly of former adherents of Judaism. Neither is there any evidence that the first day was regarded in Apostolic times as a day for general rest from secular pursuits. On the other hand, it is probable that the early Christians held special worship on the Lord's day, for, according to *Acts 20:7*, Paul preached at Troas "upon the first day of the week when the disciples came together to break bread," and the Apostle continued to speak "till the break of day." This, of course, may have been only a special meeting. The association of Sunday with the true Sabbath and its development as a day of rest came later. In the first century St. Ignatius wrote that Christians no longer observed the Sabbath but the Lord's day instead. St. Justin, writing in the second century, was probably the first Christian writer to refer to the Lord's day as Sunday. "On the Lord's day," wrote Tertullian in 202 A.D., "we ought to abstain from all habit and labor of anxiety, putting off even our business." This tendency to observe the first day of the week as a day of general cessation from work was further confirmed in 321 A.D., when the Roman emperor Constantine issued the following civil decree: "On the venerable day of the sun let the magistrates and people residing in cities rest, and let all workshops be closed. In the country, however, persons engaged in agriculture may freely and lawfully continue their pursuits; because it often happens that another day is not so suitable for grain sowing or for vine planting; lest by neglecting the proper moment for such operations, the bounty of heaven should be lost." Constantine had by this time become converted to Christianity. This edict, which excepted farmers, was a good stroke of policy, because the pagan "day of the sun" and the Christian "Lord's day" both fell on the first day of the week and both Christians and pagans were pleased. It seems that in the fourth century at Rome Saturday was observed as a fast day in the spirit of the Jewish Sabbath, whilc at Milan the day was kept as a feast day. St. Ambrose, bishop of Milan, wrote in the fourth century that even during Lent "not only the Lord's Day, but every Sabbath, except the great Sabbath before Easter, are observed as festivals and days of relaxation in the Milan churches." St. Monica, the mother of St. Augustine of Hippo (354-430), paid her son a visit at Milan while he was a teacher of rhetoric there. She was a conscientious Christian and was greatly perplexed whether she should fast on Saturday as the Romans did or follow the Milanese custom of feasting. St. Augustine says in one of his epistles that he submitted the problem to St. Ambrose on behalf of his mother. The Bishop replied that he could give them no better advice than to follow his own practice in reference to the point raised. "When I am at Rome," wrote St. Ambrose, "I fast as the Romans do; when I am at Milan I do not fast." Some authorities believe that the proverb, "When in Rome do as the Romans do," was suggested by this observation of St. Ambrose. Later the Roman church prescribed the hearing of mass and rest from work on Sunday. The Council of Laodicea, which met during the fourth century in one of the cities of "the seven churches of Asia," transferred many of the obligations and solemnities of the Jewish Sabbath to the Christian Sunday. At first it was not pretended that Sunday observance was based on any specific passage in the New Testament. But about this same time it became customary to refer the obligation of observing the Lord's day to the Decalogue. As centuries passed and the Christian church grew in numbers and strength, the majority of Christians paid less and less attention to the Jewish Sabbath and more and more to the Lord's day, until finally observance of the Jewish Sabbath was virtually abandoned by all but certain sects of Christians. In time the Lord's day, or Sunday, largely supplanted the Sabbath in their eyes, and many began to take the position that the first day of the week had some kind of divine sanction and that the commandment about the Sabbath was applicable to it instead of to the Scriptural Sabbath of the Israelites. It even became customary among English-speaking people to speak of Sunday as the Sabbath. Even as early as the reign of Elizabeth fines were imposed on persons who did not attend church on Sunday. Later persons were subject to a fine or a certain number of hours in the stocks for carrying on their trade on the Lord's day. John Richard Green, in his *History of the English People,* says: "A more galling means of annoyance was found in the different views of the two religious parties on the subject of Sunday. The Puritans identified the Lord's day with the Jewish Sabbath, and transferred to the one the strict observances which were required for the other. The Laudian clergy, on the other hand, regarded it simply as one among the holidays of the church, and encouraged their flocks in the pastimes and recreations after service which had been common before the Reformation." Thomas Babington Macaulay says on the same subject: "In defiance of the express and reiterated declarations of Luther and Calvin, they (the Puritans) turned the weekly festival by which the church had, from the primitive times, commemorated the resurrection of the Lord, into a Jewish Sabbath." Some Christian sects, such as the Seventh Day Adventists and the Seventh Day Baptists, still adhere to the practice of observing Saturday, the seventh day of the week, instead of Sunday, the first day, as the true Sabbath.

Was Paul an epileptic?

The New Testament indicates that Paul suffered chronically or intermittently from some serious physical ailment but does not clearly describe its nature. Authorities have variously surmised that Paul's physical affliction was epilepsy, malaria, cramps and the eye ailment known as ophthalmia. It is generally inferred from several allusions in Paul's writings that his disease was a neurotic disorder of some kind. That his illness was distressing and repulsive and that it affected his eyes are indicated. According to *Acts 9*, when "suddenly there shined round about him a light from heaven" Paul "fell to the earth" and "when his eyes were opened, he saw no man" but "was three days without sight." In *Galatians 4:13-15* Paul says: "Ye know how through infirmity of the flesh I preached the gospel unto you at the first. And my temptation which was in my flesh ye despised not, nor rejected; but received me as an angel of God, even as Christ Jesus. Where is then the blessedness ye spake of? for I bear you record, that, if it had been possible, ye would have plucked out your own eyes, and have given them to me." Paul appears to refer to his physical affliction also in *II Corinthians 12:7* when he says: "And lest I should be exalted above measure through the abundance of the revelations, there was given to me a thorn in the flesh, the messenger of Satan to buffet me, lest I should be exalted above measure." That Paul was an epileptic is as good a guess as any, but available information is insufficient to settle the question definitely. Despite his affliction, the Apostle must have been a man of strong physique, for he traveled almost continually and underwent imprisonments, scourgings, stonings, shipwrecks, fights with beasts, exposure to cold and hunger and many other perils.

How did the fish become the symbol of Christianity?

There are several reasons why the fish became one the earliest symbols of the Saviour and of Christianity in general. Fish and fishing played an important part in the daily lives of Jesus and his disciples. *Mark 1:16-20* says: "Now as he walked by the sea of Galilee, he saw Simon and Andrew his brother casting a net into the sea: for they were fishers. And Jesus said unto them, Come ye after me, and I will make you to become fishers of men. And straightway they forsook their nets, and followed him. And when he had gone a little further thence, he saw James the son of Zebedee, and John his brother, who also were in the ship mending their nets. And straightway he called them: and they left their father Zebedee in the ship with the hired servants, and went after him." The reader will recall the miraculous multiplication of the loaves and fishes and the miracle of the draught of fishes, as well as the repast after the resurrection on the shores of the sea of Galilee, when some of the disciples ate fish caught by following the instructions of the Lord, and, according to *Luke 24:42-43,* "they gave him a piece of a broiled fish, and of a honeycomb, and he took it, and did eat before them." One of the most remarkable incidents relating to a fish is told in *Matthew 17:24-27,* which reads: "And when they were come to Capernaum, they that received tribute money came to Peter, and said, Doth not your master pay tribute? He saith, Yes. And when he was come into the house, Jesus prevented him, saying, What thinkest thou, Simon? of whom do the kings of the earth take custom or tribute? of their own children, or of strangers? Peter saith unto him, Of strangers. Jesus saith unto him, Then are the children free. Notwithstanding, lest we should offend them, go thou to the sea, and cast an hook, and take up the fish that first cometh up; and when thou hast opened his mouth, thou shalt find a piece of money; that take, and give unto them for me and thee." The fish as an emblem of Christianity was further popularized by the coincidence that the Greek word for fish, which we render *ichthys,* is spelled in Greek in five letters, corresponding to I-CH-TH-U-S, which form what is known as an acrostic; that is, the component letters of the word for fish are the initial letters of *Iesous CHristos, THeou Uios, Soter,* meaning "Jesus Christ, Son of God, Saviour." The sign of the fish was used as a password by early Christians during the days of their persecution and it has been found drawn on the walls in the catacombs of Rome. Later this sacred sign was explained by the theory that the fish, because it touches opposite shores of the sea, symbolized the great gulf between life and death. Fish became associated with Friday in a roundabout way. Friday corresponds to the day of the week on which Jesus was crucified and many of the early Christians observed it as a weekly fast day, that is, a day on which they abstained from eating flesh meats. Pope Nicholas (858-867) declared that abstinence on Friday was obligatory on all communicants of the Roman church. Nowadays many Protestants and other non-Catholics follow the Catholic practice of serving fish almost exclusively on Friday. This is partly out of respect for the numerous Catholics found in most communities; but fish dealers report that many housewives buy fish to be served on Friday because they feel that they can obtain fish of better quality at that time of the week because of the prevailing custom. Eating fish on Friday may also have been influenced to some extent by an ancient Norse custom. Friday was named for Freya, the Scandinavian goddess of marriage, fruitfulness and prosperity. It is said that a fish was her sacred emblem and that her devotees ate fish on her day in her honor. A signet ring bearing the papal seal and used for stamping official Vatican documents is known as the Fisherman's Ring because the device represents St. Peter drawing a net full of fish. The device on the signet dates from the thirteenth century and is one of the emblems of papal investiture. When a Pope dies the Cardinal Camerlengo or high chamberlain of the Holy See turns the ring over to the Sacred College of Cardinals under whose supervision it is broken and destroyed. A new signet ring with the same device is provided for the new Pope. "The Fisherman" is one of the titles of the Pope in allusion to the original profession of St. Peter. Certain catfishes belonging to the genus *Arius* and abounding along the coasts and in the rivers of the West Indies and South and Central America are known as crucifix fish because an outline in the skull and backbone bears a remarkable resemblance to the conventional pictures of Jesus nailed on the cross. On each side of the main outline are figures faintly suggesting two weeping women present at the crucifixion. The small bones known as the *Weberian ossicles* form what appears to be a halo. Many devout people in the regions where these fishes are found hold them in a sort of reverential awe and employ them as charms against danger and sickness. Prepared specimens, often ingeniously painted and decorated, are sold in the curio shops of the West Indies and of South and Central America. There is a legend that when Jesus was crucified all fishes except the pike dived under the waters in fright. Out of curiosity this species lifted up its head and witnessed the whole terrifying scene. Accordingly, in the pike's head all phases of the crucifixion are fancied to be represented—the cross, the nails and a sword. In the Old Testament fishes are several times mentioned, but there are few allusions to fishing. Fish, however, were an important article of food among the Israelites and later Jews, and one of the gates of Jerusalem was known as the

Fish Gate. After the first captivity the Jews bought fish of the coastal peoples. *Nehemiah 13:16* says: "There dwelt men of Tyre also therein, which brought fish, and all manner of ware, and sold on the sabbath unto the children of Judah, and in Jerusalem." But Nehemiah, as governor of the Jews, cracked down on these fishmongers and put a stop to this violation of the sabbath.

What was Paul's occupation?

Acts 18:3, speaking of Aquila and his wife Priscilla at Corinth, says because Paul "was of the same craft, he abode with them, and wrought; for by their occupation they were tentmakers." The Greek word here rendered *tentmaker* is associated with the making of goats-hair cloth. Paul was probably a weaver by trade. The cloth he wove would be used in making tents, sails, saddles, clothing, etc. Several passages in his letters show that Paul worked at his trade in Thessalonica and Ephesus and perhaps in other places as well as in Corinth. In *II Thessalonians 3:8* he wrote: "Neither did we eat any man's bread for nought: but wrought with labour and travail night and day, that we might not be chargeable to any of you; not because we have not power, but to make ourselves an ensample unto you to follow us." According to *II Corinthians 12:14,* he assured the Corinthians that he would not be "burdensome" to them; and in *Acts 20:24* he told the Ephesians, "ye yourselves know, that these hands have ministered unto my necessities, and to them that were with me." Paul probably worked as a weaver also at Philippi, for *Acts 16* informs us that he stayed in the house of "a certain woman named Lydia, a seller of purple." He is regarded as the patron saint of tentmakers, ropemakers and preachers.

How did the Jordan get its name?

Jordan, the name of the most famous small river in the world, is of unknown origin. Some authorities derive it from Hebrew *yaradh,* meaning "to go down," with the ending *an* for *en.* If this theory is correct, the name literally signifies "the descender." Others suppose *Jordan* to be derived from a pre-Semitic word, the true significance of which has been completely lost. In the fifth century Jerome, the great Latin scholar, supposed *Jordan* to be a compound of Hebrew *y'or* and *Dan* and to signify literally "the river of Dan." This theory was probably suggested by the fact that the town of Dan in northern Palestine was near one of the sources of the Jordan. Jerome's theory, however, is now generally rejected as untenable. In the Bible the

Jordan is referred to by that name in patriarchal times and long before the exodus of the Israelites out of Egypt. In *Genesis 13:10* we are told that "Lot lifted up his eyes, and beheld all the plain of Jordan, that it was well watered every where." The Jordan, though the largest stream in the Holy Land, is only 135 miles long in a straight line. Because of its tortuous channel its total length is about 250 miles. Between the Sea of Galilee and the Dead Sea, a distance of only 65 miles as the crow flies, the actual length of the Jordan is 200 miles. The fall of the stream from source to mouth is about 3,000 feet, or an average of 22 feet to the mile. Its width varies between 70 and 180 feet and its depth from 5 to 12. Near its mouth it narrows down to a sluggish stream only about 70 feet wide. The Jordan is not navigable. There are many shallow places used as fords since ancient times. Neither *bridge* nor any equivalent word occurs in the Bible and it is not known whether there were any bridges over the Jordan in Biblical times. Jesus was baptized by John the Baptist in the waters of the Jordan and the stream is associated with many other important events in the Bible.

What does *Galilee* mean?

Galilee, the name of the region and lake in northern Palestine, is a Hebrew word meaning "circuit." The name is supposed to allude to the fact that in ancient times Galilee was inhabited by non-Israelites, so that the Israelites passed around instead of through the district. In *Isaiah 9:1* the prophet speaks of it as "Galilee of the nations," and in *Matthew 4:15,* which is a quotation from *Isaiah,* it is referred to as "Galilee of the Gentiles." The Sea of Galilee, because of its association with the ministry of Jesus, is one of the most famous small lakes in the world. In the Bible it is first mentioned in *Numbers 34:11,* where it is called "the sea of Chinnereth." *Joshua 19:35* gives *Chinnereth* as the name of one of the fenced cities in the territory allotted to the tribe of Naphtali, but in *Joshua 11:2* "the plains south of *Chinneroth*" are mentioned. *Chinnereth,* or *Chinneroth,* is supposed to signify "lyre" and to have been the name of an ancient town on the lake. The first mention of the region under its most famous name is in *Joshua 20:7,* where we are told that one of the cities of refuge was "Kedesh in Galilee in mount Naphtali." Galilee was in Bible times, and still is, one of the most fertile sections of Palestine. In the New Testament the lake is variously called the Sea of Galilee, from the name of the province; the Lake of Gennesaret, from the fertile plain on the northwest, and the

Sea of Tiberias, from the Roman city on its shores. The Sea of Galilee, the largest body of fresh water in Palestine, is one of a series of lakes through which the Jordan flows on its way to the Dead Sea. It is pear-shaped, 13½ miles long, 7½ miles wide, 160 feet deep and lies 682 feet below the level of the Mediterranean. The surrounding region is subject to earthquakes and the lake itself is noted for its sudden and violent storms. There are hot springs on its shores and in the time of Jesus the Sea of Galilee was a favorite summer resort.

What does the Bible say is the root of evil?

The Bible does not say, as is popularly supposed, that money is the root of all evil. It says that the *love* of money is the root of all evil, which is a different thing. *I Timothy 6:10* says: "For the love of money is the root of all evil: which while some coveted after, they have erred from the faith, and pierced themselves through with many sorrows." The author of *I Timothy* may have been quoting a classical saying. Diogenes Laertius, who lived about 200 A.D., quoted Diogenes, who lived about 300 B.C., as having said: "The love of money is the metropolis of all evil."

How did the Dead Sea get its name?

Dead Sea does not occur in the Bible. That name was first given to the lowest body of water in the world by the Apostolic Fathers and other early post-Biblical writers. In the Bible it is called "the salt sea," "the eastern sea" and "the sea of the plain." *Genesis 14:3* says: "All these were joined together in the vale of Siddim, which is the salt sea." *Siddim*, not found elsewhere in the Bible, was probably a valley at the southern end of the sea, for Verse 10 of the same chapter tells us that "the vale of Siddim was full of slimepits; and the kings of Sodom and Gomorrah fled, and fell there." A tradition dating back at least 1800 years says the Dead Sea covers the site of the wicked cities destroyed by Jehovah with brimstone from heaven. Josephus refers to the Dead Sea as "the lake called Asphaltitis." Our word *asphalt* is believed to be of Semitic origin. The Arabs call this body of water *Bahr Lut*, "lake of Lot," in allusion to the fact that Lot's wife was turned into a pillar of salt on its desolate and barren shores. The Dead Sea deserves that name. Its waters are so salty that no fish, animal or plant life except a few algae is able to live in them. The water is about four times more salty than ordinary sea water. It is so buoyant that a human body will not sink in it. The sea receives the Jordan and other streams, but has no outlet, and consequently the salinity of its waters is constantly increasing. It has an extreme length of about 47 miles and an extreme width of about 10. Its normal level is nearly 1,300 feet below the level of the Mediterranean, and in the deepest places the water is 1,300 feet deep, which means that the bottom is nearly 2,600 feet below sea level and is the deepest natural depression on the face of the earth. Because of the dryness, pressure, heat, salt, rocky surface, scarcity of vegetation and sparseness of population, the shores of the Dead Sea are one of the most desolate and dreary regions in the world.

What does *Asia* in the Bible mean?

Asia occurs nowhere in the Old Testament or in the Gospels. In *Acts,* in several of the Epistles and in *Revelation* the term is used in the sense of the Roman province of Asia in part of what is now known as Asia Minor. There was little conception in Biblical times of Asia as one land mass or continent. The ancient Hebrews, like their neighbors, conceived the civilized world as consisting chiefly of the lands bordering on the Mediterranean or "the Great Sea." The notion that the grand land mass of Eurasia consists of two separate divisions grew out of the terminology used by the ancient Assyrians who dwelt east of the Mediterranean. It was natural that they should have considered Europe and Asia as two continents because civilization in both first developed, so far as they then knew, in those parts separated by large bodies of water. *Europe* and *Africa* are not in the Bible and *Asia* occurs in the New Testament as the name of a comparatively small territory. The Assyrians called the Greek peninsula *Irib* or *Ireb,* meaning "west" or "sunset," to distinguish it from Asia Minor, which they called *Assu,* meaning "east" or "sunrise." *Irib* was corrupted by Westerners into *Europe* and *Assu* into *Asia.* In time these names were extended, the one from Greece to all Europe, and the other from Asia Minor to all Asia. Homer applied *Asia* only to a meadow near Troy. But the last king of Pergamos bore the title "king of Asia." When the Romans about 130 B.C. conquered his kingdom as well as surrounding kingdoms, they formed the territory into a province and called it Proconsular Asia. The New Testament writers invariably refer to this Roman province when they use the term *Asia.* The "seven churches that are in Asia"—Ephesus, Smyrna, Pergamos, Thyatira, Sardis, Philadelphia and Laodicea—were all in Proconsular Asia. It was that same territory that was meant when, according to *Acts 16:6,* Paul and Timothy "were forbidden of the Holy Ghost to preach the word in Asia." *Acts 19:10* tells us that "all they which dwelt in Asia heard the word of the lord Jesus, both Jews and Greeks."

Paul, according to *Acts 19:22,* sent Timothy and Erastus into Macedonia, "but he himself stayed in Asia for a season." Shortly thereafter Demetrius, a silversmith who made shrines for the goddess Diana, told his fellow workmen that Paul had persuaded and turned away much people "not alone at Ephesus, but almost throughout all Asia." In his first letter to the Corinthians, written from Philippi in Greece, Paul says "the churches of Asia salute you," and in *Acts 2,* where the homelands of those present at Jerusalem on the day of Pentecost are listed, *Asia* is used specifically for the Roman province of Asia, while other places in Asia Minor are mentioned separately, such as Phrygia, Cappadocia and Pontus. Later all of what is now Asia Minor became known as Asia. When the term was gradually extended to comprise the entire continent, "Old Asia" came to be called Asia Minor to distinguish it from "Asia Major."

Why is Jesus called "The Man of Sorrows"?

Jesus is nowhere referred to as "The Man of Sorrows" in the New Testament. Even the phrase does not occur in New Testament writings. It was suggested by *Isaiah 53:3,* which reads: "He is despised and rejected of men; a man of sorrows, and acquainted with grief: and we hid as it were our faces from him; he was despised, and we esteemed him not." This part of prophecy was interpreted as applicable to the Messiah and after the crucifixion of Jesus it was naturally applied by Christian writers to him.

Is *a law unto themselves* in the Bible?

This proverbial phrase is in the Bible, but is used in a favorable rather than an unfavorable sense. In *Romans 2:14* St. Paul says: "For when the Gentiles, which have not the law, do by nature the things contained in the law, these, having not the law, are a law unto themselves."

Does *all things to all men* occur in the Bible?

The phrase *all things to all men* is of Biblical origin. *I Corinthians 9:22* says: "To the weak became I as weak, that I might gain the weak: I am made all things to all men, that I might by all means save some."

Who said that God loves a cheerful giver?

In *II Corinthians 9:6-7* St. Paul wrote: "But this I say, He which soweth sparingly shall reap also sparingly; and he which soweth bountifully shall reap also bountifully. Every man according as he purposeth in his heart, so let him give; not grudgingly, or of necessity: for God loveth a cheerful giver." The same idea occurs in the Old Testament. *Exodus 25:1-2* says: "And the Lord spake unto Moses, saying, Speak unto the children of Israel, that they bring me an offering: of every man that giveth it willingly with his heart, ye shall take my offering." Later Moses, in *Exodus 35:5*, told the Israelites: "Take ye from among you an offering unto the Lord: whosoever is of a willing heart, let him bring it, an offering of the Lord."

How long is a Sabbath day's journey?

Under the Mosaic law the Israelites were forbidden to travel on the Sabbath day. *Exodus 16:29* says, "See, for that the Lord hath given you the Sabbath, therefore he giveth you on the sixth day the bread of two days; abide ye every man in his place, let no man go out of his place on the seventh day." It is evident, however, that the Israelites were permitted to go a certain distance on the Sabbath. For instance, they could go to the tabernacle or temple from the remote parts of the camp or city. In the course of centuries the rabbinical authorities found ways, by legal fictions, to increase the distance that an Israelite might travel on the Sabbath day in order to make the restriction less burdensome. At first a Sabbath day's journey, the distance an Israelite might travel on the Sabbath from the walled limits of a town or city, was fixed at 2,000 cubits. This particular distance was probably based upon *Joshua 3:4-5*, which reads: "And they commanded the people, saying, When ye see the ark of the covenant of the Lord your God, and the priests the Levites bearing it, then ye shall remove from your place, and go after it. Yet there shall be a space between you and it, about two thousand cubits by measure; come not near it, that ye may know the way by which ye must go: for ye have not passed this way heretofore." Later the rabbinical authorities interpreted "place" to mean town or city, so that an Israelite might travel 2,000 cubits outside the limits of his city on the Sabbath. Still later the Pharisees doubled the length of the Sabbath day's journey by another legal fiction. They laid down the rule that if an Israelite deposited food at a definite place for the Sabbath he by that act made that figuratively the place of his abode and accordingly might travel 2,000 cubits farther on the Sabbath, making a Sabbath day's journey 4,000 cubits. It appears that the Hebrew cubit was a linear measure generally equivalent to 17.58 English inches, although there is evidence that the Hebrew word so translated may sometimes refer to a measure equivalent to as much as 20 or more inches. The standards of measures in the Bible were long ago lost and it is very difficult to reproduce them. In later times the Jews adopted the measurements of the people by whom they were subjugated or among whom they lived and at the same time retained the names of their own measurements that approximated them most nearly. Consequently the length of the Hebrew cubit probably varied at different times. This probably accounts for such expressions as "the cubit of a man" and "the great cubit" in the Bible. It is customary to assume, for convenience, that the Hebrew cubit was 18 inches in length. On that assumption, the Sabbath day's journey of 4,000 cubits would have been 6,000 feet. An English statute mile is 5,280 feet. In post-Biblical times the Pharisees stretched the Sabbath day's journey again, making it 8,000 cubits, on the theory that a person, after going a distance of 4,000 cubits, would have to return. There are few allusions to the Sabbath day's journey in the New Testament. In *Matthew 24:20* Jesus is quoted as saying: "But pray ye that your flight be not in the winter, neither on the Sabbath day." In *Acts 1:12* it says, "Then returned they unto Jerusalem from the mount called Olivet, which is from Jerusalem a Sabbath day's journey." According to Josephus, the Mount of Olives was 6 furlongs, or about 3,495 feet from Jerusalem. Thus it would seem that a Sabbath day's journey in New Testament times was considerably less than one statute mile. But it seems probable that the last quotation should be construed, "which is *within* a sabbath day's journey of Jerusalem." Under an old Puritan law in England it was permissible in the event of necessity to make a journey of 10 miles on Sunday. That distance, according to medieval legal practice, was one half of an ordinary or week-day journey, namely, 20 miles.

Was King Agrippa almost persuaded to be a Christian?

Acts 26:27-29 of the King James Version says: "King Agrippa, believest thou the prophets? I know that thou believest. Then Agrippa said unto Paul, Almost thou persuadest me to be a Christian. And Paul said, I would to God, that not only thou, but also all that hear me this day, were both almost, and altogether such as I am, except these bonds." Does this mean that King Agrippa was almost persuaded by Paul's eloquence to become a Christian? Many Bible critics insist that this rendering of the passage in the King James Version is faulty. They say that the original Greek indicates clearly that Agrippa interrupted Paul to warn him that he was going too far in presuming that he was admitting his argument. "Too eagerly art thou persuading thyself that thou canst make me a Christian," it is argued, would be a more satisfactory rendering of the original of Agrippa's words. Henry Alford, dean of Canterbury and English Biblical scholar, rendered this passage, "Lightly art thou persuading thyself that thou canst make me a Christian," and the Revised Version of 1881 rendered it, "With but little persuasion thou wouldest fain make me a Christian." This King Agrippa before whom Paul appeared at Caesarea is known in history as Herod Agrippa II. He was a son of Herod Agrippa I and a great-grandson of Herod the Great, who reigned in Jerusalem when Jesus was born. Although Herod Agrippa II was nominally a Jew, like all the Herods he was merely a puppet king and took the side of the Romans in all important controversies between them and his own people. His sister Bernice is mentioned as being present at the trial of Paul. After Paul had spoken, Agrippa agreed with the Roman governor Festus that "This man doeth nothing worthy of death or of bonds" and that he "might have been set at liberty, if he had not appealed to Caesar." This probably does not mean that Agrippa was inclined to accept Paul's interpretation of the Scriptures, but merely that he saw nothing in the Apostle's position that warranted action by the government.

Does the Bible mention the Mediterranean Sea?

Mediterranean Sea does not occur in the Bible, but that body of water is frequently referred to under such names as "the great sea," "the sea of the Philistines," "the hinder sea," "the western sea," "the sea of Joppa" and simply "the sea." In *Numbers 34:6* Moses, in defining the boundaries of the Promised Land, says "as for the western border, ye shall even have the great sea for a border." Back in *Exodus 23:21* God through Moses had told the Israelites: "And I will set thy border from the Red Sea even unto the sea of the Philistines, and from the wilderness unto the river." In *Deuteronomy 11:24* the Mediterranean is called "the uttermost sea," and in *Deuteronomy 34:2,* "the utmost sea." The Israelites thought of the Dead Sea as the "eastern," "former" or "front" sea and the Mediterranean as the "western" or "hinder" sea. According to *Joshua 1:4,* the Lord spake unto Joshua after the death of Moses and said: "From the wilderness and this Lebanon even unto the great river, the river Euphrates, all the land of the Hittites, and unto the great sea toward the going down of the sun, shall be your coast." It was on the Mediterranean, the sea of Joppa, that Jonah was sailing when he was thrown overboard by the mariners and swallowed by a great fish. This sea also figured largely in the many journeys of St. Paul. The cedar and cypress wood from

Lebanon used in Solomon's Temple was shipped part of the way on the Mediterranean. The Greeks, like the Israelites, generally called it simply "the sea" or "the great sea," but the Romans called it *mare nostrum,* "our sea." In the Old Testament "from sea to sea" signified from the Red Sea to the Mediterranean. *Psalms 72:8,* which by some is regarded as Messianic, reads: "He shall have dominion also from sea to sea, and from the river unto the ends of the earth." The motto in the coat of arms of the Dominion of Canada is *a mari usque ad mare,* "from sea to sea," which is taken from the Latin version of this verse.

Are *cherubim* and *seraphim* correct forms?

Cherubim and *seraphim* are the Hebrew plurals of *cherub* and *seraph,* the names of heavenly angel-like beings or their representations. The English translators of the King James Version of the Bible, like their predecessors, erroneously treated *cherubim* and *seraphim* as singular and added an *s* to make the plural. Strictly speaking, *cherubims* and *seraphims* are double plurals. *Genesis 3:24* says the Lord "placed at the east of the garden of Eden Cherubims." *Exodus 25:18* says: "And thou shalt make two cherubims of gold, of beaten work shall thou make them, in the two ends of the mercy seat." This usage was adopted in the New Testament also. *Hebrews 9:5* says: "And over it the cherubims of glory shadowing the mercy seat; of which we cannot speak particularly." Likewise *seraphim* was construed as a singular and an *s* added to form the plural in *Isaiah 6:2,* which reads: "Above it stood the seraphims: each one had six wings; with twain he covered his face, and with twain he covered his feet, and with twain he did fly." In the Latin Vulgate occurs the form *cherubin,* which was followed by some early English translators. Although *cherubims* and *seraphims* were originally erroneous, cherubim and seraphim have been construed as singulars so long that the double plural forms generally pass unchallenged in English usage. In later Christian lore seraphim and cherubim were regarded as the first and second orders of angels in the celestial hierarchy.

Does the Bible say that angels have wings?

Nowhere in the King James Version of the New Testament are angels spoken of as having wings, although in his vision on Patmos, according to *Revelation 8:13* and *14:6,* St. John the Divine "heard an angel flying through the midst of heaven." The popular notion that faithful Christians after death are transformed into angels with two wings is hardly justified by any passage in the Bible. Isaiah describes seraphim with six wings each (*Isaiah 6:2*), and the cherubim that Ezekiel saw had four wings (*Ezekiel 1:11*). In his vision Zechariah saw two women, with wind in their wings, "for they had wings like the wings of a stork" (*Zechariah 5:9*). The cherubs of gold at the ends of the Mercy Seat on the Ark of the Covenant (*Exodus 25:20*), had two wings each. These latter references to images of cherubs, and the reference in *Zechariah*, appear to be the only instances in which angels of any order are referred to in the Bible as two-winged creatures. Some authorities suppose that the Hebrews borrowed their conception of winged seraphim and cherubim from the Assyrians and Persians, who depicted winged men with heads of hawks on the walls of their buildings, and whose palaces were guarded by sculptured winged bulls and lions. Both the Greek word from which *angel* is derived, and the Hebrew word so translated in the Bible, signify "messenger." In the Old Testament angels were the messengers of God. In the New Testament Jesus is substituted for the angels as the intermediary between God and man.

How many angels are referred to by name in the Bible?

Only two angels are mentioned by name in the Bible. They are Gabriel and Michael. In *Daniel 8:16* Gabriel is the name of the revealing angel who appeared to Daniel in a dream to interpret his vision, although *angel* is not used in that particular connection. *Daniel 9:21* says: "Yea, whiles I was speaking in prayer, even the man Gabriel, whom I had seen in the vision at the beginning, being caused to fly swiftly, touched me about the time of the evening oblation." Gabriel is not again referred to by name until *Luke 1*, where we are told that an angel of the Lord appeared to Zacharias while he executed the priest's office and burned incense in the temple. After the angel had foretold that the priest's wife Elizabeth should bear him a son, whose name should be called John, Zacharias asked, "Whereby shall I know this?" According to *Luke 1:19*, the angel answered and said to him: "I am Gabriel, that stand in the presence of God; and am sent to speak unto thee, and to shew thee these glad tidings." Later Gabriel also appeared to Mary. *Luke 1:26-27* says: "And in the sixth month the angel Gabriel was sent from God unto a city of Galilee, named Nazareth, to a virgin espoused to a man whose name was Joseph, of the house of David; and the virgin's name was Mary." Michael is not called an angel in *Daniel*. In *Daniel 10:13* we read: "But the prince of the kingdom of Persia withstood me one and twenty days: but, lo,

Michael, one of the chief princes, came to help me; and I remained there with the kings of Persia." According to Verse 21 of the same chapter the guardian angel of Judah says to Daniel: "But I will shew thee that which is noted in the scripture of truth: and there is none that holdeth with me in these things, but Michael your prince." Michael reappears in *Jude* as an archangel. Verse 9 of that book, which is too short to be divided into chapters, says: "Yet Michael the archangel, when contending with the devil he disputed about the body of Moses, durst not bring against him a railing accusation, but said, The Lord rebuke thee." Michael is mentioned also in the role of an archangel in *Revelation 12:7-8,* which reads: "And there was war in heaven: Michael and his angels fought against the dragon; and the dragon fought and his angels, and prevailed not; neither was their place found any more in heaven." *Lucifer,* popularly regarded as a fallen angel, occurs in the Bible only once. *Isaiah 14:12* says: "How art thou fallen from heaven, O Lucifer, son of the morning! how art thou cut down to the ground, which didst weaken the nations!" But Lucifer, Satan and the Devil, under various names, are referred to in the Bible as commanding angels rather than being angels themselves. *Revelation 12:9* says: "And the great dragon was cast out, that old serpent, called the Devil, and Satan, which deceiveth the whole world: he was cast out into the earth, and his angels were cast out with him." The Hebrew word translated *Lucifer* signifies "day star," while that translated *Satan* means "adversary." Two angels are mentioned by name in the Old Testament Apocrypha. *Tobias 12:15* refers to Raphael as one of the seven angels which present the prayers of the saints, while Uriel is the angel who appears to Ezra in *II Esdras 4:1.* The ancient Hebrews did not think of angels as individual entities with names, but merely as the messengers of God. Jewish authorities say that the Jews learned the names of angels during their sojourn in Babylon.

What does putting one's hand to the plow mean?

To put one's hand to the plow means to undertake a task or to begin work in earnest. The saying is of Biblical origin. *Luke 9:61-62* says: "And another said, Lord, I will follow thee; but let me first go bid them farewell, which are at home at my house. And Jesus said unto him, No man, having put his hand to the plough, and looking back, is fit for the kingdom of God." This saying of Jesus is peculiar to *Luke.* It is interesting in this connection to note that Elisha, who was actually plowing when Elijah cast his mantle on him, made and was granted a similar request. *I Kings 19:19-21* says: "So he departed thence, and found Elisha the son of Shaphat, who was plowing with twelve yoke of oxen before him, and he with the twelfth: and Elijah passed by him, and cast his mantle upon him. And he left the oxen, and ran after Elijah, and said, Let me, I pray thee, kiss my father and my mother, and then I will follow thee. And he said unto him, Go back again: for what have I done to thee? And he returned back from him, and took a yoke of oxen, and slew them, and boiled their flesh with the instruments of the oxen, and gave unto the people, and they did eat. Then he arose, and went after Elijah, and ministered unto him."

What is a scrip?

Scrip is used in the King James Version of the Bible in the sense of a small bag, wallet or *satchel.* In the Old Testament the term is used to render *yalqut,* from a verb meaning "to gather together" and applied by the Israelites to a bag carried by shepherds. Referring to David's preparation for his fight with Goliath, the giant of Gath, *I Samuel 17:40* says: "And he took his staff in his hand, and chose him five smooth stones out of the brook, and put them in a shepherd's bag which he had, even in a scrip; and his sling was in his hand: and he drew near to the Philistine." In the New Testament the English translators employed *scrip* to render a Greek word meaning a knapsack or provision pouch carried by travellers. Jesus, according to *Matthew 10:9-10,* commanded the twelve when he sent them forth: "Provide neither gold, nor silver, nor brass in your purses, nor scrip for your journey, neither two coats, neither shoes, nor yet staves: for the workman is worthy of his meat." *Scrip* is believed to be derived from Old French *escrepe,* meaning "wallet." At the time the King James Version was made it was applied particularly to the small bag carried by pilgrims, palmers, shepherds and beggars. Shakespeare uses *scrippage* in the sense of the contents of a scrip. He formed *scrip* and *scrippage* after the model of *bag* and *baggage.* In *As You Like It,* in Act III, Scene 2, Touchstone says: "Come, shepherd, let us make an honourable retreat; though not with bag and baggage, yet with scrip and scrippage." *Scrip* in the sense of a bag or pouch is often confused with *scrip* in the sense of a small piece of paper or a scrap of writing. Shakespeare, who was contemporaneous with the translators of the King James Version, also uses this word. In *A Midsummer Night's Dream,* Act 1, Scene 2, Bottom the weaver, speaking of the scroll containing the list of the names of those scheduled to play in their interlude before the duke, says to Quince the carpenter: "You were best to call them generally, man by man, according to the scrip." In this sense *scrip* is believed to be a corruption of *scrap,* perhaps influenced by *script,* which is derived from Latin *scriptum,* "writing," from which we also get *scripture. Scrip* and *script* are continually confused in origin and use and often are almost indistinguishable from each other. During and after the Civil War fractional United States currency and postal stamps used as currency were called scrip. *Scrip* is also applied to private money, paper which is not money but which is used as such, particularly paper issued to employees by companies to be used instead of cash in making purchases at company stores and commissaries. In England *scrip* is used as a shortened form of *subscription receipt,* and refers to a "provisional document" exchangeable for a formal certificate when the holder has received full payment. Although often confused with *scrip, script* in the sense of theatrical, radio and movie writing is derived from *manuscript* and was originally written *'script.* Literally *manuscript* means "hand writing."

What was the function of a prophet?

It is a common mistake to suppose that the sole function of the prophets in ancient Israel was to foretell the future. *Prophet* is from a Greek word meaning "to announce" or "to forth-tell" and that was the general significance of the Hebrew words rendered *prophet* in the Old Testament. Originally the prophets were men and women who established themselves in the theocracy as spiritual leaders, preachers, orators, writers, poets, teachers, priests and statesmen. Prophesying in the later sense of the term was only incidental to their general functions. It was the later apocalyptical prophets who caused the word to be associated mainly with future sayings rather than with practical matters. Abraham, Isaac, Jacob, Moses, Aaron, Miriam and other early civil and spiritual leaders are all referred to as prophets and prophetesses. Deborah, for instance, did not foretell the future but was called a prophetess because she was inspired to direct the Israelites in a crisis. *Deuteronomy 34:10* says "there arose not a prophet since in Israel like unto Moses." The prophets were the inspired spokesmen of the Lord. In *Deuteronomy 18:20-22* Moses himself laid down a rule for judging true and false prophets: "But the prophet, which shall presume to speak a word in my name, which I have not commanded him to speak, or that shall speak in the name of other gods, even that prophet shall die. And if thou say in thine heart, How shall we know the word which the Lord hath not spoken? When a prophet speaketh in the name of the Lord, if the thing follow not, nor come to pass, that is the thing which the Lord hath not spoken, but the prophet hath spoken it presumptuously: thou shalt not be afraid of him." Jesus, who, like John the Baptist, was called a prophet, laid down a similar rule. According to *Matthew 7:15-16* Jesus said in the Sermon on the Mount: "Beware of false prophets, which come to you in sheep's clothing, but inwardly they are ravening wolves. Ye shall know them by their fruits. Do men gather grapes of thorns, or figs of thistles?" Some of the writing prophets were literary men of great power and energy. Hardly a serious crisis arose in ancient Israel without one great prophet or more emerging to speak the words of the Lord to both rulers and people. Established prophets were privileged persons. They were permitted to enter even the palace and to pour their messages from heaven into the ears of the king on his throne. *I Samuel 9:9* says: "Beforetime in Israel, when a man went to inquire of God, thus he spake, Come, let us go to the seer: for he that is now called a Prophet was beforetime called a Seer." This suggests that some sort of change in the function of prophets was taking place in the time of Samuel. Apparently, however, *seer* and *prophet* have become transposed in this passage, because *seer* is never once used before, while *prophet* is used often in the earlier books of the Old Testament. A seer was one who could *see* past, present or future things that were hidden or secret to others. Through one of his prophets, according to *Joel 2:28,* the Lord said in the time to come he would pour out his spirit upon all flesh and "your sons and your daughters shall prophesy, your old men shall dream dreams, and your young men shall see visions." Amos, according to *Amos 7:14,* told Amaziah: "I was no prophet, neither was I a prophet's son."

How many prophetesses are mentioned in the Bible?

Prophetess is applied to five persons in the Bible in the sense of women who exercised the function of a prophet. Four of these are in the Old Testament and one in the New. The first is in *Exodus 15:20,* where the sister of Moses and Aaron is referred to as "Miriam the prophetess." The second is in *Judges 4:4,* which says: "And Deborah, a prophetess, the wife of Lapidoth, she judged Israel at that time." Incidentally, Deborah is the only woman referred to as one of the judges of Israel. She inspired Barak and helped him plan the campaign that ended in the defeat of the Canaanites at the battle of Kishon. This victory is the subject of "The Song of Deborah," found in *Judges 5,* a song of great fervor and vivid imagery. The third prophetess mentioned in the Bible is Huldah who, according to *II Kings 22:14*, "dwelt in Jerusalem in the college" and with whom Hilkiah and his associates communed. The fourth Old Testament prophetess is mentioned in *Nehemiah 6:14*, which says: "My God, think thou upon Tobiah and Sanballat according to these their works, and on the prophetess Noadiah, and the rest of the prophets, that would have put me in fear." *Luke 2:36-37* says of the only New Testament prophetess: "And there was one Anna, a prophetess, the daughter of Phanuel, of the tribe of Aser: she was of a great age, and had lived with an husband seven years from her virginity. And she was a widow of about fourscore and four years, which departed not from the temple, but served God with fastings and prayers night and day." *Isaiah 8:3* uses *prophetess* in the simple sense of the wife of a prophet. The prophet says: "And I went unto the prophetess; and she conceived, and bare a son." Likewise, among Moslems, Aveshah, second wife of Mohammed, is known as the Prophetess. It is a title of honor comparable to Sultana for the wife of the Sultan. Since Mohammed is the Prophet of Islam, his most beloved wife is spoken of as the Prophetess or Madame Prophet. *Prophetess* is employed in a figurative sense in *Revelation 2:20*, which reads: "Notwithstanding, I have a few things against thee, because thou sufferest that woman Jezebel, which calleth herself a prophetess, to teach and to seduce my servants to commit fornication, and to eat things sacrificed unto idols." In *Acts 21:9* we are told that Philip the evangelist, whom Paul visited at Caesarea, "had four daughters, virgins, which did prophesy," but these women are not specifically referred to as prophetesses.

How do major and minor prophets differ?

The division of Old Testament prophets into major and minor is merely a conventional and arbitrary classification. No such distinction is made in the Bible. This division came about in a roundabout way. The books of the Hebrew Scriptures were grouped in three sections—The Law, The Prophets and The Writings. The Prophets were divided into "The Former Prophets," *Joshua, Judges, Samuel and Kings*, and "The Latter Prophets," *Isaiah, Jeremiah, Ezekiel* and *The Twelve*. The Twelve prophets were sometimes referred to as the lesser or minor prophets. They were called minor not because they were inferior in rank or importance but because the books bearing their names were smaller in size than those of "The Former Prophets." Later, for convenience, it became customary to classify the prophets themselves as major and minor. The major prophets are generally regarded as

Abraham, Moses, Samuel, Nathan, Elijah, Elisha, Isaiah, Jeremiah and Ezekiel, and the minor prophets as Hosea, Joel, Amos, Obadiah, Jonah, Micah, Nahum, Habakkuk, Zephaniah, Haggai, Zechariah and Malachi. Daniel is sometimes regarded as a major and sometimes as a minor prophet. After the division into major and minor prophets had grown up, there developed a notion that the major prophets had the divine power to command obedience while the minor prophets did not have that power. The term *major* and *minor* have never been applied to New Testament persons referred to as prophets.

Why is the Bible so called?

Bible as the name of the Jewish-Christian sacred writings as a whole is comparatively new. This term would have meant nothing to a Jew in the time of Jesus. In those days the Hebrew scriptures were thought of not as one book but as many books. The canonization of the Old Testament was a gradual process and was not completed until forty or fifty years after the crucifixion of Jesus. At that time the Jews divided their sacred writings into three grand divisions: "The Law," the first five books of Moses; "The Prophets," *Joshua, Judges, Samuel, Kings, Isaiah, Jeremiah, Ezekiel* and the twelve minor prophets, and "The Writings," the rest of the sacred books. That "The Writings" were not yet canonized then is indicated by the fact that Jesus referred to the sacred writings as "the law and the prophets." *Bible* comes to us from ancient Egypt by way of Greece, Italy and France. *Biblos* was the Greek name for the inner bark of the Egyptian papyrus reed, the material from which paper was first made and on which books were written in New Testament times. In process of time *biblos* came to signify not only paper but a book, roll or scroll in general. The diminutive of *biblos* is *biblion,* and the plural of *biblion* is *biblia,* meaning "little books." But at an early date the singular and plural were used interchangeably. For instance, in the Greek of *Matthew 1:1* *biblos* occurs in "the book of the generation," while in the Greek of *Luke 4:17* *biblion* occurs in "the book of the prophet Esaias." The Latins borrowed this word, transcribed it *biblia* and treated it as a singular. In *I Maccabees,* which is regarded as canonical by Catholics and Apocryphal by Protestants, *biblia* is employed in reference to the Hebrew sacred writings. John Chrysostom, patriarch of Constantinople, in the fourth century A.D. referred to the general collection of Jewish and Christian writings as *biblia,* "the books," but which was probably construed as a singular. But Greek and Latin *biblia* still had a long way to go before it became English *bible.* In Old English *bibliepece* alone occurs as a name for the sacred writings. Not until the thirteenth century did the English form *bible* occasionally occur as the name of the Old and New Testament as a whole, and even then it was still used in the general sense of "the book" or "the book of books." Chaucer, writing in the fourteenth century, continued to use the term in the sense of any book, and the original meaning is retained in such compounds as *bibliography,* "a list of books," *bibliophile,* "a lover of books," and *bibliopole,* "a seller of books." In all of the some million words attributed to Shakespeare *Bible* does not occur once, although *Holy Writ, Scripture, Scriptures, Gospel* and similar terms do. Neither is *bible* used in either the text or in the Epistle Dedicatory of the King James Version of *The Holy Bible. Scriptures* was at that time the most common name for the *Bible.* The Jews had generally referred to their sacred writings by a name meaning "the books," but the New Testament writers referred to them by the Greek *hai graphai,* "the writings." In Latin this became *scripturae,* whence our *scriptures.* It came to be applied to the Bible without qualification because that book or collection of books was looked upon as "*the* writings." Likewise *Koran,* the name of the Moslem sacred writings, comes from an Arabic word signifying "to read." In olden times, when reading and writing were rare accomplishments, the mere fact that something was written bestowed upon it a measure of sacredness. "Search the scriptures," said Jesus in *John 5:39,* and in *Matthew 22:29* he told the Sadducees: "Ye do err, not knowing the scriptures." In *Romans 16:26* Paul refers to "the scriptures of the prophets, according to the commandment of the everlasting God, made known to all nations for the obedience of faith." *Book,* often used in the King James Version for sacred or inspired writings, is derived from Teutonic *boc,* meaning "writing tablet." It may be related to the root from which is derived *beech,* the name of the tree from whose smooth inner bark a writing material was made.

What is the longest verse in the Bible?

The longest verse in the Bible is *Esther 8:9,* which contains ninety words and which reads: "Then were the king's scribes called at that time in the third month, that is, the month Sivan, on the three and twentieth day thereof; and it was written according to all that Mordecai commanded unto the Jews, and to the lieutenants, and the deputies and rulers of the provinces which are from India unto Ethiopia, an hundred and twenty and seven provinces, unto every province according to the writing thereof, and unto every people after their language, and to the Jews according to their writing, and according to their language." The shortest verse in the Bible is *John 11:35,* which says simply "Jesus wept." *Revelation 20:4* is the longest verse in the New Testament.

How many chapters does the Bible contain?

The King James Version of the Bible contains 1,189 chapters, 929 of which are in the Old Testament and 260 in the New Testament. *Psalms 117,* the shortest chapter in the Bible, is also the middle chapter, being preceded by 594 and followed by the same number.

How many verses does the Bible contain?

There are 23,214 verses in the Old Testament and 7,959 in the New Testament—a total of 31,173 in the Bible. *Psalms 18:8* is the middle verse, being preceded by 15,586 verses and followed by the same number.

How many words does the Bible contain?

According to the best estimate available, the King James Version of the Bible contains 773,692 words, of which 592,439 are in the Old Testament and 181,253 in the New Testament. Computations of the exact number of words in the Bible vary considerably. Apparently all of those who have undertaken to count the words in the Bible did not agree on just what constitutes a word in every particular case. Although German generally contains more syllables than English, Luther's German Bible contains approximately the same number of words as the King James Version. *Psalms,* with 43,743 words, is the longest book in the Bible. The shortest book in the Bible is *III John,* which contains only 299 words. *Luke,* with 25,944 words, is the longest book in the New Testament, while the shortest book in the Old Testament is *Obadiah,* with 670 words. Of the some 181,253 words in the New Testament, it is estimated that the number attributed to Jesus is about 36,450.

What is the neck verse?

In the Middle Ages clergymen, monks and nuns were exempted in England from the jurisdiction of the secular courts. Any clergyman accused of a crime other than high treason could appeal to the ecclesiastical authorities. This privilege was called "benefit of clergy," which is a rough rendering of the Latin legal phrase *privilegium clericale.* It appears to have been based largely on *I Chronicles 16:22,* which reads: "Touch not mine anointed, and do my prophets no harm." This in turn is a quotation from *Psalms 105:15*. The privilege of benefit of clergy was first officially recognized in England in 1087, during the reign of William Rufus, second of the Norman kings. An ordinance was enacted entitled *Privilegium Clericale,* "Benefit of Clergy," and providing that any person in holy orders condemned to die for certain offenses could save his life by demonstrating that he could read and therefore was capable of being a clergyman. Naturally many persons not in holy orders sought the same privilege and attempted to pass as clergymen. Therefore, it became a practice, when a plea for benefit of clergy was made, to bring out a book in Latin and ask the accused to read. In those days reading was limited almost entirely to the clergy and Latin was the language of the church. If the accused could read from the book, the plea was admitted; if he could not, it was denied. If the accused demonstrated to the satisfaction of the magistrate or clergyman appointed to make the test that he could read, the magistrate or clergyman announced, "He reads like a clerk," whereupon the accused was given the benefit of clergy or learning and liberated. A statute enacted in 1489, during the reign of Henry VII, distinguished between persons actually in holy orders and others who could read, the latter being restricted to one plea in benefit of clergy; that is, a person who was not a clergyman but who could read was permitted to make the plea only once. For identification in future cases the accused was branded on the left thumb with a hot iron. *Psalms 51:1,* because of its sentiment, was generally selected as the "trial verse." It reads: "Have mercy upon me, O God, according to thy loving kindness: according unto the multitude of thy tender mercies blot out my transgressions." It is estimated that between the thirteenth and the nineteenth centuries nearly a million persons were saved from the gallows by being able to read this passage from the Bible in Latin. Popularly it came to be known as the "neck verse," because ability to read it saved the neck of the accused. After Ben Jonson was sentenced to be hanged for killing Gabriel Spencer in a duel he claimed the right of benefit of clergy. Being one of the best Latin scholars in England, he easily scanned the neck verse to the satisfaction of the court and so escaped hanging. Benefit of clergy was abolished in 1512 in respect to persons charged with murder and other grave crimes. British soldiers convicted of manslaughter for firing on the Boston mob in "the Boston Massacre" on March 5, 1770, were permitted to plead benefit of clergy and were let off with having their left thumbs branded with hot irons. It was not until 1827, during the reign of George IV, that benefit of clergy was abolished altogether in England. Although the English Colonies in America recognized the benefit of clergy, in 1790 the first Congress passed an act barring such pleas in the Federal courts. *Psalm 51,* which contains the neck verse, is called *Miserere* because its opening words in Latin are *Miserere mei Deus,* "Have mercy upon me, O God." One of the evening services of Lent is also called *Miserere* from the fact that this penitential psalm is sung on the occasion.

How many letters are there in the Bible?

It is estimated that the King James Version of the Bible contains 3,566,480 letters—2,728,100 in the Old Testament and 838,380 in the New Testament. As in the case of the number of words in the Bible, the estimates vary somewhat. The few letters compared with the number of words is indicative of the simplicity and shortness of the words selected by the translators of the English Bible.

What is the longest word in the Bible?

The longest word in the King James Version of the Bible is *Mahershalalhashbaz,* which contains eighteen letters. It occurs in *Isaiah 8:1-4,* which reads: "Moreover the Lord said unto me, Take thee a great roll, and write in it with a man's pen concerning Mahershalalhashbaz. And I took unto me faithful witnesses to record, Uriah the priest, and Zechariah the son of Jeberechiah. And I went unto the prophetess; and she conceived, and bare a son. Then said the Lord to me, Call his name Mahershalalhashbaz. For before the child shall have knowledge to cry, my father, and my mother, the riches of Damascus and the spoil of Samaria shall be taken away before the king of Assyria." Although printed in the English Bible as a word and a name, *mahershalalhashbaz* is really a Hebrew sentence literally meaning "the booty hastens, the spoil speeds." The prophet so named one of his sons either actually or figuratively to indicate the impending doom of Syria and Samaria.

What do italics in the Bible signify?

In the King James and several other early English translations of the Bible many words not intended to be emphasized are printed in italic type. This was done because the translators of the Scriptures were unable to find English words equivalent to some of the words in the Hebrew, Greek and Latin texts. Whenever they were compelled to insert extra words to make the translation intelligible to English readers they put these additional words in italics to indicate the insertions. The Geneva Bible of 1560 was the first English Bible in which italics were used for such explanatory and connective words. This practice appears to have been borrowed from a Latin version of the New Testament published in 1556 by Theodore Beza, a French Protestant theologian and scholar. In some modern translations italics are used for emphasis. Italic letters, originally called *Aldine* letters, were invented by Aldus Manutius (Aldo Manuzio), an Italian printer, who established his "Aldine Press" at Venice about 1490. Manutius originated the practice of printing books in small format and he devised Aldine letters to make it possible to print much matter in small space. In his *Curiosities of English Literature* Isaac Disraeli says on this subject: "The invention of what is now called the *Italic* letter in printing was made by Aldus Manutius, to whom learning owes much. He observed the many inconveniences resulting from the vast number of abbreviations, which were then so frequent among the printers, that a book was difficult to understand; a treatise was actually written on the art of reading a printed book, and this addressed to the learned! He contrived an expedient, by which these abbreviations might be entirely got rid of, and yet books suffer little increase in bulk. This he effected by introducing what is now called the *Italic* letter, though it formerly was distinguished by the name of the inventor, and called the *Aldine*." Italic type, in which the letters slope up toward the right, was first used by Manutius in 1501 to print small, compact editions of Virgil and the *Satires of Juvenal and Persius*. According to tradition, Manutius designed his Aldine letters in imitation of the handwriting of the Italian poet Petrarch.

Why aren't quotation marks used in the Bible?

Quotation marks originated in France during the latter part of the sixteenth century but had not generally been adopted by English printers when the King James Version of the Bible was first issued in 1611. Although quotation marks have been introduced in later English versions, they have never been inserted in the King James Version. Before the introduction of quotation marks there were no uniform signs in writing and printing to mark the beginning and end of matter borrowed from other books or sources. Quotations in the Bible are often introduced by such phrases as, "It is written," "It is said," "The scripture saith," "It saith," "It was said by them of old time," "Those of old time said," etc. The number of explicit quotations from the Old Testament in the New Testament is estimated at 275. In the King James Version it is often difficult to tell exactly just where a quotation begins and where it ends. The introduction of quotation marks in the Bible sometimes leads to ludicrous results, because strict quotation was alien to the authors of the sacred writings and for the most part they quoted the general sense from memory.

What chapter in the Bible ends with a comma?

Acts 21 is the only chapter in the King James and most other recognized English versions of the Bible that ends with a comma. It closes with the following words: "And when there was made a great silence, he spake unto them in the Hebrew tongue, saying," In the standard French translations this chapter closes with a colon. Most of the chapters in English versions end with periods, although there are several that end with question marks or exclamation points. The *Book of Jonah,* for instance, ends with a question mark.

How many times does *and* occur in the Bible?

The conjunction *and* occurs in the King James Version of the Bible 46,227 times—35,543 times in the Old Testament and 10,684 in the New Testament. The monotonous repetition of *and* in the English Bible is owing to the fact that the translators attempted to render the Hebrew and Greek originals as literally as possible.

How many personal names are from the Bible?

There are no statistics on this subject, but it has been estimated that about one half of all first or Christian names used in Europe and the New World are either Bible names or modifications of Bible names. Masculine names from the Bible outnumber feminine names from the same source about seventeen to one.

Does *its* occur in the Bible?

It is surprising how many centuries the English language got along without *its,* the possessive form of the neuter pronoun *it. Its* does not occur once in the King James Version of the Bible as originally printed in 1611. In that work the first part of *Leviticus 25:5* was translated: "That which groweth of *it* own accord of thy harvest thou shalt not reap." In later printings the *it* in this passage was changed to *its* and that is the only occurrence of *its* in the Authorized Version today. *His, her, of it, thereof* and even longer circumlocutions were used where we now employ *its.* In some instances the very idea of the possessive was avoided altogether because of the want of a possessive form of the neuter pronoun *it. Its* began to appear about 1600 during the latter Elizabethan period, but many writers resisted the innovation as an illegitimate pretender. Although *it* had been on the lips of Englishmen for a thousand years, most writers at first shunned *its* as the plague. They gradually eased into the new usage by writing the word *it's*. *Its* does not occur in any of Shakespeare's writings published during his lifetime. In the folio of 1623, published seven years after the dramatist's death, *its* occurs only once, although *it* occurs fifteen times and *it's* nine times as the possessive of the neuter pronoun *it*. Ben Jonson used *its* a few times in his writings, but did not refer to this form of the pronoun in his *Grammar*. Even Milton, who wrote much later, used *its* only two or three times in *Paradise Lost*. About 1550 English writers had begun to use *it* or the older form *hit* as the possessive of the neuter. In 1770 the eighteen-year-old English poet Thomas Chatterton produced some poems that he ascribed to a monk named Thomas Rowley in the fifteenth century. A long literary controversy over the authenticity of the Rowley poems might have ended immediately had the critics observed the line, "Life and *its* goods I scorn," in which the youthful author used a word unknown to the English language until more than a century after the time when the forgeries were alleged to have been composed.

How does the Bible end?

It is often said that the Old Testament ends with a curse, while the New Testament ends with a blessing. The last verse in the Old Testament is *Malachi 4:6*, which reads: "And he shall turn the heart of the fathers to the children, and the heart of the children to their fathers, lest I come and smite the earth with a curse." The last verse in the New Testament and in the whole Bible is *Revelation 22:21*, which reads: "The grace of our Lord Jesus Christ be with you all. Amen." The first verse in the Old Testament and in the whole Bible is *Genesis 1:1*, which reads: "In the beginning God created the heaven and the earth." The first verse in the New Testament is *Matthew 1:1*, which reads: "The book of the generation of Jesus Christ, the son of David, the son of Abraham."

Did the King James Version contain the letter *J*?

J in English is a comparatively late variant of the Latin *I* and was not regarded as a separate letter in the alphabet at the time the King James Version of the Bible was printed. For instance, in Alexander Cruden's famous *Concordance of the Bible*, published in 1737, words beginning with *I* and *J* are printed under *I* as if they were the same letter. The letters were not entirely differentiated until the nineteenth century. Colonel Charles K. Gardner, the author of the system of using letters to designate companies in the United States Army, omitted the letter *J* to avoid confusion, because when the system was established in 1816 *I* and *J* were still often written exactly alike. For the same reason there is no *J* street in Washington, D. C. *Ezra 7:21* is often cited as a Bible verse containing all the letters of the English alphabet, but this verse does not contain *J*, a fact that indicates that this verse was first pointed out for this distinction before *J* and *I* were differentiated. That verse reads: "And I, even Artaxerxes the king, do make a decree to all the treasurers which are beyond the river, that whatsoever Ezra the priest, the scribe of the law of the God of heaven, shall require of you, it be done speedily." This same fact explains why the Christian symbol *JHS* is also written *IHS*.

Can one converse in Hebrew?

Like Aramaic and Greek, the other two original languages of the Scriptures, Hebrew is a dead language and is nowhere a spoken language in its ancient form. Because of the limited vocabulary it would be impossible for anybody to carry on a satisfactory conversation on modern topics in pure Hebrew. But Hebrew has continued to be a sacred, literary and ritual language among the Jews, and after the First World War it was revived in a modernized form as a vernacular in Palestine. Hebrew, with an enlarged vocabulary from other languages, and not Yiddish, is regarded as the national language of the Palestine Jews. It is widely spoken by the younger generation and many of their elders, and is the usual language in industry, commerce, schools and colleges, the synagogues, political speeches and scientific lectures. Aramaic in its ancient form is a dead language, but dialects closely akin to it are still spoken by the Samaritans in Palestine and by various groups in Syria. Greek is still the ritual language in some of the Eastern Orthodox churches. Roman Catholic clergymen speak and write what is known as ecclesiastical or church Latin, which is based on classic models grammatically, but which contains words from the Greek, Italian and other modern languages in addition to the regular Latin vocabulary. These words from other languages, of course, are given Latin forms and pronunciations. Through this medium priests and churchmen from different countries can converse freely with one another and church Latin serves for them as an international language. Most of the official documents of the church are written in ecclesiastical Latin. Hebrew as spoken and written in Palestine at the present time has been modernized and reshaped somewhat in the same manner.

Are there any original Biblical manuscripts in existence?

There are no original manuscripts of the Bible in existence. The oldest known Biblical manuscripts are copies, not originals. Probably in the case of most of the books of the Bible there never were original copies in the handwriting of the authors. We are told in *Jeremiah 36* that the prophet dictated his book to Baruch. That was the usual custom of writers in ancient times. Even the first copies of the Epistles of Paul were not autographs of the Apostle. Paul was in the habit of dictating the body of his letters to a secretary and of then adding a salutation or few words in his own hand so his correspondents would know them to be authentic. In *I Corinthians 16:21* he says, "The salutation of me Paul with mine own hand," and in *II Thessalonians 3:17*, "The salutation of Paul with mine own hand, which is the token of every epistle: so I write." This was his way of saying that "this is my handwriting" and evidence that the letter was genuine. In *Romans 16:22* Paul's amanuensis identifies himself, "I Tertius, who wrote this epistle, salute you in the Lord." It is probable that virtually all the books of the Bible were dictated to scribes by their authors. There are no known first or original copies of the books of the Bible in existence, nor any manuscript copies dating back even to Biblical times. When the authors of the King James Version said they "translated out of the original tongues," they did not mean they had access to "original manuscripts," but rather that they consulted copies in Hebrew, Greek and perhaps other ancient languages instead of relying merely upon previous translations in English and other modern European languages. The date when a Bible book was composed and the date of the oldest copy of that book are two entirely different matters.

On what material was the Bible originally written?

The writing of the Bible extended over a period of about a thousand years and different writing materials were used at different times. It is possible that the very earliest parts of the Old Testament reduced to writing were engraved on stones with a chisel or on clay tablets with a wooden style. We are told that the Ten Commandments were written on "tables of stone." *Jeremiah 20:10-12* appears to allude to a deed of sale on clay tablets such as the Babylonians used. Most of the Hebrew scriptures were probably first written with pen and ink on skins, papyrus and parchment. The first complete Old Testament books were written on tanned skins sewed together in large rolls or scrolls. About 700 B.C. the Hebrews began to use papyrus for their sacred writings. This material, the closest ancient approach to modern paper, was made of the stems of the Egyptian papyrus plant or reed. The "ark of bulrushes" in which the child Moses was placed was probably made of these reeds. The Egyptians supplied the ancient world with paper for more than a thousand years. It is probable that virtually all of the New Testament books were originally written on papyrus. The sheets, like the earlier skins, were joined to form rolls or scrolls. *Volume* is derived from Latin *volumen,* a roll. In the second century B.C. Egypt forbade the export of papyrus, with the result that a substitute writing material was developed at Pergamum in Asia Minor, center of the skin and leather business. Sheep and goat skins were dressed in such a manner that both sides could be used for writing. This writing material came to be called *Pergamene, from Pergamum,* which in English became *parchment.* A specially fine grade of parchment came to be called *vellum,* from Latin *vitellus,* "little calf," also the source of *veal.* Parchment and vellum did not become common until the third century A.D. and did not supplant papyrus until the fifth centrury A.D. The writers of the New Testament books could hardly have appreciated the importance of what they were writing and is is probable that they wrote on papyrus rather than on the more costly parchment and vellum, After about the second and third centuries it became customary to copy the sacred writings on the more durable materials.

What was the first Bible printed in North America?

The translation of the New and Old Testament into the Massachusetts dialect of the Algonquian Indian language, issued at Cambridge in 1661 and 1663 respectively, was the first Bible printed in North America and the first translation of the Scriptures into any Indian tongue. This translation was made by John Eliot (1604-1690), a Puritan clergyman and missionary in Colonial times, who was known as "The Apostle to the Indians." He was assisted in his linguistic labors by his two sons and by several Indians, particularly by Cockenoe, the Montauk interpreter, without whose aid the monument to missionary endeavor would probably never have been completed. Near Canton, Massachusetts, in the shade of Blue Hill, Eliot began his missionary work in 1646, at first speaking to the Indians in

English. Many converts were drawn from the subjected and broken tribes and Eliot induced many of them to separate from their people and live in Christian communities, the first such community being established at Natick in 1650. These natives were known as "the praying Indians." Twenty-three villages with an aggregate population of twenty-five hundred professed Christian Indians were organized in eastern Massachusetts and the adjacent parts of New England before King Philip's war scattered them and gave the work of the missionaries a decided setback. The total number of converts made by Eliot and his helpers is estimated as high as four thousand. But most of Eliot's work was undone by the war of 1676. King Philip himself told the old missionary that he cared no more for his gospel than for the button on his coat. The praying Indians were caught between the devil and deep blue sea. By the whites they were distrusted and suspected of being secret allies of the enemy, while by the hostile Indians they were hated as renegades and traitors to their own people. A majority of the praying Indians joined the hostiles under King Philip. The loyalty of many of those who offered their services to the English colonists was rewarded by imprisonment on an island in Boston harbor, where they were held until the return of peace and where all but three hundred died of restiveness, exposure, starvation and disease. On the other hand, a company of praying Indians enlisted under the Colonial commander-in-chief, Major Daniel Gookin, and rendered valuable service to the whites against the hostiles as scouts and spies. Gookin was very friendly toward the missionary work of Eliot, had been chosen "ruler over the praying Indians," and became very unpopular during the war hysteria for speaking in their defense. This conflict practically ended the work of the missions in New England. At the close of the war the two races were so embittered toward each other that little could be done in that direction. Although only a few hundred of the praying Indians remained in the Christian communities, the venerable Eliot continued his labors until his death in 1690. About one thousand copies of his famous Indian Bible were printed, twenty of which were dedicated to King Charles II, and about fifty copies are known to be still in existence. Copies of this interesting book, particularly those dedicated to the King, are highly coveted by collectors. The difficulties with which Eliot was confronted in translating the Scriptures into the Natick dialect are illustrated by the fact that the phrase "kneeling down to him" in *Mark 1:40* was rendered by the thirty-four-letter word, *Wutteppesittukgussunnoowehtunkquoh*. The people who spoke the language of

Eliot's Bible—and his Indian grammar and other works—have vanished from the face of the earth, and today no man can read the Bible translated by "the Apostle to the Indians." Since Eliot's time the Bible has been translated and printed, in part or in whole, in thirty-one languages of Indians north of Mexico. The complete Bible, Old and New Testaments, has been printed in four other Indian languages—Cree, Santee Dakota, Labrador Eskimo and Tukkauth-kutchin. The first Bible printed in North America in a European language was an edition of Luther's German Bible issued at Germantown, Pennsylvania, in 1743 by Christopher Sauer (or Sower), who came from Germany in 1724 and who used type imported from the Rhineland. Second and Third editions of this German Bible were printed at Germantown in 1763 and 1776 respectively by his son of the same name.

How old are the oldest Bible manuscripts?

Papyrus sheets containing *Numbers* and *Deuteronomy* found in Egypt and dating back to the second century A.D. are believed to be the earliest known Bible manuscripts. The earliest known manuscript copies of the Bible substantially complete are the Vaticanus and Sinaiticus codices. *Codex* as applied to a book is derived from Latin *caudex*, "the trunk of a tree," and alludes to the ancient writing tablets of waxed wood. The Vaticanus and Sinaiticus codices are believed to be copies made in the fourth century A.D. They are in Greek and contain the Septuagint Version of the Old Testament and the Eusebio-Origen version of the New Testament. Some authorities suppose these copies on beautiful vellum were among fifty that Eusebius, bishop of Caesarea, made for Emperor Constantine for use in the churches of Constantinople. The Codex Vaticanus was listed in the first Vatican catalogue made in 1475 and probably had been in the Vatican library since it was established in 1448. The Codex Sinaiticus was found in the fortress-like convent of St. Catherine on "Mt. Sinai" in 1859 by the German Bible critic Tischendorf and taken by him to Russia. In 1934 the British government bought this manuscript from Russia for 100,000 pounds and placed it in the British Museum. Another manuscript copy of the Bible in the British Museum dates from the fifth century. It is known as the Codex Alexandrinus and was presented to Charles I in 1628 by Cyril Lucar, Patriarch of Constantinople. In the libraries of Christendom there are several thousand manuscript copies of the Bible or parts of it dating from the sixth century to the invention of printing in the fifteenth century.

Ancient manuscripts do not bear dates and it is often very difficult to determine when they were made. The approximate dates are determined by a careful scientific study of the material, ink, form of letters, style of writing and the text itself. There are several reasons why none of the original or first copies of the Bible manuscripts were preserved. In the first place, the Jews made a regular practice of recopying and destroying all sacred writings when they were mutilated or worn out. In the second place, the New Testament books were originally written on papyrus, which was brittle, fragile and generally short-lived. Such perishable manuscripts were worn out by use, destroyed by fire and climatic changes, and, in many cases, destroyed deliberately by the persecutors of the church. Contrary to a popular notion, the discovery of early Biblical manuscripts in recent centuries has added little knowledge of the Bible of interest to the general reader. Here and there some additional light has been shed on the Biblical text by these discoveries, but for the most part the texts that have been handed down through successive recopyings have proved as accurate as the early manuscripts. Some years ago it was announced that a complete codex of the Four Gospels dating back at least to the third century had been discovered. It was stated at the time that the discovery of these papyri, supposedly prepared little later than 200 A.D., would make it necessary to move closer to the time of Jesus the dates when the Gospels were composed. Yet the majority of scholars have always supposed that the Gospels were largely completed before the year 200 A.D., the earliest date assigned to the newly discovered manuscripts. The fact that such copies contain passages not in later copies, or omit passages in later copies, proves very little.

What is the Apocrypha?

Apocrypha is from a Greek word meaning "hidden." Strictly speaking, it is a plural, but in common usage it is construed as a singular with *apocryphas* as the plural. *Apocrypha* was first applied to books or writings that were put away and withdrawn from general use because they were worn out or faulty copies. Next the term was applied to books regarded as unsuitable for general or public reading. Then it was applied to books containing mysterious, esoteric, secret or hidden things for the favored few. Cyril of Jerusalem, a fourth-century Syrian churchman, is believed to have been the first to apply *apocrypha* to Biblical books of doubtful origin and authority. The original Apocrypha in this sense consisted of certain books and parts of books in the Greek Septuagint which were not found in Hebrew and which the Jews did not recognize as part of their canon. Now the term is applied specifically to the following fourteen books and fragments of books: *Tobit, Judith,* additions to *Esther, Wisdom of Solomon, Ecclesiasticus* or *Wisdom of Jesus, Son of Sirach, Baruch, Song of the Three Children, Susanna, Bel and the Dragon, I Maccabees, II Maccabees, I Esdras, II Esdras,* and the *Prayer of Manasses.* Following Martin Luther, the Church of England gave these Apocryphal books "inferior authority" and classed them as non-canonical. They are not recognized in any manner by other Protestant churches, but the Anglican church prints them between the two Testaments in its Bibles and reads them for instruction, inspiration and edification, although it does not use them in fixing points of doctrine. The Old Testament Apocrypha is not anywhere specifically recognized in the New Testament according to the King James Version, although there are several striking parallels between passages in the New Testament and in the Old Testament Apocrypha. There is also a New Testament Apocrypha, which is the same for both Roman Catholics and Protestants. It covers a wide range of literature and contains many books and fragments of gospels, acts and epistles. Some of the best known of these are: gospels according to the Hebrews, the Egyptians, the Ebionites, Peter, Thomas, Philip, and Nicodemus; the acts of John, Peter, Thomas, Andrew and Paul; the Preaching of Peter; the Birth of Mary; the Oxyrthynchus Logia; the Agrapha; the Abgarus Letters; the Shepherd of Hermas; the Protevangelium of James; the Epistle of Paul to the Laodiceans; the Apocalypse of Peter and a number of others. The New Testament Apocrypha is for the most part distinct from the body of second century Christian writings known as the Apostolic Fathers. Most of the New Testament Apocryphal books have been at one time or other regarded as canonical by one Christian sect or another. They are the source of many sacred legends and ecclesiastical traditions.

What English version of the Bible do Jews use?

The English version of the Old Testament now most widely used by English-speaking Jews is the Jewish Version, published in 1917 by the Jewish Publication Society of America. Although parts of the Hebrew scriptures had been previously translated into English for Jewish use, the first complete English Old Testament for that purpose was translated by Isaac Leeser and published in Philadelphia in 1853. Leeser followed the style of the King James Version but made so many changes in text that his work is essentially an independent translation. This monumental work held its place in English and American synagogues until it began to be replaced by the Jewish Version of 1917. In 1851, two years before Leeser's complete Bible was published, Abraham Banisch brought out the first volume of his four-volume "Jewish School and Family Bible," the last volume of which was not issued until 1861. When the project for a new English Hebrew Bible was conceived at the second biennial convention of the Jewish Publication Society in 1892, the plan called for a revision based on Leeser's translation. As the work proceeded, however, it became a new and independent translation based not only on Leeser's Bible but also on the King James Version of 1611, the English Revised Version of 1885 and the work of many eminent Jewish authorities. In the King James Version the Old Testament consists of thirty-nine books, but in the Hebrew Bible there are only twenty-four books. *I* and *II Samuel, I* and *II Kings* and *I* and *II Chronicles* are each reckoned as one book, as are also *Ezra, Nehemiah* and the twelve so-called minor prophets.

What is the Jefferson Bible?

The Jefferson Bible is a compilation made by Thomas Jefferson and consists of passages from the Four Gospels cut out and pasted in a book according to a scheme of his own. Before beginning the work himself Jefferson tried to get Dr. Benjamin Rush to compile such a work. He sent Dr. Rush a comparative outline of the moral teachings of Jesus and those of certain ancient philosophers, and explained to his friend why his name should not be associated with the enterprise. During his early political campaigns Jefferson had been widely denounced as an atheist and unbeliever because he showed little interest in formal and conventional church work. So the man who was the author of the Statute for Religious Freedom in Virginia and who more than any other was responsible for the provision in the Bill of Rights guaranteeing to Americans the free exercise of religion, wrote to Dr. Rush as follows: "And in confiding it to you, I know it will not be exposed to the malignant perversions of those who make every word from me a text for new misrepresentations and calumnies. I am, moreover, averse to the communication of my religious tenets to the public, because it would countenance the presumption of those who have endeavored to draw them before that tribunal, and to seduce public opinion to erect itself into that inquest over the rights of conscience, which the laws have so justly proscribed. It behooves every man who values liberty of conscience for himself to resist invasions of it in the case of others, or their case may, by change of circumstances, become his own." Unable to get another to do it, Jefferson, then serving his first term as President of the United States, began the work in 1804. He bought two copies of the English Bible and spent two evenings at home in the White House cutting out and pasting in a blank book the words attributed to Jesus and some other passages in close accord with the words of the great teacher. This work he found an agreeable and profitable escape from the affairs of state. He thought this first abridgment might be adapted for the use of the Indians. We learn from a letter to a friend that Jefferson was in the habit of reading from this volume every night before going to bed. In 1813 he wrote from Monticello to John Adams: "We must reduce our volume to the simple Evangelists; select, even from them, the very words only of Jesus, paring off the amphibologisms into which they have been led, by forgetting often, or not understanding, what had fallen from him, by giving their own misconceptions as his dicta, and expressing unintelligibly for others what they had not understood themselves. There will be found remaining the most sublime and benevolent code of morals which has ever been offered to man. I have performed this operation for my own use, by cutting verse by verse out of the printed book, and arranging the matter which is evidently his and which is as easily distinguished as diamonds in a dunghill. The result is an octave of forty-six pages." In 1816 Jefferson wrote to Charles Thomson: "I, too, have made a wee little book from the same materials, which I call the philosophy of Jesus; it is a paradigma of his doctrines, made by cutting the texts out of the book, arranging them on the pages of a blank book, in a certain order of time and subject. A more beautiful or precious morsel of ethics I have never seen; it is a document in proof that I am a real Christian, that is to say a disciple of the doctrines of Jesus." The Sage of Monticello in his letter to Thomson added: "If I had time I would add to my little book the Greek, Latin and French texts, in columns side by side." About 1819 Jefferson found the time to complete the work by cutting out and pasting in parallel columns in a blank book the corresponding passages from New Testaments in Greek, Latin and French, three languages that the scholarly statesman read with ease. The finished work he entitled *The Life and Morals of Jesus of Nazareth.* There are no notes or commentaries in the book except the section of the Roman law under which Jesus was supposed to have been brought to trial. The lists of passages, the title pages and the references are in Jefferson's handwriting. Two maps, one of Palestine and another of the ancient world, are pasted in front. Jefferson never published his Bible. "I not only write nothing on religion," he said, "but rarely permit myself to speak on it." In 1895 the Federal Government purchased this curious book from the Jefferson heirs and the original is now in the National Museum at Washington. Nine years later the Fifty-seventh Congress issued a limited edition of the English section of the Jefferson Bible for distribution to its members. Since then this interesting work, compiled in the White House by a President of the United States, has been printed by private publishers and is available to the public.

What is the Gideon Bible?

Gideon Bible is not the name of a version of the Bible but merely the popular name for Bibles distributed by *The Gideons, the Christian Commercial Men's Association of America*. This association was organized July 1, 1899, at Janesville, Wisconsin, by three commercial traveling men—John H. Nicholson, W. J. Knights, and S. E. Hill. It is a non-denominational religious association. According to its original declaration, its purpose is to band together the Christian travelers and through them to win the commercial travelers for the glory of God; to supply every hotel in America with a Bible in each guest room, and to prepare the hearts of travelers for salvation. The name, which was suggested by Knights, is derived from Gideon, one of the judges of Israel, whose history is related in *Judges 6* and *7*. He was a man who did exactly what God wanted him to do irrespective of his own judgment as to methods and results. A pitcher with a lamp inside it was selected as the emblem of the Gideons, in allusion to the pitchers and lamps carried by Gideon and his three hundred followers when the Midianites were delivered into their hands. Only commercial traveling men who are professing Christians and in good standing as members of a church or religious society are eligible to membership. The headquarters of *The Gideons, The Christian Commercial Men's Association of America* is in Chicago, and in 1944 the organization had 12,000 active members. Funds for purchasing Bibles are raised by the members in their local churches or in the towns and cities where they spend their Sundays while covering their itinerary. This work is done gratis and those performing it are not permitted to use any of the money collected for personal expenses. The national headquarters is maintained by contributions made specifically for that purpose and by money paid as dues by the regular and associate members of the society. Both the King James and the American Revised versions are used by the Gideons. Between 1899, when the society was organized, and 1941, when the United States entered the Second World War, the Gideons placed nearly 2,000,000 complete Bibles in hotels, hospitals, penal institutions and public schools. After the outbreak of the war the association concentrated chiefly on making Testaments available to members of the armed forces. Up to January 31, 1944, the Gideons had distributed 6,408,000 Testaments and Psalms bound together in the hands of soldiers and sailors in a program calling for the distribution of 10,000,000 such books. Local units of the Gideons are called *Camps.*

What is the Printers' Bible?

The Printers' Bible is an edition of the King James Version printed in 1702. It received its popular name from a *printers'* error par excellence. In *Psalms 119:161* the psalmist is made to complain, "Printers have persecuted me without a cause," instead of, "Princes have persecuted me without a cause."

How many copies of the Bible have been printed?

Of course there are no reliable statistics available as to the total number of Bibles printed throughout the whole world since the first Bible was printed about 1456. It has been roughly estimated, however, that more than a billion copies of the Bible have been printed up to the present time.

Has the Bible been printed in every language?

Mark 13:10 quotes Jesus as saying that before certain things come to pass "the gospel must first be published among all nations." The Bible has been printed in all of the important living languages of the world. Up to 1944, the entire Bible had been printed in about 180 languages and dialects and substantial parts of it in nearly 1,100, and the number has been increasing at the rate of about eight or ten a year. Nobody knows how many languages there are in the world. The estimates given by various authorities differ widely because no two agree on just what constitutes a language. It is difficult to determine when a system of speech should be classed as a separate and distinct language or merely as a sub-language or dialect. Many known languages are dead, many have been completely lost, and many have not yet been studied. The French Academy computed the number of languages spoken in the world at 2,796. In their *The Languages of the World,* published in 1924, Meillet and Cohen indexed 6,760 named tongues and systems of writing. A few years ago the Smithsonian Institution reported that there are more than 1,000 distinct languages in the world. The number of languages and distinct dialects has been estimated as high as 7,000. Thus it is seen that there are still thousands of "near-languages," sub-languages and dialects in which the Bible or any substantial part of it has not yet been printed.

Is the Bible copyrighted?

Only new translations of the Bible are copyrightable in the United States. Anybody may print the King James or other old versions without permission. In Great Britain, however, a copyright on the King James Version of the Bible rests perpetually in the crown. This version was translated and published at the expense of the crown for the use of the established church of which the sovereign is the head. At the time the British Copyright Act of 1911 went into effect the crown exercised its prerogative to perpetuate its copyright in the Authorized Version of the Bible and the Book of Common Prayer, with the result that this version occupies the same position in the British Empire as other copyrighted books, except the ownership of the copyright rests in the crown. The copyright is controlled in England on behalf of the crown by Eyre & Spottiswoode Limited, who are appointed King's Printers of the Bible and Book of Common Prayer by royal letters patent, the constitutional instrument under which the crown copyright is perpetuated. The Oxford and Cambridge Presses have the right under their charters to print the King James Version, but they do not have the right to grant permission to others to print it. Control of the copyright in England rests solely with the King's Printers. Requests for permission from other printers or publishers to print the Authorized Version generally are not granted. When permission is granted to reproduce extensive extracts or quotations from the King James Version it is generally required that the actual printing be done by one of the "Privileged Presses" in order to safeguard the accuracy of the text. Separate regulations apply in Scotland, where the crown copyright is administered by a body known as the Scottish Bible Board, who can issue a license to anybody whom they choose to print the King James Version in Scotland, but Bibles so printed cannot legally be imported into England or into any other part of the British Empire, except by special agreement. In fact, the prohibition against the importation of copies of the Authorized Version into England is rigidly enforced. Of course, these regulations governing the printing of the King James Version in England do not apply to publishers in the United States and other countries. The printing of the Authorized Version in the American Colonies was prohibited before the Revolution. In 1782, six years after the signing of the Declaration of Independence, Robert Aitkin, of Philadelphia, published the first whole English Bible printed in America. The title-page says the project was "approved and recommended by the U. S. Congress, assembled September 12, 1782." This edition of the King James Version, known as "the Bible of the Revolution," is more rare than even the Gutenberg Bible.

What did King James have to do with the English Bible?

King James I of England had considerable to do with the production of the version of the Bible that bears his name. In 1604 King James as head of the Church of England called a conference at Hampton Court to consider ecclesiastical matters. At that meeting John Rainolds, one of the four Puritan delegates, suggested a new revision and translation of the English Bible to take the place of the half dozen or more versions then in use. The king approved the suggestion and took a keen personal interest in the project. He drafted the scheme and appointed the scholars who executed it. The revisers represented all shades of opinion in the established church, but of the fifty-four appointed only forty-seven accepted and served. King James also asked the bishops to advise him whenever a living worth twenty pounds a year fell vacant so he could recommend one of the revisers for the place. The revisers worked in three main groups, one at Oxford, one at Cambridge and one at Westminster. These groups were further subdivided to act as checks and counterchecks on one another. Every part of the Bible was gone over at least fourteen times and the whole was then reviewed by Dr. Myles Smith. Many eminent scholars were called upon for special help and all the bishops kept the clergy of their dioceses advised on the progress of the work. Although the revisers had been enjoined to follow the Bishop's Bible as closely as possible, they also leaned heavily upon Tyndale's, Matthew's and Coverdale's Bibles, the Great Bible, the Geneva Bible and other English Bibles as well as on Bibles in ancient and modern tongues. The expenses of the project, about 3,500 pounds, were paid by the king's printer. The actual work was begun in 1607 and completed in 1610. It was published in 1611, four years after the Jamestown colony in Virginia was established, five years before the death of Shakespeare and nine years before the Pilgrims landed at Plymouth. This Bible, which included the Apocrypha, is popularly known as the King James Version. It was dedicated to King James and "appointed to be read in churches." Although there is no record of any decree making it the official version of the Anglican church, it rapidly supplanted earlier English versions and came to be known as the Authorized Version. The King James or Authorized Version has continued to hold its own against the some 250 versions that have been published in England since 1611. This version is often erroneously referred to as the *Saint* James instead of the *King* James Version. The James after whom it was named was hardly a saint.

Has the King James Version been changed?

The King James Version of the Bible as it is published at the present time is not an exact reprint of the first editions of 1611. Apparently the king's printers felt from the beginning that they were authorized to correct obvious errors and make minor changes in succeeding editions. As later editions were printed typographical errors were corrected, spelling and punctuation were altered and modernized, and italics and capital letters were varied. These alterations were made so gradually that it is difficult now to say just who made them. When the King James Version first appeared in 1611 it contained a notice to the readers, a calendar and the Apocrypha. All these have been eliminated from most modern editions. At the time the first edition was issued *J* and *I* on the one hand and *V* and *U* on the other were not differentiated. *Jesus* was printed *Iesus* and *Joseph* was printed *Ioseph*. The following is an exact transcript of the first two verses in "The First Booke of Moses called Genesis": "In the beginning God created the Heauen, and the Earth. And the earth was without forme, and voyd, and darkenesse was vpon the face of the deepe: and the Spirit of God mooued vpon the face of the waters." And here is an exact transcript of the Lord's Prayer as printed in *Matthew 6:9-13* of the original edition: "After this manner therefore pray yee: Our father which art in heauen, hallowed be thy name. Thy kingdome come. Thy will be done, in earth, as it is in heauen. Giue vs this day our daily bread. And forgiue vs our debts, as we forgiue our debters. And lead vs not into temptation, but deliuer vs from euill: For thine is the kingdome, and the power, and the glory, for euer, Amen." In some cases, of course, the old f-shaped or long *s* was used in the original edition. According to the original editions, *I Corinthians 28* read: "And God hath set some in the church, first apostles, secondarily prophets, thirdly teachers, after that miracles, then gifts of healings, *helps in governments,* diversities of tongues." *Helps in governments* was obviously a misprint. After running through several successive editions this was corrected and *helps, governments* substituted. By whose authority this justified change was made is now hard to say. In the first of the two editions issued in 1611 the last clause in *Ruth 3:15* was printed, "And he went into the city." Consequently this edition is sometimes known as "the He Bible" or "the Great He Bible." In the second edition of 1611 the passage in *Ruth* was changed to read, "And she went into the city," and that reading has been retained to this day. That edition is known as "the She Bible." Oddly enough, *He* is the correct translation of the Hebrew original and the Revised Version prints the passage, "And *he* went into the city," like the Great He Bible of 1611.

When was the Bible translated into English?

Small parts of the Bible were rendered into Anglo-Saxon and Old English at a very early date, probably in the seventh century. These first efforts to translate the Bible into the vernacular consisted of little more than poetical paraphrases of parts of the Gospels and *Psalms.* Aldhelm (640-709), churchman and scholar, abbot of Malmesbury and bishop of Sherborne, seems to have translated parts of the Bible into the everyday language of his day. The Venerable Bede (673-735), known as the most learned man in Western Europe in his time, and Ecberth, who was archbishop of York when he died in 766, did likewise. There is a tradition that King Alfred the Great (840-899?) translated some of the Scriptures into early English. Aelfric (c.955-1020), churchman and scholar, known as "Grammaticus," translated more substantial parts of the Bible into Old English. About 1215, the year King John granted the Great Charter, a metrical paraphrase of parts of the Gospels and *Acts* was made. Soon thereafter William of Shoreham and Richard Rolle of Hampole translated *Psalms* into the southern and northern dialects of England. All these early translations of parts of the Bible into the English vernacular were based on the Latin Vulgate and were done in the orthodox manner by recognized churchmen. The first translation of the entire Bible into English is associated with the name of John Wycliffe (c.1320-1384), who belonged to the anticlerical party, who was an energetic reformer and who was, in a sense, a forerunner of the Protestant Reformation. Just what part, if any, Wycliffe himself took in translating the Bible that bears his name is uncertain. His work, also based on the Vulgate, was begun in 1379 and was completed about 1382. The tradition is that the work of translation was done by Wycliffe with the help of Nicholas of Hereford, John Purvey and perhaps other associates. Wycliffe had proclaimed that the Bible itself, not the Church and Catholic tradition, was man's supreme authority in spiritual matters. He sympathized with the common people and the lower clergy as against the hierarchy and was determined that they should have a Bible in the vernacular that they could read and understand. Wycliffe was twice condemned as a heretic, in 1380 and 1382, but he was not molested personally in his retirement at Luttersworth, where he died of a paralytic stroke in 1384. Four years after his death, in 1388, a revised version of his Bible was completed. It is known as the "Later Version" and was probably the work of John Purvey and other of Wycliffe's former associates and followers. In 1395 Parliament began to take steps to destroy the Wycliffe Bible. Six years later it ordered all copies that could be found burned. By 1407 a license was required to have a Wycliffe Bible in one's possession. On May 4, 1415, the council of Constance decreed that Wycliffe's remains should be dug up and burned. This decree was finally carried out in 1428 by Bishop Richard Fleming at the command of Pope Martin V. After the body was burned the ashes were thrown into the river Swift. Notwithstanding the attempts to destroy the Wycliffe Bible, Early and Later versions, about 170 manuscript copies are still in existence. Most of them are the Later Version. This Bible, translated long before the invention of printing, remained only in manuscript form for centuries. The New Testament was first printed in 1731 and the Old Testament in 1850. Wycliffe's Bible is interesting now chiefly because it is a landmark in the history of the English language.

What is the Revised Version?

The Revised Version is a liberal revision of the King James Version. In 1870, in response to a widespread demand for an up-to-date version of the English Bible, both convocations of the Anglican church adopted a resolution calling for such a revision. The plan was to preserve the unsurpassed English of the King James Version and at the same time to modernize its language and to correct its inaccuracies in the light of modern scholarship. The work was done by seventy-five Anglo-American scholars, divided into Old and New Testament groups in both England and America. About 36,000 major and minor changes in the English of the King James Version were made. The New Testament was published in 1881, the Old Testament in 1885, and the Apocrypha in 1895. In some cases beauty of style was sacrificed for accuracy and in others stilted Latinisms were substituted for time-honored English phraseology. Because many of the changes were not acceptable to English-speaking Protestants generally, the Revised Version, though widely accepted, has never supplanted the King James Version. The American groups continued their work and in 1901 published the American Standard or the American Revised Version. These revised versions are now almost as *dated* in their English as is the older version on which they were based. Although there are many archaic words in the King James Version, it contains comparatively few obsolete words. This is because the revisers and translators of the version of 1611 were careful to choose words already firmly fixed in the language and because the popularity of the work has had a tendency to keep alive all words in it.

What is the Septuagint?

The Septuagint is a Greek translation of the Hebrew scriptures made at Alexandria between 275 and 150 B.C. This first translation of the sacred writings of the Jews into a foreign language was one of the most momentous events in the history of civilization. *Septuagint* is from Latin *septuaginta*, "seventy," and the version received its name from the tradition that it was translated by seventy-two Jewish scholars brought from Palestine by Ptolemy Philadelphus, who reigned over Egypt from 285 to 247 B.C. Seventy is used for the round number of seventy-two. The version is generally denoted simply LXX, the Latin numerals for seventy. Aristeas, Philo, Josephus and other ancient Jewish writers say that Demetrius Phalerius, keeper of the books, desired copies of the Hebrew scriptures to complete the king's library. Upon the request of Ptolemy the high priest at Jerusalem sent seventy-two scholars, six from each of the twelve tribes—to Alexandria at the king's expense to transcribe the scriptures into Greek. Part of the story is that the seventy-two Jewish scholars, conversant alike with Greek and Hebrew, worked in seclusion and separately on the island of Pharos and that after seventy-two days they compared their completed translations and found that each agreed word for word and in every particular with the others. It is said that for centuries the Alexandrian Jews held an annual festival on Pharos to commemorate the translation of the Bible into Greek. Many authorities discount this story and believe that the project was initiated by the Hellenistic Jews in Alexandria, many of whom could no longer understand Hebrew and who felt the need of a Greek version of their scriptures. Perhaps both contentions contain some of the truth. Ptolemy Philadelphus is known to have been a patron of learning and there is nothing improbable that he desired to add the Hebrew scriptures to his collection and that he brought translators from Palestine to transcribe them. The Greek kings of Egypt at that time governed Palestine and there must have been at least 100,000 Jews in Egypt. Greek was already a familiar language to many of the Jews even in Jerusalem. The original project started by Ptolemy Philadelphus may have included only the Jewish law, the five books of Moses, which eminent scholars familiar with both languages could translate in a short time. Naturally the Greek-speaking Jews would desire Greek copies of the rest of their sacred writings for their own use as well as to demonstrate to the classical world that they had a culture and literature rivaling that of Greece in antiquity and quality. The sponsors also would naturally obtain royal sanction for the undertaking and would present their king copies for his famous library. At any rate, it appears that a century or more passed before all the Old Testament books were translated into Greek at Alexandria. The liberal Greek-speaking Jews recognized a larger number of sacred books than the conservative authorities in Jerusalem and consequently the Septuagint contains most of the books now called Apocrypha by Jews and Protestants. Through the Septuagint Jewish literature was introduced to the classical world. Wherever there was a colony of Jews, the Old Testament in Greek was available. Paul and many other founders of the church appear to have read the scriptures only in Greek. Possibly Jesus did likewise. The Greek version was the common Bible of the Christians when most of the converts were Jews, and it was the first Bible of the church even in Rome. The general use of the Hebrew scriptures in Greek had much to do with the fact that the New Testament books were composed or translated at an early date into the "international" language of the Roman Empire. Without the Septuagint the conversion of Europe to Christianity would have been a much more difficult task. The first translation of the Hebrew scriptures into a foreign tongue also had a profound influence on all later translations.

What English version of the Bible do Catholics use?

The authorized English translation of the Catholic Bible is the Douay Version and that is the version most commonly used by English-speaking Catholics. This was the first English translation of the Catholic Bible and was made in France by a group of English Catholic scholars who fled from England upon the accession of Queen Elizabeth. It was originally designed chiefly for the use of English boys preparing for the priesthood. Most of the actual translating was done by Gregory Martin, who followed Jerome's Latin of the Vulgate so closely that his English was somewhat stilted and burdened with Latinisms. But he and his associates sought accuracy rather than beauty of style and diction. This Bible is sometimes called the Rheims-Douai Version, because the New Testament was published at Rheims in 1582 and the Old Testament at Douai in 1609, two years before the King James Version was published. A complete revision of the Douay Version was published in 1749 by Bishop Richard Challoner, of London, and there have been several later revisions. In 1941 a revised and modernized version of the Douay New Testament was published, and a similar edition of the Old Testament is in process of preparation. The Douay Version of today approximates the King James Version in language and style much more closely than did the original Rheims-Douai Version.

What is the Gutenberg Bible?

The Gutenberg Bible was not only the first Bible printed but also the first large book of any kind printed from movable type. Johann Gutenberg is generally credited with the invention of printing from movable type about 1452. How he hit upon the idea, how and of what material he made his type and what kind of a press he used are all equally unknown. Although the first printed Bible is generally called the Gutenberg Bible, it is not known for certain what if any direct connection he had with it. About 1450 Johann Fust advanced Gutenberg funds to start a printing business at Mainz, Germany. Gutenberg and his financial backer soon quarreled and separated and it is not known whether they printed any books during their partnership. A few years later Fust transferred his patronage to Peter Schoffer and the best information is that they printed what is now known as the Gutenberg Bible. Some authorities think that possibly the project was started by Gutenberg and Fust and completed by Schoffer and Fust. The production of this first important printed book may have required four or five years. This remarkable Bible bears no date, but is believed to have been printed in 1456 and possibly as early as 1455. Bibliographers call it the Forty-two Line Bible, because it contains forty-two lines to the page. It is also sometimes called the Mazarin Bible, because the first copy described in later times was found in 1760 in the library of Cardinal Mazarin in Paris. Since then about forty-five copies of this Bible, in varying degrees of preservation, have been found—more than forty copies printed on rag paper and three copies printed on vellum. The vellum copies are in the British Museum, London; the Bibliotheque Nationale, Paris; and the Library of Congress, Washington, D. C. The beautifully printed and well preserved three-volume vellum copy in the Library of Congress is appraised at $1,000,000 and is known as "the choicest book in christendom." The text is the Vulgate Version and it is in Latin. The letters are an imitation of those found in manuscripts of the time. It is a 1,262-page folio, with two columns to the page and with spaces that were illuminated by hand. Although not the rarest Bible in point of numbers extant, the Gutenberg Bible is one of the most highly prized. Even the paper copies, many of which are incomplete and greatly damaged, have brought large prices. Seventy years or more ago a copy sold for $8,000 in New York. Shortly thereafter the Earl of Ashburnham paid twice that amount for one. A copy presented to Yale University in 1926 by Edward S. Harkness was purchased at a New York auction for $106,000. A few years later a copy brought $123,000. Books printed during the infancy of printing, the period from the supposed date of the invention of printing to the end of the fifteenth century, are known as cradle books or *incunabula,* the plural of a Latin word meaning "cradle," "origin" or "birthplace." Naturally enough, nearly fifty percent of the incunabula consist of Bibles and religious books.

What is the Vulgate Version?

The Vulgate is one of the most important versions of the Bible in existence and is the standard and official Latin text of the Roman Catholic church. *Vulgate,* from Latin *vulgus,* "the common people," means "current" or "commonly used." The earliest Greek text of the New Testament was originally known as the Greek Vulgate. In the fourth century, in response to a demand for an authorized revision of the old Latin text, Pope Damasus I initiated and sponsored the project and commissioned Jerome to undertake the work. The eminent Latin scholar, who studied Hebrew under Jewish teachers, began his translation in Rome in 383 A.D. After the death of Pope Damasus about a year later, Jerome went to the Holy Land and continued his work in a monastic cave near Bethlehem. His work was completed in 385 A.D. It was a new translation in classical Latin rather than a mere revision of the earlier Latin text. Jerome used not only the Old Latin and the Greek Vulgate, but also various other "ancient copies" of

Hebrew and Greek manuscripts available at the time. In the course of time this version appropriated the name of the earlier Vulgate in Greek and is now universally known as "the Vulgate." On April 8, 1546, the Council of Trent, which held sessions for eighteen years from 1545 to 1563, pronounced Jerome's Vulgate the only authentic and authorized translation of the Church. In 1592 Pope Clement VIII forbade any further change in its text.

What was the Idle Bible?

That is the popular name given to an edition of the Bible printed in England in 1809 in which *Zechariah 11:17* was erroneously printed, "Woe to the *idle* shepherd that leaveth the flock!" instead of "*idol* shepherd," as it had been printed in the King James and earlier English versions. In the seventeenth century *idol* was used as an adjective in the sense of worthless, self-seeking, counterfeit. The underlying thought was that an idol is merely a worthless and meaningless figure or form. In the polemical writings of those days *idol shepherd* was employed in the sense of a sham, pretender or impostor. The Revised Version of 1885 substituted *worthless* for *idol* in the passage in *Zechariah.*

What was the Breeches Bible?

The Breeches Bible, more properly the Geneva Bible, was an English translation of the Bible printed in Geneva, Switzerland, between 1557 and 1560. It received its popular name from the fact that *Genesis 3:7* was translated as follows: "The eyes of them bothe were opened, and they knew that they were naked; and they sewed figge-tree leaves together and made themselves breeches." In the King James Version the Hebrew original is rendered *aprons.* At the time the Geneva Bible was translated *breeches* was applied to any garment covering the thighs and loins and the term had not yet acquired the specific meaning it has today. As a matter of fact, *breeches* was used in the same passage in the fourteenth-century English translation of the Latin Vulgate made by John Wycliffe, Nicholas of Hereford and John Purvey, but that Bible was not printed until many centuries later. The quaint term occurs also in this passage in the version of the Pentateuch in Caxton's edition of Voragine's *Golden Legend,* printed in 1483. But *breeches* occurred in *Genesis 3:7* in every reprint of the Geneva Bible and not in any other version printed. Consequently that work has come down through the centuries as the Breeches Bible. It was largely the work of William Whittingham, Anthony Gilby and Thomas Sampson and several other exiles from England. Printing and publication costs were borne by the congregation at Geneva. The Breeches Bible became immensely popular among the English people. Between 1560 and the outbreak of the Civil War in the time of Charles I, about 160 editions of it were printed, and in private homes it soon completely supplanted the Great Bible, the unwieldy volume then used in English churches. This Bible also has other nicknames. It is called the Goose Bible because a goose was the device of the press at Dort in the Netherlands where several editions were printed. It is also called the Place-Makers Bible, because the second edition printed in 1563 contained an odd printer's error. *Matthew 5:9* was printed, "Blessed are the placemakers," instead of the "peacemakers." For the same reason it was jokingly called the "Whig Bible."

Why was Tyndale's Bible important?

William Tyndale, whose translation was the first English Bible printed, probably did more than any other one person to fix the tone and style of the English Bible. He brought the wrath of the authorities down upon his head because he was an energetic reformer and pamphleteer as well as a great churchman, scholar and translator. Stymied in his work in England, Tyndale went to the continent, where he began to print his English New Testament at Cologne in 1525 and completed it at Worms in 1526. He based his Testament on Erasmus's Greek and Latin, the Vulgate and Luther's German versions. Some six thousand copies were smuggled into England, where the authorities, who objected to a Bible in the vernacular, burned every copy they could lay their hands on. William Warham, archbishop of Canterbury, and Cuthbert Tunstall, bishop of London, even bought up copies on the continent in order to have them destroyed. But within the next four years six editions were printed, all of them on the continent and some of them unauthorized by the translator. Tyndale continued his work but did not live to complete the entire Bible. He did, however, leave manuscript copies of his translation of the Old Testament as far as the end of *II Chronicles* and *Jonah*. Upon the instigation of the English authorities, Tyndale was arrested at Antwerp by imperial officers in 1535, confined in Vilvorde Castle, the state prison of the Low Countries about six miles from Brussels, tried on charges of heresy, found guilty, strangled to death and burned at the stake. He was an accomplished Hebrew scholar and had a keen appreciation of the rhythm of that language. At the time when printing was crystallizing the various English dialects he set the standard of English diction, and his work has had a profound influence in shaping and forming the English of later Bibles, particularly the King James Version.

What is the Wicked Bible?

An edition of the King James Version printed by the Stationers' Company in London in 1631 is known as the Wicked Bible because the printers inadvertently left *not* out of one of the Commandments, making *Exodus 20:14* read: "Thou shalt commit adultery." Archbishop Laud summoned the printers, Barker and Lucas, before the court of High Commission, which ordered every copy of the edition destroyed and fined the printers $300, one of the heaviest penalties ever imposed on the Company of Stationers in the annals of literary history. The incident resulted in a long controversy between the University of Cambridge and the London Stationers over the right to print English Bibles. Several copies of the Wicked Bible escaped the public executioner and are now very valuable. One of the four or five copies known to be still in existence sold for $155 at a London auction in 1944. The Devil's Bible and the Adulterous Bible are other names given to the Wicked Bible of 1631. These names are also sometimes applied to the Unrighteous Bible, an edition of the King James Version printed at Cambridge in 1653 and so called from the fact that through a printer's error the second *not* was omitted from the first part of *I Corinthians 6:9,* making the passage read, "Know ye not that the unrighteous shall inherit the kingdom of God?" Devil's Bible is the name also given to a curious manuscript copy of the Bible that turned up in Stockholm about the time of the Thirty Years' War. It contains the entire Bible in beautiful handwriting on three hundred asses' skins. According to legend, this Devil's Bible was written by a monk in compliance with the terms of a compact with Satan by which his life was spared on condition he copy the Bible on asses' skins in one night.

What is the Bug Bible?

The Bug Bible is an English translation of the Bible printed in 1551 by John Daye. A copy of the original is, or was until the outbreak of war in 1939, in the library of Southampton, England. William Tyndale himself wrote an introduction to the book. It received its popular name from the peculiar rendering of the first part of *Psalms 91:5,* which reads: "So that thou shalt not need to be afraid for any bugs by night." The King James Version renders this passage: "Thou shalt not be afraid for the terror by night." In the sixteenth century the primary meaning of *bug* was still ghost, goblin or bogey, a sense that survives in *bugbear* and *bugaboo*. *Bug* had been used in *Psalms 91:5* in both Coverdale's Bible and Matthew's Bible. The former was the first complete Bible to be printed in English. It was the work of Myles Coverdale and was based on Luther's German, the Latin Vulgate, Tyndale's English and various other Bibles. The first edition of Coverdale's Bible was printed at Antwerp, but the second edition, the first complete English Bible printed on English soil, was issued at Southwark in 1535. Two years later there was issued, probably at Antwerp, an English version of the Bible whose sponsors declared that it had been "truly and purely translated into English by Thomas Matthew," which was a pseudonym adopted for purposes of safety by John Rogers, an assistant of William Tyndale. But it is generally referred to as Matthew's Bible. This Bible was largely based on Coverdale's Bible. This Matthew's Bible should not be confused with what is known as Matthew Parker's Bible, a popular name of the Bishop's Bible, which was undertaken in 1562 by a company of English divines, most of them bishops, upon the suggestion and under the leadership of Archbishop Matthew Parker, a man notable for his learning. Each member of the company was assigned a part of the Bible for translation into English. Archbishop Parker then edited the whole and saw it through the press in 1568. It was really a revision of the Great Bible, which was Coverdale's revision of his own Bible of 1535 collated with Tyndale's and Matthew's and which was printed in Paris in 1539. The Great Bible, so called because its format was larger than any previous edition, is sometimes called Cromwell's Bible because it was undertaken at the direction of Thomas Cromwell. Every parish in England was required to buy a copy. It is also called Cranmer's Bible because the edition printed in 1540 contained a wood-cut title-page by Holbein representing Henry VIII seated with Cromwell and Thomas Cranmer, the famous prelate. The Bishop's Bible, notwithstanding eighteen editions of it were printed between 1568 and 1602, failed to supersede the popular Breeches Bible. Popularly the Bishop's Bible was nicknamed the Treacle Bible because the first part of *Jeremiah 8:22* was rendered, "Is there no treacle in Gilead" instead of, "Is there no balm in Gilead." The Douai Bible of 1609 has been called the Rosin Bible because it renders the same passage, "Is there no rosin in Gilead?" *Rosin* for *balm* is given as a marginal alternative reading in some later English versions. *Treacle* originally was applied to an antidote against poison, but as applied to sugar syrup it may be a corruption of *trickle,* alluding to the fact that the syrup trickled through small holes when being strained.

What is the Vinegar Bible?

The Vinegar Bible is an edition of the King James Version printed by the Clarendon Press at Oxford in 1717. It received its name from a curious printer's error. The title over *Luke 20* reads "The Parable of the Vinegar" instead of "The Parable of the Vineyard." Copies of this edition are very rare. Christ Church at Shrewsbury, New Jersey, is said to possess one of the few known copies of this edition.

What does *canon* mean in connection with the Bible?

Canon is a Greek and Latin word meaning "rule" or "measure," such as a carpenter's rule. By extension it came to signify "a standard," "a model," "a criterion" or "an ordinance." The term does not occur in either the Old or the New Testament, but as early as the fourth century it began to be used in the specific sense of the Biblical writings received and accepted as genuine and inspired. The sacred canon, also called the canonical books, consists of the whole list, collection or body of books of the Bible that are accepted as genuine and inspired Holy Scriptures; that is, the whole Bible from *Genesis* to *Revelation,* exclusive of the Apocrypha. But the exact books of the sacred canon are not identical for all churches. The sacred canon of the Jews, of course, includes only the Old Testament. So far as the Jews were concerned, the Old Testament canon was fixed at an early date. The Roman Catholic canon of the whole Bible was finally fixed by the Council of Trent, which sat from 1545 to 1563, although it had been substantially fixed long before. This sacred canon contains certain Old Testament books not accepted by the Jews and the Protestants. The canon as included in the King James Version and later versions based on it is the canon of the Church of England and the overwhelming majority of Protestant churches.

What does *Catholic* mean?

Catholic, which does not occur in the Bible, is derived from Greek *kata,* "concerning" or "according to," and *holos,* "whole." It signifies "universal," "general" or "all embracing," and began to be applied about the second century A.D. to distinguish the Church at large from the local units or from heretical or schismatic sects. In the course of time the word was interpreted as referring to the world-wide extension, doctrinal completeness, adaptation to the needs of all people and the moral and spiritual perfection of the Mother Church. The various groups that sprang from the original church or that originated independently of it and that were denounced by the Popes as unorthodox or heretical refused to abandon the use of the term *catholic*, with the result that it is still employed by many churches besides the Roman Catholic. Several small denominations use the term in their names, and Roman Catholics, Episcopalians, Methodists, Presbyterians and other denominations alike declare their belief in "the Holy Catholic Church" when they recite the Apostles' Creed. *Catholic* is still used in its original sense, and a person with broad and liberal views is said to have a catholic mind. The Epistles of *James, Peter I, Peter II, John I, John II, John III,* and *Jude* are sometimes known as the Catholic Epistles. These seven epistles are not addressed to specifically named churches or individuals, and all of them except *John II* and *John III* deal for the most part with general rather than with local or individual questions. Hence the early church fathers considered them as addressed to the general, universal or catholic church; that is, the church at large. Following the late Greek manuscripts, the translators of the King James Version expressed this idea in the titles of five of these books—*The General Epistle of James, The First Epistle General of Peter, The Second Epistle General of Peter, The First Epistle General of John* and *The General Epistle of Jude*.

How did *Protestant* originate?

Protestant, of course, is not of Biblical origin. In 1521 the Diet of Worms, called by Emperor Charles V of the Holy Roman Empire, met to consider the recalcitrant behavior of Martin Luther, who had been condemned by the Pope. This Diet demanded that Luther retract his teachings. When he refused to yield he was condemned as a heretic and asked to leave the city. In 1529 the Diet of Spires (Speyer) reaffirmed this action and issued an edict against the dissemination of the Reform doctrines. Certain dissenters, including a number of German princes, deputies and representatives of free cities in sympathy with Luther and the Reformers, submitted a *protestatio,* or solemn declaration of protest against the Edict of Spires. From this circumstance the adherents of the Reformed doctrines in Germany came to be called *protestants. Protest,* from Late Latin *protestari,* originally signified "to state formally, to aver, to declare or to affirm solemnly something about which a doubt is stated or implied." That is the sense the term has in the English Bible. For instance, according to *Genesis 43:3*, Judah said to his father concerning Joseph and Benjamin: "The man did solemnly *protest* unto us, saying, Ye shall not see my face, except your brother be with you." The word occurs only once in the entire New Testament. In *I Corinthians 15:31* Paul says: "I *protest* by your rejoicing which I have in Christ Jesus our Lord, I die daily." By 1553 *Protestant* was already applied loosely to a member or adherent of any Western church outside the communion of Rome. It is now sometimes applied retroactively even to dissenting sects that pre-date the Reformation, such as the Albigenses, the Waldenses and the adherents of John Wycliffe and John Huss. *Protestant* in its religious sense is of general application, and we properly speak of "the Protestant churches" but not of "the Protestant Church." The religious body in the United States corresponding to the Anglican church in England is officially the Protestant Episcopal church, and the word is used in the names of other denominations; as, the Methodist Protestant church. In its religious sense *Protestant* is pronounced *PROT-e-stant,* but when used as an adjective or a noun in the same sense of one who protests, without reference to its special religious significance, it is often pronounced *pro-TEST-ant*.

How large is the vocabulary of the English Bible?

The vocabulary of the English Bible is small compared to the total number of words in the English language. It is generally estimated that the total number of different words, exclusive of proper names, in the King James Version is only about 7,000, 5,642 of which are in the Old Testament. Naturally a vocabulary cannot be numbered with mathematical accuracy. Estimates of the number of different words in the Bible vary widely because authorities differ as to just what ought to be regarded as a separate word. For instance, one authority will reckon *work* and *worked* as two words, while another will reckon them as one word. This accounts for the fact that estimates of the size of the vocabulary of the English Bible range all the way from 7,000 to 10,000 words.

What language did Adam speak?

Traditionally Hebrew was the original language of Adam and Eve and continued to be the only language of the human race until the confusion of tongues at Babel. Many Jewish scholars have maintained that the sacred tongue of the Scriptures was the first and original language of mankind and accordingly have regarded Hebrew as the most important of human tongues, the language of languages. The fact is that nobody knows which was the first language and which is the oldest among the recorded dead and living languages. There is even no general agreement on the origin of human language. All of the many conjectures on the subject are impossible of positive proof. As far back as we can go in the history of the human race we find complete and developed linguistic systems spoken by everyone in the community and learned by every child as a matter of course. Among the Persians there is a legend that Arabic, Persian and Turkish are the three primitive languages. All three of them, according to the story, were spoken in the Garden of Eden. The seductive serpent spoke Arabic, the most persuasive language; Adam and Eve spoke Persian, the most poetic language; and the angel of the Lord spoke Turkish, the most awesome and menacing language. Herodotus tells how Psammetichus, king of Egypt about 600 B.C., made a curious experiment to determine whether the Egyptians were correct in believing themselves to be the most ancient of mankind. "He took two children of the common sort, and gave them over to a herdsman to bring up at his folds, strictly charging him to let no one utter a word in their presence, but to keep them in a sequestered cottage, and from time to time introduce goats to their apartment, see that they got their fill of milk, and in all other respects look after them," wrote the Father of History. "His object herein was to know, after the indistinct babblings of infancy were over, what word they would first articulate. It happened as he had anticipated. The herdsman obeyed his orders for two years, and at the end of that time, on his one day opening the door of their room and going in, the children both ran up to him with outstretched arms, and distinctly said *Becos*. When this first happened the herdsman took no notice; but afterwards when he observed, on coming often to see after them, that the word was constantly in their mouths, he informed his lord, and by his command brought the children into his presence. Psammetichus then himself heard them say the word, upon which he proceeded to make inquiry what people there was who called anything *Becos,* and hereupon he learned that *Becos* was the Phrygian name for bread. In consideration of this circumstance, the Egyptians yielded their claims, and admitted the greater antiquity of the Phrygians."

When was the Bible written?

The Bible is the work of many writers over a period of more than a thousand years. There is no general agreement as to the exact dates of composition of the books of the Bible and probably never will be.

Authorities differ widely on even the approximate dates of composition of the various books. Tables showing the exact dates are not reliable. It is doubtful whether the date of composition of a single book of the Bible is known within several years. Probably few of the authors of the Old Testament *wrote* the books bearing their names in the modern sense of the term. The usual process of writing the Scriptures appears to have been one of consecutive addition and elaboration. Ancient writers had no conception of literary ownership. Succeeding generations of scribes felt free to annotate, to elaborate and to make additions to old books and to republish them under the old titles. The earliest parts of the sacred writings were transmitted orally or preserved in brief form on stones or clay tablets. Consequently the composition of the books of the Old Testament was a gradual process. The Hebrews are believed to have begun to reduce their sacred literature to systematic writing on some kind of parchment about the eighth century B.C. Undoubtedly certain fragments of very old oral and written oracles were incorporated into these more complete documents. Some parts of the five books of Moses, *Joshua, Judges* and other early books may date from the time of the events that they describe. For instance, the song sung by Moses and the Israelites after their deliverance from Pharaoh at the Red Sea and the song of Deborah and Barak after the victory over Sisera may be among the oldest fragments of the Bible. Likewise, the *Ten Commandments* and other parts of the Mosaic law may actually have been handed down orally from the time of the great lawgiver. Many of the Biblical books, such as *Psalms* and *Proverbs,* were collected and edited through many centuries and are the work of numerous unknown authors as well as of David and Solomon. *Psalms* did not reach its present form until about 100 B.C. The first part of *Isaiah* may have been composed in the time of the prophet of that name, but other parts probably were composed by various writers through succeeding centuries. Most authorities suppose that *Daniel* was composed about 165 B.C. and was one of the last, if not the last, Old Testament book in point of the date of composition. The larger part of the New Testament is believed to have been composed during the latter half of the first century A.D. In all probability some additions were made later. The Epistles of Paul, which form a considerable part of the New Testament, were composed between 50 and 68 A.D. The earliest of these, *I Thessalonians,* is supposed to have been composed about 50 A.D., some twenty years after the crucifixion of Jesus. There is no positive evidence that Paul ever saw any of the Gospels or other parts of the New Testament that he did not himself write. Assuming that *Daniel* was composed in 165 B.C., and *I Thessalonians* in 50 A.D., the spread between the last book of the Old Testament and the first of the New would be 215 years. Authorities disagree widely on the date of composition of the Gospels. *Mark* is generally believed to have been the earliest. There is a bare possibility that all the Gospels and most of the other New Testament books had reached substantially their present form before 70 A.D. In that year the Romans completely destroyed Jerusalem and the temple and broke up the Jewish commonwealth. *Luke 19:41-44* says: "And when he was come near, he beheld the city, and wept over it, saying, If thou hadst known, even thou, at least in this thy day, the things which belong unto thy peace! but now they are hid from thine eyes. For the days shall come upon thee, that thine enemies shall cast a trench about thee, and compass thee round, and keep thee in on every side, and shall lay thee even with the ground, and thy children within thee; and they shall not leave in thee one stone upon another; because thou knewest not the time of thy visitation." In *Mark 13:1-2* and *Luke 21:5-6* Jesus is also quoted as foretelling the doom of Jerusalem and the temple. This was one of the most profound events in the history of both Jews and Christians up to that time. By it the central organization of Judaism and the mother church were both scattered. Although the authors of the Gospels generally were given to mentioning the fulfillment of prophecy, neither they nor any other New Testament writer so much as alludes to the destruction of Jerusalem and the temple. Notwithstanding this negative evidence to the contrary, it is generally believed that *Revelation*, the *Gospel According to St. John*, the three Epistles of John and several other Epistles in the New Testament were written toward the end of the first century or even later. But this view is not accepted by all competent scholars. Some modern investigators believe that *John* was the first Gospel in point of composition and that instead of being the least authentic historically it is the most authentic. They maintain that *John*, stripped of later interpolations and additions, contains internal evidence that it was composed only ten or fifteen years after the death of Jesus.

In what language was the Bible originally written?

All of the sixty-six books of the Bible are believed to have been originally composed in one of three ancient languages—Hebrew, Aramaic or Greek. Most of the Old Testament was composed in Hebrew before Aramaic began to supplant Hebrew as the everyday language of the Jews. Parts of *Ezra*, *Jeremiah* and *Daniel* are written in Aramaic, and isolated words and phrases in Aramaic occur in other parts of the Old Testament. For instance, the famous handwriting on the wall in Daniel—*Mene, Mene, Tekel, Upharsin*—is in Aramaic instead of Hebrew. These cases may be merely owing to careless copyists. Possibly a few of the later books may have been originally composed in part or in whole in Aramaic, although this is a disputed question. Even after Aramaic had become the usual spoken and written language of the Jews in Palestine, Hebrew continued to be the sacred, literary and ritual language. For that reason it is difficult to determine whether some of the later Old Testament books were composed in Hebrew and translated into Aramaic or composed in Aramaic and translated into Hebrew. Most of the New Testament books are believed to have been composed in Greek, which in the first and second centuries, when the New Testament assumed its present form, was the literary and "international" language of the Roman Empire. Even many of the upper-class Jews in Jerusalem spoke and wrote Greek. Paul undoubtedly wrote his Epistles in Greek and all of the earliest copies of the rest of the New Testament books are in that language. Many passages in the Gospels indicate that they were from Aramaic sources. Since Greek was the universal language of the Roman Empire at that time, again it is difficult to determine whether these books were composed in Aramaic and rendered into Greek or composed in Greek from Aramaic and Hebrew sources. It is not at all improbable that parts of the Gospels first appeared in sketchy Aramaic originals. So far as known none of the Twelve Apostles ever wrote a line. It is not even known whether any of them could read and write. In *Acts 4:13* Peter and John are referred to as "unlearned and ignorant men." According to tradition, the second Gospel was dictated in Rome by Peter to Mark, who was not one of the Twelve. It is possible that Peter dictated in Aramaic and that Mark wrote in Greek, which would account for any of the Aramaic traces in this Gospel. *Matthew* may have been composed at Antioch in a similar manner. It is generally supposed that *Mark*, the most fragmentary of the Four Gospels, was written the earliest. Some authorities date its composition as early as 65 A.D., which would be about thirty-five years after the crucifixion of Jesus. *Luke* and *Acts* also in places bear unmistakable traces of having had an Aramaic basis. *John* more likely was composed in Greek. The composition of the sixty-six books of the Bible extended over a period of about a thousand years and they are said to represent about fifty different authors. The period between the composition of the latest book of the Old Testament and the earliest book of the New Testament was between two and three hundred years. During the first century after the crucifixion of Jesus the only Bible used by the Christians was the Septuagint Version of the Old Testament. The New Testament did not begin to assume its present form and to be accepted as part of the Bible until about the middle of the second century A.D. Since Jesus and his disciples all spoke Aramaic, some authorities are of the opinion that all of the sayings of Jesus and his disciples as well as the story of the life of Jesus were originally collected and written in Aramaic and translated into Greek a generation or two later.

What is meant by the Lost Books of the Bible?

A number of books that are quoted, referred to or hinted at in the Bible and about which nothing whatever is known are sometimes called the Lost Books. These books should not be confused with the Apocrypha, which are extant but not included in the canon. The Lost Books, so far as known, no longer exist. For instance, *Numbers 21:14* says: "Wherefore it is said in the book of the wars of the Lord, what he did in the Red Sea, and in the brooks of Arnon, and at the stream of the brooks that goeth down to the dwelling of Ar, and lieth upon the border of Moab." There is no other mention of "the book of the wars of the Lord" in the Bible. Apparently it was a collection of war ballads and songs celebrating what Jehovah did for the Israelites by the hand of Moses. *Joshua 10:13* says: "And the sun stood still, and the moon stayed, until the people had avenged themselves upon their enemies. Is not this written in the book of Jasher? So the sun stood still in the midst of heaven, and hasted not to go down about a whole day." According *to II Samuel 1:18,* David "bade them teach the children of Judah the use of the bow: behold, it is written in the book of Jasher." It is believed that the book of Jasher was an ancient collection of Hebrew poetical compositions celebrating the earlier heroes and conquests of Israel. *I Chronicles 29:29* says: "Now the acts of David the king, first and last, behold, they are written in the book of Samuel the seer, and in the book of Nathan the prophet, and in the book of Gad the seer." Samuel's books we have, but not Nathan's and Gad's. *II Chronicles 9:29* says: "Now the rest of the acts of Solomon, first and last, are they not written in the book of Nathan the prophet, and in the prophecy of Ahijah the Shilonite, and in the visions of Iddo the seer against Jeroboam the son of Nebat?" The prophecy of Ahijah, and the visions of Iddo, if they were separate books, have been completely lost. *I Kings 14:19* says: "And the rest of the acts of

Jeroboam, how he warred, and how he reigned, behold, they are written in the book of the chronicles of the kings of Israel." This reference obviously is to neither *I Kings* and *II Kings* or to *I Chronicles* and *II Chronicles* in the Bible. *I Kings 16:5* says: "Now the rest of the acts of Baasha, and what he did, and his might, are they not written in the book of the chronicles of the kings of Israel." Similar references to "the book of the chronicles of the kings of Judah" and to "the book of the chronicles of the kings of Judah and Israel" occur in connection with other reigns. They probably refer to the annals based on the official documents kept by the national recorder. One authority estimates that there are about thirty books quoted, mentioned or alluded to in the Bible that are not included in either the canon or the Apocrypha. In a few cases, however, these allusions may be to mere passages found in the Bible or to Biblical books known to us by other names. *Jude 9* says: "Yet Michael the archangel, when contending with the devil he disputed about the body of Moses, durst not bring against him a railing accusation, but said, The Lord rebuke thee." This appears to be an allusion to the *Assumption of Moses,* but the original part or separate book describing the ascension of Moses to heaven is not found in the Apocrypha. From the fourth book of Ezra, Philo and some of the church fathers we learn of a number of books that are supposed to have been given to Moses at the time he received the Pentateuch.

How do *Ecclesiastes* and *Ecclesiasticus* differ?

Ecclesiastes and *Ecclesiasticus* are often confused. They are the names of two different books. The title of the former in the King James Version is *Ecclesiastes; Or, The Preacher*. Among the Hebrews the names of the books of the Bible were derived from the initial words and they called this book "The words of Qoheleth, son of David, king in Jerusalem." Nobody today knows for certain what *Qoheleth* means. The Greek translators of the Septuagint thought it meant "one who is a member of, or who addresses an *Ecclesia,* an assembly of people of any kind," and accordingly they named the book *Ecclesiastes.* In the book *Qoheleth* is used as a masculine proper name, as a nickname, and as a name for Solomon. It probably alludes to a story about Solomon now lost. Popular renderings of the Hebrew term as "wisdom personified by Solomon," "collector of sayings," "great orator" and "convener" have little basis in fact. *Ecclesiastes; Or, The Preacher* is accepted by both Catholics and Protestants as one of the essential and canonical books of the Bible. *Ecclesiasticus,* also known as *Wisdom of Jesus, Son of Sirach* and as *Wisdom of Sirach,* is the name of a book in the Catholic Bible. It was included in the canon fixed by the Council of Trent (1545-1563), and is classified as one of the deuterocanonical books. The Greek fathers called it *The All-Virtuous Wisdom* and the Jews of the Talmudic period *The Book of Ben Sira,* but the Latin church fathers referred to it as *Ecclesiasticus,* the "church book," whence its present name. Protestants regard *Ecclesiasticus* as one of the most important books in the Old Testament apocrypha and accordingly read it for inspiration and edification, but do not use it to fix points of doctrine.

Do Moslems believe the Bible?

Mohammed based his teachings largely upon the Old and New Testaments, upon Arabic tradition and upon his own philosophy. It is generally supposed that Mohammed obtained his sketchy knowledge of the Scriptures orally by conversing with Arabic Jews and Christians rather than from reading the Bible. The Bible plays a very minor role in Islam. Moslem authorities hold that wherever the *Koran* differs from the Bible the Jews and Christians have corrupted or perverted the Biblical text. Moslems recognize six prophets—Adam, Noah, Abraham, Moses, Jesus and Mohammed. Mohammed regarded himself as the successor of Jesus and the last of the prophets. Of the other five prophets of Islam, Abraham and Jesus are regarded as the principal ones. Islam, like Judaism, is a strictly monotheistic religion, and Moslems do not worship Mohammed or any of the other prophets as a deity. The essence of Islam is: "There is only one God, Allah, and Mohammed is his prophet." Consequently the Moslems, while they accept Jesus as one of the six prophets, do not worship him as Christians do. Like the Gnostics of old, Moslems believe that Jesus was not himself crucified but another in his likeness.

What is the Pentateuch?

Pentateuch is of Greek origin and literally means "the five books." It is derived from *penta,* "five," and *teuchos,* "tool," "implement" or "vessel," and by extension, "book." The term has been applied for many centuries by Bible critics and students to the first five books of the Old Testament—*Genesis, Exodus, Leviticus, Numbers* and *Deuteronomy*. Since this part of the Bible is traditionally ascribed to Moses, it is often referred to as "the five books of Moses." The Jews call it "The Torah." *Torah* is a Hebrew word with a two-fold meaning. On the one hand it connotes "the law" and on the other it means "doctrine in the sense of teaching." In later usage the first six books of the Old Testament are sometimes called the *Hexateuch,* signifying "the six books," because the sixth book, *Joshua,* continues the same general account of the Israelites and is believed to be a part of the same literary production. All five of the books of the Pentateuch received their current names from the Septuagint, the pre-New Testament Greek translation. For the most part the ancient Hebrew as well as the modern Jewish names for these books are quite different from the names that they bear in our English copies. In many cases the Jewish names of the books of the Old Testament are merely the opening words. This same practice is followed by the Vatican in naming certain bulls and edicts. The meaning of the names of the books of the Pentateuch are as follows: *Genesis,* "creation"; *Exodus,* "the departure"; *Leviticus,* "the Levitical (book)," that is "the priestly book"; *Numbers,* "pertaining to the numbering of the Israelites," and *Deuteronomy,* "the second law." The original Greek names have been somewhat Latinized and even Anglicized in our English versions.

Who was the first woman to translate the Bible?

Julia Evelina Smith (1792-1886), of Glastonbury, Connecticut, translated the Bible into English from Latin, Greek and Hebrew and was the first woman to translate the entire Bible into any language. She started the project when she was seventy-seven and completed it when she was eighty-four. Her translation of the Bible was published at Hartford in 1876 at her own expense. She and her sister, Abby Hadassah Smith, were prominent abolitionists and advocates of women's rights. When Julia was eighty-seven she married Amos A. Parker, who was eighty-six. Their father, Zephaniah Smith, was originally a Congregational minister but quit the ministry because he decided preaching for pay was wrong.

What are the Synoptics?

Synoptics is the name that Bible scholars and critics apply to the Gospels according to Matthew, Mark and Luke. This term, like *synopsis,* is derived from two Greek words meaning "general view." The first three Gospels are called the Synoptics or the Synoptic Gospels because they agree in many respects in subject matter, language, manner of treatment and point of view. Mark relates the public ministry of Jesus chiefly in Galilee and within a period of about a year, while Matthew and Luke, in the same general spirit, repeat much of Mark with many additional sayings of Jesus, incidents in his life and other information. The fourth Gospel is written from an entirely different viewpoint and in a different style and spirit. John, unlike the Synoptics, places the scene chiefly in Jerusalem, emphasizes the Jewish feasts in connection with the public ministry of Jesus, and casts the subject matter in the form of symbolic discourses.

Why are the two parts of the Bible called Testaments?

Testament, from Latin *testamentum,* is used in the English New Testament to render Greek *diatheke,* which signifies primarily "a disposition of property by will" and secondarily "a compact, agreement or covenant." The phrases *old testament* and *new testament* both occur in the King James Version, where they are used in a general rather than a specific sense. At the Last Supper, according to *Matthew 26:28,* Jesus said: "For this is my blood of the new testament, which is shed for many for the remission of sins." The same phrase occurs in the corresponding passages in *Mark 14:24* and *Luke 22:20.* In *II Corinthians 3* Paul refers to both the new testament and the old testament. Verse 6 says that God "hath made us able ministers of the new testament," and Verse 14 reads: "But their minds were blinded; for until this day remaineth the same vail untaken away in the reading of the old testament; which vail is done away in Christ." And in *Hebrews 7:22* we find: "By so much was Jesus made a surety of a better testament." But in *Hebrews 9:15-20* the term is used in both its primary and secondary meanings: "And for this cause he is the mediator of the new testament, that by means of death, for the redemption of the transgressions that were under the first testament, they which are called might receive the promise of eternal inheritance. For where a testament is, there must also of necessity be the death of the testator. For a testament is of force after men are dead: otherwise it is of no strength at all while the testator liveth. Whereupon neither the first testament was dedicated without blood. For when Moses had spoken every precept to all the people according to the law, he took the blood of calves and of goats, with water, and scarlet wool, and hyssop, and sprinkled both the book, and all the people, saying, This is the blood of the testament which God hath enjoined unto you." The Israelites referred to the compact made between God and his chosen people as *Berith,* which is rendered covenant in the English version of the Old Testament. But the Israelites themselves never conceived the sacred books themselves as a single covenant, will or testament. The Jewish religion was based on a series of covenants between God and his people. To the Jews in the time of Jesus the idea of an "Old Testament" would have been incomprehensible. Even for several generations after the crucifixion of Jesus, Christians and Jews alike continued to use the same Bible. At first the Christians did not think of their early writings as parts of the Scriptures. None of the New Testament books were consciously written for a place in a "New Testament." But most if not all of the New Testament writings had been completed and were in possession of the churches by the second century, and gradually Christians began to place these writings on an equal footing with the Hebrew Bible. It was not till then that Christians began to think in terms of the New and the Old Testaments, the sacred writings that made up the Bible of the Church. At the council of Carthage in 397 the canon of the New Testament was fixed substantially in its present form. The Old Testament covers a period of history extending from creation to about 400 B.C., while the New Testament covers a period of only about seventy years, from shortly before the birth of Jesus until shortly before the death of Paul in the time of Nero.

Who was Josephus?

Flavius Josephus, often quoted in this book, was one of the greatest of ancient historians. His original name was Joseph Ben Matthias. He was born in Jerusalem of a priestly family about 37 A.D., seven or eight years after the crucifixion of Jesus. After playing a dubious part in the Jewish rebellion of 66-70, which ended in the destruction of Jerusalem and the Jewish commonwealth, he received the patronage of Vespasian and his son Titus and settled in Rome as a man of letters. The present titles of his extant works and the probable dates of their composition are as follows: *Wars of the Jews,* 80 A.D.; *Antiquities of the Jews,* 93; *Against Apion,* 94, and *Autobiography,* 95. In compliment to his first great patron, Emperor Titus Flavius Sabinus Vespasianus, he adopted the Romanized name Flavius Josephus. His monumental history of the Jews from the creation of the world to his own time appears to have been written to present the history and culture of his people to the Roman and Greek world. He probably thought and composed in his native Hebrew or Aramaic and then had Greek scholars render his work into Greek under his immediate direction. It is often thought smart to refer to Josephus as unreliable. But historical standards in those days were flexible, to say the least, and he perhaps was as accurate and trustworthy as any historian up to that time. His writings are as controversial as the Bible itself. In most instances he followed the Hebrew scriptures closely, while in others he departed materially from them. This may have been owing to several reasons. He may have had sources now lost; some of the scriptures may not have been available to him in Rome where he wrote; he may have slanted many incidents to appeal to his classical audience, and his original compositions may have been somewhat corrupted by editors and copyists as they were handed down from generation to generation in manuscript form. Josephus did not continue to receive the patronage of Emperor Domitian, the second son of Vespasian and the third and last of the Flavian line. In disfavor at the court, he is believed to have died in obscurity in Rome or Judaea about 95 A.D. or shortly thereafter.

What does *by and by* in the Bible mean?

By and by now means "a little time hence," "in due time," or "in the more or less remote future." When the King James Version of the Bible was made the phrase meant "now," "directly," "instantly," "immediately," "at once," "right away," or "the nearest possible future." For instance, in *Matthew 13:21* Jesus, in expounding the parable of the sowers, is quoted as saying: "Yet hath he not root in himself, but dureth for a while: for when tribulation or persecution ariseth because of the word, by and by he is offended." But in *Mark 4:17* Jesus, in expounding the same parable, is quoted as saying: "And have no root in themselves, and so endure but for a time: afterward, when affliction or persecution ariseth for the word's sake, immediately they are offended." According to *Mark 6:25*, the daughter of Herodias "came in straightway with haste unto the king, and asked, saying, I will that thou give me by and by in a charger the head of John the Baptist." *Luke 11:7* has Jesus say: "But which of you, having a servant plowing or feeding cattle, will say unto him by and by, when he is come from the field, Go and sit down to meat?" Again in *Luke 21:9*: "But when ye shall hear of wars and commotions, be not terrified: for these things must first come to pass; but the end is not by and by."

What is the Talmud?

Talmud, from a Hebrew root meaning "to learn or to teach," is the name of a vast body of Jewish literature. It is not a book, as commonly supposed, but a large collection of books. The entire Talmud translated and printed in English would make a library of some four hundred volumes of ordinary size. It contains all the Jewish law, tradition, interpretation, legend, knowledge, literature, ritual, ceremony, commentary and homiletic comment that the ancient rabbis and scholars deemed worthy of preservation for future generations. After the Romans destroyed the temple and Jewish commonwealth in 70 A.D., the rabbis in Palestine and Babylonia began to compile and edit the Jewish law and tradition to preserve Judaism as a religion and way of life. The Pharisees, the spiritual leaders of the Jews, believed that God gave Moses many administrative laws that were not included in the Pentateuch but were handed down orally through the centuries. Fearing that the loss of these laws and traditions would result in the dissolution of Judaism, the rabbis set to work to reduce them to writing along with the authoritative interpretations and their own comments. The result of their labors was two bodies of literature now known as the Talmud. There are really two Talmuds, the Palestinian, completed in the fourth century A.D., and the Babylonian, completed in the fifth century A.D. These Talmuds consist of Mishna, text, and Gemara, commentary. The Mishna of the two Talmuds is substantially the same, but the Gemara of the Babylonian Talmud is about three times as extensive as that of the Palestinian Talmud, which it has largely superseded.

Is there any humor in the Bible?

There is probably no intentional humor in the Bible. If the many authors of the books of the Bible had a sense of humor they did not reveal it in their writings. There are no jesters, no court fools, no clowns, no funny men in the Bible. References to laughter are almost invariably associated with scorn, mockery and derision rather than with merriment and mirth. Such was the laughter of Abraham and Sarah. "He that sitteth in the heavens shall laugh: the Lord shall have them in derision," says the psalmist. In *Ecclesiastes 3:4* the Preacher says there is "a time to weep, and a time to laugh," but later he adds that "Sorrow is better than laughter." We are told that Jesus wept, but not that he laughed. According to *Luke 6:21,* Jesus said: "Blessed are ye that weep now: for ye shall laugh." But in Verse 25 of the same chapter he said: "Woe unto you that laugh now! for ye shall mourn and weep." If Jesus told any humorous stories or uttered any witty sayings, the serious-minded authors of the Gospels failed to record them. Perhaps a slight tinge of sarcasm or irony may be detected in some of the sayings of Jesus, but no humor as such. In the Bible there are plays on words, but no puns for humorous effect. The nearest approach to intentional humor in the Bible is found in *I Kings 18,* which relates a spectacular and impressive test between Elijah and the prophets of Baal on Mt. Carmel. According to *I Kings 18:27*, when the pagan prophets called in vain upon their god to enkindle the sacrificial bullock, Elijah "mocked them, and said, Cry aloud: for he is a god; either he is talking, or he is pursuing, or he is in a journey, or peradventure he sleepeth, and must be awaked." Here and there in the Bible are bits of unconscious and unintentional humor. The quaint language of the old translators, sudden changes in sequence and odd associations of ideas may make us moderns smile. In *II Chronicles 16:12-13* we are told that "Asa in the thirty and ninth year of his reign was diseased in his feet, until his disease was exceeding great: yet in his disease he sought not the Lord, but to the physicians. And Asa slept with his fathers." *Mark 5:25-26* tells of "a certain woman, which had an issue of blood twelve years, and had suffered many things of many physicians." *Judges 8:30* says: "Gideon had threescore and ten sons of his body begotten: for he had many wives." In *II Kings 19:35* we read: "And it came to pass that night, that the angel of the Lord went out, and smote in the camp of the Assyrians an hundred fourscore and five thousand: and when they arose early in the morning, behold, they were all dead corpses." And in *Numbers 19:13* is the quaint clause: "Whosoever toucheth the dead body of any man that is dead."

What was the Queen of Sheba's nationality?

The nationality of the Queen of Sheba has long been a favorite subject of historical speculation. We know nothing whatever about the lady herself except what is given in the Bible. *I Kings 10:1-10* says: "And when the queen of Sheba heard of the fame of Solomon concerning the name of the Lord, she came to prove him with hard questions. And she came to Jerusalem with a very great train, with camels that bare spices, and very much gold, and precious stones: and when she was come to Solomon, she communed with him of all that was in her heart. And Solomon told her all her questions: there was not any thing hid from the king, which he told her not. And when the queen of Sheba had seen all Solomon's wisdom, and the house that he had built, and the meat of his table, and the sitting of his servants, and the attendance of his ministers, and their apparel, and his cupbearers, and his ascent by which he went up unto the house of the Lord: there was no more spirit in her. And she said to the king, It was a true report that I heard in mine own land of thy acts and of thy wisdom. Howbeit I believed not the words, until I came, and mine eyes had seen it: and, behold, the half was not told me: thy wisdom and prosperity exceedeth the fame which I heard. Happy are thy men, happy are these thy servants, which stand continually before thee, and that hear thy wisdom. Blessed be the Lord thy God, which delighteth in thee, to set thee on the throne of Israel: because the Lord loved Israel for ever, therefore made he thee king, to do judgment and justice. And she gave the king an hundred and twenty talents of gold, and of spices very great store, and precious stones: there came no more such abundance of spices as these which the queen of Sheba gave to king Solomon." Then *I Kings 10:13* adds: "And king Solomon gave unto the queen of Sheba all her desire, whatsoever she asked, beside that which Solomon gave her of his royal bounty. So she turned and went to her own country, she and her servants." It is generally assumed that *Sheba,* also called *Seba* in the Bible, is merely a variation of *Saba,* the ancient name of a country on the Red Sea in southwestern Felix Arabia and now known as Yemen. The only other Biblical allusions to the Queen of Sheba are in the New Testament. *Matthew 12:42* quotes Jesus as saying: "The queen of the south shall rise up in the judgment with this generation, and shall condemn it: for she came from the uttermost parts of the earth to hear the wisdom of Solomon: and, behold, a greater than Solomon is here." *Luke 11:31* quotes the same saying with slight variations. But there are several references to *Sheba* and the *Sabeans* elsewhere in the Old Testament. In *Genesis 10:28-29* Sheba is referred to as a son of Joktan, and in *Genesis 25:3* as the son of Jokshan, which may be slightly variant ways of indicating the same relationship. From *I Kings 10:15* we learn that Solomon obtained gold "of all the kings of Arabia." *Job 1:14-15* tells us that "the Sabeans" fell upon the oxen and asses of the patriarch and killed the servants attending them, and *Job 6:19* says "the companies of Sheba waited for them." *Psalm 72:10* informs us that "the kings of Sheba and Seba shall offer gifts." According to *Ezekiel 22,* "the merchants of Sheba" dealt at the fairs in spices, precious stones, gold, blue clothes, embroidered work, rich apparel, and "all sorts of things." Apparently the Sabeans also dealt in slaves, for we read in *Joel 3:8* "And I will sell your sons and your daughters into the hand of the children of Judah, and they shall sell them to the Sabeans, to a people far off." By piecing this Biblical information together, and adding to it certain facts from other sources, we arrive at the conclusion that the Sabeans were a Semitic people belonging to the Keturah group of Arabian tribes. They at first lived in North Arabia but before the time of Solomon had moved southward and established themselves in southwestern Arabia, where they built a great empire and became noted as merchants. The Sabeans were no doubt dark complexioned people and belonged to the same general family as the Arabs and the Hebrews. It is barely possible that the Queen of Sheba who made herself famous by her spectacular visit to King Solomon in Jerusalem was the same person known to archaeologists as Queen Balkis of the Sabeans. The Sabeans extended their conquests across the Red Sea in Africa, established colonies there and intermarried with the inhabitants of Ethiopia and parts of Egypt, a fact that probably misled Josephus as well as other ancient writers into supposing that the Queen who visited Solomon was a "queen of Egypt and Ethiopia." But the author of Isaiah distinguished between Ethiopia and *Seba*. *Isaiah 43:3* says: "I gave Egypt for thy ransom, Ethiopia and Seba for thee." And in *Isaiah 45:14*: "Thus saith the Lord, the labour of Egypt, and merchandise of Ethiopia and of the Sabeans, men of stature, shall come over unto thee, and they shall be thine." It was only natural that many later writers should have confused the Sabeans of the Bible and the Ethiopians. All evidence, however, points to the conclusion that the Biblical Queen of Sheba came from the distant parts of Arabia rather than from any part of Africa. According to Abyssinian tradition, the Queen of Sheba was a monarch of ancient Ethiopia and the present reigning family of that country claims descent from Menelik, who they maintain was a son of the Queen of Sheba by King Solomon. *Sheba* occurs in the Bible in other connections. It occurs in *I Chronicles 5:13* as the name of the ancestral head of a Gadite family; in *II Samuel 20:1-20* as the name of a Benjamite who led an unsuccessful revolt against David, and in *Joshua 19:2* as the name of a place in the territory of the tribe of Simeon.

What metal was the brass mentioned in the Bible?

Brass in the modern sense of the term was unknown to the ancient Israelites. There was only one Hebrew word for copper and bronze and this word was rendered *brass* in the King James Version. At that time the word *bronze* had not been introduced into the English language. Formerly an alloy of copper and a base metal, particularly tin, was called *brass*, a word of Old English origin and found in no other language. Where *brass* occurs in English versions of the Bible, it refers either to pure copper or to an alloy of copper and tin. Palestine proper produced virtually no metals and the Israelites obtained copper from the Edomites to the south and tin from the Phoenicians, who got it from *Tarshish,* supposed by some to have been Spain. Traces of ancient copper works are still found in Lebanon and Edon. In *Deuteronomy 8:9* Moses described the Promised Land as "a land whose stones are iron, and out of whose hills thou mayest dig brass." According to *Job 28:1-2,* Job in his parable says: "Surely there is a vein for the silver, and a place for gold where they fine it. Iron is taken out of the earth, and brass is molten out of the stone." *Ezra 8:27* tells us that when Ezra went from Babylon to Jerusalem to restore the Israelitish nation he carried with him "two vessels of fine copper, precious as gold." Copper in one form or other was used by the Israelites to make weapons, knives, household utensils, works of art and sacred vessels, and large quantities of it were used in constructing the temple. *Bronze,* derived from Italian *bronzo,* was introduced into the English language during the eighteenth century to distinguish the alloy of copper and tin from alloys of copper and other metals. Thus in early usage *bronze* embraced *brass* in its definition. Now *brass* is applied specifically to an alloy of copper and zinc, a combination of metals unknown to the ancient Israelites.

Does the Bible say we shall get weaker and wiser?

There seems to be a quite common impression that the Bible says that each generation will grow weaker and wiser. The saying, however, does not occur in the Bible and its source is unknown. No doubt it is perpetuated largely because of the alliteration. In The *Old Man's Wish* Walter Pope (1630-1714) wrote:

> May I govern my passion with absolute sway,
> And grow wiser and better as my strength wears way.

What does *Jesus* mean?

Jesus is merely the Latin form of *Joshua,* a common Hebrew name. In Greek *Joshua* became *Iesous* and in Latin *Jesus.* The Aramaic form of this name was *Jeshua* or *Yeshua* and that is probably the form of the name by which Jesus was known among his own people. Originally in English this name occurred in the Old French objective form *Iesu* or *Jesu.* It was not until the sixteenth century that the Latin nominative form *Iesus* or *Jesus* became the established English form of the name. Even as late as 1740 Charles Wesley's now famous hymn was published under the title *Jesu, Lover of My Soul.* Joshua, one of the really great men in the Bible, is first mentioned in *Exodus 17,* where he won a brilliant victory over Amalek, while Aaron and Hur held up the hands of Moses. Joshua's original name was *Oshea* or *Hoshea,* which in Hebrew literally signifies "He has helped." As a representative of the tribe of Ephraim, Joshua was one of the twelve sent out by Moses to spy out the Promised Land. *Numbers 13:16* tells us that "Moses called Oshea the son of Nun Jehoshua." By prefixing *J,* the first letter of the Divine name, to Joshua's original name, Moses made the name mean "Jehovah is salvation." Hosea, the name of one of the minor prophets, is merely a variation of Joshua's original name. When the twelve spies returned with discouraging reports about the strength of the people in the Promised Land, Joshua joined with Caleb in urging an immediate advance upon the enemy. Because of this exhibition of courage and because they "wholly followed" the Lord, Joshua and Caleb, according to *Numbers 14:30,* were rewarded with long life and exempted from the commandment of the Lord that none of that generation of Israelites who came out of Egypt "from twenty years old and upward" should enter the Promised Land. In *Numbers 11:28* Joshua the son of Nun is referred to as "the servant of Moses, one of his young men." We are told in *Exodus 33:11*: "And the Lord spake unto Moses face to face, as a man speaketh unto his friend. And he turned again into the camp: but his servant Joshua, the son of Nun, a young man, departed not out of the tabernacle." The Hebrew word rendered *young man* in these passages may also mean an unmarried man. It may be that Joshua, being without a family of his own, was thereby able to devote his entire time to the immediate service of Moses. No children of Joshua are mentioned in the genealogical list of the tribe of Ephraim in *I Chronicles 7:27,* which says simply: "Non his son, Jehoshua his son." *Deuteronomy 31:7-8* says: "And Moses called unto Joshua, and said unto him in the sight of all Israel, Be strong and of a good courage: for thou must go with this people unto the land which the Lord hath sworn unto their fathers to give them; and thou shalt cause them to inherit it. And the Lord, he it is that doth go before thee; he will be with thee, he will not fail thee, neither forsake thee: fear not, neither be dismayed. Eventually Moses appointed Joshua his successor. *Numbers 27:18-23* says: "And the Lord said unto Moses, Take thee Joshua the son of Nun, a man in whom is the spirit, and lay thine hand upon him; and set him before Eleazar the priest, and before all the congregation; and give him a charge in their sight. And thou shalt put some of thine honour upon him, that all the congregation of the children of Israel may be obedient. And he shall stand before Eleazar the priest, who shall ask counsel for him after the judgment of Urim before the Lord: at his word shall they go out, and at his word they shall come in, both he, and all the children of Israel with him, even all the congregation. And Moses did as the Lord commanded him: and he took Joshua, and set him before Eleazar the priest, and before all the congregation: and he laid his hands upon him, and gave him a charge, as the Lord commanded by the hand of Moses." *Deuteronomy 34:9* says: "And Joshua the son of Nun was full of the spirit of wisdom; for Moses had laid his hands upon him: and the children of Israel hearkened unto him, and did as the Lord commanded Moses." Starting as the humble servant of Moses, Joshua became first the loyal lieutenant, then the victorious soldier and finally the wise ruler. He led his people into the Promised Land and spent his latter years dividing the territory among them by lot. Joshua, "the servant of the Lord," finally died at the age of 110 and they buried him in the border of his inheritance in Mount Ephraim on the north side of the hill of Gaash. After "the Lord had given rest unto Israel from all their enemies round about" and Joshua was old and stricken in age, he gathered his people together at Shechem and made them a farewell address, in which, according to *Joshua 24:15*, he said: "And if it seem evil unto you to serve the Lord, choose you this day whom ye will serve; whether the gods which your fathers served that were on the other side of the flood, or the gods of the Amorites, in whose land ye dwell: but as for me and my house, we will serve the Lord." Twice in the King James Version of the Bible Joshua is referred to by the Latinized Greek form of his name. *Acts 7:45* says: "Which also our fathers that came after brought in with Jesus into the possession of the Gentiles, whom God drave out before the face of our fathers, unto the days of David." In *Hebrews* 4:8 it is said: "For if Jesus had given them rest, then would he not afterward have spoken of another day." Clearly in both of these passages it is Joshua, not Jesus, who is meant. The literal meaning of *Jesus* is alluded to in *Matthew 1:21-23*, where the angel of the Lord appears to Joseph in a dream and says: "And she shall bring forth a son, and thou shalt call his name JESUS: for he shall save his people from their sins. Now all this was done, that it might be fulfilled which was spoken of the Lord by the prophet, saying, Behold, a virgin shall be with child, and shall bring forth a son, and they shall call his name Emmanuel, which being interpreted is, God with us." Since the Hebrew *Joshua* literally means "God is salvation," it might be said that the Greek form of the name means "Saviour." The prophecy here linked with Jesus as the Saviour occurs in *Isaiah 7*. The Lord spake unto

Ahaz, king of Judah, saying, "Ask thee a sign of the Lord thy God; ask it either in the depth, or in the height above. But Ahaz said, I will not ask, neither will I tempt the Lord." "Therefore," says *Isaiah 7:14*, "the Lord himself shall give you a sign; Behold, a virgin shall conceive, and bear a son, and shall call his name Immanuel." The name *Jesus* is not mentioned in the prophecy. Only in *Matthew* is this prophecy of Isaiah interpreted as alluding to Jesus under the name *Emmanuel*, which is a Hebrew term signifying "God with us." *Jesus* appears to have been a common name among the Jews in ancient times. Josephus mentions a score or more persons who bore the name.

What was the Holy of Holies?

Holy of Holies is not a Biblical phrase. It occurs in neither the Old nor the New Testaments of the King James Version. *The Holy of Holies* is the popular name given to *the most holy place* in the tabernacle and in the first, second and third temples. It was a perfect cube in dimensions and was separated from the holy place or sanctuary by a veil. In the tabernacle the Holy of Holies was ten cubits (fifteen feet) in height, width and breadth, while the corresponding dimensions in the three temples were twice that, twenty cubits (thirty feet). The only furniture in the Holy of Holies in the time of the tabernacle of Moses and the temple of Solomon was the Ark of the Covenant. No person was permitted to enter this sacred chamber except the high priest and he was permitted to do so only once a year —on the day of Atonement, which was observed on the tenth of the seventh month. After the destruction of the first temple by the Babylonians and the loss of the Ark of the Covenant, the Holy of Holies contained nothing except a marble stone upon which the high priest laid the censer. *Leviticus 16:2* says: "And the Lord said unto Moses, Speak unto Aaron thy brother, that he come not at all times into the holy place within the vail before the mercy seat, which is upon the ark; that he die not; for I will appear in the cloud upon the mercy seat." The Mosaic law specified in detail under what conditions the high priest might come into the most holy place. *Leviticus 16:11-14* says: "And Aaron shall bring the bullock of the sin offering, which is for himself, and shall make an atonement for himself, and for his house, and shall kill the bullock of the sin offering which is for himself: and he shall take a censer full of burning coals of fire from off the altar before the Lord, and his hands full of sweet incense beaten small, and bring it within the vail: and he shall put the incense upon the fire before the Lord, that the cloud of the incense may cover the mercy seat that is upon the testimony, that he die not: and he shall take of the blood of the bullock and sprinkle it with his finger upon the mercy seat eastward; and before the mercy seat shall he sprinkle the blood with his finger seven times." In *Numbers 18:7* the Lord tells Aaron that "thou and thy sons with thee shall keep your priest's office for every thing of the altar, and within the vail." In *Exodus 26:33-34* the Lord, after instructing Moses how to make the vail, says that "the vail shall divide unto you between the holy place and the most holy. And thou shalt put the mercy seat upon the ark of the testimony in the most holy place." The Hebrew term rendered "the most holy place" literally means "innermost" or "rear." The Holy of Holies was the most hallowed place known to the Israelites. When Pompey, after conquering Palestine, went to Jerusalem, he insisted upon entering the Holy of Holies. Expecting to find some curious object of worship, or perhaps a vast store of treasure, the Roman was disappointed to find nothing whatever in the sacred chamber within the veil. For generations before the final destruction of the temple the enemies of the Jews had circulated a report that the Holy of Holies contained an ass's head. Knowing that the Jews would not permit any unauthorized person, whether Jew or Gentile, to enter this sacred room to disprove the malicious charge, anti-Jews in Alexandria, Rome and elsewhere in the Roman Empire repeatedly taunted the Jews with worshipping an ass's head in their temple. Just before the final destruction of the temple, after it had already been set on fire by the Roman soldiers, Titus is reported to have entered the Holy of Holies, but saw nothing there but bare, hewn rock, the top of the hill on which the edifice stood. According to *Matthew 27:51* and *Mark 15:38*, "The vail of the temple was rent in twain from the top to the bottom" at the moment Jesus yielded up the ghost on the cross. *Luke 23:45* says "the vail of the temple was rent in the midst." This event is not mentioned by Josephus and other early secular historians. Christian commentators offer various interpretations of these passages. Some say that the rending of the veil signifies that the old covenant was ended and the new begun, that sacrifices were abolished and that the divine presence had been withdrawn from the temple, even the Holy of Holies being made common ground and open to the whole world. Others say that the Holy of Holies was a type of heaven and the rest of the temple a type of earth and the rending of the veil symbolized the removal of the barrier between heaven and earth and the reconciliation of God and man through the death of Jesus. *Hebrews 10:18-20* says: "Now where remission of these is, there is no more offering for sin. Having therefore, brethren, boldness to enter into the holiest by the blood of Jesus, by a new and living way, which he hath consecrated for us, through the veil, that is to say, his flesh." In the King James Version *vail* and *veil* are used interchangeably in this connection and are not uniform even in current editions. Figuratively *behind, beyond* or *within the veil* is applied to heaven, the next world, beyond the grave or out of the reach of sense perception. This usage was probably suggested by *Hebrews 6:19,* which reads: "Which hope we have as an anchor of the soul, both sure and stedfast, and which entereth into that within the veil." The Latin equivalent of *Holy of Holies* is *Sanctum Sanctorum.* This latter phrase is often applied in a light vein to a private room, apartment or office of an important person. For instance, the inner and strictly private retreat of an editor is called his Sanctum Sanctorum.

How many are a few?

This question owes its popularity to the fact that many people think the Bible defines *a few* as eight. The King James translation of *I Peter 3:20* is as follows: "Which sometime were disobedient, when once the long suffering of God waited in the days of Noah, while the ark was a preparing, wherein *few,* that is, eight souls were saved by water." Note that *few,* not *a few,* is here used. The Concordant version, however, refers to "the days of Noah while the ark was being constructed, in which *a few,* that is *eight* souls were conveyed safely through water." Thus there is Scriptural authority for the statement that *few* and *a few* mean eight! The idiomatic phrase *a few,* which dates back in English usage at least to the thirteenth century, means a small number, usually more than two; not many; some but not none. It is relative in respect to the number to which it is compared. If ten persons attend a meeting where a hundred are expected, ten are a few; on the other hand, if a hundred attend when several thousand are expected, a hundred are a few. *A few* denotes a more considerable number than the simple adjective *few,* which means barely any. The indefinite article *a* destroys the restrictive sense that *few* possesses when used alone. This distinction is purely a matter of idiom. Like other collective nouns, *a few* takes a plural verb and is referred to by a plural pronoun; as, "A few answer to their names." In his life of Mohammed Sir William Muir, the Scottish Orientalist, says that in the *Koran* the Arabic word translated *few* ordinarily signifies from three to ten. After twenty minutes of calm deliberation an English judge decided that seven is the extreme limit of *a few*. An old English nursery rhyme says:

Two is a couple,
Three is a few,
Four is too many.
And five won't do.

What is a joseph?

Joseph used to be applied to a great coat. During the seventeenth and eighteenth centuries a large riding cloak for women, provided with a cape and buttoned down the front, was called a joseph. A person who will not be seduced from continency in the face of the severest temptation is also known as a Joseph. Both of these usages were suggested by the story of Joseph and his experience with the wife of Potiphar, the captain of Pharaoh's guard, who had bought him from the Ishmeelites. *Genesis 39:7-20* says: "And it came to pass after these things, that his master's wife cast her eyes upon Joseph; and she said, Lie with me. But he refused, and said unto his master's wife, Behold, my master wotteth not what is with me in the house, and he hath committed all that he hath to my hand; there is none greater in this house than I; neither hath he kept back any thing from me but thee, because thou art his wife: how then can I do this great wickedness, and sin against God? And it came to pass, as she spake to Joseph day by day, that he hearkened not unto her, to lie by her, or to be with her. And it came to pass about this time, that Joseph went into the house to do his business; and there was none of the men of the house there within. And she caught him by his garment, saying, Lie with me: and he left his garment in her hand, and fled, and got him out. And it came to pass, when she saw that he had left his garment in her hand, and was fled forth, that she called unto the men of her house, and spake unto them, saying, See, he hath brought in an Hebrew unto us to mock us; he came in unto me to lie with me, and I cried with a loud voice: and it came to pass, when he heard that I lifted up my voice and cried, that he left his garment with me, and fled, and got him out. And she laid up his garment by her, until his lord came home. And she spake unto him according to these words, saying, The Hebrew servant, which thou hast brought unto us, came in unto me to mock me: and it came to pass, when his master heard the words of his wife, which she spake unto him, saying, After this manner did thy servant to me; that his wrath was kindled. And Joseph's master took him, and put him into the prison, a place where the king's prisoners were bound: and he was there in the prison." *Joseph's-coat,* the name of two American ornamental plants with variegated foliage, was suggested from another garment of this same Joseph. *Genesis 37:3* tells us that Jacob "loved Joseph more than all his children, because he was the son of his old age: and he made him a coat of many colours." Before Joseph's brethren cast him into an empty pit in Dothan "they stript Joseph out of his coat, his coat of many colours that was on him." *Genesis 27:31-33* says: "And they took Joseph's coat, and killed a kid of the goats, and dipped the coat in the blood; and they sent the coat of many colours, and they brought it to their father; and said, This have we found: know now whether it be thy son's coat or no. And he knew it, and said, It is my son's coat; an evil beast hath devoured him; Joseph is without doubt rent in pieces." During the American Civil War cloth was so scarce that rugs and carpets were cut up and made into overcoats. Men who wore such coats were called *Josephs* in allusion to Joseph's coat of many colors.

Does the Bible mention the wandering Jew?

The wandering Jew, of course, does not occur in the Bible, but the legend of the wandering Jew may have been suggested by an obscure passage in the New Testament. We are told that Jesus, after his resurrection, showed himself to the disciples at the sea of Tiberias. In connection with this incident *John 21:20-24* says: "Then Peter, turning about, seeth the disciple whom Jesus loved following; which also leaned on his breast at supper, and said, Lord, which is he that betrayeth thee? Peter seeing him saith to Jesus, Lord, and what shall this man do? Jesus saith unto him, If I will that he tarry till I come, what is that to thee? follow thou me. Then went this saying abroad among the brethren, that that disciple should not die: yet Jesus said not unto him, He shall not die; but, If I will that he tarry till I come, what is that to thee? This is the disciple which testifieth of these things, and wrote these things: and we know that his testimony is true." In *Matthew 16:28* it is recorded that Jesus said to his disciples: "Verily I say unto you, There be some standing here, which shall not taste of death, till they see the Son of man coming in his kingdom." The most generally accepted tradition is that John was the only one of the twelve disciples of Jesus who died a natural death and that he died a very old man at Ephesus during the reign of Trajan (98-117 A.D.). But in spite of what John said in his Gospel, the opinion long persisted that Jesus had said this disciple would not taste of death until the second advent of Christ. One story was that John was finally translated like Elijah. Even St. Augustine appears to have given some credence to a legend that John continued to breathe in his grave. At any rate, the legend that John would not die, but would tarry until the return of Jesus probably gave rise to the later legend of the wandering Jew. Nothing is heard of the later legend until 1228, when Roger of Wendover wrote in his *Flores Historiarum*, a chronicle beginning at the creation and extending to 1235 and often referred to as the Chronicles of St. Albans Abbey, that an Armenian bishop visiting England at the time reported that Joseph of Arimathaea, the honorable counseller who craved the body of Jesus, was still alive under the name of Kartaphilos. Matthew of Paris, who continued the chronicles of Roger of Wendover at St. Albans Abbey, elaborated upon this report and said that every hundred years Kartaphilos fell into a trance and woke up a man of about thirty. All the later details and elaborations of the legend of the wandering Jew appear to stem from these chronicles. A pamphlet alleged to have been printed at Leyden in 1602 relates that Bishop Paulus von Eizen of Schleswig had met at Hamburg in 1542 a Jew named Ahasuerus, who claimed to be "eternal," and that he had been condemned, because of an act of ungraciousness to Jesus, to wander over the earth until Judgment Day. From these reports several versions of the story of the Eternal and the Wandering Jew evolved. In the centuries following the legend of a Jew condemned to perpetual punishment and restless wandering became the theme of numerous poems, plays, paintings and prose works. Perhaps the theme appealed to Christians because it symbolized the dispersion and wanderings of the Jewish people as a whole. The most popular version of the story is to the effect that in going to the place of crucifixion Jesus passed the workshop of a Jew and stopped to seek a moment's rest. But the Jew drove him from his door, saying, "Go, why dost thou tarry?" Jesus replied: "I go, but thou shalt tarry till I come." In some of the stories the Jew is a carpenter, in others a cobbler, and in still others a servant of Pontius Pilate. The Eternal and Wandering Jew bears different names —Kartaphilos, Ahasuerus, Malchus, Isaac, Joannes Buttadeus, the last being Latin for "John the God-smiter," alluding to the fact that the Jew is supposed to have struck Jesus. In some of the stories the Wandering Jew, finding his eternal life on earth unbearable, continually courts death, but is unable to die, while in others he is repentant and goes about doing good to expiate his offense. Up until nearly a century ago there were what purported to be authentic reports of the Wandering Jew having been actually seen at different times in various parts of the world. The best known work employing the legend of the Wandering Jew as a theme is Eugene Sue's *Le Juif Errant,* published in 1844. Goethe in a fragment, Shelley in *Queen Mab,* Croly in *Salathiel,* as well as Schlegel, Muller and Quinet, have also used the theme.

Is *Macedonian cry* in the Bible?

Macedonian cry does not occur in the Bible, but the phrase was suggested by a Biblical passage. *Acts 16:8-10* says: "And they passing by Mysia came down to Troas. And a vision appeared to Paul in the night; There stood a man of Macedonia, and prayed him, saying, Come over into Macedonia, and help us. And after he had seen the vision, immediately we endeavoured to go into Macedonia, assuredly gathering that the Lord had called us for to preach the gospel unto them." From this passage we get *Macedonian cry* in the sense of a call for succor or an outcry for help. Troas was a city on the Asia Minor mainland and Macedonia a Roman province in northeastern Greece. From the context of *Acts 16:9* we get the impression that it was at Troas, where Paul in a vision saw a man of Macedonia praying for help, that the Apostle to the Gentiles first met Luke, the author of *Acts.* Troas is supposed to have stood on the ruins of ancient Troy.

What domestic animals are mentioned in the Bible?

The domestic animals mentioned in the Bible are sheep, camels, horses, oxen, goats, swine, dogs, asses and mules. Many people suppose that the sheep was the first domestic animal, because in *Genesis* we are told that Abel was "a keeper of sheep" and that he brought an offering unto the Lord "of the firstlings of his flock and of the fat thereof." That the camel, ox, sheep and ass were supposed by the Hebrews to have been domesticated at a very early date is indicated by the *Book of Job,* in which these animals are listed as part of the wealth of the patriarch, who is represented as having lived in primitive times. It is an interesting fact that few new species of animal of great economic importance have been domesticated in the last two thousand years. All of our more important domestic animals were already domesticated four or five thousand years ago and nobody has been able to determine with any degree of certainty which ones were tamed and used for domestic purposes first. Dogs, horses, hogs, sheep, camels, oxen, asses, goats and cats appear to have been domesticated from the earliest time of which we have authentic record. It is impossible to arrange them in the chronological order of their subjugation and domestication. All are agreed that the dog was one of the earliest of human associates. It was domesticated at a very remote date in nearly all parts of the inhabited world.

Who said, "Man does not live by bread alone"?

According to *Matthew 4:4,* when the devil tempted Jesus during his forty days' fast in the wilderness and said, "If thou be the Son of God, command that these stones be made bread," Jesus answered: "It is written, Man shall not live by bread alone, but by every word that proceedeth out of the mouth of God." In *Luke 4:4* this reply to the tempter is given in substantially the same words: "It is written, That man shall not live by bread alone, but by every word of God." Jesus was quoting the words of Moses as recorded in *Deuteronomy 8:3,* which reads: "And he humbled thee, and suffered thee to hunger, and fed thee with manna, which thou knewest not, neither did thy fathers know; that he might make thee know that man doth not live by bread only, but by every word that proceedeth out of the mouth of the Lord doth man live."

Does *science* occur in the Bible?

Science occurs twice in the King James Version, once in the Old Testament and once in the New. In *Daniel 1:4* we find: "Children in whom was no blemish, but well favored, and skilful in all wisdom, and cunning in knowledge, and understanding *science,* and such as had ability in them to stand in the king's palace, and whom they might teach the learning and the tongue of the Chaldeans." The Hebrew word here translated *science* signifies "insight" or "understanding." *I Timothy 6:20* reads: "O Timothy, keep that which is committed to thy trust, avoiding profane and vain babblings, and oppositions of *science,* falsely so called." Here *science* is the English translation of Greek *gnosis,* meaning "knowledge." It refers to pseudo-science, false knowledge, the speculative systems of those claiming to possess superior esoteric learning.

Does the Bible say, "God tempers the wind to the shorn lamb"?

Contrary to popular belief, the saying, "God tempers the wind to the shorn lamb," does not appear in the Bible. It occurs in Laurence Sterne's *Sentimental Journey through France and Italy,* published in 1768, but it is quoted, showing that Sterne did not claim the authorship. In *Jacula Prudentum,* a work published in 1640, by the English churchman and poet, George Herbert, we find the proverb in the following form: "To close shorn sheep, God gives the wind by measure," which in turn is merely a translation of a proverb in *Les Premices,* published in 1594 by Henri Estienne, noted French scholar and printer. Since Estienne regarded it as a proverb, presumably it dates back long before his time.

Does *prodigal son* occur in the Bible?

The word *prodigal* and the phrase *prodigal son* occur nowhere in the text proper of the generally accepted English translations of the Bible. In *Luke 15,* where the story popularly known as the parable of the prodigal son is related, the chief character is referred to simply as "the younger son," who took his journey into a far country and there "wasted his substance with riotous living." In the chapter heading of some versions this passage is referred to as the parable of the prodigal son, because *prodigal* means wasteful, lavish or profusely liberal. The chapter headings found in many Bibles are not part of the text; they are added by the different editors and may vary considerably with different editions even of the same translation.

Does the Bible say, "Spare the rod and spoil the child"?

It is commonly but erroneously supposed that the familiar proverb, "Spare the rod and spoil the child," is in the Bible. The nearest thing to it in the Bible is *Proverbs 13:24*: "He that spareth his rod hateth his son: but he that loveth him chasteneth him betimes." No doubt the familiar English proverb was suggested by the Bible passage. Ralph Venning, in his *Mysteries and Revelations,* published in 1649, said: "They spare the rod and spoyle the child." In slightly varying forms the proverb has been traced back in English to about the year 1000.

What does *Sabaoth* mean?

Sabaoth (pronounced *SABB-a-oath* or *sa-BAY-oath*) occurs only twice in the King James Version, both times in the New Testament, and is a Hebrew word meaning "armies" or "hosts." "The Lord of Sabaoth" signifies "the Lord of hosts" and has no relation to *Sabbath,* which literally means "rest." For some reason or other the English translators of the New Testament saw fit to let *Sabaoth* remain untranslated in *Romans 9:29* and *James 5:4.* In other parts of the Bible the Hebrew form of *Jehovah Sabaoth* is rendered by *the Lord of hosts* or an equivalent English phrase. *Sabaoth* is often confused with *Sabbath.* This mistake is not new. It was made by many noted writers of the past. For instance, in the last stanza of the *Faerie Queene* Edmund Spenser wrote:

> All that moveth doth in change delight:
> But thenceforth all shall rest eternally
> With Him that is the God of Sabaoth hight:
> O! that great Sabaoth God, grant me that Sabbath sight!

Sabaoth for *Sabbath* occurs in the second folio of Shakespeare's *The Merchant of Venice*. In the first edition of his dictionary Dr. Samuel Johnson treated the two words as if they were identical, and in *Ivanhoe* Sir Walter Scott refers to "the gains of a week, aye the space between two Sabaoths."

What is the name of the last book in the Bible?

The correct title of the last book in the Protestant Bible is *The Revelation of St. John the Divine*. In popular usage it is variously called the *Book of Revelation* and the *Apocalypse*. Roman Catholics prefer to call it the *Apocalypse*, while Protestants generally call it the *Book of Revelation*. Often it is erroneously called the *Book of Revelations* or simply *Revelations*. In this connection *Revelation* should be singular, not plural, but the plural *Revelations* has been used so long and so widely in ordinary speech that it would be little short of pedantry to take exception to it now. *The Revelations* is the result of a confusion with the correct *The Revelation* and the popular *Revelations*. *Apocalypse* comes to us through Latin from a Greek verb meaning "to uncover," "disclose" or "reveal" and is virtually synonymous with *revelation*.

What does *Mizpah* mean?

Mizpah is a Hebrew word literally meaning "watch tower." Originally it was applied to places where a watch or garrison was maintained and it became the name of several towns and places in ancient Palestine. The term is spelled in the Hebrew Bible both *Mizpah* and *Mizpeh,* without any difference of meaning. But when spelled *Mizpah* it is invariably preceded by the definite article—*the Mizpah*—except in *Hosea 5:1*. The name is particularly applied to the pillar set up and the heap of stones gathered on Mt. Gilead by Jacob and his brethren as a witness of the covenant made there with Laban. In modern usage Mizpah or "the Mizpah Benediction" signifies a parting salutation, a meaning suggested by *Genesis 31:49,* which contains Laban's prayer at Mizpah: "The Lord watch between me and thee, when we are absent one from another." The use of *Mizpah* as an inscription on memorial rings is based on the same passage. The context, however, indicates that Laban's words were more in the nature of a mutual warning than they were a blessing.

Does the Bible mention Easter?

Easter occurs once in the King James Version, but not in its present sense. *Acts 12:4* tells us that Herod, after arresting Peter and delivering him to the soldiers, intended "after Easter to bring him forth to the people." Here *Easter* clearly refers to the Passover and is so rendered in the Revised Version. *Easter* is supposed to be derived from Anglo-Saxon *Eostre,* the name of a Norse goddess whose festival was celebrated by the pagans at the vernal equinox. The root of the term probably signified "rising" or "rebirth" and Easter was the pagan festival to welcome the return of spring, the season of new birth and growth. The Anglo-Saxons called April "easter-month" because it was the month in their clime when the buds began to open. In the course of time *Easter* became the English name for the festival commemorating the resurrection of Jesus. It is to the Christians what the Passover is to the Jews and what the spring festival was to the pagans.

Why did the Israelites face the temple when praying?

After the construction of Solomon's temple in Jerusalem that sacred edifice became the place of prayer par excellence for the Israelites. We are told in *I Kings 8* that when the temple was dedicated "Solomon stood before the altar of the Lord in the presence of all the congregation of Israel, and spread forth his hands toward heaven," and, among other things, said: "And hearken thou to the supplication of thy servant, and of thy people Israel, when they shall pray toward this place." There are other references in the Bible to the fact that the ancient Israelites, if at a distance from Jerusalem, turned their faces toward the temple when praying. *Psalms 5:7* says: "But as for me, I will come into thy house in the multitude of thy mercy: and in thy fear will I worship toward thy holy temple." After the destruction of the temple by the Babylonians its site retained the same significance for the dispersed Jews. *Daniel 6:11* says: "Now when Daniel knew that the writing was signed, he went into his house; and his windows being open in his chamber toward Jerusalem, he kneeled upon his knees three times a day, and prayed, and gave thanks before his God, as he did aforetime." After the destruction of Herod's temple and the final dispersion, pious Jews throughout the Roman Empire continued to turn their faces toward the site of the temple when praying. Even in orthodox synagogues at the present time the ark, the case in which the scrolls of the law are kept, is generally orientated in such a way that the congregation faces the site of the temple in Jerusalem.

Who said: "Be sure your sin will find you out"?

This saying, which has become proverbial, is attributed to Moses in the Bible. Moses agreed to permit the children of Reuben and Gad and the half-tribe of Manasseh to settle permanently east of the Jordan provided their fighting men would help the other tribes conquer and claim the Promised Land. *Numbers 32:20-23* says: "And Moses said unto them, If ye will do this thing, if ye will go armed before the Lord to war, and will go all of you armed over Jordan before the Lord, until he hath driven out his enemies from before him, and the land be subdued before the Lord: then afterward ye shall return, and be guiltless before the Lord, and before Israel; and this land shall be your possession before the Lord. But if ye will not do so, behold, ye have sinned against the Lord: and be sure your sin will find you out."

Where does the Bible say, "The Lord is a man of war"?

Exodus 15:3 says: "The Lord is a man of war: the Lord is his name." This is part of the song that Moses and the children of Israel sang after the miraculous crossing of the Red Sea and the destruction of the Egyptian army.

Does the Bible mention a league of nations?

Shortly after the first World War Jan Christian Smuts, South African soldier and statesman and one of the chief architects of the Covenant of the League of Nations, said that "the League of Nations was first of all the vision of a great Jew, almost 3,000 years ago—the prophet Isaiah." General Smuts alluded particularly to *Isaiah 2:1-4*, where the prophet says: "The word that Isaiah the son of Amoz saw concerning Judah and Jerusalem. And it shall come to pass in the last days, that the mountain of the Lord's house shall be established in the top of the mountains, and shall be exalted above the hills: and all nations shall flow unto it. And many people shall go and say, Come ye, and let us go up to the mountain of the Lord, to the house of the God of Jacob; and he will teach us of his ways, and we will walk in his paths: for out of Zion shall go forth the law, and the word of the Lord from Jerusalem. And he shall judge among the nations, and shall rebuke many people: and they shall beat their swords into plowshares, and their spears into pruninghooks: nation shall not lift up sword against nation, neither shall they learn war any more." While these words of Isaiah may not be exactly a vision of a league of nations, they do constitute perhaps one of the earliest, if not the earliest, recorded visions of world-wide peace.

What is the meaning of *prove* in the Bible?

When the King James Version of the Bible was made *prove* had not yet generally acquired the sense of "to establish the truth of." Generally in the English Bible *prove* retains some of its primary Latin meaning of "to try, to make trial of, to test or to examine a person or thing to determine his or its goodness, worth or genuineness." In *Exodus 15:25* it is said, after Moses sweetened the bitter waters of Marah, that the Lord "proved them." *Exodus 16:4* says: "Then said the Lord unto Moses, Behold, I will rain bread from heaven for you; and the people shall go out and gather a certain rate every day, that I may prove them, whether they will walk in my law, or no." *Deuteronomy 8:2* quotes Moses as saying: "And thou shalt remember all the way which the Lord thy God led thee these forty years in the wilderness, to humble thee, and to prove thee, to know what was in thine heart, whether thou wouldest keep his commandments, or no." In *I Kings 10:1* we are told that the Queen of Sheba "came to prove" Solomon with hard questions. "Prove all things; hold fast that which is good," says Paul in *I Thessalonians 5:21.* In *II Corinthians 13:5* Paul says: "Examine yourselves, whether ye be in the faith; prove your own selves." The modern sense of *prove,* "to make manifest by argument," is approached in *Acts 9:22,* which says: "But Saul increased the more in strength, and confounded the Jews which dwelt at Damascus, proving that this is very Christ." But in *Luke 14:19* one of those bidden to a wedding feast said: "I have bought five yoke of oxen, and I go to prove them: I pray thee have me excused." We have a survival of this original meaning of *prove* in *proving ground,* which is a place where military equipment or ammunition is proved or tested. *Prove* also probably retains its original meaning of "to try" or "test" in the proverbial saying, "The exception proves the rule," an apparently senseless maxim that is often quoted to baffle us when we point out an exception to a general statement that we think covers too much ground. As popularly understood the saying is absurd. It is generally accepted as implying that a rule is not a true rule unless it has an exception, or that the existence of an exception in particular somehow demonstrates the correctness of the rule in general. In the modern sense of *prove,* an exception would not prove a rule, but rather would tend to disprove it. "The exception proves the rule" is probably a descendant of the ancient Latin legal maxim—*Exceptio probat regulam de rebus non exceptis*—which, freely translated, means that an exception or exclusion tests the rule as to things not excepted. The common expression, "the exception proves the rule," is merely a popularized technicality and ignores the true meaning of the original. Likewise *proof* does not always mean "convincing evidence" or "that which is found to be so." Sometimes it retains its older meaning of "a trial" or "the act of testing." For instance, the proofs submitted by a photographer to the subject from which selections may be made are *test* prints.

Does the Bible mention a person named Dives?

Dives (*DI-vees*) is the name popularly given to "a certain rich man" who figures in Jesus' parable of the rich man and Lazarus, recorded in *Luke 16:19-31*. The word *dives,* however, does not occur in any English translation of the Bible, either as a proper name or as a common word. It is merely the Latin word for "rich," and accordingly it occurs as an adjective in the Vulgate, a Latin version of the Scriptures translated at the close of the fourth century largely by Jerome and declared by the Council of Trent to be the official text of the Catholic church. Even in that version *dives* is not employed as a noun or proper name. As a matter of fact, in no version of the Bible is the rich man in the parable given any name. Apparently it was during the Middle Ages that it became customary to apply the names Dives to the rich man at whose gate Lazarus begged crumbs. This no doubt arose from the fact that the parable was referred to in Latin as *Dives et Lazarus,* which literally means simply "the rich man and Lazarus." It could just as well be written *Lazarus et dives,* in which case *dives* is not capitalized. Since the fourteenth century the word has been used as a proper name even in theological literature. *Dives* is often employed to signify "a rich man" or "a rich worldling."

Who was Deutero-Isaiah?

It is generally agreed that *The Book of the Prophet Isaiah,* the twenty-fourth book of the Bible and the first of the major prophets, is not the work of one author. Enough has been written about the authorship of this one book to form a sizeable library. Isaiah lived in the eighth century B.C. and obviously could not have composed those parts of the book referring to later events. Higher critics say that Isaiah himself may have been the author of the first thirty-nine chapters of the book that bears his name. The remainder of the book, supposed to have been written about 546 B.C. in the time of Cyrus of Persia, is ascribed to an unknown prophet and seer who for convenience is called Deutero-Isaiah, which means "the Second Isaiah." Some authorities say that Deutero-Isaiah composed only chapters forty to fifty-five inclusive and that chapters fifty-six to sixty-six were the work of still another unknown prophet and seer whom they designate Trito-Isaiah, which means "the Third Isaiah." But the subject is too abstruse for the average Bible reader. What seems probable is that a book originally written by Isaiah was enlarged and edited by later writers during a period of several hundred years. Isaiah as a whole contains some of the most sublime poetry in the Bible and is dear to Jew and Christian alike.

What is angels' food?

Angels' food occurs in the Bible only once and there it refers to manna. *Psalm 78:24-25* says that the Lord "had rained down manna upon them to eat, and had given them of the corn of heaven. Man did eat angels' food: he sent them meat to the full."

What was the Sanhedrin?

Sanhedrin occurs nowhere in the King James Version of the Bible. The term is an Aramaic corruption of Greek *synedrium,* from *syn,* "together," and *hedra,* "a seat," and literally signifies "a sitting together." In the King James Version it is generally rendered *council.* For instance, *Mark 15:1* says: "And straightway in the morning the chief priests held a consultation with the elders and scribes and the whole council, and bound Jesus, and carried him away, and delivered him to Pilate." *Acts 5:21* tells us that "the high priest came, and they that were with him, and called the council together." The Great Sanhedrin or Grand Council at Jerusalem, established after the return from the Babylonian captivity, exercised executive, legislative and judicial powers and was the national parliament of the Jews. It was probably modeled after the council of "seventy men of the elders of Israel" chosen to stand with Moses in the wilderness, according to *Numbers 11:17-17.* Although *Deuteronomy 17:8-9* suggests that some such body of priests and judges was contemplated as a continuing institution, there is no further reference to a grand council or great sanhedrin until after the captivity. The Great Sanhedrin at Jerusalem reached its highest development under the Maccabees, when Judaea was virtually an independent nation. This Grand Council was composed of seventy-one elders, priests and scribes in about equal numbers and was generally, although not always, presided over by the high priest. The number seventy-one appears to have been suggested by the fact that the council appointed by Moses in the wilderness consisted of seventy in addition to himself, making a total of seventy-one. This council of ancients or Jewish senate held its meetings in "The Hall of Hewn Stones" in the temple. It was not only the supreme legislative, executive and judicial council of the Jews, but also exercised all functions of religious, educational and social administration in the theocracy. The Great Sanhedrin was conceived as the human agency that carried out the will of Jehovah. There were smaller sanhedrins, consisting of twenty-three members, in the provincial towns and even in Jerusalem itself. Although the Great Sanhedrin was stripped of many of its powers under Roman rule, it continued, subject to the limitations of the Roman authorities, to administer the Jewish religious, moral and political law. It collected taxes and had the power to make arrests and conduct investigations and trials within the limitations of its jurisdiction, which varied with the whims of the Romans. On matters pertaining to the Jewish religion, the Great Sanhedrin was acknowledged as the supreme authority by the four million Jews scattered throughout the Empire. The Great Sanhedrin in the time of Jesus, because of Roman interference, was probably only a shadow of the Great Sanhedrin that existed in earlier days. Some authorities suppose that the selection of the high priest and the other members of the Great Sanhedrin was entirely controlled by the Roman procurators. It has even been contended that at that time there were two Great Sanhedrins, one religious and the other political.

What is kosher food?

Kosher is the term generally applied to food prepared according to orthodox ritual. The term, which is not in the Bible, is the Yiddish form of a Hebrew word literally meaning "proper" in the sense of fit to use. All kosher regulations are based directly or indirectly on the Mosaic laws. Food forbidden to orthodox Jews is called *tref*, a Yiddish form of a Hebrew word literally meaning "torn flesh." In *Leviticus 17:15* "that which died of itself, or that which was torn of beasts" is strictly forbidden as food. The Hebrews called the flesh of an animal that died of itself *nevelah,* and that of an animal torn by beasts, *terefah.* In the course of centuries these terms were extended in meaning. *Nevelah* was applied to the flesh of any animal killed not strictly in the prescribed manner, while *terefah* was applied to the flesh of any animal ritually slaughtered but found to contain injuries or organic diseases. Moses in the Pentateuch did not prescribe specific methods of slaughtering animals for food, but the rabbis say that he taught the Israelites such methods and that they were handed down orally for centuries. Several considerations enter into the Jewish method of slaughter known as Schechitah and the preparation of kosher food. All flesh determined by rabbinic inspection to be unsound is forbidden. The Jewish method of slaughter is designed to cause the least pain to the animal and to remove all possible blood. Jews are forbidden to torment the animal by killing it in a clumsy or slow manner. To meet the orthodox requirements kosher meat must be from an animal that has been slaughtered with a skillful stroke by a specially trained and pious Jew who has been approved by rabbinical authorities. The skillful operator kills the animal with a very sharp knife with which he severs all the great blood vessels of the neck, which produces instantaneous insensibility and prevents unnecessary suffering. Kindness to animals is repeatedly emphasized in the Mosaic law and the rabbis have always insisted that these provisions of the law apply to the slaughtering of animals for food. *Leviticus 3:17* says: "It shall be a perpetual statute for your generations throughout all your dwellings, that ye eat neither fat nor blood." *Leviticus 7:26-27* adds: "Moreover ye shall eat no manner of blood, whether it be of fowl or of beast, in any of your dwellings. Whatsoever soul it be that eateth any manner of blood, even that soul shall be cut off from his people." In *Deuteronomy 12:23-24* it is stated: "Only be sure that thou eat not the blood: for the blood is the life; and thou mayest not eat the life with the flesh. Thou shalt not eat it; thou shalt pour it upon the earth as water." Again in *Leviticus 17:10*: "And whatsoever man there be of the house of Israel, or of the strangers that sojourn among you, that eateth any manner of blood; I will even set my face against that soul that eateth blood, and will cut him off from among his people." This command against the eating of blood in any form is older even than the Mosaic law. *Genesis 9:3-4* says: "Every moving thing that liveth shall be meat for you; even as the green herb have I given you all things. But flesh with the life thereof, which is the blood thereof, shall ye not eat." Blood was emphatically withdrawn from use as an article of food and set aside for sacred and symbolical purposes. Some authorities suppose the purpose of this ban upon the eating of blood was to suppress the instinct of violence in man by weaning him from blood and instilling in him a horror of bloodshed. Whatever the original purpose, the ultimate effect was to remove from the ordinary Israelite the slaying of animals for food and the placing of this function in the hands of specially trained persons. Even today no orthodox Jewish housewife would think of killing a chicken with her own hands for her dinner table. It is said that this attitude toward the shedding of blood has resulted in a lower homicide rate among Jews than among any other group of people. Some authorities hold that many of the kosher dietary laws are directly traceable to health and sanitary measures that were desirable in ancient Palestine. At any rate, the prohibitions against cruelty to animals and the eating of blood are the general basis of many Jewish ritualistic rules for the slaughtering of animals and the preparation and inspection of kosher meat. The Jewish method of slaughter is always designed to cause the least pain to the animal and to produce the maximum effusion of blood. Every vestige of remaining blood is drained away or extracted by means of washing and salting the meat. But some of the kosher practices have an entirely different origin. Jacob wrestled all night with an angel of God, according to *Genesis 32*. "And when he saw that he prevailed not against him, he touched the hollow of his thigh; and the hollow of Jacob's thigh was strained, as he wrestled with him." And again: "And the sun rose upon him as he passed over Penuel, and he halted upon his thigh. Therefore the children of Israel eat not the sinew of the hip which is upon the hollow of the thigh, unto this day; because he touched the hollow of Jacob's thigh in the sinew of the hip." As a constant reminder of the intervention of Divine Providence in behalf of the Patriarch, orthodox Jews are required to remove the thigh-vein and other arteries and tendons from the slaughtered animal before that part can be ritually prepared for consumption. It is stated in *Exodus 34:26* and in two other places that "Thou shalt not seethe a kid in his mother's milk." Just what the original intent of this commandment was is now unknown, but the rabbis interpret it to mean that meat and milk should not be cooked, used or eaten together in any way or form whatever. Kosher fish are those having scales and fins; mollusks and eels are *tref* ("terefah"), that is, forbidden, ritually unclean. The ritual rules applying to the kosher killing of fowls are similar to those for animals. Even the use of a kitchen, table utensils or other facilities that have been used in preparing "unkosher" food are forbidden. In 1944 there were about forty-five hundred kosher shops in New York City alone. Kosher meat, because of the special methods of slaughter, preparation and inspection, is generally more expensive than other meat, and for that reason, when food rationing was introduced after the entrance of the United States into the second World War, the Office of Price Administration prepared a special schedule of ration point values for kosher meats.

Does the Bible mention China?

It is barely possible that the prophet referred to China in *Isaiah 49:12* which says: "Behold, these shall come from far: and, lo, these from the north and from the west; and these from the land of *Sinim.*" "The land of Sinim" here obviously refers to a distant country to the east or south of Palestine. Most authorities question the suggestion that Isaiah was speaking of China. The Greek geographer Ptolemy, who lived in the second century A.D., mentioned an Oriental people under the name *Sinai,* supposedly the Chinese. *Sinai* as used by Ptolemy and by later Greek and Roman writers may have been a Western corruption of the Chinese *Tsin,* which occurs in many place names and which is the source of *Tsing,* one of the native names of China. Both the Arabs and the Syrians, close lingual kinsmen of the Hebrews, referred to China as *sin* or *tsin.* It is possible that Ptolemy merely adapted this word to his vocabulary. The Septuagint, a Greek translation of the Old Testament made at Alexandria long before Ptolemy's time, translates *Sinim* in *Isaiah 49:12* as "Persians." There is a tribe of people called *Sina* who live on the foothills of the Hindu Kush mountains in Afghanistan. Despite the similarity in names, it is not believed that Isaiah referred to Mt. Sinai or the Wilderness of Sin to the southwest of Palestine and comparatively near. Nor is it probable that the prophet had in mind *the Sinite,* a tribe in near-by Phoenicia mentioned in *Genesis 10:17.* At any rate, *Sino,* used instead of *Chinese* in such combinations and words as *Sino-Japanese, Sino-Soviet, Sino-Russian, sinology, sinologist* and *sinologue,* is derived from the Greek and Latin *Sinai,* and is preferred to *Chino* because it is more euphonious.

What bird did Noah first send out from the ark?

Noah sent out a raven from the ark before he did the dove. *Genesis 8:6-7* says: "And it came to pass at the end of forty days, that Noah opened the window of the ark which he had made: and he sent forth a raven, which went forth to and fro, until the waters were dried up from off the earth." The raven, a common bird in the land of Israel, figures in several other Biblical passages. In *Leviticus 11* and *Deuteronomy 14* "every raven after his kind" is listed among the unclean fowls that were an abomination and not to be eaten. But, according to *I Kings 17,* the Lord commanded the ravens to feed Elijah the Tishbite while he hid himself by the brook Cherith. "And," says Verse 6, "the ravens brought him bread and flesh in the morning, and bread and flesh in the evening." In *Job 38:41* the Lord asked the patriarch out of the whirlwind: "Who provideth for the raven his food?" *Psalms 147:9* tells us that the Lord "giveth to the beast his food, and to the young ravens which cry." Jesus no doubt was thinking of these passages in the Old Testament when, according to *Luke 12:24,* he said: "Consider the ravens: for they neither sow nor reap; which neither have storehouse nor barn; and God feedeth them: how much more are ye better than the fowls?"

What are the Ten Commandments?

Few people are able to quote the Ten Commandments for the simple reason that no set of commandments is specifically listed and numbered as the Ten Commandments in the Bible. Consequently there is no general agreement as to what exactly constitutes the Ten Commandments. The phrase, *ten commandments,* however, occurs several times in the Old Testament. *Exodus 34:28* says of Moses: "And he was there with the Lord forty days and forty nights; he did neither eat bread, nor drink water. And he wrote upon the tables the words of the covenant, the ten commandments." *Deuteronomy 4:13* quotes Moses as saying: "And he declared unto you his covenant, which he commanded you to perform, even ten commandments; and he wrote them upon two tables of stone." Again in *Deuteronomy 10:4* Moses tells us: "And he wrote on the tables, according to the first writing, the ten commandments, which the Lord spake unto you in the mount out of the midst of the fire in the day of the assembly: and the Lord gave them unto me." It is generally assumed that the law as a whole revealed by God to Moses on Sinai shortly after the Exodus from Egypt was written down by Moses, while the Ten Commandments were inscribed by God himself on the two tables of stone. But "the ten commandments" are nowhere listed in the Bible as ten distinct and separate commandments. They are not found in the Scriptures arranged in the simple and orderly form in which they are usually circulated for popular use. By general agreement these Ten Commandments that God wrote on the two tables of stone are contained in

Exodus 20:2-17, which says that God spake all these words, saying: "I am the Lord thy God, which have brought thee out of the land of Egypt, out of the house of bondage. Thou shalt have no other gods before me. Thou shalt not make unto thee any graven image, or any likeness of any thing that is in heaven above, or that is in the earth beneath, or that is in the water under the earth: Thou shalt not bow down thyself to them, nor serve them: for I the Lord thy God am a jealous God, visiting the iniquity of the fathers upon the children unto the third and fourth generation of them that hate me; and shewing mercy unto thousands of them that love me; and keep my commandments. Thou shalt not take the name of the Lord thy God in vain; for the Lord will not hold him guiltless that taketh his name in vain. Remember the sabbath day, to keep it holy. Six days shalt thou labour, and do all thy work: but the seventh day is the sabbath of the Lord thy God: in it thou shalt not do any work, thou, nor thy son, nor thy daughter, thy manservant, nor thy maidservant, nor thy cattle, nor thy stranger that is within thy gates: for in six days the Lord made heaven and earth, the sea, and all that in them is, and rested the seventh day: wherefore the Lord blessed the sabbath day, and hallowed it. Honour thy father and thy mother: that thy days may be long upon the land which the Lord thy God giveth thee. Thou shalt not kill. Thou shalt not commit adultery. Thou shalt not steal. Thou shalt not bear false witness against thy neighbour. Thou shalt not covet thy neighbour's house, thou shalt not covet thy neighbour's wife, nor his manservant, nor his maidservant, nor his ox, nor his ass, nor any thing that is thy neighbour's." In *Deuteronomy 5:6-18* Moses, speaking to all Israel, repeats the Ten Commandments with some modifications in language. That passage reads: "I am the Lord thy God, which brought thee out of the land of Egypt, from the house of bondage. Thou shalt have none other gods before me. Thou shalt not make thee any graven image, or any likeness of any thing that is in heaven above, or that is in the earth beneath, or that is in the water beneath the earth: thou shalt not bow down thyself unto them, nor serve them: for I the Lord thy God am a jealous God, visiting the iniquity of the fathers upon the children unto the third and fourth generation of them that hate me, and shewing mercy unto thousands of them that love me and keep my commandments. Thou shalt not take the name of the Lord in vain: for the Lord will not hold him guiltless that taketh his name in vain. Keep the sabbath day to sanctify it, as the Lord thy God hath commanded thee. Six days thou shalt labour, and do all thy work: but the seventh day is the sabbath of the Lord thy God: in it thou shalt not do any work, thou, nor thy son, nor thy daughter, nor thy manservant, nor thy maidservant, nor thine ox, nor thine ass, nor any of thy cattle, nor thy stranger that is within thy gates; that thy manservant and thy maidservant may rest as well as thou. And remember that thou wast a servant in the land of Egypt, and that the Lord thy God brought thee out thence through a mighty hand and by a stretched out arm: therefore the Lord thy God commanded thee to keep the sabbath day. Honour thy father and mother, as the Lord thy God hath commanded thee; that thy days may be prolonged, and that it may go well with thee, in the land which the Lord thy God giveth thee. Thou shalt not kill. Neither shalt thou commit adultery. Neither shalt thou steal. Neither shalt thou bear false witness against thy neighbour. Neither shalt thou desire thy neighbour's wife, neither shalt thou covet thy neighbour's house, his field, or his manservant, or his maidservant, his ox, or his ass, or anything that is thy neighbour's." From these two passages, which are practically identical, it will be seen how difficult it is to divide the words and thoughts into ten separate commandments. It is small wonder that different authorities have differed on the subject through the ages. Naturally the form of the Ten Commandments given in *Exodus* is assumed to be older than that given in *Deuteronomy,* because the latter is in the nature of a recapitulation. Even Jewish authorities themselves have differed as to exactly which commandment should be regarded as the tenth. Jewish authorities, following Philo and Josephus, generally regard *Exodus 20:2* as the first of the Ten Commandments: "I am the Lord thy God, which have brought thee out of the land of Egypt, out of the house of bondage." On the other hand, the Catholic church, as did St. Augustine and Martin Luther, regards the first commandment as extending from Verses 2 to 6: "I am the Lord thy God, which have brought thee out of the land of Egypt, out of the house of bondage. Thou shalt have no other gods before me. Thou shalt not make unto thee any graven image, or any likeness of any thing that is in the heaven above, or that is in the earth beneath, or that is in the water under the earth: thou shalt not bow down thyself to them, nor serve them: for I the Lord thy God am a jealous God, visiting the iniquity of the fathers upon the children unto the third and fourth generation of them that hate me; and shewing mercy unto thousands of them that love me, and keep my commandments." Likewise Jewish authorities generally regard the whole of *Exodus 20:17* as constituting the tenth commandment, while the Catholic church regards that verse as comprising both the ninth and tenth commandments. That verse reads: "Thou shalt not covet thy neighbour's house, thou shalt not covet thy neighbour's wife, nor his manservant, nor his maidservant, nor his ox, nor his ass, nor any thing that is thy neighbour's." Under the division of the Ten Commandments made by the Catholic church the coveting of a neighbor's wife is distinguished from coveting his property. Technically the commandment, "Thou shalt not commit adultery," as translated into English does not apply to single persons, because legally only married persons can commit adultery. The Ten Commandments, related in 120 Hebrew words, have exercised a profound influence on the religious, moral and social life of man.

What is *The Psalter*?

The Book of Psalms is sometimes known as *The Psalter*, although the term does not occur in the Bible. *Psalm* is from the Greek and literally signifies "sound of a stringed instrument." The Hebrew word for *psalm* corresponds to *Praises*. The 150 psalms or hymns were composed to be sung to the psaltery, an ancient ten-stringed instrument of the zither type. Some of the most beautiful sentiments ever expressed in writing are found in *The Book of Psalms*. Seventy-three of them are attributed to King David, who in *II Samuel 23:1* is referred to as "the sweet psalmist of Israel," although whether David actually composed any of the psalms has long been a controversial subject among Bible scholars.

Does the Bible require priests to be celibate?

Celibacy was unknown to the ancient Israelites and would probably have been incomprehensible to them. "Be fruitful, and multiply, and replenish the earth," in *Genesis 1:28* was one of the first pre-Mosaic commandments given to mankind. Judaism has always emphasized the duty of building a home and of rearing a family. The rabbis have always taught that the celibate life is an unblessed life. Israel from the first had a married priesthood. Not only did the Levites and priests marry, but the office passed down from father to son. By the Mosaic law, the tribe of Levi was set apart as the priestly class in the theocracy of Israel. Marriage laws and customs for the Levites and priests were stricter than for others because of the importance of preserving the priestly lineage. There is no evidence in the Bible that even the vow taken by the Nazarite prohibited the marriage relation. Samson, though a Nazarite, was married. Certain prophets, priests and other individuals may have taken the vow of celibacy in ancient Israel, and this practice appears to have been quite common among the Jews in Palestine in the time of Jesus. There was a sect of Jews at that time called Essenes who abstained from marriage in violation of the law of Moses and the usual Jewish conception of life. Although the Essenes are not mentioned by name in the Bible, it is believed that many of their teachings had a profound influence upon the doctrines of John the Baptist, Jesus and his disciples and many of the early Christians. Some authorities even suppose that almost the entire Essene sect was absorbed by the early Christian church in Palestine. John the Baptist is generally supposed to have been a celibate. Of the twelve disciples of Jesus, there is no definite evidence that any of them was married except Peter, whose "wife's mother" is referred to in *Matthew 7:14* as well as in *Mark* and *Luke*. Eusebius records a tradition that Peter's wife accompanied him to Rome and suffered martyrdom a short time after her husband did. "Philip the evangelist," whom Paul visited at Caesarea and who "had four daughters, virgins, which did prophesy," was probably not the same person as Philip, one of the Twelve Apostles. Paul apparently never married, but vowed himself to lifelong celibacy and held up absolute celibacy as an ideal. He did not require celibacy on the part of Christians but regarded marriage as perhaps necessary and a lesser evil than license. In *I Corinthians 7* Paul said: "It is good for a man not to touch a woman. Nevertheless, to avoid fornication, let every man have his own wife, and let every woman have her own husband." And again: "For I would that all men were even as I myself. But every man hath his proper gift of God, one after this manner and another after that. I say therefore to the unmarried and widows, It is good for them if they abide even as I. But if they cannot contain, let them marry: for it is better to marry than to burn." In the early days of the Christian church the clergy were permitted to marry. The growth of celibacy, first as a custom and then as a rule of discipline, was gradual among the clergy of the Roman Catholic church. Even in modern times some Eastern churches under jurisdiction of Rome have had a married priesthood. Many bishops and priests, perhaps in imitation of St. Paul, voluntarily began to practice celibacy at an early date. Second marriages of priests began to be questioned; then marriage of priests was restricted to virgins. The first church council that definitely forbade marriage to the higher clergy was the local synod of Elvira in 305 A.D. Eighty years later—385 A.D.—Pope Siricius issued a decretal enjoining strict celibacy upon all bishops, priests and deacons. He insisted on the immediate separation of those who were married and prescribed expulsion as the penalty for disobedience. This may be regarded as the real beginning of universal compulsory sacerdotal celibacy in the Catholic church as a rule of discipline. This rule was later extended to subdeacons. For several centuries, however, the rules against the marriage of clerics in sacred orders were widely violated both openly and secretly. Even many bishops continued to have wives. In the eleventh century several Popes turned their attention to the question and took stringent measures to enforce the injunctions against marriage among the clergy. Pope Gregory VII, who was Pope from 1073 to 1085, especially distinguished himself in this respect. He enforced the celibacy rules so stringently that he is still often erroneously credited with being their author. *Celibacy*, which does not occur in the Bible, is derived from Latin *caelebs*, meaning "unmarried" or "single."

Is "the end justifies the means" in the Bible?

The saying, "the end justifies the means," is not in the Bible in those words, but the principle expressed by it is referred to by St. Paul in *Romans 3:7-8*, which reads: "For if the truth of God hath more abounded through my lie unto his glory; why yet am I also judged as a sinner? And not rather, (as we be slanderously reported, and as some affirm that we say,) Let us do evil, that good may come? whose damnation is just." The thought conveyed by the words, "the end justifies the means"—that an action bad in itself becomes good if done for a good purpose—dates back further than the time of St. Paul. Ovid, the Roman poet, who died 17 A.D., gave us *Exitus acta probat*, "the result justifies the action." "The end justifies the means" is a free translation of one of the maxims in the *Sententiae* of Publilius Syrus, a Latin writer of mimes who lived in the first century A.D. The author has been unable to trace to any definite source the exact phraseology now generally employed to express the principle. Matthew Prior (1664-1721), English poet and diplomatist, wrote in *Hans Carvel* that "The end must justify the means." For centuries the Jesuits have been accused by their enemies of originating, teaching and practicing the maxim. They vigorously repudiate it as immoral and deny that it was ever taught by the Society of Jesus. More than once they have offered large monetary rewards to any person who could point out in the writings of the Order any approval or assent to the doctrine. In Germany and Hungary, according to newspaper reports, courts have awarded damages against men who publicly repeated the common libel. Some authorities suppose that "the end justifies the means" became associated with the Jesuits from a passage in *Medulla Theologiae,* written about 1645 by Hermann Busenbaum, a prominent German Jesuit theologian who taught at Cologne. This book contains the words, *Cum finis est licitus, etiam media sunt licita,* which, roughly translated, means "When the end is lawful, the means are also lawful." It is also said that the unjustified accusation against the Jesuits (that they taught the doctrine that the end justifies the means) arose from Blaise Pascal's *Provinciales,* which began to circulate in Latin about 1656. The verse quoted above from *Romans* indicates that the same charge was made against St. Paul and his followers fifteen centuries before the Society of Jesus was formed bv Ignatius Loyola in 1540. One Jesuit writer says that if some members of the Order do practice the maxim it is certain that they have no monopoly on it.

What was "the great river" in the Bible?

The Euphrates, named as one of the rivers of Eden, is "the river" and "the great river" of the Bible. The chief root word in *Euphrates* is *Phrat* and signifies "abounding." It is about 1,780 miles long, is the largest river in Southwestern Asia and was regarded by the later Hebrews as the ideal, though not actual, northeastern boundary of Israel. Like the Nile, the Euphrates overflows its banks every year and rises as high as twelve feet. When the later Hebrew prophets spoke of "this side the river" they referred to one side or the other of the Euphrates. *I Kings 4:21* says that "Solomon reigned over all kingdoms from *the river* unto the land of the Philistines, and unto the border of Egypt."

What does *dying in harness* mean?

To the average person *dying in harness* conjures up a picture of a faithful old horse, toiling to the very last and finally dropping dead in its tracks with its draught gear on its back. Such is not the original and true meaning of the phrase, although it may be said to have acquired that significance through almost universal misunderstanding. The original meaning of *harness* was "equipment, furniture, outfit, gear, trappings, particularly a suit of mail or defensive armor." That was the sense in which the term was used by the translators of the King James Version of the Bible. In *I Kings 22:34* we are told that an archer smote King Ahab of Israel "between the joints of the harness." "Let not him that girdeth on his harness," says *I Kings 20:11,* "boast himself as he that putteth it off." Even when *harness* is used in the English Bible in connection with beasts of burden it retains its original sense. *Jeremiah 46:3-4* says: "Order ye the buckler and shield, and draw near to battle. Harness the horses; and get up, ye horsemen, and stand forth with your helmets; furbish the spears, and put on the brigandines." The war horses as well as the warriors wore armor. In *Exodus 13:18* we read that "the children of Israel went up harnessed out of the land of Egypt." *II Chronicles 9:23-24* says: "And all the kings of the earth sought the presence of Solomon, to hear his wisdom, that God had put in his heart. And they brought every man his present, vessels of silver, and vessels of gold, and raiment, harness, and spices, horses, and mules, a rate year by year." In the days of Shakespeare and the English translators of the Bible *dying in harness* meant "to die on the battlefield while fighting," "dying in one's boots or with one's boots on." When Macbeth says that "at least we'll die with harness on our back" he means that he will die fighting in full military regalia. Harness in the sense of draught gear for horses came later.

Does the Bible mention the wedding ring?

The wedding ring is not mentioned in the Bible, but the original practice from which it got its significance probably is. Some authorities suppose that the wedding ring is a survival of savage servitude and was at first a symbol of the bondage pledged to their husbands by primitive women. It is more probable, however, that the wedding ring had a later and nobler origin and grew out of the use of signet rings, which are rings bearing seals. "And Pharaoh took off his ring from his hand," says *Genesis 41:42*, "and put it upon Joseph's hand." In *Esther 3:10* we read that Ahasuerus took his ring from his hand and gave it to Haman, an act which gave the latter full authority to carry out his wicked design of destroying the Jews within the Empire. The ancient Hebrews themselves are known to have used seal rings. His signet and bracelets were among the pledges that Judah gave to his daughter-in-law Tamar when she played the role of a harlot, according to *Genesis 38:18*. In ancient times it seems to have been customary for a man to authorize important transactions by giving the signet ring to the agent instead of merely stamping the necessary papers or the equivalent. Entrusting another with one's signet ring was a token of complete confidence in him. A woman could issue commands in her lord's name after she received his ring. Possession of his ring made an Egyptian woman in every respect her husband's representative. The natural inference is that the wedding or marriage ring developed out of this practice. If this is correct, the wedding ring was not originally a badge of slavery, but the symbol of common authority over the household. The giving of an engagement ring was a later elaboration and at first was intended merely as a pledge or earnest that authority over the household would be given in due time. The fact that the ring is in its form a symbol of eternity added a sentimental touch to the significance of the transaction.

What is meant by the *quick and the dead*?

Quick is derived from Anglo-Saxon *cwic,* meaning "living" or "animate." The quick and the dead are the living and the dead. In this sense *quick* is now regarded as archaic or dialectical, except in the phrase under consideration. In *Acts 10:42* we find: "And he commanded us to preach unto the people, and to testify that it is he which was ordained of God to be the Judge of quick and dead." St. Paul, in *II Timothy 4:1,* refers to Jesus Christ "who shall judge the quick and the dead at his appearing and his kingdom." The Apostles' Creed, as said in the Roman Catholic church, declares that "from thence He shall come to judge the living and the dead." In the Protestant Episcopal version the older words "the quick and the dead" are retained. *Quick* for *living* was still in common use when the King James Version of the Bible was translated. Shakespeare has Hamlet tell the clown that the grave "is for the dead, not for the quick," and later the Prince of Denmark says to Laertes, "Be buried quick with her, and so will I," which means, "Be buried alive with her," not "Be buried at once with her." *Quick* in such words as *quicksand, quicklime* and *quicksilver* retains a degree of this earlier meaning of the term.

When did the nineteenth century end?

The nineteenth century ended with December 31, 1900. All the year 1900 was included in the nineteenth century. The twentieth century began with January 1, 1901. A century begins with the beginning of the first day of its first year and does not end until the close of the last day of its one hundredth year. This question gives many people considerable trouble and it has been the subject of much controversy. The problem is simplified by going back to the beginning of the Christian Era. Theoretically the Christian Era began with the birth of Jesus. Since a century is one hundred full years the first century must have ended with the end of the year 100. It consisted of the years 1 to 100 inclusive. Anything that happened less than a year after the birth of Jesus was born is said to have occurred in the year 1. Those who mistakenly suppose that the nineteenth century ended with the year 1899 allow only ninety-nine years for the first century, for if the nineteenth century ended with the year 1899 the first century must have ended with the year 99, which leaves only ninety-nine years for that century. The popular confusion on this subject probably arises from the common method of stating a person's age. A person born at the beginning of the Christian Era would be called one year old during his second year, namely, during the course of the year 2; he would be called two years of age during the year 3, and so on. A person thirty years old is in his thirty-first year. There are those, however, who contend that the year 1 did not begin until one year after the birth of Jesus. This would leave an intervening period without date, known for convenience as the Zero Year. This contention appears to have little merit and is not generally accepted. Each century as ordinally named (the first century and the nineteenth century) contains only one year (1 and 1900) beginning with the number that names it, and 99 (1-99 and 1801-1899) beginning with a number lower by one. Accordingly the years 100, 200 and 1900 belong to the first, second and nineteenth centuries. We are now in the twentieth century, which will end with December 31, 2000, and the twenty-first century will begin with January 1, 2001. Italian writers on art use a different system of referring to past centuries, which further confuses the question. For instance, they employ *trecento, quattrocento* and *cinquecento,* which literally mean three hundred, four hundred and five hundred, as abbreviations for the centuries of the years 1300-1399, 1400-1499 and 1500-1599. Their trecento (1300-1399) corresponds to our fourteenth century; their quattrocento (1400-1499), to our fifteenth century, and their cinquecento (1500-1599), to our sixteenth century. When an Italian writer on art refers to a painter as being a *cinquecentist* he means that he belongs to what we call the sixteenth, not the fifteenth century. This is doubly confusing to those not familiar with the system of referring to centuries, because, as said before, *cinquecento* is used as an abbreviation and truly means five hundred and not fifteen hundred. This question is closely related to another. *Teens* refers to the years of a person's age or the numbers ending in *teen* and is correctly written without the apostrophe, *teens,* not *'teens.* It is merely the plural form of the termination of the cardinal numbers from thirteen to nineteen inclusive and signifies *and ten. Sixteen,* for instance, literally means *six and ten.* A person twelve years of age is in his thirteenth year, but he is not yet in his teens. He enters his teens on his thirteenth birthday and leaves them on his twentieth birthday, when he enters his twenties, which he leaves on his thirtieth birthday. The apostrophe is not correctly placed before *teens* because no word, syllable, letter or figure is omitted. We properly write *'70's* or *'seventies,* when we refer to the decade from 1870 to 1880, because *1800* or *eighteen hundred* is understood to precede it. But in reference to a person's age we would write that he was in his *70's* or *seventies,* there being no omission. To speak of the fourth decade of the twentieth century and of the *'40's* are two different things. A decade is a period of ten years. The fourth decade of the twentieth century began January 1, 1841, and ended December 31, 1850. But the *40's* does not correspond exactly with the fourth decade. It means the years from 1840 to 1849 inclusive, whose numbers contain *4* as their third digit. Our system of reckoning time, with an assumed birth date for Jesus as the base point, ignores all other methods of chronology and time and applies to dates before as well as after the beginning of the Christian Era. The year immediately preceding 1 A.D. is reckoned as 1 B.C., the year preceding that as 2 B.C., and so on.

Does *Reverend* occur in the Bible?

The word *reverend* occurs in the Bible only once and then it refers to God. *Psalms 111:9* says: "He sent redemption unto his people: he hath commanded his covenant forever: holy and *reverend* is his name." *Reverend* is from the same Latin root as *revere* and signifies, when applied to persons, "worthy of deep respect or reverence because of age, ability, character, piety, learning or rank." It was so used in England at the time the King James Version was translated and was not then a title. *Reverend* appears to have been first applied to the English clergy as a respectful epithet during the fifteenth century. The form, "The Reverend Mr. Robert Wilson, minister of Tamworth," was employed in 1727 and has been general ever since. Before *Reverend* became a specific title, clergymen in England were customarily addressed as "Master" or "Sir."

What woman's exact age is given in the Bible?

In all the Bible the exact age of only one woman is given. She is Sarah, the half-sister and wife of Abraham. *Genesis 17:17* says: "Then Abraham fell upon his face, and laughed, and said in his heart, Shall a child be born unto him that is an hundred years old? and shall

Sarah, that is ninety years old, bear?" In *Genesis 23:1* we read that Sarah was one hundred and twenty-seven years old when she died. Although Abraham was "old and well stricken in age" at one hundred, he survived Sarah thirty-eight years and lived to the ripe old age of one hundred and seventy-five. When Abraham went down into Egypt he was seventy-five and his wife sixty-five. Sarah was so "fair to look upon" that her husband told the Egyptians that she was his sister in order to keep them from taking her for themselves. This ruse, based on a half truth, did not work. In the New Testament the approximate age of a prophetess named Anna is given. *Luke 2:36-37* says: "And there was one Anna, a prophetess, the daughter of Phanuel, of the tribe of Aser: she was of a great age, and had lived with a husband seven years from her virginity; and she was a widow of about fourscore and four years, which departed not from the temple, but served God with fastings and prayers night and day." In Chapter 8 of the same book we learn that Jairus, the ruler of the synagogue, had a daughter "about twelve years of age." Thus it will be seen that even in Biblical times there was a tendency to suppress information relative to the age of women.

Who cut Samson's hair?

It is a common mistake to suppose that Delilah with her own hands cut off the hair of Samson. Delilah did not do it herself but had somebody else do it for her while the strong man slept on her knees. The incident is related in *Judges 16:19* as follows: Delilah "made him sleep upon her knees; and she called for *a man*, and she *caused him* to shave off the seven locks of his head; and she began to afflict him, and his strength went from him."

What causes the teeth to be set on edge?

Jeremiah 31:29-30 says: "In those days they shall say no more, The fathers have eaten a sour grape, and the children's teeth are set on edge. But every one shall die for his own iniquity: every man that eateth the sour grape, his teeth shall be set on edge." In *Ezekiel 18:2-3* is a similar reference: "What mean ye, that ye use this proverb concerning the land of Israel, saying, The fathers have eaten sour grapes, and the children's teeth are set on edge? As I live, saith the Lord God, ye shall not have occasion any more to use this proverb in Israel." Both prophets were warning the Israelites not to excuse their own sins by relying on a proverb saying that their calamities were a punishment for the sins of former generations. Very sweet or very tart foods frequently *set the teeth on edge* and make it painful to chew. The same sensation is sometimes caused by grit in the food. This phenomenon is one of the anomalies of sensibility. Obviously it is impossible for the acids in the food to attack the enamel or even the exposed dentine so rapidly as to produce this pain in perfectly sound teeth. There is certainly no direct nerve contact. Therefore most modern dental scientists believe the sensation is due to a peculiar reflex nervous action that has never been satisfactorily explained. This theory is supported by the fact that persons who have had all their teeth extracted also sometimes experience the sensation popularly called *the teeth on edge.*

What Bible book does not mention God?

The words *God, Lord, Almighty* and corresponding terms do not occur in the *Book of Esther* and the deity is not anywhere so much as alluded to in that portion of the Old Testament. *Esther,* so far as known, was never quoted by any pre-Christian writer, and it is not referred to by Jesus or any of the New Testament writers. The deity is not specifically mentioned in *The Song of Solomon,* but that book is generally supposed to be allegorical and the deity is continually alluded to. Some authorities, however, recognize this book as a collection of wedding songs. The deity, under one name or other, is mentioned in all the other books of the Bible.

Did the Israelites ever offer human sacrifices?

Human sacrifices were offered by the primitive Greeks, Romans, Slavs, Celts, Germans, Scandinavians and many other ancient peoples. The practice was also common among the heathen Semitic peoples among whom the Israelites lived. The Phoenicians and Moabites sacrificed their first-born to their gods, and child sacrifices were an essential part of Moloch worship. It is probable that in primitive times the Hebrews themselves offered human sacrifices. In *Genesis 22* it is related that God, to test Abraham's faith and obedience, commanded the patriarch to take his only son Isaac into the land of Moriah and to offer him for a burnt offering. Abraham, without questioning the command, took his son up on a mountain and was about to offer him as a sacrifice, but an angel stayed him as he stretched forth his hand to slay the bound child with a knife. The patriarch, after being commended by an angel of the Lord for his willingness to offer his only son as a sacrifice, lifted up his eyes and saw a ram caught in a thicket by its horns. Accordingly he of fered the ram for a burnt offering in the stead of his son. This indicates that the practice of child sacrifice, although not common, was occasional in the earliest days of Hebrew tradition. The intervention of the angel apparently was interpreted by Abraham as a direction not to follow this abomination of the Canaanites. Some authorities suppose that the story of Abraham and Isaac was calculated to remind the Israelites that God was opposed to human sacrifices. The Mosaic law specifically forbade the practice. Under it the Israelites were to dedicate their first-born sons "alive" to the service of the Lord. *Deuteronomy 12:31* says: "Thou shalt not do so unto the Lord thy God: for every abomination to the Lord, which he hateth, have they done unto their gods; for even their sons and their daughters they have burnt in the fire of their gods." *Deuteronomy 18:10* commands that "There shall not be found among you any one that maketh his son or his daughter to pass through the fire." In *Leviticus 18:21* it is asserted that "thou shalt not let any of thy seed pass through the fire to Molech," and *Leviticus 20:1-2* elaborates and adds the penalty: "Whosoever he be of the children of Israel, or of the strangers that sojourn in Israel, that giveth any of his seed unto Molech; he shall surely be put to death: the people of the land shall stone him with stones." But the Israelites had a long uphill fight against child sacrifices and many of their own people violated these commandments and did after the manner of the heathen around about them. Jephthah, who judged Israel six years, gave his only child as a burnt offering to the Lord. It is related in *Judges 11* that Jephthah the Gileadite, before setting out against the Ammonites, vowed a vow unto the Lord that if the ancient enemies of Israel were delivered into his hands he would offer up for a burnt offering to the Lord whatever came out of his house to meet him upon his return. After smiting the Ammonites with great slaughter he returned to his home in Mizpeh and was met at the gate by his daughter with timbrels and dances. The stern old judge and warrior was very sorrowful when he saw what his vow had brought him to, for his daughter, according to *Judges 11:34*, "was his only child; beside her he had neither son nor daughter." But the Lord had kept his part of the covenant by delivering the Ammonites into Jephthah's hands, and the daughter insisted that her father keep his vow, asking only that she be let alone two months to go up and down the mountains to bewail her virginity with her companions. Then she "returned to her father, who did with her according to his vow which he had vowed," and thereafter it was a custom in Israel for young women to go out to lament the daughter of Jephthah four days each year. Some writers insist this language is figurative and means that Jephthah did not actually sacrifice his daughter but merely consecrated her as a virgin to the Lord. But most of the Jewish commentators from Josephus to the present time have interpreted the story as meaning that Jephthah offered his daughter as a burnt sacrifice, and that undoubtedly is the intent of the language. The fact that Jephthah's daughter died unmarried made her death doubly tragic in the eyes of the Israelites. It should be borne in mind that this event is supposed to have occurred during the barbarous period of the Judges, when Israelites and heathen were intermingled and when moral standards in Israel were at a low ebb. Many later backsliding Israelites committed the same offense against the Mosaic law. According to *II Kings 3:27*, during the war between Israel, Judah and Edom on the one hand and Moab on the other, the king of Moab, after the battle went sore against him, "took his eldest son that should have reigned in his stead, and offered him for a burnt offering upon the wall." In *II Kings 16:3* we are told that Ahaz, king of Judah, "walked in the way of the kings of Israel, yea, and made his son to pass through the fire, according to the abominations of the heathen, whom the Lord cast out from before the children of Israel." It is related in *II Kings 21:6* that King Manasseh of Judah also "did that which was evil in the sight of the Lord, after the abominations of the heathen" and "made his son pass through the fire." *Jeremiah 7:31* says that the children of Judah "have built the high places of Tophet, which is in the valley of the son of Hinnom, to burn their sons and their daughters in the fire; which I commanded them not, neither came it into my heart." This indicates that some of those in Israel who offered their children as sacrifices distorted the commands against human sacrifices and cited the Scripture to suit their own purposes. In *Jeremiah 19:4-5* the prophet quotes the Lord as saying that the kings of Judah "have filled this place with the blood of innocents; they have built also the high places of Baal, to burn their sons with fire for burnt offerings unto Baal, which I commanded not, nor spake it, neither came it into my mind: therefore, behold, the days come, saith the Lord, that this place shall no more be called Tophet, nor The valley of the son of Hinnom, but The valley of slaughter." It is believed that *Topheth* is of Aramaic origin and means "place of burning." Apparently it was the fireplace where human beings were sacrificed by the imitators of the abominations of the heathen. *Isaiah 30:33* says: "For Tophet is ordained of old; yea, for the king it is prepared; he hath made it deep and large; the pile thereof is fire and much wood; the breath of the Lord, like a stream of brimstone, doth kindle it." Molech was the god of one of the forbidden Israelitic cults to whom children, particularly the first-born, were sometimes offered in Old Testament times. The phrase, *pass through the fire,* is a translation of a Hebrew expression literally meaning "to transfer" and alluding to the fact that the offering was made to pass through the fire from the offerer to the god. The exact character of the rite of human sacrifice in Israel is not made clear by the Biblical references. Excavations in Palestine have revealed the skeletons of scores of infants in cemeteries around heathen altars. These skeletons show traces of partial consumption by sacrificial fire. Although it appears to be clear that human bodies were actually sacrificed, it is not known whether the victims were killed before passing through the fire. *Psalms 106: 37-38* says: "Yea, they sacrificed their sons and their daughters unto devils, and shed innocent blood, even the blood of their sons and of their daughters, whom they sacrificed unto idols of Canaan: and the land was polluted with blood." In *Ezekiel 16:20-21* the prophet cries: "Moreover thou hast taken thy sons and thy daughters, whom thou hast borne unto me, and these hast thou sacrificed. Is this of thy whoredoms a small matter, that thou hast slain my children, and delivered them to cause them to pass through the fire for them?" *Micah 6:7* says: "Shall I give my first-born for my transgression, the fruit of my body for the sin of my soul?" The death of Jesus on the cross is conceived by many as the sacrifice of the only begotten son of God for the sins of the whole world.

Did Israelitish women take part in religious services?

Just to what extent the women took part in religious services in ancient Israel is hard to say. They probably played only a minor part in such services. Presumably God created woman as well as man in his own image, for *Genesis 1:27* says: "God created man in his own image, in the image of God created he him; male and female created he them," although in *Genesis 3:16* the wife is made subject to the husband. Hebrew women enjoyed a much higher status and a greater degree of equality with men than did the women of surrounding peoples. Although the Mosaic law contains many provisions applicable to women that are not applicable to men and vice versa, in a general way the sexes were treated as equals in their relation to God and in religious matters. Miriam shared the leadership of the Exodus with her brothers Moses and Aaron, and there were women prophets and judges, but no women priests. In *Samuel 1* we are told that Hannah went up to the temple in Shiloh and "prayed unto the Lord." The eighty-four-year-old prophetess Anna, according to *Luke 2:37,* "departed not from the temple, but served God with fastings and prayers night and day." In later Judaism, after the final dispersion, the Talmudists recognized 365 commandments, as many as there are days in the year, and 248 prohibitions, as many as there are bones in the human body. It is said that Jewish women were obliged to observe the prohibitions but not to keep the commandments. While all men were required to learn the laws and commandments in Hebrew, it was sufficient for women to acquire a general knowledge of them in their mother tongue. In *Galatians 3:28* Paul declared "there is neither male nor female: for ye are all one in Christ Jesus."

What is the law of retaliation?

The Mosaic law imposing the penalty of an eye for an eye and a tooth for a tooth is known as *lex talionis,* or "the law of retaliation." In the Bible this law is first stated in *Exodus 21:23-25,* which says: "And if any mischief follow, then thou shalt give life for life, eye for eye, tooth for tooth, hand for hand, foot for foot, burning for burning, wound for wound, stripe for stripe." This statute now strikes us as cruel and barbaric. Actually it was a progressive step in legal justice at the time it was written. It substituted legal punishment for unrestricted personal revenge and established a rule of "measure for measure" in dealing out punishment to rich and poor, great and little alike. Under this law an injured person could no longer claim two eyes for one, two teeth for one, etc. Apparently the law of retaliation was presumed to apply only to Israelites and not to strangers until a test case on the subject was brought before and decided by Moses himself. The case involved a fight between a man of Israel and the son of an Egyptian by an Israelite woman named Shelomith, the daughter of Dibri, of the tribe of Dan. During the fight the half Egyptian blasphemed the name of the Lord and cursed. The offender was brought before Moses and then put in ward "that the mind of the Lord might be shewed them." What followed and the decision is told in *Leviticus 24:13-22*: "And the Lord spake unto Moses, saying, Bring forth him that hath cursed without the camp; and let all that heard him lay their hands upon his head, and let all the congregation stone him. And thou shalt speak unto the children of Israel, saying, Whosoever curseth his God shall bear his sin. And he that blasphemeth the name of the Lord, he shall surely be put to death, and all the congregation shall certainly stone him: as well the stranger, as he that is born in the land, when he blasphemeth the name of the Lord, shall be put to death. And he that killeth any man shall surely be put to death. And he that killeth a beast shall make it good; beast for beast. And if a man cause a blemish in his neighbour; as he hath done, so shall it be done to him; breach for breach, eye for eye, tooth for tooth: as he hath caused a blemish in a man, so shall it be done to him again. And he that killeth a beast, he shall restore it: and he that killeth a man, he shall be put to death. Ye shall have one manner of law, as well for the stranger, as for one of your own country, for I am the Lord your God." Since blasphemy rather than bodily harm was the offense at issue, that part of the decision of Moses relating to the law of retaliation and the applicability of the law to strangers was in the nature of what lawyers call dicta. The context of *Exodus 21:23-25* quoted above shows that there were some exceptions to these drastic penalties even from the beginning. It is probable that the law of retaliation was not construed or applied literally except in primitive times. In fact, its literal application was excluded in the administration of Hebrew law in Rabbinic times and there is no case in all Jewish history in which it was literally applied in the sense of an eye for an eye, a tooth for a tooth, a hand for a hand, and a foot for a foot. As a matter of fact, in some cases it would have been impossible of application. For instance, a toothless person who had knocked out the teeth of another could not be compelled to give tooth for tooth. Obviously the law of retaliation was regarded as a standard to measure monetary damages. "Thou shalt not bear false witness against thy neighbour," is one of the Ten Commandments, and Hebrew law provided that false witnesses should suffer the penalties that would have been imposed upon those they sought to convict by false testimony. *Deuteronomy 19:18-21* says: "And the judges shall make diligent inquisition: and, behold, if the witness be a false witness, and hath testified falsely against his brother; then shall ye do unto him, as he had thought to have unto his brother: so shalt thou put the evil away from among you. And those which remain shall hear, and fear, and shall henceforth commit no more any such evil among you. And thine eye shall not pity; but life shall go for life, eye for eye, tooth for tooth, hand for hand, foot for foot." Many passages in the law of Moses point clearly that the law of retaliation was carried out only in the case of capital punishment, life for life. *Lex talionis* is derived from Latin *lex,* and *talio,* "retaliation" or "compensation." The *lex talionis* is based on the principle of like for like, repayment in kind, fair compensation. It was a part not only of the ancient Hebrew law, but also of the Roman and other early legal systems. Under the Roman *lex talionis* the same penalty was imposed on the accuser who could not prove his case as would have been imposed upon the accused if found guilty. Jesus referred to the Mosaic law of retaliation both literally and figuratively. *Matthew 5:38* says: "Ye have heard that it hath been said, An eye for an eye, and a tooth for a tooth." In verses 29 and 30 of the same chapter Jesus is quoted as saying: "And if thy right eye offend thee, pluck it out, and cast it from thee: for it is profitable for thee that one of thy members should perish, and not that thy whole body should be cast into hell. And if thy right hand offend thee, cut it off, and cast it from thee: for it is profitable for thee that one of thy members should perish, and not that thy whole body should be cast into hell." Again in *Matthew 18:8-9*: "Wherefore if thy hand or thy foot offend thee, cut them off, and cast them from thee: it is better for thee to enter into life halt or maimed, rather than having two hands or two feet to be cast into everlasting fire. And if thine eye offend thee, pluck it out, and cast it from thee: it is better for thee to enter into life with one eye, rather than having two eyes to be cast into hell fire." The *Koran* says: "O true believers, the law of retaliation is ordained you for the slain: the free shall die for the free, and the servant for the servant, and a woman for a woman." In his *Table-Talk,* written in 1689, John Selden said: "An eye for an eye, and a tooth for a tooth. That does not mean that if I put out another man's eye, therefore I must lose one of my own (for what is he the better for that?), though this be commonly received; but it means, I shall give him what satisfaction an eye shall be judged to be worth."

Is *from Dan to Beer-sheba* in the Bible?

The saying, "from Dan to Beer-sheba," does not occur in the King James Version in that exact form. Wherever it is used it is rendered "from Dan *even* to Beer-sheba." After the Israelites occupied the Promised Land under Joshua the Danites were at first unable to conquer the Canaanites in the territory assigned to them and they were compelled to live in fortified camps. Part of the tribe of Dan migrated northward, according to *Judges 17* and *18*, and by surprise seized the Phoenician village of Laish in the far north of Palestine near the source of the Jordan in territory allotted to the tribe of Naphtali. The Danites changed the name of Laish to Dan and made it a new rallying point for the tribe. Dan thus came to be regarded as the northern limit of the country. Beer-sheba (literally "well of Sheba") was one of the chief towns in the south in the territory allotted to the tribe of Simeon. In the course of time part of the territory of Simeon was reclaimed by the desert peoples and part of it was gradually absorbed by Judah. According to *I Kings 19:3,* Beer-sheba belonged to Judah already in the time of Elijah and Ahab. At any rate, Beer-sheba was situated on the border of the southern desert and was regarded as the southern limit of the land of Israel. The Israelites referred to the whole extent of their country from north to south as "from Dan even to Beer-sheba," in the same manner that Americans speak of the extent of the United States from east to west as "from Portland, Maine, to Portland, Oregon," or that the British speak of the extent of Britain from south to north as "from Land's End to John O'Groat's House." *Judges 20:1* says: "Then all the children of Israel went out, and the congregation was gathered together as one man, from Dan even to Beer-sheba, with the land of Gilead, unto the Lord in Mizpeh." *I Samuel 3:20* tells us that "all Israel from Dan even to Beer-sheba knew that Samuel was established to be a prophet of the Lord." But in the Chronicles *Dan* and *Beer-sheba* are reversed in the saying. *I Chronicles 21:2* says: "And David said to Joab and to the rulers of the people, Go, number Israel from Beer-sheba even to Dan." Again *II Chronicles 30:5*: "So they established a decree to make proclamation throughout all Israel, from Beer-sheba even to Dan, that they should come to keep the passover unto the Lord God of Israel at Jerusalem: for they had not done it of a long time in such sort as it was written." It is possible that the Israelites living in the southern part of the country said "from Beer-sheba even to Dan," while those living in the northern part said "from Dan even to Beer-sheba." The smallness of the land of Israel is indicated by the fact that the total distance from Dan to Beer-sheba as the crow flies is only about 125 miles.

Is *the good Samaritan* in the Bible?

The good Samaritan is not in the Bible. In the sense of a person who lends a helping hand to a fellow being in distress, the phrase was suggested by one of the most popular of all the parables of Jesus. This parable, recorded only by Luke, might appropriately have been called the Parable of the Good Neighbor, but it is universally known as the Parable of the Good Samaritan. *Luke 10:25-37* says: "And, behold, a certain lawyer stood up, and tempted him, saying, Master, what shall I do to inherit eternal life? He said unto him, What is written in the law? how readest thou? And he answering said, Thou shalt love the Lord thy God with all thy soul, and with all thy strength, and with all thy mind; and thy neighbour as thyself. And he said unto him, Thou hast answered right: this do, and thou shalt live. But he, willing to justify himself, said unto Jesus, And who is my neighbour? And Jesus answering said, A certain man went down from Jerusalem to Jericho, and fell among thieves, which stripped him of his raiment, and wounded him, and departed, leaving him half dead. And by chance there came down a certain priest that way: and when he saw him, he passed by on the other side. And likewise a Levite, when he was at the place, came and looked on him, and passed by on the other side. But a certain Samaritan, as he journeyed, came where he was: and when he saw him, he had compassion on him, and went to him, and bound up his wounds, pouring in oil and wine, and set him on his own beast, and brought him to an inn, and took care of him. And on the morrow when he departed, he took out two pence, and gave them to the host, and said unto him, Take care of him; and whatsoever thou spendest more, when I come again, I will repay thee. Which now of these three, thinkest thou, was neighbour unto him that fell among the thieves? And he said, He that shewed mercy on him. Then said Jesus unto him, Go, and do thou likewise." The real point of this story lies in the fact that *neighbour* in "Love thy neighbour as thyself" had up to that time been interpreted by the Jews as applying only to an Israelite. Jesus, by making the hero a Samaritan, extended the application of the term to foreigners.

Did the Jews ever burn their dead?

Burial was the only normal method of disposing of the dead recognized by Hebrew law and custom, and cremation is still repugnant to orthodox Jews. Virtually all ancient peoples around the Mediterranean except the Egyptians and Hebrews burned their dead. Embalming and burial were practiced by the Egyptians because they believed the soul could not survive the dissolution of the body. Even the Chinese anciently burned their dead, a practice that they later abandoned in favor of burial. The Roman historian Tacitus thought it worthy of mention that the Jews buried instead of burned their dead in accordance with the almost universal practice of the time. Burial is first mentioned in the Bible in *Genesis 23*, where it is related that Abraham, after Sarah's death, paid Ephron the Hittite four hundred shekels of silver for the cave of Machpelah for a family burial place. Whether the Hebrews originally cremated their dead is not known. If they did, it is possible that Abraham, who had lived in Egypt, borrowed the burial custom from the Egyptians. Sometimes the

Israelites embalmed their dead after the Egyptian manner. When Jacob died in Egypt Joseph "commanded his servants the physicians to embalm his father: and the physicians embalmed Israel," after which Joseph took the body to Palestine for burial. Of Aristobulus, one of the Maccabees whom Pompey's partisans poisoned, Josephus says: "For a long while, he had not so much as a burial vouchsafed him in his own country; but his dead body lay, preserved in honey, until it was sent to the Jews by Antony, in order to be buried in the royal sepulchre." When Moses led the Israelites out of Egypt he took the body of Joseph with him. Even after the destruction of Jerusalem and the temple by the Romans in 70 A.D., many Jews scattered throughout the Empire continued to take their dead back to Judaea for burial. Belief in the resurrection of the body did much toward perpetuating the historic Hebrew practice of burying instead of burning the dead among both Jews and Christians. There are, however, references to cremation in the Old Testament. In *II Samuel 31:12-13* we are told that the valiant men burnt the bodies of Saul and his sons and buried the bones under a tree at Jabesh. *II Chronicles 16:14* says "they made a very great burning" for Asa, but the context shows it was not the king's body that was burned but the "sweet odours and divers kinds of spices prepared by the apothecaries' art" in which the body lay. This custom is alluded to by the prophet in *Jeremiah 34:5* when he tells King Zedekiah of Judah "thou shalt die in peace: and with the burnings of thy fathers, the former kings which were before thee, so shall they burn odours for thee." Apparently the bodies of criminals were sometimes cremated in Israel as a posthumous indignity or addition to the death penalty. According to *Joshua 7:25*, all Israel stoned Achan with stones "and burned them with fire, after they had stoned them with stones." *Leviticus 20:14* says: "And if a man take a wife and her mother, it is wickedness: they shall be burnt with fire, both he and they." *Leviticus 21:9* says: "And the daughter of any priest, if she profane herself by playing the whore, she profaneth her father: she shall be burnt with fire." These passages probably mean that the culprits were to be burnt after being stoned to death.

How did *maudlin* originate?

Maudlin, meaning "drunk to the point of silliness," is an English corruption of *Madgalene,* the surname of one of the most faithful followers of Jesus. She was one of the persons whom Jesus cured of some kind of infirmity. *Luke 8:1-3* says: "And it came to pass afterward, that he went throughout every city and village, preaching and shewing the glad tidings of the kingdom of God: and the twelve were with him, and certain women, which had been healed of evil spirits and infirmities, Mary called Magdalene, out of whom went seven devils, and Joanna the wife of Chuza Herod's steward, and Susanna, and many others, which ministered unto him of their substance." Elsewhere Mary Magdalene is mentioned in the New Testament only in connection with the crucifixion and the resurrection. *Matthew, Mark* and *John* say that Mary Magdalene was among the women who followed Jesus from Galilee and who witnessed the crucifixion from afar. According to the Gosepls, Mary Magdalene was also among the women who watched the burial of Jesus and who returned to the sepulchre early upon the first day of the week with spices and ointments, and according to *John* she was the first person to whom the risen Lord manifested himself. This is all that is positively known about Mary Magdalene. It is supposed she was so called because she was from a town named Magdala on the shores of the Sea of Galilee. According to tradition, Mary Magdalene was no other than the unnamed woman, mentioned in *Luke 7,* who was a sinner and who stood behind Jesus weeping, kissed his feet, washed them with her tears, wiped them with her hair and anointed them with ointment, while he ate meat in the house of Simon the Pharisee. Although the master of the house marveled that one who pretended to be a prophet should not know what manner of woman she was, Jesus forgave her sins and said, "Thy faith hath saved thee; go in peace." The association of Mary Magdalene with this unnamed woman no doubt arose from the common interpretion that the seven devils cast out of the former refer to immorality, which is sheer speculation. In Christian art Mary Magdalene is conventionally represented with a forlorn look on her face and with her eyes swollen and red from much weeping, which is based on *John 20,* where we are told that "Mary stood without at the sepulchre weeping and that first the two angels and then Jesus himself asked her, Woman, why weepest thou?" Because of the dubious association of the name of Mary Magdalene with the sinful woman, in England a reformed woman of ill-fame used to be called a *magdalen* and homes for such women were known as *magdalens.* The English pronounced and sometimes wrote this word *maudlin.* First it meant simply tearful or weeping in allusion to the repentant sinner, then effusively sentimental and finally drunk enough to be silly or demonstratively affectionate. The names of Magdalen College, Oxford, and Magdalene College, Cambridge, are widely pronounced *MAUD-lin* and in consequence the students of those schools are often made the butts of puns and jokes based on the name. Thus, by a strange trick of etymology and a fanciful theory, a word denoting a disgusting condition was corrupted from the beautiful surname of a woman who was healed of an infirmity by Jesus, who was one of his most faithful followers thereafter, who looked on when he was crucified, who saw him buried and who was the first to see him after he rose from the dead.

How did the Adam's apple get its name?

The Adam's apple, which is a movable projection or enlargement formed on the forepart of the human throat by the thyroid cartilage of the larynx, received its name from the old belief that when Adam ate the forbidden fruit, which is reputed to have been an apple, part of it lodged in his throat. The legend was apparently confirmed by the fact that the Adam's apple is much more prominent in men than in women. In the Japanese system of fighting known as jujitsu, the Adam's apple is one of several particular points singled out for attack by the assailant.

Did the Israelites believe in life after death?

There is not a single direct reference to the immortality of the soul, the resurrection of the body or future rewards and punishments in the five books of Moses, and there are very few allusions to these subjects in the entire Old Testament. The religion of the ancient Hebrews and Israelites was one of life, not death. They believed that a person received what he deserved while he was alive and that obedience and disobedience to God's will were rewarded and punished in this world. This is the more remarkable since the Israelites had lived for centuries among the Egyptians, who emphasized the after life in their religion. There are only hints in the Pentateuch that the Israelites may have had a vague conception of life beyond the grave. Although Abraham was buried far from his original home and people, according to *Genesis 25:8* he "was gathered to his people." The frequent occurrence of such death notices as "he slept with his fathers" and "he was gathered to his people" suggest a separation of body and soul at death and a reunion of those who had died. The later rabbis interpreted these as intimations of a belief in the immortality of the soul. Elijah's and Enoch's *translations* are other hints of a heaven as the abode of the dead. Even in the time of David and Solomon and centuries later the Israelites appear not to have looked beyond the grave. A blissful eternity or an everlasting torment was alien to their philosophy and religion. The Preacher, in *Ecclesiastes 3,* thought: "that which befalleth the sons of men befalleth beasts; even one thing befalleth them: as the one dieth, so dieth the other"; "all go unto one place: all are of the dust, and all turn to dust again," and "a man hath no preeminence above a beast." In *Ecclesiastes 9* the Preacher says: "For to him that is joined to all the living there is hope: for a living dog is better than a dead lion. For the living know that they shall die: but the dead know not anything, neither have they any more a reward." These passages indicate that the question of what becomes of man after death was discussed among the Israelites at an early date. Saul must have had some notion of a spirit world, for he was confident that the woman at Endor with a familiar spirit could call up the spirit of Samuel. In *Psalms, Isaiah, Job, Lamentations* and *Ezekiel* occur vague allusions to a nether world for the spirits of the dead, Sheol, hell, the pit and the place of silence and shadows. There are also hints of a better place after death, such as in *Psalms 73:24*: "Thou shalt guide me with thy counsel, and afterward receive me to glory." The Jews are believed to have acquired their belief in the Messiah and the resurrection of the body from the Persians and Babylonians during their exile. In *Job 19:25-26* the patriarch says: "For I know that my redeemer liveth, and that he shall stand at the latter day upon the earth: and though after my skin worms destroy this body, yet in my flesh shall I see God." *Daniel 12:2,* probably the latest part of the Old Testament, says: "And many of them that sleep in the dust of the earth shall awake, some to everlasting life, and some to shame and everlasting contempt." Similar allusions to a resurrection occur in *Isaiah 25.* The physical and spiritual in man were interwoven and the resurrection was dependent upon the coming of the Messiah. By the time of the Maccabees, when *Daniel* is believed to have been written, belief in the resurrection of the bodies of both the just and the unjust was almost universal among the Jews. About that time many of the Hellenistic Jews began to adopt the Greek idea of the immortality of the soul as distinguished from the resurrection. The two concepts are mutually exclusive. By the time of Jesus virtually all Jews believed in either the resurrection or in immortality, except the small group of Sadducees, who rejected both and adhered strictly to the Mosaic concept. Sometime between the writing of the last books of the Old Testament and of the first of the New the Pharisees had begun to teach that future rewards and punishments applied to the soul, not to the body, and that the righteous would be rewarded and the wicked punished in after life. After the Romans destroyed the Jewish commonwealth, Judaism began to emphasize Israel as "the kingdom of God" rather than as a nation. Technically orthodox Jews still believe in the resurrection and they do not emphasize the immortality of the soul as a doctrine, but the Reform Jews have adopted belief in immortality in place of the resurrection.

Was King Herod a Jew?

Herod the Great, who was king when Jesus was born, was a nominal Jew in religion but not in race. The founder of the Herod dynasty was an Idumaean named Antipas, who was governor of his province under Alexander Jannaeus, the Jewish king and high priest at Jerusalem. In 109 B.C. John Hyrcanus, then Jewish king and high priest, conquered Idumaea (Edom) and compelled the inhabitants to submit to circumcision and the Mosaic law. After that Idumaea was politically part of Judaea and the Idumaeans were nominally Jews. Josephus described them as "half-Jews." Antipater, the son of Antipas, after the Romans under Pompey conquered the country, played along with various Roman factions and became procurator of Judaea about 48 B.C. His son, Herod the Great, reigned as a Roman vassal from 37 B.C. to 4 B.C. He was the King Herod who rebuilt the temple, inquired about Jesus of the wise men and ordered the slaughter of the innocents. Herod the Great pretended friendliness toward the Jews in Judaea and to the Greeks and Romans in the rest of his rather extensive kingdom. Partly to strengthen his hold on the Jewish population, he married Mariamne, a princess of a line of Jewish kings and high priests. As a result of this marriage some of the later Herods were partly Jewish in blood as well as in religion. Three of the sons of Herod the Great are mentioned in the Bible. Archelaus was tetrarch of Judaea from shortly after his father's death until he was deposed by the Romans in 6 A.D. Disturbances attending his reign caused Joseph and Mary to take Jesus to Galilee instead of to Judaea when they returned from Egypt. A second son was tetrarch of Galilee and Perea throughout the adult life of Jesus. He figures largely in the Gospel narratives. This was the Herod who had John the Baptist beheaded because the prophet criticized him for marrying Herodias, the divorced wife of his brother Philip. Herodias was a daughter of Aristobulus, son of Herod the Great by Mariamne, and therefore part Jewish in blood. She was also a niece of both of her husbands, who were brothers. Herod Antipas was also the Herod whom Jesus alluded to in "that fox" and "the leaven of Herod." This Herod was "perplexed" about Jesus, and he questioned

Jesus at the final trial in Jerusalem. A third son of Herod the Great is mentioned in *Luke 3:1* as "Philip tetrarch of Ituraea and of the region of Trachonitis." This is presumably the Philip to whom Herodias was first married. From 41-44 A.D. Herod Agrippa I reigned as a Roman vassal over a Jewish kingdom almost as large as that of Solomon. He was a grandson of Herod the Great and Mariamne and therefore partly Jewish in blood. This "Herod the king" vexed certain of the church, slew the Apostle James and imprisoned Peter. *Acts 12:21-23* relates the manner of his death: "And upon a set day Herod, arrayed in royal apparel, sat upon his throne, and made an oration to them. And the people gave a shout, saying, It is the voice of a god, and not of a man. And immediately the angel of the Lord smote him, because he gave not God the glory; and he was eaten of worms, and gave up the ghost." One son, two daughters and a son-in-law of Herod Agrippa I are mentioned in the Bible. Herod Agrippa II was only seventeen when his father died, but the Romans later made him king of a small part of his father's domain. He was the Agrippa before whom Paul pleaded at Caesarea. Bernice, who was present on the occasion, was his sister. Another sister, Drusilla, "which was a Jewess," was the wife of the "most noble Felix," governor of Judaea, before whom Paul also appeared. After the destruction of Jerusalem in 70 A.D., Herod Agrippa, last of the Jewish kings, retired to Rome, where he is supposed to have lived until about 100 A.D. It seems that many of the Herod women were devout adherents of Judaism, but most of the Herod men were Romans first and Jews second.

When did the Israelites capture Jerusalem?

After Adonizedek, the Jebusite king of Jerusalem, and his four royal Canaanite allies were defeated and killed by Joshua, the Israelites apparently made no immediate attempt to capture Jerusalem. Under the name Jebus it remained the capital and stronghold of the Jebusites, a foreign fortress in the very heart of Israel. When the Promised Land was divided by lot among the twelve tribes, Jerusalem fell to Benjamin and lay on the very border of Judah. *Judges 1:21* says "the children of Benjamin did not drive out the Jebusites that inhabited Jerusalem." So Judah, aided by Simeon, tried to remove this enemy stronghold on its border. The children of Judah took the city, burned it and put many of the inhabitants to the sword, but they were unable to take the citadel on Mt. Zion. The result was that Jerusalem was rebuilt by the Jebusites and remained in their hands throughout the days of the judges and the reign of Saul. One of the first things that David did after becoming king of all Israel about the year 1000 B.C., was to attack and to take the city and citadel of Jerusalem. According to *I Chronicles 11:4-5*, "David and all Israel went to Jerusalem, which is Jebus," and "took the castle of Zion, which is the City of David." David had the ark of the covenant removed to Jerusalem and made that mountain stronghold his capital. When Solomon built the temple on Mount Moriah the Benjamin border was pushed back just far enough so that the sacred edifice stood entirely within Judah territory. A legend says that the temple was built on the very spot where Abraham offered his son, Isaac, as a burnt offering to the Lord. The capture of Jerusalem by David and the building of the temple there by Solomon made it, in the course of centuries, the Holy City of three great religions—Judaism, Christianity and Islam.

How did *Jerusalem* originate?

The origin of *Jerusalem* is not known for certain. It is generally derived from Hebrew *yarah*, "city," and *shalem*, "peace," and taken to signify "city of peace." In the Bible it is first mentioned under the name Salem. In *Genesis 14:18-20* we are told that "Melchizedek king of Salem," priest of the most high God, blessed Abraham and received tithes from him. But after the exodus from Egypt the place was called Jebus, after the Jebusites, a small but warlike tribe of Canannites who dwelt there and gave the Israelites considerable trouble. *Jerusalem* first occurs in *Joshua 10*, where it is related that Adonizedek, king of Jerusalem, made a league with four other kings to oppose the advance of the Israelites into their territory under Joshua. The Lord "cast down great stones from heaven upon them" and made the sun stand still in the midst of heaven about a whole day during the battle at Beth-horon, with the result that Joshua won a complete victory over the allies and put the five kings to death. Some authorities suppose *Jerusalem* is merely a corruption of *Jebus-Shalem*, but the cuneiform tablets found in 1888 in the ruins of Tel-el-Amarna in Egypt indicate that the place was known as *Uru-salim* in the fourteenth century, B.C. This name may mean "city of peace," but it is probable that it is of pre-Israelite origin and that its real significance is lost beyond recovery.

Have Jews lived in Jerusalem continuously?

Jerusalem has been without Israelite or Jewish inhabitants several times since David captured the city from the Jebusites more than twenty-eight hundred years ago. Since then the Holy City has suffered many sieges and captures and undergone numerous reconstructions.

In some places the level of the Jerusalem in the time of Jesus lies from twenty to eighty feet below the present surface, and the level of the city in the time of David and Solomon is buried still deeper. About 940 B.C., during the reign of Rehoboam, Solomon's son and successor, Shishak of Egypt captured the city and stripped it of much of its wealth. When Jehoram was king of Judah, perhaps about 845 B.C., the Philistines, Edomites and Arabians plundered Jerusalem. About 790 B.C. the northern kingdom of Israel under Joash took the city, plundered it, pulled down the walls, ravished the temple and carried "the treasures of God" to Samaria. Pharaoh Nechoh of Egypt subdued Judah about 600 B.C. and subjected it to tribute, although it is not clear that his army entered the capital. In 586 B.C. Nebuchadnezzar's Babylonians took Jerusalem by storm after a long siege, completely destroyed the temple, pulled down the walls, carried the inhabitants into captivity and left the city in ruins. For fifty years after this there were probably virtually no inhabitants on the site. In 586 B.C. a remnant of the captive Jews, under Persian protection, returned to Jerusalem and in the years following rebuilt the temple and the walls of the city and re-established a Jewish commonwealth. Ptolemy Soter, Greek king of Egypt, took Jerusalem in 320 B.C. In 203 B.C. it was taken by Antiochus, Greek king of Syria. After a revolt the city was retaken by his son Antiochus Epiphanes in 169 B.C. Pompey's Roman legions captured it in 63 B.C. after a long siege. In 41 B.C. the Parthians occupied it for a brief time. Three years later Herod besieged and captured Jerusalem with a Roman army. At the close of the Jewish rebellion of 66-70 the Romans under Titus razed the temple and city and ploughed under the ground. For years after this Jews were banned from Jerusalem and could not even visit the site without special permission. It was probably virtually without inhabitants for the next fifty years, for there is no mention of it in history. Later, however, it was rebuilt and some Jews drifted back. In 132-135 A.D. the Jews in Palestine made their last attempt to throw off the Roman yoke and to rebuild the temple. This uprising was led by Bar Cockhba, who was proclaimed the Messiah and whose forces temporarily occupied Jerusalem. The Romans crushed the rebellion with terrific slaughter and again banned Jews from approaching the site of the Holy City. Later Emperor Hadrian built a pagan city on the site and named it Aelia Capitolina. A temple to Jupiter was erected on the temple site and no Jew was permitted to enter the city. Of course, Jews who had become Christians were permitted to live there. The ban against Jews in Jerusalem remained in effect until the Roman Empire became dominantly Christian. Constantine the Great, the first Christian emperor, restored the ancient name about 336 A.D., and his mother, Helena, visited the city and did much toward making it the Holy City of Christianity. In 362 A.D. Julian, the last pagan emperor, who hated the Christians, undertook to rebuild the Jewish temple and make the city once more a Jewish center, but it is said his efforts were defeated by earthquakes and mysterious subterranean fires. About 529 A.D. Emperor Justinian built a church in Jerusalem and Christians began to make pilgrimages to the city. In 614 A. D. Chosroes II of Persia captured Jerusalem, demolished the churches and slew many priests and monks. Fourteen years later the Eastern Emperor Heraclius retook Jerusalem and again made it a Christian city. In 637 A.D. Caliph Omar and his Arab host took Jerusalem, which was regarded almost as sacred in Moslem eyes as Mecca and Medina. According to Moslem legend, Mohammed was translated into heaven at Jerusalem. The Arabs made it the first *quibleh,* "point of adoration," and named it *El Quds,* "the Holy." At first the Christians were not molested by the Arabs, but later they were pillaged by various petty Arab rulers. In 1099 the Crusaders captured Jerusalem and it became the capital of a small Christian kingdom. Benjamin of Tudela, the Jewish traveler, reported in 1170 A.D. that he found only about fifteen hundred Jews in all Judaea. Saladin defeated the Christians and took Jerusalem in 1187 A.D. When Moses ben Nahman Girondi visited Jerusalem in 1267 A.D. the only Jews in the city were two families of dyers. He had an old synagogue rebuilt, established a rabbinical college and induced Jewish families to settle there. A considerable number of Jews from central Europe began to emigrate to Jerusalem in the fifteenth and sixteenth centuries, as did also many of those who had been expelled from Spain and Portugal. By 1600 A.D. the number of Jews in Jerusalem was several thousand. The Jewish population of Jerusalem began to increase more rapidly after 1880 when Jewish immigration into Palestine began on a considerable scale. A census taken in 1939 gave Jerusalem a total population of 129,800, 79,000 of whom were Jews. In view of this record, it is small wonder scholars and investigators find it hard to identify places in Jerusalem mentioned in the Bible.

Does *charity* occur in the Old Testament?

Charity occurs nowhere in the Old Testament. Neither does it occur in the Four Gospels or in the *Acts of the Apostles. Charity* is derived from Latin *caritas,* meaning "dearness" or "high esteem." It found its way into the English Bible from the Latin Vulgate in which *caritas* was often employed to render a Greek word meaning "love," particularly love for one's fellow men. In the King James Version *charity* is employed to translate this Greek word for love in some twenty-eight passages in the Epistles and *Revelation.* St. Paul, in *I Corinthians 13:13,* says: "And now abideth faith, hope, charity, these three; but the greatest of these is charity." Here *love* would more approximate the meaning of the original, because in modern English *charity* is not synonymous with *love* in the broad sense of the Greek word.

What book of the Bible was burned when published?

The original version of *The Book of the Prophet Jeremiah* was officially burned by the king of Judah when it was first published. During Jehoiakim's reign, Jeremiah prophesied that Nebuchadnezzar, whose army was besieging Jerusalem, would destroy the city and carry the king to Babylon. He also advised acceptance of the terms offered by the Chaldeans as the only practical guarantee of safety. Although Jeremiah's motives were good, he was charged with being an appeaser and shut up in the state prison attached to the palace. The prophet then dictated everything he had said to his secretary, Baruch, who wrote them "with ink" in the "roll of a book." Since Jeremiah's own liberty was restricted, he sent Baruch to the temple to read the book in the ears of all the people. Michaiah, who heard the book read, reported the incident to the king's counselors, who directed Jehudi to bring Baruch before them. After having Baruch read the book to them, the counselors told Baruch to hide and to tell Jeremiah to do likewise. Then they went in and read the roll to the king and all the princes who stood beside him. The pathetic story of the burning of Jeremiah's book is told in *Jeremiah 36:22-23*: "Now the king sat in the winterhouse in the ninth month: and there was a fire on the hearth burning before him. And it came to pass, that when Jehudi had read three or four leaves, he cut it with the penknife, and cast it into the fire that was on the hearth, until all the roll was consumed in the fire that was on the hearth." Elnathan, Delaiah and Gemariah begged King Jehoiakim not to burn the book, "but he would not hear them," and commanded three officials "to take Baruch the scribe and Jeremiah the prophet: but the Lord hid them." Fortunately Jeremiah's book was not lost to posterity. The prophet and his scribe, with the Lord's help, defeated the purpose of the book-burners. *Jeremiah 36:32* concludes the story: "Then took Jeremiah another roll, and gave it to Baruch the scribe, the son of Neriah; who wrote therein from the mouth of Jeremiah all the words of the book which Jehoiakim king of Judah had burned in the fire: and there were added besides unto them many like words." The present book of *Jeremiah* is believed to contain the substance of the second book dictated by Jeremiah to Baruch. The only other reference to burning of books in the Bible is *Acts 19:19,* where it is related that, after hearing Paul preach, many of those at Ephesus "which used curious arts brought their books together, and burned them before all men: and they counted the price of them, and found it fifty thousand pieces of silver." This book burning, however, was voluntary.

Did the Israelites practice kissing?

Kissing on the lips between the sexes as it is known today is a product of Western civilization. Europeans are believed to have taught the world the kiss of affection and passion. Apparently it began in the early stages of Caucasian culture but developed very slowly. There is nothing in the Bible to indicate that it was known among the ancient Israelites or their neighbors. The Israelites kissed one another on the cheek, forehead, neck, hands and feet, but not on the lips. *Proverbs 24:26* says, "Every man shall kiss his lips that giveth a right answer," but that is believed to be a faulty translation. In *Proverbs 7:13* Solomon may have hinted at the kiss of passion when he said the woman attired like a harlot caught the young man void of understanding and kissed him; but even that may be an allusion only to the customary kiss of greeting prevalent in that part of the world. In the Bible the kiss is the token of many different sentiments, such as friendship, reverence, homage, greeting, sorrow at parting, adoration and worship. Aaron kissed his brother, Moses, when he met him in the mount of God; Moses kissed his father-in-law, Jethro; Isaac asked Jacob to kiss him before receiving his blessing; Laban embraced and kissed Jacob and kissed his sons and daughters; Jacob kissed Rachel when he first met her at the well; he also "kissed all his brethren" as well as Joseph's sons; Naomi kissed her daughters-in-law, and Orpah kissed her mother-in-law, but Ruth "clave unto her"; Samuel kissed Saul when he anointed him; David and Jonathan "kissed one another"; David kissed his son, Absalom, while Absalom "kissed any man that came nigh unto him"; in the Pharisee's house the woman that was a sinner kissed the feet of Jesus; the prodigal son's father "fell on his neck, and kissed him"; at Ephesus Paul's followers fell on his neck and kissed him; Paul several times admonishes the faithful to salute or greet one another with a holy kiss, and the author of *I*

Peter asks those addressed to greet one another with "a kiss of charity." All these references are to formal kisses of friendship or salutation. Until they came in contact with Europeans, the North and South American Indians, the Orientals, the Negroes of Africa, the Malays and the Polynesians not only did not practice kissing between the sexes but looked upon it with disgust. Richard Steele, the British essayist, speaking of the kiss of intimate affection, declared that "nature was its author and it began with the first courtship." But the fact that lip kissing is unknown even today to millions of the inhabitants of the earth disproves the common notion that it is the natural way of expressing physical love and kindred emotions. Cato, according to Pliny, believed that husbands started kissing to determine whether their wives had been imbibing wine! Some peoples, including the Eskimos and Polynesians, practice what is known as pressing or rubbing noses, but this practice, while it may be related to the kiss of salutation, bears no relationship to the kiss of affection and passion between sexes.

What are phylacteries?

In *Matthew 23:5* Jesus is quoted as saying that the Pharisees and scribes, to be seen of men, "make broad their phylacteries, and enlarge the borders of their garments." Phylactery (pronounced *fi-LACK-ter-i*) is derived from Greek and literally signifies "means of preservation," "amulet" or "charm." The phylacteries referred to by Jesus were small cases containing strips of parchment inscribed with scriptural texts and worn on the persons of pious Jews. They have a curious history. *Exodus 13:9* says: "And it shall be for a sign unto thee upon thine hand, and for a memorial between thine eyes, that the Lord's law may be in thy mouth: for with a strong hand hath the Lord brought thee out of Egypt." *Exodus 13:16* says: "And it shall be for a token upon thine hand, and for frontlets between thine eyes." *Numbers 15:38-39* says in part: "Speak unto the children of Israel, and bid them that they make them fringes in the borders of their garments throughout their generations, and that they put upon the fringe of the borders a ribband of blue: and it shall be unto you for a fringe, that ye may look upon it, and remember all the commandments of the Lord, and do them." Speaking of the commandments, statutes and judgments of the Lord, *Deuteronomy 6:8-9* says: "And thou shalt bind them for a sign upon thine hand, and they shall be as frontlets between thine eyes. And thou shalt write them upon the posts of thy house, and on thy gates." Again in *Deuteronomy 11:18*: "Therefore shall ye lay up these my words in your heart and in your soul, and bind them for a sign upon your hand, that they may be as frontlets between your eyes." There appears to be no evidence that the ancient Israelites interpreted these passages literally and wore anything corresponding to phylacteries. But about the second century B.C. the Jews began to construe them literally and to wear scriptural passages on their persons. The New Testament reference suggests that in the time of Jesus some of the Jews wore unusually large phylacteries and fringes for purposes of display and ostentation, as if the size of the sacred devices was a badge of importance and distinction. The Jews call these reminders on the arm and forehead *tephillin,* the plural of a Hebrew word variously believed to mean "prayer" or "prayer-band." Talmudic law directs every male Jew who has attained his religious majority—thirteen—to wear tephillin at morning prayers except on Sabbaths and festivals. The tephillin consists of two leather pouches attached by bands to the head and the arm. Four parchments in the pouches contain four sections of the Torah—*Exodus 13:1-10, Exodus 13:11-16, Deuteronomy 4:4-9,* and *Deuteronomy 9:13-21*—which are said to epitomize the Mosaic law and contain the fundamental doctrines of Judaism, namely, the kingdom of heaven, unity of the creator and the exodus from Egypt. The fringed four-cornered shawl and the parchments placed on the door are associated in origin and significance with the same ritual.

Do the Jews practice baptism?

Baptism of converts in living water is of Jewish origin. Purificatory washings played an important part in the rites of the Hebrew religion from earliest times. The fact that John the Baptist began his public ministry by baptizing in the Jordan appears to have attracted no special attention among the Jews. Yet the fact that he became known as "the Baptist" suggests that the kind of baptism he practiced was different from that generally prevalent in Judaea. While the Jews had baptized only Gentiles who became converts to Judaism, John baptized Jews as a symbol of their spiritual regeneration. His baptism apparently was performed on each individual only once in life and therefore differed from the periodic purificatory washings of the Jews. It symbolized a change in heart through repentance and a cleansing or rebirth preparatory to entrance into the kingdom of God that the Baptist proclaimed as being nigh at hand. The ancient Jewish rite known as Jewish baptism or proselyte baptism naturally bears a striking similarity to Christian baptism, of which it was undoubtedly the forerunner, but it differed in significance. When a pagan became a convert to Judaism he was required, after submission to the Abrahamic rite of circumcision, to go through a purificatory washing, which symbolized the removal of all pagan impurity. No stranger who sojourned among the Israelites could become completely one of them without complying with this rite of baptism. Although baptism as it is understood by Christians is not practiced by Jews today, orthodox Jews still require the purificatory washing when Gentiles become converts to Judaism. But in Judaism it is circumcision rather than the rite of baptism that corresponds to Christian baptism as a symbol of conversion.

Can a Christian become a Jew?

Christians and other Gentiles may and do become Jews in the religious sense. Orthodox Judaism recognizes two classes of proselytes. A proselyte of the gate (from "stranger that is within thy gates") is a Gentile who accepts the Noachian laws of humanity and adheres to Jewish law and custom but who remains outside of Jewish religious life. Such proselytes are sometimes called "half-Jews." A proselyte of righteousness (or justice) is a Gentile who submits to circumcision, undergoes baptismal purification, adheres to the entire Jewish law and agrees to rear children in the tenets of the Jewish faith. No distinction whatever is made between a born Jew and a proselyte of righteousness. The Reform or Liberal Jews do not require circumcision. From the earliest days the Israelites accepted proselytes of the gate, who generally were aliens who lived in Palestine or in neighboring countries. Ruth, a Moabitess, entered the fold of Israel and became the ancestress of David. It was, however, always easier for a Gentile woman than for a Gentile man to enter the house of Israel through marriage. Many of the great men in the Bible married foreign women. During the Babylonian captivity the Jews became a religious rather than a national community and proselytizing became common. We are told in *Esther 8:17* that "many of the people of the land became Jews." Jonah carried the message of the Lord to the Gentiles of Nineveh. Several of the prophets alluded to the universal mission of Israel and forecast the time when the whole world would recognize the God of Israel. Isaiah obviously anticipated the salvation of the Gentiles through the Messiah and adherence to Judaism. *Isaiah 49:6* says in part: "I will also give thee for a light to the Gentiles, that thou mayest be my salvation unto the end of the earth." In 109 B.C., during the Maccabean period, King John Hyrcanus of Judaea subdued

Idumaea and compelled the inhabitants to be circumcised and to adhere to Judaism or to leave their country. "They were hereafter no other than Jews," wrote Josephus. Throughout the early Greek and Roman dominance of Palestine the Jews carried on an extensive proselytizing propaganda and made many converts to their faith, particularly among the Greeks, who were especially attracted by the synagogue services and the one day of rest out of seven. Even during the height of the Jewish persecutions under Nero, Domitian and Hadrian, many Romans, some of them of high social standing, became Jewish proselytes. In *Matthew 23:15* Jesus tells the scribes and Pharisees that they "compass sea and land to make one proselyte," and rabbinical authorities say in those days it was a rule for zealous Jews to try to make at least one proselyte each year. For a considerable period after the crucifixion of Jesus the Romans regarded the Christians merely as a Jewish sect that was more active than other Jews in making proselytes among Gentiles. In fact the early Jewish Christians at Jerusalem insisted that Gentiles must submit to circumcision and adhere to Judaism before they could be full-fledged members of the Christian community. They still believed that the only way into the kingdom of heaven was through Judaism as modified by the teachings of Jesus. Proselytizing by the Jews was checked first by the Roman state and then by the Christian church. Rome in Domitian's time forbade Jews to circumcise anybody but members of their own race. Because of interference proselytizing activity among the Jews was gradually discontinued until today it is virtually non-existent.

What did Josephus say about Jesus?

In Book XVIII of our present copies of Josephus's *Antiquities of the Jews* occurs this passage: "Now there was about this time Jesus, a wise man, if it be lawful to call him a man; for he was a doer of wonderful works, a teacher of such men as receive the truth with pleasure. He drew over to him both many of the Jews, and many of the Gentiles. He was Christ. And when Pilate, at the suggestion of the principal men amongst us, had condemned him to the cross, those that loved him at the first did not forsake him: for he appeared to them alive again the third day; as the divine prophets had foretold these and ten thousand other wonderful things concerning him. And the tribe of Christians, so named from him, are not extinct at this day." In Book XX of the same work Josephus wrote, according to present copies, that Ananus, the high priest at Jerusalem, "assembled the sanhedrin of judges, and brought before them the brother of Jesus, who was called Christ, whose name was James, and some others; and when he had formed an accusation against them as breakers of the law, he delivered them to be stoned." Whether these references to Jesus in Josephus are genuine or merely later Christian interpolations has been the subject of a long and spirited controversy not yet definitely settled. Some authorities state flatly that these passages were not in the original copies of Josephus, while others insist that they were. The one about James, the brother of Jesus, was mentioned by Origen about 230 A.D., and the one about Jesus was mentioned by Eusebius about 324 A.D. Since no original copies of Josephus are known to be extant, and since there are no known contemporaneous quotations of the passages, the point cannot be determined for certain. If the passages are genuine, they are the earliest references to Jesus in secular writings, for the brief mentions of Christ and the Christians in Tacitus and Suetonius are of somewhat later date. The writings of Josephus, like the New Testament itself, were handed down for nearly fifteen hundred years in manuscript before the invention of printing. During all that time, and much longer, Josephus was copied by generation after generation of scribes and naturally many errors, interpolations and alterations crept into his works. What seems probable is that Josephus in his original copies did refer to Jesus and his brother James, as well as John the Baptist. When Josephus wrote about 93 A.D. Christians must have become quite numerous in the Roman Empire. Paul had long since completed his missionary work and much of the New Testament had been written by that time. There is nothing improbable in the belief that the historian of the Jews, who had been born and brought up in Jerusalem, made brief mention of the rising sect among the Jews and of their founder. In fact it would be strange if he had failed to do so. But it is equally probable that what Josephus wrote on this subject was later altered either accidentally or deliberately by Christian editors, for the passage about Jesus in particular, as it now stands, does not ring true in all details. It is highly improbable that Josephus described Jesus as "a wise man, if it be lawful to call him a man," or that he stated positively that Jesus was the Christ. Some authorities go even so far as to contend from internal evidence in his writings that Josephus himself became a Christian in his latter days, but this is entirely conjectural and very doubtful. All evidence points to the conclusion that Josephus, though a Roman citizen and liberal in his views, was born, lived and died in the Jewish faith. Whatever the truth, the references to Jesus, James and John the Baptist have done more to preserve and popularize the writings of

Josephus than any other one factor. Generally speaking, Christians give more credence to the great Jewish historian than do the Jews themselves.

Did the Catholic church ever baptize by immersion?

Baptism in the Latin or Roman Catholic church was originally by immersion and that method prevailed until about the twelfth century. In some places individual Catholic churches continued to baptize by immersion until a few hundred years ago. According to the ritual now authorized by the Catholic church baptism is performed by laving the candidate's head. Immersion is unquestionably the most ancient form of Christian baptism. *Baptism* is derived from Greek *baptizein,* which may signify either "to immerse" or "to wash," and which occurs in the Old Testament only in the Septuagint Version of *II Kings 5:14,* where it is related that Naaman, the Syrian leper, "*dipped* himself seven times in Jordan." *Matthew 3:16* tells us that Jesus, when he was baptized by John, "went up straightway out of the water." In *John 3:23* we are told that "John also was baptizing in Aenon near to Salim, because there was much water there."

How did swearing on the Bible originate?

Putting the hand on the Bible while taking an oath is indirectly of Jewish origin. In the earliest times the Hebrews probably touched some sacred object, such as a pillar of stone or altar dedicated to Jehovah, when taking solemn oaths. Later the Jews swore by touching their phylacteries or by placing a hand on the roll of the law. Defendants in legal proceedings were required to take an oath, but oaths in the modern sense were never administered to Hebrew witnesses. According to *Genesis 14:22,* when Abram swore to the king of Sodom he lifted up his hand unto the Lord. *Genesis 24:2* tells us that Abraham required his eldest servant to put his hand under his thigh when he swore, which may be a survival of phallic worship. The Mosaic law emphasizes the sinfulness of swearing falsely and the importance of keeping an oath after making it. Jephthah, according to *Judges 11:35,* sacrificed his only child because he had opened his mouth unto the Lord and could not go back. From *Matthew 14:7* we learn that Herod delivered the head of John the Baptist to the daughter of Herodias "for the oath's sake." Oaths were common among the Israelites and even Jehovah confirmed his promises with oaths. The oath is a solemn invocation of God to bear witness to the honesty of one's motives in making a promise. But in later times oaths were made so freely and recklessly that some of the Jewish philosophers questioned the wisdom of making oaths at all. This abuse of oaths was referred to by Jesus in *Matthew 5:33-37,* when he said: "Again, ye have heard that it hath been said by them of old time, Thou shalt not forswear thyself, but shalt perform unto the Lord thine oaths: but I say unto you, Swear not at all; either by heaven; for it is God's throne; nor by the earth; for it is his footstool: neither by Jerusalem; for it is the city of the great King. Neither shalt thou swear by thy head, because thou canst not make one hair white or black. But let your communication be, Yea, yea; Nay, nay: for whatsoever is more than these cometh of evil." *James 5:12* says: "But above all things, my brethren, swear not, neither by heaven, neither by the earth, neither by any other oath: but let your yea be yea; and your nay, nay; lest ye fall into condemnation." Members of several Christian sects interpret these and other passages literally and refuse to take oaths of any kind. The custom of taking oaths, however, had become so widespread and was so firmly fixed that Christians generally adopted it. Kissing the cross to attest an oath is believed to have started in Russia and to have spread to other parts of Europe. During the Middle Ages persons taking an oath were required to touch a prayer book, missal, New Testament, the Gospels or the whole Bible. Since these sacred books generally bore a cross as the symbol of Christianity the next step was to require the kissing of the book. To confirm an oath the Israelites used such expressions as "Jehovah is a witness between me and thee forever"; "God do so to me and more also"; "As Jehovah liveth"; and "Amen, Amen."

Why was straw used in bricks?

"To make bricks without straw" means to do something without the necessary material. In *Exodus I* it is related that the new king of Egypt who knew not Joseph set taskmasters over the Israelites to afflict them with their burdens and to build "treasure cities." The Egyptians made the children of Israel "to serve with rigour" and made "their lives bitter with hard bondage, in morter, and in brick, and in all manner of service in the field." Because Moses and Aaron asked permission to take their people three days' journey into the wilderness to worship the Lord, Pharaoh, according to *Exodus 5:7-8,* accused them of idleness and commanded the taskmasters: "Ye shall no more give the people straw to make brick, as heretofore: let them go and gather straw for themselves. And the tale of bricks, which they did make heretofore, ye shall lay upon them; ye shall not diminish ought thereof." After that the Israelites "were scattered abroad throughout all the land of Egypt to gather stubble instead of straw." The context indicates that it required a great deal more labor to prepare the stubble than the straw for the bricks. Straw or stubble is not used in the modern brick-making process. Ancient Egyptian bricks were made of Nile mud and it has generally been assumed that straw was used as a binder to hold the sun-dried bricks together. It is now known, however, that the straw was not used as a binder at all. The Hebrew word rendered *straw* does not mean straw in the modern sense of the English word, but rather stalks of grain broken, chopped or cut into short pieces. The Hebrew word rendered stubble signifies dry field rubbish, twigs, stems, roots of withered grass or chaff. It is easy to see that more work would be required to provide such stubble than to provide such straw, but it is hard to see how such stubble would serve as an effective binding material in making sun-dried bricks. Close examination of ancient Egyptian bricks shows that the straw in them was shredded and chopped fine and could not have acted as a binder. In recent years scientists have discovered that chopped straw and stubble were used in ancient brick because it is a source of tannic acid, which tempers clay and gives it consistency. Treating clay with tannin is now a valuable commercial process and is known as "Egyptianizing clay." Tannic acid in the clay increases the strength of bricks, reduces breakage and generally improves their quality. The Egyptians also tempered their pottery with finely chopped stubble, and some of the North American Indians achieved the same results with grass and bark fiber.

Who were the scribes?

Scribe is from Latin *scribere,* "to write," and is used in the English Bible to render Hebrew *sopher,* "writer." Apparently at first in ancient Israel the scribes were merely Levites and priests who could write and who acted as clerks, copyists, editors and students of the sacred writings. By virtue of their ability to write they naturally in the course of time became the annalists, chroniclers, secretaries, interpreters of the scriptures, expounders of the law, and ultimately lawyers in the sense of being doctors and teachers of the law. But in the Old Testament the term does not always refer to persons with the same functions. Some of the scribes were men of princely rank and members of the king's official family. According to *II Samuel* Sheva and Seraiah were the scribes in David's time. "Shebna the scribe, and Joah the son of Asaph, the recorder" are mentioned in *II Kings 18:18.* Perhaps some of the scribes were bookkeepers and auditors, for in *II Kings*

22:3 we are told that King Josiah sent Shaphan, the scribe, to tell the high priest to sum the silver brought into the house of the Lord. According to *I Chronicles 27:32*, "Jonathan David's uncle was a counsellor, a wise man, and a scribe." *Ezra 4:8* says "Rehum the chancellor and Shimshai the scribe wrote a letter against Jerusalem to Artaxerxes the king." Baruch the scribe seems to have acted as amanuensis to the prophet, for we are told in *Jeremiah 36:4*: "Then Jeremiah called Baruch, the son of Neriah: and Baruch wrote from the mouth of Jeremiah all the words of the Lord, which he had spoken unto him, upon a roll of a book." *Ezra 7:6* says: "This Ezra went up from Babylon; and he was a ready scribe in the law of Moses, which the Lord God of Israel had given." This last reference seems to accord somewhat with the use of the word in the New Testament, where the scribes are often linked with the Pharisees as the upholders of Jewish tradition and ceremony. It appears that during the Babylonian captivity and the early Greek period in Palestine the scribes developed into a class of men who devoted themselves to the study and exposition of the law and consequently became its professional interpreters. By New Testament times many of the scribes were probably the equivalent of modern jurists, because under the theocracy there was little distinction between secular and sacred law. Some of them had places in the judicial courts and others occupied seats in the Sanhedrin. It is supposed that they did not receive pay for their services as scribes but had to making their living by other work if they were without private means. Jesus often coupled the scribes and the Pharisees together in his condemnations, and the scribes were among his most persistent enemies. *Matthew 23:2* says that Jesus told the multitude and his disciples that "The scribes and the Pharisees sit in Moses' seat: All therefore whatsoever they bid you observe, that observe and do; but do not ye after their works: for they say, and do not." According to *Luke 20:46-47* Jesus in the audience of all the people said: "Beware of the scribes, which desire to walk in long robes, and love greetings in the markets, and the highest seats in the synagogues, and the chief rooms at feasts; which devour widows' houses, and for a shew make long prayers: the same shall receive greater damnation." *Matthew 5:20* quotes Jesus as saying: "That except your righteousness shall exceed the righteousness of the scribes and Pharisees, ye shall in no case enter into the kingdom of heaven." *Matthew 22:34-36* says: "But when the Pharisees had heard that he had put the Sadducees to silence, they were gathered together. Then one of them, which was a lawyer, asked him a question, tempting him, and saying, Master, which is the great commandment in the law?" *Mark 12:28* says: "And one of the scribes came, and having heard them reasoning together and perceiving that he had answered them well, asked him, Which is the first commandment of all?" "For he taught them as one having authority, and not as the scribes," says *Matthew 7:29.* According to *Matthew 23:15,* Jesus said: "Woe unto you, scribes and Pharisees, hypocrites! for ye compass sea and land to make one proselyte, and when he is made, ye make him twofold more the child of hell than yourselves." *Mark 2:16* says: "And when the scribes and Pharisees saw him eat with publicans and sinners, they said to his disciples, How is it that he eateth and drinketh with publicans and sinners?" And *Luke 5:30,* referring to the same occasion, says "but their scribes and Pharisees murmured against his disciples." Apparently *doctor of the law* and *teacher of the law* in the New Testament mean about the same as *scribe.* There is probably only a shade of difference in meaning between *lawyer* and *scribe* in the Bible. *Luke 5:17* says: "And it came to pass on a certain day, as he was teaching, that there were Pharisees and doctors of the law sitting by, which were come out of every town of Galilee, and Judaea, and Jerusalem." But in *Acts 5:34* Gamaliel, a Pharisee who had been Paul's teacher, is referred to as "a doctor of the law." *Matthew 16:21* says: "From that time forth began Jesus to shew unto his disciples, how that he must go unto Jerusalem, and suffer many things of the elders and chief priests and scribes, and be killed, and be raised again the third day." *Matthew 21:15* says: "And when the chief priests and scribes saw the wonderful things that he did, and the children crying in the temple, and saying, Hosanna to the Son of David; they were sore displeased." *Mark 14:1-2* tells us: "After two days was the feast of the passover, and of unleavened bread: and the chief priests and the scribes sought how they might take him by craft, and put him to death. But they said, Not on the feast day, lest there be an uproar of the people." When Jesus was before Herod, according to *Luke 23:10,* "the chief priests and scribes stood and vehemently accused him." The scribes persisted in their persecution of Jesus to the end. *Matthew 27:41-43* says: "Likewise also the chief priests mocking him, with the scribes and elders, said, He saved others; himself he cannot save. If he be the King of Israel, let him now come down from the cross, and we will believe him. He trusted in God; let him deliver him now, if he will have him: for he said, I am the Son of God." We read of little more about the scribes in the New Testament. It appears that a person could be a scribe and at the same time a Pharisee or a Sadducee. The Pharisees believed in the resurrection, while the Sadducees did not. Accordingly, after the crucifixion of Jesus, some of the Pharisees were inclined to be more lenient toward the believers in Jesus as the Christ than were the Sadducees. *Acts 23:9,* referring to Paul's appearance before the council in Jerusalem, says: "And there arose a great cry: and the scribes that were of the Pharisees' part arose, and strove, saying, We find no evil in this man: but if a spirit or an angel hath spoken to him, let us not fight against God." This is taken by some to signify that there were also scribes representing the Sadducees, who at that particular time may have been in control of the Sanhedrin. Long afterwards, in *I Corinthians 1:20* Paul asked: "Where is the wise? where is the scribe? where is the disputer of this world? hath not God made foolish the wisdom of this world?" Under the Hebrew legal system there were no lawyers, advocates or solicitors—either private or state—in the modern sense of professional persons who accept fees to prosecute or defend cases. There had to be at least three judges in each case and they acted as judges, jurors, prosecutors and defense counsel.

Is *wheels within wheels* in the Bible?

Wheels within wheels has been a common English phrase since the seventeenth century. It is not in the Bible, but is believed to have been suggested by *Ezekiel 1:16,* which reads: "The appearance of the wheels and their work was like unto the colour of a beryl: and they four had one likeness: and their appearance and their work was as it were a wheel in the middle of a wheel." The prophet employs the same comparison in *Ezekiel 10:10*: "And as for their appearance, they four had one likeness, as if a wheel had been in the midst of a wheel."

Did the Jews originate the idea of a regular rest day?

The ancient Hebrews gave to the world, if they did not actually invent, the seven-day week with one day of rest. The ancient Assyrians observed the seventh, fourteenth, twenty-first and twenty-eighth day of each lunar month as rest days, but it is not known whether they borrowed the idea from the Hebrews or the Hebrews borrowed it from them. A regular rest day was unknown to the classical world. Adoption by the early Christians of the Jewish seven-day week with one rest day out of every seven has had immense religious, moral, social and economic effects upon human society. This proportion of one day's rest in seven, which now prevails throughout the world, appears to be justified by thousands of years of experience. The first French Republic substituted one day of rest in ten, and Soviet Russia one in five, but these attempts to change the historic Jewish system were not particularly successful. *Sabbath* is from a Hebrew root meaning "desisting from" or "rest." *Genesis 2:3* says "God blessed the seventh day, and sanctified it: because that in it he had rested from all his work which God created and made." According to *Exodus 20:11,* when Moses ordained Sabbath observance he based it on the fact that the Lord made the heaven and earth in six days and rested on the seventh; but in *Deuteronomy 5:15* the Sabbath seems to be associated with the deliverance of the Israelites from bondage in Egypt.

What does *sister-in-law* in the Bible mean?

Many authorities restrict the term *sister-in-law* to mean the sister of one's husband or wife, or the wife of one's brother. Strictly speaking, two women who marry brothers do not thereby become sisters-in-law. Popular usage, however, ignores this restriction and in common English and American usage *sister-in-law* also includes the wife of one's wife's or husband's brother. It is so used by the translators of the King James Version in the only passage in which the term occurs. According to *Ruth I,* Orpah and Ruth, two Moabites who were probably not related by blood, married the two sons of Naomi; that is, they married brothers. In *Verse 15* of that Chapter Naomi says to Ruth: "Behold, thy sister in law is gone back unto her people, and unto her gods: return thou after thy sister in law." The same general principle applies to the use of *brother-in-law,* which does not occur in the English Bible. According to the restricted definition, a brother-in-law is the brother of one's husband or wife, or the husband of one's sister. According to this definition, when two men marry sisters they do not thereby become brothers-in-law. But here again popular usage ignores the restricted definition and the term is extended to include the husband of one's wife's or husband's sister.

Why did the patriarchs live so long?

The chronologies, genealogies and ages in the Old Testament present many problems that have never been satisfactorily solved. None of the various theories offered to explain the great ages of the patriarchs in the Bible are entirely adequate. Whether this longevity was supposed to be peculiar to those individuals named or was common to all men in those days is unknown. Some of the remarkable antedeluvian ages are as follows: Adam, 930 years; Seth,

912; Enos, 905; Cainan, 910; Mahalaleel, 895; Jared, 962; Enoch, 365; Methuselah, the oldest of all, 969; Lamech, 777; Noah, 950; and Shem, 600. This is particularly curious in view of the fact that in *Genesis 6:3* the Lord said the days of man "shall be an hundred and twenty years." Some of the remarkable post-deluvian ages are as follows: Abraham, 175 years; Isaac, 180; Ishmael, 137; Jacob, 147; Joseph, 110; Moses, 120; and Aaron, 123. When Jacob was 130 Pharaoh asked him how old he was and the patriarch replied: "Few and evil have been the days of the years of my life." *Deuteronomy 34:7* says: "Moses was a hundred and twenty years old when he died: his eye was not dim, nor his natural force abated." In his *Antiquities of the Jews* Josephus wrote: "Now Terah hating Chaldea, on account of his mourning for Haran, they all removed to Haran of Mesopotamia, where Terah died, and was buried, when he had lived to be two hundred and five years old; for the life of man was already, by degrees, diminished, and became shorter than before, till the birth of Moses; after whom the term of human life was one hundred and twenty years; God determining it to the length that Moses happened to live." Yet *Psalms 90:10* says: "The days of our years are threescore years and ten; and if by reason of strength they be fourscore years, yet is their strength labour and sorrow." The Old Testament is very age conscious and its genealogies frequently give ages; but very few ages are given in the New Testament. One writer explains the great ages in the Bible by saying that before the flood, when human beings were vegetarians, the food was more nutritious than it was later and consequently the normal life span gradually decreased from nearly one thousand years to fewer than one hundred. Another theory is that *years* in the early part of *Genesis* really means moons, seasons or some other periods shorter than years. This theory is unsatisfactory because the longevity of the patriarchs appears to have decreased gradually. Still another theory is that the long periods mentioned as the ages attained by individuals were really equivalent to dynasties or the number of years that one family continued in the ascendancy. The most plausible theory is that the history in *Genesis* is merely legendary and that the Hebrews, like most other ancient peoples, had a tradition that their forefathers were much longer lived than their descendants. This question was raised already in the time of Josephus, and perhaps his explanation is as good as any. "But let no one, upon comparing the lives of the ancients with our lives," wrote the historian of the Jews, "think that what we have said of them is false; or make the shortness of our lives at present an argument, that neither did they attain to so long a duration of life, for those ancients were beloved of God, and recently made by God himself; and because their food was then fitter for the prolongation of life, might well live so great a number of years; and besides God afforded them a longer time of life on account of their virtue, and the good use they made of it in astronomical and geometrical discoveries, which would not have afforded the time of foretelling the periods of the stars unless they had lived six hundred years; for the great year is completed in that interval." Josephus then proceeded to cite Egyptian, Greek, Phoenician, Chaldean and other Gentile historians to prove that all the ancients believed that the longevity of their ancestors was a thousand years. "But as to these matters," he concluded quaintly, "let every one look upon them as he thinks fit."

Why do small *x*'s signify kisses?

Probably few persons sometime in their lives have not written letters in which they put several small crosses to signify kisses—"love and xxxx." Although there is no positive evidence on the subject, it is believed that the origin of this symbol dates back to the time when the cross-mark was equivalent to an oath. Signatures on wills, deeds and other documents were followed by a cross, then in vogue as a general religious symbol. After having made the cross after his name the signer often would kiss it as a pledge of good faith and as an act of reverence. The gesture was comparable to putting the hand on a Bible or crucifix while taking an oath or attesting a statement. A person who could not write merely placed a cross—"his mark"—after his name written by another. It is not true, as often stated, that the use of the cross-mark after a signature was invariable evidence that the signer was illiterate. In Anglo-Saxon times in England the mark of the cross was required after the signatures of those who could write as well as after that of those who could not write. At any rate, it was customary to complete the transaction by kissing the cross-sign, and by this means the cross on paper became associated with the kiss. As explained elsewhere in this book, *X* was the Greek abbreviation of *Christos* and already associated with the cross. One writer suggests that it was from motives of reverence that the shape of the cross used in making one's mark on paper was that of the cross of St. Andrew, which resembles the letter *X*, and not that of the cross of Calvary. It is more probable, however, that the form of the cross used in signatures took no definite form at first. Soon after the outbreak of the second World War the British government issued regulations forbidding sailors to sign letters with the traditional "love and xxx" on the ground that these crosses might be used by spies for code messages. In 1942 American military censors forbade soldiers stationed abroad to use such symbols in letters to their people at home.

How did *Hebrew* originate?

Hebrew first occurs in the Bible in *Genesis 14:13,* where it is related that, after the battle between "four kings with five" in the vale of Siddim, "there came one that had escaped, and told Abram the Hebrew." Even Hebrew scholars are divided as to the origin of the term. There are three theories. One is that *Hebrew* is from *Habiri,* the name of a nomadic people mentioned in ancient tablets found at Tel-el-Amarna. Another is that *Hebrew* was formed from *Eber,* the name of a great-grandson of Shem and an ancestor of Abraham. This was the theory accepted by Josephus, who referred to "Heber, from whom they originally called the Jews Hebrews." Still another theory is that *Hebrew* is derived from a root meaning "one from the other side" and originally alluded to the fact that Abraham crossed the Euphrates, "the great river." This theory was accepted by the translators of the Septuagint who rendered the term in "Abram the Hebrew" by a Greek term signifying "passer-over," "passenger" or "immigrant." Whatever the reason, the descendants came to be called Hebrews to distinguish them as a people and the term was employed particularly by foreigners or in speaking of them to foreigners.

What is the origin of *Israel*?

The earliest occurrence of Israel in the Bible is in *Genesis 33:28,* where the angel who wrestled all night with Jacob says: "Thy name shall be called no more Jacob, but Israel: for as a prince hast thou power with God and with men, and hast prevailed." *Israel* is from a Hebrew root literally meaning "he that strives or prevails with God." According to *Genesis 33:20,* when Jacob settled with his family in a parcel of a field at Shalem "he erected there an altar, and called it El-elohe-Israel," which literally signifies "God the God of Israel." As Jacob became Israel, so his descendants through his twelve sons became the tribes of Israel and the Israelites. *Israel* was the name that the Hebrews applied to themselves as a compact and organized religious, social and political group. After their occupation of the Promised Land their country was known as Israel. But the term is also used in the Bible in a narrower sense. When Israel was divided by civil war in the time of Rehoboam and Jereboam, the northern kingdom alone retained the name Israel, while the southern kingdom was called Judah. From that time on we read of the kings of Israel and the kings of Judah, although the inhabitants of both kingdoms continued to be called Israelites in the older and broader sense of the inhabitants of the old land of Israel.

What Israelite invented his own musical instrument?

David, the sweet psalmist of Israel, invented the musical instrument on which he played. It is supposed to have been a kind of harp. In *Amos 6:5* one of the earliest of the prophets of Israel refers to those "That chant to the sound of the viol, and invent to themselves instruments of musick, like David."

How did *Jew* originate?

Jew is derived from *Yehuda* (Judah), the name of the fourth of Jacob's twelve sons. The territory in Palestine occupied by the tribe of Judah was called Judah and its inhabitants the children of Judah. After Israel split into two kingdoms, the southern section, comprising Judah, Benjamin and Simeon, was known as the kingdom of Judah. About 586 B.C. the kingdom of Judah was destroyed and many of the inhabitants carried away into captivity by the Babylonians. Sixty years later, under the protection of Persia, a remnant of the children of Judah returned from Babylonia and established a Hebrew commonwealth at Jerusalem. This state, like its predecessor, was called Judah. Since it was the only independent Hebrew state in existence it became the sole representative and repository of the religion of the Israelites. The inhabitants of Judah (Yehuda) called themselves *Yehudim* in Hebrew and *Yehudaye* in Aramaic. To the Greeks and and Romans *Yehuda* became *Iouda* and *Judaea* and the inhabitants *Ioudaios* and *Judaei*. The name of the inhabitants of the Hebrew commonwealth passed through the following successive linguistic stages: Hebrew *Yehuda,* Greek *Ioudaios,* Latin *Judaeus,* Old French *Juieu,* and English *Jew*. One of the earliest known uses of the English form *Jew* is dated 1175 A.D. The term occurs only a few times in the King James Version of the Old Testament and then only in connection with the later historical period. Its first occurrence is in *II Kings 18:26-27,* where the tongue spoken by the people in Jerusalem, then besieged by the Syrians in the time of Hezekiah, is referred to as the *Jews' language*. Another early use of the term is in *Jeremiah 34:9*. Even in *Ezra* and *Nehemiah* the terms *Israel* and *men of Israel* are used interchangeably with *Judah* and *Jews*. Josephus, in his *Antiqui-*

ties of the Jews, begins to refer to the Hebrews and Israelites as *Ioudaioi* (Judaeans or Jews) in the time of Samuel. "So the Jews," wrote Josephus, "prepared for the work: that is the name they are called by from the day that they came up from Babylon, which is taken from the tribe of Judah, which came first to these places, and thence both they and the country gained that appellation." For centuries adherents of the Mosaic faith who lived in Judaea were called Jews, while those of the dispersion were called Israelites. *Jew* is used in the New Testament in both the specific and the general sense. For instance, *John 7:1* says, "After these things Jesus walked in Galilee: for he would not walk in Jewry, because the Jews sought to kill him." Since Jesus himself and all his disciples were Jews, this clearly means that Jewry was Judaea proper and the Jews were the Judaeans. In the course of time, however, *Jew* came to be applied to any adherent of the Mosaic faith, regardless of the tribe from which he was descended. Beginning as the most specific and restricted of the three terms *Hebrew, Israelite* and *Jew,* the last ultimately became the most general in its application, and at the present time it is applied to the descendants of all the Hebrews and Israelites who have retained their religious, racial and lingual characteristics.

Does *Jewess* occur in the Bible?

Jewess (*Jew* with the suffix *ess* to denote a Jewish woman) occurs only twice in the King James Version, both times in *Acts.* Referring to Paul in Syria and Cilicia, *Acts 16:1* says: "Then came he to Derbe and Lystra: and, behold, a certain disciple was there, named Timotheus, the son of a certain woman, which was a Jewess, and believed; but his father was a Greek." *Acts 24:24,* in connection with Paul's detention in Herod's judgment hall at Caesarea, says: "And after certain days, when Felix came with his wife Drusilla, which was a Jewess, he sent for Paul and heard him concerning the faith of Christ." *I Chronicles 4:18* refers to the wife of Mered, the Calebite, as "Jehudijah," which is an attempt to render Hebrew *yehudiyyah* literally. The Revised Version renders this "the Jewess." According to *I Chronicles 4:18,* the woman "which Mered took" was "Bithiah the daughter of Pharaoh." Why a daughter of Pharaoh should have been specially designated "the Jewess" is not clear. It may have meant that Bithiah, though a daughter of Pharaoh, adhered to Judaism; that is, she was a Jewess from the standpoint of the Egyptians because she was married to a Jew. Some authorities suppose the text here has become dislocated and that the real meaning is that Mered had two wives, one being Bithiah the daughter of Pharaoh and the other "the Jewess." The suffix *esse* was formerly more widely used in English than at present to denote female persons or animals. *Jewess* was used in Wycliffe's fourteenth-century translation of the Bible. It is applied once to Jessica in Shakespeare's *The Merchant of Venice*.

How do *Jew, Hebrew* and *Israelite* differ in meaning?

In modern English usage *Jew, Hebrew* and *Israelite* are often used interchangeably to denote the adherents of the Mosaic faith, and it is hard to differentiate them. Yet they do express slightly different shades of meaning. *Hebrew,* the oldest of the three, connotes the Israelitish or Jewish people of the distant past in respect to their race rather than their religion. We speak properly of the Hebrew race, the Hebrew language, Hebrew history and Hebrew literature. *Israelite* connotes the Hebrews as an organized political, religious and social group or nation. *Jew* is a popular substitute for both the others but places more emphasis on religion. *Hebrew* and *Israelite* were formerly used much more by both Jews and Gentiles than they are today. Jewish organizations can almost be dated by the occurrence of *Hebrew, Israelite* and *Jewish* in their names and titles. George Washington wrote letters to Israelites and Hebrews, but not to Jews. In the early days of the United States *Hebrew* was regarded as more aristocratic than *Jew* by *Jews* themselves. At that time *Jews* was often avoided and one of the other terms substituted because it had certain traditional implications that were felt to be objectionable and because it emphasized religion more than was desired. The religious emphasis of *Jew* is illustrated by the fact that we hear of Gentiles becoming Jews, but not Israelites or Hebrews. Nowadays, however, Jews generally prefer to regard themselves and have others regard them as a religious rather than a racial and cultural group, and *Jew* has largely supplanted *Hebrew* and *Israelite* as the designation of adherents of Judaism except in the historic senses.

What is meant by *sackcloth and ashes*?

In *Matthew 11:21* Jesus is quoted as saying that if the mighty works done in Chorazin and Bethsaida "had been done in Tyre and Sidon, they would have repented long ago in sackcloth and ashes." When the ancient Israelite heard of the death of a relative or important person he rent his garments, put on sackcloth, sprinkled ashes or dust on his head and fasted. Even at the present time the Arabs put ashes on their heads as a sign of grief and mourning. Our word *sack* is of pure Hebrew origin. Sackcloth was a coarse fabric used in prehistoric times for loincloths and later in making sacks and bags. The Israelites also put on sackcloth and sprinkled ashes on their heads as a sign of distress, remorse or national calamity. In *II Samuel 1:2* we are told that a man came to David at Ziklag "out of the camp from Saul with his clothes rent, and earth upon his head." When David learned of the defeat and death of Saul and Jonathan, according to *II Samuel 1:11*, he "took hold on his clothes, and rent them: and likewise all the men that were with him." *II Samuel 3:31* tells us that "David said to Joab, and to all the people that were with him, Rend your clothes, and gird you with sackcloth, and mourn before Abner." After Job had been deprived of his sons and property and was smitten with sore boils from head to foot, according to *Job 2:8*, "he took him a potsherd to scrape himself withal; and he sat down among the ashes." In *Job 42:6* it is related that Job told the Lord: "I abhor myself, and repent in dust and ashes." The inhabitants of that great city of Nineveh, when they heard Jonah proclaiming their destruction within forty days, "believed God, and proclaimed a fast, and put on sackcloth, from the greatest of them even to the least of them." Even the king, *Jonah 3:6* tells us, "arose from his throne, and he laid his robe from him, and covered him with sackcloth, and sat in ashes." According to *Esther 4*, after Ahasuerus ordered the destruction of the Jews, Mordecai "rent his clothes, and put on sackcloth with ashes," but he did not go into the palace "for none might enter into the king's gate clothed with sackcloth. There was great mourning among the Jews, and fasting, and weeping, and wailing; and many lay in sackcloth and ashes." *Leviticus 21:10* forbade the high priest to "rend his clothes," but, according to *Mark 14:63*, after Jesus had admitted that he was the Christ, Caiaphas the high priest "rent his clothes," which is explained by the fact that by the time of Jesus it was customary for any devout Jew to rend his garment as a sign of horror and execration upon hearing what he regarded as blasphemy.

Who was the second king of Israel?

It is generally supposed that Saul was the first king of Israel and that David was the second. That is not strictly true, according to the Bible. After Saul and his three oldest sons lost their lives in the battle with the Philistines at Mt. Gilboa, David proclaimed himself king of Judah, but not of all Israel. Sometime later Abner, captain of the host of the northern kingdom, had Ishbosheth, Saul's fourth son, proclaimed king of Israel. Ishbosheth was a weak ruler and after Abner's desertion to David was murdered in his bed by two of his captains in the hope of receiving a reward from David. The reign of the second king of Israel was a brief and unhappy one. It was only after Ishbosheth's death, seven years after the death of Saul, that David proclaimed himself king of all Israel. The two kingdoms were then reunited and remained one until after the death of Solomon and Jereboam's rebellion against Rehoboam.

Were all the Benjamites left-handed?

No passage in the Bible justifies the belief that all the members of the tribe of Benjamin were left-handed, but left-handedness seems to have been exceptionally common among the Benjamites. *Judges 20:15-16* says: "And the children of Benjamin were numbered at that time out of the cities twenty and six thousand men that drew sword, beside the inhabitants of Gibeah, which were numbered seven hundred chosen men. Among all this people there were seven hundred chosen men left-handed; every one could sling stones at an hair breadth, and not miss." In *Judges 3:15* we read: "But when the children of Israel cried unto the Lord, the Lord raised them up a deliverer, Ehud the son of Gera, a Benjamite, a man left-handed." *I Chronicles 12:2,* however, indicates that the Benjamin archers and sling-shot men were ambidextrous rather than simply left-handed: "They were armed with bows, and could use both the right hand and the left in hurling stones and shooting arrows out of a bow, even of Saul's brethren of Benjamin." Left-handedness is mentioned nowhere else in the Bible. The interesting thing about this is that *Benjamin* in Hebrew signifies "son of the *right* hand." Benjamin was the youngest of the twelve sons of Jacob and Rachel died in giving him birth. *Genesis 35:18* tells us: "And it came to pass, as her soul was in departing, (for she died) that she called his name Benoni: but his father called him Benjamin." *Benoni* means "son of my sorrow." The tribe of Benjamin was always one of the smallest of the tribes of Israel in numbers and it received the smallest allotment of territory, but its fighting men were noted for their martial spirit and deeds.

When did the Hebrews begin to offer sacrifices?

Sacrifice is derived from Latin *sacer,* "holy," and *ficare,* "to make." A sacrifice is an offering made to a deity. Animal and vegetable sacrifice as a recognized religious institution existed in one form or other among virtually all races of men. The Hebrews, like nearly all other peoples in that part of the world, were offering sacrifices when they first appeared upon the stage of recorded history. In *Genesis 4:2-5* we are told: "Abel was a keeper of sheep, but Cain was a tiller of the ground. And in process of time it came to pass, that Cain brought of the fruit of the ground an offering unto the Lord. And Abel, he also brought of the firstlings of his flock and of the fat thereof. And the Lord had respect unto Abel and to his offering: but unto Cain and to his offering he had not respect." According to the Bible, Noah was the first person to build an altar and offer sacrifices on it. *Genesis 8:20* says that Noah, after going forth from the ark, "builded an altar unto the Lord; and took of every clean beast, and of every clean fowl, and offered burnt offerings on the altar." It is related in *Genesis 12:7* that one of the first things Abraham did in the land of Canaan was to build "an altar unto the Lord, who appeared unto him." Presumably the Israelites continued to offer sacrifices during their long stay in Egypt. In *Leviticus* Moses prescribed in considerable detail the ritual for offering sacrifices by the Israelites. Some authorities suppose that animal sacrifices developed from the practice of slaying captives taken in war to gain the favor of the gods. If this supposition is correct, human sacrifices antedated animal sacrifices. According to this theory, as civilization developed the human captives were spared and oxen, sheep and other animals were slain as substitutes.

What is the legend of Mohammed and the Mountain?

"If the mountain will not come to Mohammed, Mohammed must go to the mountain," has been a familiar English proverb since the seventeenth century. It is said of one who, unable to have things his own way, bows to the inevitable. Apparently the proverb was suggested by a passage in Francis Bacon's essay entitled "Of Boldness," in which he says: "You shall see a bold fellow many times do Mahomet's miracle. Mahomet made the people believe that he would call an hill to him, and from the top of it offer up his prayers, for the observers of his law. The people assembled; Mahomet called the hill to come to him, again and again; and when the hill stood still, he was never a whit abashed, but said: If the hill will not go to Mahomet, Mahomet will go to the hill." No earlier reference to the story of Mohammed and the mountain has been produced, and no counterpart of it has been found in Moslem or Arabic literature. The New Testament contains several references to mountain-removing faith: "If ye have faith as a grain of mustard seed, ye shall say unto this mountain, Remove hence to yonder place; and it shall remove"—*Matthew 17:20*; "If ye have faith, and doubt not, ye shall not only do this which is done to the fig tree, but also if ye shall say unto this mountain, Be thou removed and be thou cast into the sea; it shall be done"—*Matthew 21:21*; "That whosoever shall say unto this mountain, Be thou removed, and be thou cast into the sea; and shall not doubt in his heart, but shall believe that those things which he saith shall come to pass; he shall have whatsoever he saith"—*Mark 11:23*; and "Though I have all faith, so that I could remove mountains, and have not charity, I am nothing"—*II Corinthians 13:2*: but there is no known occurrence of this figure of speech in the *Koran* or in pre-seventeenth century Moslem writings. A story, of later date than that of Bacon and probably also of English origin, says that when Mohammed first began to teach his doctrine to the Arabs, they demanded, as a sign of his divine authority, some miracle such as Moses, Jesus and other prophets had performed. Mohammed at first replied that any such pretension to miraculous powers on his part would be displeasing to God. The Arabs, however, persisted in their demand, whereupon Mohammed, to satisfy them, called to Mt. Safa (a mountain near Mecca sacred to pagan Arabs) to come to him. When the mountain paid no attention to the prophet's command, he said: "God is merciful; for had the mountain obeyed my words and come to me, it would have fallen on us to our destruction; therefore I will go to the mountain, and give thanks to God for showing mercy to a stiffnecked generation."

Is total abstinence mentioned in the Bible?

There were at least two groups of people in ancient Israel who practiced total abstinence from all alcoholic drinks. *Numbers 6:1-4* says: "And the Lord spake unto Moses, saying, Speak unto the children of Israel, and say unto them, When either man or woman shall separate themselves to vow a vow of a Nazarite, to separate themselves unto the Lord: he shall separate himself from wine and strong drink, and shall drink no vinegar of wine, or vinegar of strong drink, neither shall he drink any liquor of grapes, nor eat moist grapes, or dried. All the days of his separation shall he eat nothing that is made of the vine tree, from the kernels even to husk." The Rechabites were also total abstainers from strong drink. According to *Jeremiah 35:6,* when the prophet set pots of wine before the Rechabites, gave them cups and said, "Drink ye wine," the Rechabites replied: "We drink no wine: for Jonadab the son of Rechab our father commanded us, saying, Ye shall drink no wine, neither ye, nor your sons forever." In the time of Jeremiah the Rechabites lived in Jerusalem, where they went to seek safety from the Chaldean and Syrian armies. The prophet held up their loyalty to their founder's ideals as worthy of emulation by the Israelites generally. Jacob brought wine to Isaac, who drank it before eating the venison, and generally it may be said that the Hebrews regarded wine as a necessary and essential part of every meal. Some authorities suppose that John the Baptist was a Nazarite, because the angel of the Lord, according to *Luke 1:15,* told Zacharias that his son "shall drink neither wine nor strong drink." And in *Matthew 11:18-19* Jesus is quoted as saying: "For John came neither eating nor drinking, and they say, He hath a devil. The Son of man came eating and drinking, and they say, Behold a man gluttonous, and a winebibber, a friend of publicans and sinners. But wisdom is justified of her children."

What was a tetrarch?

In *Matthew 14:1* the petty king of Galilee and Peraea is referred to as "Herod the tetrarch." This term is derived from Greek *tetra,* "four," and *archos,* "ruler," and literally means "the ruler of one of the four divisions of a country or province." Herod the Great was the vassal king of a domain roughly equivalent to the kingdom of David and Solomon. After the death of Herod the Great in 4 A.D., the Romans' in conformity with the king's will, divided his domain into four parts known as "tetrarchies." Archelaus, Herod's oldest son, became tetrarch of Judaea and Samaria; Herod Antipas, the second son, became tetrarch of Galilee and Peraea; Herod Philip, Herod's third son, became tetrarch of a domain east of the Jordan and the Sea of Galilee; and Lysanias II, who may have been related to Herod by marriage, became tetrarch of Abilene, a comparatively small district between Mount Hermon and Damascus. Herod Antipas remained tetrarch or petty king of Galilee and Peraea throughout the entire life of Jesus. It was he who put John the Baptist to death because he condemned the tetrarch for marrying his brother's divorced wife; it was he whom Jesus called "that fox"; and it was he who took part in the trial of Jesus.

Who said: "As thy days, so shall thy strength be"?

This saying is from *Deuteronomy 33:25* and is one of the most widely quoted passages in the Bible. It has served as the text for many a Christian sermon. The context in which the passage occurs is interesting. We are told that before Moses "went up from the plains of Moab unto the mountain of Nebo, to the top of Pisgah, that is over against Jericho" and saw the Promised Land in the distance, "the man of God blessed the children of Israel before his death." According to *Deuteronomy 33:24-25,* when Moses in his blessings came to the tribe of Asher he said: "Let Asher be blessed with children; let him be acceptable to his brethren, and let him dip his foot in oil. Thy shoes shall be iron and brass; and as thy days, so shall thy strength be." This is one of those passages in the Old Testament where the translators of the King James Version sacrificed strict accuracy for beauty, simplicity and power. Asher's territory was in the far north and on the seacoast, exposed to many foreign enemies, and Hebrew scholars say that the "iron and brass" is an allusion to the strong fortifications that would be necessary to make the territory impregnable. "Thy bars shall be iron and brass" is how the passage is rendered in some versions. Others render it, "Under thy shoes shall be iron and brass." The Hebrew word translated *strength* here is not found elsewhere in the Bible and is of doubtful meaning. It is believed to signify "rest" or "security" and to suggest that Asher's rest and security will not be disturbed. In his English Hebrew Bible of 1853 Isaac Leeser rendered the famous passage, "As thy younger days, so shall thy old age be." But it is almost universally taken to mean, "May your strength last like your days" or "May your strength be equal to the occasion."

How many plagues of Egypt does the Bible mention?

Contrary to the popular notion, the Bible mentions *ten* plagues of Egypt instead of *seven.* It is a common error to speak of the *seven plagues of Egypt.* The plagues were as follows: the turning of the Nile into blood, covering the land with frogs, turning the dust into lice, sending swarms of flies, killing of the cattle by a murrain, afflicting the Egyptians with boils, raining fire and hail, covering the land with locusts, covering the land with a thick darkness for three days, and the destruction of the first born of man and beast.

What is the meaning of, "To your tents, O Israel!"?

"To your tents, O Israel!" is often quoted as a call to united military action. That is not exactly its meaning in the Bible. In ancient Israel it was a rallying cry for rebellion and refusal to follow a leader. According to *II Samuel 20,* a man of Belial named Sheba started a rebellion against King David after his return to Jerusalem following his victory over Absalom. Sheba, the Benjamite leader of the rebels, "blew a trumpet, and said, We have no part in David, neither have we inheritance in the son of Jesse: every man to his tents, O Israel. So every man of Israel went up from after David, and followed Sheba the son of Bichri: but the men of Judah clave unto their king, from Jordan even to Jerusalem." Again, after King Solomon died his son Rehoboam succeeded to the throne, but the northern tribes rebelled and chose Jeroboam the son of Nebat as their king. The followers of Jeroboam, however, made a last-minute effort to avoid a complete and final split between Judah and the rest of Israel. But Rohoboam, rejecting the counsel of the old men that stood before Solomon his father and accepting that of the young men that grew up with him, answered roughly, saying: "My father made your yoke heavy, and I will add to your yoke: my father also chastised you with whips, but I will chastise you with scorpions." *I Kings 12:16* says: "So when Israel saw that the king hearkened not unto them, the people answered the king, saying, What portion have we in David? neither have we inheritance in the son of Jesse: *to your tents,* O Israel: now see to thine own house, David. So Israel departed unto their tents." Their departure to their tents meant that they would no longer follow the king of Judah. It was symbolical of rebellion and refusal to go along with the son of Solomon. "To your tents, O Israel!" was a rallying cry for revolt. The same thought is expressed in *Deuteronomy 1:26-27,* where Moses, speaking of the refusal of the Israelites to enter the Promised Land because of the unfavorable report of the majority of the twelve spies, says: "Notwithstanding ye would not go up, but rebelled against the commandment of the Lord your God: and *ye murmured in your tents,* and said, Because the Lord hated us, he has brought us forth out of the land of Egypt, to deliver us into the hand of the Amorites, and to destroy us." Here remaining in the tents is clearly associated with rebellion and refusal to co-operate with the leader. The proverbial phrase, *sulking in one's tent* has a similar significance. In *Deuteronomy 5:30* "Get you into your tents again" is employed in the sense of standing by. Likewise, in *Judges 7:8* we are told that Gideon "sent all the rest of Israel every man unto his tent, and retained those three hundred men."

What is meant by *evil communications*?

"Be not deceived: evil communications corrupt good manners," says St. Paul in *I Corinthians 15:33.* The Apostle to the Gentiles was either consciously or unconsciously quoting from Menander, an Athenian dramatist who lived from 342 to 291 B.C. and who wrote more than a hundred comedies. Menander was author of "Whom the gods love die young," which occurs in his *Dis Exapaton,* a fragment of which is still extant. In his *Thais,* which also survives only in fragmentary form, the Athenian dramatist said: "It must be that evil communications corrupt good manners" (disposition or character). Menander was noted for the great number of moral maxims that became proverbial. The authors of the Bible frequently quoted the sacred writers by name, but never classical writers. "Evil communications corrupt good manners" is one of the few classical quotations in the Bible that can be specifically identified as to source. The Greek word translated *communications* in this instance probably signifies conversations or disputings rather than *companionships,* as it is rendered in the Revised Version. According to *Acts 17:28,* in his discourse on Mars Hill Paul said: "For in him we live, and move, and have our being; as certain also of your own poets have said, For we are also his offspring." This thought is found in the writings of two Greek stoic poets. It occurs in the *Phaenomena* of Aratus and in the *Hymn to Zeus* of Cleanthes. In *Titus 1:12* Paul says: "One of themselves, even a prophet of their own, said, The Cretians are always liars, evil beasts, slow bellies." This appears to be a quotation from Epimenides, a Cretan poet who lived in the 6th century B.C.

Who said: "Seven women shall take hold of one man"?

In *Isaiah 1:4* the prophet says: "And in that day seven women shall take hold of one man, saying, We will eat our own bread, and wear our own apparel: only let us be called by thy name, to take away our reproach." Isaiah refers to a coming famine and day of judgment after which the women will greatly outnumber the men. It was a disgrace for a woman of Israel to go through life without having children. According to *Genesis 30:23,* after Rachel had borne a son, she said: "God hath taken away my reproach." The thought in *Isaiah 1:4* seems to be that the surplus women would not claim to become wives, but only ask the man to take away the reproach of being childless.

Which famous Biblical characters lived in Egypt?

Abraham and Sarah lived for a time in Egypt. Jacob and his twelve sons settled in Egypt and died there. Joseph married the daughter of an Egyptian priest. The twelve tribes developed into a great people during their sojourn in Egypt, and Moses, Aaron and Miriam were born and reared near the banks of the Nile. Solomon married a daughter of a pharaoh. Jereboam, the first king of the northern tribes as a separate kingdom, was a refugee for a time in Egypt. The prophet Jeremiah died in Egypt and was buried there. Joseph and Mary took Jesus to Egypt to escape from the wrath of Herod.

How did the Israelites pronounce *Jehovah*?

Jehovah in that form was unknown to the ancient Israelites. In fact, Hebrew scholars say that *Jehovah* would have been impossible according to the strict principles of Hebrew vocalization. The God of Israel was known by a name approximately rendered into English as *Yahweh*. This divine name comes from the same root as the Hebrew verb "to be" and originally expressed the idea that God was, is and always shall be. Sometimes in Hebrew the Supreme Being was referred to as *Adonay Yahweh*, literally meaning "the Lord Yahweh," and it was this combined title and name that became *Jehovah* in English through an arbitrary transliteration of the vowels in the two words. Before vowels were introduced into Hebrew about the fifth century A.D., the divine name was written *YHWH*. But many centuries before that the divine name of four letters had become so sacred that no devout Jew would pronounce it. Even to attempt it was regarded as mortal sin. Consequently the true pronunciation of *YHWH* has been completely lost. This "incommunicable" and "unpronounceable" and "ineffable" word among the Jews is sometimes called *Tetragrammaton*, from Greek *tetra*, "four," and *gramma*, "letter," which refers to the four consonants forming the divine name. By the time of Jesus the sacredness of *YHWH* was emphasized to the extent that it was considered profanation to pronounce it even during divine services. So long as the temple in Jerusalem stood, the pronunciation of the divine name of four letters was the exclusive privilege of the priests. Only once a year, on the Day of Atonement, did the High Priest call upon God by his real name in the presence of the congregation. The congregation did not follow the High Priest in uttering the ineffable name of the invisible God, but fell upon their knees and responded with the words, "Blest be his glorious name!" The Jews never wrote or pronounced the divine name even when reading. When reading the sacred books they always pronounced it *Adonay*, meaning Lord. Likewise in the synagogues *Adonay* was substituted for *YHWH*. This reverence for the divine name of four letters led to the invention of many substitute names and titles for the Supreme Being, such as: God, the Lord, the Almighty, the Mighty One, the Lord of Hosts, the Ancient of Days, the Most High, the Holy One, and many others.

In the English Bible the Hebrew *Elohim* is generally rendered "God" and *Adonay*, "Lord." The scrupulousness of the Israelites in pronouncing the sacred name has its counterpart among other people. For instance, *God* is correctly pronounced with the *o* short as in *cod*, *pod* and *plod*. It is often pronounced *gawd* by some people because they seem to feel that when so pronounced the name is more suggestive of sacredness and awe. Likewise many devout persons have a tendency to pronounce *Amen* "AYE-men" in ordinary conversation and reading, but to pronounce it "AWE-men" in singing hymns and in solemn religious ceremonies and services. *Jehovah* is the principal name of the supreme deity of Israel in the English Bible and occurs nearly seven thousand times.

Where did Noah's ark land?

The average person in replying to this question will say that Noah's ark landed on Mt. Ararat. It is not so stated in the King James Version of the Bible. *Genesis 8:4* says: "And the ark rested in the seventh month, on the seventeenth day of the month, upon the mountains of Ararat." In the Vulgate and Douay versions this is translated the "mountains of Armenia." The name *Mt. Ararat* occurs nowhere in the Scriptures. It is only a legend that the ark landed on the highest peak of the mountains of Ararat or Armenia. Moreover, there is no single peak in this range called simply Mt. Ararat, although the highest peak is known as Great Ararat and its nearest rival in height Little Ararat. *Genesis 8:4* suggests that Noah's ark landed somewhere on this mountain range rather than on a particular peak. The altitude of Great Ararat is about 17,300 feet and that of Little Ararat about 13,000 feet. The upper reaches of both these peaks are continually covered with snow and ice. Tradition differs widely as to the exact place where Noah's ark landed. The Kurds, Syrians and Nestorians generally hold that the resting place of the ark was on Mt. Judi in southern Armenia, while from time immemorial the Jews and Armenians have held that it was on Great Ararat. Josephus, who frequently departs from the Biblical versions, says in his *Antiquities of the Jews*: "After this, the ark rested on the top of a certain mountain in Armenia; . . . the Armenians call this place, The Place of Descent: for the ark being saved in that place, its remains are shown there by the inhabitants to this day." In some modern English translations of the Bible the phrases "mountains of Ararat" or "mountains of Armenia" are rendered "Mt. Ararat" in conformity with the popular notion. The Hebrew *ararat* is believed to be derived from an Armenian word meaning "super-eminence." In *Jeremiah 51:27* the prophet summons "the kingdoms of Ararat, Minni and Ashchenaz" to fight against Babylon. To the Armenians Great Ararat is *Masis,* signifying sublime. The Turkish name *Agri-dagh,* means "steep mountain." Only the Persian name alludes to the Hebraic and Christian tradition. To the Persians the highest peak of the "mountains of Ararat" is *Koh-i-Nuh,* Noah's mount. In only one instance in the King James Version is the Hebrew *ararat* translated *Armenia. II Kings 19:36-37* says in part: "So Sennacherib king of Assyria departed, and went and returned, and dwelt at Nineveh. And it came to pass, as he was worshipping in the house of Nisroch his god, that Adrammelech and Sharezer his sons smote him with the sword: and they escaped into the land of Armenia." Tradition says Armenia was settled by Haik, a grandson of Japhet, and the earliest history refers to it as a tributary of Assyria.

How many stars can be seen?

According to *Genesis 15:5,* the Lord brought Abram forth abroad in a vision and said: "Look now toward heaven, and tell the stars, if thou be able to number them: and he said unto him, So shall thy seed be." *Deutronomy 1:10* quotes Moses, in his discourse to "all Israel on this side Jordan in the wilderness," as saying: "The Lord your God hath multiplied you, and, behold, ye are this day as the stars of heaven for multitude." Again in *Deuteronomy 10:22* Moses tells the Israelites: "Thy fathers went down into Egypt with threescore and ten persons: and now the Lord thy God hath made thee as the stars of heaven for multitude." In *Deuteronomy 28:62* Moses, in warning the Israelites what will happen if they fail to keep the law and commandments, says: "And ye shall be left few in number, whereas ye were as the stars of heaven for multitude." "Their children also multipliedst thou as the stars of heaven," says *Nehemiah 9:23,* and in *Jeremiah 33:22* we find, "As the host of heaven cannot be numbered." This same figure of speech occurs in the New Testament. In *Hebrews 11:12* it is said: "Therefore sprang there even of one, and him as good as dead, so many as the stars of the sky in multitude." The actual number of stars that can be seen with the naked eye is not so great as one might suppose. Astronomers tell us that all the stars visible to the unaided eye from all points on the earth number only five or six thousand. Not more than two thousand or twenty-five hundred stars can ever be seen with the naked eye from any one point, because the other lucid stars are either below the horizon or are so close to it that they cannot be seen. Abram (Abraham's original name) therefore probably could see fewer than three thousand stars if he had normally good vision. But the stars visible to the naked eye give one the impression of being much more numerous. Nevertheless the figure used by the authors of the Hebrew scriptures to signify a great number is scientifically sound. Stars that can be seen with the naked eye are called *lucid* to distinguish them from *telescopic* stars. Millions of stars can be seen with the aid of powerful telescopes. So far there is no sign of any limit to the number of stars in the celestial sphere. St. Paul alludes to the magnitudes of stars. In *I Corinthians 15:41* he says: "There is one glory of the sun, and another glory of the moon, and another glory of the stars: for one star differeth from another star in glory."

Does the Bible mention Gabriel's horn?

The Bible does not describe Gabriel as the angel of death, and the idea of his announcing the day of final judgment with a trumpet or horn seems to be a combination of several conceptions in the Bible and Jewish tradition. From the days in the wilderness the children of Israel were regularly called to their assemblies by trumpeters. St. John the Divine, in the Apocalypse, tells of angels sounding trumpets, and St. Paul, in *I Corinthians 15:52*, says that we shall all be changed "at the last trump: for the trumpet shall sound, and the dead shall be raised incorruptible, and we shall be changed"; but in neither connection is Gabriel mentioned. As a matter of fact explicit references to Gabriel are very few in the Scriptures. In the Old Testament he is the heavenly messenger sent to Daniel to interpret the vision of the ram and the rough goat and to communicate the prediction of the Seventy Weeks; in the New Testament he foretells to Zacharias the birth of John the Baptist and to the Virgin Mary the birth of Jesus. According to the Book of Enoch, one of the Apocryphal books, and *Tobias*, one of the deuterocanonical books of the Catholic Bible as well as the rabbinical and Talmudic writings, Gabriel is one of the archangels. Christian, Jewish and Moslem sacred writings attribute to him different characteristics and functions. Literally *Gabriel* is Hebrew for "hero" or "man of God." As a general rule Gabriel is regarded by Christians as the angel of mercy and good tidings. He is the angel of death only in the sense that the call of death is good tidings to the faithful. The function of messenger and trumpeter of death attributed to him is commemorated among the miners of northern England in the popular superstition of Gabriel's hounds, a pack of phantom dogs that are supposed to be the souls of unbaptized children doomed to wander through the air until Judgment Day and that are believed to foretell death by their unearthly howling at night. In the same region certain night sounds, probably made by wild geese in flight, are known as Gabriel's ratchets.

How many times does the Bible refer to ants?

There are only two references to ants in the Bible and both of them are in the Old Testament. Solomon, the wisest of the Israelites, says in *Proverbs 6:6-8*: "Go to the ant, thou sluggard; consider her ways, and be wise: which having no guide, overseer, or ruler, provideth her meat in the summer, and gathereth her food in the harvest." He tells us that the ants are among the "four things which are little upon the earth" but which are "exceeding wise." *Proverbs 30:25* says: "The ants are a people not strong, yet they prepare their meat in the summer." Ants are probably the most numerous and widespread insects that crawl on the face of the earth and they are common in all the territory known to the Israelites.

What is the Ananias Club?

A person who deliberately tells untruths is said to be a member of the Ananias Club. It is an old phrase that President Theodore Roosevelt popularized by applying it to persons who knowingly distorted the truth. In colloquial speech an Ananias is a liar. Ananias was a follower of the Apostles and a member of the first Christian community at Jerusalem. The Bible says that these early Christians "had all things common." According to *Acts 5*, Ananias sold a piece of land and conspired with his wife Sapphira to keep back part of the price instead of contributing it all to the common fund and taking an equal chance with the others. For their falsehood and hypocrisy both of them were miraculously punished by Peter with sudden death.

What two Bible characters never died?

The prophet Elijah and Enoch, father of Methuselah, never saw death, according to the Bible. *II Kings 2:11* says: "And it came to pass, as they (Elijah and Elisha) still went on and talked, that, behold, there appeared a chariot of fire, and horses of fire, which parted them both asunder; and Elijah went up by a whirlwind into heaven." This, it is presumed, is merely a figurative way of saying that the prophet passed from earth by miraculous translation instead of through the gates of death. Likewise Enoch never saw death, according to *Hebrews 11:5*. "By faith," that passage says, "Enoch was translated that he should not see death; and he was not found, because God translated him: for before his translation he had this testimony, that he pleased God." This is the basis for the popular but misleading statement that "Methuselah, the oldest man mentioned in the Bible, died before his father did." As a matter of fact, according to the Biblical account, Methuselah's father never died at all. *Genesis 5:25* says simply: "And Enoch walked with God: and he was not: for God took him." On this subject Josephus says simply: "And indeed, as to Elijah, and as to Enoch, who was before the deluge, it is written in the sacred books that they disappeared, but so that nobody knew that they died."

Does *sweat of thy brow* occur in the Bible?

Many people suppose that "Ye shall earn thy bread by the sweat of thy brow" is a Biblical quotation. It has been attributed to the Bible for two centuries or more, but it does not occur anywhere in the Scriptures, the nearest thing to it being the following from *Genesis 3:19*: "In the sweat of thy face shalt thou eat bread, till thou return unto the ground; for out of it wast thou taken." The source of the homespun Scripture is unknown. Milton wrote: "Let us go forth and resolutely dare with sweat of brow to toil our little day."

Does the Bible mention soap?

Soap occurs only twice in the King James Version of the Bible, where it was originally spelled *sope*. *Jeremiah 2:22* says: "for though thou wash thee with nitre, and take thee much soap, yet thine iniquity is marked before thee, saith the Lord." In *Malachi 3:2* the messenger of the Lord is said to be "like a refiner's fire, and like fullers' soap." Soap in the modern sense of a compound of fatty acids and potash or soda was not known until about the beginning of the Christian Era. Before that time there was no soap even in the famous Roman baths. The Hebrew word *borith*, translated *sope* or *soap* in the English Bible, probably refers to the ashes of plants and other simple substances used as cleansing agents. Among the ancients the juice of various plants, shrubs and trees was used for that purpose. The early inhabitants of Europe washed with the juice of the common plant known as soapwort, which makes a fairly good lather and which will even remove grease stains. *Nitre* as used in the passage from *Jeremiah* is not what we now call by that name, that is, saltpeter or potassium nitrate, but common washing soda, which consists of sodium carbonate and which is properly called *natron,* not *nitre.* The Revised Version substitutes *lye* for *nitre* in *Jeremiah 2:22.* It is generally supposed that real soap, both as a cleansing and as a medicinal agent, was first made by the ancient Gauls or Germans. In his *Natural History* Pliny the Elder says: "Soap, too, is very useful for this purpose (curing scrofulous sores), an invention of the Gauls for giving a reddish tint to the hair. This substance is prepared from tallow and ashes, the best ashes for the purpose being those of the beech and yoke-elm. There are two kinds of it, the hard soap and the liquid, both of them much used by the people of Germany, the men, in particular, more than the women." Some authorities, however, believe that the Gauls learned the art of soap-making from the Phoenicians, close kinsmen and neighbors of the Israelites. There is a legend that soap was accidentally discovered when grease from animal sacrifices seeped through the altars and mingled with the ashes from the burning logs underneath. Before they learned how to make soap from the Gauls or Germans, the Romans used fuller's earth as a cleansing agent. Later they greatly improved upon the crude method of soap-making described by Pliny. A complete soap shop was found in the ruins of Pompeii, which was covered with ashes from Mt. Vesuvius in 79 A.D. *Savon* became the French word for soap, supposedly from its having been manufactured at an early date at Savona, near Genoa. A factory for making soap from olive oil was established at Marseilles in the thirteenth century, and the manufacture of this product on a large scale was begun in London in the sixteenth century, many years before the translation of the King James Version of the Bible.

What was Eve's last name?

The surname of Eve, like that of her husband, was Adam. *Genesis 5:1-2* says: "This is the book of the generations of Adam. In the day that God created man, in the likeness of God made he him; male and female created he them; and blessed them, and called their name Adam, in the day when they were created." *Adam* is merely a Hebrew word meaning "man" in the sense of a human being. It is derived from *adamah,* "earth," and is akin to a Hebrew verb meaning "to build" or "to produce." *Adam* was not at first a proper name, but was originally applied to the human race. In the verses just quoted, as well as elsewhere in the Bible, *Adam* is applied both to the first man and to mankind. The Revised Version translates *adam* as *man* or *the man* in all cases except where it clearly means the first man, where it is rendered *Adam. Genesis 1:26-27* says: "And God said, Let us make man in our image, after our likeness: and let them have dominion over the fish of the sea, and over the fowl of the air, and over the cattle, and over all the earth, and over every creeping thing that creepeth upon the earth. So God created man in his own image, in the image of God created he him; male and female created he them." In *Genesis 2* it is related that God formed the first man "of the dust of the ground" and the first woman of one of the ribs of the first man. Some have supposed that this is another account of the creation of the human race, but it is more probable that it was intended to supply additional details about the same event. *Genesis 2:22-23* says: "And the rib, which the Lord God had taken from man, made he a woman, and brought her unto the man. And Adam [the man] said, This is now bone of my bones, and flesh of my flesh: she shall be called Woman, because she was taken out of Man." This is an attempt to render into English the thought of the Hebrew original. In Hebrew the usual word for man as an individual is *Ish,* while that for woman as an individual is *Ishshah,* and the similarity in sound in both Hebrew and English emphasizes the spiritual relationship between *Ish* and *Ishshah,* man and woman. In *Genesis 3* the first man is referred to both as Adam, as if that were his name, and as "the man," while the first woman is referred to as "the woman" and as the wife of Adam or the man, until Verse 20, which says: "And Adam called his wife's name Eve; because she was the mother of all living." Of course, the last part of this verse does not mean the mother of all living things, but the mother of all mankind after the creation of the first pair. The Hebrew word *hawwah,* here translated *Eve,* is of doubtful meaning, some authorities supposing it to signify "life" and others "serpent."

Is *sacrilege* in the Bible?

Sacrilege occurs only once in the King James Version. In *Romans 2:22* St. Paul says. "Thou that sayest a man should not commit adultery, dost thou commit adultery? thou that abhorrest idols, doest thou commit sacrilege?" The Greek term here translated *commit sacrilege* is translated *rob temples* in the Revised Version. *Sacrilege* is derived from Latin *sacrilegium,* composed of *sacer,* "sacred," and *legere,* "to gather" or "pick up," and literally means "to gather or pick up sacred things." In the most general sense of the term *sacrilege* is "the crime of stealing, misusing, violating or desecrating things that are holy or dedicated to sacred purposes." *Sacrilegious,* an adjective formed from *sacrilege,* is one of the most commonly misspelled as well as mispronounced words in the English language. It really should be pronounced *sak-ri-LEE-jus,* although the pronunciation *sak-ri-LIJ-us* has become so common through error that it generally passes unchallenged. The two main elements of *sacrilegious* are not *sac* and *religious,* as many seem to think, but *sacri* and *legious.* Literally the word means "relating to the carrying away of sacred things." The underlying thought behind the Latin *religio,* the source of English *religion,* is taboo or restraint.

Which is correct, *raise cane* or *raise Cain*?

Raise Cain is the original and correct form of the common slang phrase, which means "to create a disturbance, start a quarrel or cause trouble in general." M. Schele de Vere, writing in 1871, said that "when the rowdy is in earnest and his blood is up, he has a terrible term by which to designate the nature of his action; he raises Cain." The phrase is of American origin and has been traced back to about 1850. Early examples of its use indicate that it was first used in the West and probably alluded to the fact that Cain killed Abel. There is no evidence to support the presumption, insisted upon by some writers, that the phrase refers to the cultivation of the plant known as cane and should therefore be written *raise cane.*

What is meant by *the law of the Medes and Persians*?

Persia and Media were united under the same ruler after the conquest of Media by Cyrus of Persia about 550 B.C. In *Daniel* and *Esther* the laws of the Medes and Persians are referred to as being unalterable and irrevocable after once they were promulgated. This does not mean necessarily that the edicts of the king himself were irrevocable and beyond modification or repeal, but rather that laws and decrees agreed to by his council of princes and signed and sealed by him could not be altered capriciously by the king. It probably means that the joint kindgom of the Medes and Persians in those days was not an absolute monarchy and that the king was checked by certain constitutional limitations on his authority. A law was unalterable by the king in the same sense that an act of Congress is unalterable by the President of the United States and an act of Parliament is unalterable by the King of Great Britain. The only way such a law can be changed is by passing another law in due form. Apparently this system of government was sufficiently unusual in those ancient days of absolute monarchs to attract particular attention by the authors of *Daniel* and *Esther.* That such is the true explanation of the inalterability of the laws of the Medes and Persians is made abundantly clear by *Daniel 6.* We are told that it pleased Darius to set over the whole kingdom 120 princes, "and over these three presidents; of whom Daniel was first." This is another way of saying that Darius established a sort of house of princes or lords of 120 members and also a privy council composed of three presidents, with Daniel as prime president or premier. Because "an excellent spirit was in" Daniel "the king thought to set him over the whole realm." But Daniel's enemies in the council of princes, jealous of the esteem in which he was held by the king, conspired to destroy him. Knowing that Daniel was a faithful Jew, who would refuse to commit idolatry, they passed a law making it illegal for any subject of the kingdom to ask a petition of any god or man except King Darius himself. *Daniel 6:7-9* says: "All the presidents of the kingdom, the governors, and the princes, the counsellors, and the captains, have consulted together to establish a royal statute, and to make a firm decree, that whosoever shall ask a petition of any God or man for thirty days, save of thee, O king, he shall be cast into the den of lions. Now, O king, establish the decree, and sign the writing, that it be not changed, according to the law of the Medes and Persians, which altereth not. Wherefore king Darius signed the writing and the decree." In other words, the king gave his royal consent to the measure and made it an official act. When the Bible says "all the presidents" it obviously means only two of them, because Daniel himself was one of the three. The plotting presidents and princes then watched Daniel and found him "praying and making supplication before his God" in violation of the statute. To make certain that the decree was actually in effect they asked the king whether he had signed it. The king answered and said, "The thing is true, according to the law of the Medes and Persians, which altereth not." Then the lawmakers proceeded to impeach Daniel and said, "Know, O king, that the law of the Medes and Persians is, That no decree nor statute which the king establisheth may be changed." Although the king loved Daniel, he had no choice under the law but to carry out the sentence, just as the President of the United States, as chief executive, must execute many laws of which he does not personally approve. *Esther 1:19* says: "If it please the king, let there go a royal commandment from him, and let it be written among the laws of the Persians and the Medes, that it be not altered, That Vashti come no more before king Ahasuerus." According to *Esther 8*, the king said to Queen Esther and Mordecai: "Write ye also for the Jews, as it liketh you, in the king's name, and seal it with the king's ring: for the writing which is written in the king's name, and sealed with the king's ring, may no man reverse." This indicates either that the king issued decrees on his own or that he had a more pliant council than the king had in the days of Daniel. At any rate, King Ahasuerus found a way to circumvent the decree ordering the destruction of all the Jews in his kingdom. The decree could not be revoked, but a royal order was sent out warning the Jews and giving them permission to defend themselves and to avenge themselves on their enemies. We are told that even the rulers of the provinces, and the lieutenants, deputies and officers of the king helped the Jews.

What does *martyr* in the Bible mean?

Martyr is a Greek word that originally meant simply "a witness" in the legal sense. It occurs frequently in the Greek text of the New Testament, but in the King James Version it is translated *witness* in every case except three. For instance, *Matthew 18:16* is translated, "But if he will not hear thee, then take with thee one or two more, that in the mouth of two or three *witnesses* every word may be established," where the Greek is *martyrs*. But, according to *Acts 22:20*, Paul speaking to the people from the stairs of the castle in Jerusalem, related that he had said to Jesus in the vision that he was standing by "when the blood of thy martyr Stephen was shed." Stephen is often referred to as the first true Christian martyr. The original martyrs were merely witnesses to Jesus. Since faithfulness to this testimony was often punished with violent treatment, the term gradually lost its significance of a witness or spectator and acquired that of one who undergoes torture or suffers death for his firm belief in the gospel. The original meaning of *martyr* is still obvious in *Revelation 2:13*, where John on Patmos was bidden to write to the angel of the church in Pergamos: "I know thy works, and where thou dwellest, even where Satan's seat is: and thou holdest fast my name, and hast not denied my faith, even in those days wherein Antipas was my faithful martyr, who was slain among you, where Satan dwelleth." And again in *Revelation 17:6*: "I saw the woman drunken with the blood of the saints, and with the blood of the martyrs of Jesus."

What is meant by *feet of clay*?

Feet of clay comes from Biblical usage. Figuratively it is applied to the more earthly and baser side of human nature. "He has learned that his idol has feet of clay," is said of one who is disappointed or disillusioned. *Daniel 2:32-34* says: "This image's head was of fine gold, his breast and his arms of silver, his belly and his thighs of brass, his legs of iron, his *feet* part of iron and part of *clay.* Thou sawest till that a stone was cut out without hands, which smote the image upon his *feet* that were of iron and *clay,* and brake them to pieces." In the holy city of Benares, India, there is a god whose feet of clay, after being washed away by the Ganges, are replaced each year by the priests.

How did *by the skin of the teeth* originate?

To escape *by* or *with the skin of the teeth,* meaning to escape by the narrowest possible margin, is the literal translation of an ancient Hebrew phrase which occurs in the Bible only once. "My bone cleaveth to my skin and to my flesh," says the patriarch in *Job 19:20,* "and I am escaped with the skin of my teeth."

What does *Selah* in the Bible mean?

Selah as used in the Bible is a Hebrew word of unknown origin, meaning and use, and it has given translators considerable trouble. It occurs seventy-one times in *Psalms* and three times in *Habakkuk 3,* which is also really a psalm. Generally it is placed at the end of a verse, after an obvious break and not at the end of a psalm, but there are exceptions. The most widely accepted interpretation of *Selah* is that it was some kind of musical or liturgical direction to readers or singers, perhaps indicating a pause, rest, silence, or interlude. The Septuagint, which is a Greek translation made by Hebrew scholars at Alexandria before the Christian Era, rendered *Selah* by a word that signifies "interlude," "break" or "transition." The pre-Christian Aramaic version known as the Targum and the Vulgate of Jerome translate *Selah* with words meaning "always" or "for ever." Perhaps, it has been suggested, these two renderings are different aspects of the same thing, "interlude" denoting the point where the benediction was sung and the psalm ended for that service, and "for ever" giving the last word of the benediction. At any rate, *Selah* clearly is not an essential part of the psalms in which it occurs. Other interpretations and explanations that have been offered are as follows: It is an abbreviation for an unknown expression; it is derived from *sallem,* "supplement," and merely indicated a point where the manuscript was supplemented from another manuscript; it means "a step or advance in the act of performance" and is analogous with *ma'alah* in the title "A Song of Degrees"; it is derived from a root meaning to "lift up" and is a rubric calling for a fresh outburst of instruments or voices; it is equivalent to the musical term *da capo,* which is a direction to repeat; it is a synonym of *Amen*; it means *think of that* or words of similar import; it is an Arabic word meaning "peace," or it is a musical direction indicating when the choir is to rest while the instruments play an interlude. *Selah* occurs in one other place in the King James Version, *II Kings 14:7* tells us that Amaziah, King of Judah, "slew Edom in the valley of salt ten thousand, and took Selah by war, and called the name of it Joktheel unto this day." Here *Selah* is believed to be merely an incorrect rendering of *Sela*, which means "rock" and which is used several times in the Old Testament as a proper name. *Sela* probably refers to Petra (also meaning rock), the famous rock-fortress in northern Arabia.

Where did Cain get his wife?

According to *Genesis 4*, after Cain slew his brother, Abel, he became a fugitive and vagabond in the earth with a mark set upon him lest any finding him should kill him. "And Cain went out from the presence of the Lord, and dwelt in the land of Nod, on the east of Eden. And Cain knew his wife; and she conceived, and bare Enoch: and he builded a city, and called the name of the city, after the name of his son, Enoch." The location of the land of Nod is not known, the Bible merely saying that it was east of the Garden of Eden. "Where did Cain get his wife?" presents a classical problem that Bible students have attempted to solve with more ingenuity than success. Some suppose that Cain's marriage occurred at a much later period than the murder of Abel, and that he married one of his sisters, or perhaps even a more distant relative, for we are told that after Adam had begotten Seth "he begat sons and daughters." Others regard the story of Cain as a composite of several traditions relating to different persons named Cain who lived at different periods. Still others hold that, according to the Bible, Adam and Eve were not the first two persons on the earth, but the first two *named* persons. They maintain that the first chapter of Genesis gives the account of the general creation of human beings, while the second chapter of the same book gives the process of creation of Adam and Eve. It was then that man first became *a living soul*. If this theory is correct, there may have been millions of human beings on the earth when Adam and Eve were created, and there would be many women from whom Cain could choose a wife. According to Jewish folklore, Adam had a wife before Eve was created for him. The name of this first wife of Adam was Lilith. She refused to submit to the authority of her husband and was so obstreperous that she was expelled from Eden, whereupon she became an Assyrian goddess of night and the mother of demons. Some writers have identified Adam's first wife Lilith with "the queen of heaven" referred to in *Jeremiah 44:17-25,* where the prophet tells the Jews in Egypt that evil days had fallen upon them because they and their fathers had burned incense and poured out drink offerings "unto the queen of heaven" in the cities of Judah and in the streets of Jerusalem. Commentators generally, however, regard this as a reference to the Assyrian or Babylonian moon goddess. Another folktale is that Lilith, after Adam repudiated her, took to the air, which she haunted as a specter and from which she swooped down to kill small children. Lilith appeared in the legends and superstition of the Middle Ages as a famous witch, and it is said that Jewish children were provided with amulets to protect them from the demon. Some authorities have assumed, apparently without good reason, that *lullaby,* the name of a refrain used to soothe infants and to put them to sleep, is a corruption of *Lilla, abi,* a signifying "Begone, Lilith." It is more probable, however, that *lullaby* is of onomatopoeic origin.

What does IHS mean?

Since the Middle Ages, IHS has been used as a symbol or monogram of the name of Jesus. It is derived from a frequent abbreviation or contraction of the name of Jesus in the Greek manuscripts of the New Testament. IHS is composed of the first three, or the first two and the last, letters of the Greek word for Jesus, which in Roman letters is written IHSOUS or IESOUS. In the Greek alphabet there are two signs for the letter corresponding to our *e.* The capital of one of these forms is similar to the Latin *H.* IHS would be a closer approximation in Latin letters to the original Greek. During the Middle Ages the correct origin and meaning of IHS were lost sight of and the Romanized letters were interpreted erroneously as the abbreviation of *Jesus, Hominum Salvator,* which is Latin for "Jesus, the Saviour of Men." This is still regarded as the popular meaning of IHS. Strictly speaking, these three letters or symbols represent a contraction of one word rather than the initials of separate words and accordingly should not be followed by periods, although usage differs and they are often written I.H.S. Variant forms of the monogram are IHC and JHC. On the mistaken assumption that IHS represents the initial letters of Latin or English words, the symbol is also popularly but incorrectly supposed to stand for various phrases; as, *In Hoc Signo (Vinces),* "In this sign (thou shalt conquer)," *In Hac Salus,* "In this (cross) is salvation," "Jesus Heavenly Saviour," and "I have suffered." *Monogram,* derived from two Greek words meaning "single letter," is a cipher, character or symbol composed of one or more letters interwoven or combined so as to represent a name or a part of it. Monograms are used on seals, rings, buttons and pins and by artists and artisans to distinguish their work. In Christian art IHS, surrounded by a glory in the sky or on a tablet borne by angels, is used to distinguish St. Ignatius Loyola, founder of the Society of Jesus, and as the monogram of the order of Jesuits itself. Paper of a large size, about 28½ by 21½ inches, used chiefly for engravings, is called *Jesus paper* because it was formerly watermarked with the letters *I.H.S.*

Why is *Christmas* written *Xmas*?

The derivation of *Xmas* for *Christmas* has long been a subject of controversy. Some authorities maintain that X here stands for the cross, symbol of Christ and Christianity. But *Xmas* had an origin somewhat similar to that of IHS, the monogram of Jesus. The Greek word for Christ is *XPIΣTOΣ,* which in Latin letters is rendered *Christos.* In the Greek alphabet the *k* sound is represented by the character *X* (chi). *X* was the usual abbreviation of *Christos* in the Greek manuscripts of the Bible. Since Chrismas, originally the mass of Christ, was a mass-day, it was at first called *Christ-mass.* This was abbreviated either *Ch-mass* or *X-mas,* depending on whether the writer preferred the Greek or the Latin form. In process of time the final *s* (Ε) was dropped and the word was written *Christmas,* with *Xmas* as the abbreviation. Many devout persons regard it as almost sacrilegious to abbreviate the name of this Christian festival as *X-mas,* and particularly to pronounce the abbreviated name as "*EKS-mas.*" Formerly *Christmas* was also commonly abbreviated *XP-mas, Xt-mas, X't-mas* and *Xst-mas,* and *Christian* and *Christianity* were abbreviated *Xtian* and *Xtianity.* Like IHS, discussed elsewhere in this work, XP is used as the Christian monogram, often inclosed in a circle. While IHS is derived from the Greek form of the name of Jesus, XP is derived from the Greek form of the word *Christ*. Here again the monogram is not composed of the English letters *X* and *P,* but of the Greek characters *X* (chi) and *P* (rho), which are the first two letters of *XPIΣTOΣ, Christos.*

What does *chamois* in the Bible mean?

Many people may be surprised to learn that the chamois is among the animals mentioned in the Bible. *Deuteronomy 14:4-5* says: "These are the beasts which ye shall eat: the ox, the sheep, and the goat, the hart, and the roebuck, and the fallow deer, and the wild goat, and the pygarg, and the wild ox, and the *chamois*." The Hebrew word here rendered *chamois* is of doubtful meaning and the animal referred to has never been definitely identified. It was probably a species of wild sheep. There is little probability that it was the true chamois, a species of goat-antelope inhabiting the mountains of Europe and Asia.

Does the Bible say, "Beware of dogs"?

The expression, "Beware of dogs," occurs in the Bible once. *Philippians 3:2* says: "Beware of dogs, beware of evil workers, beware of the concision." Here *dogs* is used figuratively by St. Paul to warn the Christians at Philippi against certain adversaries. A comparable use of *dogs* occurs in *Psalm 22:16*, which reads: "For dogs have compassed me: the assembly of the wicked have inclosed me: they pierced my hands and my feet." *Concision* occurs nowhere in the Bible except in *Philippians 3:2*, quoted above. It is the translation of a Greek word meaning "incision" or "cutting up." St. Paul apparently uses the term in scorn of certain Christian Jews and as a play upon circumcision. From the context his thought appears to be that some Jewish unbelievers practiced circumcision without any spiritual significance or relation to the ancient Abrahamic rite. The underlying idea seems to be that this was no better than the body mutilations or the cutting of the flesh practised by the heathen. *Leviticus 21:6* forbade the priests to "make any cuttings in their flesh." In *I Kings 18:28* we read that the prophets of Baal "cut themselves after their manner with knives and lancets, till the blood gushed out upon them." *Concision* was merely a scornful reference to circumcision that had no true spiritual significance.

Why were Adam and Eve driven from the Garden of Eden?

No idea is more firmly fixed in the popular mind than that Adam and Eve were expelled from the Garden of Eden as a punishment for eating the forbidden fruit. Yet the Bible says nothing of the kind. In *Genesis 3:22-23* it is specifically stated that God sent the first man forth from the Garden of Eden to till the ground whence he was taken "lest he put forth his hand, and take also of the tree of life, and eat, and live forever." Originally there was no ban on eating of the tree of life, for God had commanded Adam, saying, "Of every tree of the garden thou mayest freely eat: but of the tree of knowledge of good and evil, thou shalt not eat of it: for in the day that thou eatest thereof thou shalt surely die." Presumably, had not Adam and Eve eaten of the forbidden fruit, they might have partaken of the fruit of the tree of life and lived forever. The threatened death sentence, however, was not carried out. All three principals in the forbidden fruit episode were meted out punishments, but expulsion from the Garden of Eden was not among them. The serpent, cursed above all cattle and every beast of the field, was condemned to crawl on its belly and eat dust all the days of its life. Eve, made the chief antagonist of the serpent, was doomed to bring forth children in sorrow and to be ruled over by her husband. Adam, relieved of his office as gardener, was condemned to make his livelihood by tilling the stubborn ground and to eat his bread in the sweat of his face. Thus it will be seen that our first parents were not driven from paradise for eating the forbidden fruit, but to prevent them from eating the fruit of eternal life.

Who was King Lemuel?

Lemuel is the name of a king mentioned in *Proverbs 31:4.* That chapter begins: "The words of king Lemuel. The vision wherewith his mother instructed him." The name occurs again in *Verse 4*: "It is not for kings, O Lemuel, it is not for kings to drink wine; . . ." Chastity and temperance are the themes of the discourse that follows. Nothing else whatever is known of King Lemuel. Some authorities have supposed that he was King Solomon himself, while others believe that he was an ancient king of Massa, a small kingdom somewhere in Arabia, although that is mere speculation. Massa is mentioned in *Genesis 25:14* as being one of the sons of Ishmael. *Proverbs 31* is often referred to as the only chapter in the Bible written by a woman about women. Although there is no complete chapter in the Scriptures written by a woman about women, this chapter consists largely of the things that King Lemuel's mother taught him and much of it is about the virtues of women. *Judges 5* and *Ruth 2* are also sometimes so referred to, but with less reason.

Where does the Bible mention kissing the hand?

The practice of throwing a kiss is alluded to in *Job 21:27*, where, in his parable, the patriarch says: "And my heart hath been secretly enticed, or my mouth hath kissed my hand." Kissing idols was a common practice among the heathen. In *I Kings 19:18* the Lord says to Elijah: "Yet I have left me seven thousand in Israel, all the knees which have not bowed unto Baal, and every mouth which hath not kissed him." This is also referred to in *Hosea 13:1-2* "When Ephraim spake trembling, he exalted himself in Israel; but when he offended in Baal, he died. And now they sin more and more, and have made them molten images of their silver, and idols according to their own understanding, all of it the work of the craftsmen; they say of them, Let the men that sacrifice kiss the calves." Our common custom of throwing a kiss is believed to come from the ancient practice of kissing the hand to a god whose statue was too tall to be reached. If the statue of the god was low enough the worshipper kissed it; if not, he kissed his hand and waved it toward the image. Kissing the black stone is still one of the rites of the Moslem pilgrims at Mecca.

How long is a generation in the Bible?

Generation is used in the Bible in several different senses. The term literally means "genesis," "origin," "genealogy," or "descent." Adam was of the first generation, Seth the second, Enos of the third, and so on. According to *Genesis 15:16,* the Lord told Abram in a deep sleep that "in the fourth generation they [Abram's descendants] shall come hither again." In *Genesis 50:23* we are told that "Joseph saw Ephraim's children of the third generation." *Deuteronomy 23:2* says: "A bastard shall not enter into the congregation of the Lord: even to his tenth generation shall he not enter into the congregation of the Lord." In this latter use, however, "even to his tenth generation" is probably only a figurative way of saying "never." In process of time a generation came to be regarded as the average lifetime of man or the ordinary period of time at which the father was succeeded by his son. It was only natural that the generation should become the basis of a period of chronology. The ancient Hebrews, like many other ancients, sometimes computed the passage of time by generations, although they do not appear to have made extensive use of generations for that purpose. The generation did not represent a definite period, and there is nothing uniform or settled in this method of computing chronology. By the ancients the generation was variously fixed at periods of time ranging from twenty years to one hundred and ten years. Naturally a generation was much longer in the days when men were reputed to live nearly one thousand years than in later times when one hundred years was considered a ripe old age. *Matthew 1:17* says: "So all the generations from Abraham to David are fourteen generations; and from David until the carrying away into Babylon are fourteen generations; and from the carrying away into Babylon unto Christ are fourteen generations." In the preceding genealogy there are only thirteen names in the list from the captivity to Jesus, which indicates that one name has been dropped out. It should be borne in mind that genealogy was much more important to the Israelites than it is to us. Under the Mosaic law all sorts of property and other legal rights depended upon tribe and family relationship. *Ezra 2:59* says some of those who reported to return from Babylon to Jerusalem in the time of Cyrus "could not shew their father's house, and their seed, whether they were of Israel," and Josephus tells us that 662 persons who wanted to go with Zerubbabel's party and who "said they were of the Israelites" were rejected because they "were not able to show their genealogies." Many of the genealogies and "generations" in the Bible are probably the work of later pedigree-makers who did their best in filling up gaps in the fragmentary records to prove their point. Paul, writing as a former Pharisee, says in *II Timothy 3:9*: "But avoid foolish questions, and genealogies, and contentions, and strivings about the law; for they are unprofitable and vain." The problem is further complicated by the fact that the whole body of individuals born about the same period are called a generation; and, by extension, the term is applied to the time covered by their lives. In this sense, a generation is an ever-changing and not a static thing. "Verily I say unto you, This generation shall not pass, till all these things be fulfilled," says Jesus in *Matthew 24:34*. This means that all who are at present living shall not be dead when this shall come to pass, or there are some now living who shall witness these things. "This generation" and "the men of this generation" in *Luke 11:31-32* signify those now alive. In *Ezekiel 29:11* the prophet says of Egypt that it shall not "be inhabited forty years," where "forty years" probably is a round number indicating a generation. Herodotus, referring to the kings and high priests of Egypt, wrote that "three generations fill up a century." Josephus, in his chronology of the Hebrews from Joseph to Moses, estimated a generation at forty-two or forty-three years. Today a generation is generally regarded as being from thirty to thirty-three and one-third years in length, there being about three in a century. The basis of the generation as a period in modern chronology is the average interval of time between the birth of parents and that of children, although some chronologists base the generation upon the average lifetime of all persons of synchronous age who survive infancy. Formerly thirty-three years was regarded as a fair average of the length of life of man. But the foregoing observations will show that generation as a period of time is largely meaningless. In 1815 Thomas Jefferson made this interesting statement: "By the tables of mortality, of the adults living at one moment of time, a majority will be dead in about nineteen years. At the end of that period, then, a new majority is come into place; or, in other words, a new generation. Each generation is as independent of the one preceding, as that was of all which had gone before. It has, then, like them, a right to choose for itself the form of government it believes most promotive of its own happiness; consequently, a solemn opportunity of doing this every nineteen or twenty years should be provided by the Constitution." David Brewster has this to say in his *Life of Sir Isaac Newton*: "M. Freret concludes that the Argonautic expedition took place 532 years earlier than Sir Isaac made it. His second objection as to the new system of chronology relates to the length of generations, which he says is made only eighteen or twenty years. Sir Isaac, on the contrary, reckons a generation at thirty-three years, or three generations at 100; and it was the length of the reigns of kings that he made eighteen or twenty years. This deduction he founded on the reigns of sixty-four French kings. Now the ancient Greeks and Egyptians reckoned the length of a reign equal to that of a generation; and it was by correcting this mistake, and adopting a measure founded on fact, that Sir Isaac placed the Argonautic expedition forty-four years after the death of Solomon, and fixed some of the other points of his system."

What is the first book mentioned in the Bible?

The earliest use of *book* in the Bible is in *Genesis 5:1*, which says in part: "This is the book of the generations of Adam." The term there signifies a register in which events are recorded. The earliest mention of writing in the Bible is in *Exodus 17:14*, where, after Joshua defeated Amalek, the Lord said to Moses: "Write this for a memorial in a book, and rehearse it in the ears of Joshua." *Exodus 24:4* says that Moses, after coming down from Sinai, "wrote all the words of the Lord, and rose up early in the morning, and builded an altar under the mount, and twelve pillars, according to the twelve tribes of Israel." Since writing in those days often consisted of inscribing characters on clay or stone tablets, some authorities suppose that Moses may have written all the words of the Lord upon the pillars of stone that he set up, although there may be no connection between the writing and the pillars.

Why did Job want his adversary to write a book?

Job 31:35 says: "Oh that one would hear me! Behold, my desire is that, the Almighty would answer me, and that mine adversary had written a book." *Book* there is used in the sense of a writing and probably means an indictment or a bill of particulars. Job merely expresses the wish that his adversary, who is God, had charged him with specific wrongdoing, because he feels that he could then easily establish his innocence. In *Job 19:23-24* the patriarch says: "Oh that my words were now written! oh that they were printed in a book! that they were graven with an iron pen and lead in the rock for ever." The thought seems to be that Job longed to have his protestations of innocence inscribed in a book or engraved on some durable and imperishable material such as rock.

Who said: "Of making many books there is no end"?

This famous quotation is from *Ecclesiastes 12:12,* which says: "And further, by these, my son, be admonished: of making many books there is no end: and much study is a weariness of the flesh." *Ecclesiastes; Or, The Preacher,* which is the full title of this book, is popularly ascribed to Solomon. Internal evidence, however, indicates that it was composed at a much later period than the time of Solomon. He lived in the tenth century B.C., when books were comparatively rare in Palestine, and it is highly improbable that the King of Israel ever saw enough books to surfeit his intellect or to weary his flesh. *Ecclesiastes* bears decided traces of a knowledge of Greek culture, which was introduced into the entire Mediterranean world by Alexander the Great and his successors. From the death of Alexander in 323 B.C. to the conquest of Palestine by the Romans under Pompey in 63 B.C., the Jews were subjected to the influence of the Greeks of Syria and of Egypt. It was not until then that the Jews came into intimate contact with Greek thought and Greek books. The Greeks were the first people to produce books in large numbers. Undoubtedly it was the great number of books written by the Greek philosophers that wearied and bewildered The Preacher in *Ecclesiastes.*

How many Popes are mentioned in the Bible?

The Roman Catholic church regards the Apostle Peter as the first Bishop of Rome and accordingly as the first Pope. He is the only person whose name appears in the list of the Popes who is known definitely to be mentioned in the Bible. According to a list generally accepted by Catholic authorities, Pope Pius XII, who assumed the tiara in 1939, was the 262nd Pope. There is, however, a wide difference of opinion among Catholics themselves as to the exact number. Many names in the list are doubtful. According to a tradition, St. Linus succeeded St. Peter as Pope and reigned twelve years—from 67-79 A.D. St. Irenaeus, who wrote during the latter part of the second century, was of the opinion that the second Pope was the Linus mentioned by St. Paul in *II Timothy 4:21,* which reads: "Do thy diligence to come before winter. Eubulus greeteth thee, and Pudens, and Linus, and Claudia, and all the brethren." Although Catholics regard St. Peter as the first Pope and head of the Roman Catholic Church, there have been no later Popes named Peter. It is supposed that no later Popes assumed the name because they felt that it would be presumptuous to style themselves Peter II, Peter III, etc. There have been many Popes named John and Paul, but none named Matthew or Luke, and only one named Mark. Each Pope changes his name when he assumes the pontificate. This custom is said to have grown up after Sergius IV, who sat in the Papal chair from 1009-12 A.D., abandoned his own homely name in favor of a more dignified one. Originally he was known as Peter Bucca Porci (Peter Pig's Snout), and he took the name Sergius IV because his surname was too plain and because he feared that it might be deemed arrogance on his part to style himself Peter II.

What is meant by *Urim and Thummim*?

The real significance of *Urim and Thummim* has been lost for thousands of years and is one of the fascinating mysteries of the Bible. Hebrew scholars are generally agreed that *Urim* signifies "lights" and *Thummim,* "perfections." They are the names used to designate mysterious objects connected with the breastplate of the high priest. These sacred symbols are first mentioned in *Exodus 28:30,* where the Lord said to Moses: "And thou shalt put in the breastplate of judgment the Urim and Thummim; and they shall be upon Aaron's heart, when he goeth in before the Lord: and Aaron shall bear the judgment of the children of Israel upon his heart before the Lord continually." *Numbers 27:21* says Joshua "shall stand before Eleazar the priest, who shall ask counsel for him after the judgment of Urim before the Lord." *Leviticus 8:8* tells us that Moses put the breastplate upon Aaron and "put in the breastplate the Urim and Thummim." According to *Deuteronomy 33:8,* Moses in blessing the tribe of Levi said: "Let thy Thummim and thy Urim be with thy holy one." *I Samuel 28:5* says "when Saul inquired of the Lord, the Lord answered him not, neither by dreams, nor by Urim, nor by prophets," whereupon the discredited king of Israel sought out the woman at Endor. From *Ezra 2:63* and an identical passage in *Nehemiah* we learn that some of the Jews who returned to Jerusalem from the Babylonian captivity thought "they should not eat of the most holy things, till there stood up a priest with Urim and with Thummim." That is the last clear reference to these mysterious sacred objects. The high priest of Israel used the Urim and Thummim in communicating with God, but what the procedure was is unknown. Some authorities suppose that the twelve precious stones in the high priest's breastplate and the Urim and Thummim were identical. The most plausible theory, however, is that the Urim and Thummim were oracular objects, perhaps precious gem stones, carried in the breastplate of the high priest and used by him in casting lots to determine the will of Jehovah on difficult questions of national importance. There are many references in the Bible to casting lots and that was a common method of divination. According to *Leviticus 16:8*, Aaron was to "cast lots upon the two goats" to determine which was for Jehovah and which was to be sent into the wilderness as a scapegoat. The Promised Land was divided among the tribes by lot. Lots were cast to decide the various functions of the priests in the temple. This is alluded to in *Luke 1:8*, which, referring to Zacharias, says: "According to the custom of the priest's office, his lot was to burn incense when he went into the temple of the Lord." The mariners on the ship on which Jonah was sailing cast lots to determine whose evil conduct had brought on the tempest. At the crucifixion the soldiers cast lots for the garments of Jesus, and the eleven Apostles chose a successor to Judas Iscariot by lot. *Nehemiah 10:34* says: "And we cast the lots among the priests, the Levites, and the people, for the wood offering, to bring it into the house of our God." According to *Nehemiah 11:1*, "the rest of the people also cast lots, to bring one of ten to dwell in Jerusalem the holy city, and nine parts to dwell in other cities."

Why are rich merchants called merchant princes?

A merchant prince is a merchant who has princely wealth. The name was probably suggested by *Isaiah 23:8*, which reads: "Who hath taken this counsel against Tyre, the crowning city, whose merchants are princes, whose traffickers are the honorable of the earth?"

What does *anathema* in the Bible mean?

Anathema occurs only once in the King James Version of the Bible. *I Corinthians 16:22* says: "If any man love not the Lord Jesus Christ, let him be Anathema Maranatha." Here *anathema* means "an accursed thing." It is derived from a Greek word signifying "offering" and originally meant "a thing devoted." A remarkable thing about *anathema* in modern English is the fact that its meaning varies with the pronunciation. When it is accented on the second syllable and pronounced *a-NATH-e-ma* it means "a curse"; but when it is accented on the third syllable and pronounced *an-a-THEE-ma* it means "something consecrated or devoted to sacred purposes." The English translators of the Bible appear to have erroneously taken *Maranatha* as a portentously intensified anathema or curse. Bible scholars inform us that *Maranatha* is really an Aramaic phrase meaning "the Lord has come" or "Our Lord, come." *Maranatha* really should form a separate sentence. Correctly translated, *I Corinthians 16:22* would read: "If any man love not the Lord Jesus Christ, let him be accursed. The Lord has come." Some authorities suppose that *Maranatha* was used as a sort of watchword by the early Christians.

What does *venison* in the Bible mean?

Venison occurs five times in the King James Version of the Bible, but only in the story of Isaac and his twin sons, Esau and Jacob, where the term probably refers to the flesh of kids or young goats. It is a common mistake to suppose that Esau, "a cunning hunter, a man of the field," went out to hunt a deer to make his father "a savoury meat," while his brother, Jacob, "a plain man, dwelling in tents," slipped out upon his mother's suggestion and fetched two good kids of the goats from the family flock. There is every reason to suppose that the savoury meat in both cases was made of the flesh of young goats. Jacob's offering to Isaac was domestic kid, while that of Esau was wild kid. At the time the English Bible was translated *venison* was applied to the flesh of any wild animal or bird killed in the chase or by hunting and used for food. It was applied equally to the flesh of wild boars, hares, deer, pheasants, ducks, geese, quail and other game animals and birds. According to the usage of that day the flesh of a hunted hare was more properly termed *venison* than was that of a tame deer killed in a park by a gamekeeper. *Venison* is derived from Latin *venation,* meaning "hunting." The limitation of *venison* to the flesh of the deer kind is comparatively modern. This limitation of the term was natural owing to the fact that the deer gradually became the most important game animal in England.

What did Jacob pay Esau for his birthright?

Many people will be surprised to learn that the phrase *mess of pottage* occurs nowhere in the text of the King James Version of the Bible and that there is nothing in the Old Testament saying specifically that the pottage eaten by Esau was the price paid by Jacob for the birthright. Esau and Jacob were the twin sons of Isaac and Rebekah. Isaac was partial to Esau, his first born, who was a cunning hunter and a man of the field and who used to take his quiver and bow and kill venison, which his father loved when made into a "savoury meat." But Rebekah loved Jacob, a plain man, who dwelt in tents and who was not red and hairy like Esau. The story of the sale of the birthright is told in *Genesis 25:29-34*: "And Jacob sod pottage: and Esau came from the field, and he was faint. And Esau said to Jacob, Feed me, I pray thee, with that same red pottage; for I am faint: therefore was his name called Edom. And Jacob said, Sell me this day thy birthright. And Esau said, Behold, I am at the point to die: and what profit shall this birthright do to me? And Jacob said, Swear to me this day; and he sware unto him: and he sold his birthright to Jacob. Then Jacob gave Esau bread and pottage of lentiles; and he did eat and drink, and rose up, and went his way: thus Esau despised his birthright." This account tells us merely that Esau sold his birthright to Jacob and that Jacob gave Esau bread and pottage of lentiles, but it does not say in so many words that the pottage was the price paid for the birthright, which presumably carried with it the headship of the family and the double inheritance of the first-born in accordance with *Deuteronomy 21:17*. From this account it is difficult to determine whether the food was the price paid or whether Jacob only took advantage of his brother's hunger, thirst and faintness to drive a good bargain. That the food was the price paid for the birthright is a natural and legitimate inference. In *Genesis 27* Esau complains of his scheming brother that "he took away my birthright." The only specific Biblical authority for the statement that the pottage was the price paid for the birthright is found, not in the Old, but in the New Testament. *Hebrews 12:16* refers to "Esau, who for one morsel of meat sold his birthright." Formerly some editors of the Bible inserted in the chapter heading of *Genesis 25* the words, "Esau selleth Jacob his birthright for a mess of pottage." That undoubtedly accounts for the popularity of the phrase and the common notion that it is in the Bible.

What did the bears do to the children who mocked Elisha?

Contrary to a widespread impression, the Bible does not say that bears ate the children who mocked the prophet Elisha while he was on his way to Bethel after assuming the mantle of Elijah at Jericho. *Tare*, not *ate*, is the word used by the translators of the Authorized Version in this connection. The incident is related in *2 Kings 2:23-24* in the following language: "And he went up from thence unto Bethel: and as he was going up by the way, there came forth little children out of the city, and mocked him, and said unto him, Go up, thou bald head; go up, thou bald head. And he turned back, and looked on them, and cursed them in the name of the Lord. And there came forth two she bears out of the wood, and tare [tore] forty and two children of them."

What is meant by "the burial of an ass"?

"The burial of an ass" means no decent burial at all. The expression is from *Jeremiah 22:19*, which says: "He shall be buried with the burial of an ass, drawn and cast forth beyond the gates of Jerusalem." Jehoiakim, who was one of the last kings of Judah and who "did that which was evil in the sight of the Lord," was the man of whom the prophet spoke. In *II Kings* and *II Chronicles*, where the story of Jehoiakim is related, there is no intimation that the prophecy was literally fulfilled and that the unfortunate King was denied decent burial. We are told simply that he "slept with his fathers."

Why is a taxi driver called a Jehu?

A taxicab driver, especially one who drives fast and recklessly, is called a Jehu. This is an allusion to *II Kings 9:20*, which in part reads: "And the driving is like the driving of Jehu the son of Nimshi; for he driveth furiously." Jehu, not to be confused with the prophet of the same name, was an officer in the Israelite army who led a successful rebellion against King Jehoram and then assumed the royal title with the blessing of the prophet Elisha. As Jehu in his chariot approached Jezreel, the Samarian capital, King Jehoram sent a messenger on horseback to learn whether Jehu's intentions were peaceful or warlike. But the messenger fell in behind Jehu and joined the rebels. A second horseman did the same, whereupon a watchman standing on the tower at Jezreel said to King Jehoram: "He came even unto them, and cometh not again: and the driving is like the driving of Jehu the son of Nimshi; for he driveth furiously." In the ensuing battle on the field of Naboth near Jezreel Jehu personally killed King Jehoram and his men mortally wounded King Ahaziah of Judah, who happened to be visiting his royal uncle. Then Jehu as king trapped and slew the priests of Baal, destroyed the house and images of that god, killed the seventy sons of Ahab and virtually exterminated all members of the royal family of Israel. It was Jehu who induced two or three eunuchs to throw the wicked Jezebel, Ahab's Phoenician wife, out of a window to be trampled underfoot by horses and eaten by dogs. At the time of the rebellion Jehu is pictured in the Bible as being bold, decisive, able, swift, bloodthirsty and fanatically righteous in the cause of the faith of Israel. Josephus seems to differ with the Bible respecting the driving of Jehu. The Jewish historian says that when the rebel officer approached Jezreel he "marched slowly, and in good order." Although in *II Kings 9:20* the founder of the fifth dynasty of Israel is called "the son of Nimshi," *II Kings 9:14* tells us he was the son of Jehoshaphat and the grandson of Nimshi. But in the end Jehu "departed not from the sins of Jeroboam, which made Israel to sin," lost large portions of his territory to the Syrians and had to pay them tribute. The earliest use of *Jehu* in the sense of a driver or coachman recorded by the Oxford dictionary is dated 1682.

How did "holier than thou" originate?

"Holier than thou," which is applied to persons who profess to be more virtuous than other people, is taken from the Old Testament. According to *Isaiah 65:5*, the Israelites, who rebelled against Jehovah and went after their own thoughts, said: "Stand by thyself, come not near to me; for I am holier than thou." Jesus gives a good description of the holier-than-thou type in the parable of the Pharisee and the publican who went up into the temple to pray. In his prayer the self-righteous Pharisee bragged of his compliance with the technical requirements of his religion and thanked God that he was not like other men.

Why does a jury generally consist of twelve?

There is reason for believing that the fixing of twelve as the proper number of persons on a petit jury was indirectly the result of Biblical influence. Twelve was one of the sacred numbers of the ancient Hebrews and it figured largely in the symbolism of the Israelites. There were twelve months in the Hebrew calendar; Jacob had twelve sons; there were twelve tribes of Israel, and Jesus had twelve apostles. The real origin of the English jury system is lost in the obscurity of the past. Twelve as the number of a jury may have begun as an accident that was sanctioned by experience. Under the Anglo-Saxon legal system each defendant and each plaintiff in a trial was permitted to have six witnesses, a total of twelve. Charles of Burgundy set up committees of twelve men to levy taxes, and William the Conqueror named committees of the same number to take the first census in England. In 1166, in the time of King Henry II, the Constitutions of Clarendon designated twelve men in each hundred to present for trial by ordeal all those known or suspected to be violators of the law. At first the jurymen performed the functions of both judges and witnesses. The jury system as we know it today was the product of legal evolution. It was in its infancy at a time when church and state were closely identified and when religious considerations affected civil as well as ecclesiastical law. Undoubtedly twelve as the ideal number on a jury was perpetuated, if it was not actually suggested, by the symbolical significance of that number in the Bible.

Did the ancient Israelites shave?

Although it is not probable that shaving was a general practice among the ancient Israelites, the allusions to shaving and razors in the Bible are numerous. The earliest mention of shaving occurs in *Genesis 41:4*, where it is recorded that Joseph "shaved himself, and changed his raiment" when summoned from the dungeon to appear before Pharaoh. *Job 1:20* says: "Then Job arose, and rent his mantle, and shaved his head, and fell down upon the ground, and worshipped." The Hebrew word here translated *shave* is elsewhere rendered *shear* in the King James Version. It is not always clear when shaving and when shearing is meant. Israelite men were accustomed to wear full beards, which were not shaved or sheared except in particular cases. The hair and beard were regarded as symbols of vital power. Under the law of Moses shaving was a means of purification from the plague, leprosy and defilement. *Numbers 6:5* says of the Nazarite that "all the days of the vow of his separation there shall no rasor come upon his head." *According to Judges 13:5*, the angel of the Lord who appeared to the mother of Samson declared that "no rasor shall come on his head: for the child shall be a Nazarite unto God from the womb." Samson appears to have been a Nazarite of a special kind and his great strength is attributed to his hair. In *Samuel 1:11* Hannah, mother of Samuel, promises the Lord that if he will give her a man child she would give him to the Lord "all the days of his life, and there shall no rasor come upon his head." The very fact that the Nazarites were forbidden to shave suggests that other Israelites were in the habit of doing so. *Numbers 6:18* says the temporary Nazarite, after having fulfilled his vow, "shall shave the head of his separation at the door of the tabernacle of the congregation, and shall take the hair of the head of his separation, and put it in the fire which is under the sacrifice of the peace offering." In *Acts 18:18* we are told that Paul sheared his head in Cenchrea because of a vow, and this shaving or shearing of the head of Nazarites after fulfilling the vow is mentioned again in *Acts 21* in connection with Paul's return to Jerusalem. The idea seems to be that the hair on the head of the Nazarite represented his dedication with all his strength and powers to the service of God. According to *Deuteronomy 21:12,* a woman taken captive in war and claimed as the wife of an Israelite was to "shave her head, and pare her nails," as a sign that her forlorn condition was ended. It is said that among the Arabs it is still the practice of a widow to terminate her period of mourning by a similar act. *Deuteronomy 14:1* says "Ye shall not . . . make any baldness between your eyes for the dead," which appears to forbid the shaving of the head and face as a sign of mourning; but *Jeremiah 41:5* tells us of fourscore men who had "their beards shaven, and their clothing rent." *Leviticus 19:27* says: "Ye shall not round the corners of your heads, neither shalt thou mar the corners of thy beard." The Lord, according to *Leviticus 21:5,* told Moses that the priests "shall not make baldness upon their head, neither shall they shave off the corner of their beard." No doubt these prohibitions refer to Canaanitish practices that were deemed heathenish and unworthy of imitation by the Israelites. We learn from *II Samuel 10:4* and *I Chronicles 19:4* that shaving off the beard was a badge of shame in ancient Israel. Hanun, king of the Ammonites, suspected David's good-will messengers of being spies and "shaved off the one half of their beards." They were not permitted to shave off the other half and in consequence they were "greatly ashamed." David, not wishing them to become a laughing-stock, sent them word to tarry at Jericho until their beards were grown. Under the Czars of Russia persons exiled to Siberia often had one side of their heads shaved for easy identification in the event they escaped. There are two curious references to this subject in *Ezekiel.* According to *Ezekiel 5:1,* the prophet was told in his vision: "And thou, son of man, take thee a sharp knife, take thee a barber's rasor, and cause it to pass upon thine head and upon thy beard: then take thee balances to weigh, and divide the hair." In *Ezekiel 44:20* it is said of the priests: "Neither shall they shave their heads, nor suffer their locks to grow long: they shall only poll their heads." The practice of removing part or all the hair from the face dates back to prehistoric times and seems to have been begun in the earliest stages of civilization. Before the use of metal razors the hairs were pulled out individually or cut by means of flints or other small stones with sharp edges. The earliest drawings found in Egypt and Assyria depict men clean shaven. The American Indians, who resemble Orientals in having light beards, religiously removed all the hair from their faces with sharp flints. Some of the savages of Polynesia still shave with pieces of flint, while others shave with pieces of shells or sharks' teeth ground to a fine edge. Metal razors of some kind or other were probably employed by the Egyptians and Assyrians as far back as 3500 B.C. Generally speaking, it may be said that razors were first made of flint, then of bronze and finally of steel. Shaving did not become a common practice until after all of the Old Testament books were written. It is said that Alexander the Great ordered his soldiers to shave off their beards in order to remove possible appendages for the enemy to seize in battle. Pliny tells us that Scipio Africanus, who lived a century after Alexander, was the first Roman to shave regularly every day. Shaving in all probability was still uncommon in the Roman Empire during the first century A.D. Although the New Testament is silent on the subject, the general presumption that Jesus and his disciples had beards is undoubtedly correct. When Father Garnier, the French missionary among the Hurons, showed the Indians a picture of the Saviour the sight of the beard threw them into convulsions of laughter. "Send me," wrote the Jesuit in 1640 to a friend in France, "a picture of Christ without a beard."

When did the synagogue originate?

Curiously enough, *synagogue* is of Greek, not of Hebrew, origin. Another curious fact is that the synagogue is not once mentioned in the Old Testament or the Old Testament Apocrypha, while it is frequently mentioned in the New Testament. *Synagogue* is from Greek *syn*, "together," and *agein*, "to lead" or "to bring," and literally signifies "a meeting or assembly." This term was introduced to the Jews by its use in the Septuagint, the Greek translation of the Hebrew scriptures made at Alexandria long before New Testament times, where it was used to render the Hebrew words for assembly and congregation. Nobody knows for certain just when or where the synagogue originated. It is supposed that the synagogue as a place of Jewish religious worship and instruction grew up among the Jews of the dispersion after the destruction of Solomon's temple by the Babylonians. There is no evidence that the ancient Israelites had local institutions corresponding to the later synagogues. After the destruction of the first temple the synagogue became almost a necessity for the scattered communities of Jews. Even after the first dispersion the Jews constituted a religious democracy, and most authorities are of the opinion that the Babylonian captivity was the crucible from which the synagogue evolved as a local house of God for the people. The synagogue probably had its most rapid growth during the Greek and Maccabean period, and that may account for the fact that it has a Greek rather than a Hebrew name. When the second temple was built it appears that the Jews in Palestine as well as elsewhere continued the use of local synagogues as supplementary to the temple worship. References in the New Testament indicate that virtually every town and village in Palestine had its synagogue. The small town of Nazareth, where Jesus spent his boyhood and early manhood, had its synagogue, and there were synagogues even in Jerusalem almost under the shadows of the temple. The Synagogue of the Libertines, whose members disputed with Stephen according to *Acts 6:9,* was so called from the fact that its membership was composed of Cyrenian, Alexandrian and Cilian *Libertini,* freedmen or emancipated slaves. Since the destruction of Herod's temple by the Romans in 70 A.D., the synagogues have constituted the sole place of public worship by the Jews. The "rulers" of the synagogues mentioned in the New Testament were officials charged with the supervision of the building, the external order of public worship, selection of teachers and readers, examination of the discourses of speakers and the general conduct of the services. Christianity was first taught outside Palestine in the synagogues of the various Jewish communities scattered throughout the Roman Empire, and the Jewish synagogue was the mother of the Christian church and the Moslem mosque. Perhaps no human institution has had a longer continuous history than the Jewish synagogue. It has existed continually since ancient times in one place or another despite frequent suppressions and persecutions. Judaism was always a literature-sustained religion and it led the way in universal elementary education for all the children in the community. "All thy children shall be taught of the Lord," declared the prophet in *Isaiah 54:13*. Universal education, in obedience to this principle, was carried out through the synagogue. The Jews are known to have had Sabbath schools for young people in connection with their synagogues as early as 70 B.C., and these Sabbath schools were the forerunners of the later Christian Sunday schools. Among Reform Jews *temple* is preferred to *synagogue* as the name of a Jewish house of worship.

What does the number 666 signify?

Six hundred and sixty-six, often called the apocalyptic number, is the number given to one of the allegorical beasts seen by St. John the Divine in his vision on Patmos. *Revelation 13:18* says: "Here is wisdom. Let him that hath understanding count the number of the beast: for it is the number of a man; and his number is Six hundred threescore and six." This verse probably has given rise to more speculation and discussion than any other single passage in the Bible.

The interpretations are legion. The symbolical and mystic number of the beast is often identified with the antichrist. It appears that at the time *Revelation* was composed there was a tradition that an adversary of Christ known as the antichrist would appear. For instance, *I John 1:18* says: "Little children, it is the last time: and as ye have heard that antichrist shall come, even now are there many antichrists: whereby we know that it is the last time." There are allusions, though not direct references, to antichrist in Paul's Epistles. Probably the author of *Revelation* intended the number 666 as an allusion to a particular person who would be recognizable to an inner circle of readers, but not to outsiders. The cryptic number is most often identified with the Roman Emperor Nero. For generations after the death of Nero there was a persistent belief that he was not actually dead and that he would return to govern the Roman Empire. In Greek Nero was known as *Neron Kaisar,* "Nero Caesar." In the almost vowelless Hebrew of that day this name became *Nron Ksr.* These letters correspond to the numerals 50, 200, 6, 50, 100, 60 and 200, and added they total 666, the number of the beast. This ingenious device was accepted by many as conclusive proof that the beast was Nero. Some, however, despite the statement in *Revelation* that "it is the number of a man," took the mystic number to refer to Rome itself rather than any particular person. Before the Reformation some of the Waldensians and Albigensians, as well as John Wycliffe and John Hus, referred to the papacy, in a more or less figurative sense, as the antichrist. After the Reformation the Pope was often identified specifically with the antichrist and the beast in *Revelation.* According to some early Lutheran writers, antichrist began to reign over the Church in the year 607 A.D., when Pope Boniface III obtained from the Eastern emperor the privilege of calling the Roman church "Head of all the Churches." From this there grew up a curious and absurd belief among anti-Catholics that the number 666 actually appears on the tiara worn by the Pope. They supported their charge by an odd but far-fetched coincidence. The title of the Pope is Vicar of Christ. On some of the tiaras worn by the Pope this title was written *VICARIVS FILII DEI,* Latin for "Vicar of the Son of God." When those letters in this title that are used as Roman numerals are given their respective values and added together, and those not so used are excluded or given the value of zero, the total is 666. This roundabout method of converting *VICARIVS FILII DEI* into the apocalyptic number is accepted by some people even to this day as conclusive evidence of the identity of the papacy with the beast and antichrist. A similar method of applying cryptic numerology to the Greek letters of *Lateinos*, as pagan Rome was often called, brings the same result and identifies ancient Rome with the number of the beast.

What long fasts are mentioned in the Bible?

In *Exodus 34:28* we are told that Moses was on Mt. Sinai with the Lord "forty days and forty nights" and that "he did neither eat bread, nor drink water." From other allusions in the Pentateuch we gather that Moses fasted forty days and nights on the mount at three different times—first, when he received the original Ten Commandments; second, when he interceded for the people after the golden calf sin; and third, when he received the Ten Commandments the second time. Elijah on one occasion went forty days and forty nights on the strength of two meals eaten at the same time. In *I Kings 19:5-8* it is related that as the prophet lay and slept under a juniper tree in the southern desert "an angel touched him, and said unto him, Arise and eat. And he looked, and, behold, there was a cake baken on the coals, and a cruse of water at his head. And he did eat and drink, and laid him down again. And the angel of the Lord came again the second time, and touched him, and said, Arise and eat; because the journey is too great for thee. And he arose, and did eat and drink, and went in the strength of that meat forty days and forty nights unto Horeb the mount of God." *Matthew 4:1-2* says: "Then was Jesus led up of the Spirit into the wilderness to be tempted of the devil. And when he had fasted forty days and forty nights, he was afterward an hungred." Scientists say that ordinarily forty days is about the limit that a human being can live without food. Total abstinence from both food and drink leads to death by starvation in eight days or more, depending on the original physical conditions of the individual. One of the most prolonged fasts in history was that of Terence MacSwiney, Lord Mayor of Cork, Ireland, who in 1920 was sentenced to two years in prison on charges of possessing seditious documents. As a protest against his confinement in Brixton Prison, London, MacSwiney on August 12 went on a "hunger strike" and refused to eat food of any kind while in prison. He did not, however, refuse water and medicines. His death from hunger occurred October 25 of the same year—the seventy-fourth day of his fast. Although from time to time he was subject to fits of delirium, he retained consciousness until within a few days of his death. Most fasts notable for their length have been contingent upon the use of water. In 1942 a conscientious objector to military service in a Maryland camp went on a hunger strike that lasted forty-six days. A doctor who examined him at the end of the forty-six-day period pronounced him in remarkably good physical and mental condition, although considerably "dehydrated and underweight." Mohandas Gandhi, the Indian Nationalist leader, always took water and some other nourishment in his famous fasts. It is said that Frederick August, eighteenth century duke of Anhalt-Zerbat in Germany, died of starvation after a fast that lasted forty-three days. The length of time that a human being could go without food would also be affected by the physical activity of the individual and his mental state. Some religious devotees in the Orient seem to be able in their fasts to simulate a condition comparable to hibernation in animals, in which the low rate of metabolism prevents starvation. In 1943 Professor J. P. Bhansali, a Gandhi follower and a Yogi, fasted for sixty-one days, but doctors kept him alive during the last week of the fast by "forced feeding," that is, they injected glucose into his body.

How did *Passover* originate?

Moses ordained the Passover before the Israelites left Egypt more than three thousand years ago, and this feast has probably been observed continuously longer than any other elaborate religious rite. All the first-born in Egypt were condemned to die in the last of the ten plagues. Moses told each family of Israelites to kill a lamb and sprinkle the blood on their doors and to remain in their houses until they received orders to leave Egypt. *Exodus 12:23* says: "For the Lord will pass through to smite the Egyptians; and when he seeth the blood upon the lintel, and on the two side posts, the Lord will *pass over* the door, and will not suffer the destroyer to come in unto your houses to smite you." *Pass over* here is only a rough English equivalent of the Hebrew original. The Hebrew *pasach,* translated *pass over* in English, signifies "to protect," "to deliver" or "to pass by or over in the sense of to spare." The application of *pasach* to the sacrificial lamb killed and eaten at this feast may have been influenced by the fact that the Assyrian *pasahu* meant "to propitiate." The English translators in turn may have been influenced by the fact that Anglo-Saxon *opher* meant "a sacrifice" or "victim" and *pasch-opher* meant "paschal offering." Moses commanded the Israelites to observe the Passover forever to commemorate their exodus from Egyptian bondage. This seven-day festival begins on the fourteenth day of the first month of the Hebrew calendar and lasts until the twenty-first. Leavened bread is the symbol of ceremonial pollution and uncleanness, and the eating of unleavened bread during the Passover and the feast of unleavened bread was suggested by the fact that the Israelites left Egypt in such haste they had no time to leaven their bread. *Exodus 12:34* says: "And the people took their dough before it was leavened, their kneading troughs being bound up in their clothes upon their shoulders." Again *Exodus 12:39*: "And they baked unleavened cakes of the dough which they brought forth out of Egypt, for it was not leavened; because they were thrust out of Egypt, and could not tarry, neither had they prepared for themselves any victual." Some authorities suppose the Passover and the feast of unleavened bread were originally separate feasts and that they were later fused into one; but it seems more probable that the feast of unleavened bread was at first one ceremonial event during the feast of seven days now known as the Passover. Mosaic law prescribed that the Passover lamb be a male yearling without blemish, roasted whole and eaten at one meal. It was eaten as a peace offering, its blood was sprinkled as in the ritual of atonement, and the remains were consumed as in burnt offerings. The Passover has been kept by the Israelites and the Jews down through the ages. "And they kept the passover on the 14th day of the first month at even in the wilderness of Sinai," says *Numbers 9:5*. *Joshua 5:10* says: "And the children of Israel encamped in Gilgal, and kept the passover on the fourteenth day of the month at even in the plains of Jericho." In *II Chronicles 30* we are told that in the time of King Hezekiah of Judah, after Israel had been carried away into captivity, "there assembled at Jerusalem much people to keep the feast of unleavened bread in the second month, a very great congregation," and "then they killed the passover on the fourteenth day of the second month." *II Chronicles 35:1* says Josiah, one of the last kings of Judah before the captivity, "Kept a passover unto the Lord in Jerusalem: and they killed the passover on the fourteenth day of the first month." Of this Passover we are told in *II Kings 23:22*: "Surely there was not holden such a passover from the days of the judges that judged Israel, nor in all the days of the kings of Israel, nor of the kings of Judah." The Jews did not forget this important and memorable feast when a remnant of them returned to Jerusalem from the captivity. *Ezra 6:19* tells us that "the children of the captivity kept the passover upon the fourteenth day of the first month." The last supper eaten together by Jesus and his disciples was in observance of the Passover. "Now," according to *Matthew 26:17*, "the first day of the feast of unleavened bread the disciples came to Jesus, saying unto him, Where wilt thou that we prepare for thee to eat the passover?" We are told that the disciples did as Jesus appointed them, they made ready the passover, and "when even was come, he sat down with the twelve." To the Christians the death of Jesus became symbolical of the killing of the sacrificial lamb at the Passover. In *I Corinthians 5:7* Paul says: "Purge out therefore the old leaven, that ye may be a new lump, as ye are unleavened. For even Christ our passover is sacrificed for us." In the course of time the Hebrew *pasach,* Passover, became Latin *pascha,* Easter.

Is *Lent* mentioned in the Bible?

Lent, a period of penance set apart by the Christian church, is only indirectly of Biblical origin. Some of the church fathers of the fifth and sixth centuries were of the opinion that Lent was of Apostolic origin, although most modern authorities reject this view. It is quite certain, however, that what we call Lent was observed by the Christian Church within 150 years after the crucifixion of Jesus. At first the number of days of the fast was not specified. In the fourth century the number of fast days in Lent was fixed at thirty-six. Pope Felix II added four fast days to Lent in 487 A.D. to make the total correspond to the number of days that Jesus fasted in the wilderness. During the eighth or ninth century the Lenten period was fixed as it is observed today in the Roman Catholic, Greek Catholic and Anglican churches. It begins with Ash Wednesday and ends with Easter Sunday. The Sundays are a part of the Lenten season, but since they are feast days they are not included among the forty days of fasting or abstinence. Therefore Lent proper is the forty days preceding Easter, exclusive of Sundays. *Lent* is derived from Anglo-Saxon *lenct,* meaning "long." Spring was called *Lencten-tide* because at that time of the year the days noticeably increase in length. Later *Lencten-faesten,* "spring fast," was shortened to *Lent* and became the name of the great Christian fast period in the spring.

Does *senators* occur in the Bible?

Senate and *senators* both occur once in the King James Version. Speaking of Joseph in Egypt, *Psalms 105:21-22* says that Pharaoh "made him lord of his house, and ruler of all his substance: to bind his princes at his pleasure; and teach his senators wisdom." *Acts 5:21* reads: "And when they heard that, they entered into the temple early in the morning, and taught. But the high priest came, and they that were with him, and called the council together, and all the senate of the children of Israel, and sent to the prison to have them brought." *Senate* as the name of a legislative body was borrowed from Roman usage. It is derived from Latin *senex*, meaning "old." The Roman *Senatus*, literally signifying "a council of elders or old men," was originally an advisory body, but in the process of centuries it acquired legislative and administrative powers and functions. *Senator* and *senile* are from the same Latin root, and *senior* is from the same source.

What was the sabbatical year?

The Mosaic law required the Israelites to let their land lie idle every seventh year for twelve months. This, essentially a soil conservation measure, is known as the sabbatical year. During the sabbatical year all debts between Israelites were remitted, the poor and dumb animals were treated with special consideration, and all bondmen were freed and given liberal parting gifts by their masters. *Exodus 23:10-11* says: "And six years thou shalt sow thy land, and shalt gather in the fruits thereof: but the seventh year thou shalt let it rest and lie still; that the poor of thy people may eat: and what they leave the beasts of the field shall eat. In like manner thou shalt deal with thy vineyard, and with thy oliveyard." *Leviticus 25:3-7* elaborates on this: "Six years thou shalt sow thy field, and six years thou shalt prune thy vineyard, and gather in the fruit thereof; but in the seventh year shall be a sabbath of rest unto the land, a sabbath for the Lord: thou shalt neither sow thy field, nor prune thy vineyard. That which groweth of its own accord of thy harvest thou shalt not reap, neither gather the grapes of thy vine undressed: for it is a year of rest unto the land. And the sabbath of the land shall be meat for you; for thee, and thy servant, and for thy maid, and for thy hired servant, and for thy stranger that sojourneth with thee, and for thy cattle, and for the beast that are in thy land, shall all the increase thereof be meat." The seventh year was also called the year of release. *Deuteronomy 15:1-3* says: "At the end of every seven years thou shalt make a release. And this is the manner of the release: Every creditor that lendeth ought unto his neighbour shall release it; he shall not exact it of his neighbour, or of his brother; because it is called the Lord's release. Of a foreigner thou mayest exact it again: but that which is thine with thy brother thine hand shall release." The Mosaic law took notice of the fact that some persons might take advantage of the approach of the year of release by withholding loans. So *Deuteronomy 15:9* says: "Beware that there be not a thought in thy wicked heart, saying, The seventh year, the year of release, is at hand; and thine eye be evil against thy poor brother, and thou givest him nought; and he cry unto the Lord against thee, and it be sin unto thee." *Leviticus 25:20-22* explains how the Israelites were to live during the sabbatical years: "And if ye shall say, What shall we eat the seventh year? behold, we shall not sow, nor gather in our increase: Then I will command my blessing upon you in the sixth year, and it shall bring forth fruit for three years. And ye shall sow the eighth year, and eat yet of old fruit until the ninth year; until her fruits come in ye shall eat of the old store."

How did *jubilee* originate?

Jubilee in its modern sense has a dual origin. The year of jubilee, a sabbatical year of sabbatical years set aside every fifty years by the Mosaic law, received its name from *jobel*, the Hebrew name of the ram's horn used as a trumpet to announce the beginning of the year of jubilee. From this usage *jubilee* came to signify any observance of a fiftieth anniversary or the anniversary of any long period. But there is also a native Latin word *jubilum*, unrelated in origin to the Hebrew *jobel*, and meaning "a shout" or "wild cry." A fusion of these two terms gave us *jubilee* in the sense of a joyous celebration, and occasion of exultation, or the observance of an anniversary with great rejoicing. The Hebrew year of jubilee was held as a sacred commemoration of the deliverance of the Israelites from Egypt and was a solemn event. *Leviticus 25:8-9* says: "And thou shalt number seven sabbaths of years unto thee, seven times seven years; and the space of the seven sabbaths of years shall be unto thee forty and nine years. Then shalt thou cause the trumpet of the jubilee to sound on the tenth day of the seventh month, in the day of atonement shall ye make the trumpet sound throughout all your land." During the jubilee year Hebrew slaves were set free, mortgaged property in the country and villages was restored to the original owners or their heirs, the fields were left untilled, debtors were released from their obligations, even crops that grew of their own accord were not gathered but left to the poor, prices of products were raised or lowered in relation to the year of jubilee, and many other religious, economic and social adjustments were made. Some have supposed that the forty-ninth rather than the fiftieth year was the year of jubilee, because otherwise two sabbatical years would come together and no crops would be harvested for two consecutive years, but the traditional view is that it was the fiftieth year. To what extent the year of jubilee was actually carried out in the elaborate form specified in *Leviticus* is not known. The Talmud says it was observed so long as the Holy Land was inhabited and ruled chiefly by Israelites, but it was permitted to lapse after the Israelites were dispersed. The prophet apparently refers to the institution in *Ezekiel 46:17*, where he speaks of "the year of liberty." The sabbatical years and the year of jubilee were based on God's command in *Leviticus 25:23*, which says that "the land shall not be sold for ever: for the land is mine." They were periods of emancipation, restoration and economic and social readjustment to prevent power and wealth from being concentrated indefinitely in the hands of a few. Even at the time the Mosaic law was written it was recognized that the sabbatical and jubilee economic adjustments would be difficult to apply to commercial transactions. Accordingly the owners of houses in walled cities were given an opportunity to redeem their property within a year, and the cancellation of debts did not apply to foreigners; that is, commercial debts.

How did *hang as high as Haman* originate?

Hang as high as Haman, a phrase that owes much of its popularity to its alliteration, is not in the Bible, but it was suggested by the story of Haman and Mordecai in *Esther*. Ahasuerus (identified as Xerxes, son of Darius Hystaspis), was king of the Medes and Persians and Haman was his chief minister of state and as such sat above all the princes of the empire. Mordecai, who apparently occupied some minor office at court, was a Jew who had been carried away a captive from Jerusalem when the Holy City was taken by Nebuchadnezzar of Babylon. He was a cousin of Esther, Ahasuerus's queen, whom he had brought up as his own daughter. Mordecai, being a faithful Jew, refused to bow to and reverence Haman as the king had commanded all his subjects to do. Haman conceived a mortal enmity not only against Mordecai for his insolence but against all the Jews scattered throughout the 127 provinces of the empire stretching from India to Ethiopia. Accordingly the prime minister got the king to grant him authority to have the Jews all destroyed. After obtaining this royal decree, Haman left the palace joyful and with a glad heart, but when he "saw Mordecai in the king's gate, that he stood not up, nor moved for him, he was full of indignation against Mordecai." Haman, full of wrath, went home and told his friends and his wife Zeresh that all his splendor, riches, multitude of children and high office availed him nothing so long as Mordecai the Jew sat at the king's gate and refused to bow to him or reverence him. "Then," according to *Esther 5:14*, "said Zeresh his wife and all his friends unto him, Let a gallows be made of fifty cubits high, and to morrow speak thou unto the king that Mordecai may be hanged thereon: then go thou in merrily with the king unto the banquet. And the thing pleased Haman, and he caused the gallows to be made." Mordecai's plight was relieved somewhat by the fact that a short time before he had exposed a plot against the king's life by two of his chamberlains and had received no honor or reward for this generous and patriotic act. King Ahasuerus, being unable to sleep, had the chronicles read to him and was reminded how Mordecai had saved his life without receiving any honor or dignity. At the very moment that the king decided to honor Mordecai "Haman was come into the outward court of the king's house, to speak unto the king to hang Mordecai on the gallows that he had prepared for him." Haman, instead of being honored himself as he expected, was compelled by the king to put on Mordecai the royal apparel that the king used to wear, seat him on the horse that the king rode, place on his head the crown royal, and bring him on horseback through the street of the city, proclaiming before him, "Thus shall be done unto the man whom the king delighteth to honour." Queen Esther, who had not "shewed her kindred nor her people," was then able to humiliate Haman and get the doom against her people reversed. *Esther 7:9-10* says: "And Harbonah, one of the chamberlains, said before the king, Behold also, the gallows fifty cubits high, which Haman had made for Mordecai, who had spoken good for the king, standeth in the house of Haman. Then the king said, Hang him thereon. So they hanged Haman on the gallows that he had prepared for Mordecai." Mordecai became prime minister in Haman's stead and the Jews were given permission to defend themselves against their enemies. In the fighting that followed, the Jews slew the ten sons of Haman. Queen Esther made one more request of the king. "Then said Esther," according to *Esther 9:13-14*, "If it please the king, let it be granted to the Jews which are in Shushan to do to morrow also according unto this day's decree, and let Haman's ten sons be hanged upon the gallows. And the king commanded it so to be done: and the decree was given at Shushan; and they hanged Haman's ten sons." It is popularly supposed that Haman's ten sons were hanged upon the same gallows that their father had prepared for Mordecai, but the account does not make that clear. Since Haman's ten sons were already dead, it is probable that their bodies were impaled and exposed to public view after the custom of the time. Assuming the cubit to have been eighteen inches in length, Haman's gallows would have been seventy-five feet high. The Bible says the gallows stood "in the house of Haman." It is unlikely that even the princely chief minister had a house tall enough for such a purpose. This passage probably means merely that the gallows were erected on his extensive grounds. The greater the crime the higher the gallows appears to have been at one time a practical maxim of law. That seems to have been the idea of the extremely high gallows prepared by Haman for Mordecai. We find an echo of this notion in Great Britain as late as the seventeenth century. The English equivalent of *hang as high as Haman* is to *hang as high as Gilderoy's kite*. To hang a person as high as Gilderoy's kite means to punish him very severely, and *higher than Gilderoy's kite* signifies very high indeed. Gilderoy was the nickname of a notorious robber named Patrick MacGregor, who plied his trade in Perthshire, Scotland. He was the "Billy the Kid" of his day and boasted that he had hanged a judge, robbed Oliver Cromwell, and picked the pocket of Cardinal Richelieu in the presence of the king. Gilderoy, who was noted for the beauty of his person, is the subject of several old ballads. In 1636 he and a number of his followers were hanged at Edinburgh. On the principle, the greater the crime the higher the gallows, Gilderoy was hanged on a gallows much higher than those used for his fellow highwaymen. Tradition says it was thirty feet high. Just what *kite* refers to in connection with Gilderoy is not clear. Some authorities suppose the word alludes to the fact that the robber's body was hung so high that it "looked like a kite in the clouds." One writer, however, advances the theory that *kite* here may be the old north Scotch dialect word *kyte* or *kite,* meaning "belly," "stomach" or "paunch." By extension, he says, it was applied to the entire body, especially in a derogatory or contemptuous sense. If this is correct, the old phrase *high as Gilderoy's kite* is equivalent to *high as Gilderoy's carcass.*

Does the Bible say bread is the staff of life?

Bread is the staff of life is not in the Bible, but the saying is undoubtedly of Biblical origin. *Leviticus 26:26* says: "When I break your staff of bread, ten women shall bake your bread in one oven, and they shall deliver your bread again by weight; and ye shall eat, and not be satisfied." *Break your staff of bread* is the English rendering of a Hebrew expression meaning to diminish or to cut off the supply of food. Alluding to the famine in Egypt in the time of Joseph, *Psalms 105:16* says: "Moreover he called for a famine upon the land:

he brake the whole staff of bread." *Ezekiel 4:16* says: "Moreover he said unto me, son of man, behold, I will break the staff of bread in Jerusalem: and they shall eat bread by weight, and with care; and they shall drink water by measure, and with astonishment." In *Ezekiel 5:16* the Lord says through the prophet that he will increase "the famine upon you, and will break your staff of bread." And *Ezekiel 14:13*: "Son of man, when the land sinneth against me by trespassing grievously, then will I stretch out mine hand upon it, and will break the staff of the bread thereof, and will cut off man and beast from it." We find a similar figure of speech in *Isaiah 3:1*, where we are told that the Lord "doth take away from Jerusalem and from Judah the stay and the staff, the whole stay of bread, and the whole stay of water." The earliest occurrence of the English saying, *bread is the staff of life*, recorded by the Oxford dictionary is dated 1638, but it is probably much older than that, for in 1624 Edward Winslow, in *Good Newes from New England*, referred to "Corn, which is the staff of life." *Staff of life* signifies not only bread in the strict sense of the term, but any staple food that is the equivalent of bread.

Who was the first efficiency expert?

A good executive is one who knows how to choose assistants and how to delegate authority. Even Moses did not at first understand this important principle of administering government. How the great Hebrew leader learned to delegate authority is related in *Exodus 18*. A few months after Moses had led the Israelites out of Egypt, his father-in-law, Jethro, the priest of Midian, paid him a visit at his camp in the wilderness. The next day Jethro saw his son-in-law sitting alone from morning until evening judging all the people. Moses was obviously hard pressed and wearied by his attempt to judge every individual case under the laws that he had given his people. "What is this thing that thou doest to the people?" asked the father-in-law. "Why sittest thou thyself alone, and all the people stand by thee from morning unto even?" "Because," answered Moses, "the people come unto me to inquire of God. When they have a matter, they come unto me: and I judge between one and another, and I do make them know the statutes of God, and his laws." "The thing that thou doest is not good," replied Jethro. "Thou wilt surely wear away, both thou, and this people that is with thee; for this thing is too heavy for thee; thou art not able to perform it thyself alone." Then the father-in-law counseled the son-in-law to choose from the people "able men, such as fear God, men of truth, hating covetousness; and place such over them, to be rulers of thousands, and rulers of hundreds, rulers of fifties, and rulers of ten. And," continued Jethro, "let them judge the people of all seasons: and it shall be, that every great matter they shall bring unto thee, but every small matter they shall judge: so shall it be easier for thyself, and they shall bear the burden with thee." Moses, a wise as well as a meek man, hearkened to the voice of his father-in-law and did all that he had said. What Moses did was to establish a system of higher and lower courts, with himself as Chief Justice of the Supreme Court. After taking the advice of Jethro, his efficiency expert, the Moses administration of public affairs ran more smoothly. "Moses," we are told, "chose able men out of all Israel, and made them heads over the people, rulers of thousands, rulers of hundreds, rulers of fifties, rulers of tens. And they judged the people at all seasons: the hard cases they brought to Moses, but every small matter they judged themselves." But later the burden became too great for Moses alone. *Numbers 11:16-17* says: "And the Lord said unto Moses, Gather unto me seventy men of the elders of Israel, whom thou knowest to be the elders of the people, and officers over them; and bring them unto the tabernacle of the congregation, that they may stand there with thee. And I will come down and talk with thee there; and I will take of the spirit which is upon thee, and will put it upon them; and they shall bear the burden of the people with thee, that thou bear it not thyself alone." This senate of seventy elders apparently assisted Moses only temporarily during the crisis, when the people were weeping and murmuring against his leadership, for there is no allusion down through the centuries to such a body until the Great Council or Sanhedrin was established after the captivity.

Does the Bible mention weaning?

Weaning is mentioned several times in the Bible. *Genesis 21:8* says: "And the child grew, and was weaned: and Abraham made a great feast the same day that Isaac was weaned." In the East the usual age of weaning is two or three years, and the weaning of a child is still made the occasion of a feast. Apparently in Israel offerings to the Lord were made when a child was weaned. *I Samuel 1:21-24* says: "And the man Elkanah, and all his house, went up to offer unto the Lord the yearly sacrifice, and his vow. But Hannah went not up; for she said unto her husband, I will not go up until the child be weaned, and then I will bring him, that he may appear before the Lord, and there abide for ever. And Elkanah her husband said unto her, Do what seemeth thee good; tarry until thou have weaned him; only the Lord establish his word. So the woman abode, and gave her son suck until she weaned him. And when she had weaned him, she took him up with her, with three bullocks, and one ephah of flour, and a bottle of wine, and brought him unto the house of the Lord in Shiloh: and the child was young." We are also told in this connection that Hannah at that time dedicated her child to the Lord. The child grew up to be the great judge and prophet Samuel. In *Kings 11:19-20* we learn that Pharaoh gave Hadad, the Edomite, "to wife the sister of his own wife, and the sister of Tahpenes the queen. And the sister of Tahpenes bare him Genubath his son, whom Tahpenes weaned in Pharaoh's house." Other references to weaning in the Bible are for the most part figurative. For instance, in *Psalms 131:2* David says: "Surely I have behaved and quieted myself, as a child that is weaned of his mother: my soul is even as a weaned child." *Isaiah 11:8* says: "And the sucking child shall play on the hole of the asp, and the weaned child shall put his hand on the cockatrice's den." And *Isaiah 28:9*: "Whom shall he teach knowledge? and whom shall he make to understand doctrine? them that are weaned from the milk, and drawn from the breast."

Is "God Save the King" in the Bible?

Many may be surprised to learn that "God Save the King" is in the Bible. That was the popular acclamation of the Israelites at Mizpeh when the prophet Samuel proclaimed Saul the son of Kish their first king. *I Samuel 10:23-24* says: "And they ran and fetched him thence: and when he stood among the people, he was higher than any of the people from his shoulders and upward. And Samuel said to all the people, See ye him whom the Lord hath chosen, that there is none like him among the people? And all the people shouted, and said, *God save the king*." The Israelites regarded Saul as God-chosen and the acclamation was peculiarly appropriate and applicable to the new monarch of a nation that had always been a theocracy. In the Latin Vulgate this passage is translated *Vivat rex*, which means, "May the king live." *II Samuel 16:16*, referring to the time that Absalom revolted against his father and set himself up as king in Jerusalem, says: "And it came to pass, when Hushai the Archite, David's friend, was come unto Absalom, that Hushai said unto Absalom, God save the king, God save the king." In *I Kings 1:33-34* King David is quoted as saying: "Take with you the servants of your lord, and cause

Solomon my son to ride upon mine own mule, and bring him down to Gihon: and let Zadok the priest and Nathan the prophet anoint him there king over Israel: and blow ye with the trumpet, and say, God save the king Solomon."

Who was Melchizedek?

Melchizedek is a fascinating figure who vanishes from the Biblical narrative as abruptly and mysteriously as he appears. After Abraham with his followers made a successful surprise attack by night on King Chedorlaomer of Elam and the kings with him, he returned with the spoils to the valley of Shaveh, "which is the king's dale," supposedly near Jerusalem. *Genesis 14:18-20* says: "And Melchizedek king of Salem brought forth bread and wine: and he was the priest of the most high God. And he blessed him, and said, Blessed be Abram of the most high God, possessor of heaven and earth: and blessed be the most high God, which hath delivered thine enemies into thy hand. And he gave him tithes of all." Volumes have been written about this interesting passage. In Hebrew *Melchizedek* is a title rather than a name and signifies "king of righteousness." Jewish legend identifies Melchizedek with no other than Shem, eldest son of Noah, who lived to be six hundred. The curious thing about this passage is that Abraham, traditionally the first monotheist, at this early date met a priestly king who acknowledged the one and only God. There is nothing to indicate whether Melchizedek was a Hebrew. He may have been a convert to Abraham's faith or Abram may have been a convert to his, or possibly, like Balaam, Melchizedek may have worshipped the true God independently of the Hebrews. There is no other mention of Melchizedek in the Old Testament except in *Psalms 110:4,* which reads: "The Lord hath sworn, and will not repent, Thou art a priest for ever after the order of Melchizedek." This psalm of David was interpreted by later writers as an allusion to the future descendant of David who should reign over Israel as the ideal king and high priest. Consequently Melchizedek became a type of the Messiah. In *Hebrews* this idea is elaborated as applied to Jesus. The author of that book says Christ was "Called of God an high priest after the order of Melchisedec" and supplanted the Levitical priesthood as the true high priest. *Hebrews 7:1-4* says: "For this Melchisedec, king of Salem, priest of the most high God, who met Abraham returning from the slaughter of the kings, and blessed him: to whom also Abraham gave a tenth part of all; first being by interpretation King of righteousness, and after that also King of Salem, which is, King of peace; without father, without mother, without descent, having neither beginning of days, nor end of life; but made like unto the Son of God; abideth a priest continually. Now consider how great this man was, unto whom even the patriarch Abraham gave the tenth of the spoils." Josephus says "this Melchisedek supplied Abraham's army in an hospitable manner, and gave them provisions in abundance." The Jewish historian also tells us that Melchisedek built a temple at Salem and called the city Jerusalem. The statement in *Hebrews* that Melchisedek was "without father, without mother, without descent, having neither beginning of days, nor end of life" has been variously interpreted. Samuel Butler, author of *Hudibras,* wrote in his *Note-Book*: "Melchisedec was a really happy man. He was without father, without mother and without descent. He was an incarnate bachelor. He was a born orphan." Some of the early church fathers supposed Melchisedek to have been an angel, or even the incarnation of the Holy Spirit.

Is *Hallelujah* in the Bible?

Hallelujah in that form is not in the King James Version of the Bible. In its Greek form *Alleluia* it occurs in *Revelation 19:6,* which reads: "And I heard as it were the voice of a great multitude, and as the voice of many waters, and as the voice of mighty thunderings, saying, Alleluia: for the Lord omnipotent reigneth." The Hebrew original of *Hallelujah* literally means "praise ye Yah," where *Yah* is the shortened form of the divine name. In the Hebrew texts of the Old Testament it occurs at the opening of eleven Psalms and at the close of thirteen, but in each case the King James Version renders it "Praise ye the Lord," which is an approximation to the literal meaning. From its frequent occurrence in the Hebrew original of the Psalms, *Hallelujah* has been widely adopted in Christian hymns and liturgies. It is supposed that it was not originally an integral part of the Psalms in which it now occurs, but rather a liturgical or traditional ejaculation used with them.

Was Herod's temple the second or third temple?

Authorities differ as to whether there were three or only two successive temples in Jerusalem. The temple which stood in the time of Jesus and which is frequently mentioned in the New Testament is called the Second Temple by some writers and the Third Temple by others. Solomon's temple, dedicated about 950 B.C., is known by all as the First Temple. It stood until 585 B.C., when it was completely destroyed by the Babylonians under Nebuchadnezzar. Zerubbabel's temple, begun in 535 B.C. under Persian auspices and completed twenty years later, is known by all as the Second Temple. This temple stood with few substantial alterations until Herod the Great became king of Judaea in 37 B.C. The Second Temple is supposed to have been inferior in size and architecture to the First Temple, which was the most monumental and magnificent structure of the ancient Israelites. Herod the Great, a noted builder, began about 20 A.D. to model, renovate and reconstruct the Second Temple. Authorities differ as to whether this was a completely new temple or merely a restoration, enlargement and improvement of the old one. Herod's workmen appear to have torn down the Second Temple in sections and to have rebuilt the new one part by part. Some authorities say that this structure was so completely rebuilt that no remains of the original edifice were recognizable. It seems that in one sense it was a remodeling and renovation of the Second Temple; but in another sense it was a new edifice, larger, grander, more magnificent and more beautiful than either of its predecessors. At any rate, some authorities persist in referring to this as the Second Temple, while others call it the Third Temple. Popularly it is more easily identified as Herod's Temple. Apparently it was not completed until long after Herod's death in 4 B.C. There seems to have been a tradition that the reconstruction work begun by Herod took many years, for according to *John 2:20*, the Jews said to Jesus: "Forty and six years was this temple in building." It was finally completely destroyed in 70 A.D. by the Romans under Titus and later attempts to rebuild it were unsuccessful. The site is now occupied by "The Dome of the Rock," often erroneously called the Mosque of Omar.

What is the oldest city in the world?

It is generally supposed that Damascus, the chief city of Syria, is the oldest city in the world. Although positive evidence is wanting, there is some reason for believing that its site has been occupied longer and more continuously by a city than has any other spot on the earth. The Jewish historian Josephus, who probably based his assertion on Hebrew tradition, attributed the foundation of Damascus to Uz, the son of Aram and the great-grandson of Noah. In *Genesis 14* it is related that Abraham pursued the routed kings to Hobah, "which is on the left hand of Damascus." While this statement is not conclusive, the evidence indicates that Damascus was a place of importance already in the time of Abraham, who, it is supposed, lived two thousand years or more before Christ. Damascus and the part of Syria of which it was the capital was placed under tribute to the Israelites under David.

Why are the Ten Commandments called the Decalogue?

The Hebrew words in the Bible rendered *ten commandments* in English literally signify "ten words." In the Septuagint, the Greek version of the Old Testament made at Alexandria in the second century B.C., this phrase was translated *dekalogoi,* from *deka,* "ten," and *logos,* "word." From this circumstance, the Ten Commandments collectively as a body of law and as the basis of the moral system and religion of both Judaism and Christianity came to be known in the Western world as the Decalogue.

What is a Jeremiad?

Jeremiah, the Hebrew prophet of doom and judgment, is unique among the great Biblical prophets in having a popular noun formed from his name. Although Jeremiah's preaching, teaching and prophesying are recorded in *The Book of the Prophet Jeremiah* and *The Lamentations of Jeremiah,* it is chiefly from the latter book that a lament, a doleful story, a denunciation, complaint, tirade or a writing or speech in a strain of grief or distress came to be known as a *Jeremiad. Ad* or *ade* is a suffix of Greek origin often added to a specific noun to make it collective. *Jeremiad* was no doubt originally formed after the manner of such words as *Iliad, Dunciad* and *Columbiad.*

Why are the hands clasped in prayer?

Clasping the hands in prayer is merely a conventional form of holding up the hands toward heaven. The earliest intimation of the posture assumed by the Israelites during prayer is found in *Exodus 17,* where Moses held up his hands during a battle between his people and Amalek. *Leviticus 9:22* says Aaron, the high priest, "lifted up his hand toward the people, and blessed them." The offering of sacrifice and prayer were at first associated. *Psalms 141:2* says, "Let my prayer be set forth before thee as incense; and the lifting up of my hands as the evening sacrifice," and *Psalms 143:6,* "I stretch forth my hands unto thee." According to *Nehemiah 8:6,* when Ezra blessed the Lord "all the people answered, Amen, Amen, with lifting up their hands: and they bowed their heads, and worshipped the Lord with their faces to the ground." Stretching out the hands seems to be a natural attitude assumed by inferiors when asking favors of, presenting petitions or doing homage to, superiors and is apparently one of the primitive instincts of the human race. No particular posture of prayer is prescribed in the Bible. The bodily attitudes assumed during prayer are standing, sitting, kneeling, bowing toward the ground and prostrating oneself. All these postures imply humility, respect and reverence. Isaac Disraeli, in *Curiosities of Literature,* wrote: "To bend and prostrate one's self to express sentiments of respect, appears to be a natural motion; for terrified persons throw themselves on the earth when they adore invisible beings." According to *I Samuel 1:26,* Hannah, the mother of Samuel, stood when she prayed to the Lord, and *I Kings 8:22* says that "Solomon stood before the altar of the Lord in the presence of all the congregation of Israel, and spread forth his hands toward heaven." In the parable of the Pharisee and the publican, who went up into the temple to pray, both stood, but the publican "would not lift up so much as his eyes unto heaven, but smote upon his breast." *II Samuel 7:18* tells us that David "sat before the Lord" when he prayed. In Hebrew the term for *to kneel* also means to bless and to pray. Kneeling, bowing the head and prostrating the body were gestures of honor and respect as well as of worship and prayer. *Genesis 43:26* says Joseph's brethren "bowed down their heads, and made obeisance" to their brother. When Joseph rode in Pharaoh's second chariot they "cried before him, Bow the knee." *Isaiah 45:23* says, "That unto me every knee shall bow." In *Genesis 24:26* we are told "the man bowed down his head, and worshipped the Lord." "Let us kneel before our Lord our Maker," says *Psalms 95:6.* According to *Daniel 6:10,* Daniel "kneeled upon his knees three times a day, and prayed." Ezra, in *Ezra 9:5,* says: "I fell upon my knees, and spread out my hands unto the Lord my God." Jesus, according to *Luke 22:41,* "kneeled down, and prayed," and *Acts 7:60* says Stephen "kneeled down" and cried to the Lord with a loud voice. *Luke 17:16* tells us that the Samaritan leper who had been healed "fell down on his face" at the feet of Jesus and gave him thanks.

Who were the hewers of wood and drawers of water?

There is a popular notion that the Bible says all the descendants of Ham were condemned to be hewers of wood and drawers of water. This notion is owing to a confusion of two different passages in the Bible. In *Genesis 9:18* we are told that Ham, youngest of the three sons of Noah, was the father of Canaan. *Genesis 9:25* tells us that

Noah, upon waking from a drunken sleep and learning that his youngest son had treated him with indignity, said: "Cursed be Canaan; a servant of servants shall he be unto his brethren." At the same time Noah, because his two older sons had treated him with respect while he was drunk, blessed Shem and Japheth, but followed each blessing with the words, "and Canaan shall be his servant." Ham had four sons, Cush, Mizraim, Put and Canaan. Presumably Noah's curse applied only to the descendants of Ham through his son Canaan. There is nothing in the Bible about all the descendants of Ham being condemned to be hewers of wood and drawers of water. "Hewer of wood and drawer of water" was applied to any *stranger* or slave who performed menial duties for the Israelites. *Deuteronomy 29:10-11* says: "Ye stand this day all of you before the Lord your God; your captains of your tribes, your elders, and your officers, with all the men of Israel, your little ones, your wives, and thy stranger that is in thy camp, from the hewer of thy wood unto the drawer of thy water." In other words, everybody, including non-Israelite servants and slaves. In *Joshua 9* it is related that the inhabitants of Gibeon, upon learning what the Israelites had done to Jericho and Ai, disguised ambassadors in old clothes and sent them to Joshua at Gilgal under the pretense that they were from a far country and had come a great distance to make a league with the victorious Israelites. Joshua, deceived by the ruse, made peace with the Gibeonites, promised to let them live and had the league confirmed with an oath by the princes of the congregation. Three days later, however, the Israelites learned that the Gibeonites were their neighbors and that their rulers had been the victims of a trick. When the Israelites occupied Gibeon and its allied cities they did not smite the inhabitants, but let them live because of the oath. Nevertheless the people murmured against the princes of Israel for having been deceived by the wily Gibeonites. The princes replied that they could not touch the Gibeonites because of the oath they had sworn but promised the Israelites that these people should be "hewers of wood and drawers of water unto all the congregation." The rest of the story is told in *Joshua 9:22-27*: "And Joshua called for them, and he spake unto them, saying, Wherefore have ye beguiled us, saying, We are very far from you: when ye dwell among us? Now therefore, ye are cursed, and there shall none of you be freed from being bondmen, and hewers of wood and drawers of water for the house of my God. And they answered Joshua, and said, Because it was certainly told thy servants, how that the Lord thy God commanded his servant Moses to give you all the land, and to destroy all the inhabitants of the land from before you, therefore we were sore afraid of our lives because of you, and have done this thing. And now, behold, we are in thine hand: as it seemeth good and right unto thee to do unto us, do. And so did he unto them, and delivered them out of the hand of the children of Israel, that they slew them not. And Joshua made them that day hewers of wood and drawers of water for the congregation, and for the altar of the Lord, even unto this day, in the place which he should choose." From this passage comes *Gibeonite* in the sense of a slave, menial or drudge. The Gibeonites, like the other Canaanites, were no doubt descendants of Ham, but there is nothing in the Bible to justify the popular belief that all the descendants of Ham were condemned to be hewers of wood and drawers of water.

Does the Bible say, "God helps those who help themselves"?

"God helps those who help themselves" is not in the Bible, as many suppose. It is a proverb in many languages in many parts of the world. The earliest occurrence of the proverb in English in its present form that we have been able to find is in Algernon Sidney's *Discourses Concerning Government,* published in 1698. "God helps him who helps himself" is one of the precepts in Benjamin Franklin's *Poor Richard's Almanack* for 1733, and in the maxims prefixed to the same almanac for 1757 "God helps them that help themselves" occurs. In his collection of proverbs entitled *Jacula Prudentum* George Herbert (1593-1633) said: "Help thyself, and God will help thee." A similar idea was expressed by Cervantes (1547-1616) in *Don Quixote,* and by La Fontaine (1621-1695) in his fables. Even some of the ancient Greek writers of the fifth century before the Christian Era, particularly Aeschylus, Sophocles and Euripides, hinted at the proverb. For instance, in *Persae* Aeschylus wrote: "To the man who himself strives earnestly, God also lends a helping hand."

Why is a hunter called a Nimrod?

Nimrod for a hunter was suggested by *Genesis 10:8-9,* which reads: "And Cush begat Nimrod: he began to be a mighty one in the earth. He was a mighty hunter before the Lord: wherefore it is said, Even as Nimrod the mighty hunter before the Lord." Bible scholars are not agreed as to just what is meant by Nimrod's being "a mighty hunter before the Lord." Some commentators accept the description in the literal sense of one who hunts animals, because many of the ancient Assyrian kings were noted for their prowess in the chase of wild beasts. But *gibbor*, the Hebrew word rendered "hunter" in the English Bible, also means "hero" and therefore some authorities interpret the phrase as signifying simply that Nimrod was a great warrior. In *Genesis 10:10* we are told that the beginning of Nimrod's kingdom was Babel in the land of Shinar, which was Babylon in Assyria. *Micah 5:6* mentions "the land of Nimrod" as being in the "entrances" of Assyria. The inference is that Nimrod, Ham's grandson, was the originator of the military state, based on arbitrary force. Many attempts have been made to identify him with various historical or legendary personages known through other sources, but no equivalent of the name has ever been found on any of the cuneiform records excavated in Assyria. Several Babylonian monuments depict monarchs in the act of hunting. At any rate, *Nimrod* has become the romantic name for any hunter. What is said to be Nimrod's tomb is pointed out to travelers in Damascus, and according to Moslem legend no dew ever falls on it.

Are chickens mentioned in the Bible?

It is doubtful whether the Israelites had domestic fowls during the historic period covered by the Old Testament. Eggs have been used for food since the dawn of history and nobody knows who first ate them. Undoubtedly they were one of the original natural foods of the human race. The Book of Job, which deals with an early period of Hebrew history, contains one of the earliest references to eggs as food. In *Job 6:6* the patriarch asks: "Can that which is unsavory be eaten without salt? or is there any taste in the white of an egg?" This, however, does not prove that domestic poultry was known to the Hebrews at that time, for obviously the eggs of wild fowls were gathered and eaten long before any fowls were domesticated. The law of Moses refers only to wild birds. For instance, *Deuteronomy 22:6-7* says: "If a bird's nest chance to be before thee in the way in any tree, or on the ground, whether they be young ones, or eggs, and the dam sitting upon the young, or upon the eggs, thou shalt not take the dam with the young: but thou shalt in any wise let the dam go, and take the young to thee; that it may be well with thee, and that thou mayest prolong thy days." The species of the "peacocks" mentioned in the Bible has never been identified. In *I Kings 10:22* and *II Chronicles 9:21* the name of fowls brought to King Solomon by the navy of Hiram is translated "peacocks." The only other place in the Bible where "peacocks" occurs is *Job 39:13*, which reads: "Gavest thou the goodly wings unto the peacocks? or wings and feathers unto the ostrich?" There the Hebrew word translated "peacocks" really means "ostriches." It is not known whether the Israelites ever regarded the ostrich as a domestic bird. The peafowl, a member of the pheasant family, is native to the hill regions of India and Ceylon, where it is still found in large numbers in the wild state. It is believed that all domestic chickens are descended from the wild jungle fowls of India and the Malay Peninsula. Apparently domesticated chickens were already common in many parts of the Roman Empire in the time of Jesus. *Hen, cock* and *chicken* all occur in the King James Version of the New Testament. According to *Matthew 23:37,* Jesus cried: "O Jerusalem, Jerusalem, thou that killest the prophets and stonest them which are sent unto thee, how often would I have gathered thy children together, even as a hen gathereth her chickens under her wings, and ye would not!" After Peter on the Mount of Olives had protested he never would be offended because of Jesus, the Master said: "Verily I say unto thee, That this night, before the cock crow, thou shalt deny me thrice." Later it came to pass that, while waiting in the outer room of the high priest's palace, Peter, because of his Galilean speech, was accused three different times of having been with Jesus. The first time he simply denied it; the second time he denied it with an oath, and the third time he began "to curse and to swear, saying, I know not the man. And immediately the cock crew." According to *Mark 13:35,* Jesus said: "Watch ye therefore: for ye know not when the master of the house cometh, at even, or at midnight, or at the cockcrowing, or in the morning." This indicates the four watches in which the night was divided under the Roman regime. Cockcrowing was the third watch and included the three hours from 12:00 P.M to 3:00 A.M.

What was "the river of Egypt"?

The "river of Egypt" mentioned several times in the Old Testament was not the Nile, as popularly supposed. According to *Genesis 15:18,* "the Lord made a covenant with Abram, saying, Unto thy seed have I given this land, from the river of Egypt unto the great river, the river Euphrates." In *Numbers 34:5* the Lord, speaking to Moses about the boundaries of the Promised Land, says: "And the border shall fetch a compass from Azmon unto the river of Egypt." This "river of Egypt" has been identified with the broad and shallow watercourse known to the modern Arabs as the Wady el-'Arish, which runs north and northwest from the Sinaitic peninsula and flows into the Mediterranean about fifty miles southwest of Gaza. It is a typical *wadi* or "flash stream," being virtually dry except during the rainy season, when it becomes a swift river. *I Kings 8:65* says: "And at that time Solomon held a feast, and all Israel with him, a great congregation, from the entering in of Hamath unto the river of Egypt." This "river of Egypt" was regarded by the Israelites as the border of Egypt and the southern boundary of Solomon's kingdom. It may surprise some to learn that the Nile is nowhere mentioned by that name in the King James Version of the Bible. *Nile* is the Anglicized form of the classical name of this great river. The Egyptians never knew it by that name and there is no corresponding word for it in Hebrew. In the story of Moses in *Genesis* and elsewhere in the King James Version the Nile is referred to simply as "the river." Some authorities conjecture that Gihon, one of the "four heads" of the "river that went out of Eden to water the garden," was the Nile, for *Genesis 2:13* says: "And the name of the second river is Gihon: the same is it that compasseth the whole land of Ethiopia."

Did the Israelites have conscription for military service?

The earliest known registration of men for military conscription occurred among the ancient Israelites. The first registration in the Bible, however, was essentially for the purpose of collecting a poll-tax rather than for military purposes. *Exodus 30:11-16* says: "And the Lord spake unto Moses, saying, When thou takest the sum of the children of Israel after their number, then shall they give every man a ransom for his soul unto the Lord, when thou numberest them; that there be no plague among them when thou numberest them. This they shall give, every one that passeth among them that are numbered, half a shekel after the shekel of the sanctuary: (a shekel is twenty gerahs:) an half shekel shall be the offering of the Lord. Every one that passeth among them that are numbered, from twenty years old and above, shall give an offering unto the Lord. The rich shall not give more, and the poor shall not give less than half a shekel, when they give an offering unto the Lord, to make an atonement for your souls. And thou shalt take the atonement money of the children of Israel, and shalt appoint it for the service of the tabernacle of the congregation; that it may be a memorial unto the children of Israel before the Lord, to make an atonement for your souls." It is believed that this first numbering of the men in Israel was the basis of military service as well as of paying the poll-tax. The military age in Israel began at twenty. *Plague,* in "that there be no plague among them, when thou numberest them" is the English rendering of a Hebrew word that comes from the same root as the Hebrew word for "slaughter in battle." Jewish commentators tell us that the ransom for every man of military age was required as an atonement because the soldier who is ready to fight is in the eyes of the Lord a potential taker of life, though not a deliberate murderer. It is an interesting fact that this poll-tax paid by the Israelites was the same for rich and poor and was not based on capacity to pay. *Exodus 37:24-26* gives us the number of men over twenty in Israel and the amount of money collected from the poll-tax: "All the gold that was occupied for the work in all the work of the holy place, even the gold of the offering, was twenty and nine talents, and seven hundred and thirty shekels, after the shekel of the sanctuary. And the silver of them that were numbered of the congregation was an hundred talents, and a thousand seven hundred and threescore and fifteen shekels, after the shekel of the sanctuary. A bekah for every man, that is, half a shekel, after the shekel of the sanctuary, for every one that went to be numbered, from twenty years old and upward, for six hundred thousand and three thousand and five hundred and fifty men." The fourth book of Moses, called *Numbers* received its present name from the fact that part of it is the report of two registrations or numberings of the Israelites. The oldest Hebrew name for this book was "The Fifth of the Musterings"; that is, one of the five books of Moses describing the numbering of the Israelites. Later the Jews called it *In the Wilderness*, from the opening phrase. Its present name first occurred in the Septuagint, the Greek version of the Old Testament made at Alexandria in the second century B.C. *Numbers 1:2-4* says: "Take ye the sum of all the congregation of the children of Israel, after their families, by the house of their fathers, with the number of their names, every male by their polls; from twenty years old and upward, all that are able to go forth to war in Israel: thou and Aaron shall number them by their armies. And with you there shall be a man of every tribe; every one head of the house of his fathers." Then follows a list of the chief census-takers for each tribe and the results of the census by tribes. *Numbers 1:46* gives the total: "Even all they that were numbered were six hundred thousand and three thousand and five hundred and fifty." This number is exactly the same as the number required to pay the poll-tax under the previous numbering. This suggests that the second numbering was merely a classified return of the census already taken. The time had come when Moses and Joshua would require a certified list of men to be called to the colors as they were needed to fight the battles necessary to conquer the Promised Land. But the tribe of Levi, which provided the priests and those charged with other strictly religious functions, were exempted from this registration. The Levites were not numbered for war in Israel. So a separate census of them was taken. *Numbers 1:47-49* says: "But the Levites after the tribe of their fathers were not numbered among them. For the Lord had spoken unto Moses, saying, Only thou shalt not number the tribe of Levi, neither take the sum of them among the children of Israel." The Levites were enumerated on a different basis. *Numbers 3:39* gives us the results of this census of the clergy: "All that were numbered of the Levites, which Moses and Aaron numbered at the commandment of the Lord, throughout their families, all the males from a month old and upward, was twenty and two thousand." Then Moses was commanded to number all the first-born of the males of the children of Israel from a month old and upward. The total of this census, according to *Numbers 3:43,* was "twenty and two thousand two hundred and threescore and thirteen." It will be seen that the first-born of all Israel numbered 273 more than the number of Levites. Since the Levites were to be devoted to the service of the Lord in place of the first-born, the extra 273 first-born had to be redeemed independently by paying five shekels apiece. Some authorities suppose that since the total number of first-born males was only 22,273 out of a total population of 603,550 adult males, only the first-born males under twenty years of age at the time the census was taken is meant. According to *Deuteronomy 20:5-8,* four classes were exempted from military service. "What man is there that hath built a new house, and hath not dedicated it? let him go and return to his house, lest he die in the battle, and another man dedicate it. And what man is he that hath planted a vineyard, and hath not yet eaten of it? let him also go and return unto his house, lest he die in the battle, and another man eat of it. And what man is there that hath betrothed a wife, and hath not taken her? let him go and return unto his house, lest he die in battle, and another man take her. . . . What man is there that is fearful and faint-hearted? let him go and return unto his house, lest his brethren's heart faint as well as his heart." Newly married men were exempt from conscription for one year. *Deuteronomy 24:5* says: "When a man hath taken a new wife, he shall not go out to war, neither shall he be charged with any business: but he shall be free at home one year, and shall cheer up his wife which he hath taken." Nearly forty years after the first census, when the Israelites were camped on the plains of Moab by Jordan near Jericho, it became necessary to take another census, because the Promised Land was about to be divided by lot among the tribes. A plague had greatly diminished their numbers. *Numbers 26:1-2* says: "And it came to pass after the plague, that the Lord spake unto Moses and unto Eleazar the son of Aaron the priest, saying, Take the sum of all the congregation of the children of Israel, from twenty years old and upward, throughout their fathers' house, all that are able to go to war in Israel." This census, according to *Numbers 26:51,* showed "six hundred thousand and a thousand seven hundred and thirty," a decrease of 1,820 of the Israelites from twenty years old and upward that were able to go to war. According to *Numbers 26:62,* the number of Levites from a month old and upward was "twenty and three thousand," an increase of 1,000 compared with the census taken nearly forty years earlier in the wilderness. Apparently the Israelites, like other Oriental peoples, looked upon such enumerations with superstitious feelings. For thousands of years most people, civilized and primitive, were superstitious about being counted, and census-takers were resisted at first in all parts of the world. This was probably because such enumerations were generally associated with military service, taxes or other governmental regulations and requirements. There was not another census in Israel until the reign of David. *II Samuel 24:1-4* says: "And again the anger of the Lord was kindled against Israel, and he moved David against them to say, Go number Israel and Judah. For the king said to Joab the captain of the host, which was with him, Go now through all the tribes of Israel, from Dan even to Beersheba, and number ye the people, that I may know the number of the people. And Joab said unto the king, Now the Lord thy God add unto the people, how many soever they be, an hundredfold, and that the eyes of my lord the king may see it: but why doth my lord the king delight in this thing? Notwithstanding the king's word prevailed against Joab, and against the captains of the host. And Joab and the captains of the host went out from the presence of the king, to number the people of Israel." In *II Samuel 24:8-9* we are told: "So when they had gone through all the land, they came to Jerusalem at the end of nine months and twenty days. And Joab gave up the sum of the number of the people unto the king: and there were in Israel eight hundred thousand valiant men that drew the sword; and the men of Judah were five hundred thousand men." But David acknowledged to Jehovah that he had done wrong in taking the census. *II Samuel 24:10* says: "And David's heart smote him after that he had numbered the people. And David said unto the Lord, I have sinned greatly in that I have done; and now, I beseech thee, O Lord, take away the iniquity of thy servant; for I have done very foolishly." Through his seer Gad, David, as punishment for taking the census, was given the choice of having seven years of famine, three months of constant military defeats at the hands of the enemy, or a three days' pestilence in the land. "So the Lord," says *II Samuel 24:15*, "sent a pestilence upon Israel from the morning even to the time appointed: and there died of the people from Dan even to Beersheba seventy thousand men." Ezra, according to *Ezra 8*, took a census of those who went with him from Babylon to Jerusalem, and a similar census was taken of the Jews in the time of Nehemiah, according to *Nehemiah 7*. Only one census is mentioned in the New Testament. Jesus was born at Bethlehem instead of in his father's house at Nazareth because of a Roman census. This registration, however, was purely for taxing purposes and not for military service. *Census* is derived from Latin *censere*, meaning "to value" or "to tax." *Luke 2:1-5* says: "And it came to pass in those days, that there went out a decree from Caesar Augustus, that all the world should be taxed. (And this taxing was first made when Cyrenius was governor of Syria.) And all went to be taxed, every one into his own city. And Joseph also went up from Galilee, out of the city of Nazareth, into Judaea, unto the city of David, which is called Bethlehem; (because he was of the house and lineage of David:) to be taxed with Mary his espoused wife, being great with child." Another such enrollment is alluded to in *Acts 5:37*, where we are told that after Theudas "this man rose up Judas of Galilee in the days of the taxing."

Did Moses marry a Negro woman?

Numbers 12:1 says: "And Miriam and Aaron spake against Moses because of the Ethiopian woman whom he had married: for he had married an Ethiopian woman." Since *Ethiopian*, like *African*, is now applied to the Negro race, many readers of this passage assume that Moses married a Negro woman. The passage is puzzling because there is no other hint in the Bible that Moses ever married any woman other than Zipporah, one of the seven daughters of Jethro, priest of Midian, who dwelt somewhere on the Sinai peninsula. The word rendered *Ethiopian* in the King James Version is *Cushite* in Hebrew. *Ethiopian* and *Cushite* are employed so loosely in the Bible that it is hard in many cases to determine what people they refer to. When the English Bible was translated it was supposed that *Cush*, the name of Ham's eldest son, always referred to Ethiopia. Some authorities suppose that Moses had only one wife and that the *Ethiopian woman* in *Numbers 12:1* refers to Zipporah, because *Cushan* is used in *Habakkuk 3:7* as synonymous with *Midian,* home of a North Arabian Semitic people known as Kusi. Yet it seems improbable that Miriam and Aaron at this late date would have started a rebellion in protest against the marriage of their younger brother to Zipporah. For her part in the family quarrel Miriam was stricken with leprosy and shut out of the camp for seven days. This suggests that jealousy over the superior position of Moses was the real cause of the strife. It appears that in some cases *Ethiopia* and *Cush* refer to a region in southwestern Arabia. Accordingly some authorities suppose that Moses married a second time and that his second wife was from southern Arabia and was Semitic or Hamitic in race. It is not probable she was an Ethiopian woman in the modern sense of the term. The Hamites, the race to which the ancient Egyptians belonged, were a Caucasian people with dark skins, wavy hair and oval faces who invaded North Africa at a very early date and drove the original darker-skinned inhabitants southward. Ethnologically the term *Hamite* is difficult to define, because most of the Hamitic peoples have become so mixed by inter-marriage with Semites, Aryans, Negroes and even earlier races that their original characteristics have almost disappeared. The fellahs of the Nile Valley, the Nubians and the Ethiopians show traces of Hamitic origin, but the original race is said to be best preserved in the Berbers of the Atlas Mountains and a few roving tribes in the Sahara.

Was circumcision peculiar to the Hebrews?

Circumcision was practiced by many ancient peoples. Herodotus said the Colchians, Egyptians and Ethiopians were the only peoples who practiced circumcision from earliest times. "The Phoenicians and the Syrians of Palestine (presumably the Jews) themselves confess they learned the custom of the Egyptians," wrote the Father of History. The truth, however, seems to be that virtually all ancient Semitic peoples and many of their neighbors practiced circumcision. It was also practiced to some extent by some North American Indians, natives of Australia and the Hawaiians. The original purpose of circumcision is lost in obscurity. Among some peoples it was probably adopted to safeguard health. Herodotus said the Egyptians practiced it "for the sake of cleanliness, considering it better to be cleanly than comely." Among others it appears to have originally been a sacrificial rite designed to secure fertility. Among still others it was supposed that circumcision restrained carnal lust. Some authorities believe that among the Hebrews it was originally a purificatory ceremony and symbolized the casting off of uncleanness preparatory to admission to membership in the tribe. Whatever the original purpose, the Hebrews adopted circumcision as the token of their covenant with God and as the badge to distinguish themselves from other peoples. According to *Genesis 17:10-12*, God said to Abraham: "This is my covenant, which ye shall keep, between me and you and thy seed after thee; Every man child among you shall be circumcised. And ye shall circumcise the flesh of your foreskin; and it shall be a token of the covenant betwixt me and you. And he that is eight days old shall be circumcised among you, every man child in your generations, he that is born in the house, or bought with money or any stranger, which is not of thy seed." The soul that is not circumcised "shall be cut off from his people; he hath broken my covenant." Apparently Abraham's family had not practiced circumcision previously, for *Genesis 17:24-26* informs us that the patriarch, then ninety-nine, and his thirteen-year-old son Ishmael were circumcised on the same day. The Moslem Arabs, who claim descent from Ishmael, still administer the rite at the age of thirteen. At first the Abrahamic rite was performed by the father, but later it was done by a physician or special officer. In the Bible there are many curious references to circumcision. *Genesis 34* says a Canaanite named Shechem violated Jacob's daughter Dinah. When Shechem wanted to marry her the brothers agreed provided all male members of the tribe were circumcised. But on the third day after the Canaanites were circumcised, Simeon and Levi attacked them "and slew all the males." It appears that for some reason or other Moses postponed the circumcision of one of his sons. While he and his family were on the way from Jethro's home in Midian to Egypt, he became very ill, and, according to *Exodus 4:25-26*, his wife, Zipporah, administered the Abrahamic rite to the son. All the male Israelites that went out of Egypt had been circumcised, but the rite was suspended during the forty years in the wilderness. *Joshua 5:2-8* says the Lord commanded Joshua, after the Israelites had reached the borders of the Promised Land, to circumcise all males born since they had left Egypt. According to *I Samuel 18*, David, who was "a poor man," gave the foreskins of two hundred Philistines to King Saul as a dowry for his daughter, Michal. Saul had made this a condition of the marriage in the hope his young rival would be killed while trying to kill the Philistines. During the latter part of the nineteenth century the khedive of Egypt levied a tax on the circumcision of all boys in the Sudan. Josephus says two of the Maccabean kings of Judaea, John Hyrcanus and Aristobulus, compelled all the male inhabitants to be circumcised when they conquered Idumaea and Ituraea respectively. When Rome under Domitian forbade circumcision, Jews and Egyptian priests were exempted from the edict. Moslems not only practice circumcision but perform a similar ritualistic operation on women. Whether circumcision should be required of all Christians was a subject of controversy in the early church. The mother church at Jerusalem, according to *Acts 15*, decided that Gentile converts need not submit to the Abrahamic rite, and later it was abandoned even by the Jewish Christians, although the rite survives to the present time among the Copts of Egypt and the Abyssinian Christians.

What was manna?

Manna was the food supplied miraculously to the Israelites during their sojourn in the wilderness. No natural substance found anywhere in the world answers the description of Biblical manna. When the Israelites murmured for want of food and yearned for the fleshpots of Egypt, the Lord told Moses he would "rain bread from heaven for you." *Exodus 16:14-15* says: "And when the dew that lay was gone up, behold, upon the face of the wilderness there lay a small round thing, as small as the hoar frost on the ground. And when the children of Israel saw it, they said one to another. It is manna: for they wist not what it was. And Moses said unto them, this is the bread which the Lord hath given you to eat." The Hebrew form of the word is *man*. In Aramaic *man-hu* signifies "what is it?" The idea seems to be that the Israelites, not having before seen the miraculous substance, asked, "What is it?" and then applied to it a word meaning "What is it?" This, however, may be sheer folk-etymology. Some authorities derive *manna* from Egyptian *mennu*, their name for gum-like exudations from certain trees, while others derive it from *mannah*, a Hebrew term meaning "to divide" or "to measures." *Exodus 16:31* says: "And the house of Israel called the name thereof Manna: and it was like coriander seed, white: and the taste of it was like wafers made with honey." *Numbers 11:7* says that "the colour thereof" was "as the colour of bdellium." Coriander seeds are small, grayish white in color and have a pleasant spicy flavor. Bdellium is generally supposed to be a sparkling precious stone, although Josephus says it was "one of the sweet spices." Manna was the first food to be rationed by measure. The Israelites were commanded to "gather of it every man according to his eating, an omer for every man, according to the number of your persons." An omer was a tenth of an ephah or slightly less than two quarts. In *Exodus 16* we are told that no matter how much manna each person gathered, when he measured it there was only an even omer for each member of his family. Paul alludes to this in *II Corinthians 8:15* when he says: "As it is written, He that had gathered much had nothing over; and he that had gathered little had no lack." Moses commanded the Israelites to eat every bit of the manna before morning. "Notwithstanding they hearkened not unto Moses; but some of them left of it until morning, and it bred worms, and stank: and Moses was wroth with them. And they gathered it every morning, every man according to his eating; and when the sun waxed hot, it melted." Elsewhere we are told that "when the dew fell upon the camp in the night, the manna fell upon it." But no manna fell upon the sabbath. Each person gathered a double portion on the sixth day to tide the family over the seventh. "And it did not stink, neither was there any worm therein." Manna was prepared both by baking and seething. *Numbers 11:8* says the people "ground it in mills, or beat it in a mortar, and baked it in pans, and made cakes of it: and the taste of it was as the taste of fresh oil." Manna apparently was not a substantial diet and the Israelites grew weary of eating it. They said, "now our soul is dried away: there is nothing at all, beside this manna, before our eyes," and they complained that "our soul loatheth this light bread." But "the children of Israel did eat manna forty years, until they came to a land inhabited." Speaking of their arrival at Gilgal, *Joshua 5:12* says: "And the manna ceased on the morrow after they had eaten of the old corn of the land; neither had the children of Israel manna any more; but they did eat of the fruit of the land of Canaan that year." According to *Exodus 16:32-34*, Aaron, upon the command of Moses, laid away an omer of manna "before the Testimony" so future generations might see the bread with which the Lord fed their ancestors in the wilderness, and *Hebrews 9:4* tells us the ark of the covenant contained "the golden pot that had manna." In most of the Old Testament miracles God is represented as having used natural phenomena and substances for special purposes. He did not create special substances for the miracles but employed materials already existing. For instance, the "quails that came up and filled the camp" to supply the Israelites with fresh meat on the same occasion are presumed to have been ordinary quails known to that part of the world. But apparently the quails were sent only once and did not constitute a recurring miracle. For this reason those who think all Biblical miracles can be explained by natural phenomena have sought to find in nature a counterpart of manna. Various different vegetable and animal substances have been *identified* with the Biblical manna, such as lichens and the honey dew secreted by aphids, but none of these answers the description of manna in the Bible. The modern Arabs apply *man* (manna) to the sweet, sticky-gum-like drops exuded from tamarisk shrubs on the Sinai peninsula, but this substance, although it contains medicinal qualities, is found only in small quantities and is not a satisfactory food. It is difficult to see how this gum or any other known natural product could have been made to fall every night except on the sabbath wherever the Israelites happened to be for a period of forty years. In *Deuteronomy 8:3* Moses himself tells the Israelites that the Lord "suffered thee to hunger, and fed thee with manna, which thou knewest not, neither did thy fathers know." The manna of modern medicine is made from the juice of a European ash. The conclusion seems to be inescapable that the authors of the Old Testament believed that manna was a miraculous substance, not a natural substance supplied in a miraculous way. In *Psalms 78:24* we are told that the Lord "rained down manna upon them to eat, and had given them of the corn of heaven," and *Psalms 105:40* says the Lord "satisfied them with the bread of heaven." According to a Jewish tradition, the ark of the covenant, including the pot of manna, was hidden by Jeremiah and would be restored when the Messiah came. Jesus alluded to manna when he compared himself to the bread of life. *Revelation 2:17* says: "To him that overcometh will I give to eat of the hidden manna."

How many tribes of Israel were there?

It is commonly supposed that the tribes of Israel were all named after sons of Jacob and that they numbered twelve. That is not quite correct. There were really thirteen instead of twelve tribes. Jacob, who was called Israel, had twelve sons by his two wives and his two concubines, Leah, Rachel, Zilpah and Bilhah. The names of the twelve sons were: Reuben, Simeon, Levi, Judah, Issachar, Zebulon, Gad, Asher, Dan, Naphtali, Joseph and Benjamin. According to *Genesis 49:28*, after Jacob had blessed all of his twelve sons in succession, he said: "All these are the twelve tribes of Israel." But Jacob had already indicated that no tribe would bear Joseph's name. By Asenath, daughter of an Egyptian priest, Joseph had two sons. In

Genesis 48:5-6 Jacob said to Joseph: "And now thy two sons, Ephraim and Manasseh, which were born unto thee in the land of Egypt before I came unto thee into Egypt, are mine; as Reuben and Simeon, they shall be mine. And thy issue, which thou begettest after them, shall be thine, and shall be called after the name of their brethren in their inheritance." Consequently there were really thirteen tribes, eleven named after sons and two after grandsons of Jacob. When the Israelites settled in the Promised Land only twelve tribes were allotted separate territory. The tribe of Levi was consecrated as a tribe of hereditary priests and they were assigned dwelling privileges in forty-eight cities scattered in the territory allotted to the other twelve tribes. Nevertheless the Levites continued to be referred to as the tribe of Levi. Twelve was a sacred number among the ancient Hebrews and when the tribe of Levi was withdrawn as a separate political and military unit, an additional tribe was created by subdividing the tribe of Joseph into Ephraim and Manasseh. This respect for the number twelve apparently survived among the Jews down to New Testament times. Jesus had twelve disciples, but after Judas Iscariot betrayed his master and committed suicide, the remaining eleven chose a successor by lot so the number of apostles would again be twelve. While Judas was still in good standing, according to *Matthew 19:28,* Jesus said to his disciples that "ye which have followed me, in the regeneration when the Son of man shall sit in the throne of his glory, ye also shall sit upon twelve thrones, judging the twelve tribes of Israel."

How tall do cedars of Lebanon grow?

Ever since King Solomon raised a levy of men to cut cedars and firs of Lebanon for use in his temple these trees have been proverbial for their height. It is believed that cedars of Lebanon were not, even in the time of Solomon, particularly tall trees, comparatively speaking, although they were probably taller than any other trees familiar to the subjects of the King of Israel. For many years it was supposed that a few hundred trees about fifteen miles from Beirut were the only cedars of Lebanon left in their original habitat. But an inspection made in 1922 revealed that many thousand specimens still grow on the slopes of Lebanon and neighboring mountains in Syria. The cedars now growing on the Lebanon mountains comprise only the scattered and possibly the stunted remains of the magnificent forests known to the ancients. Nonetheless, it is believed that cedars of Lebanon normally grow only from fifty to eighty feet high. They are noted rather for their large trunks and widespreading branches. Numerous horizontal branches extend from the main trunk, tier upon tier, often covering an area as great in diameter as the height of the trees. There is reason for supposing that various kings who reigned in the territory between the Mediterranean and the Euphrates used wood to decorate their palaces long before the time of David and Solomon. From *I Kings 5* we learn that Solomon raised a levy of 30,000 Israelites and sent them to Lebanon to cooperate with the subjects of King Hiram of Tyre to obtain beams and boards of cedar for the new temple at Jerusalem. These men went to Lebanon "ten thousand a month by courses: a month they were in Lebanon, and two months at home." But from *II Chronicles 2:17-18* we learn that for this purpose Solomon numbered all the strangers in the land of Israel and found the number to be 153,600. "And," says that passage, "he set threescore and ten thousand of them to be bearers of burdens, and fourscore thousand to be hewers in the mountain, and three thousand and six hundred overseers to set the people to work." This and other passages indicate that Solomon supplied 193,600 men for the task, in addition to the workmen supplied by the king of Tyre. Solomon paid Hiram in yearly contributions of wheat, barley, oil and wine. King Hiram had the trees cut, hewed, carried down to the sea and transported "in floats by sea to Joppa," from where they were taken up to Jerusalem by Solomon's "bearers of burdens." This wood was also used in making ship masts, chariots and other articles. *The Song of Solomon 3:9* says: "King Solomon made himself a chariot of the wood of Lebanon." Cedars of Lebanon were used in rebuilding the temple after the return of the Jews from the first captivity and in repairing it from time to time down through the centuries. *Ezra 3:7* says: "They gave money also unto the masons, and to the carpenters; and meat, and drink, and oil, unto them of Zidon, and to them of Tyre, to bring cedar trees from Lebanon to the sea of Joppa, according to the grant that they had of Cyrus king of Persia." Josephus quotes a letter of Antiochus the Great to Ptolemy of Egypt in which he "who ruled over all Asia" said in reference to the temple at Jerusalem: "And for the materials of wood, let it be brought them out of Judea itself, and out of the other countries, and out of Lebanus, tax free." In connection with the building of the second temple Josephus says: "The Sidonians also were very willing and ready to bring the cedar trees from Lebanus, to bind them together, and to make a united float of them, and to bring them to the port of Joppa, for that was what Cyrus had commanded at first, and what was now done at the command of Darius." The cedar of Lebanon is an evergreen tree, reaches a great age, produces hard, durable and fragrant wood and was regarded by the Israelites as the most beautiful and majestic of all trees. Accordingly, in the Bible cedar of Lebanon is used figuratively as the symbol of greatness, strength, regal power, glory and even eternal life. In the Scriptures *cedar* always refers to this tree, except possibly in *Numbers 24:6*—"as cedar trees beside the waters"—where the translation is doubtful. The highest peak in the Lebanon mountains is Dhor el Khorib, with an altitude of about 10,050 feet, and cedars there are seldom found at altitudes lower than 5,000 or 6,000 feet above sea level. Yet cedars of Lebanon seem to thrive in lower altitudes. In 1902 some of these trees were planted in the Arnold Arboretum of Harvard University at Boston. More recently some cedars from the Lebanon mountains were presented by the American University at Beirut to the United States in appreciation of the aid extended to Syria through the Near East Relief. These trees were transplanted in Arlington National Cemetery near Washington and seem to be thriving.

Does the Bible call the Israelites *the chosen people*?

The phrase *the chosen people* is not in the Bible, but it was suggested by various Biblical passages. According to *I Chronicles 16:13*, David sang a psalm in which he said: "O ye seed of Israel his servant, ye children of Jacob, his chosen ones." *Psalms 33:12* says: "Blessed is the nation whose God is the Lord; and the people whom he hath chosen for his own inheritance." Verse 6 of *Psalms 89* says, "O ye seed of Abraham his servant, ye children of Jacob his chosen," and Verse 43 of the same Psalm, "And he brought forth his people with joy, and his chosen with gladness." The same thought is expressed in the New Testament. In *Acts 13:17* Paul says: "The God of this people of Israel chose our fathers, and exalted the people when they dwelt as strangers in the land of Egypt."

What does *giving up the ghost* mean?

This phrase was first introduced in the English Bible printed at Geneva in 1560 by William Whittingham and his assistants, and was retained by the translators of the King James Version. The Hebrew word so rendered in the Old Testament signifies literally "to come to an end" and figuratively "to die." It is employed in connection with the deaths of several of the patriarchs. *Genesis 25:8* says: "Then Abraham gave up the ghost, and died in a good old age, and full of years; and was gathered to his people." According to *Genesis 35:29*,

Isaac "gave up the ghost, and died, and was gathered to his people." *Genesis 49:33* tells us that "when Jacob had made an ending of commanding his sons, he gathered up his feet into the bed, and yielded up the ghost, and was gathered unto his people." And Ishmael, according to *Genesis 25:17*, "gave up the ghost and died; and was gathered to his people." The phrase is also used elsewhere in the Old Testament. For instance, *Job 10:18* says: "Wherefore then hast thou brought me forth out of the womb? Oh that I had given up the ghost, and no eye had seen me!" This usage was adopted with variations in translating the Greek of the New Testament into English. Mark, Luke and John say that Jesus "gave up the ghost," while in Matthew "yielded up the ghost" is employed. In *Acts 5* it is related that "Ananias hearing these words fell down, and gave up the ghost," but shortly thereafter his wife Sapphira "yielded up the ghost." Some modern English versions have substituted "died," "expired" and similar phrases in all of these passages.

Where does the Bible mention the green bay tree?

Psalms 37:35 says: "I have seen the wicked in great power, and spreading himself like a green bay tree." Bible scholars differ as to the exact meaning of the Hebrew original rendered "a green bay tree" in the King James Version. In the Septuagint Version this passage in the psalms of David was rendered by the Greek equivalent of "the cedars of Lebanon." The editors of the American Revised Version, under the impression apparently that they were improving this beautiful passage, translated it "a green tree in its native soil."

Does the Bible forbid suicide?

Suicide as distinguished from murder is nowhere specifically forbidden in either the New or Old Testament. Since suicide is self-slaughter it is naturally prohibited by the commandment, "Thou shalt not kill" (in Hebrew literally *murder*). Oddly enough, however, the Talmudic writers did not base their prohibition against suicide so much on this commandment as they did upon the pre-Mosaic commandment in *Genesis 9:5*, which says in part: "And surely your blood of your lives will I require." Generally speaking, Judaism has never emphasized suicide as a crime and sin to the extent that the Christian church has, although orthodox Jews segregate suicides in burial. Josephus tells us that when his companions in the pit at Jotapata were contemplating suicide he said to them: "Our laws determine that the bodies of such as kill themselves should be exposed until the sun be set, without burial." In this connection it is an interesting fact that in ancient Greece and Rome the bodies of persons struck by lightning, unteethed children and suicides were denied the privilege of cremation and were buried. In 1190 A.D. the Jews of York, England, committed suicide en masse and perished almost to a man in anticipation of a general massacre at the hands of a mob that attacked them on the eve of the Passover on the charge that they used human blood in their services. Only five specific cases of suicide are mentioned in the King James Version of the Bible, one in the New Testament and four in the Old. Judas Iscariot hanged himself; Ahithophel, a counselor of David, did likewise; Saul, after being wounded and defeated by the Philistines, killed himself by falling upon his sword, although the young Amalekite who brought the news to David claimed that he had slain the king at the latter's request; Saul's armour-bearer did likewise; and Abimelech, the "Bramble King," after being wounded by a woman, was thrust through by his armor-bearer upon his own request. In a sense Samson and Zimri also committed suicide. Samson brought destruction upon himself and his enemies by wrecking the house of the Philistines. His object, however, was vengeance rather than suicide. Zimri, who was king of Israel only seven days, preferred death to capture and died in the ruins of his palace, which he himself had set on fire. The early Christian church placed more emphasis upon the sinfulness of killing oneself than upon killing another. This was probably owing in part to the fact that the pagans of the classical world at that time looked upon suicide as legal. It is also probably owing in part to the fact that if the persecuted Christians had resorted to suicide instead of facing martydom for their faith it would have been impossible to have spread and established the Christian religion. Shakespeare makes several references to the special sinfulness of suicide. For instance:

> Or that the Everlasting had not fix'd
> His canon 'gainst self-slaughter.
> —*Hamlet,* Act 1, Scene 2

> Against self-slaughter
> There is a prohibition so divine,
> That cravens my weak hand.
> —*Cymbeline,* Act 3, Scene 4

The Roman Catholic church condemns deliberate self-slaughter and refuses Christian burial to suicides. "Direct suicide is intrinsically evil and is forbidden by the natural and positive law of God," says *The*

New Catholic Dictionary, published in 1929. Pope Leo XIII, in General Decrees Concerning the Prohibition and Censorship of Books, issued January 25, 1897 said: "Those books are prohibited which defend suicide as lawful." At one time in England the property of a suicide was forfeited to the crown, and the body, with a stake driven through it, was buried ignominiously on a public highway without Christian rites. Under the law of the land a person who died by his own hand committed *felo de se,* "felony upon himself." Suicide is derived from Latin *sui,* "of oneself," and *caedere,* "to kill," and literally means "self-killing."

Does the Bible mention butter?

Butter occurs a number of times in the Bible. Referring to the three angels who visited Abraham at his tent in the plains of Mamre, *Genesis 18:8* says: "And he took butter, and milk, and the calf which he had dressed, and set it before them; and he stood by them under the tree, and they did eat." This is the only place in the Bible where celestial beings are portrayed as partaking of food. It is not probable that the Hebrews at that time understood the art of churning milk to produce butter. The Hebrew word rendered *butter* here signifies "curdled milk." In a hot climate like Palestine fresh milk quickly sours and acquires a pleasant acid flavor suggesting lemon cream. Curd and milk is a refreshing and thirst-quenching drink and is still widely drunk in that part of the world. Although the later Israelites had olive oil to take its place, butter in the modern sense of the term was probably known to them. It is supposed that churning milk for butter was originally suggested by the occurrence of this substance in the goatskin bags of milk carried over the desert on camel back by the Arabs. Even at the present time the Arabs churn a soft, rancid butter by putting cream in a goatskin bag suspended between two poles and pressing or shaking it. Milk, especially milk from cows and goats, was an important food in ancient Palestine. The camel was an unclean animal, according to the Mosaic law, and only the Arabs used camel's milk. In the Bible it is not always clear when real butter, cheese or "thick milk" is meant. The ancients appear to have been familiar with cheese as a foodstuff long before they learned the art of making butter. In *Job 10:10* the patriarch asks: "Hast thou not poured me out as milk, and curdled me like cheese?" Moses, in *Deuteronomy 32:14,* refers to "butter of kine, and milk of sheep." Zophar the Naamathite, in *Job 20:17,* says that the wicked and the hypocrite shall not see "the rivers, the floods, the brooks of honey and butter." When Sisera asked Jael, wife of Heber the Kenite, for a little water to drink, she, according to *Judges 4:19,* "opened a bottle of milk, and gave him drink." But *Judges 5:25* has Deborah and Barak say in their song: "He asked water, and she gave him milk; she brought forth butter in a lordly dish." We are told in *I Samuel 17:18* that "ten cheeses" were part of the food that Jesse asked David to carry to the Israelite army encamped opposite the Philistines. According to *II Samuel 17:29,* sympathizers brought David and his people at Mahanaim "honey, and butter, and sheep, and cheese of kine." "Surely," says Solomon in *Proverbs 30:33,* "the churning of milk bringeth forth butter." In *Psalms 55:21* David says, "The words of his mouth were smoother than butter, but war was in his heart," and in *Job 29:6* the patriarch in his parable says, "When I washed my steps with butter, and the rock poured me out rivers of oil." And finally, *Isaiah 7:15,* in the prophecy of Immanuel, who was to be the son of a virgin, says: "Butter and honey shall he eat, that he may know to refuse the evil, and choose the good." Oddly, there are no references to butter and cheese in the New Testament.

Why did Gideon choose men who lapped water like dogs?

The real significance of the drinking test used by Gideon to choose three hundred men from ten thousand is one of the unsolved Bible puzzles. Thirty-two thousand responded to Gideon's call for volunteers to fight the Midianites. The Lord told the "mighty man of valour" that the number was too great, lest the Israelites fail to attribute their victory to the Lord and boast they had won it with their own hands. What was wanted was a mere handful of dependable men for a dangerous mission. The strategy was to confuse and defeat the host of the enemy by an early morning surprise attack with trumpets and pitchers containing lamps. *Judges 7:4-7* says: "And the Lord said unto Gideon, The people are yet too many; bring them down unto the water, and I will try them for thee there: and it shall be, that of whom I say unto thee, This shall go with thee, the same shall go with thee; and of whomsoever I say unto thee, This shall not go with thee, the same shall not go. So he brought down the people unto the water: and the Lord said unto Gideon, Every one that lappeth of the water with his tongue, as a dog lappeth, him shalt thou set by himself; likewise every one that boweth down upon his knees to drink. And the number of them that lapped, putting their hand to their mouth, were three hundred men: but all the rest of the people bowed down upon their knees to drink water. And the Lord said unto Gideon, By the three hundred men that lapped will I save you, and deliver the Midianites into thine hand: and let all the other people go every man unto his place." Some authorities suggest that this may have been only an arbitrary test. They say it is as easy to think of reasons for choosing those who stooped down and drank in long draughts as it is for rejecting them. It seems more probable, however, that this drinking test had some psychological basis on which Gideon formed his opinion as to the fitness of the men for the particular undertaking he had in mind. More than eighteen hundred years ago Josephus wrote the following version of this incident: "Now that they might not pass God over, but ascribe the victory to him, and might not fancy it obtained by their own power, because they were a great army, and able of themselves to fight their enemies, but might confess that it was owing to his assistance, he advised him to bring his army about noon, in the violence of the heat, to the river, and to esteem those that bent down on their knees, and so drank, to be men of courage; but for all those that drank tumultuously, that he should esteem them to do it out of fear, and as in dread of their enemies. And when Gideon had done as God had suggested to him, there were found three hundred men that took water with their hands tumultuously; so God bid him take these men, and attack the enemy." In other words, according to Josephus, Gideon chose from the ten thousand a handful of three hundred who evidenced fear and dread of the enemy. The theory seems to be that the exploit was calculated to demonstrate not only that "there is no restraint to the Lord to save by many or by few" but also that even the least courageous would serve the purpose so long as the Lord was with Gideon. This construction of the drinking test is just the opposite of the generally accepted one, which is that Gideon reduced the unwieldy mob of Israelites to a small but trusty band of energetic and courageous men.

Does the Bible mention looking glasses?

Looking glasses or mirrors are several times referred to in the Bible. The earliest reference to them is in connection with the making of the tabernacle in the wilderness. *Exodus 38:8* tells us that Bezaleel, the master workman, "made the laver of brass, and the foot of it of brass, of the looking-glasses of the women assembling, which assembled at the door of the tabernacle of the congregation." These mirrors contributed by the women of Israel were probably made of polished or burnished molten copper, brass or bronze. There is a rabbinic tradition that Moses at first was loath to accept this offer of mirrors on the ground that they ministered to feminine vanity. But God reminded the great

Lawgiver that the women of Israel had shared the burden of their husbands' bondage in Egypt and had done everything in their power to cheer them in the wilderness, whereupon Moses changed his mind to the extent of permitting the metal from the mirrors to be used in making the laver. In *Job 37:18* Elihu, speaking on God's behalf, asks rhetorically: "Hast thou with him spread out the sky, which is strong, and as a molten looking glass?" According to *Isaiah 3:23,* "glasses" were among the vain ornaments that the Lord would take away from the haughty daughters of Zion, but some authorities question that translation of the original Hebrew word. There are several allusions to mirrors in the New Testament. *James 1:23* says: "For if any be a hearer of the word, and not a doer, he is like unto a man beholding his natural face in a glass." Paul, in *II Corinthians 3:18,* says: "But we all, with open face beholding as in a glass the glory of the Lord." The Apostle to the Gentiles, in *I Corinthians 13:12,* also says that "now we see through a glass darkly; but then face to face," where the allusion is probably to the fact that the reflection of the ancient burnished metal mirrors was indistinct.

Why did the Jews discontinue sacrifices?

The Jewish law forbade the offering of sacrifices everywhere except in the temple at Jerusalem, and the custom of offering sacrifices was necessarily discontinued after the temple was destroyed by the Romans in 70 A.D. Originally the Hebrews offered their sacrifices wherever the opportunity presented itself and generally a temporary altar was erected on an elevated site for the purpose. In the wilderness the Israelites offered their sacrifices in the tabernacle wherever it was set up. *Deuteronomy 12:4-7* shows that the law of Moses contemplated an ultimate central sanctuary. It was to be "the place which the Lord your God shall choose out of all your tribes to put his name there." The location of the tabernacle or temple was regarded as the place chosen by the Lord. After reaching the Promised Land, the Israelites sacrificed successively at Gilgal, Nob, Gideon, Mount Ebal, Shiloh and finally Jerusalem. The law of Moses did not designate Jerusalem for the site of the temple. This subject was a controversial one until David took the ark of the covenant there and settled the matter. In time Jerusalem came to be regarded as the only proper place for the sacrificial rites. When the northern tribes separated from Judah, the fact that the central sanctuary was at Jerusalem was a decided advantage to the latter. Jeroboam established places for sacrificing within his dominions, but with indifferent success. When the Babylonians destroyed Jerusalem and the temple, all sacrifices were suspended by the Jews and not resumed until the temple was rebuilt in Jerusalem during the reign of Cyrus. But the Samaritans, who were descended from Medes and Persians and who affected to observe the Hebrew religious rites, built a temple on Mt. Gerizim and offered sacrifices there according to the Mosaic law. This old controversy about the proper place for religious worship is alluded to in what the Samaritan woman at Jacob's well said to Jesus in *John 4:20*: "Our fathers worshipped in this mountain; and ye say, that in Jerusalem is the place where men ought to worship." Several times during the turbulent periods under the Syrians, Greeks, Egyptians and other conquerors the temple services were interrupted. Although orthodox Jews hold that the laws providing for sacrificial rites have been only suspended and not repealed, there is not at present, and has not been for centuries, any active movement to rebuild the temple and to resume sacrifices. There is reason for believing that the bloodier forms of animal sacrifice had fallen into disuse by the beginning of the Christian Era. Many of the prophets had cried out against the sordid side of the sacrificial system and emphasized the importance of justice, mercy and other spiritual values over the grosser forms of the Jewish ritual. "To do justice and judgment is more acceptable to the Lord than sacrifice," says *Proverbs 21:3*. Samuel, Isaiah, Micah, Amos and several other prophets, while not condemning sacrifices as such, condemned the hypercritical character of some of those who offered them. To some extent at the present time various prayers and symbolical observances take the place of the sacrifices formerly offered.

Is the penknife mentioned in the Bible?

Penknife occurs in the English Bible only in connection with the account of the burning of the roll of a book dictated by Jeremiah to Baruch and read by the latter to the congregation in the house of the Lord. *Jeremiah 36:23*, describing the scene when King Jehoiakim sat before a fire on the hearth in his winterhouse, says: "And it came to pass, that when Jehudi had read three or four leaves, he cut it with the penknife, and cast it into the fire that was on the hearth, until all the roll was consumed in the fire that was on the hearth." *Penknife* is a holdover from the days when steel pens were unknown. The original penknife was a small knife used in making and mending quill pens and in erasing writing from the rolls of papyrus. Now almost any kind of small pocketknife is called a penknife. We find *penknife* used in English as early as the middle of the fifteenth century. At that time it referred to a blade fitted in a sheath and carried in the pocket for the purpose of sharpening quills for writing. It was not until much later that penknives were made with jointed blades fitting inside a handle.

Does the Bible mention handling snakes?

In 1942 three members of a backwoods church in Kentucky were held to a grand jury on a murder charge for participating in a meeting at which another member of the congregation was fatally bitten by rattlesnakes. The judge ordered the sheriff's deputies to kill four large rattlesnakes that were alleged to have bitten the "murdered" man while being "handled" at a religious meeting in the church. Incidents of this kind often occur in certain sections of Virginia, North Carolina, Tennessee and Kentucky, and they became so frequent in Kentucky that the legislature in 1940 passed a law making it illegal to use snakes in religious ceremonies. The religious groups who make a practice of handling snakes in church are sometimes referred to as a "snake cult." This creates the impression that these people are snake worshippers and that they indulge in "snake charming." But snake charming and snake worship are not involved in this particular practice. These people are fundamentalists and interpret very literally, and undertake to put into practice, certain passages in the New Testament. In *Mark 16* it is related that Jesus after the Crucifixion, appeared to the eleven Apostles as they sat at meat and upbraided them with their unbelief and hardness of heart, because they believed not them who had seen him after he had risen from the grave. Jesus told the eleven that certain signs would follow them that believe, and one of these signs would be: "They shall take up serpents; and if they drink any deadly thing, it shall not hurt them." According to *Luke 10:10,* Jesus said to the seventy after they returned: "Behold, I give unto you power to tread on serpents and scorpions, and over all the power of the enemy: and nothing shall by any means hurt you." The viper story in *Acts 28* is also in point. When Paul was being taken in bonds from Jerusalem to Rome the "ship of Alexandria sailing into Italy" from "Myra, a city of Lycia" was run aground during a storm on the shores of Melita, modern Malta, and broken with the violence of the waves. All members of the crew and the prisoners saved their lives by swimming to land. *Acts 28:2-6* says: "And the barbarous people shewed us no little kindness: for they kindled a fire, and received us every one, because of the present rain, and because of the cold. And when Paul had gathered a bundle of sticks, and laid them on the fire, there came a viper out of the heat, and fastened on his hand. And when the barbarians saw the venomous beast hang on his hand, they said among themselves, No doubt this is a murderer, whom, though he hath escaped the sea, yet vengeance suffereth not to live. And he shook off the beast into the fire, and felt no harm. Howbeit they looked when he should have swollen, or fallen down dead suddenly: but after they had looked a great while, and saw no harm come to him, they changed their minds, and said that he was a god." Some authorities have questioned this story on the ground that there are no venomous reptiles of any kind on the island of Malta at the present time. Be that as it may, the snake handlers of the mountains of Kentucky and neighboring states accept these passages in the Bible literally and they sincerely believe that if their Christian faith is firm enough they can "tread on" and "take up" with their bare feet and hands rattlesnakes, copperheads and other poisonous snakes without being harmed. They do not worship the snakes, nor do they pretend to charm them or exercise any power over them, but simply use them to put their own faith to the utmost test, according to their understanding of the passages quoted above from the Scriptures. Snake charming is alluded to in the Bible. *Jeremiah 8:17* says: "For, behold, I will send serpents, cockatrices, among you, which will not be charmed, and they will bite you, saith the Lord." "Surely," says *Ecclesiastes 10:11*, "the serpent will bite without enchantment."

Is selling dogs condemned in the Bible?

Many people have a decided prejudice against selling dogs. Some go so far as to regard the sale of a dog as positively sinful. This writer once knew of an elderly woman who severely condemned a neighbor who engaged in the business of raising dogs for sale. She branded his business as sinful and protested against her church accepting contributions of his money, which she said was *tainted* because it was received in violation of *Deuteronomy 23:18*, which says in part: "Thou shalt not bring . . . the price of a dog into the house of the Lord God for any vow." Whether the prejudice against trafficking in dogs is based on this Mosaic passage is hard to say. Many commentators accept *dog* in that passage in the literal sense and suppose that Moses declared dogs unclean and prohibited traffic in them. The Talmudic writers and Josephus interpret *dog* literally and take it to mean anything obtained in exchange for a dog. Others, however, take a different view of the passage, although they do not deny that the Hebrews regarded the dog as ritually unclean. The Semitic term for a male person who practiced immoral conduct as a religious rite was the same as that for dog, and accordingly they say that *dog* in the passage under consideration does not refer to the animal, but to a person who has prostituted himself by committing any abominable act, such as sodomy. The context seems to confirm this latter opinion, for *Deuteronomy 23:17-18* reads: "There shall be no whore of the daughters of Israel, nor a sodomite of the sons of Israel. Thou shalt not bring the hire of a whore, or the price of a dog, into the house of the Lord thy God for any vow: for even both these are abomination unto the Lord thy God." In all probability *dog* here denotes a person who practiced immoral conduct as an idolatrous rite. There are echoes of this usage in the New Testament. *Revelation 22:15* says "For without are dogs, and sorcerers, and whoremongers, and murderers, and idolaters, and whosoever loveth and maketh a lie."

Are there any dog stories in the Bible?

There are no dog stories in the Bible. In ancient Palestine, as in the Orient generally, the dog was for the most part regarded as filthy and was looked upon with loathing and aversion. Even today in the East the dog is not looked upon as the affectionate pet and faithful companion of man that it is in the West. The dog is mentioned more than forty times in the Bible, and with few exceptions is referred to with contempt. The Hebrew equivalent of *dog* was one of the most contemptuous terms in the vocabulary of the Israelite. Moslems still speak of *Christian dogs*. In ancient Palestine street-cleaning was practically unknown and garbage was thrown into the streets of the cities to be disposed of by homeless dogs which roamed at will and which were the accepted scavengers. These dogs, regarded as ritually unclean and accordingly treated badly, were generally vicious and unfriendly to man. *Exodus 22:31* says: "And ye shall be holy men unto me; neither shall ye eat any flesh that is torn of beasts in the field; ye shall cast it to the dogs." According to *Exodus 11:7*, the Lord said unto Moses: "But against any of the children of Israel shall not a dog move his tongue, against man or beast." That was a proverbial expression indicating safety and peace. In *Psalms 59:6* we read: "They return at evening: they make a noise like a dog, and go round about the city." In *II Kings 8:13* Hazael asked Elisha: "Is thy servant a dog, that he should do this great thing?" It is related in *II Kings 9:10* that "the dogs shall eat Jezebel in the portion of Jezreel, and there shall be none to bury her." Jehu induced two or three eunuchs to throw the wicked woman out of a window to be trampled underfoot by horses and eaten by dogs. To compare a man with a dead dog was one of the most offensive expressions an ancient Israelite could use. The persecuted David, according to *I Samuel 24:14,* said to Saul: "After whom is the king of Israel come out? After whom doest thou pursue? after a dead dog, after a flea." Although there is no certainty on this point, it is supposed that the common dogs in ancient Palestine were of two types—the pariah dog of the cities and villages and a dog of the Scotch Collie type originally introduced by the nomadic shepherds. The dog fares little better in the New Testament. Speaking to the woman of Canaan who besought him to cure her daughter who was grievously vexed with a devil, Jesus, according to *Matthew 15:26,* said: "It is not meet to take the children's bread, and to cast it to dogs." The woman pathetically replied: "Truth, Lord: yet the dogs eat of the crumbs which fall from their masters' table." In *Matthew 7:6,* in the Sermon on the Mount, Jesus is quoted as saying: "Give not that which is holy unto the dogs." But in the parable of the rich man and Lazarus, Jesus refers to dogs without any indication of contempt. *Luke 16:20-21* says: "And there was a certain beggar named Lazarus, which was laid at his gate, full of sores, and desiring to be fed with the crumbs which fell from the rich man's table: moreover the dogs came and licked his sores."

Why did the Jews particularly abhor pork?

In every instance except one hogs and pigs are mentioned in the King James Version only under the name *swine.* The ancient Israelites were forbidden by the law of Moses to eat the flesh of the swine or to touch its carcase. In *Leviticus 11:3-8* it is stated: "Whatsoever parteth the hoof, and is cloven footed, and cheweth the cud, among the beasts, that shall ye eat. Nevertheless these shall ye not eat of them that chew the cud, or of them that divide the hoof: as the camel. . . . the coney. . . . the hare. . . . and the swine, though he divide the hoof, and be clovenfooted, yet he cheweth not the cud; he is unclean to you. Of their flesh shall ye not eat, and their carcase shall ye not touch; they are unclean to you." Here the swine is not singled out as being specially unclean and no emphasis is placed on this animal among the forbidden beasts. At first the Israelites probably were acquainted with no swine except the wild boar. But the Syrians and Canaanites both used wild and domesticated swine for food and sacrifice. The later Israelites and Jews probably came to regard this animal with particular abhorrence because it was a favorite of their historic enemies, because it was loathsome to them in appearance and in its manner of living, and, perhaps, because badly cooked pork in that climate often produced trichinosis. The Phoenicians alone among the ancient inhabitants of Palestine seem to have shared this aversion to the hog with the Israelites. Very few if any swine were raised in a country where the animal was held in such abhorrence, and consequently the authors of the books of the Bible had little occasion to mention it. Besides that in *Leviticus*, there are only four references to swine in the entire Old Testament. In *Proverbs 11:22* Solomon says: "As a jewel of gold in a swine's snout, so is a fair woman which is without discretion." And in *Isaiah 65:4* and *66:3* and *17* the prophet associates "swine's flesh" and "swine's blood" with other abominations. By the time of Jesus pious Jews so loathed the swine that they would not utter its name and preferred death to touching or eating pork. In the New Testament the swine is referred to with similar contempt. At that time Palestine was governed by Gentiles and the Jews were more familiar with the detested animal. According to *Matthew 7:6*, Jesus said in the Sermon on the Mount: "Give not that which is holy unto the dogs, neither cast ye your pearls before swine, lest they trample them under their feet, and turn again and rend you." We are told in *Luke 15:15* that the prodigal son became so reduced in circumstances that he went into the fields of the citizen of a far country "to feed swine." Equally familiar is the incident, related in the Synoptics, when Jesus cast the evil spirits into a herd of about two thousand swine, which then ran violently down a steep place and were choked in the sea. In *II Peter 2:22* those who believe in Jesus and then backslide are compared to "the sow that was washed to her wallowing in the mire." This is the only instance in the Bible where the hog is referred to by any name other than swine. Mohammed forbade the eating of swine's flesh and the Moslems abhor pork with a vehemence equal to that of the Israelites.

Is *besetting sin* in the Bible?

Besetting sin is not in the Bible, but was undoubtedly suggested by *Hebrews 12:1*, which refers to "the sin which doth so easily beset us."

What Biblical character made iron float?

The Bible says that the prophet Elisha made an iron ax head float in the waters of the river Jordan. This interesting incident is related in *II Kings 6:1-7*, which reads: "And the sons of the prophets said unto Elisha, Behold now, the place where we dwell with thee is too strait for us. Let us go, we pray thee, unto Jordan, and take thence every man a beam, and let us make us a place there, where we may dwell. And he answered, Go ye. And one said, Be content, I pray thee, and go with thy servants. And he answered, I will go. So he went with them. And when they came to Jordan, they cut down wood. But as one was felling a beam, the ax head fell into the water: and he cried, and said, Alas, master! for it was borrowed. And the man of God said, Where fell it? And he shewed him the place. And he cut down a stick, and cast it in thither; and the iron did swim. Therefore said he, Take it up to thee. And he put out his hand, and took it."

Is *turning one's face to the wall* of Biblical origin?

A person on his deathbed and conscious of the approaching end is said to turn his face to the wall. This expression is of Biblical origin. *II Kings 20:1-3* says: "In those days was Hezekiah sick unto death. And the prophet Isaiah the son of Amoz came to him, and said unto him, Thus saith the Lord, Set thine house in order: for thou shalt die, and not live. Then he turned his face to the wall, and prayed unto the Lord, saying, I beseech thee, O Lord, remember now how I have walked before thee in truth and with a perfect heart, and have done that which is good in thy sight. And Hezekiah wept sore." But the king of Judah did not die at that time. The Lord told Isaiah to tell Hezekiah that he had heard his prayer and seen his tears and would heal him and add fifteen years to his life. *II Kings 20:7* informs us what the malady was and reveals the method of the cure. It says simply: "And Isaiah said, Take a lump of figs. And they took and laid it on the boil, and he recovered." This story is also told with slight variations in *Isaiah 38*. Incidentally, this lump of figs laid "for a plaister upon the boil" is one of the few medical remedies found in the Bible.

Who sold Joseph into slavery?

The popular notion that Joseph was sold into slavery by his brethren may not be entirely correct. According to *Genesis 37,* when Joseph's brethren saw him afar off they conspired to kill him. However, upon the suggestion of Reuben who wanted to save his seventeen-year-old brother and return him unharmed to their father, Joseph was stripped of his coat of many colors and cast into an empty pit. While the brethren were eating and debating what to do next, "a company of Ishmeelites came from Gilead with their camels bearing spicery and balm and myrrh, going to carry it down to Egypt." Judah suggested that instead of killing Joseph they sell him to the Ishmaelites (the present spelling of the word). But before the suggestion could be accepted and acted upon "there passed by Midianites merchantmen; and *they* drew and lifted up Joseph out of the pit, and sold Joseph into Egypt." Whether the pronoun *they* refers back to the Midianites or to Joseph's brethren is not entirely clear; but that the Midianites and not Joseph's brethren sold him to the Ishmaelites is indicated by *Genesis 37:29-30,* which says: "Reuben returned unto the pit; and, behold, Joseph was not in the pit; and he rent his clothes. And he returned unto his brethren, and said, the child is not; and I, whither shall I go?" That it was the Midianites and not his brethren who sold him seems to be further borne out by *Genesis 40:41,* where Joseph in prison tells the chief butler that he "was stolen away out of the land of the Hebrews." The account is confused somewhat by the fact that *Genesis 37:36* says "the Midianites sold him into Egypt unto Potiphar." This, however, may be only a telescoped way of saying that the Midianites sold him to the Ishmaelites who resold him in Egypt. The Ishmaelites and Midianites, though sometimes confused, were different peoples. Some authorities attribute these seemingly inconsistent statements about the Midianites and Ishmaelites to the supposed fact that in this story of Joseph and his brethren the final compiler of *Genesis* wove together two different narratives that represented two different traditions as to the nationality of the caravan that bought Joseph. Hebrew scholars say that the Hebrew copies of *Genesis* contain the same difficulties in connection with this story as do our English copies. It is a point that probably never can be settled definitely to the satisfaction of all Bible students. At any rate, we have the authority of no other than St. Paul that it was Joseph's brethren who sold him. In *Acts 7:9* Paul is quoted as saying that "the patriarchs, moved with envy, sold Joseph into Egypt."

What is the millennium?

Millennium is not a Biblical word. It was coined during the latter Middle Ages from Latin *mille,* "a thousand," and *annus,* "a year," after the fashion of *biennium,* "a period of two years." Specifically *millennium* is applied to the thousand years mentioned by St. John the Divine in the Apocalypse. *Revelation 20:1-7* says: "And I saw an angel come down from heaven, having the key of the bottomless pit and a great chain in his hand. And he laid hold on the dragon, that old serpent, which is the Devil, and Satan, and bound him a thousand years, and cast him into the bottomless pit, and shut him up, and set a seal upon him, that he should deceive the nations no more, till the thousand years should be fulfilled: and after that he must be loosed a little season. And I saw thrones, and they sat upon them, and judgment was given unto them: and I saw the souls of them that were beheaded for the witness of Jesus, and for the word of God, and which had not worshipped the beast, neither his image, neither had received his mark upon their foreheads, or in their hands; and they lived and reigned with Christ a thousand years. But the rest of the dead lived not again until the thousand years were finished. This is the first resurrection. Blessed and holy is he that hath part in the first resurrection: on such the second death hath no power, but they shall be priests of God and of Christ, and shall reign with him a thousand years." This was interpreted by many theologians as signifying that holiness would be triumphant and Christ would reign in person on earth for a thousand years. In everyday speech *millennium* is used figuratively to mean an extended period of great happiness, good government, or freedom from wickedness.

What is meant by Alpha and Omega?

In the Bible *Alpha and Omega* occurs only in the Apocalypse. *Revelation 1:8* says: "I am Alpha and Omega, the beginning and the ending, saith the Lord, which is, and which was, and which is to come, the Almighty." In *Revelation 21:5-7* we read: "And he that sat upon the throne said, Behold, I make all things new. And he said unto me, Write: for these words are true and faithful. And he said unto me, It is done. I am Alpha and Omega, the beginning and the end. I will give unto him that is athirst of the fountain of the water of life freely. He that overcometh shall inherit all things; and I will be his God, and he shall be my son." And in *Revelation 22:13* the angel said to St. John the Divine: "I am Alpha and Omega, the beginning and the end, the first and the last." In all these passages *Alpha and Omega* is used figuratively of God himself. *Alpha,* A, is the first letter in the Greek alphabet, and *Omega,* O, is the last, and the phrase literally means "from first to last." We express the same thought in our "from A to Z." *Alphabet* itself is derived from *Alpha* and *Beta,* B, the second letter in the Greek alphabet. The word is equivalent to our *ABC's.*

Does the Bible say, "There is none good, no, not one"?

"There is none good, no, not one" is a common saying generally ascribed to the Scriptures. It appears to be merely a fusion of several Biblical passages. In *Psalms 14:1* we find, "There is none that doeth good," and in the third verse of the same Psalm, "There is none that doeth good, no, not one." *Psalms 53* is substantially the same as *Psalms 14* and both of these passages are repeated there. *Romans 3:10* says: "As it is written, There is none righteous, no, not one." In *Matthew 19:17* and *Mark 10:18* Jesus says: "Why callest thou me good? there is none good but one, that is, God."

What is meant by the evil eye?

Evil eye is used in the Bible in the sense of covetousness and envy. *Proverbs 23:6* says: "Eat thou not the bread of him that hath an evil eye, neither desire thou his dainty meats." And in *Proverbs 28:22* we are told: "He that hasteth to be rich hath an evil eye, and considereth not that poverty shall come upon him." In *Baba Metzia,* written about 200 B.C., one of the Talmudic scribes says: "For one that dies of natural causes ninety-nine die of the evil eye." "Is thine eye evil, because I am good?" asked Jesus in *Matthew 20:15.* In other words, "Are you jealous and envious because I am kind and generous." In *Mark 7:22* Jesus includes "an evil eye" with covetousness, wickedness, deceit and other evil things that come from within and defile a man. Belief in the evil eye was one of the most common and widespread of all ancient superstitions and many customs and practices are traceable to it. The evil eye was one of the basic principles of demonism, sorcery and witchcraft. A primitive form of the superstition was that the eyes of some persons darted noxious rays on objects which they glared upon and the first morning glance of such eyes was sure to blight with bad luck both man and beast. Virgil tells of an evil eye that made kine lean. All sorts of amulets, names, phrases, garments and gestures were devised to ward off the blight of the evil eye. The veiling and cloistering of women, eating in private, the covering of certain parts of the body regardless of comfort, style or necessity are among the customs that may be traceable to the superstition of the evil eye. One of the notions of the evil eye was that a person should not praise, admire or in any way encourage those that were prosperous or lucky. Belief in the evil eye is still prevalent among many primitive peoples. In modern usage *evil eye* survives in the sense of jealousy, envy or malice.

Did the Israelites help build the pyramids?

The great pyramids in lower Egypt are believed to have been built many centuries before Joseph and his brethren went down into Egypt. The history of ancient Egypt is generally divided into three periods. Of these the earliest is known as "The Old Kingdom," which comprised the first ten dynasties and which began about 3500 B.C. and ended about 2375 B.C. This was the period of the great pyramid-builders. The largest of these pyramids is that of Cheops (Khufu), who belonged to the fourth Egyptian dynasty, and it is believed to have been built about 2900 or 3000 B.C. There are now about seventy-five pyramids in Egypt in varying stages of preservation. It is supposed that all of these structures were completed before the end of the Old Kingdom. Although Old Testament chronologies are indefinite to say the least, historians are generally agreed that the Israelites went to Egypt about 1800 or 1900 B.C. and remained there for four or five hundred years. If these dates are approximately correct, all of the pyramids had been constructed many centuries before the arrival of the Israelites in Egypt. In the time of the Israelites the building of pyramids was no longer in fashion. The pyramid at Cheops, perhaps the oldest existing man-made structure in the world, was more than fifteen hundred years old when Moses was born.

What is the present name of Mt. Sinai?

The peak in the Sinaitic mountains of the peninsula between the gulfs of Akabah and Suez where Moses received the law has never been identified beyond question. In the Old Testament *Sinai* and *Horeb* appear to be used interchangeably, although some authorities suppose that the former refers to the entire chain and the latter to a single peak. Volumes have been written to prove that this or that peak in the Sinaitic mountains is the original "Mountain of the Law," where Moses received the Ten Commandments. The majority of Bible scholars incline to the belief that the ancient Horeb or Sinai was the peak now known by the Arabs as *Jebel Musa*, "mountain of Moses." This peak is more than 6,000 feet high and near the top is a chapel dedicated to Elijah in allusion to the fact that it was on Horeb that the prophet heard "a still small voice," as related in *I Kings 19*. Near *Jebel Musa* is another peak of similar altitude known to the Arabs as *Ras Sufsafeh*, "peak of the willow," where Moses is supposed to have cut his rod. Some authorities suppose that *Ras Sufsafeh* rather than *Jebel Musa* was the actual Horeb and Sinai of the Israelites. One reason for this supposition is that there is an extensive plain at the base of *Ras Sufsafeh* where the Israelite host might have camped, whereas there is no such satisfactory camping site for so large a number of people around *Jebel Musa*. That the general location of these two peaks should be identified with the Horeb and Sinai of the Bible is supported not only by local tradition but also by the fact that

Justinian I, Roman emperor of the East in the sixth century, had a Christian church in honor of the Virgin built there on the assumption that one of the two peaks was the original Horeb and Sinai. But the evidence identifying either of these peaks with "the mount of God" is not conclusive. Eusebius, a native of Palestine, who died about 340 A.D., recorded a tradition identifying Horeb and Sinai with *Jebel Serbal,* a 6,750-foot peak fifteen or twenty miles northwest of *Jebel Musa.* This tradition, however, is rejected by many authorities because there is no space in the vicinity that would have provided a satisfactory camping site for the Israelite host. Several eminent investigators have sought to locate the sacred mountain of Moses in Arabia proper. There is scant probability that the Biblical Horeb and Sinai will ever be positively identified.

What is a shibboleth?

Nowadays we often hear *shibboleth* used in the sense of "a battle cry," "party slogan" or "pet phrase." That is not the original application of the term. The original meaning of the term as used in English was "test," "criterion," "password" or "watchword." *Shibboleth* occurs in different passages in the Hebrew Bible with different meanings. In some places it is translated "stream" or "flood," in others "ear of corn," and in still others "branch." It should be borne in mind that Hebrew as written in ancient times contained only consonants. Originally the language had no vowels, which were not introduced until the sixth century A.D. to preserve the traditional pronunciation. Accordingly it is often difficult to distinguish certain Hebrew words from one another. The modern application of *shibboleth* comes from its use as a test word in *Judges 12.* Jephthah, who judged Israel six years, was a native of Gilead, but was expelled by his own people because he was the son of a strange woman. Gilead lay east of the Jordan, perhaps in part of the territory originally assigned to Gad, and its inhabitants were largely descended from fugitives of other tribes, particularly Ephraimites and Manassites. Later Jephthah was called from his exile in the land of Tob by the Gileadites to lead them against the Ammonites. With an army of Gileadites he marched across the territory of Ephraim and smote and overcame the ancient enemy of Israel. In accordance with a vow he had made the Lord before setting out, he gave his daughter, an only child, as a burnt offering. Naturally he was in no trifling mood when the Ephraimites gathered themselves together and threatened to burn his house over his head because he had not called them to go with him against the Ammonites. The Gileadites, fighting on their own soil, scattered the men of Ephraim and took possession of the fords across the Jordan. When the stragglers reached the river and sought to pass over, the Gileadites asked each the question: "Art thou an Ephraimite?" If the answer was "Nay," he was asked by the Gileadites to say "Shibboleth." If he was an Ephraimite he "could not frame to pronounce it right," but said "Sibboleth." The penalty for being unable to pass the test was death, and forty-two thousand Ephraimites were slain at the passages of the Jordan. It appears that the people west of Jordan had developed a dialect different in many respects from the language spoken east of that river, and one of the differences was in the pronunciation of the sibilant sounds represented by *s* and *sh*. The Gileadites merely took advantage of this dialectical peculiarity to identify the Ephraimite fugitives. Any other Hebrew word beginning with *sh* would probably have served the purpose of the Gileadites just as well, and very likely *shibboleth* is given in the Bible as a typical word rather than the only one used. On the other hand, *shibboleth* may have been chosen as a watchword at the Jordan crossings because one of its meanings was "flood" or "stream." There are parallels to this story in later history. Both in the case of the Sicilian Vespers in 1282 and the Flemish revolt in 1302 the inability of Frenchmen to pronounce certain foreign phrases was the signal for their slaughter. When the Germans invaded the Netherlands in 1940 the Dutch resorted to this method of identifying persons suspected of being Germans masquerading as Hollanders. The suspects were asked to pronounce "Scheveningen," the name of a Dutch town near The Hague. Native Hollanders pronounce the first syllable with almost a sibilant *s* sound, while Germans give it a hard *sh* sound. Any Dutch word beginning with *sch* would have served just as well for the purpose.

Why do artists depict Moses with horns?

Many medieval painters depicted Moses with horns protruding from his head. Michelangelo's masterpiece of sculpture, the colossal figure of Moses in the Church of St. Pietro in Vincoli at Rome, also represents the leader of the Israelites with horns. This figure was designed for the mausoleum of Pope Julius II and was intended as a compliment to that Pope's warlike prowess. It portrays the painfully restrained wrath and majestic indignation of Moses when he descended from Mt. Sinai and found his people worshipping the golden calf. Although the horns undoubtedly heighten the effect desired, they were really owing to a mistake in Biblical translation. In *Exodus*

34:29-30 it is stated: "And it came to pass, when Moses came down from Mount Sinai with the two tables of testimony in Moses' hand, when he came down from the mount, that Moses wist not that the *skin of his face shone* while he talked with him. And when Aaron and all the children of Israel saw Moses, behold, the *skin of his face shone*; and they were afraid to come nigh him." In Hebrew the word for this shining is *qaran* or *karan*, which means "rays of light darting out" or "sending forth beams." The Hebrew word for horn is *qeren*. The translators of the Latin version of the Old Testament known as the Vulgate rendered the phrase *quod cornuta esset facies sua*, which means "his face was horned." Since *horn* is frequently used in the Bible for *strength*, the medieval artists represented Moses with horns, thinking the horns were mentioned in the Bible to symbolize power. The error was perfectly understandable, because the Vulgate version was made in the fourth century A.D. before vowels had been introduced into Hebrew. Perhaps the original idea in *Exodus* about the face of Moses shining alluded to what later became known as the halo, nimbus and aureole.

What is a scapegoat?

A scapegoat is a person who is blamed or punished for the shortcomings of another, a "whipping boy." Both the term and the idea were borrowed from the Bible. *Scape* in *scapegoat* is merely a shortened form of *escape*. The original scapegoat was a goat that was permitted to escape into the wilderness after the high priest of the Israelites had symbolically transferred to it the sins of the people. It is believed that *scapegoat* was coined by William Tyndale, who in translating the Bible into English used the term to render the Hebrew *Azazel*, a rare Hebrew common noun meaning "dismissal" or "entire removal." *Azazel*, misconstrued by early translator as a proper name, was the ancient Hebrew technical term applied to the entire removal of the sin and guilt of the congregation or community. Later it was mistakenly supposed variously to refer to the goat itself, to the place to which it was sent, or to an evil spirit that inhabited the desert. The Latin Vulgate rendered *Azazel* as "goat," which became Tyndale's "scapegoat." But the Greek Septuagint had rendered it as "the one to be sent away." Release of a goat was part of the solemn ritual prescribed by the Mosaic law for the Day of Atonement, observed by the Israelites each year on the tenth day of the seventh month. In *Leviticus 16* it is related that the Lord, through Moses, commanded Aaron as high priest to "take of the congregation of the children of

Israel two kids of the goats for a sin offering. . . . And he shall take the two goats, and present them before the Lord at the door of the tabernacle of the congregation. And Aaron shall cast lots upon the two goats; one lot for the Lord, and the other lot for the scapegoat. And Aaron shall bring the goat upon which the Lord's lot fell, and offer him for a sin offering. But the goat, on which the lot fell to be the scapegoat, shall be presented alive before the Lord, to make atonement with him, and to let him go for a scapegoat into the wilderness. . . . And when he hath made an end of reconciling the holy place, and the tabernacle of the congregation, and the altar, he shall bring the live goat: And Aaron shall lay both his hands upon the head of the live goat, and confess over him all the iniquities of the children of Israel, and all their transgressions in all their sins, putting them upon the head of the goat, and shall send him away by the hand of a fit man into the wilderness. . . . And he that let go the goat for the scapegoat shall wash his clothes, and bathe his flesh in water, and afterward come into the camp." *Wilderness* here means a wild and uninhabited place sufficiently separated from the Israelite camp to make it impossible for the sin-laden animal to wander back. Later, when it became impossible to send the scapegoat to a place from which it would not return to inhabited parts, the animal was cast down a precipice. This ritual was not peculiar to the ancient Israelites. Similar ceremonies with similar significance have been practiced by many different people in different parts of the world at different times. Among some the scapegoat was an animal, among others a person, and among still others a material object. For instance, the scapegoat of the ancient Athenians was a young man, that of the Arabs a camel, and that of the aborigines of Borneo a canoe. In each case the scapegoat was laden with the sins, crimes, ill luck or misfortunes of the people and sent or driven away as a symbolic dispelling of the evils. In modern democracies it is customary to choose a scapegoat from the members of the cabinet, the military commanders or other high public officials.

Does *navy* occur in the Bible?

Navy occurs in the English Bible five times, each time in connection with the story of Solomon and Hiram. *I Kings 9:26-27-28* says: "And King Solomon made a navy of ships in Eziongeber, which is beside Eloth, on the shore of the Red sea, in the land of Edom. And Hiram sent in the navy his servants, shipmen that had knowledge of the sea, with the servants of Solomon. And they came to Ophir, and fetched from thence gold, four hundred and twenty talents, and brought it to King Solomon." In *I Kings 10:11* we are told that "the navy also of Hiram, that brought gold from Ophir, brought in from Ophir great plenty of almug trees, and precious stones." The only other occurrence of the word in the Bible is in *I Kings 10:22,* which reads: "For the king had at sea a navy of Tharshish with the navy of Hiram: once in three years came the navy of Tharshish, bringing gold, and silver, ivory, and apes, and peacocks." The ancient Israelites, confined for the most part to the highlands of Palestine, concerned themselves little with ships and navigation. On the other hand, Tyre and Sidon were seaports, and the Phoenicians were noted for their sea commerce. *Navy* is derived from Latin *navis,* meaning simply "ship," and originally the term referred to all of a nation's ships, whether for commerce or for war. The use of the term in *I Kings* shows clearly that the English translators referred to merchant ships.

Why is a wife called a *helpmate*?

Genesis 2:18-20 says: "And the Lord God said, It is not good that the man should be alone; I will make him an help meet for him. And out of the ground the Lord God formed every beast of the field, and every fowl of the air; and brought them unto Adam to see what he would call them: and whatsoever Adam called every living creature, that was the name thereof. And Adam gave names to all cattle, and to the fowl of the air, and to every beast of the field; but for Adam there was not found an help meet for him." Here *help* means "helper" and *meet* means "fit" or "suitable." The second clause of *Genesis 2:18* is equivalent to, "I will make him a helper suitable for him." *Help* and *meet* were at an early date absurdly combined to make a compound word, first into *help-meet,* and then into *helpmeet,* and taken to signify "helper" or "companion." *Helpmeet* in turn was perverted into *helpmate* on the mistaken theory that *meet* was an erroneous form of *mate.* As a result of this double error we now have two words, *helpmeet* and *helpmate,* which in modern usage are used interchangeably as synonyms of "wife" or "husband."

Does *boys and girls* occur in the Bible?

The phrase *boys and girls* occurs in the King James Version of the Bible once. *Zechariah 8:5,* one of the most beautiful and appealing verses in the Scriptures, says: "And the streets of the city shall be full of boys and girls playing in the streets thereof." *Joel 3:3* says: "And they have cast lots for my people; and have given a boy for an harlot, and sold a girl for wine, that they might drink." *Girl* occurs only in these two passages, once in the singular and once in the plural. The term is of obscure origin. Originally it signified a child or young person of either sex, but by the time the King James Version was made it had already acquired its present sense of a young unmarried woman. *Boy,* equally obscure in origin, occurs in only one other Biblical passage. *Genesis 25:27* says: "And the boys grew: and Esau was a cunning hunter, a man of the field; and Jacob was a plain man, dwelling in tents."

What does *the apple of the eye* mean?

The apple of the eye is the symbol of that which is cherished and most precious and the phrase refers to anything extremely dear, greatly beloved or highly valued. It is very old and occurs a number of times in the King James Version of the Bible. *Deuteronomy 32:10* says that the Lord found Jacob "in a desert land, and in the waste howling wilderness; he led him about, he instructed him, he kept him as the apple of his eye." In *Psalms 17:8-9* the psalmist asks the Lord to keep him "as the apple of the eye, hide me under the shadow of thy wings, from the wicked that oppress me, from my deadly enemies, who compass me about." Solomon, according to *Proverbs 7:2* says: "Keep my commandments, and live; and my law as the apple of thine eye." "Their heart cried unto the Lord," says Jeremiah in *Lamentations 2:18,* "O wall of the daughter of Zion, let tears run down like a river day and night: give thyself no rest; let not the apple of thine eye cease." And *Zechariah 2:8*: "For thus saith the Lord of hosts; after the glory hath he sent me unto the nations which spoiled you: for he that toucheth you toucheth the apple of his eye." In other words, Israel was the apple of the eye of the Lord. The original application of *the apple of the eye* is not entirely clear, some supposing it to be a perversion of *the pupil of the eye,* and others adhering to the theory that it originated in the notion that the pupil of the eyes is a round object resembling an apple. In all probability the latter theory is correct, because in German the eyeball is called "*Augapfel,*" literally meaning "eye apple," and it is used in the German Bible where *the apple of the eye* is used in English translations. The Hebrew word for apple is *Tappuach,* which means "fruit of fragrance" and which is often applied to the peach, apricot, quince and other fruits as well as the apple. Although *apple, apple-tree* and *apples* all occur in our English translations, it is not known for certain that the apple was known to the Hebrews in ancient times. The Hebrew *tappuach* does not occur in any of the Hebrew phrases generally translated *the apple of the eye,* as in *Psalms 17:8,* for instance. Three other Hebrew words, *ishon, bath* and *babah,* are rendered *apple,* and they signify respectively "little man," "little daughter" and "hollow or hole," the latter being equivalent to "gate" or "door." Thus we might have *little man of the eye, little daughter of the eye,* and *little gate of the eye.* The phrase, according to this theory may therefore have originally referred to what seems to be the image of a human being reflected in the eye. But the figurative sense of the Hebrew phrase rendered "as the apple of his eye" is equivalent to English "as his very life" and accordingly is a close approximation of the original.

When was a man stoned to death for gathering sticks?

In *Numbers 15:32-36* is told the story of a man who was stoned to death for gathering sticks on the Sabbath. That passage reads: "And while the children of Israel were in the wilderness, they found a man that gathered sticks upon the sabbath day. And they that found him gathering sticks brought him unto Moses and Aaron, and unto all the congregation. And they put him in ward, because it was not declared what should be done to him. And the Lord said unto Moses, The man shall be surely put to death: all the congregation shall stone him with stones without the camp. And all the congregation brought him without the camp, and stoned him with stones, and he died; as the Lord commanded Moses."

What Biblical city was sown with salt?

Abimelech, one of the first Israelites to make himself a king, sowed Shechem with salt after he had captured and destroyed the place following a revolt of the people. *Judges 9:45* tells us: "And Abimelech fought against the city all that day; and he took the city, and slew the people that was therein, and beat down the city, and sowed it with salt."

Does the Bible say that rabbits chew the cud?

Whether rabbits and hares chew the cud is an oft-asked question. The popular notion that they do arose from two passages in the English Bible. *Leviticus 11:5* says: "And the coney, because he cheweth the cud, but divideth not the hoof; he is unclean unto you." And *Deuteronomy 14:7*: "Nevertheless these ye shall not eat, of that that chew the cud, or of them that divide the cloven hoof; as the camel, and the hare, and the coney: for they chew the cud, but divide not the hoof; therefore they are unclean unto you." These passages present a classical difficulty. *Coney,* also spelled *cony,* is an old English name for the rabbit and it is a well-known fact that there are several species of hare in Palestine. But rabbits and hares are rodents, not ruminants, and do not chew the cud. Clearly there is some error either in fact or in translation. Bible scholars are generally agreed that the word *coney* in the English Bible refers to the Syrian hyrax, a small animal about the size of a rabbit. By the Arabs of the Near East this animal is called *daman Israil,* "the sheep of Israel." It is now variously called badger, bear-rat and rock rabbit, but there was no common English name for it when the early translations of the Bible were made. This fact, however, does not solve the diffiiculty, because the Syrian hyrax does not chew the cud either. Where the English translations use *rabbit* and *coney,* the Greek text used *cherogrillus,* meaning "porcupine," and the Hebrew text uses *shaphan,* which undoubtedly refers to the hyrax or daman. It has been suggested that the ancient writers erroneously thought that the hare and the coney chew the cud because they move their jaws as if ruminating or re-chewing. The Syrian hyrax is a small, thick-set animal with short legs and ears, rudimentary tail and a peculiar gland on the back. Hyraxes belong to the order or sub-order known as *Hyracoidea.* Their feet have soft pads and broad nails, and their molar teeth resemble those of the gigantic rhinoceros, but their incisors suggest those of rodents, to which group the hyraxes have a superficial resemblance. They are regarded by scientists as the survivors of an ancient and generalized type of *ungulates,* or hoofed animals. Hyraxes are very timid and live in rocky places. In *Psalms 104:18* David tells us that "the rocks" are a refuge "for the conies," and *Proverbs 30:26* says "the conies are but a feeble folk, yet make they their houses in the rocks." When a litter of hyraxes (Biblical conies) was born in the Philadelphia zoo in 1941 the event was proclaimed as a rare occurrence in the history of zoological gardens.

Who said: "What hath God wrought!"

The words, "What hath God wrought!" are famous chiefly because they were the first message sent over the electric telegraph perfected and built by Samuel F. B. Morse and his partners. This telegraph line, constructed with $30,000 appropriated by Congress in 1843, was completed in the spring of 1844 and ran between Washington, D. C., and Baltimore, Maryland. On May 24 of that year Morse, operating his apparatus in the Supreme Court chamber in the Capitol at Washington, sent the following simple Bible quotation over the telegraph line to his partner, Alfraid Vail, in Baltimore: "What hath God wrought!" This message, chosen by Annie Ellsworth, daughter of the commissioner of patents, was taken from *Numbers 23:23,* according to which Balaam said to Balak: "Surely there is no enchantment against Jacob, neither is there any divination against Israel: according to this time it shall be said of Jacob and of Israel, What hath God wrought!"

Does *advertise* occur in the Bible?

Advertise occurs twice in the King James Version of the Bible, but in the sense of "to warn," "admonish" or simply "to make known." *Numbers 24:14* quotes Balaam as saying to Balak: "And now, behold, I go unto my people: come therefore, and I will advertise thee what this people shall do to thy people in the latter days." According to *Ruth 4:4,* Boaz said to Naomi's kinsman concerning a parcel of land: "And I thought to advertise thee, saying, Buy it before the inhabitants, and before the elders of my people."

What was the corn mentioned in the Bible?

The nature of the corn mentioned in the Bible is only conjectural, but there is little doubt that it was a kind of "small grain," probably wheat and barley. In Great Britain and on the Continent *corn* is applied to all kinds of grain, such as wheat, oats, rye and barley, and that is the sense in which the term was used in the King James Version of the Bible. Americans, used to thinking of corn as maize, are particularly prone to go wrong on Biblical corn. The cereal variously known as maize, Indian corn, or simply corn, is undoubtedly a native of some part of the New World, although kernels of corn found in ancient ruins at Athens and representations resembling maize plants in ancient Chinese books have led some to suppose that this cereal may have been indigenous to Asia also. If Indian corn was ever known to the Asiatics and Europeans before the discovery of America, which is highly improbable, it had not been cultivated for many centuries prior to its introduction into Europe by the Spanish. For many years after the introduction of maize into western Europe it was called *Turkey corn* or *Turkey wheat* because, like the Turkey fowl, it was erroneously supposed to have come from Turkey. The British always speak of American corn as Indian corn or maize to distinguish it from their corn, which comprises wheat, barley, oats and rye. The editors of the American Revised Version of 1881 substituted *grain* for *corn* throughout the Bible except in the passage that says wild asses in the desert "reap every one his corn in the field." Jesus, according to *John 12:24*, said: "Verily, verily, I say unto you, Except a corn of wheat fall into the ground and die, it abideth alone: but if it die, it bringeth forth much fruit." As used in this passage, *corn* is an old English noun meaning a small, hard particle, such as a grain or seed. It is the Teutonic equivalent of *grain* and some authorities suggest, that the two words may be derived from the same root, akin to the verb *to grow* and originally "seed." *Peppercorn* and *barleycorn* are survivals of this old usage. The barleycorn was at one time used as a unit of measure of length. Among the ancient Hebrews the smallest dimension of length was the barleycorn. Two barleycorns laid endways made a finger-breadth, equivalent to two-thirds of an inch. In 1607, four years before the King James Version was published, it was ordained in England "that three barley cornes, dry and round, shall make up the measure of an inch." But in 1611, the year the King James Version was published, we find a barleycorn defined as one-fourth of an inch. *Kernel* is merely a modification of *cornel*, signifying little corn. At one time *kernel of corn* was redundant, because literally it meant "a little corn of corn." *Corn* was applied very early as a generic name to cereal grains, the most useful seeds and the chief breadstuff. It is an interesting fact that in northern countries *corn* is generally applied to the particular cereal grain that is most important in the rural economy. In England corn is wheat; in the Scandinavian countries, barley; in most parts of Germany, rye; and in the United States, maize.

Does the Bible say bats are birds?

Leviticus 11:19 lists "the bat" among the "fowls" that the Israelites were not to eat, but to "have in abomination." *Deuteronomy 14:18* reiterates this classification of the bat among the unclean fowls and birds. Bats, of course, are animals, not birds. They suckle their young at the breast and are classed by zoologists as flying mammals. The belief that bats are birds persisted until comparatively modern times.

What is meant by *Armageddon*?

Armageddon occurs in the Bible only once. *Revelation 16:12-16* says: "And the sixth angel poured out his vial upon the great river Euphrates; and the water thereof was dried up, that the way of the kings of the east might be prepared. And I saw three unclean spirits like frogs come out of the mouth of the dragon, and out of the mouth of the beast, and out of the false prophet. For they are the spirits of devils, working miracles, which go forth unto the kings of the earth and of the whole world, to gather them to the battle of that great day of God Almighty. Behold, I come as a thief. Blessed is he that watcheth, and keepeth his garments, lest he walk naked, and they see his shame. And he gathered them together into a place called in the Hebrew tongue Armageddon." From this passage *Armageddon* has come to signify the place of the last great battle between the powers of good and evil on the Day of Judgment. In common speech *Armageddon* is applied figuratively to any decisive battle, final contest on a grand scale, or scene of slaughter. In *Rantoul* John Greenleaf Whittier wrote:

> We seemed to see our flag unfurled,
> Our champion waiting in his place
> For the last battle of the world,
> The Armageddon of the race.

During the First World War (1914-1918) the term was revived in popular usage and was often applied to that conflict. Nobody knows for certain why St. John the Divine employed *Armageddon* in *Revelation*. The generally accepted opinion is that the author of the Apocalypse alluded to Megiddon, a place in Palestine proverbial for the decisive battles fought there. According to the Song of Deborah and Barak in *Judges 5*, "the kings came and fought, then fought the kings of Canaan in Taanach by the waters of Megiddo." In *II Kings 9:27* we are told that Ahaziah, after being defeated by Jehu, "fled to Megiddo, and died there." In *II Kings 23:29* it is related, "In his days Pharaoh-nechoh king of Egypt went up against the king of Assyria to the river Euphrates: and king Josiah went against him; and he slew him at Megiddo, when he had seen him." King Josiah's servants "carried him in a chariot dead from Megiddo, and brought him to Jerusalem, and buried him in his own sepulchre." Perhaps the author of *Revelation* had in mind *Zechariah 12:11*, which reads: "In that day shall there be a great mourning in Jerusalem, as the mourning of Hadadrimmon in the valley of Megiddon." Some authorities suppose that *Armageddon* is a Greek corruption of Hebrew *Har-Magedon*, "mountain of Megiddo," and it is so rendered in some modern versions.

How many of each species did Noah take into the ark?

According to *Genesis 7:2-3*, God said to Noah: "Of every clean beast thou shalt take to thee by sevens, the male and his female; and of beasts that are not clean by two, the male and his female. Of fowls also of the air by sevens, the male and the female; to keep seed alive upon the face of the earth." In other words, one pair of every species of unclean animals and seven pairs of every species of clean animals were to be taken into the ark. This is the first mention in the Bible of clean and unclean animals and the passage as translated in English seems to be at variance with the context. In *Genesis 6:19-20* God had commanded Noah: "And of every living thing of all flesh, two of every sort shalt thou bring into the ark, to keep them alive with thee; they shall be male and female. Of fowls after their kind, and of cattle after their kind, of every creeping thing of the earth after his kind, two of every sort shall come unto thee to keep them alive." *Genesis 7:8-9* says: "Of clean beasts, and of beasts that are not clean, and of fowls, and of every thing that creepeth upon the earth, there went in two and two unto Noah into the ark, the male and the female, as God had commanded Noah." Again, in *Genesis 7:15-16,* we read: "And they went in unto Noah into the ark, two and two of all flesh, wherein is the breath of life. And they that went in, went in male and female of all flesh, as God had commanded him; and the Lord shut him in." In *Genesis 8:20* we are told that one of the first things that Noah did after the flood was to build an altar to the Lord and offer on it burnt offerings of every clean beast and every clean fowl. If Noah had only one pair of each kind of animal and bird he certainly would not kill any of them for sacrificial purposes. Therefore he must have taken more than two of each species into the ark or they increased in number during the voyage. The Bible narrative does not say whether any animals or birds died on the ark, or whether any young were born. Since the story of Noah and the ark relates to a period long before the promulgation of the Mosaic law dealing with sacrifices and defining clean and unclean animals, some authorities suppose that the references to clean and unclean beasts and birds were inserted in the ancient account long after the original story was written. Students of ancient history tell us that the distinction between clean and unclean animals for sacrificial purposes antedates the Mosaic law and was observed in Egypt, Assyria and other parts of the world centuries before Moses lived. The apparent conflict between the quoted passages in Genesis may be explained by the fact that few species of animals and fowls were used for sacrifice at that early date and the author of the ancient narrative did not take the trouble to distinguish between clean and unclean beasts and fowls in every passage in which reference to the subject is made. Another theory is that the story of the flood is a composite one and that the references to clean and unclean creatures and to the offering of clean beasts and fowls as sacrifices were inserted in the ancient story at a comparatively late date. The probability is that the final compiler of *Genesis* wove together two or more different narratives that represented different traditions.

Does the Bible mention the leopard's spots?

The prophet Jeremiah refers to the changing of the spots of the leopard, an age-old symbol of the impossible. *Jeremiah 13:23* says: "Can the Ethiopian change his skin, or the leopard his spots? Then may ye also do good, that are accustomed to do evil." When early European travellers in Asia first met with this animal they supposed it to be a cross between the lion and the panther, and so they called it leopard, from Latin *leo*, "lion," and *pardus*, "panther."

What does *brimstone* in the Bible mean?

Brimstone used to be the common English name for sulphur. It literally signifies "burning stone" and refers to the inflammable character of the element. Brimstone or sulphur was probably the first chemical element discovered and used by primitive man. It is mentioned by Homer and the ancient Greeks used it as a fumigator and as a "pest averter." Mentions of brimstone in the Bible are numerous. *Genesis 19:24* says: "Then the Lord rained upon Sodom and upon Gomorrah brimstone and fire from the Lord out of heaven." Echoing this passage, Jesus, according to *Luke 17:29*, said: "But the same day that Lot went out of Sodom it rained fire and brimstone from heaven, and destroyed them all." Moses in his farewell message to his people, according to *Deuteronomy 29:23*, foretold that if the children of Israel departed from the covenant with God future generations and strangers from a far land would see "the whole land thereof is brimstone, and salt, and burning." In *Job 18:15* the patriarch says "brimstone shall be scattered upon his habitation." *Psalm 11:6* says: "Upon the wicked he shall rain snares, fire and brimstone, and an horrible tempest: this shall be the portion of their cup." In *Ezekiel 38:22* the Lord says through the prophet: "And I will plead against him with pestilence and with blood; and I will rain upon him, and upon his bands, and upon the many people that are with him, an overflowing rain, and great hailstones, fire, and brimstone." *Isaiah 30:33* tells us: "for Tophet is ordained of old; yea, for the king it is prepared; he hath made it deep and large; the pile thereof is fire and much wood; the breath of the Lord, like a stream of brimstone, doth kindle it." Again in Chapter 34, Verse 9, Isaiah says:

"And the streams thereof shall be turned into pitch, and the dust thereof into brimstone, and the land thereof shall become burning pitch." In *Revelation* St. John "saw the horses in the vision, and them that sat on them, having breastplates of fire, and of jacinth, and brimstone: and the heads of the horses were as the heads of lions; and out of their mouths issued fire and smoke and brimstone." Elsewhere in that book we find the expressions "tormented with fire and brimstone" and "a lake of fire, burning with brimstone." Brimstone in the Bible is symbolic of hell fire. The Hebrew word for sulphur, translated *brimstone* in English, is believed to be related to the word for *bitumen,* the name of a substance that abounds in the Jordan Valley and especially around the Dead Sea. The rain of brimstone and fire when Sodom and Gomorrah were destroyed may refer to the combustion of sulphur or petroleum in the vicinity. Solyman (or Suleiman), the name of a famous 16th century sultan of Turkey, signified "sulphur eater."

What does the Bible say about swords and plowshares?

Isaiah 2:4 says: "And he shall judge among the nations, and shall rebuke many people: and they shall beat their swords into plowshares, and their spears into pruninghooks: nation shall not lift up sword against nation, neither shall they learn war any more." *Micah 4:3* repeats this thought almost verbatim. But *Joel 3:9-10* reverses the figure: "Proclaim ye this among the Gentiles: Prepare war, wake up the mighty men, let all the men of war draw near; let them come up: beat your plowshares into swords, and your pruninghooks into spears: let the weak say, I am strong."

Are mules mentioned in the Bible?

Mule and *mules* occur many times in the Old Testament, but not once in the New Testament. It is probable that in some instances *mule* is employed in the English Bible where *ass* or *donkey* would have been the more exact translation. The mule, which is a cross between a mare and a male ass, has been bred since the dawn of history. The inhabitants of Mysia, Paphlagonia and Cappadocia, ancient countries in Asia Minor, are said to have been the first people to raise mules. This, while not definitely established, is borne out by Homeric tradition. Mules were raised in large numbers by both the ancient Greeks and Romans. The Israelites were forbidden to raise mules by *Leviticus 19:19,* which says: "Thou shalt not let thy cattle gender with a diverse kind." Evidently, however, the Israelites either imported hybrids or broke the Mosaic law, because early in their history they possessed large numbers of mules, which were preferable to horses and asses in a hilly country like Palestine. Mules are first mentioned in the Bible in the time of David. *Genesis 36:24* says: "This was that Anah that found the *mules* in the wilderness, as he fed the asses of Zibeon his father." But in this particular case the Hebrew *yemin* was incorrectly translated *mules* when it should have been *warm springs*. It is surprising how many people think the mule is a distinct species of animal capable of reproduction. The mule is merely a hybrid produced by breeding a female horse to a male ass. So far as known all male mules, and most females, are sterile. There is no authentic record of a jenny mule giving birth to a foal sired by a male mule. Since mules are incapable of reproducing their kind it is impossible to raise mules from mules. There are a few authentic cases on record of female mules giving birth to young when bred to male asses and stallions. But in such cases the foals are not true mules, being three-fourths either ass or horse. Not only is the male mule sterile in reference to female mules, but there are no cases on record of she-asses or mares giving birth to foals when bred to male mules. When the she ass gives birth to a foal sired by a stallion the offspring is called a *hinny*, not a mule. The hinny, which is also sterile, resembles the horse more than the mule does.

How is *saith* in the Bible pronounced?

Saith as used by the translators of the English Bible is an archaic form of the verb *say* in its present tense, singular number, third person and indicative mode and corresponds to modern *says*. It is correctly pronounced *seth* to rhyme with *beth* in *Macbeth*. Many people erroneously pronounce it in two syllables, *SAY-eth*. *Sayest* is also used in the King James Version as the archaic and solemn form of *say* in its present tense, singular number, second person and indicative mode and corresponds to modern *say*. Accordingly we have "He saith" and "Thou sayest."

Why is *shew* instead of *show* used in the Bible?

Shew and *show* are merely variations of the same word and are pronounced the same. When the King James Version of the Bible was translated *shew* was still the preferred spelling of the word both as a noun and a verb, particularly in books written in a solemn style. *Shew* is now used in America only as an old-fashioned spelling.

Some British writers still use *shew* as a verb, but not as a noun. For instance, they might write, "Shew me the way to the show," but not, "Show me the way to the shew." In the Bible the *shewbread* consisted of the twelve loaves placed every Sabbath "before the Lord" on a table beside the incense altar and eaten at the end of the week by the priests alone. For any other person to eat this hallowed bread was regarded as sacrilegious. But, according to *I Samuel 21:6* David and his young men were permitted to satisfy their hunger with the shewbread in the sanctuary to Jehovah at Nob on condition that they were ritually clean.

Does the Bible call the lion the king of beasts?

Nowhere in the Bible is the lion referred to as the king of beasts, but *Proverbs 30:30* says: "A lion, which is strongest among beasts, and turneth not away for any." The title "king of beasts" was conferred on the lion at an early date, but by whom is not known for certain. The ancients so called the animal because of its strength, courage and majestic appearance.

Who said: "All men are liars"?

In *Psalms 116:11* King David says: "I said in my haste, All men are liars." *Romans 3:4* says: "yea, let God be true, but every man a liar." In *John 8:44* quotes Jesus as saying: "Ye are of your father the devil, and the lusts of your father ye will do. He was a murderer from the beginning, and abode not in the truth, because there is no truth in him. When he speaketh a lie, he speaketh of his own: for he is a liar, and the father of it."

Does the Bible mention chimneys?

Chimney occurs only once in the English Bible. *Hosea 13:3* says: "Therefore they shall be as the morning cloud, and as the early dew that passeth away, as the chaff that is driven with the whirlwind out of the floor, and as the smoke out of the chimney." The chimney, taken for granted by moderns, does not date back so far in civilization as one might suppose. It was unknown to the ancient Hebrews, Egyptians, Greeks and Romans. Originally English *chimney* signified hearth or fireplace. In early times the fire for heating a room or house was built in the center and the smoke escaped through a hole in the roof. It was not until about the twelfth century in England that the fire was moved to the side of one of the walls and a tube of some sort provided to carry the smoke and fumes from the house. In

Biblical times in Palestine rooms were heated in the winter by means of braziers, pans for live coals. *Jeremiah 36:22* says: "Now the king sat in the winterhouse in the ninth month: and there was a fire on the hearth burning before him." It is probable that the smoke from the fire of King Jehoiakim of Judah escaped from the room through openings either in the walls or in the roof.

What does *leasing* in the Bible mean?

Leasing occurs twice in the Bible. *Psalms 4:2* says: "O ye sons of men, how long will ye turn my glory into shame? how long will ye love vanity, and seek after leasing? Selah." And *Psalms 5:6*: "Thou shalt destroy them that speak leasing: the Lord will abhor the bloody and deceitful man." *Leasing*, pronounced "*LEEZE-ing*," is an old English word signifying "lying," "falsehood" or "a lie." It is one of the few words that has become completely obsolete in spite of its inclusion in the King James Version of the Bible.

Where does the Bible refer to a six-toed man?

I Chronicles 20:6-7 says: "And yet again there was war at Gath, where was a man of great stature, whose fingers and toes were four and twenty, six on each hand, and six on each foot: and he also was the son of the giant. But when he defied Israel, Jonathan the son of Shimea David's brother slew him." Having six fingers on each hand and six toes on each foot is known as *hexadactylism*. Many cases of hexadactylism have been reported by science, and it appears that in some instances it is hereditary in certain families.

What is the Holy Grail?

Holy Grail is not in the Bible. It is the popular name of the legendary cup or chalice that Jesus blessed and passed to his disciples at the Last Supper. *Matthew 26:27* says: "And he took the cup, and gave thanks, and gave it to them, saying, Drink ye all of it." *Mark 14:23* says: "And he took the cup, and when he had given thanks, he gave it to them; and they all drank of it." According to *Luke 22:17-20*: "And he took the cup, and gave thanks, and said, Take this, and divide it among yourselves: for I say unto you, I will not drink of the fruit of the vine, until the kingdom of God shall come. And he took bread, and gave thanks, and brake it, and gave unto them, saying, This is my body which is given for you: this do in remembrance of me. Likewise also the cup after supper, saying, This cup is the new testament in my blood, which is shed for you." Nothing whatever is said in the Bible about the disposition of the actual cup or chalice used by Jesus on this occasion. The most usual version of the legend of the Holy Grail, related in the apocryphal gospel of Nicodemus, is that Joseph of Arimathea, the honorable counselor who craved the body of Jesus from Pilate, took the sacred cup from the table after the Last Supper and afterward caught in it some of the blood of Jesus at the crucifixion. After Joseph's death the holy vessel was taken to England by one of his relatives and handed down in the family for generations. It possessed many magic properties and with it miracles could be performed, such as multiplying a few loaves of bread into many and turning water into wine. Owing to the sinfulness of its guardians, the Holy Grail disappeared. It became the symbol of chastity and the quest for the lost Grail forms the basis of many beautiful stories, and the Medieval and modern literature woven around the theme would fill many volumes. The sacred chalice figures in the legends of King Arthur, and three of his knights—Galahad, Percival and Bors—set out in quest of it. Sir Galahad found the Holy Grail at Glastonbury and took it to the mysterious city of Serras in the East, where it vanished. Another legend has it that the Grail, after being snatched up to heaven from the descendants of Joseph, was brought down to earth again by angels and entrusted for safekeeping to a body of knights who jealously guarded it on top of a mountain, and when the spot was approached by anyone not perfect in purity the sacred vessel disappeared from sight. In some of the legends the Holy Grail is not a cup but the platter or dish from which Jesus ate at the Last Supper. When Caesarea in Palestine was taken by the Crusaders under Baldwin I in 1101 A.D., among the objects seized was a green crystal vase, which was said to have been used at the Last Supper and which figured in subsequent literature and legend as "*the* Holy Grail." In modern times *Holy Grail* has been applied to the cup known as "the great chalice of Antioch," a large silver central goblet eight inches in height sheathed in silver and gold leaf, which in 1910 was found in the ruins of a Christian edifice built in Antioch in Syria by Constantine the Great in the fourth century and destroyed by an earthquake in 526 A.D. The carving on the sheathing contains twelve figures, two of which have been identified tentatively by several archaeologists as Jesus in youth and manhood, and the others as ten of his disciples. Some authorities believe that the cup dates from the first century and that the figures are the oldest and only authentic portraits of Jesus, having been made by an artist who had either seen him or who had obtained descriptions from persons who had known him. Naturally many people readily accepted as fact the presumption that this chalice was none other than the cup used by Jesus at the Last Supper and therefore the Holy Grail itself.

Is "a little bird told me" in the Bible?

"A little bird told me," is the reply often received from a person who has been asked the source of certain information and who does not care to reveal it. The saying is very old, and, although not in the Bible, it may have been suggested by *Ecclesiastes 10:20,* which says: "Curse not the king, no not in thy thought; and curse not the rich in thy bedchamber: for *a bird of the air shall carry the voice,* and that which hath wings *tell* of the matter." In *Pericles* Shakespeare has Cleon, Governor of Tarsus, say to his wife: "Be one of those that think the pretty wrens of Tarsus will fly hence, and open this to Pericles." Ernest Ingersoll, in *Birds in Legend and Folklore,* tells us that the Breton peasants credit all birds with the power of using human language and that, according to legend in different parts of the world, all birds once had that power. The Basques have an old folk tale of a bird that always speaks truthfully and the Biloxi Indians used to say that the humming bird would not lie. Gossip, which is notorious for the celerity with which it travels, is particularly ascribed to little birds.

When did a dead man come to life by touching a dead man?

One of the little known but remarkable miracles in the Bible relates to a dead man who came to life when he came in contact with the bones of a dead man. *II Kings 13:20-21* says: "And Elisha died, and they buried him. And the bands of the Moabites invaded the land at the coming in of the year. And it came to pass, as they were burying a man, that, behold, they spied a band of men; and they cast the man into the sepulchre of Elisha: and when the man was let down, and touched the bones of Elisha, he revived, and stood up on his feet."

When was dew on wool used as a test of the Lord's wishes?

The presence and absence of dew on a sheepskin was used by Gideon, one of the judges of Israel, to determine whether the Lord wanted him to save Israel by leading his army against the Midianites, Amalekites and the children of the east who had pitched in the valley of Jezreel. *Judges 6:36-40* says: "And Gideon said unto God, If thou wilt save Israel by mine hand, as thou hast said, Behold, I will put a fleece of wool in the floor; and if the dew be on the fleece only, and it be dry upon all the earth beside, then shall I know that thou wilt save Israel by mine hand, as thou hast said. And it was so: for he rose up early on the morrow, and thrust the fleece together, and wringed the dew out of the fleece, a bowl full of water. And Gideon said unto God, Let not thine anger be hot against me, and I will speak but this once: let me prove, I pray thee, but this once with the fleece; let it now be dry only upon the fleece, and upon all the ground let there be dew. And God did so that night: for it was dry upon the fleece only, and there was dew on all the ground." It is interesting in this connection that wool is noted for its quality of retaining moisture for a long time.

What does scourging with scorpions mean?

I Kings 12:12-14 says: "So Jeroboam and all the people came to Rehoboam the third day, as the king had appointed, saying, Come to me again the third day. And the king answered the people roughly, and forsook the old men's counsel that they gave him: and spake to them after the counsel of the young men, saying, My father made your yoke heavy, and I will add to your yoke: my father also chastised you with whips, but I will chastise you with scorpions." In many places in the Bible *scorpion* is used literally and figuratively in the sense of a venomous crawling creature which belongs to the spider family but which looks more like a small flat lobster than a spider. But in the famous saying attributed to Rehoboam, son and successor of Solomon, *scorpion* means either a prickly stick resembling the stinger of a scorpion or some sort of cruel whip. The clear implication is that *scorpion* was applied to a rod or lash used in scourging.

What is a son of Belial?

Belial (pronounced *BEE-lial* or *BEEL-yal*) is an interesting word frequently found in both the Old and the New Testaments as well as in the Apocryphal and rabbinical writings. It is obscure in both origin and original meaning. As a rule we find it in such phrases as *son of Belial, daughter of Belial, children of Belial,* etc. The context generally indicates clearly that the term does not always mean the same thing. There is even doubt as to whether it should be regarded as a proper or a common noun. Some authorities attempt to trace it to *Belili,* a Babylonian goddess of the lower regions or netherworld. Others derive it from Hebrew *b'li,* "not" or "without," and *ya'al,* "profit" or "use." If the latter assumption is correct the word literally signifies "worthless," "unprofitable" or "no good." The Talmudic writers define *Belial* as "lawless one," in the sense of one who does not submit to the yoke of the law. In the Old Testament *Belial* is often associated with lawlessness or opposition to established authority, whether civil or religious. *Deuteronomy 13:13* says: "Certain men, the children of Belial, are gone out from among you, and have withdrawn the inhabitants of their city, saying, Let us go and serve other gods, which ye have not known." In many cases, however, it appears that a son or daughter of Belial is no more than a wicked or sinful person. In *I Samuel 1:16* Hannah asks Eli not to count "thine handmaid for a daughter of Belial." *Judges 19:22* refers to "the men of the city, certain sons of Belial," who "beset the house round about, and beat at the door." Occasionally *Belial* seems to have a secondary sense of destructiveness and signifies "destructive rivers under the world." In later religious literature *Belial* became synonymous with the personification of the grave, evil, hell, the devil or the prince of darkness. It occurs only once in the New Testament—*II Corinthians 6:15*—where the question is asked: "What concord hath Christ with Belial?" There the word obviously refers to Antichrist, Satan, or an evil spirit opposed to God. In Milton's *Paradise Lost* one of the fallen angels is named Belial.

What Biblical character ate grass like an ox?

Nebuchadnezzar, king of Babylon, was stricken with a strange malady by the Lord to humble his pride and for seven years he lived like a beast and ate grass like an ox. It is a common mistake to suppose that Nebuchadnezzar died in this condition. On the contrary, he is quoted in the Bible as himself telling the story of his horrible experience and of the recovery of his reason. According to *Daniel 4,* the Babylonian king, who had captured Jerusalem, destroyed the temple and carried away the inhabitants into exile, had a vision in a dream which troubled him and which his wise men, magicians, astrologers, soothsayers and Chaldeans were unable to interpret. So he called upon Daniel for an interpretation. The nature of the dream as well as the prophet's interpretation may be gathered from *Daniel 4:20-26*: "The tree that thou sawest, which grew, and was strong, whose height reached unto the heaven, and the sight thereof to all the earth; whose leaves were fair, and the fruit thereof much, and in it was meat for all; under which the beasts of the field dwelt, and upon whose branches the fowls of the heaven had their habitation: it is thou, O king, that art grown and become strong: for thy greatness is grown, and reacheth unto heaven, and thy dominion to the end of the earth. And whereas the king saw a watcher and an holy one coming down from heaven, and saying, Hew the tree down, and destroy it; yet leave the stump of the roots thereof in the earth, even with a band of iron and brass, in the tender grass of the field; and let it be wet with the dew of heaven, and let his portion be with the beasts of the field, till seven times pass over him; this is the interpretation, O king, and this is the decree of the most High, which is come upon my lord the king: that they shall drive thee from men, and thy dwelling shall be with the beasts of the field, and they shall make thee to eat grass as oxen, and they shall wet thee with the dew of heaven, and seven times shall pass over thee, till thou know that the most High ruleth in the kingdom of men, and giveth it to whomsoever he will. And whereas they commanded to leave the stump of the tree roots; thy kingdom shall be sure unto thee, after that thou shalt have known that the heavens do rule." Twelve months later all this came upon the king Nebuchadnezzar. As the king walked in his palace and gloated over the magnificent capital and great empire he had built by the might of his power and for the honor of his majesty, even while the words were in his mouth, a voice came from heaven repeating the warning of the former vision and telling him that his kingdom had departed from him. "The same hour," says *Daniel 4:33-36*, "was the thing fulfilled upon Nebuchadnezzar: and he was driven from men, and did eat grass as oxen, and his body was wet with the dew of heaven, till his hairs were grown like eagles' feathers, and his nails like birds' claws. And at the end of the days I Nebuchadnezzar lifted up mine eyes unto heaven, and mine understanding returned unto me, and I blessed the most High, and praised and honoured him that liveth for ever, whose dominion is an everlasting dominion, and his kingdom is from generation to generation: and all the inhabitants of the earth are reputed as nothing: and he doeth according to his will in the army of heaven, and among the inhabitants of the earth: and none can stay his hand, or say unto him, What doest thou? At the same time my reason returned unto me; and for the glory of my kingdom, mine honour and brightness returned unto me; and my counsellors and my lords sought unto me; and I was established in my kingdom, and excellent majesty was added unto me." Contrary to a common impression, there is nothing in the Bible about the death of Nebuchadnezzar. According to Babylonian sources, the Chaldean king died peacefully in his palace in the year 561 B.C. There is no historical record of his seven years of madness related in *Daniel*. But the type of insanity ascribed to him in the Bible is not uncommon and is recognized by medical science. It is known as *lycanthropy*, Greek for "wolf-man," and is applied to any form of madness in which the patient imagines himself to be a beast of one species or other.

Why did Judas kiss Jesus?

Any hypocritical or treacherous kiss is known as a Judas kiss. *Matthew 26:48-49*, speaking of the arrest of Jesus, says: "Now he that betrayed him gave them a sign, saying, Whomsoever I shall kiss, that same is he: hold him fast. And forthwith he came to Jesus, and said, Hail, master; and kissed him." *Luke 22:47-48* says: "And while he yet spake, behold a multitude, and he that was called Judas, one of the twelve, went before them, and drew near unto Jesus to kiss him. But Jesus said unto him, Judas, betrayest thou the Son of man with a kiss?" Kissing was a common mode of greeting and salutation in those days. There is Old Testament precedent for the kiss of treachery. In *II Samuel 20:9-10* it is related: "Joab said to Amasa, Art thou in health my brother? And Joab took Amasa by the beard with the right hand to kiss him. But Amasa took no heed to the sword that was in Joab's hand: so he smote him therewith in the fifth rib, and shed out his bowels to the ground, and struck him not again; and he died." Solomon, in *Proverbs 27:6*, warned that "the kisses of an enemy are deceitful." It is said that in the time of Jesus it was customary for a master to kiss his disciples but unusual for the disciples to kiss their master. *Matthew* and *Luke* may have emphasized the kiss in connection with the betrayal of Jesus not only because Judas abused the kiss of friendship but also because he showed insolence and bad taste in kissing his master at all.

Where was the Garden of Eden?

The location of the Garden of Eden cannot be determined from the description of it given in *Genesis 2*. Eden is the English form of a Hebrew word signifying "delight" or "pleasure." *Genesis 2:8-15* says: "And the Lord God planted a garden eastward in Eden; and there he put the man whom he had formed. And out of the ground made the Lord God to grow every tree that is pleasant to the sight, and good for food; the tree of life also in the midst of the garden, and the tree of knowledge of good and evil. And a river went out of Eden to water the garden; and from thence it was parted, and became into four heads. The name of the first is Pison: that is it which compasseth the whole land of Havilah, where there is gold; and the gold of that land is good: there is bdellium and the onyx stone. And the name of the second river is Gihon: the same is it that compasseth the whole land of Ethiopia. And the name of the third river is Hiddekel: that is it which goeth toward the east of Assyria. And the fourth river is Euphrates. And the Lord God took the man, and put him into the garden of Eden to dress it and to keep it." Adam was already in the Garden of Eden when he named the animals and fowls and when God formed Eve from one of his ribs. In the rest of the narrative the place is referred to simply as *the garden* until *Genesis 3:23-24,* which reads: "Therefore the Lord God sent him forth from the garden of Eden, to till the ground from whence he was taken. So he drove out the man; and he placed at the east of the garden of Eden Cherubims, and a flaming sword which turned every way, to keep the way of the tree of life." These passages make it clear that the garden in which God put the first man and woman was merely a pleasant place in the country or land called Eden. It is probable that the authors of *Genesis* conceived the land of Eden as comprising the then known world, probably all the territory of Assyria, Asia Minor, Armenia, Palestine, Arabia, Egypt, Ethiopia, etc. The actual location of the Garden of Eden has been the subject of much speculation. Mesopotamia, Armenia, Palestine, Syria, Kashmir, Egypt, Arabia, Mongolia, Merv, Ceylon, and even Australia and the North Pole have been suggested as the site. The description in *Genesis 2* points to Armenia or Mesopotamia as the most plausible suggestions. According to Hebrew tradition the Garden of Eden lay somewhere between the Euphrates and Tigris rivers and in accordance with that belief modern Iraq is popularly accepted in western Asia as the site of the Biblical garden. In non-Biblical usage the Garden of Eden is called *Paradise,* a term that does not occur in the King James Version of the Old Testament. *Paradise* is a Persian word meaning "inclosure" or "garden" and was applied particularly to the extensive parks and pleasure grounds of the Persian monarchs. In the Septuagint, a Greek version of the Old Testament made at Alexandria long before the time of Jesus, *garden of Eden* was translated *Paradise. Paradise* occurs only three times in the New Testament, where it is synonymous with Heaven. According to *Luke 23:43,* Jesus said to the penitent thief on the cross: "Verily I say unto thee, To day shalt thou be with me in paradise." In *II Corinthians 12:4,* Paul says: "How that he was caught up into paradise, and heard unspeakable words, which it is not lawful for a man to utter." And on Patmos, according to *Revelation 2:7,*

St. John the Divine wrote: "He that hath an ear, let him hear what the Spirit saith unto the churches; to him that overcometh will I give to eat of the tree of life, which is in the midst of the paradise of God."

What was the species of the forbidden fruit?

The Bible does not give the name of the species of the forbidden fruit that Adam and Eve ate in the Garden of Eden. It refers merely to the fruit of "the tree of knowledge of good and evil." That the forbidden fruit was an apple is only a popular tradition. In the East, however, there is a belief that the tree of knowledge mentioned in the Bible was a banana plant and that the serpent that tempted Eve hid in a bunch of the fruit. This legend obviously influenced the early classifiers of bananas, who designated two species—*Musa paradisiaca* (fruit of paradise) and *Musa sapientum* (fruit of knowledge). Some writers are of the opinion that *Musa sapientum* was originally intended to allude to a statement made by the Greek philosopher Theophrastus respecting a fruit, supposedly the banana, which served as food for the ancient wise men of India. Whether the Israelites were acquainted with the apple is a matter of debate.

Who were the Herodians?

It is not clear just who the Herodians mentioned in the Gospels were. Jesus several times linked them in name with the Pharisees. In *Mark 8:15* we are told that he charged his disciples: "Take heed, beware of the leaven of the Pharisees, and of the leaven of Herod." *Mark 3:6* says: "And the Pharisees went forth, and straightway took counsel with the Herodians against him, how they might destroy him." Again *Mark 12:13*: "And they send unto him certain of the Pharisees and of the Herodians, to catch him in his words." Some authorities suppose that these Herodians were members of a religious sect of Jews, perhaps those who believed that Herod himself was the Messiah of whom the prophets of old had spoken. But Josephus, who discussed in detail the various religious sects in Palestine at that period, does not mention the Herodians among them. He mentions only the Pharisees, Sadducees and Essenes, the last named not being referred to by name in the New Testament. It is more probable that the Herodians were members of a political party rather than a religious sect, although religion and politics in those days were difficult to differentiate. Perhaps the Herodians were those Jews who were adherents or partisans of the Herod dynasty, which ruled with various degrees of Roman authority in Jerusalem from 37 B.C. until the destruction of the city by the Romans in 70 A.D. Although the Herods were not true Jews, they professed Judaism for political purposes and observed its forms and practices while in the Jewish parts of their dominions. Several of them married Jewish women and some of the later Herods were partly of Jewish blood. Herod the Great built the third temple as a grand gesture of friendliness toward his Jewish subjects. The Herodians may have been those Jews who preferred to have their country quasi-independent under the Herod regime rather than to see it converted into a Roman province with a procurator in charge of public affairs. Under the friendly Herods the Jews enjoyed at least nominal independence. Apparently the teachings of Jesus were no more favorable to the policies of the Herodians than they were to those of the Pharisees. It seems that the Herodians were interested in getting Jesus into difficulties with the political authorities, while the Pharisees were equally desirous of embroiling him with the Sanhedrin and the religious authorities. So they conspired together "to catch him in his words." At that time the Romans, through their various puppet governments, imposed a tax or tribute upon the Jews, as they did their other subject peoples. Naturally the Jews, including the Pharisees and Herodians, objected to paying this tribute to Edom, the symbolical name they applied to Rome. But the upper classes could not openly resist this tax without risking civil war and the complete loss of what little independence they had left. The Zealots, however, composed of common people, particularly in Galilee, exercised no such restraint and openly resisted the tax on the ground that it was inconsistent with their ancient theocracy and freedom. Accordingly the Herodians and Pharisees decided to embarrass Jesus by asking him a two-edged question. They figured that if Jesus said it was lawful to pay the tribute he would incur the displeasure of the government, and if he said it was not lawful he would offend a large part of his popular following. What happened is one of the great stories in the Bible. *Matthew 22:15-22* says: "Then went the Pharisees, and took counsel how they might entangle him in his talk. And they sent out unto him their disciples with the Herodians, saying, Master, we know that thou art true, and teachest the way of God in truth, neither carest thou for any man: for thou regardest not the person of men. Tell us therefore, What thinkest thou? Is it lawful to give tribute to Caesar, or not? But Jesus perceived their wickedness, and said, Why tempt ye me, ye hypocrites? Shew me the tribute money. And they brought unto him a penny. And he saith unto them, Whose is this image and superscription?

They say unto him, Caesar's. Then saith he unto them, Render therefore unto Caesar the things which are Caesar's; and unto God the things that are God's. When they had heard these words, they marvelled, and left him, and went their way."

Who were the Samaritans?

In New Testament times Samaria was a district around the town of Samaria, ancient capital of Israel. After the majority of the Israelites were carried into captivity beyond the Euphrates, the Assyrians transplanted and settled on their lands Semitic colonists from Mesopotamia and Syria. These colonists intermarried with the remaining Israelites and produced a mixed race known as Samaritans. In *II Kings 17:27-28* we are told that the Assyrian king sent back a priest to teach the Samaritans the "manner of the God of the land." Accordingly the Samaritans acquired a diluted and lax form of Jehovah worship. Ancient writers refer to them variously as "half-Jews," "half-breed Israelites," "apostate Jews" and "semi-Gentiles." Josephus says the Samaritans professed kinship to the Jews only when it was to their political advantage to do so. When a remnant of the Jews returned from Babylon in 537 B.C., the Samaritans offered to join them in rebuilding the temple and re-establishing Judaism at Jerusalem, but their offer was rejected, with the result that the Samaritans opposed the project and gave the Jews no little trouble. The feud that then started between the Samaritans and the Jews continued for six centuries. About 420 B.C. the Samaritans built their own temple at Mount Gerizim in imitation of that at Jerusalem. The woman of Samaria at Jacob's well alluded to this controversy over the site of the temple when she said to Jesus: "Our fathers worshipped in this mountain; and ye say, that in Jerusalem is the place where men ought to worship." In New Testament times people of Samaritan stock lived all over northern Palestine but were most numerous in Samaria. Jesus frequently passed through this district on his trips between Galilee in the north and Judaea in the south. Jesus, unlike most other Jews of the time, associated with the Samaritans, but he did not regard them as Jews. In *Matthew 10:5-6* Jesus is quoted as saying to the Twelve: "Go not into the way of the Gentiles, and into any city of the Samaritans enter ye not; but go rather to the lost sheep of the house of Israel." In other words, the Samaritans were neither Gentiles nor Israelites. The Jews regarded the Samaritans as heretics, and, according to *John 8:48,* they accused Jesus of being a Samaritan. In *John 4:9* the woman of Samaria said to Jesus: "How is it that thou, being a Jew, askest drink of me, which am a woman of Samaria? for the Jews have no dealings with the Samaritans." Although Jesus said "salvation is of the Jews," we are told that "many of the Samaritans of that city believed on him" and besought him to tarry with them. The woman regarded Jacob as the father of her race but the Jews as its enemies. According to *Luke 17:16*, the only one of the ten lepers who returned to thank Jesus for being cleansed was a Samaritan and Jesus referred to him as "this stranger." A community of several hundred Samaritans still live in the vicinity of ancient Shechem. This interesting racial and religious group is the sole distinctive representative of the ancient Israelites and Jews who have lived continuously in the Holy Land since ancient times. The ancestors of all the other present inhabitants of Palestine have resided at one time or another in some other country. The Samaritans speak a dialect of Palestinian Aramaic and write with an archaic alphabet derived from Old Hebrew. Of the Bible they accept only the Pentateuch, which they read in an ancient Aramaic version known as the Targum. They do not wear phylacteries, they keep the Sabbath strictly, cling to the most ancient beliefs and practices of the Hebrew religion, have their own high priest and each year sacrifice a passover lamb on Mount Gerizim.

Who were the Sadducees and Pharisees?

The New Testament often mentions the Sadducees and Pharisees, the two chief sects or parties among the Jews at that time. *Matthew 16:1* says: "The Pharisees also with the Sadducees came, and tempting desired him that he would shew them a sign from heaven." These two parties, although deadly political enemies, regarded Jesus as a common threat and joined hands in opposing him. The Sadducees were a comparatively small group of conservatives who construed the Mosaic law literally and rejected the tradition and oral law. Their strict adherence to the Mosaic law is alluded to in *Matthew 22:24*, where some of them began a question to Jesus with the words, "Master, Moses said." Two essential differences in the religious tenets of these sects or parties are mentioned in *Acts 23:8* which says that "the Sadducees say there is no resurrection, neither angel, nor spirit: but the Pharisees confess both." *Sadducee* is variously derived from *Zadok*, the first of a line of high priests, and from a Hebrew word meaning "righteous ones." The Sadducees had at different times controlled the Sanhedrin and the temple, but were a decided minority in the time of Jesus. They were essentially politicians, who represented the wealthy and aristocratic elements, who regarded themselves as the leaders of a priestly and hereditary ruling class, who sided with the Roman conquerors and who were cordially disliked by the common people. The Pharisees are mentioned more often in the Gospels because they were the most numerous religious party among the Jews at that time. Compared to the Sadducees, they were "liberals" in religion and politics and represented the middle and poor classes. They differed from the Sadducees chiefly in the emphasis they placed on tradition and oral law and on liberal interpretations that would lighten the burdens of the people. *Pharisee* is supposed to be derived from either a Hebrew word meaning "separatist" or one meaning "interpreters." Although primarily devotees of the written and oral law and the spiritual leaders of the people, they had considerable political influence and controlled the Sanhedrin in the time of Jesus. The Pharisees are mentioned more frequently than the Sadducees because they were the dominant religious group and Jesus came into more frequent contact with them. Like all pious and zealous Jews in Palestine at that time, they taught and practiced a complicated code and ritual respecting food, dress and almost every detail of daily life. In *Mark 7:9* Jesus accuses the Pharisees of putting their tradition ahead of the Mosiac law: "Full well ye reject the commandment of God, that ye may keep your own tradition." Jesus also often denounced them for their formalism and hypocrisy. After the Romans destroyed Jerusalem and the temple, the Sadducees disappeared from the Jewish scene, but the Pharisees continued their spiritual leadership through the Talmud and modern Judaism still bears the stamp of their teachings. Many Pharisees, because of their belief in the Messiah and the resurrection, became followers of Jesus. Nicodemus, who came to Jesus by night, was a Pharisee, and Joseph of Arimathaea, who buried Jesus, was probably of the same sect. Paul was originally a Pharisee, and in *Acts 15:5* we are told that "certain of the sect of the Pharisees which believed" were present at the council in Jerusalem that ruled on whether Christians should be "circumcised after the manner of Moses." Although the Pharisees thought of themselves as liberals and progressives, and were acknowledged to be such by most of the Jews of that day, because of their opposition to Jesus and their emphasis on ceremony and ritual their name has come down through the centuries as a very synonym for stilted formalists, fussy adherents of tradition, hypocrites or self-righteous persons in general. From Philo, Josephus and other sources we learn there was a third Jewish sect, not mentioned in the Bible. They were the Essenes, a semi-monastic order, communistic and pacifistic in principles, who practiced celibacy and vegetarianism and who believed vividly in the coming Messiah and the resurrection. As vegetarians, they rejected animal sacrifices and accordingly were not permitted to take part in temple worship, although they visited the temple and brought gifts. Some authorities suppose that John the Baptist, and possibly even Jesus himself, were Essenes. If true, this might account for the fact that neither John nor Jesus, so far as known, ever offered sacrifices or even so much as alluded to the sacrificial system. One theory is that large numbers of the Essenes were ultimately absorbed by the Christian movement.

Was the patriarch Job a Hebrew?

There is nothing in *The Book of Job* or elsewhere in the Bible to indicate that Job was a Hebrew. Like Melchizedek, Jethro and Balaam, Job occurs in the Bible as one of those scattered few who worshipped the true God but who were not connected with Israel. The usual assumption is that Job was an Arab chieftain.

Who were the publicans?

Publican does not occur in the Old Testament and in the New Testament only in the Four Gospels. The early Latin translators of the Bible employed *publicani* inaccurately to render the Greek *telonai,* which means "tax-gatherers," and this erroneous usage was carried over into the English Bible. The *publicani* of classical literature were wealthy Romans, often nobles and aristocrats, who obtained exclusive contracts to collect the revenue or to construct public works in a given area and who farmed out the actual work to deputies. But the publicans (*telonai*) of the Gospels were merely small contractors and their deputies who collected only direct taxes in money. Just what was the relation of these publicans to the Roman government and to the puppet governments of the Herods is not clear. It is believed that each publican and his deputies collected only a single tax in a limited area and had nothing to do with the Jewish tithes and levies in kind. They appear to have been natives and Jews. Paying these taxes was a badge of bondage and the freedom-loving Jews, jealous of their ancient independence and liberty, despised those of their number who engaged in the occupation of collecting the taxes. The vicious system lent itself to extortion, dishonesty and unjust enrichment, and the publicans were looked upon by the people as little better than heathen, harlots, robbers, thieves, pickpockets and even traitors to their own people. No patriotic, self-respecting Jew would eat with publicans or have any social contacts with them. Despite their bad reputation and odious and hateful as they were to the people in general, Jesus entered the homes of publicans, ate with them and accepted them among his followers. The general attitude of the Jews toward the publicans is illustrated by *Luke 19:1-10*, which reads: "And Jesus entered and passed through Jericho. And behold, there was a man named Zacchaeus, which was the chief among the publicans, and he was rich. And he sought to see Jesus who he was; and could not for the press, because he was little of stature. And he ran before, and climbed up into a sycamore tree to see him: for he was to pass that way. And when Jesus came to the place, he looked up, and saw him, and said unto him, Zacchaeus, make haste, and come down; for to day I must abide at thy house. And he made haste, and came down, and received him joyfully. And when they saw it, they all murmured, saying, That he was gone to be guest with a man that is a sinner. And Zacchaeus stood, and said unto the Lord; Behold, Lord, the half of my goods I give to the poor; and if I have taken any thing from any man by false accusation, I restore him fourfold. And Jesus said unto him, This day is salvation come to this house, forasmuch as he also is a son of Abraham. For the Son of man is come to seek and to save that which was lost." While Zacchaeus was a chief publican, apparently Matthew was only a deputy. *Matthew 9:9* says: "And as Jesus passed forth from thence, he saw a man, named Matthew, sitting at the receipt of custom: and he saith unto him, Follow me. And he arose, and followed him." In the list of the Twelve Apostles given in *Matthew 10* he is specifically referred to as "Matthew the publican." In *Luke 3:12-13*, referring to John the Baptist preaching and baptizing in the wilderness, we are told: "Then came also publicans to be baptized, and said unto him, Master, what shall we do? And he said unto them, Exact no more than that which is appointed you." Jesus, according to *Matthew 21:31*, said: "Verily I say unto you, That the publicans and the harlots go into the kingdom of God before you." Again, according to *Luke 7:34-35*: "The Son of man is come eating and drinking; and ye say, Behold a gluttonous man, and a winebibber, a friend of publicans and sinners! But wisdom is justified of all her children." In *Mark 2:15* it is related: "And it came to pass, that, as Jesus sat at meat in his house, many publicans and sinners sat also together with Jesus and his disciples." And in *Matthew 18:17* Jesus is quoted as saying that if a trespassing brother "neglect to hear the church, let him be unto thee as an heathen man and a publican." It is possible that the occupation of publican was carried on only in the provinces. The only mention of a publican in Jerusalem is in Jesus' parable of the Pharisee and the Publican who went up into the temple to pray.

Does *circle* occur in the Bible?

Circle is among those words that are found only once in the King James Version of the Bible. In *Isaiah 40:22* the prophet, replying to his own question, "To whom then will ye liken God?" says: "It is he that sitteth upon the circle of the earth, and the inhabitants thereof are as grasshoppers; that stretcheth out the heavens as a curtain, and spreadeth them out as a tent to dwell in."

Why is Satan called Beelzebub?

Beelzebub as used in the New Testament as the name of the prince of devils came from Old Testament usage. The original form of the term was *Baalzebub* and it literally signifies "god of flies." *II Kings 1:2* says: "And Ahaziah fell down through a lattice in his upper chamber that was in Samaria, and was sick: and he sent messengers, and said unto them, Go, inquire of Baalzebub the god of Ekron whether I shall recover of this disease." This particular god of flies appears to have been a local deity worshipped by the Philistines at Ekron. Josephus, paraphrasing the above passage in *II Kings 1*, wrote: "Now it happened that Ahaziah, as he was coming down from the top of his house, fell down from it, and in his sickness sent to the Fly, which was the god of Ekron, for that was his name, to inquire about his recovery." In these passages, however, Baal seems to be the sun-god with power over disease rather than the god of flies. Among the Greeks and other ancients there was a god of flies whose function was both to send flies and to drive them away. He had absolute power over all flies. One of his functions was to drive flies away from the flesh of the sacrifices. At any rate, the Baalzebub of the Old Testament became the Beelzebub, the lord of the nether world, of the New Testament. Jesus, according to *Matthew 10:25*, said: "If they have called the master of the house Beelzebub, how much more shall they call them of his household?" When the Pharisees heard that Jesus had healed one possessed with a devil, Jesus knew their thoughts and, according to *Matthew 12:25-27*, said: "Every kingdom divided against itself is brought to desolation; and every city or house divided against itself shall not stand: and if Satan cast out Satan, he is divided against himself; how shall then his kingdom stand? And if I by Beelzebub cast out devils, by whom do your children cast them out?

Therefore they shall be your judges." *Mark 3:22* says: "And the scribes which came down from Jerusalem said, He hath Beelzebub, and by the prince of the devils casteth he out devils." The charge that Jesus cast out devils through Beelzebub, "the chief of the devils," occurs also in *Luke 11:15*. In *Paradise Lost* Milton makes Beelzebub, the "fly-lord," the fallen angel next to Satan himself in power and crime.

What was the handwriting on the wall?

The handwriting on the wall, now applied to any omen of impending calamity or imminent doom, does not occur in the Bible in that exact form, but the popular phrase was suggested by the writing on the palace wall at Belshazzar's feast and interpreted by Daniel as foretelling the destruction of Belshazzar and the kingdom of Babylon. This story, related in *Daniel 5,* is one of the most popular and thrilling in the Bible. Belshazzar the king made a great feast to a thousand of his lords and he and his princes, wives and concubines drank wine from the golden vessels that his father Nebuchadnezzar had taken from the temple at Jerusalem. "In the same hour," says *Daniel 5:5,* "came forth fingers of a man's hand, and wrote over against the candlestick upon the plaster of the wall of the king's palace: and the king saw the part of the hand that wrote." Then Belshazzar's countenance was changed, his thoughts troubled him, the joints of his loins were loosed and his knees smote one against another. The king cried aloud to bring in the astrologers, Chaldeans and soothsayers, and when they had arrived Belshazzar promised to the one who could read and interpret to him the writing on the wall that he should be clothed with scarlet, have a chain of gold about his neck and should be made the third ruler in the kingdom. But the wise men of Babylon could not read or interpret the mysterious writing and the king was again greatly troubled and his countenance was so changed that his lords were astonished. At that point the queen overheard the words of the king and his lords and came into the banquet house. She told Belshazzar that there was in his kingdom a man named Daniel who could interpret the writing on the wall. The king had heard of Daniel, whom Nebuchadnezzar his father had brought captive out of Judah and later made master of the magicians, astrologers, Chaldeans and soothsayers. So Belshazzar called Daniel and offered him the same reward he had offered the wise men of Babylon if he could read and interpret the writing. Daniel told the king he would make known to him the interpretation but wanted none of his gifts. First he reminded Belshazzar how the Lord had humbled the pride of Nebuchadnezzar with seven years of madness. Then he reminded Belshazzar himself that, though knowing what happened to Nebuchadnezzar, he had not humbled his heart, but instead had lifted up himself against the Lord of heaven, had desecrated the sacred vessels stolen from the temple in Jerusalem, had praised the gods of silver, gold, brass, iron, wood and stone, and had not glorified God. The part of the hand, he said, was sent from God to write the mysterious message on the wall that was so troubling the king. *Daniel 5:25-28* says: "And this is the writing that was written, MENE, MENE, TEKEL, UPHARSIN. This is the interpretation of the thing: MENE; God hath numbered thy kingdom, and finished it. TEKEL; Thou art weighed in the balances, and art found wanting. Peres; Thy kingdom is divided, and given to the Medes and Persians." In that night, we are told, was Belshazzar the king of the Chaldeans slain and Darius the Median took the kingdom. This chapter in *Daniel* has given Bible students almost as much trouble as the writing on the wall gave Belshazzar. Enough has been written on this subject to make volumes. Even Hebrew scholars have difficulty in making sense of the cryptic writing on the wall. This message, as well as other parts of *Daniel,* are in Palestinian Aramaic, while the rest of the book is in Hebrew. It is believed that the book was composed in Palestine during the latter half of the second century B.C., or nearly four hundred years after the events related in it, although some parts of it may have been in existence at a much earlier date. At that time Palestine was subject to the Greek Seleucidae at Antioch in Syria, Antiochus having wrested the Holy Land from the Greek Ptolemies of Egypt. When Daniel is supposed to have lived Aramaic in one form or other was the everyday language not only of Palestine but of large parts of the Babylonian empire. Therefore there is nothing remarkable in the fact that the writing on the wall and other parts of *Daniel* should have been written in Aramaic, and it was natural that the Palestinian writers of the second century B.C. should render the language in their particular form of the popular language. As a matter of fact, Belshazzar and his lords would have been much more likely to understand Aramaic than they would Hebrew. It was the everyday language of millions of the subjects of the Babylonian king. Some authorities go so far as to suppose that the Judaeans picked up Aramaic during the Babylonian captivity and took it back to Palestine with them when they returned to Jerusalem under the protection of the Persian conquerors of Babylon. Perhaps the literal meaning of the words of the writing on the wall have been completely lost through translation into another language. It should be borne in mind that, according to the Bible, this was a cryptic and mysterious message that Belshazzar, his lords and his wise men could neither read nor interpret. Only Daniel was able to do that. Naturally the significance of the writing was not intended to be obvious. *Mene* is the Aramaic form of Hebrew *mina,* the name of a coin or weight of money worth about sixty shekels. It was probably repeated in the cryptic writing on the wall for emphasis or to give it the meaning of the process of counting or numbering. Daniel ignored this repetition in his interpretation. *Tekel* is the Aramaic form of the Hebrew *shekel,* the name of a monetary unit by weight. *Upharsin* is more difficult to explain. *U* apparently is merely a connective particle equivalent to "and." *Pharsin* or *parsin* is believed to signify "half-minas" or "half-shekels" or "divisions." Daniel seems to have interpreted it as the plural of *Peres,* "Persian," perhaps owing to a similarity in sound. According to what appears to be the best authority, the writing on the wall seems to signify something like this: "Counted, counted (like minas), weighed (like shekels) and divided (like half-minas or half-shekels)." "Given to the Medes and Persians" was probably supplied by the similarity in sound between *Pharsin* and *Peres* and by the fact that Babylon was then at war with Persia. In popular parlance part of Daniel's interpretation is rendered, "Thou art weighed in the balance." The King James Version of the Bible renders this, "Thou art weighed in the balances," where the English *balances* is used in the sense of *scales,* a device for weighing. There are several statements in this story as related in *Daniel* 5 that do not accord with the information learned from inscriptions on Babylonian tablets and from other historical sources. But these discrepancies do not substantially differ from known history and may be due to faulty translation and copying. *Daniel* says that Nebuchadnezzar and Belshazzar were father and son, while history says they were not related. Nebuchadnezzar's regime was overthrown by a palace revolution by a leader named Nabonidus, who became the last king of Babylon before the capture of the city by the Persians. But it appears that Nabonidus was an inactive ruler and that he turned most of the administrative affairs of the government over to his eldest son, Belshazzar, who ruled as prince-regent. It is possible that Belshazzar married one of Nebuchadnezzar's daughters and therefore was his son-in-law, but of that we have no knowledge. Naturally most of the inscriptions on the clay tablets relate to affairs before the final fall of the city and contain no information of the last days of ancient Babylon. The fact that Belshazzar ruled only as prince-regent under his father, Nabonidus, may explain another interesting passage in *Daniel 5*. Referring to the promise made by Belshazzar to anybody who could read and interpret the cryptic message on the wall, Verse 29 says: "Then commanded Belshazzar, and they clothed Daniel with scarlet, and put a chain of gold about his neck, and made a proclamation concerning him, that he should be the third ruler in the kingdom." Bible scholars tell us that the phrase translated "be the third ruler" literally means "shall rule as one of three." Historically Nabonidus was first ruler and his son, Belshazzar, was second ruler. Therefore Belshazzar could not offer the first or second place in the kingdom, but only the third. In other words, he promised Daniel, as a reward for his interpretation, that his father and he would share with him the rulership of the empire. Perhaps the author of *Daniel*, if properly translated, revealed a more intimate knowledge of history than many give him credit for. Writing long after the events related, it was only natural that he should fail to mention the inactive and inconspicuous Nabonidus and regard the flashy and famous Belshazzar as the son of Nebuchadnezzar rather than as merely his successor in the active rulership. Historians tell us that it was Cyrus of Persia, not Darius, who took Babylon in 538 B.C. No ruler named Darius at that time seems to fit into the historical picture. There is good reason, however, for supposing that Belshazzar himself may have been the active commander of the Babylonian army at the time the capital was taken and the kingdom destroyed. Both Nabonidus and Belshazzar were probably put to death by the Persians. Apparently the Persian ruler respected the promise made to Daniel by Belshazzar. At any rate, we are told in the opening verses of *Daniel 6* that Darius, whoever he was, set over the kingdom 120 princes "and over these three presidents: of whom Daniel was first."

What became of the Ark of the Covenant?

It is not known for certain what became of the Ark of the Covenant after the Babylonians captured and destroyed Jerusalem about 600 B.C. There are several traditions as to its final disposition. The Ark of the Covenant was an oblong chest, two and one half cubits long by one and one half cubits wide and deep, made of acacia wood overlaid with gold. Speaking of the time when the Ark was placed in Solomon's temple, *I Kings 8:9* says "There was nothing in the ark save the two tables of stone, which Moses put there at Horeb." It may be that other sacred objects were placed in the Ark later, for

Hebrews 9:4 refers to "the ark of the covenant overlaid round about with gold, wherein was the golden pot that had manna, and Aaron's rod that budded, and the tables of the covenant." Rabbinic tradition says that Moses also put in the ark the fragments of the first tablets containing the Ten Commandments that were broken. There were golden rings at each corner of the chest through which passed bars for carrying it. On the lid was a gold plate, called the Mercy Seat or the propitiatory, with two gold cherubim at each end. It was called the Ark of the Covenant of Jehovah or the Ark of the Testimony because it contained the two stone tables on which were engraved the basic covenant between Jehovah and Israel. The Ark of the Covenant was constructed about the time the tabernacle was made. Some authorities suppose there were two arks—a temporary one made by Moses when he received the tables, and a permanent one made later by the master workman, Bezaleel. The Ark was in charge of the Levites, who, assisted by the priests, carried it at the head of the Israelites through the wilderness, at the crossing of the Jordan and in the march around the walls of Jericho. Joshua took it first to Gilgal and then to Shiloh, where it remained until the time of Samuel. After it was captured in battle by the Philistines and sent back to the Israelites, the Ark rested at Kirjath-jearim until it was taken to Jerusalem by David when he made that city his capital. It was the only piece of furniture placed in the Holy of Holies of Solomon's temple. Some suggest that *Jeremiah 3:16* implies that the Ark was still in Jerusalem in the time of that prophet. "And it shall come to pass," says Jeremiah, "when ye be multiplied and increased in the land, in those days, saith the Lord, they shall say no more, The ark of the covenant of the Lord: neither shall it come to mind: neither shall they remember it; neither shall they visit it; neither shall that be done any more." The books comprising the Protestant Bible are silent on the fate of the Ark, but a tradition on the subject is recorded in *II Maccabees,* one of the sacred books of the Catholic Bible. The passage quoted is from a writing of Jeremiah and is as follows: "The prophet (Jeremiah), being warned by God, commanded that the tabernacle and the Ark should accompany him, till he came forth to the mountain where Moses went up and saw the inheritance of God. And when Jeremiah came thither he found a hollow cave and he carried in thither the tabernacle and the Ark and the altar of incense, and so stopped the door. Then some of them that followed him, came up to mark the place; but they could not find it. And when Jeremiah perceived it, he blamed them, saying: the place shall be unknown, till God gather together the congregation of the people and receive them to mercy." This story dates back at least two centuries B.C. In 1927 Dr. A. F. Futterer, a Jewish-American, obtained permission from the Palestine authorities to search for the lost Ark on a mountain identified by him as Mt. Nebo, from which Moses surveyed the Promised Land and where Jeremiah is supposed to have concealed the sacred chest in a cave, but, needless to say, nothing ever came of the enterprise. That the original Ark of the Covenant was not in the second temple seems certain. *Ezra, Nehemiah, Maccabees* and Josephus all refer to the sacred utensils in the second temple, but none of them mentions the Ark. In fact, it appears that the absence of the sacred object was one of the particulars in which the second temple was held to be inferior to that of Solomon. Some writers suppose that a new Ark was made for the second temple, but there is no evidence whatever that such was the case. In the *Apocalypse* of *Esdras,* which is regarded as apocryphal by both Catholics and Protestants, it is related that the Ark of the Covenant was carried away as a trophy by the Babylonians. This seems probable, because the troops of Nebuchadnezzar stripped the temple of its brass, silver and gold. It should be borne in mind, however, that Jerusalem was captured and the temple despoiled several times before the final destruction of both by the Babylonians. In the reign of Rehoboam, son and successor of Solomon, the city surrendered to the Egyptian king, Shishak, who stripped the temple and the palace of many of their ornaments. Some suppose the Ark of the Covenant was either carried away or destroyed on that occasion. This agrees with a tradition among the Ethiopians, who maintain that the Ark of the Covenant finally found its way to their country, whose royal family claims descent from King Solomon and the Queen of Sheba, and a chest carefully preserved and guarded at Aksum is claimed to be nothing less than the original Ark of the Covenant. On the other hand, the editors of the Talmud say that the sacred chest was hidden by King Josiah in a secret place that had been prepared by Solomon himself in the event the temple should be captured and destroyed.

Is *grandmother* in the Bible?

Grandmother occurs only once in the King James Version. In *II Timothy 1:5* St. Paul says: "When I call to remembrance the unfeigned faith that is in thee, which dwelt first in thy grandmother Lois, and thy mother Eunice; and I am persuaded that in thee also." We are given no additional information about Timothy's grandmother Lois. It is presumed that she was the maternal grandmother of Paul's friend and companion and she was probably a Jewess either by descent or conversion. It is an interesting fact that *grandfather* is found nowhere in the King James Version.

Do maternal impressions affect unborn offspring?

The ancient Hebrews believed that the offspring could be affected by outward objects. According to *Genesis 30,* Jacob got his uncle Laban to agree to give him all the spotted, speckled, grisled and ring-straked animals as wages for his services in feeding and keeping the flocks. Apparently then as now the majority of the sheep in Syria were white and the goats black. Jacob outwitted his crafty uncle by getting all the strong and healthy females of plain colors to bear spotted, speckled, grisled and ring-straked young by putting up striped poles at the drinking troughs. The idea was that the color of the unborn young would be affected if the ewes saw these striped poles at the time they conceived. *Genesis 30:37-39* says: "And Jacob took him rods of green poplar, and of the hazel and chestnut tree; and pilled white strakes in them, and made the white appear which was in the rods. And he set the rods which he had pilled before the flocks in the gutters in the watering troughs when the flocks came to drink, that they should conceive when they came to drink. And the flocks conceived before the rods, and brought forth cattle ringstraked, speckled, and spotted." Jacob used this device only when the strongest ewes were breeding. Scientists have been unable to find any basis of fact in this notion. Likewise they reject the old theory that so-called birthmarks are caused by fear, fright, unnatural desire or other impressions made upon the mother during pregnancy. It was once generally believed, and the belief is still far from extinct, that if a pregnant woman is frightened by a beast the outline of the animal is likely to be communicated to the skin of the unborn child in the form of a birthmark. Likewise it was believed that if a woman with child had a strong desire for some fruit, such as strawberries, a birthmark resembling that fruit was likely to be impressed upon the unborn child. Scientists are firm in the conviction that there is no connection between the mental state of the mother and the birthmark of the child. Mothers have been absolved from all blame for these blemishes in the court of medical science. Nothing that they can think, see or do will produce or determine the outline of a birthmark on the skin of a child in their wombs. These disfigurements are popularly known as birthmarks, mother marks, wine marks and longing marks. *Birthmarks* is a misleading name because they are produced before rather than at birth. Technically they are called *naevi,* a Latin word meaning "moles," "warts" or "skin marks." They are always congenital and are due to an excessive development of the fibrous tissue, hair, pigments or blood vessels in a patch in the upper layer of the skin. Surgeons have numerous methods for removing these blemishes successfully.

Is *eternity* found in the Bible?

Although *eternal* occurs many times in the King James Version, *eternity* is among those words found only once. *Isaiah 57:15* says: "For thus saith the high and lofty One that inhabiteth eternity, whose name is Holy; I dwell in the high and holy place, with him also that is of a contrite and humble spirit, to revive the spirit of the humble, and to revive the heart of the contrite ones."

What was Moses's defect of speech?

When the Lord, speaking out of the midst of the burning bush on Horeb, asked Moses to appear before Pharaoh and demand that the children of Israel be permitted to leave Egypt, Moses, according to *Exodus 3:10,* replied: "O my Lord, I am not eloquent, neither heretofore, nor since thou hast spoken unto thy servant: but I am slow of speech, and of a slow tongue." In the Hebrew original the term rendered *eloquent* here literally signifies "man of words," and *"slow of speech, and of a slow tongue"* literally signifies "heavy of speech and heavy of tongue." There is no way of determining whether this passage means that Moses had an actual defect of speech, such as stammering, stuttering or lisping, or was merely not a ready speaker. Most authorities interpret it as signifying that Moses had a physical impediment of speech. This is borne out by the context. *Exodus 4:11-12* says: "And the Lord said unto him, Who hath made man's mouth? or who maketh the dumb, or deaf, or the seeing, or the blind? have not I the Lord?" Now therefore go, and I will be with thy mouth, and teach thee what thou shalt say." But Moses still insisted that he could not do it. He said: "O my Lord, send, I pray thee, by the hand of whom thou wilt send." That is, send anybody but me. The upshot of the matter was that Aaron, the older brother of Moses, was designated spokesman. *Exodus 4:14-16* tells the rest of the story: "And the anger of the Lord was kindled against Moses, and he said, Is not Aaron the Levite thy brother? I know that he can speak well. And also, behold, he cometh forth to meet thee: and when he seeth thee, he will be glad in his heart. And thou shalt speak unto him, and put words in his mouth: and I will be with thy mouth, and with his mouth, and will teach you what ye shall do. And he shall be spokesman unto the people: and he shall be, even he shall be to thee instead of a mouth, and thou shalt be to him instead of God." There is an interesting Rabbinic story that accounts for the manner in which Moses came by his heavy tongue. One day while Pharaoh was holding Moses on his knee the child reached up, took off the crown of the king of Egypt and put it on his own head. The court soothsayers and wise men were greatly alarmed and advised Pharaoh to make an experiment to determine whether it would be safe to permit the Hebrew boy to live. They suggested that two braziers, one filled with gold and the other with live coals, be placed before the child. The test was whether Moses would reach for the gold or the coals. If he reached for the gold it would be a sign that he might some day, if brought up at court, attempt to usurp the crown of Egypt. When the braziers were set before Moses he stretched out his hand toward the one containing the gold, but the angel Gabriel interfered and guided the hand toward the live coals. The child unfortunately picked up and put in his mouth one of the burning coals, which burned his tongue and impaired his speech for life.

What were the flesh pots of Egypt?

Flesh pots are vessels in which flesh is cooked. Figuratively, the term signifies food in abundance, high living, luxury, material welfare, sordid considerations, and even sensual indulgence of any kind. "Sighing for the flesh pots of Egypt" means hankering for good things no longer obtainable. The expression is of Bible origin. In *Exodus 16:2-3* we read: "And the whole congregation of the children of Israel murmured against Moses and Aaron in the wilderness: and the children of Israel said unto them, Would to God we had died by the hand of the Lord in the land of Eygpt, when we sat by the flesh pots, and when we did eat bread to the full: for ye have brought us forth into this wilderness, to kill this whole assembly with hunger." This does not necessarily mean that the Israelites were well fed while in Egypt. The Israelites remembered the food but not the bondage in Egypt. Their hunger in the desert caused them to look back to their slave-fare as the height of luxury. The fare they had when in Egypt seemed good to them after living on manna a long time in the wilderness. *Numbers 11:4-5* says: "And the mixt multitude that was among them fell a lusting: and the children of Israel also wept again, and said, Who shall give us flesh to eat? We remember the fish, which we did eat in Egypt freely; the cucumbers, and the melons, and the leeks, and the onions, and the garlick." Ancient Egypt was proverbial for the abundance and cheapness of its fish.

Who said: "As the twig is bent the tree is inclined?"

Many people think this proverbial saying is in the Bible. It is a very old proverb that occurs in varying forms in many languages in many parts of the world. The thought is expressed in *Proverbs 22:6*, which says: "Train up a child in the way he should go: and when he is old, he will not depart from it." But the thought is nowhere expressed in the Bible by comparing the child to a twig and the adult to a tree. In fact, *twig* occurs only twice in the English Bible, both times in the plural. *Ezekiel 17:4* says that a great eagle came to Lebanon, took the highest branch of the cedar, "cropped off the top of his young twigs, and carried it into a land of traffic." This figurative application of a tender twig to the Israelites is repeated later in the same chapter. Apparently the current English form of the proverb comes from Alexander Pope, who, in his *Moral Essays*, wrote: "Just as the twig is bent, the tree's inclin'd."

Are there any riddles in the Bible?

There is only one riddle in the Bible in the modern sense of the term. We are told in *Judges 14* that when Samson took his parents to Timnath to negotiate with the Philistines for a bride "a young lion roared against him." The strong man killed the insolent beast with his bare hands. Later, while on the way to claim his bride, Samson "turned aside to see the carcase of the lion: and, behold, there was a swarm of bees and honey in the carcase of the lion." He ate some of the honey and gave some of it to his father and mother. This incident gave Samson the idea for a riddle. After the custom of the young men of the time, the bridegroom made a wedding feast, at which he wagered with the Philistines present thirty sheets and thirty change of garments that they could not solve the following riddle within the seven days of the feast: "Out of the eater came forth meat, and out of the strong came forth sweetness." The Philistines, knowing nothing about the dead lion and the swarm of bees in the carcase, were unable to solve the riddle, but they got Samson's wife to pry the answer out of him and before sundown of the seventh day came forward with the correct solution. Through this trick Samson lost thirty sheets and thirty change of garments to "the men of the city." Samson said to them: "If he had not plowed with my heifer, ye had not found out my riddle." Josephus informs us that King Solomon and King Hiram had a mania for constructing riddles and that they carried on a correspondence couched entirely in the guise of sophisms, riddles, enigmatical statements and dark sayings. A great deal of money in the form of wagers on riddles passed between the King of Israel and the King of Tyre.

What is the source of *holding up the hands* of another?

A person who supports or encourages another in action is said to hold up the latter's hands. This is an allusion to the supporting of the hands of Moses by Aaron and Hur during a battle between Joshua and Amalek. *Exodus 17:8-13* says: "Then came Amalek and fought with Israel in Rephidim. And Moses said unto Joshua, Choose us out men, and go out, fight with Amalek: to morrow I will stand on the top of the hill with the rod of God in mine hand. So Joshua did as Moses had said to him, and fought with Amalek: and Moses, Aaron, and Hur went up to the top of the hill. And it came to pass, when Moses held up his hand, that Israel prevailed: and when he let down his hand, Amalek prevailed. But Moses' hands were heavy; and they took a stone, and put it under him, and he sat thereon; and Aaron and Hur stayed up his hands, the one on the one side, and the other on the other side; and his hands were steady until the going down of the sun. And Joshua discomfited Amalek and his people with the edge of the sword." The Lord then said unto Moses, "Write this for a memorial in a book, and rehearse it in the ears of Joshua: for I will utterly put out the remembrance of Amalek from under heaven," whereupon Moses "built an altar, and called the name of it Jehovah-nissi." *Jehovah-nissi* literally means "the Lord is my banner," and the Talmudic commentators explain that perhaps Moses raised his staff like a banner during the battle, and when the Israelites could see the banner they were courageous and victorious, but when they could not see it they were despondent and unable to win.

Is *Brother Jonathan* from the Bible?

Brother Jonathan occurs in the Bible in *II Samuel 1:26*, where David is quoted as saying in his lament: "I am distressed for thee, my brother Jonathan." David, however, was not Jonathan's blood brother but his brother-in-law, having married Jonathan's sister, Micah. The use of *Brother Jonathan* as a generic name for the people of the United States is of obscure origin. It was applied to the Americans by the British as early as March, 1776. Apparently *Brother Jonathan* originally was applied to New Englanders in particular rather than to Americans in general. A pamphlet published in England in 1643 contains the following curious passage: "Queene Elizabeth's monument was put up at my charge when the regal government had fairer credit among us than now, and her epitaph was one of my Brother Jonathan's best poems before he abjured the university or had a thought of New England." In 1812 James Kirke Paulding published a book entitled *The Diverting History of John Bull and Brother Jonathan*. Twelve years later Paulding published his *John Bull in America; or the New Munchausen*, in which he wrote: "John Bull christened this son of his by the name of Jonathan; but by and by when he became a man grown, his friends and neighbors gave him the nickname Uncle Sam, a sure sign they liked him, for I never knew a respectable nickname given to a scurvy fellow in my life." After the War of 1812 *Uncle Sam* gradually replaced *Brother Jonathan* as the popular nickname of the United States and of Americans. In 1846 the Norwich (Connecticut) *Courier* printed what purported to be a communication from a man then upwards of eighty years of age who had been an active participant on the Revolutionary stage. This article said in part: "When General Washington, after being appointed commander of the army of the Revolutionary war, came to Massachusetts to organize it and make preparations for the defense of the country, he found a great want of ammunition and other means necessary to meet the powerful foe he had to contend with, and great difficulty to obtain them. If attacked in such condition, the cause at once might be hopeless. On one occasion, at that anxious period, a consultation of the officers and others was had, when it seemed no way could be devised to make such preparation as was necessary. His Excellency Jonathan Trumbull the elder was then governor of the State of Connecticut, on whose judgment and aid the general placed the greatest reliance, and remarked: 'We must consult *Brother Jonathan* on the subject.' The general did so, and the governor was successful in supplying many of the wants of the army. When difficulties afterwards arose, and the army was spread over the country, it became a by-word, 'We must consult Brother Jonathan.' The term *Yankee* is still applied to a portion, but *Brother Jonathan* has now become a designation of the whole country, as John Bull has for England." So far as known this was the first association of the name of Jonathan Trumbull with *Brother Jonathan* in the sense of a typical American. It has been generally accepted ever since as the true origin of *Brother Jonathan* as applied to the United States and its people. But the historical accuracy of the story is doubtful. Jonathan Trumbull (1710-1785), whose surname was *Trumble* until he changed the spelling in 1766, was governor of Connecticut from 1769 to 1784. It is well known that Governor Trumbull and General Washington were close friends, that they were in almost continual correspondence during the early years of the Revolution and that the Governor supported the General loyally in providing supplies of food, clothing and munitions for the army. Washington said of Trumbull that his services "justly entitled him to the first place among patriots." Trumbull had three sons who distinguished themselves: Joseph, the first commissary-general of the Continental Army; Jonathan, soldier, Representative, Senator and Governor of Connecticut, and John, "the painter of the Revolution." During the latter part of the Revolution Jonathan Trumbull the younger served as secretary and aide-de-camp to General Washington, and a later story has it that it was this Jonathan Trumbull whom Washington called *Brother Jonathan* and whose nickname became the first nickname of the United States. But there is no contemporary evidence connecting either Jonathan Trumbull with the origin of *Brother Jonathan* as the national nickname. It seems more probable that *Brother Jonathan* was first applied to the New England Yankees by the British. As a national nickname it still survives to some extent in British usage, while it is almost forgotten in America.

What are Jonathan arrows?

Jonathan arrows are arrows shot to warn, not to hurt. The phrase is an allusion to the story of Jonathan and David in *I Samuel 20.* When it appeared that Saul would try to kill David if he returned to his accustomed place at the king's table, Jonathan met David in the field and suggested a method of warning him as to Saul's temper. According to *I Samuel 20:18-22*, Jonathan said to David: "To morrow is the new moon: and thou shalt be missed, because thy seat will be empty. And when thou hast stayed three days, then thou shalt go down quickly, and come to the place where thou didst hide thyself when the business was in hand, and shalt remain by the stone Ezel. And I will shoot three arrows on the side thereof, as though I shot at a mark. And, behold, I will send a lad, saying, Go find out the arrows. If I expressly say unto the lad, Behold, the arrows are on this side of thee, take them; then come thou: for there is peace to thee, and no hurt; as the Lord liveth. But if I say thus unto the young man, Behold, the arrows are beyond thee; go thy way: for the Lord hath sent thee away." Saul missed David at the table the second day and was furious when he learned that Jonathan was shielding him. The king even cast a javelin at his son to smite him. *I Samuel 20:35-42* says: "And it came to pass in the morning, that Jonathan went out into the field at the time appointed with David, and a little lad with him. And he said unto his lad, Run, find out now the arrows which I shoot. And as the lad ran, he shot an arrow beyond him. And when the lad was come to the place of the arrow which Jonathan had shot, Jonathan cried after the lad, and said, Is not the arrow beyond thee? And Jonathan cried after the lad, Make speed, haste, stay not. And Jonathan's lad gathered up the arrows, and came to his master. But the lad knew not any thing: only Jonathan and David knew the matter. And Jonathan gave his artillery unto his lad, and said unto him, Go, carry them to the city. And as soon as the lad was gone, David arose out of a place toward the south, and fell on his face to the ground, and bowed himself three times: and they kissed one another, and wept one with another, until David exceeded. And Jonathan said to David, Go in peace, forasmuch as we have sworn both of us in the name of the Lord, saying, The Lord be between me and thee, and between my seed and thy seed for ever. And he arose and departed: and Jonathan went into the city."

What is a levirate marriage?

Levirate is derived from Latin *levir,* meaning "brother-in-law" or "a husband's brother." It does not occur in the Bible, but it is the technical name of a custom among the Israelites by which a brother or the next of kin of a deceased man was bound under certain circumstances to marry the widow. In *Deuteronomy 25:5-10* Moses commanded that if a man who had a brother died his widow should "not marry without unto a stranger" but the brother should marry her and raise seed to his brother that "his name be not put out of Israel." If the brother refused to marry her and to build up his brother's house and persisted in that course, then his deceased brother's wife, in the presence of the elders might "loose his shoe from off his foot, and spit in his face." Obviously this law applied only to childless widows or at least only to widows who had no male children. *Genesis 38,* one of the most remarkable chapters in the Bible, illustrates the levirate marriage in actual practice. The levirate marriage is referred to in *Matthew 22:23-30,* which reads "The same day came to him the Sadducees, which say that there is no resurrection, and asked him, saying, Master, Moses said, If a man die, having no children, his brother shall marry his wife, and raise up seed unto his brother. Now there were with us seven brethren: and the first, when he had married a wife, deceased, and, having no issue, left his wife unto his brother: likewise the second also, and the third, unto the seventh. And last of all the woman died also. Therefore in the resurrection whose wife shall she be of the seven? for they all had her. Jesus answered and said unto them, Ye do err, not knowing the scriptures, nor the power of God. For in the resurrection they neither marry, nor are given in marriage, but are as the angels of God in heaven." The levirate marriage in various forms existed among many ancient peoples and among certain American Indian tribes. There is a common notion that even at the present time in America it is unlawful for a man to marry his former wife's sister. The notion that such marriages are forbidden by law in the United States is a hold-over from the English common law. It was once widely believed that there were biological reasons why a woman should not have children by her dead husband's brother. As late as 1907 the British Parliament passed an act that permitted a man to marry his deceased wife's sister but forbade a woman to marry the brother of her deceased husband. In 1920 Lady Astor began agitation to the end of having this prohibition removed from the statute books. No State in the Union prohibits the marriage of a man to his former wife's sister or of a woman to her former husband's brother, but every State and most foreign countries have statutes prohibiting marriages between blood relatives, such as between uncles and nieces, nephews and aunts, etc.

How large was Jerusalem in the time of Jesus?

No reliable population figures for the time of Jesus are available. From various sources it is estimated that the permanent population of Jerusalem was then somewhere between 70,000 and 100,000. Jerusalem was the religious capital of the Jews and hundreds of thousands of Jews visited the Holy City every year to attend the great religious festivals. According to Josephus, Hecataeus of Abdera wrote in the fourth century B.C. that Jerusalem "is inhabited by a hundred and twenty thousand men, or thereabouts." Josephus says there were 2,700,000 people within the walls of Jerusalem when it was besieged by the Romans in 70 A.D., and Tacitus placed it at 600,000, but these estimates are believed to be wide off the mark. When the Jewish rebellion started in the time of Nero the number of Jews in Jerusalem was increased by the presence of tens if not hundreds of thousands of refugees and visitors who sought protection within the strong walls and fortifications of the city. Josephus tells us that 1,100,000 Jews perished during the siege and 97,000 were taken captive and sold into slavery. This siege and capture of Jerusalem occurred about forty years after the crucifixion of Jesus. It is probable, however, that Josephus' figure was intended to include all the Jews put to death by the Romans for participating in the rebellion. The population of Palestine in the time of Jesus was probably about 3,000,000, including both Jews and Gentiles. At that time there were between 3,000,000 and 4,000,000 Jews in the Roman Empire, which included virtually all the lands fronting on the Mediterranean. The Roman Empire had an area of about 1,500,000 square miles—about half the territory of continental United States—and its total population is estimated at 100,000,000. Rome, the largest city, had about 1,200,000 inhabitants. Alexandria, Egypt, the second city, and Antioch, Syria, the third city, were somewhat smaller.

Does *the seven pillars of wisdom* occur in the Bible?

The phrase, *the seven pillars of wisdom,* does not occur in the Bible, but it was undoubtedly suggested by *Proverbs 9:1,* which reads: "Wisdom hath builded her house, she hath hewn out her seven pillars." Some of the ancient Rabbis supposed that *Numbers* originally consisted of three parts or books and that at one time there were seven instead of five books of Moses. If this is true, the "seven pillars" of *Proverbs 9:1* may refer to the Pentateuch, which the Jews call the Torah. Among the Hebrews seven was the sacred number par excellence. It occurs in the Bible scores of times with symbolical significance.

Why are non-Jews called Gentiles?

Gentile is from a Greek and Latin word meaning "tribe," "people" or "nation." It was used in the Latin Vulgate to render a Hebrew word signifying "nation" and applied by the Israelites to all peoples of a different race, nationality and religious faith. In the King James Version of the Bible *Gentile* is used sometimes in this restricted sense and sometimes in the sense of pagan, heathen, barbarian, stranger or sojourner in the land, foreigner, alien, an uncircumcised person, etc. The Israelites regarded themselves as living according to the terms of a covenant made between Abraham and the Lord and they considered other peoples less fortunate than themselves by reason of that fact. According to *Exodus 19:5,* the Lord said to Moses out of Sinai: "Now therefore, if ye will obey my voice indeed, and keep my covenant, then ye shall be a peculiar treasure unto me above all people: for all the earth is mine." *Isaiah 43:20* refers to the Israelites as "my people, my chosen" and as the people whom the Lord had formed for himself. In New Testament times the Jews divided the Gentiles into Greeks, who included the Romans and other civilized peoples in the Roman Empire, and the barbarians. The court of the Gentiles was an outer part of the Temple at Jerusalem beyond whose bounds no Gentile could pass without incurring the death penalty. Sometimes *Greek* and *Gentile* are used synonymously in the New Testament. For instance, in *Romans 1:16* St. Paul says: "For I am not ashamed of the gospel of Christ: for it is the power of God unto salvation to every one that believeth; to the Jew first, and also to the Greek." In *Galatians 2:7* Paul says: "the gospel of the uncircumcision was committed unto me, as the gospel of the circumcision was unto Peter," where *uncircumcision* and *circumcision* are used in the sense of *Gentile* and *Jew*. Paul is called the Apostle to the Gentiles, and Peter the Apostle to the Jews. Whether the Gentiles should be permitted to share in the promises and privileges of the Messiah was one of the first difficult questions with which the first Christian Jewish community at Jerusalem was confronted. After once this question was definitely settled the great majority of converts were made among the Gentiles rather than among the Jews. *Gentile* is often used in the general sense of unbeliever. In India the term is applied to Hindus to distinguish them from Moslems, and the Mormons regard all non-Mormons, including Jews, as Gentiles.

Is the serpent medical emblem of Biblical origin?

The traditional emblem of the medical profession consists of a single serpent coiled about a rod. This emblem may have been of Biblical origin. The serpent has been regarded as a wise and subtle creature since remote antiquity. In the Old Testament story of Adam and Eve in the Garden of Eden the serpent is referred to as "more subtile than any beast of the field," and it was condemned by God to crawl on its belly and eat dust all the days of its life for meddling in the domestic affairs of the first man and woman. Jesus, according to *Matthew 10:16,* said to his twelve disciples: "Behold, I send you forth as sheep in the midst of wolves: be ye therefore wise as serpents, and harmless as doves." We are told that when the children of Israel wandered in the wilderness their soul "was much discouraged because of the way." *Numbers 21:5-9* says: "And the people spake against God, and against Moses, Wherefore have ye brought us up out of Egypt to die in the wilderness? for there is no bread, neither is there any water; and our soul loatheth this light bread. And the Lord sent fiery serpents among the people, and they bit the people; and much people of Israel died. Therefore the people came to Moses, and said, We have sinned, for we have spoken against the Lord, and against thee; pray unto the Lord, that he take away the serpents from us. And Moses prayed for the people. And the Lord said unto Moses, Make thee a fiery serpent, and set it upon a pole: and it shall come to pass, that every one that is bitten, when he looketh upon it, shall live. And Moses made a serpent of brass, and put it upon a pole, and it came to pass, that if a serpent had bitten any man, when he beheld the serpent of brass, he lived." This brazen serpent made by Moses was preserved as an object of veneration by the Israelites. In the course of centuries, however, it became the object of idolatrous worship and was therefore destroyed by King Hezekiah, who "did that which was right in the sight of the Lord, according to all that David his father did." *II Kings 18:4* says: "He removed the high places, and brake the images, and cut down the groves, and brake in pieces the brazen serpent that Moses had made: for unto those days the children of Israel did burn incense to it: and he called it Nehushtan." *John 3:14* says: "And as Moses lifted up the serpent in the wilderness, even so must the Son of man be lifted up." The Egyptians, among whom the Israelites had lived several centuries, associated the serpent with the healing art. Among the ancient Greeks it was the symbol of renovation and was believed to have the power of revealing medicinal herbs. The serpent was sacred to Asclepius, the Greek god of medicine, and a snake coiled around a rod was his most characteristic emblem. In many parts of Greece Asclepius was worshiped under the form of a serpent, and in 293, B.C., when Rome was smitten with a pestilence, this form of worship was introduced into the Eternal City from Epidaurus. Asclepius became Aesculapius to the Romans. In later mythology Hygeia, the goddess of health, who was a daughter of Asclepius, is often represented as bearing a serpent wand. It will be recalled that in *Exodus* the rod cast down before Pharaoh by Aaron "became a serpent." The curious feature of that passage is that the wise men, sorcerers and magicians of Egypt called in by Pharaoh were able to perform the same miracles. *Exodus 7:12* says: "For they cast down every man his rod, and they became serpents: but Aaron's rod swallowed up their rods." The emblem commonly called the caduceus, strictly speaking, does not and never did symbolize the medical profession or healing art, although, owing to its confusion with the serpent as a medical emblem, it is often referred to as such. The caduceus probably had a somewhat different origin. As now generally represented the caduceus consists of a smooth rod with two wings at one end and entwined around in opposite directions by two serpents with their heads confronting each other near the wings. *Caduceus* is a Latin adaptation of Greek *kerykion,* "herald's staff," and it was the wand carried by ancient Greek heralds. The Romans did not use the caduceus as we know it. Originally the wand was a pronged stick decorated with garlands or a plain rod of olive wood entwined with cords or fillets of wood knotted at the end. The rod itself denoted power. Later two serpents were substituted for the cords to denote wisdom, and wings were added to denote speed and activity. In Greek mythology such a rod was carried as a badge of his office by the messenger of the gods, who was known as Hermes to the Greeks and as Mercury to the Romans. Since Mercury was the god of commerce his wand became the emblem of commerce, prosperity and peace, and as such it is still used. Among the Romans it was rather the badge of ambassadors. The messenger of the gods conducted the dead into the next world with the caduceus, and some of the poets declared that with it he could give sleep to whomever he touched, whence Milton's reference to the "opiate rod." Edmund Spenser mentioned the caduceus in 1591, and in *Troilus and Cressida,* written about 1606, Shakespeare has the deformed and scurrilous Thersites pray, "Mercury, lose all the serpentine craft of thy caduceus."

What became of the lost tribes of Israel?

It is popularly supposed that, after the final split in the kingdom of Israel, the northern kingdom was composed of ten tribes and the southern kingdom of two tribes, while the thirteenth tribe, the Levites, was scattered among the other twelve tribes. The fact is that, exclusive of the Levites, the kingdom of Israel was composed of only nine tribes and the southern kingdom of three tribes. Simeon is the real "lost tribe of Israel." This tribe was allotted territory in the extreme south of Palestine within the general territory of Judah. Its central town was Beersheba but its boundaries were indefinite. The Simeonites disappeared as a separate tribe at an early date and are not mentioned in the later history of Judah and Israel. Although Beersheba was in the heart of Simeon, that place is mentioned in

Elijah's time as belonging to Judah. Apparently the Simeonites were partly absorbed by Judah and partly reclaimed by the desert peoples. Judah also absorbed Benjamin. This tribe was virtually exterminated by the other tribes in the days of the judges when the Lord "made a breach in the tribes of Israel." Thus the later kingdom of Judah was composed of the territory and people of three tribes, Judah, Benjamin and Simeon. Besides, many members of the northern tribes, especially the Levites, not wishing to be separated from the temple service at Jerusalem, migrated to Judah. Therefore, if the Levites are not counted as a tribe, the northern kingdom was composed of the territory and people of only nine, not ten, tribes. Perhaps the notion that it consisted of ten tribes arose from the habit of regarding the half-tribes of Manasseh, which occupied non-contiguous territory, as two separate tribes. About 735 B.C. King Tiglath-pileser of Assyria took "all the land of Naphtali" in the north and carried the inhabitants into captivity. Fourteen years later "the king of Assyria took Samaria, and carried Israel away into Assyria." Josephus says all the "ten tribes" were transplanted, that the people as a body remained beyond Euphrates and in his day were still "an immense multitude and not to be numbered." Although Israel was annihilated as a nation, there is no reason to suppose that all its inhabitants were carried away or that those who were deported were lost in the generally accepted sense of the word. A considerable part of the population of Israel, it is believed, remained at home, while others migrated southward and joined their cousins in Judaea. Those carried away never returned to Palestine in a body. No doubt some of them intermarried with their captors, others migrated to different countries, and still others drifted back in small groups or individually to the homeland. Josephus says large numbers of Jews were being brought back from Babylon as late as the time of Antiochus the Great. Many of these so-called Jews of Babylon may have descended from the "ten tribes" as well as from Judaeans. One of the essential parts of the Messianic hope of the exilic prophets was that the "lost tribes" beyond Euphrates would be returned to the fold of Judaism. The tribes of Israel began to intermarry and intermingle with one another at an early period and tribal identity had been well-nigh lost even before the captivity. Jews of today are descended not only from Judaeans—Judah, Benjamin, Simeon and Levi—but also from the other nine tribes—Reuben, Issachar, Zebulon, Gad, Asher, Dan, Naphtali, Ephraim and Manasseh. Even after the tribal organization ceased to exist, the Jews continued to trace their descent from the thirteen tribes. For instance, Paul the Apostle tells us he was of "the tribe of Benjamin," and *Luke 2:36* says the prophetess Anna was "the daughter of Phanuel, of the tribe of Aser."

Are the Indians descended from the lost tribes?

That the American Indians are of Hebrew origin and descended from "the ten lost tribes of Israel" has been a favorite popular theory virtually ever since the discovery of the New World. The era of discovery was also one of religious fervor and both priests and laymen were fascinated by the thought that the roving bands of savages in the wilds of America might be the remnants of the scattered tribes over whom David and Solomon once ruled. This theory, which persists to the present day and crops out in pseudo-scientific and popular literature upon the slightest provocation, was particularly plausible when America was still supposed to be the eastern extremity of Asia and when information about the Indians was meager and fragmentary. As early as 1585 Father Diego Duran, in his history of the Spanish Indies, stated positively, that "these natives are of the ten tribes of Israel that Shalmaneser, king of the Assyrians, made prisoners and carried to Assyria." The notion was readily accepted by many—even William Penn thought there might be something to it—and dozens of volumes and innumerable articles have since been written in support or in contradiction of a theory that is absurd and fantastic in the light of more recent researches and a more careful analysis of the facts. Edward King Kingsborough, an Irish antiquarian who was known as "Lord Kingsborough" by courtesy, spent a fortune of about $300,000 and finally died in a debtors' prison in Dublin as a result of his attempt to identify the ancient Mexicans with the lost tribes of Israel. His *Antiquities of Mexico,* a monumental work in nine large volumes, beautifully printed and illustrated in colors, was published between 1830 and 1848 and was originally prompted by the compiler's desire to prove his pet theory. The Mormons, supported by alleged direct revelation recorded in the *Book of Mormon,* accepted the theory of the Hebrew origin of the Indians and in consequence treated the aborigines with more than ordinary consideration. Every real or fancied resemblance in religion, language, art, custom, habit and tradition between the Jews and Indians has been adduced to sustain the theory. Arguments favoring it were believed to have been greatly reinforced when it was learned that some of the Athapascan tribes, such as the Sekani and Etchareottines of the Northwest, circumcised many of their male children, although the same practice existed among the prehistoric Hawaiians as well as some non-Jewish peoples in other parts of the world, but not as a religious rite. As shown elsewhere in this book, the main premise on which the theory is based, that ten of the tribes of Israel were "lost," is itself unsupported by positive evidence. It belongs to the realms of fancy alone to picture the "lost tribes of Israel" as remaining in a body or in bodies and taking refuge in the wilderness of another continent. At one time the theory that the Anglo-Saxons were descended from these same wandering Israelites found considerable popular favor. Science and history have been greatly enriched by the numerous attempts to identify the Indians with the scattered remnants of Israel, and a vast fund of knowledge has been collected and examined as a result of these researches, but the theory has been abandoned as untenable and it does not now have the support of a single anthropologist of repute. The Jews and the aborigines of America belong racially to different types and have no striking physical characteristics in common. Similarities in language, religion, customs, art and tradition are probably only coincidences and no greater than in the case of many other peoples. Primitive man always has much in common with civilized man, no matter where found, and the progress of mankind on the different continents has passed through similar stages. The antiquity of man in America is very great—going back at least several thousand years and probably much further—and the aborigines from Alaska to Patagonia had been separated from other races so long, if they did not have a different origin, that, when first encountered by Europeans, they had become surprisingly homogeneous and had developed such marked characteristics that they are classed as a separate race. In view of overwhelming evidence to the contrary, any theory that derives the Indians from any Old World people within comparatively recent times should be looked upon with extreme skepticism.

What does *strait* in the Bible mean?

Although pronounced the same, *strait* and *straight* are different in both meaning and origin. As used in the English Bible the two words are often confused. *Matthew 3:3* says: "For this is he that was spoken of by the prophet Esaias, saying, The voice of one crying in the wilderness, Prepare ye the way of the Lord, make his paths straight." But *Matthew 7:13-14* says: "Enter ye in at the strait gate: for wide is the gate, and broad is the way, that leadeth to destruction, and many there be which go in thereat: because strait is the gate, and narrow is the way, which leadeth unto life, and few there be that find it."

The underlying thought in *straight* is "stretched" or "extended," the word being derived from the same root as *stretch*; while the idea back of *strait* is "close," "tight," "narrow," "drawn together," the word being derived from Latin *strictus*, past participle of *stringere*, "to draw tight," which is also the source of *strict* and *strain*. In the passages quoted from Matthew *strait* means "narrow," while *straight* means "not crooked," "direct." In *Philippians 1:23* Paul the Apostle says "for I am in a strait betwixt two." But, according to *Acts 9:11*, the Lord said in a vision to Ananias in Damascus, "Arise, and go into the street which is called Straight." A person in difficulty, great need or serious trouble is said to be in "bad straits," not "bad straights." Violent criminals are put in "strait-jackets," not "straight-jackets," and a person bad off is in "straitened," not "straightened," circumstances. One strict in his morals is "strait-laced," not "straight-laced." *Strait*, both singular and plural, is applied geographically to a narrow passageway of water separating two lands connecting two larger bodies of water. It occurs in many place names; as, Strait of Gibraltar, the Malacca Strait, Magellan Strait and Straits Settlements. A strait may be straight or crooked; most straits are crooked. *Straitly* in the Bible means *strictly*. For instance, *Exodus 13:19* says: "And Moses took the bones of Joseph with him: for he had straitly sworn the children of Israel, saying, God will surely visit you; and ye shall carry up my bones away hence with you."

What is meant by "the voice of the turtle"?

When John Van Druten's *The Voice of the Turtle* became a popular comedy hit on Broadway many people were under the impression that the title referred to the sound made by the reptile known as a turtle. The title is from the Bible. In the King James Version *turtle* always refers to a bird and never to a reptile. Usually it occurs in conjunction with *dove*, but in three instances *dove* is omitted. *The Song of Solomon 2:11-13* says in part: "For lo, the winter is past, the rain is over and gone; the flowers appear on the earth; the time of the singing of birds is come, and the voice of the turtle is heard in our land; the fig tree putteth forth her green figs, and the vines with the tender grapes give a good smell." Incidentally, that is one of the most beautiful descriptions of spring in the Holy Land in all literature. *Numbers 6:10* says: "And on the eighth day he shall bring two turtles or two young pigeons, to the priest, to the door of the tabernacle of the congregation." And *Jeremiah 8:7*: "Yea, the stork in heaven knoweth her appointed times; and the turtle and the crane and the swallow observe the time of their coming; but my people know not the judgment of the Lord." In all these instances the context shows clearly that *turtle* means *turtledove*. In fact, *turtle* was not generally applied to reptiles until after the King James Version was made. Throughout Shakespeare *turtle* means a dove, and that is the meaning of the term in the poem entitled *The Phoenix and the Turtle*, conventionally ascribed to Shakespeare, who did most of his writing before the King James Version was published. *The voice of the turtle* in the Bible and in the title of the play is the sweet and mournful cooing of the turtledove, not the metallic croaking of the tortoise. On the other hand, *turtle* in the fable of the turtle and the hare refers to the tortoise, not to the turtledove. Etymologists derive *turtle* from Latin *turtur*, which means "turtledove" and which probably was of imitative origin. The word was not applied to the tortoise until the sixteenth or seventeenth century. It is supposed that in the latter sense the word is a corruption of French *tortue* or Spanish *tortuga*, signifying "tortoise." *The New English Dictionary* supposes that British sailors originated the usage by assimilating the foreign word to the common *turtle*. The reptiles known variously as turtles and tortoises are not notable for the vocal sounds they utter. Common painted turtles utter a piping note; the wood turtle, when startled, makes a snakelike hissing sound; and the giant Galapagos tortoises make a loud, roaring or bellowing noise during the mating season. *Tortoise* occurs in the King James Version only once. *Leviticus 28:29* says: "These also shall be unclean unto you among the creeping things that creep upon the earth; the weasel, and the mouse, and the tortoise after his kind." The creature referred to by the original Hebrew word is not clear. The Revised Version renders the word *great lizard*.

What is meant by *the bulls of Bashan*?

Bashan was the ancient name of a district in Palestine lying east of the Sea of Galilee and the upper Jordan. It was proverbial for its fertile soil, good pasture, great timber and fine livestock. There are several references in the Bible to the cattle of Bashan. Bashan was already famous for its cattle when the Israelites took possession of the region under Moses. In *Deuteronomy 32:14* Moses referred to "butter of kine, and milk of sheep, with fat of lambs, and rams of the breed of Bashan, and goats, with the fat of kidneys of wheat." The later prophet alludes to this in *Micah 7:14* when he says: "Feed thy people with thy rod, the flock of thine heritage, which dwell solitarily in the wood, in the midst of Carmel: let them feed in Bashan and Gilead, as in the days of old." The cattle of Bashan became the type of wealthy, powerful, cruel and loud-mouthed oppressors in Israel. In *Psalms 22:12* David sang: "Many bulls have compassed me: strong bulls of Bashan have beset me round." *Amos 4:1* says: "Hear this word, ye kine of Bashan, that are in the mountain of Samaria, which oppress the poor, which crush the needy, which say to their masters, Bring, and let us drink." The oaks of Bashan were almost as famed as the cedars of Lebanon. *Isaiah 2:12-13* says: "For the day of the Lord of hosts shall be upon every one that is proud and lofty, and upon every one that is lifted up; and he shall be brought low; and upon all the cedars of Lebanon, that are high and lifted up, and upon all the oaks of Bashan." Ezekiel, in his lamentation for Tyre, according to *Ezekiel 27:5-6*, says: "They have made all thy ship boards of fir trees of Senir: they have taken cedars from Lebanon to make masts for thee. Of the oaks of Bashan have they made thine oars." And in *Zechariah 11:2* we read: "Howl, O ye oaks of Bashan; for the forest of the vintage is come down." Bashan is still one of the granaries of Palestine and is inhabited largely by the Druses, a fierce, warlike sect whose secret religion consists of a strange combination of Christian, Moslem and pagan doctrines.

What is Dead Sea Fruit?

Anything pleasing to the eye but worthless when acquired is called "Dead Sea fruit" or "apples of Sodom." These phrases do not occur in the Bible, but they may have been suggested by a Biblical passage. According to *Deuteronomy 32:32*, Moses, in the song that he spoke in the ears of all the congregation of Israel, said: "For their vine is of the *vine of Sodom*, and of the fields of Gomorrah: their grapes are grapes of gall, their clusters are bitter." Bible scholars differ as to whether this figure alludes to the inward corruption of Israel or of Israel's enemies. Several old writers mention a curious deceptive plant that was supposed to grow on the borders of the Dead Sea and that yielded "Apples of Sodom," a fruit said to be beautiful on the outside but, when mature, filled with fiber and dust and bitter to the taste. Josephus described such a fruit. "Still, too," wrote the Jewish historian, "may one see ashes reproduced in the fruits, which from their outward appearance would be thought edible, but on being plucked with the hand dissolve into smoke and ashes." Tacitus wrote as if this condition were true of all vegetation in the region of the Dead Sea. "Whatever the earth produces, whether by the prolific vigor of nature, or the cultivation of man," said the Roman historian, "nothing ripens to perfection. The herbage may shoot up, and the trees may put forth their blossoms; they may even attain the usual appearance of maturity; but with this florid outside, all within turns black, and moulders into dust." The Dead Sea fruit of Josephus can not be definitely identified. No known plant answers to his description completely. Perhaps the ancient writer merely recorded a "traveler's tale" that had but slight basis in fact. Some authorities think that Josephus referred to *Solanum sodomeum,* a prickly shrub with fruit resembling a small yellow tomato. Others suppose the original Dead Sea fruit to have been the Bussorah gall, which is produced on certain oaks. Edward Robinson, an American Biblical scholar, was of the opinion that the singular fruit known to the Arabs as *'osher* is the true apple of Sodom. This plant is the *Asclepias procera* of botanists. "Its fruit," wrote Dr. John C. Geikie in *The Holy Land and the Bible,* "is like a large smooth apple or orange. When ripe it is yellow and looks fair and attractive, and is soft to the touch, but if pressed, it bursts with a crack, and only the broken shell and a row of small seeds in a half-open pod, with a few dry filaments, remain in the hand."

Does the Bible mention the witch of Endor?

Contrary to popular belief, the phrase *the witch of Endor* does not occur in the text of the Bible, although in some English editions it is used in the chapter heading of *I Samuel 28.* The person commonly called the witch of Endor is referred to merely as "a woman that hath a familiar spirit of Endor." She brought up the prophet Samuel from the dead upon the request of Saul, who wished to inquire as to the fateful battle in which he was to lose his life. Her function was not exactly that of a witch, who is supposed to hold communion with the devil and other evil spirits, but rather that of a spiritualistic medium, who claims to have power to convey messages from the dead to the living.

What became of Lot's wife?

According to *Genesis 19,* Lot's wife was turned into a "pillar of salt" because she looked back while she and her husband and their two daughters were fleeing from Sodom. Two angels, warning Lot of the impending destruction of "the cities of the plain," had said to him, "look not behind thee . . . lest thou be consumed." "But," says the Bible, "his wife looked back behind him, and she became a pillar of salt." Lot was the son of Abraham's brother Haran, but we are not told who Lot's wife was before her marriage. The phrase, "Remember Lot's wife," is of New Testament, not of Old Testament, origin. Jesus, according to *Luke 17:28-32,* said: "Likewise also as it was in the days of

Lot; they did eat, they drank, they bought, they sold, they planted, they builded; but the same day that Lot went out of Sodom it rained fire and brimstone from heaven, and destroyed them all. Even thus shall it be in the day when the Son of Man is revealed. In that day, he which shall be upon the housetop, and his stuff in the house, let him not come down to take it away: and he that is in the field, let him likewise not return back. Remember Lot's wife." Toward the end of the first century. Josephus wrote: "But Lot's wife continually turning back to view the city as she went from it, and being too nicely inquisitive what would become of it, although God had forbidden her so to do, was changed into a pillar of salt; for I have seen it, and it remains at this day." Clement of Rome, in the first century, and Irenaeus, in the second century, both attested that this pillar of salt was standing in their day. Even at the present time credulous travellers in the Holy Land are sometimes shown what is said to be the very pillar of salt into which Lot's wife was converted. More than one tourist has been told by local guides that if a finger or other member of the pillar is broken off it is immediately replaced by some miraculous process. As one guide expressed it a few years ago: "You can slice off a piece from the pillar and it evaporates, and the blemish heals up."

Why is a gifted person said to be talented?

Talent in the sense of natural ability, mental endowment or special aptitude is traceable to the use of the term in the parable of the talents. In *Matthew 25:14-30* the following parable is attributed to Jesus: "For the kingdom of heaven is as a man travelling into a far country, who called his own servants, and delivered unto them his goods. And unto one he gave five talents, to another two, and to another one; to every man according to his several ability; and straightway took his journey. Then he that had received the five talents went and traded with the same, and made them other five talents. And likewise he that had received two, he also gained other two. But he that had received one went and digged in the earth, and hid his lord's money. After a long time the lord of those servants cometh, and reckoneth with them. And so he that had received five talents came and brought other five talents, saying, Lord, thou deliveredst unto me five talents: behold, I have gained beside them five talents more. His lord said unto him, Well done, thou good and faithful servant: thou hast been faithful over a few things, I will make thee ruler over many things: enter thou into the joy of thy lord. He also that had received two talents came and said, Lord, thou deliveredst unto me two talents: behold, I have gained two other talents beside them. His lord said into him, Well done, good and faithful servant; thou hast been faithful over a few things, I will make thee ruler over many things: enter thou into the joy of thy lord. Then he which had received the one talent came and said, Lord, I knew thee that thou art an hard man, reaping where thou hast not sown, and gathering where thou hast not strawed: and I was afraid, and went and hid thy talent in the earth: lo, there thou hast that is thine. His lord answered and said unto him, Thou wicked and slothful servant, thou knewest that I reap where I sowed not, and gather where I have not strawed: thou oughtest therefore to have put my money to the exchangers, and then at my coming I should have received mine own with usury. Take therefore the talent from him, and give it unto him which hath ten talents. For unto every one that hath shall be given, and he shall have abundance; but from him that hath not shall be taken away even that which he hath. And cast ye the unprofitable servant into outer darkness: there shall be weeping and gnashing of teeth." The Greek word translated *talent* means "weight" or "balance" and is derived from a verb signifying "to bear." In ancient times money metal of any quantity was weighed instead of counted, and the talent was originally a measure of weight rather than of value per se. Tens of thousands of words have been written in efforts to render the actual value of the Biblical talent in terms of modern money. The results vary widely and are unsatisfactory, because the value of units of money mentioned in the Bible are almost untranslatable into their modern equivalents. Often the original value is unknown, and even when it is, the relative value has changed because of the difference in purchasing power. Estimates of the value of the Biblical talent range all the way from a few hundred to several thousand dollars. As good a guess as any is that the silver talent in the time of Jesus was worth about $1,600 in modern American money, while the gold talent was worth fifteen or twenty times that amount. The task is pointless in relation to *Matthew 25:14-30*, because Jesus was merely pointing out a moral in a parable and the exact unit of money he employed for the purpose is of little importance. Any other unit of money, or the phrase "a sum of money" would have served as well. As a matter of fact, a variant version of the same parable is related in *Luke 19*, where *pound* instead of talent is used in the King James Version. The adjective *talented*, in the sense of gifted, clever, accomplished, having special aptitude, was not accepted in English usage for several centuries after the noun *talent* was well established. The earliest use of it recorded by the Oxford Dictionary is dated 1804. In 1832 the English poet, Samuel Taylor Coleridge, wrote: "I regret to see that vile and barbarous vocable *talented* stealing out of the newspapers into the leading reviews and most respectable publications of the day. Why not shillinged, farthinged, tenpenced, etc.?" Thomas Carlyle in his *Life of Sterling* quoted John Sterling as saying: "*Talented*, a mere newspaper and hustings word, invented, I believe, by O'Connell." This adjective was formed from *talent* on the same principle as *gifted* from *gift*, *lettered* from *letter*, and *bigoted* from *bigot*. It is probable that its appearance in the early nineteenth century was merely a revival of an earlier usage, for George Abbot, archbishop of Canterbury in the time of James I, wrote of "one *talented* but as a common person."

What became of the tables of stone broken by Moses?

Exodus 32:15-19 says: "And Moses turned, and went down from the mount, and the two tables of the testimony were in his hand: the tables were written on both their sides; on the one side and on the other were they written. And the tables were the work of God, and the writing was the writing of God, graven upon the tables. And when Joshua heard the noise of the people as they shouted, he said unto Moses, There is a noise of war in the camp. And he said, It is not the voice of them that shout for mastery, neither is it the voice of them that cry for being overcome; but the noise of them that sing do I hear. And it came to pass, as soon as he came nigh unto the camp, that he saw the calf, and the dancing: and Moses' anger waxed hot, and he cast the tables out of his hands, and brake them beneath the mount." The Bible is completely silent on what became of these original tables of stone containing the Ten Commandments. *Exodus 34:1*: "And the Lord said unto Moses, Hew thee two tables of stone like unto the first: and I will write upon these tables the words that were in the first tables, which thou brakest." Again *Exodus 34:4*: "And he hewed two tables of stone like unto the first; and Moses rose up early in the morning, and went up unto mount Sinai, as the Lord had commanded him, and took in his hand the two tables of stone." Later, in *Exodus 34:27-28* we read: "And the Lord said unto Moses, Write thou these words: for after the tenor of these words I have made a covenant with thee and with Israel. And he was there with the Lord forty days and forty nights; he did neither eat bread, nor drink water. And he wrote upon the tables the words of the covenant, the ten commandments." From this it appears to be clear that the commandments written on the second set of two tables were identical with those written on the two tables that were broken by Moses. According to Jewish tradition, the first five commandments, dealing with man's duties toward God, were engraved on the first table, while the second five, dealing with man's duties to his fellow-man, were engraved on the second table. These two tables of stone containing the Ten Commandments were known as the "tables of testimony" or the "tables of the covenant." In *Exodus 25:21* the Lord had commanded that "in the ark thou shalt put the testimony that I shall give thee." From *I Kings 8:9* we learn that these tables were still in the ark of the covenant when it was placed in Solomon's newly completed temple in Jerusalem. That passage says: "There was nothing in the ark save the two tables of stone, which Moses put there at Horeb, when the Lord made a covenant with the children of Israel, when they came out of the land of Egypt." Presumably these tables remained there until the ark was finally lost to history.

What is the Eleventh Commandment?

Eleventh Commandment is a popular phrase that has been applied to various maxims regarded as being on a par in importance with the Ten Commandments. It has often been applied to "Thou shalt love thy neighbour as thyself," from *Leviticus 18:19,* which Jesus called the second great commandment. It has also been applied to *John 13:34,* in which Jesus is quoted as saying: "A new commandment I give unto you, That ye love one another; as I have loved you, that ye also love one another." The Eleventh Commandment is sometimes given ironically as, "Thou shalt not be found out." In his *Memoirs* Prince de Joinville said that the "Eleventh Commandment, according to the late Lord Clarendon, sums up all the rest." In 1879 Bertha H. Buxton wrote in *Jenny of the Prince's*: "After all, the eleventh commandment [thou shall not be found out] is the only one that is vitally important to keep in these days." "Mind your own business" and "Don't tell tales out of school" are also sometimes referred to as the Eleventh Commandment.

Can a whale swallow a man whole?

This oft-asked question is prompted by the story of Jonah related in the book that bears his name. The Hebrew prophet was told by the Lord to go to Nineveh and cry out against that great city because of its wickedness. But Jonah, instead of obeying the command, fled from the presence of the Lord and went down to Joppa on the Mediterranean coast and paid his fare on a ship bound for Tarshish. "But the Lord," says *Jonah 1:4,* "sent out a great wind into the sea, and there was a mighty tempest in the sea, so that the ship was like to be broken." Then the mariners were afraid, and, crying every man unto his god, they cast the wares in the ship into the sea to lighten it. Meanwhile Jonah lay fast asleep in the sides of the ship. So the shipmaster went down to the sleeping prophet and asked him to call upon his God lest they all perish. Finally the mariners cast lots to determine "for whose cause this evil is upon us," and the lot fell upon Jonah, who then explained who he was and how he happened to be on the ship. When they asked the prophet what they should do to calm the tempestuous sea and to save their lives, Jonah replied: "Take me up, and cast me forth into the sea; so shall the sea be calm unto you; for I know that for my sake this great tempest is upon you." The mariners nevertheless rowed hard to bring the ship to land, but in vain. So they cast Jonah into the sea and the sea ceased her raging. "Now the Lord," says *Jonah 1:17*, "had prepared a great fish to swallow up Jonah. And Jonah was in the belly of the fish three days and three nights." "Then Jonah prayed unto the Lord his God, out of the fish's belly" and promised to pay what he had vowed. *Jonah 2:10* concludes the incident with these simple words: "And the Lord spake unto the fish, and it vomited out Jonah upon the dry land." In the King James Version of the Bible, *whale* nowhere occurs in *Jonah*. Only *great fish* and *fish* are used. *Whale*, however, does occur in the Old Testament several times. *Genesis 1:21* tells us that "God created great whales, and every living creature that moveth, which the waters brought forth abundantly, after their kind." According to *Job 7:12*, the patriarch asked: "Am I a sea, or a whale, that thou settest a watch over me?" In *Ezekiel 32:2* the Lord said to the prophet: "Son of man, take up a lamentation for Pharaoh king of Egypt, and say unto him, Thou art like a young lion of the nations, and thou art as a whale in the seas: and thou camest forth with thy rivers, and troubledest the waters with thy feet, and foulest their rivers." But in *Matthew 12:40* Jesus is quoted as saying: "For as Jonas was three days and three nights in the whale's belly; so shall the Son of man be three days and three nights in the heart of the earth." This is the only use of *whale* in the Bible in connection with the story of Jonah. Elsewhere such terms as *dragon* and *serpent* are used in about the same sense as *whale*. Perhaps *sea-monster* would be a more accurate rendering of the Hebrew and Greek originals. Whales are not fish, but sea mammals that bring forth perfectly formed living young that are nursed by the mother like land mammals. The Bible, however, was written when whales were regarded as fishes. Whether the *Book of Jonah* should be treated as history or merely as an imaginative work was long the subject of dispute even among theologians themselves. There seems to be little doubt that the chief character in the book was a prophet named Jonah who lived in the eighth century B.C. in the days of Jeroboam II. *II Kings 14:25* tells us that Jeroboam the son of Joash king of Israel "restored the coast of Israel from the entering of Hamath unto the sea of the plain, according to the word of the Lord God of Israel, which he spake by the hand of his servant Jonah, the son of Amittai, the prophet, which was of Gath-hepher." It is generally believed now, however, that the story of Jonah, although written in a matter-of-fact literary style, was deliberate fiction with a moral lesson, an allegory produced as a protest against narrow Jewish nationalism and as a stimulant to missionary work by the Jews, the ancient prophet Jonah having been chosen as the hero because of his anti-Assyrian bias. Whatever the correct answer to that problem may be, those interested in the questions whether a whale can swallow a human being whole and whether a person could survive such an ordeal are concerned with the physical rather than the miraculous character of the narrative of Jonah. That there are fishes and whales that can swallow a man whole is quite probable. Most whales, it is true, have small gullets, especially those that feed on Crustacea. For instance, the throat of the blue whale, probably the largest mammal that has ever inhabited the earth, is only nine or ten inches in diameter. But the sperm whale or cachalot, which feeds chiefly on squids and cuttlefish, has a throat large enough to swallow a human being whole. In 1941 Dr. Eugene Maxmillian Karl Geiling, professor of pharmacology at the University of Chicago, said that he had crawled through the gullet of a dead whale just to demonstrate that it could be done. "It was a pretty slimy trip," Dr. Geiling declared, "but there was plenty of room." The manager of a whaling station in northern Britain told Sir Francis Fox in 1914 that the largest thing ever found in a whale was the skeleton of a shark sixteen feet in length. "Whaling captains," according to Sir Francis, "say that it frequently happens that men are swallowed by whales who become infuriated by the point of the harpoon, and attack the boats." One of the largest predaceous fishes, says the American Museum of Natural History, is the white or man-eater shark, which sometimes reaches a length of thirty or forty feet. Basking and whale sharks grow longer and have larger mouths, but they feed on small creatures. A species of shark similar to the basking shark, found in the Indo-Pacific Ocean, is known to attain a length of fifty feet and is said sometimes to attain seventy. Many exaggerated reports have been published concerning a whale shark captured in 1912 near Knight's Key, off Miami, Florida, by Captain Charles H. Thompson. This specimen, when measured in the water, was thirty-eight feet long, eighteen feet in girth and about ten thousand pounds in weight. In preparing this shark for exhibition, however, the skin was stretched to a length of forty-five feet and the mouth and other parts were greatly distorted. The species, declared the United States Bureau of Fisheries, is doubtless the largest of all fishes. It feeds upon minute animal life and, although its mouth is very large, could not possibly swallow a large fish or adult human being. David Starr Jordan, an authority on fishes, stated that a fair-sized young sea lion was found whole in the stomach of a white shark. These fish, however, have vicious teeth and it is inconceivable that one could swallow a man without killing him. It is also improbable that a human being could be long retained alive in the stomach of a whale. Although the stomach of these creatures is cave-like in dimensions, the high temperature, the powerful gastric juice, and the spasmodic contraction and expansion of the stomach, would be fatal in a very short time. Certainly a man could not live in a conscious state inside a whale's stomach more than a few minutes. He might be able to live in an unconscious state considerably longer. One authority estimated the normal blood temperature of whales at 104.6° Fahrenheit. Dr. Gerrit S. Miller, formerly curator of mammals at the National Museum in Washington, was convinced that no man could survive being swallowed by a whale. That is generally the verdict of scientists, notwithstanding numerous reports that such cases do occasionally occur. On October 4, 1771, the *Boston Post Boy* reported an alleged case in which a whale swallowed a sailor, bit out part of the ship and then vomited the sailor alive on the wreckage. What is often cited as an *authentic* instance of a man being swallowed by a whale and surviving the experience is recorded in Sir Francis Fox's *Sixty-three Years of Engineering, Scientific and Social Work,* published in 1924. That account is said to be based on declarations of the captain and another officer of a whaling vessel. The incident, Sir Francis assures us, was carefully investigated by M. de Parville, scientific editor of the *Journal des Debats of Paris,* who died during the first World War and who had the original manuscripts in his possession. In February, 1891, according to Sir Francis, the *Star of the East* sent out boats to harpoon a large sperm whale in the vicinity of the Falkland Islands. A lash of the whale's tail upset one of the boats and threw the crew into the sea. One man was drowned and another, James Bartley, could not be found. The crew killed the whale, tied it alongside the ship and began to remove the blubber. The next morning the missing sailor was found unconscious in the whale's stomach after it was hoisted on deck. A sea-water bath revived Bartley, but his mind was not clear and he was placed in the captain's cabin, where he remained two weeks a raving lunatic. He gradually regained possession of his senses and at the end of three weeks was sufficiently recovered to resume his duties. The skin of his face, neck and hands, where it was exposed to the gastric juice, was bleached to a deadly whiteness and did not recover its normal appearance even after being treated in a London hospital, although his health was not unfavorably affected. Bartley affirmed that he lost his senses from fright and not from want of air. He remembered being encompassed in darkness and felt himself slipping along a smooth passage. Then the terrible heat seemed to draw out his vitality and he became unconscious. The other members of the crew thought their comrade survived because he was near the whale's throat and because the whale cooled off rapidly after being killed. Such is the strange story told by Sir Francis Fox, who pronounced it "well accredited." The incident, however, is not so well authenticated as might at first appear. Neither Sir Francis nor M. de Parville had any first-hand information, and we are given nothing about the character of the unnamed whaling captain and the other officer. Jonah and the whale is one of the most popular stories in the Bible, and it is only natural that some sea-faring people should be tempted to find counterparts of it in their actual experience. But efforts to explain all Bible miracles by natural phenomena are far from satisfactory, and perhaps it is best to leave the story of Jonah and the great fish where the author of the *Book of Jonah* left it and to regard the prophet's deliverance as a miraculous occurrence in either fact or fiction.

What was the mark set upon Cain?

Genesis 4:9-15 says: "And the Lord said unto Cain, Where is Abel thy brother? And he said, I know not; Am I my brother's keeper? And he said, What hast thou done? the voice of thy brother's blood crieth unto me from the ground. And now art thou cursed from the earth, which hath opened her mouth to receive thy brother's blood from thy hand; when thou tillest the ground, it shall not henceforth yield unto thee her strength: a fugitive and a vagabond shalt thou be in the earth. And Cain said unto the Lord, My punishment is greater than I can bear. Behold. thou hast driven me out this day from the face of the earth; and from thy face shall I be hid; and I shall be a fugitive and a vagabond in the earth; and it shall come to pass, that every one that findeth me shall slay me. And the Lord said unto him, Therefore whosoever slayeth Cain, vengeance shall be taken on him sevenfold. And the Lord set a mark upon Cain, lest any finding him should kill him." The Bible narrative does not give us the least hint as to the nature of the protective sign appointed for Cain. Numerous speculations supply us with little that is worthy of consideration. One commentator supposes that the sign or mark set on Cain was an incision in the forehead. Another suggests that it may have consisted of circumcision. Still another thinks the mark set on Cain was a tribal mark or clan totem analogous to the cattle marks used by the Bedouins and other nomadic peoples. In the East such marks or brands often had a religious significance and denoted that the bearer was a follower of a certain deity. Cain may have feared that if he left his people without a mark of identification he would be slain by members of other tribes or clans. It is difficult to see what purpose a scar or brand on the body would serve except to aid the revengeful in detecting the culprit. Therefore some have supposed that the Lord did not set an actual mark upon Cain's body, but merely gave out a protective sign to guide others. This sign, it has been suggested, consisted of the words: "Whosoever slayeth Cain, vengeance shall be taken on him sevenfold." The theory is supported by the fact that the Hebrew word for sign is *oth*, and it means "a sign set up," such as a road sign to guide travelers. Only in the passage about Cain is the word *oth* translated "mark" instead of "sign." *Tav* is the Hebrew word meaning an actual brand on the body. In Ezekiel's vision the Lord sent a man with a writer's inkhorn through Jerusalem to "set a mark [*tav*] upon the foreheads of the men" who grieved because of the wickedness of the city. Accordingly, the more correct translation of the latter part of *Genesis 4:15* is: "And the Lord appointed a sign for Cain, lest any finding him should kill him." Some of the Talmudic interpreters say that the popular expression *brand of Cain* in the sense of a mark on the body of the murderer, arises from a misunderstanding of the passage. Their contention is that Cain was a repentant sinner and that the Lord merely assured him that he would not be regarded as a common, intentional murderer. The law of Moses forebade Israelites to blemish, mutilate or cut their bodies in any manner. *Leviticus 19:28* says: "Ye shall not make any cuttings in your flesh for the dead, nor print any marks upon you." This appears to have been originally intended to forbid tattooing parts of the body, which was a common practice among neighboring idolatrous peoples, who imprinted on their bodies the representation of the deity they worshipped. According to a curious popular belief, Cain was the progenitor of the colored race and the mark set upon him consisted of Ethiopian or African characteristics. This, however, contradicts another common belief, namely, that Cain's hair and beard were yellow or reddish yellow, which gives us the term *cain-colored.*

What is Pentecost?

In the King James Version of the Bible *Pentecost* does not occur in the Old Testament and is recorded only in three passages in the New Testament. The term is derived from a Greek word signifying "fiftieth." It was applied to the Jewish harvest festival because it was held on the fiftieth day after the feast of unleavened bread. In the Old Testament it is called "the feast of weeks." *Exodus 34:22* says: "And thou shalt observe the feast of weeks, even of the first-fruits of wheat harvest, and the feast of ingathering at the turn of the year." But it is called "the feast of harvest" in *Exodus 23:16,* which says that thou shalt keep "the feast of harvest, the first-fruits of thy labours, which thou sowest in the field; and the feast of ingathering, at the end of the year, when thou gatherest in thy labours out of the field." In *Deuteronomy 16:9-10* the name "feast of weeks" is explained: "Seven weeks shalt thou number unto thee: begin to number the seven weeks from such times as thou beginnest to put the sickle to the corn. And thou shalt keep the feast of weeks unto the Lord thy God with a tribute of a freewill offering of thine hand, which thou shalt give unto the Lord thy God, according as the Lord thy God hath blessed thee." In *Leviticus 23:15-16* is explained how the seven weeks becomes fifty days: "And ye shall count unto you from the morrow after the sabbath, from the day that ye brought the sheaf of the wave offering; seven sabbaths shall be complete: even unto the morrow after the seventh sabbath shall ye number fifty days; and ye shall offer a new meat offering unto the Lord." The Greek name *Pentecost,* "the fiftieth (day)" was in general use among the Jews long before the time of Jesus. On the occasion of the second of the great annual feasts Jerusalem was visited by Jews from all over the Roman Empire. It was a day of thanksgiving, joy and mutual entertainment. But among the Christians Pentecost became associated with divine revelation and it acquired a significance that the Jews had never given to it. Speaking of the followers of Jesus in Jerusalem immediately after the crucifixion, *Acts 2:1-13* says: "And when the day of Pentecost was fully come, they were all with one accord in one place. And suddenly there came a sound from heaven as of a rushing mighty wind, and it filled all the house where they were sitting. And there appeared unto them cloven tongues like as of fire, and it sat upon each of them. And they were all filled with the Holy Ghost, and began to speak with other tongues, as the Spirit gave them utterance. And there were dwelling at Jerusalem Jews, devout men, out of every nation under heaven. Now when this was noised abroad, the multitude came together, and were confounded, because that every man heard them speak in his own language. And they were all amazed and marvelled, saying one to another, Behold, are not all these which speak Galileans? And how hear we every man in our own tongue, wherein we were born? Parthians, and Medes, and Elamites, and the dwellers in Mesopotamia, and in Judaea, and Cappadocia, in Pontus, and Asia, Phrygia, and Pamphylia, in Egypt, and in the parts of Libya about Cyrene, and strangers of Rome, Jews and proselytes, Cretes and Arabians, we do hear them speak in our tongues the wonderful works of God. And they were all amazed, and were in doubt, saying one to another, What meanest this? Others mocking said, These men are full of new wine." After Peter stood up with the eleven and spoke "the same day there were added unto them about three thousand souls." Naturally among the early Jewish Christians Pentecost became an event almost as memorable as the crucifixion and the resurrection. In *Acts 20:16* we are told: "For Paul had determined to sail by Ephesus, because he would not spend the time in Asia: for he hasted, if it were possible for him, to be at Jerusalem the day of Pentecost." Paul, according to *I Corinthians 16:8,* said: "I will tarry at Ephesus until Pentecost." As a Christian festival Pentecost is observed on the seventh Sunday after Easter in commemoration of the descent of the Holy Ghost upon the disciples on the day of Pentecost. In England it is called Whitsunday, from Old English *Hwita Sunnandaeg,* literally "white Sunday," supposedly alluding to the ancient custom of the newly baptized wearing white baptismal robes at the feast of Pentecost.

Does the Bible provide for trial by ordeal?

There are two passages in the Bible that suggest trial by ordeal. *Ordeal* is derived from an old Teutonic root signifying "to deal out," "to allot," "to decide" or "to give judgment." Trial by ordeal was an ancient Teutonic and Anglo-Saxon practice of referring disputed questions of crime to supernatural decisions. Under this mode of trial the suspected person was subjected to some physical test fraught with danger, such as plunging the hand in boiling or freezing water, carrying hot iron, walking barefoot and blindfolded between red-hot plowshares, drinking poisoned food or drink, or fighting with the accuser with deadly weapons. The result was regarded as the immediate judgment of the Deity. Trial by ordeal was based on the belief that God would defend the right, even by miraculous means if necessary. *Ordeal* does not occur in the English Bible, but a test resembling this mode of trial is provided in connection with what is called "the law of jealousies" in the law of Moses. This remarkable and interesting passage is found in *Numbers 5:11-31,* which reads: "And the Lord spake unto Moses, saying, Speak unto the children of Israel, and say unto them, If any man's wife go aside, and commit a trespass against him, and a man lie with her carnally, and it be hid from the eyes of her husband, and be kept close, and she be defiled, and there be no witness against her, neither she be taken with the manner; and the spirit of jealousy come upon him, and he be jealous of his wife, and she be defiled: or if the spirit of jealousy come upon him, and he be jealous of his wife, and she be not defiled: then shall the man bring his wife unto the priest, and he shall bring her offering for her, the tenth part of an ephah of barley meal; he shall pour no oil upon it, nor put frankincense thereon; for it is an offering of jealousy, an offering of memorial, bringing iniquity to remembrance. And the priest shall bring her near, and set her before the Lord; and the priest shall take holy water in an earthen vessel; and of the dust that is in the floor of the tabernacle the priest shall take, and put it into the water: and the priest shall set the woman before the Lord, and uncover the woman's head, and put the offering of memorial in her hands, which is the jealousy offering: and the priest shall have in his hand the bitter water that causeth the curse: and the priest shall charge her by an oath, and say unto the woman, If no man have lain with thee, and if thou hast not gone aside to uncleanness with another instead of thy husband, be thou free from this bitter water that causeth the curse: but if thou hast gone aside to another instead of thy husband, and if thou be defiled, and some man have lain with thee beside thine husband: then the priest shall charge the woman with an oath of cursing, and the priest shall say unto the woman, The Lord make thee a curse and an oath among thy people, when the Lord doth make thy thigh to rot, and thy belly to swell; and this water that causeth the curse shall go into thy bowels, to make thy belly to swell, and thy thigh to rot: and the woman shall say, Amen, amen. And the priest shall write these curses in a book, and he shall blot them out with the bitter water: and he shall cause the woman to drink the bitter water that causeth the curse: and the water that causeth the curse shall enter into her, and become bitter. Then the priest shall take the jealousy offering out of the woman's hand, and shall wave the offering before the Lord, and offer it upon the altar: and the priest shall take an handful of the offering, even the memorial thereof, and burn it upon the altar, and afterward shall cause the woman to drink the water. And when he hath made her to drink the water, then it shall come to pass, that, if she be defiled, and have done trespass against her husband, that the water that causeth the curse shall enter into her, and become bitter, and her belly shall swell, and her thigh shall rot: and the woman shall be a curse among her people. And if the woman be not defiled, but be clean; then she shall be free, and shall conceive seed. This is the law of jealousies, when a wife goeth aside to another instead of her husband, and is defiled; or when the spirit of jealousy cometh upon him, and he be jealous over his wife, and shall set the woman before the Lord, and the priest shall execute upon her all this law. Then shall the man be guiltless from iniquity, and this woman shall bear her iniquity." This trial by ordeal was prescribed in the law of Moses only in cases of doubt. Other cases of this kind fell under *Leviticus 20:10,* which provided: "And the man that committeth adultery with another man's wife, even he that committeth adultery with his neighbour's wife, the adulterer and the adulteress shall surely be put to death." Some authorities suppose that *Exodus 32:20* also alludes to some ancient trial by ordeal. There we are told that Moses took the molten calf made by Aaron for the Israelites "and burnt it with fire, and ground it to powder, and strewed it upon the water, and made the children of Israel drink of it." Since Moses called the sons of Levi and had them slay about three thousand men for their part in the molten calf incident, it is supposed that the drinking of the water in which the powdered molten calf had been strewed was to determine "whoso is on the Lord's side"; that is, who was guilty of insisting on having Aaron make the golden calf. This theory is that the water harmfully affected those who were guilty but left the innocent immune.

What are small cattle?

At the time the King James Version was translated *small cattle* was used in English for cattle smaller in size than oxen, particularly sheep. In *II Chronicles 35:8-9* we are told, in connection with the Passover kept by Josiah in Jerusalem: "And his princes gave willingly unto the people, to the priests, and to the Levites: Hilkiah and Zechariah and Jehiel, rulers of the house of God, gave unto the priests for the passover offerings two thousand and six hundred small cattle, and three hundred oxen. Conaniah also, and Shemaiah and Nethaneel, his brethren, and Hashabiah and Jeiel and Jozabad, chief of the Levites for passover offerings five thousand small cattle, and five hundred oxen." *Isaiah 43:23* says in part: "Thou hast not brought me the small cattle of thy burnt offerings; neither hast thou honoured me with thy sacrifices." In all these cases the Hebrew original means "sheep." In America wheat, oats, barley and other cereal grains are often called *small grain* to distinguish them from maize.

Why are shoes thrown at newly married couples?

The custom of throwing a shoe at a newly married couple is very old and may be a relic of the ancient practice of giving a shoe to another to symbolize the transfer of possession. Sometimes new ownership was symbolized by throwing the shoe on the property in question. "Over Edom will I cast out my shoe," says both *Psalms 60:8* and *Psalms 108:9*, meaning that the country would be subdued. "Now this," we read in *Ruth 4:7*, "was the manner in former time in Israel concerning redeeming and concerning changing, for to confirm all things; a man plucked off his shoe, and gave it to his neighbour: and this was a testimony in Israel." Accordingly, when Boaz's kinsman relinquished his rights in Ruth and her inheritance he "drew off his shoe" in the presence of witnesses. There is an interesting reference to this subject in *Deuteronomy 25*. In the law of Moses it was provided that "if brethren dwell together, and one of them die, and have no child, the wife of the dead shall not marry without unto a stranger: her husband's brother shall go in unto her, and take her to him to wife, and perform the duty of an husband's brother unto her." But "if the man like not to take his brother's wife, then let his brother's wife go up to the gate unto the elders, and say, My husband's brother refuseth to raise up unto his brother a name in Israel, he will not perform the duty of my husband's brother." If, after the elders of the city had spoken to him about the matter, he persisted in his refusal, "Then shall his brother's wife come unto him in the presence of the elders, and *loose his shoe from off his foot,* and spit in his face, and shall answer and say, So shall it be done unto that man that will not build up his brother's house. And his name shall be called in Israel, The house of him that hath his *shoe loosed.*" The author of *Ruth* refers to the custom of loosing the shoe in connection with the levirate marriage as an ancient practice that had gone out of use in his time. The later Jews referred to a prodigal as "one without sandals," because a seller gave his sandals to the buyer as a ratification of the bargain. Among the Anglo-Saxons it was customary for the father to give one of the shoes of the daughter to the bridegroom, who touched her on the head with it, the ceremony signifying the passage of authority and dominion over the daughter from parent to husband. Later, it is supposed, the custom degenerated and the shoe was thrown after the couple as they departed to their new home. Some writers, however, believe that throwing shoes at newly married pairs represents missile-throwing and is a savage survival of the days when the bride was often carried away by force from her people who attempted to drive off her abductor. This theory seems to be partially confirmed by the present practice in Turkey and other parts of the Near East, where the bridegroom alone is chased by the guests and pelted with slippers. The custom of throwing rice, grain, nuts and fruit at a newly wedded pair had a different origin and probably symbolized originally the wish that they might be blessed with children.

Why is the "plural of majesty" used in the Bible?

Several times the plural form of the pronoun is used in the King James Version when God is quoted as speaking. *Genesis 1:26* says: "And God said, Let *us* make man in *our* image, after *our* likeness." In *Genesis 3:22* we are told that the Lord God said, "Behold, the man is become as one of *us,* to know good and evil." In connection with the building of the tower of Babel, according to *Genesis 11:7,* the Lord said, "Go to, let *us* go down, and there confound their language, that they may not understand one another's speech." And the prophet, according to *Isaiah 6:8,* "heard the voice of the Lord, saying, Whom shall I send, and who will go for *us.*" This use of the plural pronoun has been interpreted by some commentators as alluding to the Holy Trinity. Such, however, would be anticipating a thought revealed only in later ages. Another interpretation has been that God was speaking as in a council of angelic beings. It seems more probable that the plural pronoun in the passages just quoted is related to what is known as the plural of majesty. God is there regarded as a super-king. Comparisons of the deity with a king and heaven with a kingdom are common in the Scriptures. The royal *we, us* and *our* were probably adopted by sovereigns because they thought the plural form of pronouns in the first person was more dignified and authoritative when speaking officially for the whole nation and its government. The sovereign, although one person, represents and speaks for many subjects. Lord Coke, in his *Institutes* says that King John was the first English king to use the plural form for one person. He, according to Coke, introduced *nos* and *noster* into grants and other legal documents, while his predecessors were content with *ego* and *meus*. In those days all official documents were written in Latin. An examination of Rymer's *Faedera,* however, shows that the royal *we* was adopted by John's brother and predecessor, Richard the Lion-Hearted. It has been suggested that the royal or majestic plural may be a survival of the time when there were two Roman rulers, who reigned at different capitals and issued identical decrees under their joint authority. Many modern sovereigns, including the king of Great Britain, have discontinued the use of the plural of majesty and speak and write officially in the first person singular. But the Pope employs the plural of majesty, as his predecessors have done since ancient times. Writers often employ *we, us* and *our* instead of *I, me* and *my* to make their style appear more impersonal and to give their writings the stamp of greater authority. It is assumed that by alluding to himself as *we, us* and *our* an author avoids the appearance of egotism that would result from the frequent repetition of the pronouns in the singlar. The editorial *we* used by editors is slightly different in origin and purpose. It is intended to impress the reader with the fact that the writer is understood to be supported in his opinions and statements by the editorial staff collectively. In *Advice to a Young Reviewer,* published in 1807, Edward Copelstan thus ridiculed the practice: "There is a mysterious authority in the plural *we* which no single name, whatever may be its reputation, can acquire." Carl Sandburg, in *Abraham Lincoln, the War Years,* says: "One secret of Lincoln's success in 'captivating the popular mind,' hazarded James R. Lowell, was his use of the capital I without any suggestion of egotism. 'There is no single vowel which men's mouths can pronounce with such difference of effect.' Some men in discourse would use the capital I with offensive challenge, a dry northeast wind giving goose flesh. 'Mr. Lincoln forgets himself so entirely in his object as to give his I the sympathetic and persuasive effect of *We* with the great body of his countrymen.' "

To what does "a Daniel come to judgment" refer?

In *The Merchant of Venice,* after Portia declares that there is no power in Venice that can alter an established decree of the state, Shakespeare has Shylock exclaim: "A Daniel come to judgment! yea, a Daniel!" Later, when the tables are turned, Gratiano takes it up and throws it in the face of the Jew. "A second Daniel, a Daniel, Jew!" he shouts. And again: "A Daniel, still say I; a second Daniel!—I thank thee, Jew, for teaching me that word." The average person would naturally assume that the Jewish merchant referred to something in the *Book of Daniel* as it is printed in the King James Version of the Bible. Such is not the case. Nothing in that book suggests Daniel as the perfect judge. There Daniel appears rather as a sage, wise man, interpreter of dreams and prophet. Among Bible characters Solomon would have been more appropriate for the purposes of the passage in Shakespeare. Shylock referred to an incident related in *The History of Susanna,* a fragment of the *Book of Daniel* that is regarded as apocryphal by Protestants and as deuterocanonical by Catholics. In the time of Shakespeare *The History of Susanna,* along with the other apocryphal books was customarily printed in English Bibles between the Old and New Testaments. This fragment relates a parable that deals with Susanna, the beautiful and virtuous wife of Joakim of Babylon, and that is calculated to illustrate the importance of cross-examining witnesses. Two elders who had been appointed judges attempted to constrain Susanna. Failing in their evil purpose they tried to cover up their own wickedness by testifying falsely that they saw Susanna cavorting with a young man in Joakim's garden. Just as the condemned but innocent woman was being led from the meeting to be thrown over the cliff, an angel of the Lord bestowed a spirit of discernment on a young man named Daniel, who stood up boldly in the midst of the people and reopened the trial. He asked each judge separately and apart what kind of tree it was he saw the couple under. One answered a mastick tree, the other a holm tree. Thus Daniel convicted the judges of false witness, cleared the good name of Susanna and dealt with the wicked ones as they had intended to deal with her. Whether this Daniel and the Daniel in the *Book of Daniel* as accepted by Protestants and Jews is one and the same person is an academic question. In Hebrew *Daniel* literally means "God is my judge," and in some of the old manuscripts *The History of Susanna* bears the subtitle *The Judgment of Daniel.*

What is a *painted Jezebel*?

A bold, flaunting, ambitious, scheming, abandoned and wicked woman is popularly referred to as a painted Jezebel. The term came into English use during the sixteenth century when painting the face was accepted as prima facie evidence that a woman was loose in morals. It was suggested, of course, by Jezebel in the Bible. In *Kings 16* we are told that Ahab, king of Israel, who "did more to provoke the Lord God of Israel to anger than all the kings of Israel that were before him," in addition to walking in the sins of his predecessors, "took to wife Jezebel the daughter of Ethbaal king of the Zidonians." As queen of the northern kingdom the pagan princess introduced Baal worship, "cut off the prophets of the Lord," had Naboth judically murdered by writing letters in the king's name to get possession of his hereditary vineyard in Jezreel, and threatened to kill Elijah and drove him temporarily into retirement. Her name became a byword for wickedness in Israel. *II Kings 9:30* says: "And when Jehu was come to Jezreel, Jezebel heard of it; and she painted her face, and tired her head, and looked out at a window." Her eunuchs tossed her out of the window and she was trampled under the feet of Jehu's horses and eaten by dogs. In later times Jezebel became the symbol of idolatrous seduction. *Revelation 2:20* says: "Notwithstanding I have a few things against thee, because thou sufferest that woman Jezebel, which calleth herself a prophetess, to teach and to seduce my servants to commit fornication, and to eat things sacrificed unto idols."

Does the Bible mention holy water?

Holy water occurs only once in the King James Version of the Bible. In connection with the exposition of "the law of jealousies" in *Numbers 5* it is said in Verse 17 that "the priest shall take holy water in an earthen vessel." Presumably this holy water was water from the tabernacle laver in which the priests performed their ritual washing before approaching the altar. In the Christian church holy water as a sacramental blessed by a priest to invoke God's blessing on those who use it is believed to date from about the second century.

What is the unpardonable sin?

Unpardonable sin does not occur in the Bible. It is the name given to the sin against the Holy Ghost because Jesus referred to it as the one sin that admitted of no forgiveness. In *Matthew 12:31-32* Jesus says: "Wherefore I say unto you, All manner of sin and blasphemy shall be forgiven unto men: but the blasphemy against the Holy Ghost shall not be forgiven unto men. And whosoever speaketh a word against the Son of man, it shall be forgiven him: but whosoever speaketh against the Holy Ghost, it shall not be forgiven him, neither in this world, neither in the world to come." Similar passages occur in *Mark* and *Luke*. Theologians differ as to the exact nature of the unpardonable sin and the subject is an abstruse one among them. The context of the passages referred to indicates that the sin against the Holy Ghost consists of assigning his works to Satan or of denying out of pure malice the divine character of such works. When Jesus made the statement just quoted the Pharisees had accused him of casting out devils by the prince of devils instead of by the spirit of God. Some commentators interpret the words "blasphemy against the Holy Ghost" in their most literal sense and define the unpardonable sin as the utterance of an insult against the Divine Spirit. By others the sin against the Holy Ghost is held to mean final impenitence or perseverance in "mortal sin" until death. A looser interpretation places in this class all sins committed in downright malice, especially those directly opposed to charity and goodness, supposedly the characteristic qualities of the Holy Ghost. "There is a sin unto death: I do not say that he shall pray for it," says the author of *I John,* and some suppose that *Hebrews 6:4-6* refers to the experience that a person must go through to commit that sin, that is, become enlightened and partake of the Holy Ghost and then fall away. The idea of unpardonable sin was borrowed from the Old Testament. For instance, *Numbers 15:30-31* says: "But the soul that doeth ought presumptuously, whether he be born in the land, or a stranger, the same reproacheth the Lord; and that soul shall be cut off from among his people. Because he hath despised the word of the Lord, and hath broken his commandment, that soul shall utterly be cut off; his iniquity shall be upon him." In other words, no sacrificial atonement was acceptable for a wilful offense and under the Mosaic law a person who sinned deliberately was not forgiven. Both in the Old and New Testaments blasphemy is the unpardonable sin. Presumably "the great transgression" mentioned in *Psalms 19:13* refers to the same offense, i.e., presuming upon God's mercy and knowingly doing what is wrong, which is held to be sin in the first degree.

Where was the land of Goshen?

The land of Goshen was the country on the eastern borders of Egypt that Pharaoh assigned to Joseph's kinsmen and where their descendants continued to dwell until the Exodus. The vast region designated Egypt on modern maps is not the Egypt of the Pharaohs. Ancient Egypt consisted only of the Nile Valley, the Fayum and the Delta—a long narrow strip of land watered each year by the inundations of the Nile. The land of Goshen lay somewhere between the Delta and the Isthmus of Suez and was not in ancient Egypt proper, although it was under the jurisdiction of the Pharaohs. Joseph told his brethren that they would be "near unto" him in the land of Goshen, and he himself "went up" to meet Jacob his father when he came down from Canaan before taking him to the Egyptian monarch. Some authorities suppose that the capital of the land of Goshen was on or near the site of the present Fakus. Jacob and his family of sixty-five were semi-nomad shepherds and they were given land that produced an abundance of grass. Whether this region was previously uninhabited or sparsely populated is difficult to say, although it appears that Pharaoh's cattle were pastured there. From the Bible we learn that the land of Goshen was fruitful in edible vegetables, that there was a good supply of fish and that ultimately it supported a population of Israelites mightier and more numerous than the Egyptians themselves. Passages in *Joshua* indicate that a city and a district in Palestine were also called Goshen. Since the land of Goshen was productive, at least from the viewpoint of the nomadic shepherds from Canaan, and since it was exempted from the ten plagues, the name is often applied figuratively to any place of plenty, a refuge from evil, or a long-desired goal. The Bible indicates clearly that the Israelites did not all continue to live in the land of Goshen, but were scattered among the Egyptians during the days of their bondage.

How did Palestine get its name?

It is an interesting fact that Palestine, the historic homeland of the Jews, did not receive its name from the Israelites, but from their ancient enemies, the Philistines. *Palestine* is derived through Greek and Latin from *Philistia,* a strip of sea-coast inhabited by the Philistines, who were a non-Semitic people supposed to have come originally from Crete and other Greek islands. *Philistia,* for the land of the Philistines, occurs several times in the Old Testament. *Psalms 60:8* says: "Moab is my washpot; over Edom will I cast out my shoe: Philistia, triumph thou because of me." *In Psalms 87:4* we read: "I will make mention of Rahab and Babylon to them that know me: behold Philistia, and Tyre, with Ethiopia." *Psalms 108:9* says: "Moab is my washpot; over Edom will I cast out my shoe: over Philistia will I triumph." Herodotus appears to have been the first to refer to Palestine by that name. The Father of History uses several phrases such as "the Phoenicians and the Syrians of Palestine" and "in the part of Syria called Palestine." Josephus in his *Antiquities of the Jews* wrote: "Now all the children of Mesraim (apparently one of the four sons of Ham), being eight in number, possessed the country from Gaza to Egypt, though it retained the name of one only, the Philistim; for the Greeks call part of that country Palestine." The Greeks naturally had more knowledge of the Philistines, a seacoast people of warriors and sea traders, than they did of the Israelites in the interior. The Latin form *Palestina* occurs several times in the King James Version of the Bible. *Exodus 15:14* says: "The people shall hear, and be afraid: sorrow shall take hold on the inhabitants of Palestina." In *Isaiah 14* the prophet says: "Rejoice not thou, whole Palestina, because the rod of him that smote thee is broken," and "Howl, O gate; cry, O city; thou, whole Palestina, art dissolved." Only once is the modern English form *Palestine* used. *Joel 3:4* says: "Yea, and what have ye to do with me, O Tyre, and Zidon, and all the coasts of Palestine?" *Palestine* in no form occurs in the New Testament. At first this region, or part of it, was called Canaan, or the land of Canaan, because it was settled by Canaan, the son of Ham and the grandson of Noah. The Canaanites were of Semitic stock. Originally *Canaanites* was applied only to the peoples inhabiting the lowland coasts of Phoenicia and Philistinia, but in time it became the general name for all the inhabitants of ancient Palestine. Canaan, where Abraham and the other patriarchs had sojourned temporarily as strangers, was promised to Abraham and his seed as a permanent abode and henceforth was called the Promised Land. *Exodus 6:4* says: "And I have also established my covenant with them, to give them the land of Canaan, the land of their pilgrimage, wherein they were strangers." Again *Exodus 12:26*: "And it shall come to pass, when ye come to the land which the Lord will give you, according as he hath promised, that ye shall keep this service." *Promised Land* in that exact form is not found in the English Bible. This was the country described in *Joshua 5:6* and elsewhere in the Old Testament as "a land that floweth with milk and honey." After the conquest of the Promised Land by the Israelites under Joshua it became known as Israel, or the Land of Israel. But the Philistine plain by the sea was never conquered by the Israelites, even under David, and it did not become a part of the country as a whole until after the Israelites were conquered by foreign foes. *Holy Land,* still widely used as a popular name for Palestine, occurs only in *Zechariah 2:12*, which reads: "And the Lord shall inherit Judah his portion in the holy land, and shall choose Jerusalem again." But in *Exodus 19:5-8* the Lord told Moses on Sinai to say to the house of Jacob and the children of Israel: "Now therefore, if ye will obey my voice indeed, and keep my covenant, then ye shall be a peculiar treasure unto me above all people: for all the earth is mine: and ye shall be unto me a kingdom of priests, and an holy nation." *Jewry* occurs once in the Old Testament, but refers to Judaea rather than to all of Palestine. "Then was Daniel brought in before the king," says *Daniel 5:13*. "And the king spake and said unto Daniel, Art thou that Daniel, which art of the children of the captivity of Judah, whom the king my father brought out of Jewry?" This term occurs twice in the New Testament. *John 7:1* says: "After these things Jesus walked in Galilee: for he would not walk in Jewry, because the Jews sought to kill him." *Luke 23:4-5* says: "Then said Pilate to the chief priests and to the people, He stirreth up the people, teaching throughout all Jewry, beginning from Galilee to this place." In this latter instance *Jewry* appears to refer to the Jews throughout Palestine rather than to the country itself.

What does *Babel* mean?

The popular phrase, *tower of Babel,* does not occur in the Bible. *Babel* is the Anglicized form of the Hebrew *Babbil,* the native name of Babylon. In Babylonian the term literally means "gate of God." It has no known Semitic root and is rendered *Babylon* in the King James Version of the Bible everywhere except in *Genesis 10* and *11*. *Genesis 10:8-10* says: "And Cush begat Nimrod; he began to be a mighty one in the earth. He was a mighty hunter before the Lord: wherefore it is said, Even as Nimrod the mighty hunter before the Lord. And the beginning of his kingdom was Babel, and Erech, and Accad, and Calneh, in the land of Shinar." In the Bible *Babel* is particularly associated with confusion and it may have originally had that meaning in Babylonian, although it is more probable that this significance was owing to what is known as folk-etymology. The building of the tower of Babel is related in *Genesis 11:1-9,* which reads: "And the whole earth was of one language, and of one speech. And it came to pass, as they journeyed from the east, that they found a plain in the land of Shinar; and they dwelt there. And they said one to another, Go to, let us make brick, and burn them throughly. And they had brick for stone, and slime had they for mortar. And they said, Go to, let us build us a city and a tower, whose top may reach unto heaven; and let us make us a name, lest we be scattered abroad upon the face of the whole earth. And the Lord came down to see the city and the tower, which the children of men builded. And the Lord said, Behold, the people is one, and they have all one language; and this they begin to do: and now nothing will be restrained from them, which they have imagined to do. Go to, let us go down, and there confound their language, that they may not understand one another's speech. So the Lord scattered them abroad from thence upon the face of the earth and they left off to build the city. Therefore is the name of it called Babel; because the Lord did there confound the language of all the earth: and from thence did the Lord scatter them abroad upon the face of all the earth." It should be noted that the Bible does not say that the children of men built merely a tower at Babel, but "a city and a tower." Babylon, among all the cities of the ancient world, was noted for its high towers, walls, palaces, buildings and other structures. From this account we get *Babel* in the sense of an impossibly lofty structure, a visionary scheme, a turbulent assemblage, a scene of utter confusion or a place of uproar. A confusion of voices, sounds and noises, in which nothing can be heard but the hubbub, is said to be a perfect Babel.

How did the Israelites pay tithes?

The payment of tithes in ancient Israel was a much more complicated procedure than most people might suppose. In fact, it was about as complicated as modern income taxes. Israel was a theocracy and religious and civil administration were essentially one and the same thing. *Tithe* is an old Anglo-Saxon word used in the Bible to translate a Hebrew word in the Old Testament and a Greek word in the New Testament meaning "a tenth." The tithe was a tenth part of a person's income. But in the early days Israel was a crude agricultural society and paying the tithe was not so simple as merely paying to the government a tenth part of a person's monetary income. It appears that there was some kind of practice of offering a tenth of one's gain to a sanctuary in Palestine in the time of Abraham, long before Moses received the law from Sinai after the Exodus from Egypt. *Genesis 14:18-20* says: "And Melchizedek king of Salem brought forth bread and wine: and he was the priest of the most high God. And he blessed him, and said, Blessed be Abram of the most high God, possessor of heaven and earth: and blessed be the most high God, which hath delivered thine enemies into thy hand. And he gave him tithes of all." This is referred to in *Hebrews 7:6*, which, referring to Melchizedek, says: "But he whose descent is not counted from them received tithes of Abraham, and blessed him that had the promises." According to *Genesis 28:22*, Jacob, on the way from Beersheba to visit Laban at Padanaram, vowed a vow to God saying that "of all that thou shalt give me I will surely give the tenth part unto thee." In the law of Moses there are several provisions dealing with tithes. *Leviticus 27:31-33* says: "And all the tithe of the land, whether of the seed of the land, or of the fruit of the tree, is the Lord's: it is holy unto the Lord. And if a man will at all redeem ought of his tithes, he shall add thereto the fifth part thereof. And concerning the tithe of the herd, or of the flock, even of whatsoever passeth under the rod, the tenth shall be holy unto the Lord. He shall not search whether it be good or bad, neither shall he change it: and if he change it at all, then both it and the change thereof shall be holy; it shall not be redeemed." The law of Moses regarded tithes as belonging to God as the real owner of the land. The tithe of the land, analogous to the firstling of sacrificial animals, was in the nature of a rent paid by the people as the tenants of God. *Deuteronomy 14:22-29* says: "Thou shalt truly tithe all the increase of thy seed, that the field bringeth forth year by year. And thou shalt eat before the Lord thy God, in the place which he shall choose to place his name there, the tithe of thy corn, of thy wine, and of thine oil, and the firstlings of thy herds and of thy flocks; that thou mayest learn to fear the Lord thy God always. And if the way be too long for thee, so that thou art not able to carry it; or if the place be too far from thee, which the Lord thy God shall choose to set his name there, when the Lord thy God hath blessed thee: then shalt thou turn it into money, and bind up the money in thine hand, and shalt go unto the place which the Lord thy God shall choose: and thou shalt bestow that money for whatsoever thy soul lusteth after, for oxen, or for sheep, or for wine, or for strong drink, or for whatsoever thy soul desireth: and thou shalt eat there before the Lord thy God, and thou shalt rejoice, thou, and thine household, and the Levite that is within thy gates; thou shalt not forsake him; for he hath no part nor inheritance with thee. At the end of three years thou shalt bring forth all the tithe of thine increase the same year, and shalt lay it up within thy gates: and the Levite, (because he hath no part nor inheritance with thee,) and the stranger, and the fatherless, and the widow, which are within thy gates, shall come, and shall eat and be satisfied; that the Lord thy God may bless thee in all the work of thine hand which thou doest." The exact difference between tithes and first-fruits is not entirely clear, except that, according to *Deuteronomy 26*, the first-fruits were offered to the priests. The tribe of Levi did not receive an allotment of territory but was given tithes instead. *Numbers 18:21* says: "And, behold, I have given the children of Levi all the tenth in Israel for an inheritance, for their service which they serve, even the service of the tabernacle of the congregation." The Levites, however, were required to give part of the tithes to the priests. *Numbers 18:26-28* says: "Thus speak unto the Levites, and say unto them, When ye take of the children of Israel the tithes which I have given you from them for your inheritance, then ye shall offer up an heave offering of it for the Lord, even a tenth part of the tithe. And this your heave offering shall be reckoned unto you, as though it were the corn of the threshing floor, and as the fulness of the winepress. Thus ye also shall offer an heave offering unto the Lord of all your tithes, which ye receive of the children of Israel; and ye shall give thereof the Lord's heave offering to Aaron the priest." The Talmud designates the tithe for the support of the Levites as the "first tithe" and that for the support of the poor and unfortunate as the "second tithe." From all this it can readily be seen that paying tithes under the Mosaic law was a rather complicated procedure. In the time of Jesus all male Jews twenty years of age or over in Palestine were expected to give one-tenth of everything they produced to maintain the temple and religious services. Since the two forms of tithes prescribed in the law of Moses were later combined it is said that the total contribution of a Jew amounted to one-fifth or twenty percent of his income. There are few references to the tithes in the later historical books of the Bible. One of these is in *II Chronicles 31:5-6,* which, referring to the passover held in Jerusalem by King Hezekiah, says: "And as soon as the commandment came abroad, the children of Israel brought in abundance the first-fruits of corn, wine, and oil, and honey, and of all the increase of the field; and the tithe of all things brought they in abundantly. And concerning the children of Israel and Judah, that dwelt in the cities of Judah, they also brought in the tithe of oxen and sheep, and the tithe of holy things which were consecrated unto the Lord their God, and laid them by heaps." In *Nehemiah 10:38* we read: "And the priest the son of Aaron shall be with the Levites, when the Levites take tithes: and the Levites shall bring up the tithe of the tithes unto the house of our God, to the chambers, into the treasure house." *Malachi 3:10* says: "Bring ye all the tithes into the storehouse, that there may be meat in mine house, and prove me now herewith, saith the Lord of hosts, if I will not open you the windows of heaven, and pour you out a blessing, that there shall not be room enough to receive it." In the time of Jesus devout Jews regarded the payment of tithes as an essential requirement of Judaism and failure to pay it was looked upon as disloyalty to Jehovah. "I give tithes of all that I possess," says the Pharisee in Jesus's parable of the Pharisee and publican who went up into the temple to pray, according to *Luke 18:12.* Apparently the Pharisees even tithed their garden herbs. *Matthew 23:23* quotes Jesus as saying: "Woe unto you, scribes and Pharisees, hypocrites! for ye pay tithe of mint and anise and cummin, and have omitted the weightier matters of the law, judgment, mercy, and faith: these ought ye to have done, and not to leave the other undone." The paying of tithes as a regular practice was discontinued by the Jews after the destruction of the temple in 70 A.D. by the Romans. Later tithing in a simpler form was adopted by the Christians in various countries but the practice is not so common now as it was formerly. Tithing, however, is still required by all members of the Mormon church.

Who killed six hundred men with an ox goad?

Judges 3:31 says that after Ehud "was Shamgar the son of Anath, which slew of the Philistines six hundred men with an ox goad: and he also delivered Israel." *Goad* is an old Teutonic word related in origin to *gad,* "a whip." The ox goad of Biblical times was a stick about nine feet long, pointed at one end or fitted with a sharp brad and used in urging oxen, especially in plowing. That the ox goads were fitted with metal tips is indicated by *I Samuel 13:19-21,* which reads: "Now there was no smith found throughout all the land of Israel: for the Philistines said, Lest the Hebrews make them swords or spears: but all the Israelites went down to the Philistines, to sharpen every man his share, and his coulter, and his axe, and his mattock. Yet they had a file for the mattocks, and for the coulters, and for the forks, and for the axes, and to sharpen the goads." In *Ecclesiastes 12:11* the Preacher says: "The words of the wise are as goads, and as nails fastened by the masters of assemblies, which are given from one shepherd." The Hebrew word rendered *goad* in the Old Testament corresponds to the Greek word rendered *pricks* twice in the New Testament. According to *Acts 9:5,* Paul near Damascus heard the voice of the Lord saying: "I am Jesus whom thou persecutest: it is hard for thee to kick against the pricks." Later, according to *Acts 26:14,* Paul said before Agrippa: "And when we were all fallen to the earth, I heard a voice speaking unto me, and saying in the Hebrew tongue, Saul, Saul, why persecutest thou me? it is hard for thee to kick against the pricks." Here Paul is pictured as in the position of a plow ox and Jesus as the driver holding the goad.

Does the Bible mention the sundial?

The sundial is referred to twice in the Bible. *II Kings 20:8-11* says: "And Hezekiah said unto Isaiah, What shall be the sign that the Lord will heal me, and that I shall go up into the house of the Lord the third day? And Isaiah said, This sign shalt thou have of the Lord, that the Lord will do the thing that he hath spoken: shall the shadow go forward ten degrees, or go back ten degrees? And Hezekiah answered, It is a light thing for the shadow to go down ten degrees: say, but let the shadow return backward ten degrees. And Isaiah the prophet cried unto the Lord: and he brought the shadow ten degrees backward, by which it had gone down in the *dial* of Ahaz." This same incident is alluded to in *Isaiah 38:7-8,* which uses the term *sun dial* and which reads: "And this shall be a sign unto thee from the Lord, that the Lord will do this thing that he hath spoken; behold, I will bring again the shadow of the degrees, which is gone down in the sun dial of Ahaz, ten degrees backward. So the sun returned ten degrees, by which degrees it was gone down." No other timepiece is mentioned in the Bible. All of the books of the Bible were written before the invention of mechanical clocks. It is believed that the sundial was developed by the Babylonians about five thousand years ago, and it was only natural that the ancient Israelites should have known of it and used it. The sundial was the earliest instrument for measuring the time of the day. Even before the invention of the sundial primitive man no doubt learned to keep track of the time roughly by his own shadow or that of some other object.

Why was the king of Egypt called Pharaoh?

Pharaoh is a Hebraized form of the title of the rulers of ancient Egypt. The term occurs as *Pheron* in the Greek of Herodotus. Etymologists are generally agreed that it is derived from Egyptian *per-'o,* meaning "the great house," which was the name the Egyptians applied to the royal establishment. There are two theories as to how *Pharaoh* became the title and generic appellation of the rulers of Upper and Lower Egypt. One is that it evolved from the name of the royal palace and gradually became identified with the chief occupant in the same way that in later times the Holy See became the designation for the Popes, the Sublime Porte for the Sultans of Turkey, and the White House for the Presidents of the United States. The other is that an early ruler of Egypt was named *Pharaoh* and that the term gradually became the name and title of his successors after the manner of Caesar and Ptolemy. This title has survived in English usage almost entirely because of its frequent occurrence in the Old Testament. In many instances *Pharaoh* is used in the Bible alone as a synonym of "king of Egypt." Occasionally it occurs in association with the name of an Egyptian ruler. The prophets sometimes used it as a symbol for Egypt rather than for a specific person. Despite the great amount of historical and archaeological research that has been done on the subject, very few, if any, of the Pharaohs mentioned in the Bible have been identified beyond question. The obscurity of the references, the differences in languages and the meagerness of chronological data all contribute to make complete identification impossible. The Israelites in the sacred books left us few clews about the identity of the Egyptian rulers, and the Egyptians in turn were silent about the Israelites. Egyptian inscriptions are generally too meager and vague to be of much help. Likewise the chronologies and names of the two peoples are confusing and difficult to reconcile. The Egyptians never knew their country by the name *Egypt*. That name was given to the country by the Greeks and was never used by the ancient Egyptians themselves. On monuments along the Nile the country is generally called *KEM*. In the Old Testament the most frequent Hebrew name for Egypt is *Mizraim,* which is a plural. The poetical books of the Bible sometimes refer to Egypt as the land of Ham and as *Rahab,* meaning "proud" or "insolent." Very few of the place names mentioned in the Bible as being in Egypt or near its borders can be definitely identified. Although some thirteen hundred different places and localities mentioned in the Bible as being in Palestine have been satisfactorily identified in modern times, there are hundreds of others that probably never can be identified with any degree of accuracy. Historians are generally of the opinion that the Egyptians did not apply *Pharaoh* or their native equivalent to their rulers until about 1000 B.C. Apparently the Hebrew writers employed the term retroactively and projected the name and title back into a period when it was unknown to the Egyptians themselves. It appears that it was restricted to male rulers and not applicable to queens. The first Biblical Pharaoh appears in connection with Abraham's visit to Egypt. This Pharaoh, as well as those of the time of Joseph, Moses, Hadad and Solomon, cannot be identified with historical individuals, although in some cases scholars have tentatively identified their dynasties. It is believed that the Hyksos or shepherd kings who reigned in Egypt at the time Joseph arrived were of Semitic stock. This fact may explain their friendliness toward Joseph and his brethren. After the expulsion of the shepherd kings, who had befriended the Israelites, the New Empire took shape. It is believed to have been formed about 1587 B.C. and to have lasted about a thousand years. It is not known whether the Pharaoh whose daughter brought up Moses was the same Pharaoh of the oppression after Moses was grown up. They may have been different rulers. "Now there arose up a new king over Egypt, which knew not Joseph," we are told in *Exodus 1:8*. In the next chapter it is related that "when Pharaoh heard this thing, he sought to slay Moses.

But Moses fled from the face of Pharaoh, and dwelt in the land of Midian." Nor is it known for certain that the same Pharaoh was ruling when Moses many years later returned to deliver the Israelites from their bondage in Egypt. According to Talmudic tradition, the name of the daughter of Pharaoh who found Moses in the bulrushes was Bathia. The greatest Pharaoh of the New Empire was Rameses II, and many suppose that he was the Pharaoh of the oppression, but not of the exodus. In two Biblical instances a personal name is used with the title. *Jeremiah 44:30* says: "Thus saith the Lord; Behold, I will give Pharaoh-hophra king of Egypt into the hands of his enemies, and into the hand of them that seek his life." This Pharaoh is believed to be the same as the historical Apries, who reigned about 588-569 B.C. Pharaoh-nechoh who, according to *II Kings 23*, captured Jerusalem, deposed King Jehoahaz, put Jehoiakim in his place and imposed tribute on the land, probably was Necho II of history, who reigned about 609-593 B.C. Shishak who, according to *I Kings 14*, despoiled the temple in Rehoboam's time, is referred to only as king of Egypt and not as Pharaoh. He is supposed to be the historical Sheshonk I, a Libyan who seized the Egyptian throne about 945 B.C. The title became defunct after the Greek Ptolemies began to rule Egypt, if it had not fallen into desuetude long before.

Where did the Israelites cross the Red Sea?

The exact point at which Moses led the Israelites across the Red Sea cannot be identified for certain. It is generally supposed that the Israelites made their famous crossing at the narrow Strait of Suez, where the distance from shore to shore is less than a mile. Emmanuel Las Cases, in his *Memorial de Ste Helene*, quotes Napoleon Bonaparte as saying that during his Egyptian campaign in 1798 he marched his army on dry land across the same place where the Israelites crossed. There is nothing particularly improbable about this statement, because in the time of Moses the Red Sea undoubtedly extended several miles farther northward than it did in the time of Napoleon. It is believed that in ancient times Lake Timsah and the Bitter Lakes were connected with each other and with the Gulf of Suez by shallow water. At that time the Gulf of Suez, an arm of the Red Sea, probably extended several miles farther north than it does at present. Those who attempt to explain the crossing by the Israelites as a practical matter without any element of the miraculous say that a strong northeast wind blowing all night and acting in conjunction with an ebbing tide may have laid virtually bare the land beneath the shallow water and left a safe path for the Israelites across the gulf with pools on each side as defensive "walls" against the Egyptians. In other words, the combined effect of wind and tide was to cause "the sea to go back" and "stand upright as a heap" in a wall-like formation. It was reported just before the Suez Canal was begun that the Red Sea at this point had so silted and become blocked with sand that a camel could hardly bathe its legs there. Even today there are little more than pools of water left on the bottom of the upper gulf when the tide is low and the prevailing northwest winds are blowing strongly. But the safe crossing of the Red Sea by the Hebrews and the complete destruction of the pursuing Egyptian army made a profound impression on the men who wrote the Old Testament and they regarded the event as miraculous. In *Exodus 14:15-28* we are told: "And the Lord said unto Moses. . . . lift thou up thy rod, and stretch out thine hand over the sea, and divide it: and the children of Israel shall go on dry ground through the midst of the sea. . . . And Moses stretched out his hand over the sea; and the Lord caused the sea to go back by a strong east wind all that night, and made the sea dry land, and the waters were divided. And the children of Israel went into the midst of the sea upon the dry ground: and the waters were a wall unto them on their right hand, and on their left. And the Egyptians pursued, and went in after them to the midst of the sea . . . . And Moses stretched forth his hand over the sea, and the sea returned to his strength when the morning appeared; and the Egyptians fled against it; and the Lord overthrew the Egyptians in the midst of the sea. And the waters returned, and covered the chariots, and the horsemen, and all the host of Pharaoh that came into the sea after them." This event, whether or not owing partly to a natural cause, was regarded by the Israelites as the greatest of all the wonders performed by Moses in Egypt. According to a Rabbinic legend, Pharaoh alone among the Egyptian host escaped with his life. A later Jewish legend says he never has and never will die, but stands at the portals of the netherworld and asks each tyrant who appears: "Why didn't you profit by my example?" Those who try to explain the Red Sea crossing, as well as many other Bible miracles, merely as a poetical account of a natural phenomenon meet with difficulties. This is not the only reference in the Bible to the miraculous dividing of waters. Something similar happened when Joshua led the Israelites across the Jordan into the Promised Land. *Joshua 3* tells us: "And as they that bare the ark were come unto Jordan, and the feet of the priests that bare the ark were dipped in the brim of the water, (for Jordan overfloweth all his banks all the time of harvest), That the waters which came down from above stood and rose up and upon an heap very far from the city Adam, that is beside Zaretan: and those that came down toward the sea of the plain, even the salt sea, failed, and were cut off: and the people passed over right against Jericho. . . . And the priests that bare the ark of the covenant of the Lord stood firm on dry ground in the midst of Jordan, and all the Israelites passed over on dry ground, until all the people were passed clean over Jordan." From *II Kings 2* we learn that both the prophets Elijah and Elisha also performed the miracle of the parting of the waters. While fifty men of the sons of the prophets who were at Jericho "stood to view afar off" Elijah and Elisha "stood by Jordan. And Elijah took his mantle, and wrapped it together, and smote the waters, and they were divided hither and thither, so that they two went over on dry ground." After Elijah had been taken by a whirlwind into heaven, Elisha "took up also the mantle of Elijah that fell from him, and went back, and stood by the bank of Jordan; and he took the mantle of Elijah that fell from him, and smote the waters, and said, Where is the Lord God of Elijah? and when he also had smitten the waters, they parted hither and thither: and Elisha went over."

Does the Bible forbid women to wear men's clothes?

The interchange of attire between men and women is forbidden in the Mosaic law. *Deuteronomy 22:5* says: "A woman shall not wear that which pertaineth unto a man, neither shall a man put on a woman's garment: for whosoever doeth these things is an abomination unto the Lord thy God." This provision may have originally alluded to certain heathen rites practiced in Syria in which men and women among the idolatrous worshippers exchanged dress. St. Paul, however, who was brought up a strict Jew and was familiar with the Mosaic law, may have been influenced by this passage in arriving at the conclusion that it was improper for women to imitate men in worshipping with their heads uncovered, as expounded in *I Corinthians 11:3-16*.

What is meant by Gog and Magog?

Gog and *Magog* are used rather obscurely in the Scriptures. *Genesis 10:2* says: "The sons of Japheth, Gomer, and Magog, and Madai, and Javan, and Tubal, and Mesheeh, and Tiras." Some authorities suppose that here *Magog* is a mistake for *Gog*. The theory is that an early scribe, in copying the passage, intended to write *Gog*, but by mistake first wrote the initial syllable of the following *Madai* and carelessly omitted to erase it. In *Chronicles 5:4* Gog is mentioned as the son of Shemaiah in the line of Reuben. But in *Ezekiel 38* and *39* Gog appears as the chief prince of Meshech and Tubal, which is also called the land of Magog. The prophet foretold that Gog of the land of Magog would be defeated and five-sixths of his army destroyed when he came "up from the north parts" and invaded "the mountains of Israel." Here it is clear that Gog and Magog are the names respectively of a king and his supposed kingdom, but the passages contain only vague and uncertain indications as to the identity of the ruler and the location of his realm. In his *Antiquities of the Jews* Josephus says that Magog, the son of Japheth, son of Noah, "founded those that from him were named magogites, but who are by the Greeks called Scythians." Some have supposed *Gog* to be merely a title of royal dignity, similar to the Pharaoh of Egypt; but since the ruler in question is represented in *Ezekiel* as being accompanied in his invasion of the land of Israel by the Persians, Ethiopians, Libyans and others, it has been suggested that the name may be a general designation for all the enemies of the Israelites. The latter theory finds some confirmation in the fact that in *Revelation 20:8-10* Gog and Magog are linked together as if they were both persons and they seem to symbolize all future enemies of the kingdom of God, particularly the hostile powers that are to manifest themselves in the world immediately before the end of things. Probably taking their cue from this passage, various writers of the seventh century identified Gog with Anti-Christ. It seems more probable, however, that the Gog mentioned in the Old Testament was actually the ruler of a non-Semitic nation lying to the north of Palestine—in Asia Minor, Armenia, Syria or Scythia. Gog and Magog also figure in English legend and are the popular or fanciful names of two gigantic wooden statues in the Guildhall in London. These effigies, which are fourteen feet in height, were carved in 1708 by Richard Saunders to replace two similar statues which were destroyed in the Great Fire of 1666 and which had been in London at least since the reign of Henry V (1387-1422). The legend of Gog and Magog is of unknown date and origin. In the medieval romance entitled *The Recuyell of the Historye of Troye,* Gog and Magog are the sole survivors of the thirty-three wicked daughters of the Emperor Diocletian, who, after being set adrift in a boat for murdering their husbands, reached the shores of England, where they formed an unnatural union with demons. Aided by his companions, Brute, a Trojan refugee and the legendary founder of London, killed all the descendants of the monstrous union except the two giants Gog and Magog, who were taken in chains to London (*Troynovant,* New Troy) and compelled to serve as porters at the royal palace, which stood on the site of the present Guildhall. This legend seems to have been confused with another. Geoffrey of Monmouth (1110?-1154), who professed to base his work on an ancient book entitled *Britannici sermonis,* says in his *Chronicles* that a giant named Goemot or Goemagot dominated the western horn of England and was slain by Corineus, one of Brute's companions. A Welsh translation spells the name *Gogmagog* and that may have been Geoffrey's original spelling. A few miles southeast of Cambridge is a knoll known as Gogmagog Hill, into which the giant is said to have been transformed after his advances had been rejected by the nymph Granta.

How did the Red Sea get its name?

The ancient Hebrews called the oceanic gulf between Egypt and Arabia *yam suph,* "sea of reeds," clearly referring to the shallow, marshy upper reaches of the gulf that were best known to the Israelites. Reeds abounded in the northern part of the Gulf of Suez and in Lake Timsah, which was connected by shallow water with the gulf in ancient times. For some unknown reason the Greek translators of the Septuagint Version of the Hebrew Scriptures translated *yam suph* ("Sea of reeds") as *He Eruthra Thalassa,* "the Red Sea." Several centuries later St. Jerome, whose work formed the basis of the Latin Vulgate version of the Bible, adopted the same translation and it finally found its way into the King James Version. There are many conjectures as to why the Hebrew scholars who translated the Old Testament into Greek at Alexandria called this body of water the Red Sea. The most logical is that the translation was influenced by the Hebrew *Edom.* The land in southeastern Palestine bordering on the Red Sea was called Edom and the inhabitants were supposed to be the descendants of Jacob's brother Esau. *Edom* is derived from a Hebrew word meaning "red." Possibly the region was called Edom because of Esau's reddish complexion. *Genesis 25:24* says: "And when her days to be delivered were fulfilled, behold, there were twins in her womb. And the first came out red, all over like an hairy garment; and they called his name Esau." But *Genesis 25:30* adds: "And Esau said to Jacob, Feed me, I pray thee, with that same red pottage; for I am faint: therefore was his name called Edom." Because the land of the Edomites bordered on this body of water it came to be called the

Sea of Edom, or the Red Sea. *Sea of Edom,* however, does not occur in the Bible. Other conjectures are that the Red Sea received that name from the color of the inhabitants on the eastern shore, from the great number of plankton, microscopic seaweed or other reddish plants growing in the water, from the reddish corals in the water, or from the reddish hue of the sandstone mountains in neighboring Edom. But the normal colors of the water of the Red Sea are green and blue, and there is no evidence that they ever have been red, notwithstanding many statements to the contrary. The Greeks and Romans extended *Red Sea* to include the Persian Gulf and all that part of the Indian Ocean touching the shores of western Asia. Josephus, for instance, says: "Euphrates also, as well as Tigris, goes down into the Red Sea." The Red Sea is referred to only twice in the New Testament. *Acts 7:36* says: "He brought them out, after that he had shewed wonders and signs in the land of Egypt, and in the Red Sea, and in the wilderness forty years." "By faith they passed through the Red Sea as by dry land: which the Egyptians assaying to do were drowned," says *Hebrews 11:29.*

How large were the Biblical giants?

Genesis 6:1-4 says: "And it came to pass, when man began to multiply on the face of the earth, and daughters were born unto them, that the sons of God saw the daughters of men that they were fair; and they took them wives of all which they chose. And the Lord said, My spirit shall not always strive with man, for that he also is flesh: yet his days shall be an hundred and twenty years. There were giants in the earth in those days; and also after that, when the sons of God came in unto the daughters of men, and they bare children to them, the same became mighty men which were of old, men of renown." This seems to suggest that supernatural beings married with human beings and produced a race of giants. According to *Numbers 13:32-33,* the men whom Moses sent to search and spy out the land of Canaan brought back "an evil report" to the children of Israel in the wilderness, saying, "The land, through which we have gone to search it, is a land that eateth up the inhabitants thereof; and all the people that we saw in it are men of a great stature. And there we saw the giants, the sons of Anak, which come of the giants: and we were in our own sight as grasshoppers, and so we were in their sight." *Anakim,* the Hebrew plural of *Anak,* literally means "long-necked ones." It comes from a Hebrew word similar to that meaning "neck" and the term may refer either to the great size or the great strength of the Anakim. *Joshua 14:15* says:

"And the name of Hebron before was Kirjath-arba; which Arba was a great man among the Anakims." Hebron was allotted by Joshua to Caleb, and in *Joshua 15:14* we are told that "Caleb drove thence the three sons of Anak, Sheshai, and Ahiman, and Talmai, the children of Anak." The Anakim also occupied a town near Hebron called *Kirjath-sepher*, which literally means "book-town" and which might be taken to indicate that the giants had a national literature of some kind. A strip of territory on both sides the Jordan north of Jerusalem and the reputed home of the giants is several times referred to as "the valley of the giants" in the Old Testament. They seem to have kept a foothold in the land even in the face of the incoming Canaanite peoples. *Judges 1:20* says that "they gave Hebron unto Caleb, as Moses said: and he expelled thence the three sons of Anak," who had been king of the giants. *Deuteronomy 2:10-11*, referring to Ar, a city of the Moabites, says: "The Emims dwelt therein in times past, a people great, and many, and tall, as the Anakims; which also were accounted giants, as the Anakims; but the Moabites call them Emims." From *Deuteronomy 3:13* we learn that the tableland of Bashan, the kingdom of Og, was called "the land of the giants." Verse 2 of that chapter says: "For only Og king of Bashan remained of the remnant of giants; behold, his bedstead was a bedstead of iron; is it not in Rabbath of the children of Ammon? nine cubits was the length thereof, and four cubits the breadth of it, after the cubit of a man." After the giants were driven from their mountain strongholds a remnant appears to have mingled with the Philistines along the seacoast. *II Samuel 5:18* says: "The Philistines also came and spread themselves in the valley of Rephaim." *Rephaim* is Hebrew for "giants." Goliath and his brothers appear to have been descendants of this race of giants. One of the most specific descriptions of a giant in the Bible is that of Goliath, the champion of the Philistines, whom David slew. *I Samuel 17:4-7* says: "And there went out a champion out of the camp of the Philistines, named Goliath, of Gath, whose height was six cubits and a span. And he had an helmet of brass upon his head, and he was armed with a coat of mail; and the weight of the coat was five thousand shekels of brass. And he had greaves of brass upon his legs, and a target of brass between his shoulders. And the staff of his spear was like a weaver's beam; and his spear's head weighed six hundred shekels of iron." Goliath is nowhere in the Bible referred to specifically as a "giant." But David was not yet through killing giants. *I Chronicles 20:4-8* says: "And it came to pass after this, that there arose war at Gezer with the Philistines; at which time Sibbechai the Hushathite slew Sippai, that was of the children of the giant: and they were subdued. And there was war again with the Philistines; and Elhanan the son of Jair slew Lahmi the brother of Goliath the Gittite, whose spear staff was like a weaver's beam. And yet again there was war at Gath, where was a man of great stature, whose fingers and toes were four and twenty, six on each hand, and six on each foot: and he also was the son of a giant. But when he defied Israel, Jonathan the son of Shimea David's brother slew him. These were born unto the giant in Gath; and they fell by the hand of David, and by the hand of his servants." From *II Samuel 21:22* we learn that there were four of these latter-day giants, but the number probably included Goliath. Several Hebrew words are rendered *giant* in the Old Testament and some of them may signify merely persons of unusual size and strength rather than members of a race of giants. The belief in races of giants prevailed among many ancient peoples. In many cases the giants were regarded as of divine or semi-divine origin. Samson is represented in the Bible as a "strong man" rather than as a giant. Since he was an Israelite, he could not have belonged to the race of giants, but the legends of the giants may have influenced many of the folk tales about his remarkable strength and deeds. Even with the weights and measures given in the Bible in connection with Goliath of Gath and King Og of Bashan it is impossible to determine how large they were, because we cannot definitely translate the cubit and shekel of that time into terms of modern measures of length and weight. The cubit seems to have varied in length at different periods and it is possible that the Israelites used more than one unit of length called a cubit at the same time. The length of the cubit is estimated at all the way from fifteen to twenty-one inches. *Cubit* is from Latin *cubitum*, "elbow," and as a measure of length it was originally the distance from the elbow to the end of the middle finger. It is believed that the average Hebrew cubit was about eighteen inches. A span is the distance between the tip of the thumb and the tip of the little finger when the hand is fully extended. The average Hebrew span was probably nine inches. Assuming the cubit of *II Samuel 17:4* to be eighteen inches, and the span to be nine inches, Goliath would have been eight feet and one inch in height. Using the same cubit, "the cubit of a man," of *Deuteronomy 3:11*, the iron bedstead of King Og would have been thirteen and a half feet long and six feet wide. Of course, it does not necessarily follow that Og was as tall as his bedstead was long. The weight of the coat of mail, helmet and spearhead carried by Goliath are equally difficult to estimate from the available information. *Shekel* is derived from a Hebrew word meaning "weigh" and it was the name of a unit of weight of Babylonian origin. The Israelites appear to have had two weights called a shekel, one being about one-sixtieth of a pound and the other twice that weight. Assuming the shekel in *I Samuel 17:5-7* to be the light shekel, Goliath's bronze coat of mail would have weighed about eighty-three pounds and his iron spearhead about ten pounds, or a total of ninety-three pounds. If the heavy shekel was meant, the total weight of the coat of mail and the spearhead would be 186 pounds. The weight of the armor worn in the Middle Ages varied from fifteen pounds to more than a hundred. In the Tower of London there is a ninety-four-pound suit of mail that belonged to Henry VIII of England. It is probable that Goliath was merely an individual warrior of unusual stature rather than a giant in the sense that King Og of Bashan was. Reliable records of the maximum height of human beings are very scarce. Stories of men of gigantic stature are generally exaggerated and due allowance should be made for the imagination of the narrators. The average height of the human species is a little less than five feet six inches and in every race the great majority of individuals do not depart far from a certain average height. Among Americans only about one man out of two hundred is six feet or more tall. No existing race of people is sufficiently tall to be described as a race of giants. The Tehuelch Indians of Patagonia are noted for their great stature, and the men have an average height of slightly over six feet, while the average height of the men of the Sara tribe on the Upper Nile is slightly less. In the folklore of nearly all primitive peoples there are legends of men who were twice as tall as the average person. Within the last few centuries there have been more or less authentic records of men between nine and ten feet in height. These individuals, however, were not the products of ordinary gigantism, but of acromegaly, which is the abnormal but permanent enlargement of certain parts of the body.

Is *a still small voice* in the Bible?

A still small voice, now generally employed to signify "conscience" or "the inner voice," is from *I Kings 18:12*. After Elijah had slain the prophets of Baal and of the groves with the sword and Jezebel had sworn to have him killed, the only surviving prophet of the Lord took refuge in a cave on Horeb, the mount of God. *I Kings 18:11-13* says: "And he said, Go forth, and stand upon the mount before the Lord. And, behold, the Lord passed by, and a great and strong wind rent the mountains, and brake in pieces the rocks before the Lord; but the

Lord was not in the wind: and after the wind an earthquake; but the Lord was not in the earthquake: and after the earthquake a fire; but the Lord was not in the fire; and after the fire *a still small voice*. And it was so, when Elijah heard it, that he wrapped his face in his mantle, and went out, and stood in the entering in of the cave. And, behold, there came a voice unto him, and said, What doest thou here, Elijah?"

What does *sitting under one's vine and fig tree* mean?

"Vine and figs" occurs often in the Old Testament as the typical food crops of the Holy Land. *Sitting under one's vine and fig tree* symbolizes happiness and security. In *Deuteronomy 8:8* the Promised Land is described as "a land of wheat, barley, and vines, and fig trees, and pomegranates; a land of oil olive, and honey." *I Kings 4:25* says: "And Judah and Israel dwelt safely, every man under his vine and under his fig tree, from Dan even to Beersheba, all the days of Solomon." From the Assyrian host in front of the walls of Jerusalem, Rabshakeh "cried with a loud voice in the Jews' language" to the people "Hearken not to Hezekiah: for thus saith the king of Assyria, Make an agreement with me by a present, and come out to me, and then eat ye every man of his own vine, and every one of his fig tree, and drink ye every one the water of his cistern."—*II Kings 18:31* Several of the prophets employed the same figure of speech. *Zechariah 9:11* says: "And I will remove the iniquity of that land in one day. In that day, saith the Lord of hosts, shall ye call every man his neighbour under the vine and under the fig tree." And *Micah 4:4* says: "But they shall sit every man under his vine and under his fig tree; and none shall make them afraid: for the mouth of the Lord of hosts hath spoken it." Joel and Habakkuk use virtually the same figure in reverse. "The vine is dried up," says *Joel 1:12*, "and the fig tree languisheth; the pomegranate tree, the palm tree also, and the apple tree, even all the trees of the field, are withered: because joy is withered away from the sons of men." *Habakkuk 3:17* says: "Although the fig tree shall not blossom, neither shall fruit be in the vines; the labour of the olive shall fail, and the fields shall yield no meat; the flock shall be cut off from the fold, and there shall be no herd in the stalls."

What are the Noachian laws?

Noachian and *Noachic* are adjectives formed from *Noah* and mean simply "pertaining to the patriarch Noah." According to *Genesis 9:1-17*, long before the Mosaic law was given to Israel through Moses on Sinai, God blessed Noah and his sons, made a covenant with them and gave them and their descendants certain commandments. The rabbinic authorities deduced from this passage what has become known as the Seven Commandments given to the descendants of Noah or the Seven Noachian Laws of Humanity. These laws are: (1) Observance of established courts of justice and the prohibition of (2) blasphemy, (3) idolatry, (4) incest, (5) bloodshed, (6) robbery, and (7) the eating of flesh cut from living animals. The seventh of these Noachian laws forbids a barbarous practice that was common among the primitive people in the time of Noah. These Seven Noachian Laws of Humanity constituted natural religion in the eyes of the Hebrews and were regarded as essential to the existence of decent human society. While the Israelites as the chosen people of God required their people to observe all the precepts of the Torah, they required non-Israelites living among them, "thy stranger within thy gates," to obey only the Seven Noachian laws. Even today Judaism recognizes persons who attach themselves to the Jewish community and who accept the Seven Noachian Laws of Humanity without becoming "proselytes of righteousness" or complete Jews as "proselytes of the gate."

Does *rainbow* occur in the Bible?

Rainbow occurs only twice in the King James Version, both times in *Revelation*. In the Old Testament the rainbow is referred to simply as *the bow*. *Genesis 9:8-17* says: "And God spake unto Noah, and to his sons with him, saying, And I, behold, I establish my covenant with you, and with your seed after you; and with every living creature that is with you, of the fowl, of the cattle, and of every beast of the earth with you; from all that go out of the ark, to every beast of the earth. And I will establish my covenant with you; neither shall all flesh be cut off any more by the waters of a flood; neither shall there any more be a flood to destroy the earth. And God said, This is the token of the covenant which I make between me and you and every living creature that is with you, for perpetual generations; I do set my bow in the cloud, and it shall be for a token of a covenant between me and the earth. And it shall come to pass, when I bring a cloud over the earth, that the bow shall be seen in the cloud: and I will remember my covenant, which is between me and you and every living creature of all flesh. And the bow shall be in the cloud; and I will look upon it, that I may remember the everlasting covenant between God and every living creature of all flesh that is upon the earth. And God said unto Noah, This is the token of the covenant, which I have established between me and all flesh that is upon the earth." Hebrew authorities do not generally interpret this passage to mean that God specially created the rainbow as a token of the covenant with Noah and his descendants. They rather interpret it as meaning that the rainbow, a natural phenomenon that existed from the creation, was then given a new significance and made the token of God's pledge that the world would never again be destroyed by water. It is an interesting fact that, despite this beautiful story about the rainbow in *Genesis,* the rainbow does not figure largely in later Hebrew sacred writings or in the folklore of Isarel. *Bow* in this sense is mentioned only once elsewhere in the Old Testament, and there it is the emblem of the glory of God, not the Rainbow of Promise. *Ezekiel 1:28,* referring to the visions seen by the prophet when he was among the captives by the river of Chebar, says in part: "As the appearance of the bow that is in the cloud in the day of rain, so was the appearance of the brightness round about. This was the appearance of the likeness of the glory of the Lord." This same figure was employed twice by John on Patmos. In *Revelation 4:2-3* we read: "And immediately I was in the spirit: and, behold, a throne was set in heaven, and one sat on the throne. And he that sat was to look upon like jasper and a sardine stone: and there was a rainbow round about the throne, in sight like unto an emerald." *Revelation 10:1* says: "And I saw another mighty angel come down from heaven, clothed with a cloud: and a rainbow was upon his head, and his face was as it were the sun, and his feet as pillars of fire." The Hebrew word translated *bow* and the Greek word translated *rainbow* both signify "bow," which is extended literally to signify "rainbow."

Who were the patriarchs?

Patriarch is derived from two Greek words meaning "ruler of a family." Although the term is applied to the progenitors of the human race in general and the Israelites in particular as recorded in the Bible, it does not occur in the King James Version of the Old Testament. The patriarchs are there referred to as "princes of the tribes," "heads of the fathers" and similar phrases. *Patriarch,* singular and plural, occurs four times in the New Testament. Speaking of Melchisedec, *Hebrews 7:4* says: "Now consider how great this man was, unto whom even the patriarch Abraham gave the tenth of the spoils." *Acts 7:8* tells us that "Jacob begat the twelve patriarchs," and the following verse says that "the patriarchs, moved with envy, sold Joseph unto Egypt." In *Acts 2:29* Peter is quoted as saying: "Men and brethren, let me freely speak unto you of the patriarch David, that he is both dead and buried, and his sepulchre is with us unto this day." In popular speech the term is generally applied to the great Biblical heroes before the time of Moses, particularly Noah, Abraham, Isaac, Jacob and the twelve sons of the last.

What prophet fed a hundred men with twenty loaves?

One of the miracles of Elisha the prophet was feeding a hundred men with twenty loaves of bread. Speaking of Elisha at Gilgal, *II Kings 4:42-44* says: "And there came a man from Baalshalisha, and brought the man of God bread of the firstfruits, twenty loaves of barley, and full ears of corn in the husk thereof. And he said, Give unto the people, that they may eat. And his servitor said, What, should I set this before an hundred men? He said again, Give the people, that they may eat: for thus saith the Lord, They shall eat, and shall leave thereof. So he set it before them, and they did eat, and left thereof, according to the word of the Lord." This miracle of Elisha was the prototype of two miracles performed by Jesus, the feeding of four thousand men, besides women and children, with seven loaves and a few little fishes, and the feeding of about five thousand men, besides women and children, with five loaves and two fishes. In all three cases there was food left over.

Does the Bible say there will always be poor people?

Deuteronomy 15:11 says: "For the poor shall never cease out of the land: therefore I command thee, saying, Thou shalt open thine hand wide unto thy brother, to thy poor, and to thy needy, in the land." This passage was quoted in substance by Jesus when it was objected that the alabaster box of very precious ointment with which Mary anointed his feet might have been sold and given to the poor. The quotation is given in substantially the same form in three of the Gospels. *Matthew 26:11* says: "For ye have the poor always with you; but me ye have not always." *Mark 14:7* gives it: "For ye have the poor with you always, and whensoever ye will ye may do them good: but me ye have not always." In *John 12:8* the language is: "For the poor always ye have with you; but me ye have not always."

Who were the Judges of Israel?

The Hebrew *shophet* translated *judge* in the *Book of the Judges* is of much wider application than the English term. *Ruler* would be a closer approximation to the Hebrew original. The judges of Israel were far from being judges in the judicial sense. During the period of about two centuries between the death of Joshua and the creation of the kingship under Saul, the Israelites had no national leader. This is known as the period of the judges. It was the dark ages of Israel, a barbaric period of anarchy, civil wars, conquests and oppressions by the Canaanites, without political or religious unity and authority. The nation created by Moses and Joshua had virtually disintegrated. "In those days," *Judges 17:6* tells us, "there was no king in Israel, but every man did that which was right in his own eyes." During this period Israel was ruled by persons who arose to leadership to meet the needs of the hour, not by hereditary succession or by official appointment, but by personal character, ability and influence. The judges of Israel for the most part appeared on the scene to repel foreign invasions, suppress uprisings among the Canaanites or to deliver the Israelites from their oppressors. Some of them ruled over only a limited territory, and probably more than one was in authority at the same time in different parts of Israel. These judges were warriors, prophets, priests, local magistrates, and persons of distinction in general. It is customary to reckon the number of the judges of Israel as fifteen—fourteen men and one woman—although several of them were hardly judges in the strict sense of the term. They were: Othniel, Ehud, Shamgar, Deborah, Gideon, Abimelech, Tola, Jair, Jephthah, Ibzan of Bethlehem, Elon of Aijalon, Abdon, Eli, Samson and Samuel. Eli was high priest as well as a judge. Samuel, who was also one of the great prophets, was the greatest and last of the judges of Israel. He supplied the leadership that drew together the loosely knit and scattered tribes and united them into a people under a king. Only in a few instances are the judges referred to as performing the functions of a judge in the generally accepted sense of the word. In *Judges 4:4-5* we are told that Deborah "judged Israel at that time. And she dwelt under the palm tree of Deborah between Ramah and Bethel in mount Ephraim: and the children of Israel came up to her for judgment." *I Samuel 7:15-17* says: "And Samuel judged Israel all the days of his life. And he went from year to year in circuit to Bethel, and Gilgal, and Mizpeh, and judged Israel in all those places. And his return was to Ramah; for there was his house; and there he judged Israel; and there he built an altar unto the Lord." The next chapter tells us that when Samuel was old "he made his sons judges over Israel" and "they were judges in Beersheba." That Israel was ultimately to have a king was anticipated by the Mosaic law. *Deuteronomy 17:14-15* says: "When thou art come unto the land which the Lord thy God giveth thee, and shalt possess it, and shalt dwell therein, and shalt say, I will set a king over me, like as all the nations that are about me; thou shalt in any wise set him king over thee, whom the Lord thy God shall choose: one from among thy brethren shalt thou set king over thee: thou mayest not set a stranger over thee, which is not thy brother." It was in keeping with this statute that Samuel would not anoint Saul and proclaim him king until the people were duly warned of the dangers involved and after they persisted in their demand.

Who said: "Woe to the land whose king is a child"?

In *Ecclesiastes 10:16-17* Solomon says: "Woe to thee, O land, when thy king is a child, and thy princes eat in the morning! Blessed art thou, O land, when the king is the son of nobles, and thy princes eat in due season, for strength, and not for drunkenness!" This quotation is perhaps better known in Shakespeare's paraphrase. In *Richard III*, Act 2, Scene 3, the Third Citizen is made to say: "Woe to that land that's govern'd by a child!"

How many wives did Solomon have?

I Kings 11:1-3, one of the most remarkable passages in the Bible, reads: "But king Solomon loved many strange women, together with the daughter of Pharoah, women of the Moabites, Edomites, Zidonians, and Hittites; of the nations concerning which the Lord said unto the children of Israel, Ye shall not go in to them, neither shall they come in unto you: for surely they will turn away your heart after their gods: Solomon clave unto these in love. And he had seven hundred wives, princesses, and three hundred concubines: and his wives turned away his heart." Josephus, paraphrasing the last part of this passage in his *Antiquities of the Jews,* wrote that Solomon "had married seven hundred wives, the daughters of princes and of eminent persons, and three hundred concubines, and these besides the king of Egypt's daughter." Solomon may have referred to his thousand wives and concubines in *Ecclesiastes 7:28* when he said: "One man among a thousand have I found: but a woman among all those have I not found." The passage in *I Kings 11* probably means that Solomon married a thousand women and that the difference between those called wives and those called concubines was one of social status. It is not necessarily true, however, that Solomon's marital establishment contained a thousand wives and concubines all at one time. Perhaps a fair interpretation of the passage is that the king of Israel had a total of a thousand wives and concubines during his life. *Judges 8:10-11* says: "And Gideon had threescore sons of his body begotten: for he had many wives." From this it is not clear that Gideon had more than one wife at one time, although he probably had several. The casualties among so many women must have been considerable and if Solomon had a thousand at one time he must have had a much larger number during his lifetime. King David, Solomon's father, had several wives at the same time and many concubines. He married two wives at one time and four at another. After several wives of David are mentioned in *II Samuel 3:1-5,* we are told in *II Samuel 5:13* that "David took him more concubines and wives out of Jerusalem, after he was come from Hebron." Solomon appears to have violated the Mosaic law in two particulars in having so many wives. First, he violated *Deuteronomy 17:17,* which says the king shall not "multiply wives to himself." Second, he violated the statute in *Deuteronomy 7* forbidding the Israelites to intermarry with the non-Israelites of Palestine. But Solomon is not condemned in the Bible for the great number of wives he had, but only for taking wives of strange and forbidden nationality. It should be borne in mind that polygamy, especially among princes and the rich, was not particularly frowned upon in the Near East. The first mention of polygamy in the Bible is in *Genesis 4:19,* which says "Lamech took unto him two wives." In its many provisions regulating domestic relations the law of Moses nowhere forbids plural marriages. On the contrary, polygamy was recognized. *Deuteronomy 21:15-17* says: "If a man have two wives, one beloved, and another hated, and they have borne him children, both the beloved and the hated; and if the firstborn son be hers that was hated: then it shall be, when he maketh his sons to inherit that which he hath, that he may not make the son of the beloved firstborn before the son of the hated, which is indeed the firstborn: but he shall acknowledge the son of the hated for the firstborn, by giving him a double portion of all that he hath: for he is the beginning of his strength; the right of the firstborn is his." In *Samuel 1* we are told that Elkanah, father of Samuel, "had two wives" and that to one of them he gave "a worthy portion." The patriarchs, like their Semitic neighbors, began to practice bigamy and even polygamy at an early date. Because she bore no children, Sarah asked Abraham to have children by her handmaid, an Egyptian, whose name was Hagar. As everybody knows, Ishmael was the offspring of that union. *Genesis 25:1* says: "Then again Abraham took a wife, and her name was Keturah." Verses 5 and 6 of the same chapter informs us that Abraham gave all he had to Isaac "but unto the sons of the concubines, which Abraham had, Abraham gave gifts and sent them away from Isaac his son, while he yet lived." Isaac apparently had no wife other than Rebekah, but Esau took to wife two women when he was forty and Jacob had two wives and two handmaids. The twelve sons of Jacob, whose descendants became the twelve tribes of Israel, were the offspring of four women who were living in Jacob's household at the same time. The father, not the mother, was the chief consideration in tracing descent in Israel. Marriage was jealously guarded by the Laws of Moses, but it was the family as a whole rather than the relationship between husband and wife that constituted the basic institution of ancient Hebrew society. Even as late as the time when Jesus was born, King Herod, a lukewarm adherent of Judaism, had nine wives at one time and he married a total of ten during his life. Nowhere in the Old Testament do we find any formal recognition of the entering into marriage as a religious or judicial covenant. Marriage in Israel was treated largely as a private matter. It did not go beyond the individual and family law and was in the nature of a private contract between the man who wished to marry and the man who controlled the woman whom he wanted to marry. The state or the people in general had no interest in a marriage as such. The Israelite was permitted to increase the number of his wives and concubines according to his desires and financial means. Custom and the law recognized concubines, handmaids and maid-servants, who were women of inferior social status and who were subject to the authority of the husband. But bigamy and polygamy were probably not so common in ancient Israel as some might suppose. In the Old Testament those mentioned as having more than one wife are generally the rich, the great, or kings. The ordinary man, particularly among the poorer classes, contented himself with one wife. It was an economic necessity. Besides, it is probable that monogamy was the original marriage ideal of the Israelites. One of the finest things ever said about monogamous marriage occurs in *Genesis* 2. We are told there that God made the first woman from a rib of the first man "and brought her unto the man." Adam said: "This is now bone of my bones, and flesh of my flesh; she shall be called Woman, because she was taken out of Man. Therefore shall a man leave his father and his mother, and shall cleave unto his wife; and they shall be one flesh." Apparently Noah and his three sons all had only one wife each. A fine appreciation of the significance of monogamy and the worth of woman is also voiced by some of the prophets. All of the ethical parts of the Old Testament seem to point to the ideal of a man and one wife. While the Mosaic law has little to say about the making of marriages, it contains many provisions relating to marriage relations and the protection of women, After the Babylonian exile polygamy gradually began to disappear among the Jews. Rabbenu Gershom, rabbi, poet, reviser of the Mishna and head a Talmudic academy at Metz, France, excommunicated polygamists among Jews in 1000 A.D. Nowhere in the New Testament is polygamy specifically forbidden, except perhaps in *I Timothy 3:2* and *12* which read in part: "A bishop then must be blameless, the husband of one wife," and "Let the deacons be the husbands of one wife," which, however, may refer to the second rather than bigamous marriages. Likewise in *Titus 1:6* Paul desired the elders to be "blameless, the husband of one wife." Monogamy appears to be taken for granted throughout the New Testament. In *Ephesians 5:28-33* Paul says: "So ought men to love their wives as their own bodies. He that loveth his wife loveth himself. For no man ever yet hated his own flesh; but nourisheth and cherisheth it, even as the Lord the church. For we are members of his body, of his flesh and of his bones. For this cause shall a man leave his father and mother, and shall be joined unto his wife, and they two shall be one flesh. This is a great mystery; but I speak concerning Christ and the church. Nevertheless let every one of you in particular so love his wife even as himself; and the wife see that she reverence her husband." It is said that adultery among men is generally considered a graver offense in polygamous than in monogamous communities because there is a wider choice and less excuse for it.

Is *grapes of wrath* in the Bible?

The phrase *grapes of wrath* is not found in the Bible, but it was suggested by Biblical passages. There are references in the Bible to "the blood of the grape" and the winepress was a common figure for the vengeance and carnage in battle. *Isaiah 63:1-6* says: "Who is this that cometh from Edom, with dyed garments from Bozrah? this that is glorious in his apparel, travelling in the greatness of his strength? I that speak in righteousness, mighty to save. Wherefore art thou red in thine apparel, and thy garments like him that treadeth in the winefat? I have trodden the winepress alone; and of the people there was none with me; for I will tread them in mine anger and trample them in my fury; and their blood shall be sprinkled upon my garments, and I will stain all my raiment. For the day of vengeance is in mine heart, and the year of my redeemed is come. And I looked, and there was none to help; and I wondered that there was none to uphold; therefore mine own arm brought salvation unto me; and my fury, it upheld me. And I will tread down the people in mine anger, and make them drunk in my fury, and I will bring down their strength to the earth." This passage in *Isaiah* undoubtedly influenced Mrs. Julia Ward Howe when she composed *The Battle Hymn of the Republic,* first published in the February issue of the *Atlantic Monthly* in 1862. The earliest known use of *grapes of wrath* occurs in the first stanza of that hymn, which reads:

> Mine eyes have seen the glory of the coming of the Lord;
> He is trampling out the vintage where the grapes of wrath are stored;
> He hath loosed the fateful lightning of His terrible swift sword;
> His truth is marching on.

Does the Bible say all men were once vegetarians?

It appears from passages in *Genesis* that mankind did not eat the flesh of animals before the flood. According to *Genesis 1:29,* God said to Adam and Eve: "Behold, I have given you every herb bearing seed, which is upon the face of all the earth, and every tree, in the which is the fruit of a tree yielding seed; to you it shall be for meat." But after the flood permission to eat animal food was granted. According to *Genesis 9:3,* God said to Noah and his sons: "Every moving thing that liveth shall be meat for you; even as the green herb have I given you all things." The term "every moving thing" obviously includes all animal life—beast, fish, fowl. This passage seems to signify that just as the green herb was granted to mankind for food at the beginning, now they are given permission to eat flesh.

Who slew a thousand men with the jawbone of an ass?

In *Judges 15* we are told that Samson, who "judged Israel in the days of the Philistines twenty years," slew a thousand men with the new jawbone of an ass. After Samson had smote the Philistines "hip and thigh with a great slaughter," the men of Judah, because the strong man had brought the wrath of the Philistines down upon them, bound Samson "with two new cords" and delivered him into the hands of the enemy. *Judges 15:14-19* says: "And when he came unto Lehi, the Philistines shouted against him: and the Spirit of the Lord came mightily upon him, and the cords that were upon his arms became as flax that was burnt with fire, and his bands loosed from off his hands. And he found a new jawbone of an ass, and put forth his hand, and took it, and slew a thousand men therewith. And Samson said, With the jawbone of an ass, heaps upon heaps, with the jaw of an ass have I slain a thousand men. And it came to pass, when he had made an end of speaking, that he cast away the jawbone out of his hand, and called that place Ramath-lehi. And he was sore athirst, and called on the Lord, and said, Thou hast given this great deliverance into the hand of thy servant: and now shall I die for thirst, and fall into the hand of the uncircumcised? But God clave an hollow place that was in the jaw, and there came water thereout; and when he had drank, his spirit came again, and he revived: wherefore he called the name thereof En-hakkore, which is Lehi unto this day." The phrase *heaps upon heaps* in this passage is an English attempt to translate a Hebrew play upon words. In Hebrew the words for *ass* and *heap* sound the same. *Lehi* is Hebrew for "jawbone." The Hebrew original does not signify that the hollow from which the water came was in the jawbone of the ass, but rather from a spring in a hollow place or basin at the place called Ramath-lehi, "height of the jawbone."

What does *Beth* in Bible names mean?

Beth in Hebrew is the name of the letter *B* and it literally means "house." In compound names of places mentioned in the Bible *Beth* signifies "house of," "place of," "abode of," or "temple of." For instance, Bethel means house of God; Bethsaida, house of fishes; Bethphage, place of figs; Beth-Shittah, place of the acacias; Beth-Dagon, temple of Dagon; Beth-Emek, place of the valley; Beth-Hoglah, place of a partridge; Beth-Anath, temple of Anath; Beth-Arbel, house of Arbel; Beth-Horon, house of a hollow; Beth-Lebaoth, place of lions; Beth-Marcaboth, place of chariots; Beth-Merhak, house afar off; Beth-Pelet, house of escape; Bethshan, house of safety; Beth-Shemesh, house of the sun; Beth-Tappuah, place of apples, and so on. *Beth-Israel,* the house of Israel, occurs several times in the Hebrew text of the Old Testament. In *John 5:2* the pool near the sheep market in Jerusalem, where Jesus healed a man on the Sabbath, was "called in the Hebrew tongue *Bethesda,*" which means "house of mercy." *Bethlehem,* the name of the birthplace of David and Jesus about five and a half miles from Jerusalem, signifies "house of bread." It is hard to believe that *Bedlam,* which is now applied to a madhouse or lunatic asylum and to an excited or turbulent crowd, is an old English corruption of the beautiful Biblical name *Bethlehem.* Eight hundred years ago the birthplace of Jesus was called *Bedlam* in England. This term was applied in particular to Bethlehem hospital, officially known as the Hospital of St. Mary of Bethlehem, in London. The institution was originally founded as a priory in 1247. We find it referred to as a hospital already in 1330, and as a hospital for lunatics in 1402. When the monasteries and religious establishments were confiscated during the reign of Henry VIII, Bedlam was given to the city of London and was established as a royal institution for the reception of lunatics. Its original site was in Bishopsgate, but later it was rebuilt near London Wall, and in 1815 it was transferred to Lambeth. In Shakespeare's *II King Henry VI,* written about 1593, Lord Clifford says of the Duke of York: "To Bedlam with him: Is the man growne mad?" Centuries ago Bedlam hospital became notorious for the ill-treatment received by its inmates. Patients were discharged partially cured and went about the country begging. In Shakespeare's *King Lear* Edgar, to escape the decree of death proclaimed by his father the Duke of Gloster, assumed the guise of a Bedlam beggar, "the basest and most poorest shape that ever penury, in contempt of man, brought near to beast." Such a beggar was known as a Bedlamite or a Tom o' Bedlam. The reports of brutal treatment of Bedlam patients, although well authenticated, are almost incredible. Sometimes inmates were placed in iron cages like wild animals and exhibited to the public who paid a fee for the privilege of seeing the unfortunate creatures.

What is a Jonathan and David friendship?

The relationship between Jonathan and David is a type of inseparable friendship between two men. Jonathan and David are the Biblical counterpart of the classical Damon and Pythias. The son of Saul is one of the most attractive and chivalrous figures in the Old Testament. Although a notable soldier and national hero in his own right, Jonathan risked the wrath of his father and sacrificed his own succession to the throne because of his unwavering love and loyalty to David. We are told in *I Samuel 17* that Saul was attracted to the youthful David because of his exploits against the Philistines. The king took him and would let him go no more home to his father's house. While Saul and David were talking, according to *I Samuel 18:1,* "the soul of Jonathan was knit with the soul of David, and Jonathan loved him as his own soul." *I Samuel 18:3-4* says: "Then Jonathan and David made a covenant, because he loved him as his own soul. And Jonathan stripped himself of the robe that was upon him, and gave it to David, and his garments, even to his sword, and to his bow, and to his girdle." One of the most beautiful passages in the Bible is David's lamentation when he learned that Jonathan had been slain in the battle of Mount Gilboa by the Philistines and that Saul had killed himself by falling on his sword. *II Samuel 1:17-27* says "And David lamented with this lamentation over Saul and over Jonathan his son: (Also he bade them teach the children of Judah the use of the bow: behold, it is written in the book of Jasher.) The beauty of Israel is slain upon thy high places: how are the mighty fallen! Tell it not in Gath, publish it not in the streets of Askelon; lest the daughters of the Philistines rejoice, lest the daughters of the uncircumcised triumph. Ye mountains of Gilboa, let there be no dew, neither let there be rain, upon you, nor fields of offerings: for there the shield of the mighty is vilely cast away, the shield of Saul, as though he had not yet been anointed with oil. From the blood of the slain, from the fat of the mighty, the bow of Jonathan turned not back, and the sword of Saul returned not empty. Saul and Jonathan were lovely and pleasant in their lives, and in their death they were not divided: they were swifter than eagles, they were stronger than lions. Ye daughters of Israel, weep over Saul, who clothed you in scarlet, with other delights, who put on ornaments of gold upon your apparel. How are the mighty fallen in the midst of the battle! O Jonathan, thou wast slain in thine high places. I am distressed for thee, my brother Jonathan: very pleasant hast thou been unto me: thy love to me was wonderful, passing the love of women. How are the mighty fallen, and the weapons of war perished."

Does the Bible mention rats?

Although rats are common in Palestine at the present time, they are nowhere mentioned in the Bible. Both the common brown and the black rat are believed to be natives of China, and it is possible that neither of these had penetrated as far westward as Palestine in Biblical times. The brown rat did not make its appearance in Europe until about 1727, when great numbers of them swam across the Volga River and established themselves in the province of Astrakhan in eastern Russia, whence they spread westward to Europe and finally to America.

Does the Bible mention the Hanging Gardens of Babylon?

The Hanging Gardens of Babylon are not specifically mentioned in the Bible, but they are probably alluded to in *Daniel 4:28-30,* which reads: "All this came upon the king Nebuchadnezzar. At the end of twelve months he walked in the palace of the kingdom of Babylon. The king spake, and said, is not this great Babylon, that I have built for the house of the kingdom by the might of my power, and for the honour of my majesty?" It is also probable that the "banquet house" in which Belshazzar made a great feast to a thousand of his lords was a compartment in the great palace and surrounding grounds of which the Hanging Gardens were a part. Nebuchadnezzar was reputed to be one of the greatest builders of ancient times. He built up Babylon on both sides of the Euphrates, and in the heart of the capital, on a low artificial hill, he built a great palace, which, with the adjoining Hanging Gardens, was regarded as one of the seven wonders of the ancient world. In his *Antiquities of the Jews* Josephus says of Nebuchadnezzar: "He also added another city to that which was there of old, and rebuilt it, that such as would besiege it hereafter might no more turn the course of the river, and thereby attack the city itself. He therefore built three walls round about the inner city, and three others about that which was the outer, and this he did with burnt brick. And after he had, after a becoming manner, walled the city, and adorned its gates gloriously, he built another palace before his father's palace, but so that they joined to it; to describe whose vast height and immense riches it would perhaps be too much for me to attempt; yet as large and lofty as they were, they were completed in fifteen days. He also erected elevated places for walking, of stone, and made it resemble mountains, and built it so that it might be planted with all sorts of trees. He also erected what was called a pensile paradise, because his wife was desirous to have things like her own country, she having been bred up in the palaces of Media." Diodorus Siculus, a Greek historian who wrote during the first century B.C., described the "pensile paradise" of Nebuchadnezzar at Babylon as a garden four hundred feet square which rose in a series of terraces from the Euphrates and which was covered with earth sufficiently deep to accommodate trees of great size. Several ancient writers refer to the tradition that the Hanging Gardens were built by King Nebuchadnezzar to gratify the whim of his wife, Amytis, who was bored by the monotonous plains of Babylonia and longed for something resembling her native hills in Media. Perhaps this Amytis was the very queen who, according to *Daniel 5*, "by reason of the words of the king and his lords, came into the banquet house" and suggested that Daniel, the captive from Judah, could read and interpret the writing on the wall. Many ancient historians mention the famous Hanging Gardens, but they differ widely as to just what they were like. Some of them even say that they were not built by Nebuchadnezzar, but by Semiramis, the Assyrian princess who is reputed to have founded Babylon. But these writers may refer to an earlier structure. The Hanging Gardens, it seems, consisted of several acres of groves, flower gardens, avenues of trees and shrubs, interspersed with bowers, fountains and banqueting rooms. It was probably a terraced structure, perhaps pyramidal in form, with the trees, flowers and fountains on the terraces. One ancient writer says it was a terrace-like structure rising up from the Euphrates on tiers of masonry arches to heights of from seventy-five to three hundred feet above the plain. Another says the Gardens were a building-like structure with the flowers and trees on the roof. Still another asserts that the Hanging Gardens were irrigated from a reservoir situated at the top and supplied with water from the Euphrates by means of a large screw-like pump at which a force of men was continually at work. It is impossible to say how much truth there is in these stories of the Hanging Gardens of Babylon. Excavations on the site of Babylon have unearthed the remains of a structure faintly answering to the ancient descriptions but of much smaller dimensions. Whatever the actual structure, its many elevated terraces created the impression of a large park suspended in mid-air and gave rise to the strange myth of the pensile paradise or Hanging Gardens of Babylon.

What became of the golden calf?

In popular speech the golden calf symbolizes wealth, riches or Mammon. A person who is greedy for money is said to worship the golden calf. This is only a figurative and not a literal application of the story of the molten calf made by Aaron for the Israelites while Moses was absent on Mount Sinai receiving the law. *Golden calf* occurs nowhere in the Bible. The incident is related to *Exodus 32.* "And when the people saw that Moses delayed to come down out of the mount, the people gathered themselves together unto Aaron, and said unto him, Up, make us gods, which shall go before us; for as for this Moses, the man that brought us up out of the land of Egypt, we wot not what is become of him. And Aaron said unto them, Break off the golden earrings which are in the ears of your wives, of your sons, and of your daughters, and bring them unto me. And all the people brake off the golden earrings which were in their ears, and brought them unto Aaron. And he received them at their hand, and fashioned it with a graving tool, after he had made it a molten calf; and they said, These be thy gods, O Israel, which brought thee up out of the land of Egypt. And when Aaron saw it, he built an altar before it; and Aaron made proclamation, and said, Tomorrow is a feast to the Lord. And they rose up early on the morrow, and offered burnt offerings, and brought peace offerings; and the people sat down to eat and to drink and rose up to play." Again: "And it came to pass, as soon as he came nigh unto the camp, that he saw the calf, and the dancing: and Moses' anger waxed hot, and he cast the tables out of his hands, and brake them beneath the mount. And he took the calf which they had made, and burnt it in the fire, and ground it to powder, and strewed it upon the water, and made the children of Israel drink of it." The last verse of the chapter tells us: "And the Lord plagued the people, because they made the calf, which Aaron made." The popular impression is that this molten calf was an image of pure gold. Some authorities believe that it is more likely that it was the wooden image of a bullock plated with gold. The account in *Numbers 32* does not make it entirely clear whether the Israelites, in demanding the molten calf, intended to worship strange gods or merely desired a visible image of their own god. Learned commentators have advanced ingenious arguments to prove that by this idolatrous act the Israelites violated the first of the Ten Commandments, which says, "Thou shalt have no other gods before me," or the second Commandment, which says, "Thou shalt not make unto thee a graven image." As a matter of fact, since Moses broke the two tables containing the Decalogue before he returned to the people, the Ten Commandments had not at that time yet been made known to the Israelites. The demand for a molten calf by the Israelites before they had received the law is explained by some as merely a resurgence of ancient image-worship, which had been common among their ancestors and which was practiced a long time afterwards by their Assyrian, Chaldean and other Semitic neighbors. The act of the Israelites may have been in imitation of the sacred cows worshipped by the Egyptians among whom they had lived for centuries. At Chichester, England, there is a curious local legend that the molten calf made by Aaron is buried in near-by Rook's Hill!

Who said: "It is more blessed to give than to receive"?

It is a remarkable fact that the saying, "It is more blessed to give than to receive," is nowhere attributed to Jesus in the Four Gospels. Its only Biblical source is St. Paul in *Acts 20:25*, which reads: "I have showed you all things, how that so labouring ye ought to support the weak, and to remember the words of the Lord Jesus, how he said, It is more blessed to give than to receive." This is regarded by some authorities as the only authentic saying of Jesus not found in the Gospels. Another, however, may be concealed in *I Thessalonians 4:15*, which reads: "For this we say unto you by the word of the Lord, that we which are alive and remain unto the coming of the Lord shall not prevent them which are asleep." *Prevent,* derived from Latin *prae,* "before," and *venire,* "to come," is used here, as elsewhere in the

King James Version, in its original sense. One gets the impression from reading the New Testament that Paul either was not familiar with the life and teachings of Jesus or that he did not concern himself very much with them. In all the writings ascribed to the Apostle to the Gentiles there is not a direct reference to the many miracles performed by Jesus. Paul emphasized Jesus as the Christ crucified for mankind rather than the doctrines taught by Jesus. The miracle that concerned Paul chiefly was that wrought by God for Jesus, which was his resurrection.

Where does the Bible mention covered wagons?

Covered wagons are mentioned in the Bible only in connection with the dedication of the altar when the newly completed tabernacle was opened for offerings in the wilderness. The dedication of the first offerings at the new tablernacle lasted twelve days, one day being devoted to the offerings of each of the heads of the twelve tribes. *Numbers 7:1-3* says: "And it came to pass on the day that Moses had fully set up the tabernacle, and had anointed it, and sanctified it, and all the instruments thereof, both the altar and all the vessels thereof, and had anointed them, and sanctified them; that the princes of Israel, heads of the house of their fathers, who were the princes of the tribes, and were over them that were numbered, offered: and they brought their offering before the lord, six covered wagons, and twelve oxen; a wagon for two of the princes, and for each one an ox; and they brought them before the tabernacle." These covered wagons are believed to have been crude and clumsy carts such as are still seen in use in the Near East. They probably had two wooden wheels and were equipped with a tongue or pole, being drawn by two oxen yoked side by side. So far as known the ancient Israelites did not have four-wheeled wagons. The Hebrew word rendered *wagon* and *chariot* stems from a root meaning "to be round" or "to roll."

What does *Amen* mean?

Amen, though used chiefly as an interjection, is one of the commonest words in human speech. It is a transcription of a Hebrew word with the root idea of confirming or supporting and signifies "So be it," or "So it is." Originally it was in the nature of an affirmation of a preceding statement. By saying *Amen* the speaker made the statement his own, and said in effect "I concur." According to *Numbers 5:22* a woman charged with infidelity to her husband was required to say "Amen, Amen." This did not mean that the woman admitted the charges, but that she solemnly agreed to abide by the results of the trial by ordeal prescribed in the law of Moses. In other words, she merely confirmed the oath. When David announced to his council that he had named Solomon to succeed him, according to *I Kings 1:35*, "Benaiah the son of Jehoiada answered the king, and said, Amen: the Lord God of my lord the king say so too." *Jeremiah 28:5-6* says: "Then the prophet Jeremiah said unto the prophet Hananiah in the presence of the priests, and in the presence of all the people that stood in the house of the Lord, even the prophet Jeremiah said, Amen: the Lord do so: the Lord perform thy words which thou hast prophesied, to bring again the vessels of the Lord's house, and all that is carried away captive, from Babylon into this place." "All the people shall say, Amen," is appended to the various commandments, preceded by "Cursed be he," proclaimed "to all the men of Israel with a loud voice," reviewed in *Deuteronomy 27:14-26*. For instance, "Cursed be he that removeth his neighbour's landmark. And all the people shall say, Amen." In *Nehemiah 5:12-13* we read: "Then I called the priests, and took an oath of them, that they should do according to this promise. Also I shook my lap, and said, So God shake out every man from his house, and from his labour, that performeth not this promise, even thus be he shaken out, and emptied. And all the congregation said, Amen." In the course of time it became customary to use *Amen* at the close of public psalms, prayers or benedictions. In the New Testament epistles *Amen* occurs as the response to public or private prayers. *Amen* is also used in the New Testament with the force of an adverb in the sense of yea, truly, verily or for a certainty. It occurs at the close of the Lord's Prayer as given in *Matthew 6:9-13*. In *I Corinthians 14:16* Paul asks rhetorically: "Else when thou shalt bless with the spirit, how shall he that occupieth the room of the unlearned say Amen at thy giving of thanks, seeing he understandeth not what thou sayest?" *II Corinthians 1:20* says: "For all the promises of God in him are yea, and in him Amen, unto the glory of God by us." In the King James Version every book closes with *Amen* except *Acts, The General Epistle of James,* and *The Third Epistle of John.* Consequently, since *Amen* is the last word in *Revelation,* the English Bible closes with that solemn word. But generally *Amen* in the Gospels is rendered "Verily." *Amen* was taken over from the Hebrew into the Greek and where the original Gospels quote Jesus as saying, "Amen, Amen, I say unto thee," The English Bible has, "Verily verily, I say unto thee," or an equivalent expression. In

Revelation 3:14, however, *Amen* is applied to the Saviour himself. That verse reads: "And unto the angel of the church of the Laodiceans write; These things saith the Amen, the faithful and true witness, the beginning of the creation of God."

Is Davy *Jones* derived from *Jonah*?

Some authorities suppose that *Jones* in *Davy Jones* is a corruption of the name of the Hebrew prophet *Jonah* or *Jonas*. Since Jonah brought a tempest upon the ship in which he sought to flee from the Lord, *Jonah* is used as a verb in the sense of to bring ill luck and as a noun in the sense of the cause of ill luck or misfortune. In sailor lore Davy Jones is the evil spirit of the sea. Sometimes sailors apply Davy Jones to the devil in general. The ocean as the grave of men drowned or buried at sea is called Davy Jones' Locker. Although it is customary to derive *Davy Jones* from Duffy, a spirit in West Indian Negro folklore, and *Jonah*, the name of the Hebrew prophet who had an unusual adventure with a great fish, there is no etymological evidence to support the theory. Jonah also occurs in slang in the sense of a tall tale, an exaggerated account, or a "whopper."

What intoxicating drinks are mentioned in the Bible?

Wine is the only intoxicating drink specifically mentioned in the Bible by name. All other intoxicating liquors are referred to under the comprehensive term *strong drink*. We have no means of determining definitely just what was the strong drink of Biblical times. It is supposed that this strong drink, a rough rendering of two Hebrew and Greek words, was made by distilling grain and honey and various fruits such as grapes, pomegranates and dates. Biblical strong drink was probably a variety of brandy. Drunkenness appears to have been a rather common vice in ancient Israel as elsewhere. Both Noah and Lot are mentioned as having been drunk. In *I Samuel 25* we are told that the foolish and churlish Nabal, first husband of Abigail, "was very drunken" after he had "held a feast in his house, like the feast of a king." *Numbers 6:3* says that any man or woman taking the vow of a Nazarite "shall separate himself from wine and strong drink, and shall drink no vinegar of wine, or vinegar of strong drink, neither shall he drink any liquor of grapes, nor eat moist grapes, or dried." Apparently women in Israel also drank strong drink, for, according to *I Samuel 1:13*, Eli thought that Hannah "had been drunken" because "only her lips moved, but her voice was not heard." Even the priests and prophets occasionally imbibed too freely of intoxicating liquor. *Isaiah 28:7* says: "But they also have erred through wine, and through strong drink are out of the way; the priest and the prophet have erred through strong drink, they are swallowed up of wine, they are out of the way through strong drink; they err in vision, they stumble in judgment." The writers of the Old Testament were familiar with the sight of men drunk. *Isaiah 19:14* says: "The Lord hath mingled a perverse spirit in the midst thereof: and they have caused Egypt to err in every work thereof, as a drunken man staggereth in his vomit." In *Proverbs 20:1* Solomon warns: "Wine is a mocker, strong drink is raging: and whosoever is deceived thereby is not wise." The wisest man in Israel understood clearly the dangers of strong drink. In *Proverbs 23:29-35* he says: "Who hath woe? who hath sorrow? who hath contentions? who hath babblings? who hath wounds without cause? who hath redness of eyes? They that tarry long at the wine; they that go to seek mixed wine. Look not thou upon the wine when it is red, when it giveth his colour in the cup, when it moveth itself aright. At the last it biteth like a serpent, and stingeth like an adder. Thine eyes shall behold strange women, and thine heart shall utter perverse things. Yea, thou shalt be as he that lieth down in the midst of the sea, or as he that lieth upon the top of a mast. They have stricken me, shalt thou say, and I was not sick; they have beaten me, and I felt it not: when shall I awake? I will seek it yet again." Solomon's father, the sweet psalmist of Israel, says in *Psalms 107:27* that they that go down to the sea in ships and see the wonders of the Lord in the deep during a storm "reel to and fro, and stagger like a drunken man, and are at their wits' end." In *Job 12:24-26* the patriarch says that God "taketh away the heart of the chief of the people of the earth, and causeth them to wander in a wilderness where there is no way. They grope in the dark without light, and he maketh them to stagger like a drunken man." *Isaiah 4:11* warns: "Woe unto them that rise up early in the morning, that they may follow strong drink; that continue until night, till wine inflame them!" According to *Ezekiel 44:21*, no priest was permitted to drink wine when he entered the inner court, but under certain circumstances the people could use wine and strong drink as a libation. *Numbers 28:7* says: "And the drink offering thereof shall be the fourth part of an hin for the one lamb: in the holy place shalt thou cause the strong wine to be poured unto the Lord for a drink offering." If the Israelite lived too far away to bring his tithe in kind to the sanctuary in person he was permitted to "turn it into money" and, according to *Deuteronomy 14:26*, could "bestow that money for whatsoever thy soul lusteth after, for oxen, or for sheep, or for wine, or for strong drink, or for whatsoever thy soul desireth: and thou shalt eat there before the Lord thy God, and thou shalt rejoice, thou and thine household." References to wine and strong drink are fewer in the New Testament than in the Old. Jesus, who miraculously converted water into wine at Cana, was himself accused of being "a man gluttonous, and a wine-bibber," because, unlike John the Baptist, he "came eating and drinking," according to *Matthew 11:19* and *Luke 7:34*. That drunkenness was not an uncommon thing in Jerusalem in the time of the Apostles is indicated by *Acts 2:13*, where it is related that some mockingly said that the followers of Jesus assembled on Pentecost day were "full of new wine." But Peter assured them that "these are not drunken, as ye suppose, seeing it is but the third hour of the day."

Are mice mentioned in the Bible?

Mice, singular and plural, occurs several times in the Old Testament. *Leviticus 11:29* says: "These also shall be unclean unto you among the creeping things that creep upon the earth; the weasel, and the mouse, and the tortoise after his kind." *Isaiah 66:17* says: "They that sanctify themselves, and purify themselves in the gardens behind one tree in the midst, eating swine's flesh, and the abomination, and the mouse, shall be consumed together, saith the Lord." This alludes to the fact that the flesh of the mouse was eaten as part of the mystic rites of a heathen cult of the time. Field mice, like many other animals, were held sacred in Egypt. Herodotus tells an interesting incident that occurred during a war between Sennacherib, king of the Assyrians and Arabians, and Sethos, king of Egypt. "Sethos, then, relying on the dream," says the Father of History, "collected such of the Egyptians as were willing to follow him, who were none of them warriors, but traders, artisans, and market people; and with these marched to Pelusium, which commands the entrance to Egypt, and there pitched his camp. As the two armies lay here opposite one another, there came in the night a multitude of field mice, which devoured all the quivers and bowstrings of the enemy, and ate the thongs by which they managed their shields. Next morning they commenced their flight, and great multitudes fell, as they had no arms with which to defend themselves. There stands to this day in the temple of Vulcan, a stone statue of Sethos, with a mouse in his hand, and an inscription to this effect—'Look on me, and learn to reverence the gods.' " Images of mice are mentioned several times in *I Samuel 6.* The priests and diviners told the Philistines that they should put in the captured ark of the covenant as a trespass offering "five golden emerods, and five golden mice," according to the number of the lords of the Philistines. "Ye shall make images of your emerods, and images of your mice that mar the land," they declared. *I Samuel 6:11* says: "And they laid the ark of the Lord upon the cart, and the coffer with the mice of gold and the images of the emerods." Later in the same chapter we are told that the golden mice were "according to the number of all the cities of the Philistines belonging to five lords, both of fenced cities, and the country villages." *Emerods* is an old English variant of *haemorrhoids,* tumorous veins causing piles. In the preceding chapter it is related that "the hand of the Lord was heavy upon them of Ashdod, and he destroyed them, and smote them with emerods." Field mice are common in Palestine today and probably were so in ancient times. One species found there is supposed by some to be the progenitor of the common house mouse.

Who was David's mother?

"Who was David's mother?" is often cited as an unanswerable question, like "How old was Ann?" and "Who hit Billy Patterson?" David was the son of Jesse, a Bethlehem shepherd and farmer, who had several sons and daughters. The name of the wife of Jesse and the mother of David is nowhere recorded in the Bible. But she is referred to. In *I Samuel 22* we are told that "his brethren and all his father's house" joined David when he took refuge in the cave of Adullam. Verses 3 and 4 of that chapter say: "And David went thence to Mizpeh of Moab: and he said unto the king of Moab, Let my father and my mother, I pray thee, come forth, and be with you, till I know what God will do for me. And he brought them before the king of Moab: and they dwelt with him all the while that David was in the hold." But *II Samuel 8:2* says: "And he smote Moab, and measured them with a line, casting them down to the ground; even with two lines measured he to put to death, and with one full line to keep alive. And so the Moabites became David's servants, and brought gifts." This is interpreted to mean that David killed two out of every three of the defeated Moabites. Although this cruel treatment of a conquered enemy was in keeping with Oriental warfare in that day, no reason for its severity is given in the Bible. Josephus says it was in revenge for the slaughter of David's father and mother by the king of Moab. It is supposed that David alludes to his mother in *Psalms*

68:16, where he says: "O turn unto me, and have mercy upon me; give thy strength unto thy servant, and save the son of thine handmaid." Also perhaps in *Psalms 116:16*: "O Lord, truly I am thy servant; I am thy servant, and the son of thy handmaid: thou hast loosed my bonds." The *Book of Ruth*, an anonymous historical romance, tells how a Moabitess woman named Ruth came to marry Boaz of Bethlehem, thus becoming the great-grandmother of King David and the ancestress of Jesus. It is believed that David reigned over Israel about 1000 B.C.

Did the Israelites have a national flag?

Although standards and ensigns for national and tribal identification are of ancient origin, national emblems in the modern sense were not known to the various Israelite and Jewish kingdoms and commonwealths of antiquity. Banners and standards were employed in ancient armies very much as they are now. References in the Bible indicate that during the forty years of wandering in the wilderness, between Egypt and the Promised Land, each of the original twelve tribes of Israel carried a banner for identification and the colors and designs corresponded to the twelve precious stones in the breastplate of Aaron and his successors in the office of high priest. *Numbers 1:52* says: "And the children of Israel shall pitch their tents, every man by his own camp, and every man by his own standard, throughout their hosts." In *Numbers 2:2-3* we read: "Every man of the children of Israel shall pitch by his own standard with the ensign of their father's house: far off about the tabernacle of the congregation shall they pitch. And on the east side toward the rising of the sun shall they of the standard of the camp of Judah pitch throughout their armies." Similar references are then made to the standards of other tribes. The design of the flag or standard of the tribe of Judah (from whom the Jews get their name), according to the Talmud, consisted of a pictorial emblem of a young rampant lion, suggested by Jacob's blessing on Judah in *Genesis 49:9*, and the following inscription from *Numbers 10:35*: "Rise up, Lord, and let thine enemies be scattered; and let them that hate thee flee before thee." In this connection the Bible mentions both standards and ensigns. Since during the march the twelve tribes were organized into grand divisions of three tribes each, some writers suppose that the standards represented the divisions while the ensigns represented the individual tribes. In latter times it appears that a cluster of grapes was regarded as the emblem of the Jewish nation. This was an allusion to the "branch with one cluster of grapes" which was cut in the land of Canaan by the representatives of the twelve tribes sent by Moses "to spy out the land" and which they brought back to Moses and Aaron as evidence that the Promised Land flowed "with milk and honey," as related in *Numbers 13*. Naturally after the destruction of Jerusalem in 70 A.D. by the Romans and the final dispersion, the Jews had no civil government to adopt a national flag. But there is evidence that some of the Jews engaged in shipping on the Mediterranean, particularly between Alexandria and Rome, used a banner with a cluster of grapes as the emblem of the Jewish people. It is said that Herod the Great, when he rebuilt the temple, had fixed above the door of the inner temple a solid-gold cluster of grapes as big as a man. This emblem of Israel was destroyed by the Romans when they burned and razed the temple. Soon after the first World War the International Council of the Zionists adopted a flag to represent the Jewish people of the world. It consists of a white ground with a blue horizontal stripe on the upper and lower edge and the star or shield of David in blue in the center. The six-pointed star or shield of David, formed by one equilateral triangle superimposed upon or interlocked with another, is now regarded as the symbol of Judaism. It is placed not only on the Zionist flag, but also upon synagogues, sacred vessels and gravestones, and it is the device of several Jewish organizations, being employed somewhat as the cross is by Christians. Often one of the triangles of the *Magem Dawid* (Hebrew for "Shield of David") is dark in color and the other light. Neither the Torah nor the Talmud recognizes images of God, and orthodox Jews are generally opposed to the acceptance of religious symbols of any kind. This symbol, however, is of considerable antiquity, although its origin is obscure. A dubious legend regards the shield as an accidental conventionalization of the Hebraic signature of King David himself. Apparently it was first used as a sign or amulet. Some have supposed that it originated among the rabbis of the Middle Ages; but the device has been found at Tarentum in southern Italy on a tombstone believed to date back to the third century A.D. The first specific mention of it in Jewish literature occurred in the middle of the twelfth century, when it was referred to as "the sign called David's shield." Through error the star of David is often called Solomon's seal, or the pentacle, which was not of Hebrew but Greek origin and which was originally a five-pointed figure, reputed to have magical powers since the days of Pythagoras. These figures, now generally formed after the fashion of the star of David, are said to symbolize the union of the body and the soul and to be charms against danger. Their original significance has been lost in antiquity and is now merely a matter of conjecture. Before the first World War the United States Government made no distinction in the markers on the graves of Jewish and Christian soldiers, sailors and marines. The headstones supplied by the American Government for veterans of the Civil War and the Spanish-American War consisted of a slab of white American marble with the top slightly rounded and an inscription within a sunken shield. The headstones placed at the graves of veterans since the beginning of the first World War also consist of a white marble slab, but each stone has a small circle on the front face near the top containing an emblem of religious faith—a Latin cross for Christian graves and a six-pointed star of David for Jewish graves.

What does *confection* in the Bible mean?

Exodus 30:34-35 says: "And the Lord said unto Moses, Take unto thee sweet spices, stacte, and onycha, and galbanum; these sweet spices with pure frankincense: of each shall there be a like weight: and thou shalt make it a perfume, a confection after the art of the apothecary, tempered together, pure and holy." This is the only occurrence of *confection* in the King James Version. *Confection* is derived from Latin *con,* "together," and *facere,* "to put," and literally signifies "something put together or compounded." As used in the English Bible *confection* means merely a compound or mixture. In *I Samuel 8:13* the prophet, warning the Israelites against the manner of king that would reign over them in the person of Saul, says: "And he will take your daughters to be confectionaries, and to be cooks, and to be bakers." In the margin of the Revised Version *confectionaries* here is rendered *perfumers.* At the time the King James Version was translated *confectionary* meant a person who compounds drugs, medicines, perfumes and the like.

Where did God come from?

In *Deuteronomy 33:2* Moses says: "The Lord came from Sinai." And in *Habakkuk 3:3* it says: "God came from Teman." These passages, without reference to their contexts and their obvious figurative allusions, are sometimes quoted to prove that the Bible says where God came from. Of course, the passages referred to are sheer symbolism and not to be taken literally. *Deuteronomy 33:1-2* says: "And this is the blessing, wherewith Moses the man of God blessed the children of Israel before his death. And he said, The Lord came from Sinai, and rose up from Seir unto them; he shined forth from mount Paran, and he came with ten thousands of saints: from his right hand went a fiery law for them." Moses merely meant that Sinai, the mount of revelation, was the starting point where God manifested himself to the Israelites and came to abide in their midst. "Rose from Seir" is a metaphor of sunrise, in which the shedding forth of God's light on his chosen people is compared to the rising and dawning of the sun. The same figure of speech is used by Habakkuk. *Habakkuk 3:1-3* reads: "A PRAYER of Habakkuk the prophet upon Shigionoth. O Lord, I have heard thy speech, and was afraid: O Lord, revive thy work in the midst of the years, in the midst of the years make known; in wrath remember mercy. God came from Teman, and the Holy One from mount Paran. Selah. His glory covered the heavens, and the earth was full of his praise." Teman, literally "on the right hand," was a district in northwestern Edom, and Paran was a mountain range between Sinai and Seir. Apparently Habakkuk used *Teman* in the sense of "a southern quarter" or "the south." He pictures the storm accompanying Jehovah's coming as beginning in Sinai and sweeping northward. In *Genesis 36:11* Teman occurs as the son of Eliphaz and grandson of Esau, who dwelt in Mount Seir in Edom. *Job 2:11* refers to Job's friend Eliphaz as "the Temanite." It appears that the Temanites had a reputation for wisdom, for *Jeremiah 49:7* says: "Concerning Edom, thus saith the Lord of hosts: Is wisdom no more in Teman? is counsel perished from the prudent? is their wisdom vanished?" In some cases in the Bible *Teman* seems to be used as synonymous with *Edom.*

Is "it depends on whose ox is gored" in the Bible?

The proverbial expressions, "It depends on whose ox is gored" and "It makes a difference whose ox is gored," have a quaint Biblical flavor about them and many people suppose they are derived from the Bible. They are not, however, of Biblical origin. The law of Moses contains two provisions having a slight bearing on the subject. *Exodus 21:28-32* provides: "If an ox gore a man or a woman, that they die: then the ox shall be surely stoned, and his flesh shall not be eaten; but the owner of the ox shall be quit. But if the ox were wont to push with his horn in time past, and it hath been testified to his owner, and he hath not kept him in, but that he hath killed a man or a woman; the ox shall be stoned, and his owner also shall be put to death. If there be laid on him a sum of money, then he shall give for the ransom of his life whatsoever is laid upon him. Whether he have gored a son, or have gored a daughter, according to this judgment shall it be done unto him. If the ox shall push a manservant or a maidservant; he shall give unto their master thirty shekels of silver, and the ox shall be stoned." *Exodus 21:35-36* deals with cases where one ox gores another: "And if one man's ox hurt another's, that he die; then they shall sell the live ox, and divide the money of it; and the dead ox also they shall divide. Or if it be known that the ox hath used to push in time past, and his owner hath not kept him in; he shall surely pay ox for ox; and the dead shall be his own." It is hard to see how either one of these passages, or any other in the Bible, could have suggested the proverbial saying, "It makes a difference whose ox is gored." This saying is believed to have been suggested by one of the fables in *The American Spelling Book,* first published by Noah Webster in 1817. *Fable VIII,* headed *The Partial Judge,* in that work is as follows: "A Farmer came to a neighboring Lawyer, expressing great concern for an accident which he said had just happened. One of your Oxen, continued he, has been gored by an unlucky Bull of mine, and I should be glad to know how I am to make you reparation. Thou art a very honest fellow replied the Lawyer, and wilt not think it unreasonable that I expect one of thy Oxen in return. It is no more than justice, quoth the Farmer, to be sure; but what did I say?—I mistake—It is *your* Bull that has killed one of *my* Oxen. Indeed! says the Lawyer, that alters the case: I must inquire into the affair—and if—And *if*! said the Farmer—the business I find would have been concluded without an *if,* had you been as ready to do justice to others as to exact it from them." Whether this fable of Noah Webster's suggested the saying, "It makes a difference whose ox is gored," or whether the fable was suggested by the saying, the wide circulation of *The American Spelling Book* and its immense popularity undoubtedly did much to make the saying proverbial in America. *Gore* in the sense of "piercing," "hurting" or "wounding with horns," is related in origin to Old English *gar,* "a spear," and the underlying idea of the term seems to refer to stabbing with a sharp weapon like a spearhead.

What were the badgers' skins mentioned in the Bible?

According to *Exodus 25,* the Lord spake unto Moses in the wilderness and enumerated the various articles that would be acceptable from the Israelites for use in building the tabernacle. Among the offerings that Moses was to take were "badgers' skins." Elsewhere in *Exodus* we learn that these badgers' skins were used in making the upper covering of the roof of the tabernacle to protect it from the weather. *Exodus 4* tells us that "a covering of badgers' skins" was used to protect various sacred vessels and articles while the Israelites were on the march. According to *Ezekiel 16:10*, the Lord caused the prophet to say to Jerusalem: "I clothed thee also with broidered work, and shod thee with badgers' skin, and I girded thee about with fine linen, and I covered thee with silk." The Hebrew *tachash*, rendered *badgers' skins* in the King James Version, has given translators considerable trouble. Nobody really knows what it means. A favorite theory is that the unknown Hebrew word refers to the skins of seal-like animals found in the Red Sea. The Revised Version renders the term *seal-skins* and in the margin suggests *porpoise-skins* as an alternative. Some authorities identify the animal as the dugong or sea-cow, a dolphin-like animal common in the Red Sea and the Indian Ocean, the skin of which is used for leather. Another theory is that the unknown Hebrew word rendered *badgers' skins* was merely an attempt to reproduce the Egyptian word for leather. Nearly all authorities admit that *badgers' skins* was a poor guess. According to Jewish legend, *tachash* referred to a unique species of sea-animal that lived in the Red Sea in the time of Moses but which is now extinct.

Is *ivory tower* in the Bible?

Ivory tower is not in the Bible, but *tower of ivory* is. The phrase is getting more and more common in everyday speech and writing. Dictionaries define *ivory tower* as a retreat or secluded place for meditation. Ivory towers, observed a recent writer, seem to be inhabited chiefly by newspaper columnists who seek perspective by avoiding facts. Some authorities have suggested that *ivory tower* in this sense may be a corruption of *ivy tower*; that is, an *ivy*-covered tower. But the phrase may have been suggested by a passage in the Bible. "Thy neck is as a *tower of ivory*," says *The Song of Solomon 7:4*. Ivory was one of the most precious substances known to the ancients and there are many references to it as a decorative material in the Scriptures. Some of the many Biblical references to ivory are: "A throne of ivory," "the ivory house which Ahab made," "ivory palaces," "his belly is as bright as ivory overlaid with sapphires," "the company of the Ashurites have made them benches of ivory, brought out of the isles of Chittim," "they brought thee for a present horns of ivory," "the houses of ivory shall perish," "beds of ivory," and "no man buyeth vessels of ivory." If houses and palaces were made of ivory, or decorated and overlaid with ivory, why not towers of ivory for seclusion and meditation? Shakespeare, the greatest word juggler of all time, had Gremio in *The Taming of the Shrew* say he had stuffed his crowns in *ivory coffers.* Although the idea of the ivory tower must be much older, the earliest direct reference that we find to it in the modern sense occurs in Charles Augustin Sainte-Beuve's *Les Consolations,* published in 1831. In that work the French literary historian and critic refers to the French poet, novelist and dramatist Count de Alfred Victory Vigny *en sa tour d'ivoire,* "in his tower of ivory." *Ivory Tower* was the title of an unfinished novel by Henry James. Pearl Buck, in her *Of Men and Women,* says of the Manchu of old China: "He was born into his ivory tower and never left it."

Does the Bible mention the Holy Shroud?

Holy Shroud does not occur in the Bible. It is merely the popular name of the winding cloth in which Jesus was buried. All four of the Gospels refer to this garment. *Matthew 27:57-60* says: "When the even was come, there came a rich man of Arimathaea, named Joseph, who also himself was Jesus' disciple: he went to Pilate, and begged the body of Jesus. Then Pilate commanded the body to be delivered. And when Joseph had taken the body, he wrapped it in a clean linen cloth, and laid it in his own new tomb, which he had hewn out in the rock: and he rolled a great stone to the door of the sepulchre, and departed." According to *Mark 15:46* Joseph of Arimathaea "bought fine linen, and took him down, and wrapped him in the linen." Luke, who describes Joseph as a counsellor, "a good man, and a just," who "himself waited for the kingdom of God," tells us that he "took it down, and wrapped it in linen, and laid it in a sepulchre that was hewn in stone, wherein never man before was laid." *John 19:38-40* says that Nicodemus, "which at the first came to Jesus by night," brought a mixture of myrrh and aloes, about an hundred pound weight" and that he and Joseph took "the body of Jesus, and wound it in linen clothes with the spices, as the manner of the Jews is to bury." The Bible tells us nothing as to what became of the grave clothes of Jesus after the Resurrection. There are several holy shrouds preserved as Christian relics. The most notable of these is the Holy Shroud at Turin, Italy. According to Catholic tradition, this is the actual "clean linen cloth" in which Joseph of Arimathaea wrapped the body of Jesus after the Crucifixion. It is an age-blackened piece of linen cloth about fourteen feet long and four feet wide. On the lower half of the cloth, front and back, is the faint but distinct image of a human body. The Holy Shroud was first heard of about 1360 A.D. at Lirey in the diocese of Troyes, France. Since 1858 it has been preserved in a gold case studded with precious stones in a chapel at the Cathedral of Turin. The relic belongs to the Italian royal house and may be mended only by the queen or a royal princess working on her knees. After Italy entered the second World War, the sacred relic was deposited for safety in a place known only to the King of Italy, the Crown Prince and the Archbishop of Turin. Naturally the genuineness of the Holy Shroud has been contested and is still occasionally the subject of controversy. Abbe Ulysse Chevalier, a Catholic clergyman and history professor at the Catholic University of Lyons, traced the history of this winding sheet and concluded that it was not made earlier than the fourteenth century. In 1901 Dr. Paul Vignom maintained that the image on the relic was beyond the skill of any medieval forger and is a natural negative of the blood-stained body of the Saviour. The authenticity of the Holy Shroud at Turin is not questioned in various pronouncements of the Holy See, and persons not duly authorized are forbidden to touch the sacred garment upon pain of excommunication. On several occasions the Holy Shroud has been removed from its gold case, carried in processions to the main altar of the cathedral and exhibited to the public. In 1931, it was reported, more than a million persons viewed the relic when it was displayed for the first time in thirty-two years.

Who was Ichabod?

Ichabod is a Hebrew word that is popularly interpreted as meaning "departed glory" or "no glory." Some authorities suppose that it literally means "Where is the glory?" but its real meaning is not known for certain. In *I Samuel 4 Ichabod* is given as a name to the posthumous son of a priest named Phinehas. There it is related that after the Israelites were overcome by the Philistines at Ebenezer, they sent to Shiloh and brought the ark of the Covenant into the camp. Hophni and Phinehas, the sons of Eli, took charge of the sacred chest. When the battle was renewed, however, the Israelites were defeated with great slaughter, Hophni and Phinehas were slain and the ark of the Covenant was captured by the enemy. This was one of the greatest calamities that had ever befallen the chosen people up to that time. Eli himself, who was ninety-eight years old, fell over backward and broke his neck when a runner from the army informed him what had happened. The wife of Phinehas, who was with child, was so shocked when she heard that her people had been defeated, the ark taken, her husband and her brother-in-law both slain and her father-in-law killed by the news, that she immediately gave birth to a son, whom she called Ichabod, saying, "The glory is departed from Israel: for the ark of God is taken." We are told nothing of the life of Ichabod and there is only one other reference to him in the Bible. From the fourteenth chapter of the same book we learn that Ahiah, who crossed over to the Philistine garrison with Jonathan, was "the son of Ahitub, Ichabod's brother." John Greenleaf Whittier applied the name Ichabod to Daniel Webster after the Massachusetts statesman had delivered his famous Seventh of March speech in the United States Senate in 1850. That is the only speech in history that is remembered by the date on which it was delivered. It is known simply as Webster's Seventh of March speech. The great orator had hoped that the adoption of the compromise measures introduced by Henry Clay would prevent a sectional war and save the Union. The abolitionists, of whom the Quaker poet was one, were very bitter toward Webster, whom they accused of selling out to the slaveholding South. Whittier's *Ichabod* is one of the most scathing poems ever written about any public man during his life and received its title from the opening stanza, which reads:

> So fallen! so lost; the light withdrawn
> which once he wore!
> The glory from his gray hairs gone
> Forevermore!

What does *Baraca* mean?

Baraca, pronounced *"ba-RAK-a,"* is the name of an international, interdenominational organization of young men's Protestant Sunday-school classes, the first of which was organized in 1890 at Syracuse, New York, by a businessman named Marshall A. Hudson. Baraca Bible classes, which were the forerunners of organized Bible classes, consist of thousands of local groups in many different religious denominations, being particularly strong among the Baptists. The name is an adaptation of a Hebrew word meaning "blessing" or "God will bless." Although spelled in different ways, it occurs several times in the Old Testament as a personal and place name. Berachah was the name of one of the Benjamites who joined David at Ziklag, according to *I Chronicles 12:3,* and *II Chronicles 20:26* says: "And on the fourth day they assembled themselves in the valley of Berachah, for there they blessed the Lord: therefore the name of the same place was called, The valley of Berachah, unto this day." According to *Matthew 23:35,* Jesus said: "That upon you may come all the righteous blood shed upon the earth, from the blood of righteous Abel unto the blood of Zacharias son of Barachias, whom ye slew between the temple and the altar." This undoubtedly refers to an episode in the reign of Joash, king of Judah, related in *II Chronicles 24:20-21,* which reads: "And the Spirit of God came upon Zechariah the son of Jehoiada the priest which stood above the people, and said unto them, Thus saith God, Why transgress ye the commandments of the Lord, that ye cannot prosper? because ye have forsaken the Lord, he hath also forsaken you. And they conspired against him, and stoned him with stones at the commandment of the king in the court of the house of the Lord." Apparently the words *son of Barachias* were mistakenly inserted in *Matthew 23:35* by a later copyist. In *Luke 11:51* the same saying is expressed without any reference to Zacharias' being the son of Barachias. There was a Jewish tradition that the blood of Zechariah could not be removed from the ground by washing, but remained bubbling where it was shed.

What is simony?

Simony, pronounced *"SIMM-i-ni,* is traffick in things sacred, especially the crime of buying or selling church offices. This form of graft and corruption is most common in state churches where ecclesiastical offices and large revenues are linked together. In Shakespeare's *King Henry VIII* the divorced Queen Katharine says that under the regime of Cardinal Woolsey "simony was fair play." The term is of Biblical origin, being derived from the name of Simon, who, according to *Acts 8,* gave out that he was some great one and who bewitched the people of Samaria with sorceries into believing that he was the great power of God. When Philip the Evangelist went to the city of Samaria and preached Christ to the inhabitants, confirming his preaching with many miracles and signs, Simon, along with the others, believed and was baptized. Peter and John were then sent to Samaria that the Holy Ghost might fall upon the new converts. Simon, seeing the Holy Ghost was given through laying on of the Apostles' hands, offered them money, saying, "Give me also this power, that on whomsoever I lay hands, he may receive the Holy Ghost." The indignant Peter replied: "Thy money perish with thee, because thou hast thought that the gift of God may be purchased with money. Thou hast neither part nor lot in this matter: for thy heart is not right in the sight of God. Repent therefore of this thy wickedness, and pray God, if perhaps the thought of thine heart may be forgiven thee. For I perceive that thou art in the gall of bitterness, and in the bond of iniquity."

The contrite Simon then asked Peter to pray to the Lord for him that none of these things that the Apostle had spoken might come upon him. This Simon was called Simon Magus, which means Simon the Magician, and it is said that he founded a sect known as the Simonians. There are two legends as to the manner of his death. According to one, he engaged in a dispute over his powers with Peter and Paul at Rome during the reign of Nero and promised to fly up to heaven to prove his point. He actually ascended to a great height in the air, but, at the prayers of the Apostles, was dashed to the ground by the evil spirits that had enabled him to ascend. According to the other legend, he offered to be buried alive and promised to arise on the third day, but his disciples waited in vain for his resurrection from the deep trench in which he had been covered with several feet of earth.

Is *king's high way* in the Bible?

The phrase, *the king's high way,* is used twice in the English Bible, both times in connection with the proposed passage of the Israelites through a foreign country. In *Numbers 20:17* it is related that Moses sent messengers from Kadesh in the wilderness to the king of Edom, saying: "Let us pass, I pray thee, through thy country: we will not pass through the fields, or through the vineyards, neither will we drink of the water of the wells: we will go by the king's high way, we will not turn to the right hand nor to the left, until we have passed thy borders." But Edom refused to give Israel passage through his dominions, wherefore Israel turned away from him. When the Israelites reached Bamoth they sent messengers with a similar request to Sihon, king of the Amorites, saying, according to *Numbers 21:22*: "Let me pass through thy land: we will not turn into the fields, or into the vineyards; we will not drink of the waters of the well; but we will go along by the king's high way, until we be past thy borders." Sihon also refused, gathered all his people together and went out against Israel in the wilderness; but Israel in a battle at Jahaz smote him with the edge of the sword and possessed his land from Arnon unto Jabbok.

Who was the only woman called great in the Bible?

The only woman called great in the Bible is an unnamed woman at Shunem who played the part of the good Samaritan to Elisha and who was rewarded manyfold for so doing. The story of the relationship between Elisha and the Shunamite woman is told in *II Kings 4* and *8* and is one of the most beautiful stories in the Bible. *II Kings 4:8-11* says: "And it fell on a day, that Elisha passed to Shunem where was a great woman; and she constrained him to eat bread. And so it was, that as oft as he passed by, he turned in thither to eat bread. And she said unto her husband, Behold now, I perceive that this is an holy man of God, which passeth by us continually. Let us make a little chamber, I pray thee, on the wall; and let us set for him there a bed, and a table, and a stool, and a candlestick: and it shall be, when he cometh to us, that he shall turn in thither. And it fell on a day, that he came thither, and he turned into the chamber, and lay there." Upon the suggestion of the prophet, his servant Gehazi called the Shunamite and said to her: "Behold, thou hast been careful for us with all this care; what is to be done for thee? wouldest thou be spoken for to the king, or to the captain of the host?" But she answered that she dwelt among her own people. "What then is to be done for her?" asked Elisha. Gehazi replied that she was old and had no child. So Elisha had the servant call the woman, and when she stood in the door, he said: "About this season, according to the time of life, thou shalt embrace a son." Although she thought the man of God mocked her, she conceived and bare a son just as Elisha had foretold. When this son was grown he was stricken in the field and died. The mother placed the dead son on the bed in the little chamber she had prepared for the prophet and shut the door. Then she and one of the young men rode as hard as they could to find Elisha, whom they found at Mount Carmel. Sending Gehazi ahead to lay his staff upon the face of the dead child, Elisha arose and followed the grief-stricken mother home. *II Kings 4:32-37* says: "And when Elisha was come into the house, behold, the child was dead, and laid upon his bed. He went in therefore, and shut the door upon them twain, and prayed unto the Lord. And he went up, and lay upon the child, and put his mouth upon his mouth, and his eyes upon his eyes, and his hands upon his hands; and he stretched himself upon the child; and the flesh of the child waxed warm. Then he returned, and walked in the house to and fro; and went up, and stretched himself upon him: and the child sneezed seven times, and the child opened his eyes. And he called Gehazi, and said, Call this Shunamite. So he called her. And when she was come in unto him, he said, Take up thy son. Then she went in, and fell at his feet, and bowed herself to the ground, and took up her son and went out." But the prophet did not forget the "great woman" when there was a threat of famine in the land. *II Kings 8:1-6* says: "Then spake Elisha unto the woman, whose son he had restored to life, saying, Arise and go thou and thine household, and sojourn wheresoever thou canst sojourn: for the Lord hath called for a famine:

and it shall also come upon the land seven years. And the woman arose, and did after the saying of the man of God: and she went with her household, and sojourned in the land of the Philistines seven years. And it came to pass at the seven years' end, that the woman returned out of the land of the Philistines: and she went forth to cry unto the king for her house and for her land. And the king talked with Gehazi the servant of the man of God, saying, Tell me, I pray thee, all the great things that Elisha hath done. And it came to pass, as he was telling the king how he had restored a dead body to life, that, behold, the woman, whose son had been restored to life, cried to the king for her house and for her land. And Gehazi said, My lord, O king, this is the woman, and this is her son, whom Elisha restored to life. And when the king asked the woman, she told him. So the king appointed unto her a certain officer, saying, Restore all that was hers, and all the fruits of the field since the day that she left the land, even until now."

What does *neesing* mean?

Neesing is an obsolete word that occurs in the King James Version once. According to *Job 41:18,* the Lord, answering the patriarch, said of the leviathan: "By his *neesings* a light doth shine, and his eyes are like the eyelids of the morning." The allusion is probably to the heavy breathing of the crocodile. *Neesing* is related to *sneezing* in origin and meaning, and the term in *Job* is rendered *sneezings* in the Revised Version. We find *sneeze* only once in the King James Version. According to *II Kings 4:35,* when Elisha restored the son of the Shunamite woman to life "the child sneezed seven times."

Is *robbing Peter to pay Paul* from the Bible?

Robbing Peter to pay Paul is not in the Bible. The proverbial saying probably was suggested by the traditional rivalry in the early Roman Christian community between Peter, "the Apostle to the Jews," and Paul, "the Apostle to the Gentiles." "As one who crucified Paul that Peter might go free," is a translation of a Latin sentence in the *Life of St. Thomas of Canterbury,* written by Herbert of Bosham about 1175 A.D. In 1383 John Wycliffe wrote: "Lord, hou schulde God approve that thou robbe Petur and gif this robbere to Poule in the name of Christ?" *Robbing Peter to pay Paul* appears to have been a familiar saying as early as the fourteenth century. In *Jacob's Well,* a work of unknown authorship written about 1440, we find: "To rob Peter, and give it Paul, it were not alms but great sin." In John

Ray's *English Proverbs*, published in 1670, occur "Praise Peter, but don't find fault with Paul" and "Peter in, Paul out," the latter being listed as a Scottish proverb. In his *Jacula Prudentum*, which antedates Ray's work, George Herbert has "Give not Saint Peter so much, to leave Saint Paul nothing" and "Who praiseth St. Peter does not blame St. Paul." Reference to the saying occurs even in the works of Francois Rabelais, who died in 1553: "By robbing Peter he paid Paul, he kept the moon from the wolves, and was ready to catch larks if ever the heavens should fall." It is often said that *robbing Peter to pay Paul*, in the figurative sense of taking something from one person to give to another, arose from the following circumstance: In 1550, during the reign of King Edward VI of England, the abbey church of St. Peter, Westminster, was advanced to the dignity of a cathedral by letters patent; but ten years later, in the reign of Mary, the church was again joined to the diocese of London and many of its estates and funds were appropriated to repair St. Paul's Cathedral. Although the saying may have been used in connection with that incident, the earlier quotations we have cited prove conclusively that it did not originate at that time. *Robbing Peter to pay Paul*, like many other sayings, survives because of the alliteration. Its true origin probably never will be ascertained.

Where is *occurrent* found in the Bible?

Occurrent is a rare old English word that is found only once in the Bible. It is an adjective which signifies "occurring," "current," "happening," "presenting itself," and, sometimes, "incidental." According to *I Kings 5:4* King Solomon sent to Hiram, saying: "But now the Lord my God hath given me rest on every side, so that there is neither adversary nor evil occurrent."

Who said: "Cleanliness is next to godliness"?

This proverbial saying is often erroneously quoted as being in the Bible. It is of disputed authorship. In his sermon on dress, delivered about 1740, John Wesley said: "Slovenliness is no part of religion; neither this [referring to the Bible] nor any text in the Scripture, condemns neatness of apparel. Certainly this is a duty, not a sin; 'cleanliness is indeed next to godliness.'" The founder of Methodism indicated by the quotation marks that he was not the author of the last part of the excerpt. Reverend Rowland Hill attributed the words to George Whitefield. Probably Hill gave the true author of the saying in its present form. The thought expressed by the proverb, however, is ancient. In one of the *Mishna* referred to in the Jewish *Talmud* is the following: "Phinehas ben Yair says, The doctrines of religion are resolved into (or are next to) carefulness; carefulness into vigorousness; vigorousness into guiltlessness; guiltlessness into abstemiousness; abstemiousness into cleanliness; *cleanliness into godliness* . . ." Perhaps the nearest English approximation to the Hebrew saying is: "Cleanliness is akin to godliness." In the *Advancement of Learning*, written about 1605, Francis Bacon said: "Cleanness of body was ever deemed to proceed from a due reverence to God, to society, and to ourselves." Personal as well as ritual cleanliness were of the very essence of the Hebrew faith. In *II Corinthians 6:16* Paul, who was brought up in that faith, says "ye are the temple of the living God," and in Verse 1, Chapter 7 of the same Epistle, "let us cleanse ourselves from all filthiness of the flesh and spirit, perfecting holiness in the fear of God."

Does the Bible mention cabins?

Cabins occurs only once in the King James Version. In *Jeremiah 27:16* we are told that the prophet entered "into the dungeon, and into the cabins." There the correct meaning is expressed by *cells*, and it is so translated in the Revised Version.

Who was the Bramble King?

Abimelech, who made the first attempt to set up a monarchy in Israel, is known as the Bramble King. His violent and ill-fated reign of three years over Israel is related in *Judges 9*. Abimelech was the natural son of Gideon, fifth Judge of Israel. After the death of Gideon, who was also called Jerubbaal, Abimelech obtained threescore and ten pieces of silver from his mother's people with which he "hired vain and light persons, which followed him. And he went unto his father's house at Ophrah, and slew his brethren the sons of Jerubbaal, being threescore and ten persons, upon one stone: notwithstanding yet Jotham the youngest son of Jerubbaal was left; for he hid himself." After this cold-blooded slaughter of his father's seventy legitimate sons, Abimelech was proclaimed king by all the men of Shechem in Ephraim. When Jotham, the only legitimate son of Gideon who survived, heard what happened he went and stood on the top of Mt. Gerizim and warned the Shechemites against Abimelech in a parable from which the nickname "Bramble King" is derived. Jotham said: "The trees went forth on a time to anoint a king over them; and they said unto the olive tree, Reign thou over us. But the olive tree said unto them, Should I leave my fatness, wherewith by me they honour God and man, and go to be promoted over the trees? And the trees said to the fig tree, Come thou, and reign over us. But the fig tree said unto them, Should I forsake my sweetness, and my good fruit, and go to be promoted over the trees? Then said the trees unto the vine, Come thou, and reign over us. And the vine said unto them, Should I leave my wine, which cheereth God and man, and go to be promoted over the trees? Then said all the trees unto the bramble, Come thou, and reign over us. And the bramble said unto the trees, If in truth ye anoint me king over you, then come and put your trust in my shadow: and if not, let fire come out of the bramble, and devour the cedars of Lebanon." Jotham then related the services of his father and the cruel murder of his own seventy brothers, and added: "If ye then have dealt truly and sincerely with Jerubbaal and with his house this day, then rejoice ye in Abimelech, and let him also rejoice in you: but if not, let fire come out from Abimelech, and devour the men of Shechem, and the house of Millo; and let fire come out from the men of Shechem, and from the house of Millo, and devour Abimelech." Shechem repented its action and revolted, whereupon the Bramble King captured the city, took the citadel by stratagem, burned it to the ground and sowed the site with salt. The turn of Thebez came next. After taking the city and while attempting to set fire to the citadel, Abimelech's skull was broken by a piece of a millstone cast from the walls by a woman. What happened to the first would-be king of Israel is related in *Judges 9:54*: "Then he called hastily unto the young man his armourbearer, and said unto him, Draw thy sword, and slay me, that men say not of me, A woman slew him. And his young man thrust him through, and he died."

What is a Jesse tree?

A genealogical tree representing the descent of Jesus from Jesse, whose youngest son was David, is known as a Jesse tree, a tree of Jesse, or simply as a Jesse. This name was suggested by *Isaiah 11:1*, which reads: "And there shall come forth a rod out of the stem of Jesse, and a Branch shall grow out of his roots." In *I Samuel 16:1* we are told: "And the Lord said unto Samuel, How long wilt thou mourn for Saul, seeing I have rejected him from reigning over Israel? fill thine horn with oil, and go, I will send thee to Jesse the Bethlehemite: for I have provided me a king among his sons." In Christian church art the Jesse tree is used as a decoration for walls, ceilings, windows and vestments. Sometimes the Jesse tree takes the form of a large candlestick with many branches; at others it represents Jesse himself in a recumbent position with a vine rising from his loins. A stained window, representing Jesse with a tree shooting from him containing the pedigree of Jesus, is called a Jesse window.

What is Yiddish?

Yiddish is an Anglicized corruption and shortened form of German *Judisch-Deutsch*, meaning "Jewish German." Yiddish is the native language of those Jews whose ancestors left the Middle Rhineland section of Germany during the fourteenth and fifteenth centuries and settled in Poland, Lithuania, Russia and other Slavic countries. These Jewish emigrants from the Rhineland area retained their medieval Lowland German dialect but wrote it in Hebrew characters. They were isolated so many centuries from those who spoke German that their language absorbed much from the languages and dialects of the people of the lands where they resided, and gradually Yiddish became irregular in grammar, spelling and pronunciation, finally evolving into a distinct folk tongue. Yiddish acquired many Hebrew, Polish, Balto-Slavic and Russian words, as well as a sprinkling of words of Latin, Greek, Romanian and Hungarian origin. Some authorities suppose that many of the Hebrew words in Yiddish may be inherent in the language, because the Jews in Eastern Europe continued to be influenced by the Scriptures and other writings in ancient Hebrew and Aramaic. Since many of the Jews who settled in Eastern Europe during the fourteenth and fifteenth centuries had resided in the Netherlands, it is also supposed that some of the original vocabulary was composed of Holland Dutch. But it is impractical to argue whether the basic elements of Yiddish are of *Low* or *High* German origin, because when Yiddish originated the German language was little more than a conglomeration of Germanic dialects. The basic elements of Yiddish were derived from the prevailing German dialects spoken in the middle Rhineland area during the late Middle Ages. Yiddish has since made so many acquisitions and undergone so many changes that it may now be properly classed as a distinct language rather than as a dialect. The Hebrew characters employed in writing and printing Yiddish give it more the appearance of Hebrew than German. Although historically Yiddish is a kind of German rather than a kind of Hebrew, and it has been defined facetiously as "crucified German," its seeds sprouted in a German dialect no longer spoken and a modern German who had not specially studied Yiddish would find it unintelligible, just as the language of Chaucer would be unintelligible to an American or Englishman of today. Roughly speaking, the vocabulary of Yiddish as spoken and written in Europe contains seventy percent of German words, twenty percent of Hebrew and Aramaic, and ten percent of Slavic. It is now so widely spoken by Jews that it serves as a sort of international language for them. In the United States, however, Yiddish has absorbed so many English words and phrases that its purity as a separate language is threatened, and Yiddish-speaking Jews newly arrived from Europe find it difficult to understand their language as spoken by Jews in America. Originally Yiddish had no consistent grammatical rules and the phonetic spelling varied widely. For centuries Jews regarded Yiddish only as a folk tongue to be used in ordinary conversation and commercial translations and Jewish scholars frowned upon it as a medium for religious and literary expression. But during the nineteenth century Yiddish grammar and spelling were made more uniform, and there is now a rich and extensive literature printed in this flexible, varied, idiomatic and expressive language. Sometimes Yiddish is referred to as *Judaeo-German.* Yiddish, like Hebrew, is written and read from the right to the left.

How is *trow* pronounced?

Trow occurs in the Bible only once. *Luke 17:9* quotes Jesus as saying: "Doth he thank that servant because he did the things that were commanded him? I trow not." *Trow* is an obsolete English word related in origin to *true* and *trust.* "I trow" is equivalent to modern "I trust" or "I think." It is correctly pronounced *tro,* with a long *o* to rhyme with *throw.* In *King Lear* the Fool sings:

Have more than thou showest,
Speak less than thou knowest,
Lend less than thou owest,
Ride more than thou goest,
Learn more than thou trowest,
Set less than thou throwest.

What is the Biblical inscription on the Liberty Bell?

"Proclaim Liberty throughout all the land unto all the inhabitants thereof," is the Biblical inscription on the Liberty Bell. This passage is among the words that "the Lord spake unto Moses in mount Sinai" and is taken from *Leviticus 25:10,* the full text of which reads: "And ye shall hallow the fiftieth year, and proclaim liberty throughout all the land unto all the inhabitants thereof: it shall be a jubilee unto you; and ye shall return every man unto his possession, and ye shall return every man unto his family." The remarkable thing about this inscription is the fact that it was ordered placed on the bell in 1751, twenty-five years before the adoption of the Declaration of Independence and many years before any Americans seriously considered a general revolt against the Mother Country. On November 1, 1751, the three superintendents of the State House at Philadelphia wrote a letter to Robert Charles, London agent of the colony, in which they commissioned him to get a bell "with the following words, well shapen in large letters round it, viz: 'By order of the Assembly of the Province of Pennsylvania for the State House in the City of Philadelphia, 1752.' And underneath: 'Proclaim Liberty throughout all the land unto all the inhabitants thereof—Lev. xxv, 10.' " The bell was originally cast in the foundry of Mears and Stainback in Whitechapel, London, and it arrived in Philadelphia in August, 1752. Because of the use of faulty bell metal, the bell had to be recast in Philadelphia twice by Pass and Stow before the Spring of 1753, when it was finally raised and fixed in the steeple of the State House, which became known as Independence Hall after the Declaration of Independence was adopted and signed there. It is believed that the Biblical inscription on the bell was suggested by Isaac Norris, who was speaker of the assembly, one of the "superintendents of the State House" and chairman of the committee instructed by the Assembly to get a bell. Apparently the bell received its popular name solely from the inscription on it and was so known long before the Revolution. The inscription proved to be prophetic and its full significance was not appreciated until the bell was rung July 8, 1776, after the Declaration of Independence had been made public and read by Colonel John Nixon to a large assemblage of people in the State House yard. There is no reliable information about bells before the Christian Era. Church bells were not used until about the fifth or six century A.D. The Jews do not now, and never have, made use of bells in connection with their synagogues. *Bell* occurs only a few times in the King James Version of the Bible. The bells upon the high priest's dress were merely tinkling ornaments and not true bells. *Exodus 28:33-35* says: "And beneath upon the hem of it thou shalt make pomegranates of blue, and of purple, and of scarlet, round about the hem thereof; and bells of gold between them round about; and a golden bell and a pomegranate, a golden bell and a pomegranate, upon the hem of the robe round about. And it shall be upon Aaron to minister: and his sound shall be heard when he goeth in unto the holy place before the Lord, and when he cometh out, that he die not." Again in *Exodus*

39:25-26: "And they made bells of pure gold, and put the bells between the pomegranates upon the hem of the robe, round about between the pomegranates; a bell and a pomegranate, a bell and a pomegranate, round about the hem of the robe to minister in; as the Lord commanded Moses." The word does not occur elsewhere in the English Bible except in *Zechariah 14:20,* which reads in part: "In that day shall there be upon the bells of the horses, HOLINESS UNTO THE LORD."

What is meant by sin-eating?

Sin-eating is said to have been a curious medieval custom of which there is little actual evidence. Certain persons known as sin-eaters are supposed to have been hired for a small fee to attend funerals and eat food that had touched the corpse. The origin of this odd practice is not known for certain, although it may be related to the scapegoat of *Leviticus 16,* discussed elsewhere in this book. Some authorities believe that sin-eating was suggested originally by a mistaken interpretation of *Hosea 4:8,* which reads in part: "They eat up the sin of my people." The context indicates that the prophet meant merely that the self-seeking priest "fed upon" the sin-offerings and enriched themselves instead of checking sin among the people. "Like people, like priest," says Hosea. At any rate, the food of medieval sin-eating represented the sins of the deceased and by eating it the sin-eater was supposed to take those sins upon himself and thus prevent them from disturbing the rest of the departed soul. Although some authorities question the authenticity of the evidence, sin-eating appears to have existed at one time in parts of the British Isles. It is said that some villages had official sin-eaters who were notified when a death occurred in the community. Upon the arrival at the home of the deceased the sin-eater, generally an old man, was provided with a low stool on which he sat just outside the door of the death chamber until the corpse was brought out. When the pall-bearers carried the corpse from the room the sin-eater was commanded to consume a loaf of bread and a bowl of ale placed on the bier by a close female relative of the deceased. After the sin-eater had eaten the bread and drunk the ale he was given a few pennies and dismissed. In the most primitive form of the custom it is probable that the sin-eater entered the death chamber and ate the bread while it was actually lying on the corpse, after which he was given his fee and then driven from the house with curses and perhaps a few kicks for good measure. John Aubrey, seventeenth-century English antiquary and folklorist, wrote that in Herefordshire it was a custom at funerals to give a sin-eater a piece of bread, a bowl of beer and sixpence over the corpse. By eating the bread and drinking the beer the sin-eater was supposed to take upon himself the sins of the deceased and free his ghost from "walking." Aubrey says the custom was known in Wales and neighboring English counties. There have been faint reminiscences of the custom in comparatively modern times. In certain rural sections of Bavaria, it is said, a cake used to be placed on the breast of the corpse and eaten by the nearest relative. The Dutch who settled in New Netherland brought with them from Holland the custom of giving attendants at a funeral *doed-koecks,* "dead cakes," marked with the initials of the deceased. Faint traces of sin-eating are said to be still found in Lincolnshire and the Scottish Highlands where "burial cakes" are occasionally served, and in parts of the Balkans where a small bread image of the deceased is sometimes made and eaten by members of the family.

Is *the sons of the wild jackass* in the Bible?

On November 7, 1929, Senator George H. Moses, of New Hampshire, made an address in Washington, D. C., before the New England Manufacturers' Association in which he said: "Mournfully I prophesy that the program of these *sons of the wild jackass* who now control the Senate will probably go forward to complete consummation." Senator Moses referred to a group of independent Republican senators who had joined the Democrats in blocking legislation providing higher tariff protection desired by the New England Republicans. The particular phrase used by Moses was resented by several of the insurgent senators and the subject was widely discussed in the newspapers. Various interpretations were placed on what the New Hampshire senator had said. The utterance of the sharp-tongued Moses was the subject of a stormy debate in the Senate the following day. A feeble and futile effort was made to unseat him as chairman of the Republican Senatorial Campaign Committee and as President Pro Tempore of the Senate. It is often said that *sons of the wild jackass* was borrowed from the Bible, but no such phrase occurs in the Scriptures, although it was undoubtedly suggested by a vague recollection and fusion of several Biblical passages. Senator Moses afterward explained that the phrase was inspired by *Jeremiah 14:6,* which says: "And the wild asses did stand in the high places, they snuffed up the wind like dragons; their eyes did fail, because there was no grass." *Jackass* does not occur in the King James Version and probably was not coined for more than a century after that version was made. *Job 11:12* says: "For vain man would be wise, though man be born like a wild ass's colt." The fact that the donkey is the popular emblem of the Democratic Party, with which the insurgent Republicans had collaborated, may have influenced the spicy phrase coined by the Republican senator from New Hampshire.

How did *peter out* originate?

The pithy and expressive slang verbal phrase *peter out,* meaning "to run out," "to fail" or "to become exhausted gradually," may have been originally suggested by an incident in the Bible. At first this colloquial term was simply *peter* and meant "to stop" or "leave off." The Oxford dictionary tells us that in England as early as 1812 *Peter that* was synonymous with *Stop that*. *Peter* was transformed into *peter out* in Western American mining slang. A promising vein of ore or placer mine that soon became exhausted of precious metal was said to peter out. The term quickly acquired a figurative sense. In 1854 H. H. Riley wrote in *Puddleford*: "He hoped this 'spectable meeting warn't going to *Peter-out*." The fact that the author capitalized *Peter-out* suggests that he associated it with the proper name *Peter*. According to the Gospels, the chief Apostle assured his Master: "Though all men shall be offended because of thee, yet will I never be offended . . . Lord, I am ready to go with thee, both into prison, and to death . . . I will lay down my life for thy sake." Jesus said to him: "I tell thee, Peter, the cock shall not crow this day, before that thou shalt thrice deny that thou knowest me." When the supreme test came that very night Peter denied his Master three times. Although etymological evidence is incomplete, it is very probable that *peter out* was suggested by Peter's failure to stand by Jesus in that critical hour, despite previous professions of loyalty.

What is the rule of John Smith?

In *II Thessalonians 3:10* St. Paul says: "For even when we were with you, this we commanded you, that if any would not work, neither should he eat." This Biblical injunction is popularly called the rule of John Smith because of an incident in the early days of the English colony at Jamestown. The colony was at first operated on a common basis; all the products of labor and trade were put in a common stock and the ignorant and lazy fared as well as the intelligent and industrious. In 1609 about forty men were supporting the whole company of some two hundred. Early in the spring of that year Captain John

Smith called the colonists together and plainly told them that as their lawfully chosen ruler he would promptly punish all infractions of discipline. "Countrymen," he said, "you see now that power resteth wholly in myself. You must obey this, now, for a law,—that 'he that will not work shall not eat.' And though you presume that authority here is but a shadow, and that I dare not touch the lives of any, but my own must answer it, yet he that offendeth, let him assuredly expect his due punishment. . . . I protest by that God that made me, since necessity hath no power to force you to gather for yourselves, you shall not only gather for yourselves, but for those that are sick." It was an old Jewish idea that every member of the community who was able, even the priests and scribes, should earn their own living by some useful occupation. Paul not only taught this but apparently practiced it during his long career as a missionary. In *I Thessalonians 4:11* the Apostle to the Gentiles urged the Christians "to study to be quiet, and to do your own business, and to work with your own hands, as we commanded you." According to *I Corinthians 4:11-12* he said: "Even unto this present hour we both hunger, and thirst, and are naked, and are buffeted, and have no certain dwelling-place; and labour, working with our own hands." In *I Timothy 3:8-9* Paul said: "Neither did we eat any man's bread for nought; but wrought with labour and travail night and day, that we might not be chargeable to any of you: not because we have not power, but to make ourselves an ensample unto you to follow us."

What is the Joshua tree?

Many seem to be under the impression that the Joshua tree is mentioned in the Bible. This name is only indirectly of Biblical origin. *Joshua tree* is the popular name of *Yucca brevifolia,* a genus of giant yuccas native to certain elevated desert regions in Utah, Nevada, Arizona and California. The trunks of some Joshua trees attain a diameter of several feet and a height of thirty-five or forty feet. These cactus-like plants have no annual rings of growth in their stems and it is hard to determine their age. They grow very slowly and naturalists have observed individual plants over a period of twenty years without detecting any measurable increase in size. A Joshua tree with a trunk three feet in diameter was estimated by botanists to be seven hundred years old. These tall, tree-like plants, with their forked branches bent like great arms as if extended heaven-ward in prayer, have a picturesque and weird appearance and made a profound impression on the first European visitors to the Far West. The early Mormons, given to adopting symbols from the Scriptures, called this "praying plant" the Joshua tree because to them it seemed to symbolize the conquest of their Promised Land. Another name for the Joshua tree is the yucca cactus. It has rigid, narrow, sharp-pointed leaves, and from March to May produces clusters of large, waxy, greenish-white blossoms. Although the Joshua tree is largely ornamental, its seeds were ground into a meal for food by the Indians, and the soft, spongy wood of the plant has been used to a limited extent in making paper pulp and packing materials.

What does Twelfth Night commemorate?

Twelfth Night is the evening before Epiphany or Twelfth Day, which is a festival celebrated January 6 or the twelfth day after Christmas. It was formerly a time of merrymaking and is supposed to commemorate the rejoicing attendant on the arrival of the wise men from the east at Bethlehem with gifts for the Christ child. Some writers say that Twelfth Night commemorates the appearance of the Star of Bethlehem to the wise men. At any rate, the festival traditionally symbolizes the manifestation of Christ to the Gentiles. One of Shakespeare's greatest plays is entitled *Twelfth-Night.* It is generally believed that the dramatist first called this play *What You Will,* but changed the title when it was selected as the chief attraction at the Twelfth-Night revels and festivities at the court of King James I. *Epiphany* is from a Greek root meaning "to show" and is applied to the Christian festival on Twelfth Day because it traditionally commemorates the "showing" or "manifestation" of Christ to the Gentiles in the persons of the Magi.

What is the Wailing Wall?

The Wailing Wall is a section of the western wall in the Dome of the Rock, the Moslem mosque standing on the site of the temple in Jerusalem. This section of the wall, about 59 by 120 feet in dimensions, is believed to be composed of stones taken from the ruins of Herod's temple when the mosque was built. It is also sometimes called Solomon's Wall, because traditionally these same stones were part of Solomon's original temple. An inclosed area near the wall, approached by a series of steps and lanes, is known as the Wailing Place of the Jews. Every year Jews from all over the Holy Land gather at the Wailing Wall to observe the anniversary of the destruction of Herod's temple by the Romans as well as the destruction of Solomon's temple by the Babylonians, which happened to be the same day of the year. After the Romans destroyed the city in 70 A.D., they permitted no Jews to visit the site without special permission; but about the twelfth century the Arab rulers of Palestine granted permission to the Jews to gather near the Wailing Wall to worship, to mourn, to pray, to lament and to read from Jeremiah's *Lamentations* on the eve of the Sabbath and of Jewish feast days and on the anniversary of the destruction of the temples. This event, together with the only remnants of the ancient sacred edifice, symbolizes the final dispersion of the Jews and their dissolution as a nation. It is also observed with appropriate ceremonies in the synagogues of orthodox Jews in other parts of the world. In 1929 a mob composed of some two thousand Moslems attacked the Jews gathered near the Wailing Wall on this melancholy anniversary. The riots spread and martial law was proclaimed, but before the British military authorities could suppress the disorders nearly one thousand Moslems, Jews and Christians were killed and about three hundred others were seriously wounded. A League of Nations commission, appointed to determine the question of the ownership of the Wailing Wall, decided in 1930 that it was part of the Dome of the Rock and legally belonged to the Moslems. The commission, however, recommended that the Jews be permitted to continue to use the Wailing Place as one of the holy places of worship provided they did so in restricted numbers and without religious propaganda calculated to excite the Moslems to disorder.

Who said: "Where the Scriptures speak, we speak"?

Many erroneously suppose this oft-quoted saying is in the Bible, but Thomas Campbell (1763-1854), a noted Protestant clergyman, was the author of the quotation. He and his son, Alexander Campbell, were the real founders of the denomination known as the Christian Church or the Disciples of Christ (sometimes as the Campbellites), although they renounced all denominationalism and always contended that they were not the founders of a religious denomination in the generally accepted sense of that term. The elder Campbell emigrated from Ireland to western Pennsylvania in 1807 and in 1809 he called a religious meeting at the house of Abraham Altars in Washington County. He made an eloquent address in which he advocated a return to the simple teachings of the Bible and the abandonment of everything in religion for which Scriptural warrant could not be produced. In Campbell's opinion the Bible could be relied on as a complete and sufficient moral and spiritual guide. He then announced the rule upon which he thought that he and those associated with him should act. "That rule, my highly respected hearers," declared the clergyman, "is this, that where the Scriptures speak, we speak, and where the Scriptures are silent, we are silent." This meeting was the actual beginning of the Campbellite reformation and it resulted in the Christian Association of Washington County, which was organized "for the sole purpose of promoting simple evangelical Christianity," and which was the forerunner of the group of Christians who refer to themselves as the Disciples of Christ. With a total membership of more than 1,600,000, the Disciples of Christ is the largest religious body having its origin in the United States.

When did a prophet use a parable to rebuke a king?

One of the most beautiful parables in the Bible was told by Nathan the prophet to King David to drive home the point that the king had sinned greviously against the Lord in having Uriah the Hittite slain in battle to get possession of the latter's wife, Bathsheba. *II Samuel 12:1-7* says: "And the Lord sent Nathan unto David. And he came unto him, and said unto him, There were two men in one city; the one rich, and the other poor. The rich man had exceeding many flocks and herds: but the poor man had nothing, save one little ewe lamb, which he had bought and nourished up: and it grew up together with him, and with his children; it did eat of his own meat, and drank of his own cup, and lay in his bosom, and was unto him as a daughter. And there came a traveller unto the rich man, and he spared to take of his own flock and of his own herd, to dress for the wayfaring man that was come unto him: but took the poor man's lamb, and dressed it for the man that was come to him. And David's anger was greatly kindled against the man; and he said to Nathan, As the Lord liveth, the man that hath done this thing shall surely die: and he shall restore the lamb fourfold, because he did this thing, and because he had no pity. And Nathan said to David, Thou art the man." What Nathan said to David figured in the counterpart of the courtship of John Alden and Priscilla Mullens in Colonial Virginia. "The John Alden of Virginia" was the Reverend Mr. John Camm, who was President of William and Mary College at Williamsburg from 1771 to 1777. The romance of the parson's life came to him when he was fifty-one years old, which was two years before he became president of the college. Among his parishioners was Miss Betsy Hansford, whom he had baptized in the early days of his ministry. A young friend, who had courted Miss Betsy unsuccessfully, asked the parson to aid him with his persuasive speech and eloquence. The clergyman, accordingly, called on the young lady and, among other authorities, cited Holy Writ as enjoining matrimony as one of the prime duties of life. But his persuasions had no effect. Finally, however, Miss Betsy told the parson that if he would go home and read *II Samuel 12:7* he would learn the reason for her refusal. Upon reaching his home he opened his Bible and found these words staring him in the face: "And Nathan said to David, Thou art the man." The marriage of Miss Betsy Hansford and the Reverend Mr. John Camm was announced soon afterwards.

Does the Bible say every tub shall stand on its own bottom?

This proverb is not found in the Bible, although many seem to think that it is. The earliest known occurrence of it is in William Bulleyn's *Dialogue Against the Fever Pestilence,* published in 1564, where it has the form: "Let every vat stand upon his own bottom." John Bunyan's *The Pilgrim's Progress,* published in 1678, contains the following: "Sloth said, Yet a little more sleep; and Presumption then said, Every fat must stand upon his bottom." *Fat* is an old English word meaning "vat" or "tub." In later usage *tub* was substituted for *vat* and *fat* in the proverb.

What Israelite threw stones and dust at his king?

Shimei (pronounced *SHIMM-e-eye*) was an Israelite about whom we know virtually nothing except that he threw stones and dust at and cursed his king. He has come down through the ages as a typical malcontent. This particular Shimei first appears in the Bible when King David was fleeing from Jerusalem after his son Absalom had revolted and occupied the city. *II Samuel 16:5-13* says: "And when king David came to Bahurim, behold, thence came out a man of the family of the house of Saul, whose name was Shimei, the son of Gera: he came forth, and cursed still as he came. And he cast stones at David, and at all the servants of king David: and all the people and all his mighty men were on his right hand and on his left. And thus said Shimei when he cursed, Come out, come out, thou bloody man, and thou man of Belial: the Lord hath returned upon thee all the blood of the house of Saul, in whose stead the Lord hath delivered the kingdom into the hand of Absalom thy son: and, behold, thou art taken in thy mischief, because thou art a bloody man. Then said Abishai the son of Zeruiah unto the king, Why should this dead dog curse my lord the king? let me go over, I pray thee, and take off his head.

And the king said, What have I to do with you, ye sons of Zeruiah? so let him curse, because the Lord hath said unto him, Curse David. Who shall then say, Wherefore hast thou done so? And David said to Abishai, and to all his servants, Behold, my son, which came forth of my bowels, seeketh my life: how much more now may this Benjamite do it? let him alone, and let him curse; for the Lord hath bidden him. It may be that the Lord will look on mine affliction, and that the Lord will requite me good for his cursing this day. And as David and his men went by the way, Shimei went along on the hill's side over against him, and cursed as he went, and threw stones at him, and cast dust." Although David would not molest Shimei at the time because his own kingly fortunes were at a low ebb and because the Lord had bidden Shimei to curse him, nevertheless he deeply resented this insult to his royal person and did not forget it. On his deathbed, according to *I Kings 2:8-9,* David charged Solomon, his son and successor: "And, behold, thou hast with thee Shimei the son of Gera, a Benjamite of Bahurim, which cursed me with a grievous curse in the day when I went to Mahanaim: but he came down to meet me at Jordan, and I sware to him by the Lord, saying, I will not put thee to death with the sword. Now therefore hold him not guiltless: for thou art a wise man, and knowest what thou oughtest to do unto him; but his hoar head bring thou down to the grave with blood." The last days and the end of Shimei are related in *I Kings 2:36-46*: "And the king sent and called for Shimei, and said unto him, Build thee an house in Jerusalem, and dwell there, and go not forth thence any whither. For it shall be, that on the day thou goest out, and passest over the brook Kidron, thou shalt know for certain that thou shalt surely die: thy blood shall be upon thine own head. And Shimei said unto the king, The saying is good: as my lord the king hath said, so will thy servant do. And Shimei dwelt in Jerusalem many days. And it came to pass at the end of three years, that two of the servants of Shimei ran away unto Achish son of Maachah king of Gath. And Shimei arose, and saddled his ass, and went to Gath to Achish to seek his servants: and Shimei went, and brought his servants from Gath. And it was told Solomon that Shimei had gone from Jerusalem to Gath, and was come again. And the king sent and called for Shimei, and said unto him, Did I not make thee to swear by the Lord, and protested unto thee, saying, Know for a certain, on the day thou goest out, and walkest abroad any whither, that thou shalt surely die? and thou saidst unto me, The word that I have heard is good. Why then hast thou not kept the oath of the Lord, and the commandment that I have charged thee with? The king said moreover to Shimei, Thou knowest all the wickedness which thine heart is privy to, that thou didst to David my father: therefore the Lord shall return thy wickedness upon thine own head; and king Solomon shall be blessed, and the throne of David shall be established before the Lord for ever. So the king commanded Benaiah the son of Jehoiada; which went out, and fell upon him, that he died. And the kingdom was established in the hand of Solomon."

What was the Biblical unicorn?

In the King James Version of the Bible *unicorn* occurs as the name of an unidentifiable animal of great size, strength and ferocity. Balaam, when he lifted up his eyes and saw Israel abiding in his tents, according to *Numbers 24:8,* took up his parable and said: "God brought him forth out of Egypt; he hath as it were the strength of an unicorn: he shall eat up the nations his enemies, and shall break their bones, and pierce them through with his arrows." According to *Job 39:9-12,* the Lord, answering the patriarch out of the whirlwind, asked: "Will the unicorn be willing to serve thee, or abide by thy crib? Canst thou bind the unicorn with his band in the furrow? or will he harrow the valleys after thee? Wilt thou trust him, because his strength is great? or wilt thou leave thy labour to him? Wilt thou believe him, that he will bring home thy seed, and gather it into thy barn?" In *Psalms 29:5-6* David sang: "The voice of the Lord breaketh the cedars; yea, the Lord breaketh the cedars of Lebanon. He maketh them also to skip like a calf; Lebanon and Sirion like a young unicorn." "But my horn shalt thou exalt like the horn of an unicorn," says *Psalms 99:10,* and *Psalms 22:21*: "Save me from the lion's mouth: for thou hast heard me from the horns of the unicorns." In *Deuteronomy 33:17* we are told that Moses, in his blessing of Joseph, said that "his horns are like the horns of unicorns: with them he shall push the people together to the ends of the earth." *Isaiah 34:7* says: "And the unicorns shall come down with them, and the bullocks with the bulls; and their land shall be soaked with blood, and their dust made fat with fatness." In all these passages the Hebrew original is *reem.* The King James Version renders *reem* as *unicorn,* the Revised Version as *wild ox,* and some Medieval versions as *rhinoceros.* Just what species the Biblical unicorn was is a question that probably never will be settled definitely. In using *unicorn* in the Bible the English translators were undoubtedly influenced by the imaginary unicorn of classical legend, and the Medieval conception of the legendary unicorn as a strong and fierce animal was in turn reinforced by the Scriptural use of the word. Many ingenious arguments have been advanced by various Biblical authorities to prove that the unicorn was the rhinoceros, a now extinct wild ox or buffalo, or an antelope. The one-horned Indian rhinoceros is scientifically called *Rhinocerous unicornis,* and the authors of the Old Testament may have heard stories of this remarkable animal. Even in some species of the two-horned Indian rhinoceros the anterior horn is so much larger than the posterior one that the animals are popularly regarded as being one-horned. English *unicorn* is derived immediately from Latin *unus,* "one," and *cornu,* "horn," and ultimately from Greek *monoceros,* which also signifies "one-horned." The unicorn of classical legend naturally has no counterpart in any existing species of animal, nor in any known prehistoric species, but the germ of the legend may have been suggested by the rhinoceros. So far as known the earliest writer to mention a unicorn was Ctesias, Greek historian and physician, who lived at the Persian court in the fifth century B.C. and who had some second-hand knowledge of India. Ctesias, however, described the Indian unicorn as a wild ass. Its horn, he explained, was a preventive of poison when used as a drinking cup. Aristotle mentioned two different one-horned animals, the oryx, a kind of antelope, and "the so-called Indian ass." Pliny added the one-horned Indian ox to the list. A modern authority feels quite certain that the Beisa antelope, found in northwest Africa, Ethiopia and Somaliland, is the very animal that in ancient times gave rise to the fabled unicorn. The unicorn of classical and Medieval legend is described as a large, swift beast with the head and body of a horse, the hind legs of an antelope, the tail of a lion, the beard of a goat and a head from which projected a long, sharp and twisted horn. This beast was said to have blue eyes, a white body and a red head. The horn itself had a white base, a black middle and a red tip. It was said that the unicorn could outrun a horse and it was often linked with the lion as its chief rival. The mythical unicorn became a favorite heraldic device. Two unicorns acted as supporters of the Scottish royal arms for about a hundred years before the union of the crowns of Scotland and England. When James VI of Scotland became James I of the United Kingdom in 1603 one of these unicorns supplanted the Red Dragon of Wales as the sinister supporter of the shield in the British coat-of-arms. The belief that the horn of the unicorn had medicinal and magical properties, especially as an antidote to or a preventive of poison, first mentioned about 400 B.C. by Ctesias, has persisted until modern times. During the Middle Ages drinking cups made of the horns of narwhales and rhinoceroses were sold at high prices as genuine unicorn. The Dukes of Burgundy kept pieces of alleged unicorn horn in their wine jugs and used others to test all the food tasted. In an inventory of the jewels and plate in the Tower of London in 1649 are listed cups and beakers of unicorn horn, including "a rhinoceras cupp, graven with figures, with a golden foot," valued at twelve pounds. Charles II of England drank from cups with figures of the unicorn engraved on the sides, symbols of the ancient belief in the efficacy of the horn of that animal as a charm against poison. In his *The Guls Horne-Booke,* published in 1609, Thomas Dekker, the English dramatist, refers to "the unicorn whose horn is worth a city." At one time this fabled infallible test of poison sold on the continent at six thousand ducats for a piece suitable for an amulet. A fable grew up that the unicorn itself, by dipping its horn into a liquid, could detect whether it contained poison. Even in recent times the Indian rhinoceros was threatened with extinction because the horns commanded high prices in China, where they are still used for medicinal purposes. In *Julius Caesar* Shakespeare has Decius Brutus say that Caesar "loves to hear that unicorns may be betrayed with trees."

Are there Negro Jews?

No reliable figures are available, but it is estimated that there are some 100,000 Negro Jews in the United States. They maintain synagogues in New York City and elsewhere. There are believed to be about 250,000 Negro Jews in Latin America, perhaps 100,000 of them in the West Indies, and a million or more in Africa. Some of these colored Jews are converts to the Jewish faith, but the majority of them are the descendants of Jews who intermixed with the colored people of Ethiopia and other parts of Africa centuries ago. Like other Jews, they are divided into two groups, orthodox and unorthodox. The orthodox colored Jews accept the Jewish religion in its entirety, deny Jesus as the Messiah, eat only kosher food, observe Saturday as the Sabbath, fast on Yom Kippur and eat unleavened bread during the Passover. Negro rabbis generally speak Hebrew or Arabic, while the members of their congregations as a rule speak the language of the country in which they reside. One congregation of colored Jews in New York City holds that its members are the original and pure Israelites of the tribe of Judah and that all white Jews are descended from the lost tribes. Some of the American colored Jews are descended from the so-called Black Jews of Ethiopia. This interesting religious and racial group was first called to the attention of the world in 1790 by James Bruce, the Scottish explorer. During the latter part of the nineteenth and the early part of the twentieth centuries several other explorers visited and studied the Black Jews of Ethiopia. About a quarter of a century ago their number was estimated at 100,000. They then lived in their own villages or in separate quarters in the towns and cities of Ethiopia, chiefly in the Addis Ababa and Lake Tana areas. The Black Jews call themselves *Falasha,* an Abyssinian word variously translated "strangers," "exiled," "emigrants" and "the misunderstood." The Falasha (the word is both singlar and plural) were reported to be Jewish in religion but Ethiopian in race, although some of them were said to possess slight Jewish racial characteristics. Their origin is lost in the obscurity of the past. One theory is that they are descended from the Lost Tribes of Israel; another that their ancestor was Menelik, Solomon's alleged son by the Queen of Sheba, and still another, which is the most probable, that they are the descendants of Jews who took refuge in Egypt thousands of years ago, perhaps in the time of Jeremiah, and finally made their way to the Abyssinian highlands, where they increased in numbers by natural growth, intermarriage with the natives and conversion. When first contacted by Europeans the Falasha knew nothing of the Hebrew language and their Bible consisted of fragments of the Old Testament in Amharic. Their Judaism had been somewhat affected by pagan and Christian influences, and the omission of certain festivals and rites in their ceremonies was taken by some as evidence that they antedated the Babylonian captivity. Their synagogues resembled Christian churches. The Falasha did not marry alien women, kept the Mosaic rules of food and ablution and purified themselves after contact with non-Jews. They sometimes owned land and worked on it, but they did no trading, neither lent nor borrowed money, and were rarely wealthy. Among Christians and Mohammedans alike they had the reputation of being industrious, generally higher in moral standards than their neighbors, and were the most useful inhabitants of the country. In fact, the Falasha were in great demand as builders, potters, masons, ironworkers, silversmiths, weavers, tanners and basketmakers, and were virtually the only skilled workers in Ethiopia. Falasha priests married, but no man was permitted to be a priest who had eaten bread with a Gentile or who was the son or grandson of one so contaminated. They were very secretive about their rituals, emblems and sacred books. When first contacted by Europeans the Falasha had their own kings, whom they claimed were descended from King David. Their royal line became extinct about 1800 A.D., when the Falashas became subjects of Abyssinia. Some authorities suppose the claim of the Ethiopians that their royal family is descended from King Solomon and the Queen of Sheba originated centuries ago when members of the Falasha and Ethiopian royal families intermarried. In this connection it is interesting to recall that there have been reports from China and India of similar small groups of Chinese and Hindu Jews; that is, Chinese and Indians with slight Jewish racial characteristics who profess a primitive form of Judaism.

What is a jorum?

A jorum is a large drinking vessel, particularly a bowl for punch. *Jorum* also signifies the contents of such a bowl as well as "a large quantity." The term is supposed to be a corruption of *Joram* in *II Samuel 8:9-11*, which reads: "When Toi king of Hamath heard that David had smitten all the host of Hadadezer, then Toi sent Joram his son unto king David, to salute him, and to bless him, because he had fought against Hadadezer, and smitten him: for Hadadezer had wars with Toi. And Joram brought with him vessels of silver, and vessels of gold, and vessels of brass: which also king David did dedicate unto the Lord, with the silver and gold that he had dedicated of all nations which he subdued." In the sense of a large drinking vessel *jorum* dates back in English at least to the early half of the eighteenth century.

Did the Israelites have cancer?

No disease identifiable as cancer is mentioned in the Bible. That Jews seldom if ever have cancer was at one time a common belief. Apparently the question of the prevalence of this disease among Jews as compared with its prevalence among other races was first discussed when the London *Lancet*, British medical journal, published a letter written by a doctor who stated that in all his practice he had never met with a Jew afflicted with cancer. Immediately many readers jumped to the conclusion that this assertion was generally applicable and it was popularly supposed that orthodox Jews are not subject to attacks of cancer because of their observance of the Mosaic laws of diet and cleanliness, particularly that forbidding the eating of pork. After the subject had been raised, investigation showed that cancer does occur among orthodox Jews, who do not eat pork, although some authorities said there was some reason for believing that the number of cases was smaller proportionately for Jewish people than for many other groups. Dr. William Roger Williams, in *The Natural History of Cancer*, published in 1908, wrote: "The liability of Jews to cancer varies with their mode of living, approximately that of the people among whom they dwell, but generally being somewhat inferior to it." In his *Mortality from Cancer Throughout the World*, published in 1915, Dr. Frederick Ludwig Hoffman gave figures indicating that Jewish women are less liable to cancer of the uterus than are women of other races. About 1930 the United States Public Health Service said: "Cancer is not generally reportable, and comparatively few statistics showing the number of cases are available. The statistics of deaths from cancer show the birthplace, sex and age, but they do not show race. For these reasons there is very little available information on the subject of cancer among Jews." Little has been heard of this controversy in recent years and it can be presumed that investigators who pursued the subject did not find sufficient evidence to justify the belief that orthodox Jews are less afflicted with cancer than other people who do not observe the Mosaic injunction against eating pork and certain other foods.

What did Jesus say about prophets without honor?

One of the most often quoted, and at the same time one of the most pathetic, sayings attributed to Jesus is what he said about a prophet having no honor in his own country. The simplest, most concise and most frequently quoted version is that given by *John 4:44*, which reads: "For Jesus himself testified, that a prophet hath no honour in his own country." *Matthew 13:54-58* says: "And when he was come into his own country, he taught them in their synagogue, insomuch that they were astonished, and said, Whence hath this man this wisdom, and these mighty works? Is not this the carpenter's son? is not his mother called Mary? and his brethren, James, and Joses, and Simon, and Judas? And his sisters, are they not all with us? Whence then hath this man all these things? And they were offended in him. But Jesus said unto them, A prophet is not without honour, save in his own country, and in his own house. And he did not many mighty works there because of their unbelief." *Mark 6* elaborates on some points in the incident. "And when the sabbath day was come, he began to teach in the synagogue: and many hearing him were astonished, saying, From whence hath this man these things? and what wisdom is this which is given unto him, that even such mighty works are wrought by his hands? . . . And they were offended at him. But Jesus said unto them, A prophet is not without honour, but in his own country, and among his own kin, and in his own house. And he could there do no mighty work, save that he laid his hands upon a few sick folk, and healed them. And he marvelled because of their unbelief." The most detailed account of this visit of Jesus to his home town is related in *Luke 4:16-30*, which reads: "And he came to Nazareth, where he had been brought up: and, as his custom was, he went into the synagogue on the sabbath day, and stood up for to read. And there was delivered unto him the book of the prophet Esaias. And when he had opened the book, he found the place where it was written, The Spirit of the Lord is upon me, because he hath anointed me to preach the gospel to the poor; he hath sent me to heal the brokenhearted, to preach deliverance to the captives, and recovering of sight to the blind, to set at liberty them that are bruised, to preach the acceptable year of the Lord. And he closed the book, and he gave it again to the minister, and sat down. And the eyes of all them that were in the synagogue were fastened on him. And he began to say unto them, This day is this scripture fulfilled in your ears. And all bare him witness, and wondered at the gracious words which proceeded out of his mouth. And they said, Is not this Joseph's son? And he said unto them, Ye will surely say unto me this proverb, Physician, heal thyself: whatsoever we have heard done in Capernaum, do also here in thy country. And he said, Verily I say unto you, No prophet is accepted in his own country. But I tell you of a truth, many widows were in Israel in the days of Elias, when the heaven was shut up three years and six months, when great famine was throughout all the land; but unto none of them was Elias sent, save unto Sarepta, a city of Sidon, unto a woman that was a widow. And many lepers were in Israel in the time of Eliseus the prophet; and none of them was cleansed, saving Naaman the Syrian. And all they in the synagogue, when they heard these things, were filled with wrath, and rose up, and thrust him out of the city, and led him unto the brow of the hill whereon their city was built, that they might cast him down headlong. But he passing through the midst of them went his way, . . ."

Is it in the Bible?

Among the many things popularly supposed to be in the Bible is the following oft-quoted saying: "The time will come when you cannot tell summer from winter except by the putting forth of the buds and the falling of the leaves." It is not in the Bible and its origin is not known. *Genesis 8:22* seems to express a contrary idea: "While the earth remaineth, seedtime and harvest, and cold and heat, and summer and winter, and day and night shall not cease." Like most other homespun Scripture, however, the quotation in question was undoubtedly suggested by certain Biblical passages. It may have originally arisen from a misconception of the words attributed to Jesus in relating the parable of the fig tree. According to *Matthew 24:32* Jesus said: "When his branch is yet tender, and putteth forth leaves, ye know that summer is nigh." There is an allegorical hint of a seasonless time in *Revelation 22:12*, which reads: "And he shewed me a pure river of water of life, clear as crystal, proceeding out of the throne of God and of the Lamb. In the midst of the street of it, and on either side of the river, was there the tree of life, which bare twelve manner of fruits, and yielded her fruit every month: and the leaves of the tree were for the healing of the nations."

Who are the Sepharadim?

Sepharadim, the Hebrew plural of *Sephardi*, is applied to the descendants of the Jews of Spain and Portugal. This usage is based on *Obadiah 20*, which reads: "And the captivity of this host of the children of Israel shall possess that of the Canaanites, even unto Zarephath; and the captivity of Jerusalem, which is Sepharad, shall possess the cities of the south." Obadiah wrote after the captivity and pronounced the judgement of the Lord upon Edom for siding with the enemies of Israel. The meaning of *Sepharad* in *Obadiah 20* is obscure. Some authorities suspect that the text is faulty. Since Jews were evidently in captivity at Sepharad when Obadiah wrote, the place has been variously identified as a district in Persia and as Sardia or some other place in Asia Minor. But the rabbinical commentators interpreted Sepharad to be Spain and called the Spanish and Portuguese Jews Sepharadim. The Sepharadim are as a rule darker than the northern Jews. After their expulsion from Spain and Portugal, the Sepharadim settled chiefly in North Africa and the Near East and their descendants still live in those places as well as in Greece, the Balkans, the Netherlands, Britain and America.

What are ember days?

Ember days are twelve days of the year, three in each of the four seasons, set apart for fasting and prayer. The ember days recognized by the Anglican and Roman Catholic churches are Wednesday, Friday and Saturday after the first Sunday in Lent, after Whitsunday, after September 14, and after December 13. Weeks in which these days fall are called ember weeks. Ember days were first instituted in the third century by Pope Clixtus primarily to prepare the clergy for ordination according to the manner set forth in *Acts 13:3*, which, referring to the ordination of Barnabas and Saul by certain prophets and teachers in the church at Antioch, says: "And when they had fasted and prayed, and laid their hands on them, they sent them away." The ember days were consecrated by the Council of Placentia in 1095 and fixed essentially as now observed. *Ember* in this connection is derived from an old English root meaning "regular period," "revolution," "time" or "season." Modern lexicographers generally reject the popular belief that ember days were so called because of the custom of penitents sitting in sackcloth and ashes (embers).

Does the Bible mention Job's comforters?

Job's comforters does not occur in the Bible, but the phrase is derived from *Job 16:2*, in which the patriarch says to the three friends who came to comfort him: "I have heard many such things: miserable comforters are ye all." Eliphaz the Temanite, Bildad the Shuhite and Zophar the Naamathite "made an appointment together to come to mourn with him and to comfort him," but they told Job that he had brought on his affliction himself and thereby in reality added weight to his sorrow. Hence a Job's comforter is one who afflicts another with words intended to comfort him. Bad news is called *Job's news* and the bringer of such news *Job's post*, in allusion to the messengers who told Job of the loss of his cattle, servants and sons.

Why was *widow woman* used in the English Bible?

II Samuel 14:5 says: "And the king said unto her, What aileth thee? And she answered, I am indeed a *widow woman*, and mine husband is dead." *Widow* now means a woman whose husband is dead and who has not married again, and *woman* in *widow woman* is redundant. But before the King James Version of the Bible was made *widow* was applicable to either a man or a woman. It is derived from an Indo-European root signifying "to be empty" or "separated," and probably is akin to Latin *viduus*, which primarily means "void" and secondarily "widow." Originally a widow was a man or a woman deprived of wife or husband. In the King James Version there are other similar holdovers from earlier usage. *II Kings 19:35* says: "And it came to pass that night, that the angel of the Lord went out, and smote in the camp of the Assyrians an hundred fourscore and five thousand: and when they arose early in the morning, behold, they were all *dead corpses*." This language, including *dead corpses*, is virtually repeated in *Isaiah 37:36*. *Corpse* now means "a dead body," and *dead* in *dead corpse* is redundant. But *corpse* is derived from Latin *corpus,* "body," and centuries ago a corpse might be either a living or a dead body. Hence *dead corpse*. Both *widow woman* and *dead corpse* are still heard occasionally in colloquial usage.

What does *froward* mean?

Froward occurs many times in the English Old Testament, particularly in *Proverbs* where private and public morals and conduct are the theme. It was an old North of England dialect form of the preposition *from-ward,* literally signifying "turned from" and used as an antonym of "toward." The King James translators employed it as a noun, adjective and adverb to render Hebrew originals meaning "turning from," "perverse," "false," "crooked," "wayward," "refractory," "naughty" and "counter to what is demanded, expected or reasonable." In *Deuteronomy 32:20* the Israelites are described as "a very froward generation, children in whom is no faith." *Isaiah 57:17* tells us "he went on frowardly in the way of his heart." According to *Proverbs 10:32,* "The lips of the righteous know what is acceptable: but the mouth of the wicked speaketh frowardness." The word occurs once in the New Testament. *I Peter 2:18* says: "Servants, be subject to your masters with all fear; not only to the good and gentle, but also to the froward."

What was the rose of Sharon?

The Song of Solomon 2:1 says: "I am the rose of Sharon, and the lily of the valleys." *Rose* occurs only once elsewhere in the King James Version and there it is also associated with Sharon. *Isaiah 35:1-2* says: "The wilderness and the solitary place shall be glad for them; and the desert shall rejoice, and blossom as the rose. It shall blossom abundantly, and rejoice even with joy and singing: the glory of Lebanon shall be given unto it, the excellency of Carmel and Sharon, they shall see the glory of the Lord, and the excellency of God." The true meaning of the Hebrew original translated *rose* in these two passages is not known for certain. It has been identified by some with a species of narcissus (*Narcissus tazetta*), by others with the meadow saffron (*Colchicum autumnale*), by still others with various species of rock rose and tulip. *Lily of the valleys* likewise cannot be definitely identified with any particular species of plant. It may have been a generic name for several plants of the lily type. Most authorities suppose it to refer to an iris common in Palestine. A number of different species bear the name *rose of Sharon* and *lily of the valley*, but these names were bestowed without any reference to the originals. *Sharon*, supposedly derived from a Hebrew root denoting "level country," was the name of an undulating plain in ancient Palestine noted for its fertility, luxuriant pastures, richly colored flowers and abundant harvests. *Isaiah 65:10* says: "Sharon shall be a fold of flocks," and in *I Chronicles 27:29* we are told that over David's "herds that fed in Sharon was Shitrai the Sharonite." This "garden of Palestine," as the plain of Sharon has been described, is about fifty miles long and from six to twelve wide. It lies northward from Joppa between the sand-dunes of the Mediterranean coast and Mt. Carmel. Throughout the centuries the sand-dunes have been extending themselves eastward and encroaching upon the plain of Sharon.

Where does the Bible mention the frying-pan?

Frying-pan occurs twice in the King James Version. *Leviticus 2:7* says: "And if thy oblation be a meat offering baken in the frying-pan, it shall be made of fine flour with oil." Again, *Leviticus 7:9*: "And all the meat offering that is baken in the oven, and all that is dressed in the frying-pan, and in the pan, shall be the priest's that offereth it." Just what the frying-pan was is not known. The Hebrew original so translated probably means simply a shallow vessel either of earthenware or metal.

What is meant by the horseleach's daughters?

Proverbs 30:14-16 says: "There is a generation, whose teeth are as swords, and their jaw teeth as knives, to devour the poor from off the earth, and the needy from among men. *The horseleach hath two daughters, crying, Give, give.* There are three things that are never satisfied, yea, four things say not, It is enough: The grave; and the barren womb; the earth that is not filled with water; and the fire that saith not, It is enough." *Horseleach* is one of a number of words used only once in the King James Version. The Hebrew *alugah* so translated is of uncertain meaning. Some authorities suppose it to signify "sucker" and to refer to a variety of the bloodsucking worms known as leeches. The context of *Proverbs 30:15* clearly associates the term with devouring, rapacity or greed. Other authorities, however, think the term is an allusion to a mythical vampire-like creature, perhaps the Lilith of Babylonian legend. *Leech*, formerly spelled *leach*, is derived from Anglo-Saxon *laece*, "one who relieves pain," from *laenian*, "to heal." A physician was formerly called a *leach* and the healing art *leach-craft*. When blood-letting was regarded virtually as a cure-all, bloodsucking worms were widely used by physicians in bleeding patients. The worms were probably called leeches because they were thought to be healers. In other words, the physician and the bloodsucking worm both received the name *leach* for the same reason. Animals as well as human beings were bled and a veterinary surgeon or horse-doctor was called a *horse-leach*, a name also applied to a European species of bloodsucking worm that was believed to attack the nose and mouth of horses while drinking but which is now known to feed chiefly on other worms. Leeches, which are generally flat in shape and which have segmented and ringed bodies, are found in the sea, in fresh-water and on the land in many parts of the world, and they were a common pest to man and beast in the Near East in Bible times. It is said that the leech is the only living creature that can survive being turned inside out.

Why is a preacher called a pastor?

Pastor in the sense of a clergyman or priest in charge of a congregation or parish was suggested by Biblical usage. It is the Latin word for a shepherd, herdsman or one who cares for a flock of sheep. The term is derived from *pascere*, "to feed," whence comes also our *pasture*. The translators of the King James Version used *pastor* to render Hebrew originals signifying "shepherd," but only when they were used figuratively to denote civil, political and spiritual rulers of the people. They did not employ the term in the literal sense of a herder of sheep or in the modern ecclesiastical sense of a local clergyman. For instance, *Jeremiah 10:21* says: "For the pastors are become brutish, and have not sought the Lord: therefore they shall not prosper, and all their flocks shall be scattered." Again in *Jeremiah 3:15*: "And I will give you pastors according to mine heart, which shall feed you with knowledge and understanding." In the New Testament *pastor* occurs only in *Ephesians 4:11*, which reads: "And he gave some apostles; and some, prophets; and some, evangelists; and some, pastors and teachers." This passage may account for the fact that *pastor* is now applied to the lower, rather than the higher, clergy.

What kind of bird was the Biblical sparrow?

As used in the King James Version *sparrow* probably refers to various small birds rather than to one particular species. The Hebrew original in the Old Testament is *tsippor*, which literally signifies "chirper" and which is undoubtedly of onomatopoeic or imitative origin. In all cases except two it is translated *bird* or *fowl. Psalms 84:3* says: "Yea, the sparrow hath found an house, and the swallow a nest for herself, where she may lay her young, even thine altars, O Lord of hosts, my King, and my God." And *Psalms 10:7*: "I watch, and am as a sparrow alone upon the house top." The bird referred to as a *tsippor* or *sparrow* may have been a lark, swallow, thrush or other species of small bird common in Palestine. The Greek equivalent in the New Testament denotes any small bird and is translated *sparrow* only four times. *Matthew 10:29* and *31* says: "Are not two sparrows sold for a farthing? And one of them shall not fall on the ground without the Father. . . . Fear ye not therefore, ye are of more value than many sparrows." In *Luke 12:6-7* this occurs as: "Are not five sparrows sold for two farthings, and not one of them is forgotten before God? . . . Fear not therefore: ye are of more value than many sparrows." *Sparrow* is now applied to scores of different species of small birds. The term may also be of imitative origin, probably originally having been an attempt to indicate the harsh, discordant note of the English or house sparrow, *Passer domesticus,* which is a member of the family of weaver finches. The house sparrow, which has been transplanted to many parts of the world, has not yet established itself in Palestine, and it is highly improbable that this bird was known there in ancient times.

Why does an anchor symbolize hope?

The anchor as the symbol of hope was suggested by *Hebrews 6:19,* which reads in part: "Which hope we have as an anchor of the soul, both sure and stedfast." "Hope" is the motto of Rhode Island and the chief figure in the design on the flag of that State is an anchor. There is only one other mention of anchors in the Bible. In connection with Paul's voyage from Caesarea to Malta, *Acts 27:30* says: "And as the shipmen were about to flee out of the ship, when they had let down the boat into the sea, under colour as though they would have cast anchors out of the foreship, . . ." Originally large stone were used to hold ships at anchor, but in Paul's time the Romans already used anchors of metal similar to those used at the present time.

Does *mile* occur in the Bible?

In the Sermon on the Mount, according to *Matthew 5:41,* Jesus said: "And whosoever shall compel thee to go a mile, go with him twain." That is the only place in the King James Version where *mile* occurs. *Mile* is derived from Latin *mille,* "thousand." The Roman mile was originally 1,000 long paces and was equivalent to nearly 5,000 feet. In the passage quoted the Greek word translated *compel* is from a Persian root signifying "impress." The same term is used in *Matthew 27:32*, where it is related that Simon of Cyrene was "compelled" to bear the cross of Jesus. Royal couriers and dispatch carriers in the ancient Persian empire were empowered to impress both men and beasts of burden along their route for the king's service. Likewise Roman soldiers and officials had the authority to compel any subject in a conquered province to carry their baggage. The exercise of this authority, a form of taxation, was one of the most galling exactions imposed on the Jews by the Romans. Without a moment's notice any Jewish subject of Rome might be called upon by a soldier or official to become a common burden-bearer. Jesus undoubtedly alluded to this practice when he said, "Whosoever shall compel you to go a mile, go with him twain." In effect he advised his followers to pay their taxes willingly and to bear their public burdens cheerfully; that is, to make their burdens lighter by doing more than was expected of them. If a Roman impressed them to carry his baggage a mile they were voluntarily to offer to carry it a second mile.

INDEX

✠